THE IRWIN SERIES IN ACCOUNTING

Consulting Editor

WILLARD J. GRAHAM, Ph.D., C.P.A.
University of North Carolina

BOOKS IN THE IRWIN SERIES IN ACCOUNTING

MANAGEMENT ACCOUNTING

Text and Cases

Management Accounting

TEXT AND CASES

By ROBERT N. ANTHONY, D.C.S.

Ross Graham Walker Professor of Management Controls
Graduate School of Business Administration
Harvard University

THIRD EDITION

1964

RICHARD D. IRWIN, INC.

HOMEWOOD, ILLINOIS

THIRD EDITION

First Printing, August, 1964
Second Printing, January, 1965
Third Printing, December, 1965

Library of Congress Catalog Card No. 64–22114

PRINTED IN THE UNITED STATES OF AMERICA

To

GRETCHEN

PREFACE

THE THIRD EDITION is intended for the same types of courses as were the previous editions: (1) a full-year or half-year course for college students with no background in accounting; (2) a half-year follow-on course, building on an introductory course in accounting principles; and (3) a course in a management development program. Of these three types, I am most interested in the first. The beginning student, whether or not he is an accounting major, should, I believe, approach the subject with the point of view of the user of accounting information rather than that of the accountant who supplies the information. Such an approach makes the subject both more interesting and more intellectually challenging than does the alternative of focusing on mechanics. As in previous editions, the text is arranged so that the student can construct and use financial statements from the very beginning of the course.

Although designed for the beginner, the book does not contain enough "pencil-pushing" material for him. The beginning college student needs also the companion volume, *Accounting Problems and Cases.*[1]

The text has been brought up to date, clarified, and somewhat reorganized. It incorporates changes and additions required by Opinions through April 1964 of the AICPA Accounting Principles Board and by the Internal Revenue Act of 1964.

Part I has been revised and retitled "The Accounting Structure." In it I have tried to emphasize the underlying rationale of accounting principles by showing that they are all explainable in terms of the criteria of objectivity, feasibility, and usefulness. The arrangement of topics is governed more by pedagogical than by logical considerations; that is, the intent is to proceed gradually from the simple to the complicated, rather than to discuss all aspects of a topic at once. Thus, the basic idea of Cost of Goods Sold is introduced in Chapter 3, but the complications of the deduction method are deferred until Chapter 5, the process of calculating Cost of Goods Sold in a manufacturing company is described in Chapter 7, and the LIFO-FIFO issue is not mentioned until Chapter 9.

---

[1] Robert N. Anthony and John Dearden, *Accounting Problems and Cases* (Homewood, Ill.: Richard D. Irwin, Inc., 1962).

Part II, "Using Information in Financial Statements" is changed considerably in detail, especially in the chapter on funds flow statements.

Part III, "Accounting in Management Control," treats the whole management control process, including budgeting, as essentially a single entity. This makes for a more coherent arrangement. Material on the behavior of costs has been expanded and brought together into a new chapter. A chapter on "The Analysis of Differences" gives a broader treatment to this important subject than does the corresponding chapter in the Revised Edition, which was restricted to standard cost variances.

Part IV, "Accounting in Business Decisions," contains a completely redone chapter on "Planning Capital Acquisitions." The subject is now introduced via the present value method, which is less time consuming and more straightforward than the time-adjusted return method previously used for this purpose. A new Table C eliminates all the arithmetic previously required to figure the tax effect of accelerated depreciation, and there is therefore no longer any need to make the unrealistic assumption of straight-line depreciation. A new chapter, "Advanced Concepts and Techniques," has been added to introduce some of the new quantitative techniques and to stimulate interest in advanced courses.

Some of the cases are new or revised, but cases from the previous edition have been retained if they seem to be more useful than any other available cases.

As I wrote in the Preface to the first edition, the cases have been selected because of their interest and educational value as a basis for class discussion. They are not necessarily intended to illustrate either correct or incorrect handling of management problems. Skill in the management use of accounting information can be acquired, I believe, only through experience. Thinking about a case, and discussing it in the classroom and in informal discussion groups, can help to provide such experience. In preparing to discuss a case in class, the student is required to *do* something—to analyze a problem, to weigh various factors involved in it, to make some calculations, to take a position, and so on. In class, the student is required to explain his point of view, to defend it, to understand and appraise the arguments of his colleagues, and to decide what arguments are the strongest. Practice in doing these things helps to increase skill and understanding; in fact, many educators believe that the really important parts of a subject can be learned only by experience of some sort, as opposed to merely hearing or reading about them. Thus, although the case material comprises only about half the pages in this book, the discussion of these cases is by far the more important part of the educational process.

Although some professors suggested that each case should be accompanied by a set of detailed questions, others felt that such questions would tend to channel the preparation and discussion of the case too narrowly. I have decided to continue, for most of the cases, the practice of giving only a few broad questions, with the thought that those who prefer the other approach can easily supplement these when making assignments.

ACKNOWLEDGMENTS

Again, for myself and on behalf of the other authors of cases, I express our gratitude to the businessmen who were willing to give their time and the benefit of their experience in the development of cases. I wish also to acknowledge again my debt to Professors Ross G. Walker and Charles A. Bliss, who were largely responsible for creating and developing the Control course at the Harvard Business School, from which this book is descended.

As can be seen from the detailed list in the Index and Sources of Cases that follows, many people participated in the process of preparing the cases included herein. I appreciate the permission that both those at Harvard and those at other institutions have given me to use their cases in this book.

Many users of the book have been good enough to make suggestions for improving it. Of these, I want especially to thank Professors Harold W. Fox, Robert K. Jaedicke of Stanford, Ralph C. Jones of Yale, Harry D. Kerrigan of the University of Connecticut, and Dwight R. Ladd of the University of New Hampshire. My colleagues, John Dearden, Robert T. Sprouse, and David F. Hawkins read sections of the manuscript and made many valuable comments.

Miss Marian V. Sears edited the manuscript and prepared the index, and Miss Carol Peterson supervised the typing and other work connected with the production of the manuscript. I am deeply grateful to them.

ROBERT N. ANTHONY

BOSTON, MASSACHUSETTS
    June 1, 1964

TABLE OF CONTENTS

16. CHARACTERISTICS OF COST 476

RELATION OF COSTS TO VOLUME: Cost-Volume Diagrams. Behavior. Formula
for the Cost Line. Unit Costs. Estimating Cost-Volume Relationship. Measures
of Volume. The Overhead Rate and Standard Volume. THE PROFITGRAPH:
Construction of a Profitgraph. Interpretation of the Profitgraph. Improving
Profit Performance. Limitations on Profitgraph Analysis. MARGINAL INCOME
ANALYSIS STATEMENT. CONTROLLABLE COSTS: Engineered Costs and Managed Costs. SUMMARY. APPENDIX: Fitting a Straight Line by Least Squares.

CASES

17. THE ANALYSIS OF DIFFERENCES 520

STRUCTURE OF ANALYSIS. NONCOMPARABLE DATA. PRODUCT CHARACTERIS-
TICS. PRICE AND QUANTITY OF INPUTS: Direct Labor. Material Cost Vari-
ances. MIX: General Use of the Mix Concept. OUTPUT PRICE AND VOLUME.
VOLUME AND COSTS: Interpretation of the Variances. MEASURING STICK
VARIANCE. AN ILLUSTRATIVE ANALYSIS: Marketing Variance. Manufacturing
Variances. SUMMARY.

CASES

PART IV. ACCOUNTING IN BUSINESS DECISIONS

18. DECIDING AMONG ALTERNATIVE COURSES OF ACTION 561

APPROACH TO ALTERNATIVE CHOICE PROBLEMS: Criteria. Outline of Ap-
proach. Definition of the Problem and of Alternative Solutions. Weighing and
Measuring the Quantitative Factors. Evaluating and Weighing the Unmeas-
ured Factors. Reaching a Decision. PROBLEMS INVOLVING COSTS: Future
Costs. Differential Costs. Mechanics of the Calculation. The Margin of Error.
Example: Operating an Automobile. Example: Economic Lot Size. PRICING:
Theoretical Considerations. Full-Cost Pricing. Contribution Pricing. SUGGES-
TIONS FOR ATTACKING CASES. SUMMARY.

CASES

GENERAL FRAMEWORK OF ANALYSIS: Essentials of a Business Investment. Concept of "Return on Investment." The Concept of Present Value. Present Value Method. Present Value of a Stream of Payments. Other Present Value Tables. Unadjusted Return on Investment. ESTIMATING THE VARIABLES: Required Earnings Rate. Earnings. Economic Life. Investment. Summary of the Process. OTHER METHODS: Time-Adjusted Return. MAPI Method. Comparison of Methods. PREFERENCE PROBLEMS: Profitability Index. Comparison of Preference Rules. Concluding Comment. SUMMARY.

CASES

STRATEGIC PLANNING: Probability Theory. Mathematical Models. MANAGEMENT CONTROL: Social Psychology. Related Disciplines. Profit Centers and Investment Centers. New Planning Devices. Cost Accounting. OPERATIONAL CONTROL: Operations Research. INFORMATION HANDLING: Automatic Data Processing. CONCLUSION.

INDEX

INDEX AND SOURCES OF CASES

The cases published in this book are listed below in alphabetical order, together with their authors and the institution with which they were associated when they wrote them. These institutions are the copyright owners. Cases without identification were written by the author of this book and are copyrighted by the President and Fellows of Harvard College. No case may be reproduced, in whole or in part, without the written permission of the copyright owner. Problems are not listed.

* Under the direction of R. N. Anthony.

* Under the direction of R. N. Anthony.

* Under the direction of R. N. Anthony.

---

* Under the direction of R. N. Anthony.

Chapter 1

MANAGEMENT'S USE OF ACCOUNTING INFORMATION

NEARLY EVERY business enterprise has an accounting system, that is, a means of collecting, summarizing, analyzing, and reporting, in monetary terms, information about the business. In studying these systems, it is useful to consider them as consisting of two parts, labeled financial accounting and management accounting, although in practice the two are not neatly separated.

Financial accounting has the primary objective of providing financial information to parties outside the business—stockholders, bankers, other creditors, and government agencies. The techniques, rules, and conventions according to which financial accounting figures are collected and reported reflect, to a considerable extent, the requirements of these outside parties.

The persons responsible for operating a business—that is, the management—also need monetary information to aid them in doing their jobs effectively. Although much of this information is the same as that contained in reports prepared for outsiders, management also needs a considerable amount of additional information. *Management accounting,* which is the focus of this book, is concerned with accounting information that is useful to management.

"Useful" always connotes some *purpose* for which the figures are to be used. The problems we shall discuss are not like textbook problems in mathematics, in which figures are often manipulated with no practical objective in mind. We are concerned with the use of accounting figures in the recognition or solution of management problems.

The terms "financial accounting" and "management accounting" are not precise descriptions of the activities they comprise. All accounting is *financial* in the sense that all accounting systems are in monetary terms, and *management* is responsible for the content of financial accounting reports. (This is the first of many problems in terminology that will be noted throughout this book. The student is cautioned against drawing inferences from the labels alone; he must learn the concepts that the labels represent.)

1

PLAN OF THE BOOK

The Structure of Accounting

A single structure underlies both financial accounting and management accounting. This structure consists of a few basic principles and concepts, a set of relationships among the elements comprising the accounting system, a terminology, and various rules and guides for the application of the principles to specific situations. This underlying structure will be described in Part I of this text.

We shall focus this description on the principles underlying the construction of financial statements because experience has shown that this provides the clearest way of describing the structure of accounting. Since these financial statements are the special concern of financial accounting, Part I, in one sense, deals with financial accounting. Our objective, however, is not to discuss financial accounting per se; rather, it is to develop the concepts and terminology that underlie all accounting.

Furthermore, we do not describe in detail the techniques used to collect and summarize accounting information. Our point of view is that of the *user* of accounting information. The user needs to know something about these techniques in order to understand the nature and limitations of the information that they produce, but he does not need the detailed knowledge that the accountant must have.

The approach to accounting taken in Part I is something like that used by an airplane pilot in learning to use his instruments. The pilot needs to know the meaning of the message conveyed by each of his instruments; that is, he needs to know such things as the fact that a clockwise movement of a certain arrow probably means one thing and that a counterclockwise movement probably means another thing, that the flashing of a red light probably means that a certain component is not functioning, that a certain sound in his earphones probably means that he is on course, and so on. The word "probably" is used because, for one reason or another, an instrument may not always give the reading that it is supposed to give; the pilot must realize this, and he must also understand something of the likelihood of, and the reasons for, these abnormalities. On the other hand, the pilot does not need to know how to design airplane instruments, how to construct them, how to check them for accuracy, how to maintain them, or how to repair them. Specialists are available for these important functions.

Similarly a person who is to make intelligent use of accounting information must understand what a given accounting figure probably means, what its limitations are, and under what circumstances it may mean something different from the apparent "signal" that it gives. He does not, however, need to know how to design, construct, operate, or check on the accuracy of an accounting system. He can rely on accountants for these important functions. The discussion of accounting in Part I is limited, then, to matters which it is believed that the *user* of accounting information needs to know.

Uses of Accounting

Knowledge of the meaning of an instrument reading is by no means all, or even a very important part of, what the pilot needs to know in order to fly his plane. In addition, he must know how to use this knowledge to solve the problems that arise during flight, and he must know a great deal about the "art" of flying, which includes many matters that have little or nothing to do with the instruments. Parts II, III, and IV of this book deal with the use of accounting information; however, there is much more to the "art" of management than the use of accounting information, and this is in no sense a book on the whole art of management.

Analyzing Financial Statements

Since the material in Part I focuses on the principles underlying the construction of financial statements, a good place to begin our examination of the use of accounting information is the use made of these statements. This is the subject matter of Part II.

The two principal financial statements are the balance sheet, which reports the financial position of a business at one moment in time, and the income statement, which summarizes its performance over a period of time. We shall discuss how the businessman can obtain from these statements useful information both about his own business and about other businesses in which he may be interested. We shall at the same time point out the inherent limitations of financial statement information, limitations which prevent these statements from providing the answers to all, or even the most important, questions that are raised about a business.

Management Control

An important process in which accounting information is used within a business is called *management control*. This is the process of assuring that resources are obtained and used effectively and efficiently in the accomplishment of the organization's objectives. In Part III, we discuss the role of accounting information in this process.

Management control has to do with the ongoing operation of the business. It consists of a more-or-less regularly recurring sequence of interrelated activities. For convenience in exposition, these activities may be classified as either control activities or planning activities. Nevertheless, the whole process is a single, indivisible one, in which the two types of activities interact and merge into one another; the same people are involved in both. Although pedagogical considerations make it desirable to discuss these activities separately, we shall throughout emphasize the relationship between them.

Control.   Control is the process by which management assures itself, insofar as is feasible, that what the organization does conforms to management's plans and policies. Accounting information is useful in control as a means of communication, of motivation, and of appraisal.

As a means of *communication,* accounting reports can assist in informing the organization about management's plans and policies and, in general, the types of action that management wishes the organization to take.

Unless the business is a one-man enterprise, it is not management's job to do the work; that is, management does not personally manufacture and sell the product. Rather, it is the responsibility of management to see to it that the work gets done by others. This requires, first, that personnel be hired and formed into an organization and, secondly, that this organization be motivated in such a way that it will do what management wants it to do. Accounting information can help (and also, unless properly used, can hinder) this *motivation* process.

Periodically, management needs to evaluate how well the employees are doing their jobs. Such an *appraisal* of performance may result in a salary increase, promotion, reassignment, corrective action of various kinds, or, in extreme cases, dismissal. Accounting information can assist in this appraisal process, although an adequate basis for judging a man's performance cannot be obtained solely from information revealed by accounting records.

Planning.   Planning is the process of deciding what action should be taken in the future. The area covered by one plan may be a tiny segment of the enterprise, or it may be the whole enterprise. Thus, a decision as to whether the price of one product should be increased 10 cents is a plan, and so is a decision to merge or not to merge the company with another company.

The essential characteristic of a plan is that it involves a decision about action to be taken in the future. Planning is therefore to be distinguished from *forecasting.* A forecast is an estimate of what will happen in the future, but the forecaster makes no attempt to influence the future by his own decisions or action. People *forecast* the weather, but they do not—except in the few areas where cloud-seeding operations are carried on—attempt to *plan* the weather.

Some businesses have planning staffs whose full-time job is to assist in making plans. The planning function, however, is much broader than the work done by these staffs; it is performed at all levels in the organization and in all organizations, whether or not they have separate planning staffs. The foreman who decides to route a certain job through Machine A rather than through Machine B is planning in the same sense as, but on a smaller scale than, the president who decides how much the company will spend on research.

A systematic form of planning, called *budgeting,* occurs as part of the management control process. Budgeting is the process of planning the overall activity of the enterprise for a specified period of time, usually a year. An important objective of this process is to fit together the separate plans made for various segments of the enterprise so as to assure that these plans harmonize with one another and that the aggregate effect of all of them on the whole enterprise is satisfactory. For example, the budgeting process might reveal that the sales organization has planned a considerable increase in the sales of one product line but that the production organization has not planned for the additional facilities and manpower necessary to turn out the increased volume; or an expansion of facilities might be planned without adequate consideration of where the funds required to build these facilities are to be obtained. In a very small business, top management may have a sufficient personal awareness of overall plans so that formal, written budgets are unnecessary, but a business of any considerable size is likely to be so complex that some systematic process of formulating and balancing the plans for the separate parts of the enterprise is essential.

Decision Making

Part IV describes how accounting information is used as an aid in making business decisions. Although in one sense all business activities involve decision making, our focus in Part IV is on the type of decision that relates to some specific segment of the business, rather than to operations as a whole. This might be a decision to buy a new machine, to enter a new market, to use a new type of raw material or a new method of manufacturing, to borrow money from a bank, or any of a host of other decisions.

All these decisions are arrived at by, essentially, recognizing that a problem exists, identifying the alternative ways of solving the problem, analyzing the consequences of each alternative, and comparing these consequences so as to decide which is best. Accounting information is useful especially in the analysis step.

SOME GENERAL CONSIDERATIONS

Before we plunge into detail, it may be well to consider briefly a few general matters that apply to all sorts of problems and to all types of figures, both accounting and nonaccounting. Although they are introduced here, it is not expected that these points will become entirely meaningful or concrete until the student has had an opportunity to examine them and to think about their relevance in specific case situations. It may therefore be desirable to refer back to these points from time to time.

Different Figures for Different Purposes

In mathematics, and in most of the physical sciences, there are definitions that are valid under a wide variety of circumstances. Such is not the case with most accounting definitions. Each of the purposes described in the preceding section requires a different kind of accounting figure. Since these different figures may superficially resemble one another and may even be called by the same name, a person who is not familiar with them may easily become confused or frustrated. The most common source of confusion is the word "cost." As will be seen in later chapters, there are historical costs, standard costs, original costs, net costs, residual costs, variable costs, differential costs, incremental costs, marginal costs, opportunity costs, direct costs, estimated costs, and full costs. Some of these terms are synonymous; others are almost but not quite synonymous; still others, although not synonymous at all, are used by some as if they were synonymous.

Accounting figures should always be discussed in terms of the particular problem that they are intended to help solve, rather than in any abstract sense. A statement that "the cost of such-and-such is $100" literally has no meaning unless those who hear this statement understand clearly which of the several possible concepts of cost was intended. A useful procedure to follow in approaching a specific problem is to define, as carefully as possible, the purpose for which figures are to be used in that problem and then to consider how the figures should be assembled and used for that specific purpose.

Accounting Figures Are Approximations

Accounting is a system for recording and summarizing measurements of business facts, and, as is the case with any measurement, an accounting figure is an approximation rather than a precisely accurate statement. Most of the data used in the physical sciences are also measurements, and like the scientists and engineers, the user of accounting information must acquire an understanding of the degree of approximation that is present in the data.

Consider, for example, the concept of temperature. With the proper instruments, the temperature of the human body is easily measured to a tenth of a degree and that of a room to a degree or so, but the temperature of the sun is measurable only in very approximate terms. Although these measurements differ widely in their degree of accuracy, each is useful for a particular purpose. Similarly, some accounting figures, such as the amount of cash on hand, may be accurate within very narrow limits, while others are only rough approximations.

There are many reasons for the roughness of accounting figures. A few are mentioned here, and others will become apparent in later chapters. One of them is simply that a business is a complicated organism which includes vastly dissimilar elements—money, buildings, morale, machines, incentives, materials, policies, and so on. There can be no precise way of adding all these diverse elements together so as to form a completely accurate picture of the whole enterprise.

The problem of obtaining reasonably accurate measurements is further complicated by management's desire to obtain information quickly. A rough approximation that is available today is often more useful to management than a more accurate figure published a year from now. For instance, consider the cost of owning and operating an automobile. This cost includes the purchase price of the automobile, plus the cost of gasoline, repairs, and other operating items, less anything that is received when the automobile is sold or traded. The total cost cannot be known exactly until after the automobile has been sold or traded. Businessmen are unwilling to wait this long for information about what an automobile costs, however; they want information every year, every month, or perhaps oftener. In order to provide this information, the accountant must work with estimates of how many years or months the automobile will be used in the future and how much will be received when it is eventually sold or traded. The accuracy of any interim figure on the cost of the automobile depends on the validity of these estimates.

For the same reason that automobile costs cannot be precisely determined until the automobile is sold, the profit of a whole company cannot be precisely determined accurately until the company goes out of business. Also, for reasons to be discussed subsequently, the profit of a division, a product, or other segment of a company usually cannot be measured with close accuracy. Nevertheless, management needs information on costs and profits for short periods of time, such as a month, and for individual divisions, products, or other segments of a business. Accounting will furnish such information, and it can be most helpful to management. (After all, one needs only a rough approximation of the outside temperature in order to decide whether to wear an overcoat.) Management must clearly understand, however, the approximations that are inherent in most accounting figures.

The degree of approximation is especially high in the case of the figures used for planning purposes. Such figures are always estimates of what will happen in the future. But businessmen are not clairvoyant; they do not *know* what will happen in the future, and the figures used for planning purposes can be no better than their estimates of what the future holds.

Working with Incomplete Data

No one could ask a person to solve a problem in mathematics without furnishing him all the information he needs. In a business problem, on the other hand, one almost never has exactly the information he would like to have. In nearly every case given in this book, you can think of additional information that would be helpful if it were available. This is what happens also in practical business situations. On the other hand, there are many business situations in which page after page of figures are available, but only a small fraction of them are at all relevant to the problem at hand, and perhaps none of them is quite what you need to solve the problem.

It is a fact of life, however, that problems must be solved, business decisions must be made, and often the decision cannot be delayed until all the pertinent information is available. One does the best he can with what he has, and then moves on to the next problem. On the other hand, a decision should not be made if a vital, obtainable piece of evidence is missing. Deciding whether or not to act on the available evidence is one of the most difficult parts of the whole decision process. As the late Dean Wallace B. Donham has put it: "The art of business is the art of making irrevocable decisions on the basis of inadequate information."

Figure Evidence Is Only Partial Evidence

Few, if any, business problems can be solved solely by the collection and analysis of figures. Usually, there are important factors that cannot be, or have not been, reduced to numbers. For example, think of how you would judge the performance of a baseball player. Every time a baseball player comes to bat, and almost every time he handles the ball in the field, a statistic is generated. Detailed records are published on his times at bat, walks, hits, slugging, two-base hits, home runs, strikeouts, putouts, fielding chances, assists, errors, earned run average, and so on. Nevertheless, when the manager of the team must decide whether A is a better ball player than B, he knows better than to rely completely on the numerical information. Such factors as how well a man gets along with his colleagues, his ability to hit in the pinches, and other unmeasurable characteristics must also be taken into account. If the question of a ball player's ability could be answered solely by an analysis of statistics, there would be no reason for the millions of man-hours of discussion by the "hot-stove league" during the winter months.

Some people act as if problems could be completely solved by numerical analysis. They have the erroneous idea that solely from a knowledge of loads, stresses, and material strengths the engineer can figure just how a bridge should look, disregarding the element of judgment completely. At the other extreme, there are those who believe that intuition is the sure guide to a sound decision, and who therefore pay no attention to the figures. Although the correct attitude is clearly somewhere between these extremes, there is no way of describing precisely where it is. Thus, an important objective of the cases in this book is to provide the student with a basis for reaching his own conclusion on the relative importance of figure and nonfigure data in the solution of management problems.

People, Not Figures, Get Things Done

An obvious fact about business organizations is that they consist of human beings. Anything that the business accomplishes is the result of the action of these people. Figures can assist the people in the organization in various ways, but the figures themselves are nothing more than marks on pieces of paper; by themselves they accomplish nothing. It is surprising how often this point is overlooked.

An accounting system may be beautifully designed and carefully operated, but the system is of no use to management unless it results in action by human beings. For instance, three companies may use exactly the same system—the same chart of accounts, the same set of records and reports, the same procedure for collecting and disseminating information—with entirely different results. In one company, the system may be *useless* because management never acts on the information collected, and the organization has become aware of this fact. In the second company, the system may be *helpful* because management uses the information as a general guide for planning and control and has educated the organization to use it in the same spirit. In the third company, the system may be *worse than useless* because management overemphasizes the importance of the figures and therefore takes unwise actions.

SUMMARY

In this book we shall discuss some powerful tools that can assist management in the tasks of operating a business. The invention and refinement of these tools have, in a significant way, made possible the creation and efficient operation of large enterprises, and it is scarcely conceivable that any business, except the smallest ones, could operate without them. At the same time we shall explore the limitations on the use of these tools. We shall see that in the real world, formulas or mechanical techniques rarely provide the complete solution to a problem. The essential reason for these limitations has been well summed up by G. K. Chesterton:

> The real trouble with this world of ours is not that it is an unreasonable world, nor even that it is a reasonable one. The commonest kind of trouble is that it is nearly reasonable, but not quite. Life is not an illogicality; yet it is a trap for logicians. It looks just a little more mathematical and regular than it is; its exactitude is obvious, but its inexactitude is hidden; its wildness lies in wait.[1]

CASES

CASE 1–1.   CONAN COMPANY

The Conan Company manufactured an inexpensive grade of men's clothing which it sold through house-to-house salesmen. A salesman took the measurements of the customer and entered them on the order blank, which the company used as a cutting order. Since the company found from experience that the measurements were usually of approxi-

---

[1] *Orthodoxy* (London: The Bodley Head, 1949 reprint), p. 131.

Exhibit 1

CUTTING RECORD

Cutting Ticket Number	Cutter	Style	Cloth	Color	Size	Yards Saved	Yards Lost
1	A	102	1073	Grey	37	...	0.10
2	B	101	1116	Blue	39	...	0.02
3	C	104	1178	Blue	37	...	0.10
4	D	103	1241	Brown	38	0.04	...
5	A	102	1073	Brown	40	...	0.14
6	B	101	1116	Brown	38	0.04	...
7	C	104	1178	Blue	38	...	0.06
8	A	103	1241	Brown	36	0.08	...
9	D	103	1241	Grey	35	0.10	...
10	B	104	1178	Grey	37	0.06	...
11	C	101	1116	Blue	36	...	0.06
12	A	101	1116	Grey	40	0.02	...
13	B	104	1178	Brown	37	0.00	0.00
14	D	104	1178	Blue	39	0.06	...
15	C	101	1116	Blue	36	...	0.08
16	A	103	1241	Brown	38	0.04	...
17	C	102	1073	Brown	40	...	0.18
18	D	103	1241	Blue	42	0.02	...
19	B	103	1241	Grey	36	...	0.04
20	A	102	1073	Brown	37	...	0.08
21	C	102	1073	Grey	37	...	0.16
22	B	102	1073	Brown	36	...	0.10
23	C	103	1241	Brown	38	0.02	...
24	A	104	1178	Grey	38	0.06	...
25	D	101	1116	Brown	36	0.04	...
26	B	104	1178	Brown	37	0.08	...
27	C	104	1178	Blue	39	0.02	...
28	A	101	1116	Grey	37	...	0.06
29	D	101	1116	Blue	42	0.08	...
30	B	104	1178	Grey	38	0.04	...
31	C	103	1241	Blue	37	...	0.12
32	A	103	1241	Grey	40	...	0.02
33	B	103	1241	Blue	38	0.02	...
34	C	101	1116	Blue	36	...	0.04
35	D	102	1073	Brown	39	...	0.06
36	B	101	1116	Grey	35	0.06	...
37	C	104	1178	Blue	44	...	0.06
38	A	102	1073	Grey	37	...	0.18
39	D	103	1241	Brown	40	0.02	...
40	C	103	1241	Brown	38	...	0.04

mately regular sizes, it cut the garments from regular-size patterns with only slight changes. The wool worsted goods used by the Conan Company cost approximately $3 per yard.

In order to insure very quick delivery the company made out cutting tickets for each garment as fast as orders were received and distributed them to the cutters together with a record of the standard yardage allowance for cutting that size of that style garment. It was expected that cutters would try to cut garments out of the least amount of cloth possible in order to keep down costs. They were, of course, also expected to cut as many garments as possible in a day. Each cutter earned $1.80 per hour and worked eight hours per day.

A careful record was kept of the garments cut each day. A transcript of the cutting record for one day is shown in Exhibit 1.[2] Yardage figures are given to the hundredth of a yard for ease in computation.

Questions

1. What conclusions can you draw from a cross-classification of yardage lost or saved according to cutters and styles? (By cross-classification is meant an orderly arrangement of the figures, grouped in column and row according to cutter, or style, or some other factor.) Who is apparently the fastest cutter? The most careful cutter? The best cutter?

2. Comment on the reliability and adequacy of the standards used to measure performance.

3. Should the most careful cutter specialize on the style for which losses are most frequent?

4. Before taking any action, what additional information would be needed?

CASE 1–2.   C. R. HAYES, INC.

Mr. F. W. Walker, the personnel manager of C. R. Hayes, Inc., a department store doing a business of approximately $30,000,000 annually, was charged with the responsibility for all matters relating to personnel in the store. He arranged for the hiring and the firing of all the store salespeople and also considered all salary increases and decreases of both selling and nonselling employees.

It was the policy of the store to review a salesperson's record every 12 months on the anniversary of his entrance into the store. On the anniversary date the salesperson's department manager received a form

---

[2] The sample used in this case is too small to be adequate. A small sample is used, however, to bring out certain points without requiring the student to spend time on mere mechanical handling of a large number of figures. For purposes of class discussion, you may assume that this record is representative.

raising the question of whether or not the weekly rate should be increased. If this form was returned with the approval of the department manager, a salesperson's record would be examined in detail. Recommendations for increases required the approval of the store manager and the vice president as well as the department head. A salesperson could ask the personnel manager directly for an increase in salary at any time, and such requests were common.

Early in March 1960, Mr. Walker had on his desk, awaiting action, three requests for increases in salary resulting from anniversary reviews. The applicants were from different departments of the store, one being from the women's better shoe department, another from the stationery department, and the third from the silverware department. In addition to these three, Mr. Walker had received a personal request for a raise from Mr. Perrin, who handled the selling of boys' shoes.

In considering the merits of requests for increases, Mr. Walker examined first the sales performance of the salespersons. The store maintained records of the salaries and sales of all salespersons in order to facilitate fair judgment of their accomplishments, since clearly the store could afford to pay higher salaries only to salespeople maintaining a high volume of sales. Greatest attention was paid to the direct selling expense ratio; that is, selling salaries plus commissions divided by sales volume. This expense ratio was recorded by months for each salesperson. Store executives regularly examined this ratio for departments and for the store as a whole. In 1952, the sales expense ratio for the store as a whole had been 6.3 per cent. Pressure was constantly maintained to reduce the selling costs of the store, and for this reason the expense ratio for individual salespeople was examined with care.

Sales and Expense Data

Of the four salespeople whose salaries were under review, the lowest expense ratio was that of Miss Marsten, who was employed in the silverware department. In the year ended January 31, 1960,[3] Miss Marsten sold $77,349 worth of merchandise. Her salary payments during the year totaled $1,880 and she earned $595 in commissions. Thus, total selling costs were $2,475, which was 3.2 per cent of sales. Miss Young in the women's better shoe department had been paid $2,530, plus commissions of $493 during the same period. The total

---

[3] Like many department stores, C. R. Hayes, Inc., maintained records for fiscal years running from February 1 through January 31, rather than for the calendar year from January 1 through December 31. The term "1959" as used in this case refers to the year ended January 31, 1960.

was 6.9 per cent of her sales volume of $43,824. Salary payments to Mr. Dagmar in the stationery department amounted to $2,016 and commissions to $251. These selling costs were 6.4 per cent of his selling volume of $35,418. Mr. Perrin, who was selling boys' shoes, was paid a salary of $2,704 and commissions of $280. His selling expense ratio was 12.2 per cent of a sales volume of $24,468.

In addition to salary and commission, shoe salespeople were able to gain extra pay by selling merchandise that the store wished to move. These special bonuses for sales of "premium merchandise" were called P.M.'s. Such premium payments were not classed with salaries and commissions in calculating expense ratios and, therefore, had no bearing on the performance record of the various salespeople. In 1959, Miss Young received $112 in P.M.'s and Mr. Perrin received $110.

In terms of service, Mr. Perrin had been with the store the longest, having come on December 4, 1931; Miss Marsten joined the store in February 1941; Miss Young came in January 1950; and Mr. Dagmar had been with the store only since December 1958.

The sales records of these four salespeople for the three years, 1957, 1958, and 1959, are shown in Exhibit 1 with similar records for other salespeople in the respective departments and in one additional department. The sales figure for each department as a whole is in every instance larger than the sum of the sales of the salespeople listed, for several reasons. C. R. Hayes, Inc., in common with many other department stores, was open for business more than 50 hours a week, whereas the regular full-time salespeople were employed for a 40-hour workweek. This required the use of short-hour and extra people, a group in which there was considerable turnover. Members of the store's flying squad also were used to supplement the regulars when additional salespeople were required. The selling expense ratio for each department reflected wage payments (including commissions and vacation pay to regulars) for all the selling man-hours used in relation to total departmental sales.

The Departments Involved

In examining the merits of the four applicants, Mr. Walker had to consider other information. For one thing, the physical arrangements for selling were by no means the same in all departments. In the better shoe department, salespeople could serve any customer at any point on the floor. Shoe salespeople were not behind counters as were the salespeople in the silverware department. Also, since selling shoes required some intimate knowledge of proper fitting, styles, and so forth, frequently the customer would ask for the services of a particular person.

Exhibit 1

DIRECT SELLING EXPENSE RATIO AND RELATED DATA, BY INDIVIDUAL SALESPEOPLE, FIVE DEPARTMENTS

Department	Direct Selling Expense Ratio			Sales			Entrance Date	Date of Last Raise	Base Rate per Week
	1957	1958	1959	1957	1958	1959			1959
Women's Better Shoe:									
Entire department..	9.4%	8.7%	9.5%	$440,091	$462,093	$464,461			
Miss Clark........	9.3	8.5	8.5	30,112	34,719	35,201	2/44	2/57	$53.50
Mr. Enders........	9.3	9.0	9.2	34,201	36,901	37,090	9/56	9/59	60.00
Mr. Elliot.........	8.8	8.3	9.1	36,540	39,712	38,076	10/47	10/59	60.00
Miss Aspinwald*...	8.3	8.0	8.2	29,211	31,019	30,180	9/26	9/56	46.00
Mr. Smith.........	8.2	7.9	8.2	39,109	40,781	41,211	2/46	2/59	60.00
Miss Sanders.......	7.8	7.4	7.4	44,921	46,753	47,063	12/49	12/56	62.00
Mr. Hanking......	9.0	9.0	9.5	34,724	35,651	36,102	5/56	5/59	60.00
Miss Johnson......	8.6	8.0	7.9	35,092	38,920	40,610	11/45	11/57	54.00
Miss Young†	7.5	7.2	6.9	39,651	41,786	43,824	1/50	1/57	55.00
Boys' Shoes:									
Mr. Perrin†	12.7	12.4	12.2	23,664	24,183	24,468	12/31	.....	52.00
Stationery:									
Entire department..	9.1	7.9	7.3	282,852	308,349	364,491			
Miss Bard.........	11.1	11.1	10.0	21,208	21,421	23,449	11/56	11/57	42.00
Miss Cox..........	9.0	8.1	7.4	25,556	27,360	29,994	3/38	3/56	42.00
Mr. Dagmar†	..	..	6.4	......	....	35,418	12/58	.....	42.00
Miss Dorn.........	..	7.0	6.4	......	33,406	36,765	9/57	.....	44.00
Miss Gorden.......	7.1	6.3	5.5	31,422	35,076	41,039	8/45	8/57	42.00
Miss Scott.........	8.3	7.7	6.6	27,490	29,600	34,868	3/50	3/56	42.00
Miss Seick	6.4	6.4	5.6	35,750	36,281	41,478	4/56	4/57	43.00
Silverware:									
Entire department..	6.0	4.8	5.0	184,123	252,098	271,002			
Miss Hitchcock....	4.2	3.6	3.6	56,027	65,039	66,811	1/40	1/56	46.00
Miss Marsten†	4.0	3.5	3.2	67,418	73,801	77,349	2/41	2/57	47.00
Miss Santos.......	..	6.3	5.3	......	34,032	40,001	1/58	.....	40.00
Miss Morse........	..	..	5.6	......	......	38,119	4/59	.....	40.00
Women's and Children's Hosiery:									
Entire department..	6.3	7.0	7.2	380,070	368,009	324,204			
Miss Austin*......	7.1	7.9	10.2	23,516	21,066	16,296	3/56	.....	40.00
Miss Banter.......	6.6	5.7	5.4	34,590	39,079	41,209	12/55	12/57	43.00
Miss Boyle........	5.3	5.2	5.9	44,501	45,333	39,190	10/56	.....	45.00
Mrs. Epstein.......	7.1	7.6	8.1	36,010	34,333	31,977	8/46	8/56	47.00
Mrs. Hawkes......	5.8	5.4	5.5	39,920	43,016	42,494	3/56	.....	45.00
Miss Moore........	6.1	6.4	7.2	39,597	37,076	33,486	10/47	10/57	45.00
Miss Oppenheimer.	5.5	5.8	6.5	40,496	38,252	34,035	12/55	12/57	42.00
Entire Store:									
All Selling Departments...........	6.4	6.4	6.9						

* Part-time worker.
† Salary under review.

The silverware department, manned regularly by four full-time salespeople, sold hollow ware, flatware, and small novelty and gift items. Whereas everyone was allowed to sell any of the merchandise, the position of the cash drawers operated by the several persons actually resulted in "station selling," with the old-timers responsible for the flat and hollow ware, and the newer people taking care of the novelty items. This department was particularly busy at certain times of the year when special promotions were made.

In the stationery department a variety of goods were sold, ranging from card tables to cameras. The arrangement of selling space in this department was not particularly good. On one side of the department were two long counters back to back with stationery displayed and sold on both sides. Access to the position behind the counters was at the ends only. To the right of this double counter were several aisle tables from which department items were sold. In addition, a facing wall counter beyond the aisle tables was provided, this position being used, as of 1959, for the sales of greeting cards at one end and cameras and related equipment and supplies at the other. Mr. Dagmar, in charge of the cameras, was the employee here whose compensation was up for review. The camera section of the stationery department had been established February 1, 1959.

Mr. Perrin was the only regular salesman in the boys' shoe department, which was a small department located next to the boys' clothing department. If a customer was waiting to be sold boys' clothing and Mr. Perrin was not busy, he could step across the aisle to make the sales in the other department and would receive credit for such sales. When Mr. Perrin had first joined the store, he had sold men's clothing. During World War II and the years following, he had been working on a straight commission basis, which, in a period of high consumer demand, yielded a substantially larger income than did the commissions received in many of the other departments. In 1955, he had been transferred to the boys' shoe department where the compensation method used was salary plus 1 per cent of sales. Thus his earnings had been considerably reduced, and he was anxious to obtain a salary increase. Mr. Walker, on inquiring of a noncompeting department store, found that its expense ratio was 11 per cent in the boys' shoe department, where two people were employed.

Merchandise sold in the various departments was priced at different levels, and the unit sales usually varied accordingly. The dollars per sales check in the silverware department averaged $15.00 in 1959; in the stationery department, the average sales check was $1.40; in the women's shoe department, it was $12.29; and in the boys' shoe department, it was $7.00.

Miscellaneous Information

The personnel department had the full history of each salesperson's performance. Records were kept on absences, tardiness, and on any infringements of the store rules. In addition, the department managers were asked to rate the salespeople in their department as to sales ability, stock care, cooperation, and general suitability. The rating of sales ability was supposed to take into account sales volume, credits (merchandise returned), merchandise knowledge, and service. "Stock care" referred to the salesperson's method of handling merchandise and keeping stock in good order. In judging cooperation the managers were supposed to consider the salesperson's record in the carrying out of store rules, compliance with instructions, punctuality, helpfulness to others, and special effort. In rating suitability the managers considered the fitness, by personality, appearance, and so forth, of the salesperson for the particular department and position from the point of view of both the customer and the store. The records on these points for the four people whose salaries were under review were satisfactory.

The employees of C. R. Hayes, Inc., had been organized into a store union since the middle of 1936. This was an independent union, not affiliated with any other labor organization, and was the outgrowth of an old cooperative union which had been established in the store. The union had taken no position in regard to the four cases being reviewed by Mr. Walker.

Questions

1. There are many "yardsticks" against which the performance of the four employees being considered for raises can be compared. For example, their selling expense ratios can be compared with the overall ratio for the store, with the average ratio for the department, with ratios for prior years, and so on. Which of these yardsticks is of most significance to Mr. Walker?

2. What action should Mr. Walker recommend with respect to each of the four employees being considered for raises?

CASE 1–3.   MASSACHUSETTS BUSINESS DEVELOPMENT
CORPORATION

At a meeting in May 1954, the executive committee of the Massachusetts Business Development Corporation was considering a request for a ten-year loan of $80,000 from the Quality Weldments Company of Quincy. The loan, which would be payable in ten annual installments, would carry interest at 6 per cent. Quality Weldments wanted the loan to help finance a move to new quarters, which it estimated would cost $118,000. It hoped to finance this amount as follows:

MBDC loan.	$ 80,000
Northeastern National Bank.	13,000
Additional loans from stockholders.	25,000
	$118,000

Massachusetts Business Development Corporation

The Massachusetts Business Development Corporation was created by a special act of the Massachusetts legislature in July 1953. Its purpose was to promote economic activity in Massachusetts by providing local industries with financing of a type otherwise not readily available. The corporation derived its funds from the sale of its stock and from loans made by cooperating financial institutions. In 1954 it had several million dollars available, which was believed to be adequate to meet all sound requests for loans that were pending at that time.

Many Massachusetts business leaders were included among the incorporators of the company. The executive committee consisted of nine men prominent in industrial and financial affairs in the state.

Quality Weldments Company

The Quality Weldments Company operated a small metal fabrication shop in Quincy specializing in the production of steel weldments. The production of weldments, which are used in many cases to replace castings, was a comparatively new industry in 1954. Six or eight firms, including Quality Weldments, produced almost all the weldments sold in the New England market. Production of weldments required a much higher degree of skill and technical knowledge than was found in the typical welding shop.

The company was formed in 1946 by two engineering graduates of Tufts College. Mr. Michael A. Cifrino, who was 36 in 1954, handled sales and administration. After graduation from Tufts, Mr. Cifrino had worked as an engineer on the Panama Canal and had served three years in the Navy. Mr. John P. Parks, who was 41, was in charge of engineering and production. Prior to joining Quality Weldments, he had worked for eight years as a welding engineer at the Boston Naval Shipyard.

The Quincy plant was the company's second location. An earlier move had been made in 1951 when the company's original quarters had become inadequate. There were 10,000 square feet of usable space in the Quincy building. The company occupied the property under a lease running until November 1955, which called for monthly rental payments of $750. Under the terms of the lease, the company was required to supply its own utilities and services and to maintain the building in good shape.

The company's sales had quadrupled between 1949 and 1952. Messrs. Cifrino and Parks expected the growth in sales to continue. They pointed out that Lincoln Electric Company, a leading producer of weldments, estimated that only one quarter of the potential New England market had been tapped.

Recent financial information about the company is given in Exhibits 1, 2, and 3.

Exhibit 1

QUALITY WELDMENTS COMPANY

Comparative Income Statements

	Fiscal Year Ending August 31			6 Mos. Ending February 28	
	1951	1952	1953	1953	1954
Net sales..........................	$174,339	$297,137	$349,540	$163,721	$249,556
Cost of goods sold (see Exhibit 2)....	139,010	270,224	300,572	130,476	208,623
Gross profit.......................	$ 35,329	$ 26,913	$ 48,968	$ 33,245	$ 40,933
Selling, administrative, and general expense.......................	11,004	19,070	26,978	12,136	19,464
Net income from operations..........	$ 24,325	$ 7,843	$ 21,990	$ 21,109	$ 21,469
Other charges against income.........	20,577	515	2,695	1,229	1,741
Net income before taxes..............	$ 3,748	$ 7,328	$ 19,295	$ 19,880	$ 19,728
Federal and state taxes on income.....	1,516	2,960	6,942	7,173	7,102
Net Income.......................	$ 2,232	$ 4,368	$ 12,353	$ 12,707	$ 12,626

Proposed Relocation

By the spring of 1954, the company had again outgrown its plant and was searching for a new location. In order to be closer to its major customers, the company looked for a site near Worcester, Massachusetts. The building selected contained about 12,500 square feet of usable space on a plot of approximately ten acres. The property, which could be purchased outright for $30,000, had recently been appraised by a local bank at $42,000. Property taxes were approximately $300 a year. Messrs. Cifrino and Parks considered the physical facilities in the new building to be ideal for their purposes.

In addition to the purchase price, the company estimated it would have to spend about $68,000 in refitting the building and in moving its equipment (see Exhibit 4). It also hoped to buy a new power shear for $20,000; this would permit it to purchase steel directly from the producers rather than through jobbers, with a consequent saving in cost.

Exhibit 2

QUALITY WELDMENTS COMPANY

Analysis of Cost of Goods Sold

	Fiscal Year Ending August 31			6 Mos. Ending February 28	
	1951	1952	1953	1953	1954
Inventory, beginning of period........		$ 14,017	$ 11,262	$ 11,262	$ 24,132
Purchase of raw materials............		103,570	102,208	43,413	73,369
Paid to subcontractors..............	Not	7,850	10,208	5,132	8,389
Paid to labor......................		90,857	118,508	54,541	91,093
Factory expense*..................	Available	65,192	82,517	33,620	57,206
Total.........................		$281,486	$324,704	$147,968	$254,189
Less: Inventory, end of period........		11,262	24,132	17,492	45,566
Cost of Goods Sold..............		$270,224	$300,572	$130,476	$208,623

* Factory expense includes Mr. Parks' salaries (about $13,000 in 1953); depreciation; rent, heat, light, and power; and maintenance and repairs. Mr. Cifrino's salary ($13,500 in 1953) was included in selling, general, and administrative expense.

If the move was made, the company expected to save approximately $26,000 annually at its present volume of sales. Of this amount, $10,000 would result from the direct purchase of steel which would be made possible by use of the power shear. The balance would result from elimination of overtime work in the new plant. Because of the crowded conditions at Quincy, it was frequently necessary to employ labor at premium rates in order to finish jobs by the time they had been promised.

The company would have to replace most of its sixty production employees if it moved to Worcester. In addition, it planned to increase its labor force by 12 to 18 employees. Since there was some unemployment in the Worcester area, no problem was expected in hiring new

Exhibit 3

QUALITY WELDMENTS COMPANY

Comparative Balance Sheets

	August 31 1951	August 31 1952	August 31 1953	Feb. 28, 1954
ASSETS				
Current Assets:				
Cash..........................	$ 8,381	$12,772	$ 16,241	$ 15,788
Accounts receivable.................	8,455	18,388	25,675	43,268
Inventories.......................	14,017	11,262	24,132	45,566
Prepaid rent......................	1,250	1,250	1,250	1,250
Total Current Assets............	$32,103	$43,672	$ 67,298	$105,872
Fixed Assets:				
Machinery and equipment...........	$19,256	$38,206	$ 42,684	$ 46,710
Jigs and tools.....................	738	850	850	850
Office equipment..................	745	955	955	955
Autos............................	.....	1,980	4,178	4,178
Total Fixed Assets..............	$20,739	$41,991	$ 48,667	$ 52,693
Less: Accumulated depreciation.......	6,022	8,872	13,604	16,435
Net Fixed Assets................	$14,717	$33,119	$ 35,063	$ 36,258
Deferred Charges......................	886	430	430	430
Total......................	$47,706	$77,221	$102,791	$142,560
LIABILITIES AND NET WORTH				
Current Liabilities:				
Notes payable to bank—unsecured.....	$ 850	$ 5,825	$ 1,750	$ 18,500
Notes payable to bank—equip. oblig...	.....	1,017	4,569	2,697
Accounts payable...................	5,305	16,951	21,130	26,841
Taxes withheld from employees.......	722	2,665	1,881	2,459
Accrued expenses..................	2,768	3,282	3,395	3,348
Federal and state income taxes........	908	2,960	6,942	9,965
Total Current Liabilities.........	$10,553	$32,700	$ 39,667	$ 63,810
Notes payable to stockholders........	19,000	22,000	23,250	26,250
Total Liabilities................	$29,553	$54,700	$ 62,917	$ 90,060
Net Worth:				
Capital stock......................	$12,500	$12,500	$ 17,500	$ 17,500
Retained earnings..................	5,653	10,021	22,374	35,000
Total Net Worth...............	$18,153	$22,521	$ 39,874	$ 52,500
Total......................	$47,706	$77,221	$102,791	$142,560

Exhibit 4

DETAIL OF MOVING AND REFITTING EXPENSES

Moving expense	$14,000
Bridges and cranes	22,500
Electrical wiring	10,000
New floor	4,500
Outside racks and cranes	4,500
Heating system	3,750
Installation of equipment	2,250
Office	2,250
Paint and blastrooms	1,500
Manifolds	1,500
Washrooms	1,250
	$68,000

workers. Most of the company's supervisory employees had expressed a willingness to move with the company.

Investigation by MBDC

In addition to the information contained in the company's loan application, the executive committee had received a report from Mr. F. P. Brennan, chief examiner of MBDC. Mr. Brennan had visited the company and was impressed by the technical and administrative abilities of Messrs. Cifrino and Parks, whom he termed "capable and aggressive." He believed that management of their caliber was unusual in a company the size of Quality Weldments.

Mr. Brennan looked over the list of the company's customers. It included many large firms with national reputations and excellent credit ratings. Many of these companies had become customers of Quality Weldments relatively recently. At the end of April, the company had unfilled orders of about $115,000.

Mr. Brennan also visited the Northeastern National Bank. The loan officer at the bank confirmed the bank's intention to finance two thirds of the cost of the power shear on a three-year basis. In addition, the bank indicated its willingness to finance the company's seasonal working capital needs. The bank did not feel that it could finance the new building and the moving expenses, however, in view of the long repayment period which would be required. The loan officer pointed out to Mr. Brennan that the size of the financing required was considerably larger than any amount the company had previously borrowed and was also large relative to the size of the company.

At Mr. Brennan's request, the bank supplied a letter to be included with the loan application. Excerpts from the letter follow:

It is our opinion that the management is well above that of comparable concerns and has used its experience and ability to make well-thought-out and sound decisions. . . .

. . . We feel that the proposed plant relocation and investment program, in spite of the resulting heavy debt to investment ratio, would be a wise move if soundly financed. . . .

Questions

1. What standards should the executive committee of MBDC apply in deciding whether to make a loan?

2. If the loan is made, does the evidence indicate that Quality Weldments Company will probably have the ability to repay it over a ten-year period? Consider both (a) the probable amount of money that will become available for this purpose, working with the information in the financial statements, and (b) other information in the case that bears on this question.

3. If you had to act only on the basis of the information available, would you recommend that the $80,000 loan request be approved?

4. Does MBDC need additional information in order to reach a decision? If so, how should it be obtained?

Part

I

THE ACCOUNTING STRUCTURE

Chapter 2 | BASIC ACCOUNTING CONCEPTS

SUPPOSE YOU were asked to keep track of what was going on in a business so as to provide useful information for management. One way of carrying out such an assignment would be to write down a narrative of important events in a diary or in a log similar to that kept by the captain of a ship. After some experience with your log or diary, you would gradually develop a set of rules to guide your efforts. For example, since it would be impossible to write down every action of every person in the business, you would frame rules to guide you in choosing between those events that were important enough to record and those that should be omitted.

You would also find that your diary would be more valuable if you standardized certain terminology. People who studied it would then have a clearer understanding of what you meant. Furthermore, if you standardized terms and definitions of these terms, you could turn the job of keeping the diary over to someone else and have some assurance that his report of events would convey the same information that you would have conveyed had you been keeping the diary personally.

In devising these rules of keeping a diary, you would necessarily be somewhat arbitrary. There might be several ways of describing a certain event, all equally good; but in order to have a common basis of understanding, you would select just one of these for use in your record-keeping system.

All the foregoing considerations were actually involved in the development of accounting, which is the name given to the most commonly used system of maintaining a record of events in a business. Accounting has evolved over a period of several hundred years, and during this time certain rules and conventions have come to be accepted as useful. If you are to understand accounting reports—the end products of an accounting system—you must be familiar with the rules and conventions lying behind these reports. The purpose of this and the next eight chapters is to describe the more common of these rules and conventions.

Accounting as a Language

Accounting has been called the "language of business," and while this may not be a completely apt phrase, you will find that the task of learning accounting is essentially the same as the task of learning a new language.

This task is complicated, however, by the fact that many of the words used in accounting mean almost, but not quite, the same thing as the identical words mean in everyday, nonaccounting usage. If you are an American learning French, you realize from the beginning that the words and the grammar in French are completely new to you and must therefore be learned carefully. The problem of learning accounting, however, is more like that of an American learning to speak English as it is spoken in Great Britain; unless he is careful, the American will fail to recognize that words are used in Great Britain in a different sense from that used in America.

> EXAMPLE: The grain that Americans call "wheat" is called "corn" by the British, and the British use the word "maize" for the grain that Americans call "corn." To complicate the matter further, a grain grown in certain parts of America is called "maize," and it is almost, but not quite, like corn. Unless he understands these differences in terminology, an American will be confused when talking with an Englishman.

Perhaps the greatest difficulty that a beginning student of accounting encounters is that of distinguishing between the accounting meaning of certain terms and the meaning that he has attached to these terms in their nonaccounting, everyday usage.

Accounting also resembles a language in that some of its rules are definite, whereas others are not, and there are differences of opinion among accountants as to how a given event should be recorded, just as there are differences of opinion among grammarians as to many matters of sentence structure, punctuation, and choice of words. Nevertheless, there are many practices that are clearly "poor English," and there are also many practices that are definitely "poor accounting." In these chapters, therefore, an attempt is made to describe the elements of "good accounting" and to indicate areas in which there are differences of opinion as to what constitutes good practice.

Finally, languages evolve and change in response to the changing needs of society, and so does accounting. The rules described here are currently in use, but it is to be expected that at least some of them will gradually be modified to meet the changing needs of business.

NATURE AND SOURCE OF PRINCIPLES

The rules and conventions of accounting are commonly referred to as "principles." The word "principle" is here used to mean "a general law or rule adopted or professed as a guide to action; a settled ground or basis of conduct or practice."[1] Note that this definition describes a principle as a *general* law or rule to be used as a *guide* to action; accounting principles do not prescribe exactly how each detailed event occurring in a business should be recorded. Consequently, there are a great many things in accounting practice that differ from one company to another. In part, these differences are inevitable because a single detailed set of rules could not conceivably apply to every company. In part, the differences reflect the fact that the accountant has considerable latitude within the "generally accepted accounting principles" in which to express his own idea as to the best way of recording and reporting a specific event.

The student should realize therefore that he cannot know the precise meaning of many of the items on an accounting report unless he knows which of several equally acceptable possibilities has been selected by the person who prepared the report. For example, as mentioned in Chapter 1, the simple word "cost" has many different meanings, and there is agreement on the definition of this word only in the broadest sense.

Criteria

Accounting principles are man-made. Unlike the principles of mathematics, physics, chemistry, and the other natural sciences, accounting principles were not deduced from basic axioms, nor is their validity verifiable by observation and experiment. Instead, they have evolved, essentially by the following process: A problem is recognized; someone works out what he thinks is a good solution to this problem; if other people agree that this is a good solution, its use gradually becomes widespread, and then it becomes an accounting principle. Moreover, some hitherto accepted principles fall from favor with the passage of time. This evolutionary process is going on constantly; accounting principles are not "eternal verities."

The general acceptance of an accounting principle or practice usually depends on how well it meets three criteria: usefulness, objectivity, and feasibility. A principle is *useful* to the extent that it results in information

---

[1] AICPA, *Accounting Terminology Bulletin No. 1*, p. 9.

that is meaningful and helpful to those who need to know something about a certain business. A principle is *objective* to the extent that the information is not influenced by the personal bias or judgment of those who furnish it. A principle is *feasible* to the extent that it can be implemented without undue complexity or cost.

We shall illustrate and expand on the significance of these criteria in connection with the discussion of the principles themselves. At this point it is sufficient to point out that these criteria usually conflict with one another. The most useful solution is likely to be the least objective and the least feasible.

In developing new principles, the essential problem is to strike the right balance between usefulness on the one hand and objectivity and feasibility on the other. Failure to appreciate this problem often leads to unwarranted criticism of accounting principles. It is easy to criticize accounting on the grounds that it is not as useful as it might be; but the critic often overlooks the fact that proposals to increase usefulness almost always involve a sacrifice of objectivity and feasibility; on balance such a sacrifice may not be worthwhile.

Sources

Accounting principles are not codified in a single source that resembles, either in the amount of detail or in its authority, the codification of legal principles on which lawyers rely so heavily. Perhaps the most widely recognized authority is the Accounting Principles Board of the American Institute of Certified Public Accountants (AICPA). The Accounting Principles Board was organized in 1959, and so far has issued few opinions of its own. However, it has adopted, until further notice, opinions issued by its predecessor organization, the Committee on Accounting Procedure, as published in the series of *Accounting Research Bulletins* and *Accounting Terminology Bulletins*. Approximately fifty of these bulletins have been published; the principles set forth in each bulletin vary in length from a paragraph to a few pages. Even briefer statements are issued by the "Standards Committees" of the American Accounting Association. A third widely used source of statements about accounting principles are publications of the U.S. Securities and Exchange Commission, particularly its *Regulation S-X* and its *Accounting Series Releases*.

The opinions of the Accounting Principles Board, although the principal source of accounting principles, are not binding even on the members of AICPA. If, however, an AICPA member uses a different principle, he must call attention to this fact, and he must find "substantial support" for his alternative. Evidence of such support usually consists of showing that several reputable companies follow the practice in question.

BASIC CONCEPTS

Listed below are seven concepts that are basic to an understanding of accounting, five of which will be discussed in this chapter and two in the next. They are so basic that most accountants do not consciously refer to them. Some of these concepts are currently undergoing a critical reexamination by the profession, but in this initial contact with them, the student is asked to understand and accept them rather than to criticize them. As is the case with a language, the student can criticize the way certain words are spelled (e.g., "bough," "cough," "doff"), but the fact remains that the words *are* spelled in a certain way, and if he is to use the language effectively, the student must understand what is done.

1. The Money Measurement Concept

In accounting, a record is made only of those facts that can be expressed in monetary terms. This concept imposes a severe limitation on the scope of an accounting report. Accounting does not record the state of the president's health; it does not record the fact that the sales manager is not on speaking terms with the production manager; it does not report that a strike is beginning; and it does not reveal that a competitor has placed a better product on the market. Accounting therefore does not give a complete account of the happenings in a business or an accurate picture of the condition of the business. It follows then that the reader of an accounting report should not expect to find therein all, or perhaps even the most important, facts about a business.

The advantage of expressing facts in monetary terms is that money provides a common denominator by means of which heterogeneous facts about a business can be expressed in terms of numbers that can be added and subtracted.

> EXAMPLE: Although it may be a fact that a business owns $10,000 of cash, 6,000 pounds of raw material, six trucks, 10,000 square feet of building space, and so on, these amounts cannot be added together to produce a meaningful total. Expressing these items in monetary terms —$10,000 of cash, $5,000 of raw material, $20,000 of trucks, and $100,000 of buildings—makes such an addition possible.

Although the common denominator concept is an essential one, and although money is probably the only practical denominator, the use of money implies a homogeneity—a basic similarity between one dollar and another—that may not in fact exist.

> EXAMPLE: In the items listed above, the cash is expressed in today's dollars, but the amounts for the other items may be stated in terms of the dollars used to purchase them some months or some years previously, when a dollar was worth substantially more than a dollar is worth today in terms of real purchasing power.

The problems created by the fact that price levels change over the years will be discussed in Chapter 9.

2. The Business Entity Concept

Accounts are kept for *business entities,* as distinguished from the *persons* who are associated with these entities. In recording facts in the accounts, the important question is: how do they affect the business?—not, how do they affect the persons who own, operate, or otherwise are associated with the business? When the owner takes cash out of his business, for example, the accounting records show that the *business* has less cash than previously, even though the real effect of this event on the *owner* himself may have been negligible; he may have taken cash from his business "pocket" and put it into his personal "pocket," but it remains his cash.

It is sometimes difficult to define the business entity for which a set of accounts is kept. Consider the case of a man and his wife who run a small unincorporated retail store. In *law* there is no distinction between the financial affairs of the store and those of the people who own it, but in *accounting* a set of accounts is kept for the store as a separate business entity, and the events reflected in these accounts must be those of the store; the nonbusiness events that affect the couple must not be included in them. Clearly, this means that the family's expenses for food, clothing, shelter, and the like should be separated from the expenses of running the store. But suppose that the couple lives on the business premises. How much of the rent, the electric light bill, and the property taxes of these premises are properly part of the business and how much are personal expenses of the family? Questions like these make the distinction between the business entity and outside interests a difficult one to make in practice.

In the case of a corporation, the distinction is often quite easily made. A corporation is a legal entity separate from the persons who own it, and the accounts of many corporations correspond exactly to the scope of the legal entity. There may be complications, however. In the case of a group of legally separate corporations that are related to one another by stockholdings, the whole group may be treated as a single business entity for certain purposes, giving rise to what are called "consolidated" accounting statements. Conversely, within a single corporation, a separate set of accounts may be maintained for each of the principal divisions of the corporation, especially when they are physically separated from the home office.

These differences in practice do not complicate matters here since in our introductory cases we shall be dealing only with situations where the definition of the business entity is reasonably clear.

There follows from the distinction between the business entity and the outside world the idea that an important purpose of financial accounting is to provide the basis for reporting on *stewardship*. The managers of a business are entrusted with funds supplied by owners, banks, and others. Management is responsible for the wise use of these funds, and financial accounting reports are in part designed to show how well this responsibility, or stewardship, has been discharged. This is a narrow view of the purpose of financial accounting, because financial accounting reports are likely to be of as much or more use to the management than to the outsider, but it does explain the reasoning behind many accounting principles.

3. The Going-Concern Concept

Unless there is good evidence to the contrary, accounting assumes that the business will continue to operate for an indefinitely long period in the future. The importance of this assumption can be indicated by contrasting it with a possible alternative; namely, that the business is about to be liquidated or sold. Under the latter assumption, accounting would attempt to measure at all times what the business *is currently worth* to a buyer, but under the going-concern assumption there is no need to do this, and it is in fact not done. Instead, a business is viewed as a mechanism for adding value to the resources it uses, and its success is measured by the difference between the value of its output (sales of goods and services) and the cost of the resources used in creating that output. Resources which have been acquired but not yet used in creating output are shown on the accounting records not at their current value to an outside buyer, but rather at their cost. Their current resale value is irrelevant, since it is assumed that they will not be sold as such, but rather that they will be used in the creation of future output values.

4. The Cost Concept

Resources (i.e., rights in tangible and intangible property) owned by a business are called, in accounting language, *assets*. A fundamental concept of accounting, closely related to the going-concern concept described above, is that an asset is ordinarily entered on the accounting records at the price paid to acquire it—that is, at its cost—and that this cost is the basis for all subsequent accounting for the asset.

Since, for a variety of reasons, the real worth of an item may change with the passage of time, the accounting measurement of assets does not necessarily—indeed, does not ordinarily—reflect what assets are worth, except at the moment they are acquired. There is therefore a considerable difference between the accounting concept of cost and the everyday, nonaccounting concept of value, since in its ordinary usage "value" means what something is currently worth.

> EXAMPLE: If a business buys a plot of land, paying $5,000 for it, this asset would be recorded in the accounts of the business at the amount of $5,000. Subsequent changes in the market value of this land would ordinarily not be reflected by changes in the accounts. If a year later the land could be sold for $10,000, or if it could be sold for only $2,000, no change would ordinarily be made in the accounting records to reflect this fact. (The word "ordinarily" is used since there are a few situations in which accounting records are changed to reflect changes in market value; these will be described subsequently.)

Thus, the amounts at which assets are listed in the accounts of a company do *not* indicate what the assets could be sold for. One of the most common mistakes made by uninformed persons reading accounting reports is that of believing that there is a close correspondence between the figure at which an asset appears on these reports and the actual value of the asset. Of course, there may well be a correspondence between accounting measurements and real market values in the case of certain assets. The asset "cash" is the best example. Readily marketable securities and inventories held by the company for only a short period of time may appear on the books at figures that are close to their actual worth. In general, it is safe to say that the longer an asset has been owned by a company, the less likely it is that the amount at which it appears on the accounting records corresponds to its current market value.

The cost concept does not mean that all assets remain on the accounting records at their original purchase price for as long as the company owns them. The figure for an asset that has a long, but nevertheless limited, life is systematically reduced over that life by the process called *depreciation,* as discussed in more detail in Chapter 6. The purpose of the depreciation process is gradually to remove the *cost* of the asset from the accounts and show it as a cost of operations; depreciation has no necessary relationship to changes in market value or in the real worth of the asset to the company.

It follows from the cost concept that if the company pays *nothing* for an item it acquires, this item will usually *not* appear on the accounting records as an asset. Thus, the knowledge and skill that is built up as the business operates, the teamwork that grows up within the organization, a favorable location that becomes of increasing importance as time goes on, a good reputation with its customers—none of these appears as an asset in the accounts of the company.

On some accounting reports, you will see the term "goodwill"; and reasoning from the everyday definition of this word, you may conclude that it represents the accountant's appraisal of what the company's name and reputation are worth. This is not so. Goodwill appears in the accounts of the company only when the company has *purchased* some intangible and valuable property right. A common case is when one company buys another company and pays more than the fair value of the tangible assets owned by that company. The amount by which the purchase price exceeds the value of the tangible assets may be called goodwill, representing the value of the name, the reputation, the location, or other intangible possessions of the purchased company. Unless the business has actually purchased such intangibles, however, no item for "goodwill" is shown in the accounts. If the item does appear, it is shown initially at the purchase price, even though the management may believe that its real value is considerably higher.

It also follows from the cost concept that an event may affect the true value of a business without having any effect on the accounting records. To take an extreme case, suppose that several key executives are killed in a plane accident. To the extent that "an organization is but the lengthened shadow of a man," the real value of the company will change immediately, and this will be reflected in the market price of the company's stock, which reflects investors' appraisal of value. The accounting records, however, will not be affected by this event.

The cost concept provides an excellent illustration of the problem of applying the three basic criteria discussed in the preceding section: usefulness, objectivity, and feasibility. If the *only* criterion were usefulness, then the cost concept would not be defensible. Clearly, investors and others are more interested in what the business is actually worth today rather than what the assets cost originally.

But who knows what a business is worth today? The fact is that any estimate of current value is just that—an estimate—and informed people will disagree on what is the right estimate. (For illustrations, see the judgments about companies that are reported in the financial press. On the same day, some people will say that the stock of a given company is "overpriced" and others will say that it is "underpriced.") Furthermore, accounting reports are prepared by the management of a business, and if they contained estimates of what the business is actually worth, these would be management's estimates. It is quite possible that such estimates would be biased.

The cost concept, by contrast, provides a relatively objective foundation for accounting. It is not purely objective, for, as we shall see, judgments are necessary in applying it. It is much more objective than the alternative of attempting to estimate current values, however. Essentially, the reader of an accounting report must recognize that it is based on the cost concept, and he must arrive at his own estimate of current value, partly by analyzing the information in the report and partly by using nonaccounting information.

Furthermore, a "market value" or "current worth" concept would be difficult to apply, because it would require that the accountant attempt to keep track of the ups and downs of market prices. The cost concept leads to a system that is much more feasible.

In summary, adherence to the cost concept indicates a willingness on the part of those who developed accounting principles to sacrifice some degree of usefulness in exchange for greater objectivity and greater feasibility.

5. The Dual-Aspect Concept

As stated above, the resources owned by a business are called "assets." The claims of various parties against these assets are called "equities." There are two types of equities: (1) *liabilities,* which are the claims of creditors, i.e., everyone other than the owners of the business; and (2) *owners' equity* (or "capital," or "proprietorship"), which is the claim of the owners of the business.[2] Since all of the assets of a business are claimed by someone (either by the owners or by some outside party) and since the total of these claims cannot exceed the amount of assets to be claimed, it follows that—

$$\text{ASSETS} = \text{EQUITIES} .$$

Accounting systems are set up in such a way that a record is made of *two aspects* of each event that affects these records, and in essence these aspects are changes in assets and changes in equities.

---

[2] Some accountants use the word "liabilities" to include both the claims of creditors and the claims of owners; when so used it is synonymous with the word "equities" as used here. The narrower meaning is used here for the sake of clarity.

Suppose that a man starts a business and that his first act is to open a bank account in which he deposits $10,000 of his own money. The dual aspect of this action is that the business now has an asset, cash, of $10,000, and the owner has a claim against this asset, also of $10,000, or—

$$\text{Assets (cash), } \$10,000 = \text{Equities (owner's), } \$10,000 .$$

If the business then borrowed $5,000 from a bank, the accounting records would show an increase in cash, making the amount $15,000, and a new claim against this cash by the bank in the amount of $5,000. At this point the accounting records of the business would show the following:

Cash..................$15,000	Owed to bank............$ 5,000
	Owner's equity........... 10,000
Total Assets.........$15,000	Total Equities........$15,000

It follows that every event that is recorded in the accounts affects at least two items; there is no conceivable way of making only a single change in the accounts. Accounting is therefore properly called a "double-entry" system.

An accounting system conceivably could be set up with some concept other than the one stated here. As a matter of fact, there is a system called "single-entry" accounting that records only one aspect of a transaction, very much like the record maintained in a ship's log or a diary. However, as will become apparent in later chapters, there are many advantages, both mechanical and conceptual, in the dual-aspect concept, and this is so universally accepted that no further mention will be made of any other possibility.

6. The Accrual Concept
7. The Realization Concept

These two concepts are mentioned here only to round out the basic list. They will be described and discussed in Chapter 3.

FUNDAMENTAL CONVENTIONS

In practice, the foregoing concepts are modified by certain widely accepted conventions. Of these, the most important are (1) consistency, (2) conservatism, and (3) materiality.

Consistency

The seven concepts just given are so broad that there are in practice several different ways in which a given event may be recorded in the accounts. For example, when a company takes a cash discount in paying bills to its vendors, this discount may be treated as being revenue to the company; it may be treated as a reduction in the purchase price of the goods purchased; or the cash discounts *not* taken may be treated as an expense. The consistency convention requires that once a company has decided on one of these methods, it will treat all subsequent events of the same character in the same fashion. If a company made frequent changes in the manner of handling a given class of events in the accounting records, comparison of its accounting figures for one period with those of another period would be difficult.

Because of this convention, changes in the method of keeping accounts are not made lightly. A company's auditors invariably include in their opinion (i.e., a letter summarizing the results of their annual examination of accounting records) the statement that the figures were prepared "in conformity with generally accepted accounting principles *applied on a basis consistent with that of the preceding year";* or if there were changes in practice, these are spelled out in the opinion.

Conservatism

The conservatism convention means that when the accountant has a reasonable choice, he ordinarily will show the lower of two asset amounts for a given item, or will record an event in such a way that owners' equity is lower than it otherwise would be. This convention is often stated as follows: "Anticipate no profit, and provide for all possible losses." It is especially important as a modifier of the cost concept. To illustrate, inventories (material held for sale, supplies, etc.) are ordinarily reported not at their cost, which is what one would expect in accordance with the cost concept, but rather at the *lower* of their cost or their current replacement value.

The conservatism convention is applied much less strongly now than was the case a few decades ago when it was a common practice to report some assets at far less than either their cost or their current market value. Nevertheless, the convention still has an important influence on accounting. Many informed persons would say that this convention is illogical and that the accountant should attempt to report the figures either consistently on the basis of cost or consistently on the basis of market value rather than choosing the more conservative of these two possible approaches. Nevertheless, few would question the fact that the convention does exist and that it is important.

Materiality

In law, there is a doctrine called *de minimis non curat lex,* which means that the court will not consider trivial matters. Similarly, the accountant does not attempt to record a great many events which are so insignificant that the work of recording them is not justified by the usefulness of the results. An example of these trivialities is the accounting treatment of pencils. A brand new pencil is an asset of the company. Every time someone writes with the pencil, part of this asset is used up, and the owners' equity decreases correspondingly. Theoretically, it would be possible to ascertain daily the number of partly used pencils that are owned by the company and to correct the records so as to show that fractional amount of the asset amount that remains, but the cost of such an effort would obviously be gigantic, and no accountant would attempt to do this. He would take the simpler, even though less exact, course of action and consider that the asset was used up at the time the pencils were purchased or at the time they were issued from inventory to the user.

There is no agreement as to the exact line separating material events from immaterial events. The decision depends on judgment and common sense. It is natural for the beginning student, who does not have an appreciation of the cost of collecting accounting information, to be more meticulous in recording events in the accounts than would the practicing accountant.

THE BALANCE SHEET

The balance sheet is the fundamental accounting report in the sense that every accounting transaction can be recorded in terms of its effect on the balance sheet. It shows the status of the business as of a given moment of time, insofar as accounting figures can show its status.[3]

A balance sheet for a hypothetical corporation is shown in Illustration 2–1. Let us examine this statement in terms of the basic concepts listed above. The figures are *expressed in money* and reflect only those matters about a corporation that can be measured in money amounts.

---

[3] A balance sheet dated "December 31" is implicitly understood to mean "at the close of business on December 31." Sometimes the identical balance sheet may be dated "January 1," meaning "at the beginning of business on January 1," which is the same moment of time. Ordinarily, the "close of business" connotation is the correct one.

Illustration 2–1

GARSDEN CORPORATION

Balance Sheet as of December 31, 1963

ASSETS		
Current Assets:		
Cash		$ 3,448,891
Marketable securities (market value, $248,420)		246,221
Accounts receivable (net)		5,943,588
Inventories		12,623,412
Prepaid expenses and deferred charges		388,960
Total Current Assets		$22,651,072
Fixed Assets:		
Land, buildings, and equipment	$26,945,848	
Less: Accumulated depreciation	13,534,069	13,411,779
Other Assets:		
Investments	$ 110,000	
Goodwill	63,214	173,214
Total Assets		$36,236,065

EQUITIES		
Current Liabilities:		
Accounts payable		$ 6,601,442
Estimated tax liability	1,672,000	
Accrued expenses payable	640,407	
Deferred income	205,240	
Total Current Liabilities		$ 9,119,089
Other Liabilities:		
Mortgage bonds payable		3,000,000
Stockholders' Equity:		
Common stock	$15,000,000	
Retained earnings	9,116,976	24,116,976
Total Equities		$36,236,065

The *business entity* involved is the Garsden Corporation, and the balance sheet pertains to that entity rather than to any of the individuals associated with the company. The statement assumes that the Garsden Corporation is a *going concern.* The asset amounts stated are governed by the *cost concept.* The *dual-aspect* concept is evident from the fact that the assets listed on one side of this balance sheet are equal in total to the equities, or claims against the assets, listed on the other side.

Incidentally, the practice of listing assets on the left-hand side and equities on the right-hand side of the balance sheet is common in the United States. An alternative practice of listing assets at the top of the page with equities underneath them is also common. The former format is called the *account* form, and the latter, the *report* form of balance sheet. In certain other countries, assets are listed on the right-hand side and equities on the left-hand side. None of these differences have any real significance.[4]

It should be emphasized that the fact that the two sides add up to the same total necessarily follows from the dual-aspect concept; it does not tell anything about the company's financial condition. This equality of the two sides of the balance sheet is always found unless a clerical error has been made.

Since the term *balance* sheet may give the erroneous impression that there is something good or something significant about this balance or equality of the totals, the Accounting Principles Board recommends that this term be replaced by "statement of financial position" or "position statement." An increasing number of companies are complying with this recommendation in their published reports, but the term "balance sheet" is still so widely used in ordinary business conversation that it is retained here.

Note also that the amounts are rounded to dollars. Pennies are eliminated in many published statements. In reports prepared for internal purposes, the amounts may be rounded even further, to thousands of dollars, or in large corporations to millions of dollars, so as to highlight the important figures.

Account Categories

Although each individual asset or equity—each building, each piece of equipment, each bank loan, etc.—could theoretically be listed

---

[4] Most of the balance sheets in the cases in this book are given in the report form for the simple reason that this fits better on a printed page. Most balance sheets typed on regular 8½ × 11 paper are in the report form for the same reason. In published annual reports, the balance sheet is often in the account form, since this makes an attractive two-page spread.

separately on the balance sheet, it is more practicable and more informative to summarize and group related items into categories or *account classifications.* There is no fixed pattern as to the number of such categories or the amount of detail reported; rather, the format is governed by the accountant's opinion as to the most informative way of presenting significant facts about the status of the business.

As in any classification scheme, the categories are defined in such a way that (1) the individual items included in a category resemble one another in some essential and significant respect and (2) the items in one category are essentially different from those in all other categories. Although the items included in a category are similar to one another, they are not identical.

> EXAMPLE: The category labeled "Cash" usually includes money on deposit at savings banks as well as money on deposit in commercial banks. These two types of money are *similar* in that they both are in highly liquid form, but they are *not identical* because certain restrictions may apply to withdrawals from savings banks that do not apply to withdrawals from commercial banks. If an accountant thought this difference was important enough to report, he would set up two separate categories. This would, however, increase the amount of detail shown on the balance sheet.

The balance sheet in Illustration 2–1 gives a minimum amount of detail. The terms used on this balance sheet are common ones, and they are described briefly below.

Assets

We shall now supersede the brief definition of "asset" given in the preceding section by the following more exact statement: *Assets are valuable resources owned by a business which were acquired at a measurable money cost.* The three key points in this definition are the following: (1) the resource must be valuable; (2) the resource must be owned; and (3) the resource must be acquired at a measurable money cost.

A resource is *valuable* either if it is cash or an item that probably will be converted into cash or if it is expected to benefit the future operation of the business. In some cases the presumed benefit for the future is rather nebulous and debatable; for example, some accountants regard the cost of organizing a corporation as an asset on the grounds that the corporate form of organization is valuable to the business, but others disagree with this reasoning.

EXAMPLE: Amounts due from customers are assets, to the extent that customers are likely to pay their bills. The protection promised by an insurance policy is an asset since the insurance provides a valuable protection against losses from future misfortunes. Worthless machines that can neither be used nor traded in for new machines are not assets.

Ownership is a legal concept, which is to be distinguished from possession or control. The accounting concept is close to, but not exactly the same as, the legal concept. Thus, when a business buys an automobile on the installment plan, the lender may own the car, in the legal sense, until the last installment has been paid; nevertheless, the automobile is regarded as substantially owned by the business and is shown as an asset. But, possession or control, without substantial ownership, is not enough to qualify the item as an asset.

EXAMPLE: A leased piece of equipment is not an asset of the lessee even though it is in his possession and he has complete control over its use. Goods on consignment are assets of the consignor who owns them, not of the consignee who has possession of them.

The *acquisition at a measurable money cost* test is usually clear-cut, but in some instances is difficult to apply. If the resource was purchased for cash or the promise to pay cash, it is an asset. If the resource was manufactured by the business, then money was paid for the costs of manufacture, and it is an asset. If the resource was acquired by trading in some other asset or by issuing stock, then the item is an asset, although there may be problems in measuring its amount because of the difficulty in valuing the traded-in item or the stock. Ordinarily, the solution to this problem is to determine what the asset would have cost had cash been paid for it; but when no objective evidence of this amount can be found, the best possible estimate is made from whatever information is available. On the other hand, as already pointed out (p. 35), a valuable reputation or an efficient organization is not an asset if it arose gradually over a period of time, rather than being acquired at a specifically measurable cost.

EXAMPLE: Both "Seagrams" and "Schenley" are valuable trade names. Nevertheless, the 1963 balance sheet for Distillers Corporation–Seagrams Ltd. shows only a nominal amount ($1.00) for "Distillery Product Trademarks, Bottling and Blending Rights, Contracts, and Goodwill," whereas the 1963 balance sheet for Schenley Industries, Inc., shows $1,854,860 for the corresponding item.

Assets are recorded at their total cost, not the company's "equity" in them.

EXAMPLE: If a business buys land for $100,000, pays $30,000 cash, and gives a $70,000 mortgage, the asset is recorded at $100,000, not $30,000.

On most business balance sheets, assets are listed in order of their liquidity; that is, in order of the promptness with which they are expected to be converted into cash. On some balance sheets, notably those of public utilities, the order is reversed, and the least liquid assets are listed first.

Current assets are almost always reported in a separate category, and there may also be other categories—the "Fixed Assets" and "Other Assets" headings appearing on the Garsden Corporation balance sheet is a frequently used breakdown.

Current Assets

The definition given by the Accounting Principles Board is a good one to follow:

For accounting purposes, the term *current assets* is used to designate cash and other assets or resources commonly identified as those which are reasonably expected to be realized in cash or sold or consumed during the normal operating cycle of the business. Thus the term comprehends in general such resources as (a) cash available for current operations and items which are the equivalent of cash; (b) inventories of merchandise, raw materials, goods in process, finished goods, operating supplies, and ordinary maintenance material and parts; (c) trade accounts, notes, and acceptances receivable; (d) receivables from officers, employees, affiliates, and others, if collectible in the ordinary course of business within a year; (e) installment or deferred accounts and notes receivable if they conform generally to normal trade practices and terms within the business; (f) marketable securities representing the investment of cash available for current operations; and (g) prepaid expenses such as insurance, interest, rents, taxes, unused royalties, current paid advertising service not yet received, and operating supplies.[5]

The distinction between current assets and noncurrent assets is important since much attention is given by lenders and others to the total of current assets. The essence of the distinction is *time*. Current assets are those that will be owned only for a short period of time, usually not more than a year from the balance sheet date, whereas noncurrent assets are those that are expected to be owned for a longer period of time.

Although the usual time limit is one year, exceptions occur in companies whose normal operating cycle is longer than one year.

---

[5] AICPA, *Accounting Research Bulletin No. 43*, p. 20. (We shall throughout attribute quotations from *Accounting Research Bulletins* to the Accounting Principles Board, even though most of them were originally prepared by its predecessor committee.)

Tobacco companies and distilleries, for example, include their inventories as current assets even though tobacco and liquor remain in inventory for an aging process that lasts two years or even longer.

Cash consists of funds that are immediately available for disbursement without restriction. Usually, most of these funds are on deposit in checking accounts in banks, and the remainder is in cash registers or other temporary storage facilities on the company's premises.

Marketable securities are investments which are both readily marketable and which are expected to be converted into cash within a year. They are investments made so as to earn some return on cash that otherwise would be temporarily idle.

Accounts receivable are amounts owed to the company, usually by its customers. Sometimes this item is broken down into *trade* accounts receivable and *other* accounts receivable; the former refers to amounts owed by customers, and the latter refers to amounts owed by employees and others. On the Garsden Corporation balance sheet, accounts receivable are reported "net." This means that the figure $5,943,588 is not the total amount owed by customers but is a smaller amount; the total amount owed has been reduced by an estimate of the amount that will not be collected.

If the amount owed is evidenced by a note or some other written acknowledgement of the obligation, it would ordinarily appear under the heading *notes receivable* rather than accounts receivable.

As defined by the Accounting Principles Board, the term *inventory* means "the aggregate of those items of tangible personal property which (1) are held for sale in the ordinary course of business, (2) are in process of production for such sales, or (3) are to be currently consumed in the production of goods or services to be available for sale."[6]

The item *prepaid expenses and deferred charges* represents certain assets, usually of an intangible nature, whose usefulness will expire in the near future. An example is an insurance policy. A business pays for insurance protection in advance, often for a three-year or a five-year period. Its right to this protection is an asset—a valuable, owned resource—but this right will expire within a fairly short period of time.

The distinction between "prepaid expenses" and "deferred charges" is not important. In some businesses, prepaid expenses and deferred charges are shown not as current assets but rather as "other assets" near the bottom of the balance sheet.

---

[6] *Ibid.*, p. 27.

Fixed Assets

Fixed assets are tangible, relatively long-lived, resources. The business has acquired these assets, ordinarily, in order to use them in the production of other goods and services. If the assets are held for resale, they are classified as inventory, even though they are long-lived assets. In the balance sheet shown in Illustration 2–1 fixed assets are lumped together into the single item, "land, buildings, and equipment," but in the balance sheets of many companies the figures for land, for buildings, and for various kinds of machinery and equipment are shown separately. In accordance with the cost concept, the figure $26,945,848 on the Garsden Corporation balance sheet represents the cost of these assets to the company at the time they were purchased. The next item, "accumulated depreciation," means that a fraction of the original cost amounting to $13,534,069 has been already allocated as a cost of doing business, as will be described in Chapter 6.

Other Assets

Investments are securities of one company owned by another for reasons other than the temporary use of excess cash. They are therefore to be distinguished from "marketable securities," which is an item in the current asset section of the balance sheet. A company acquires such securities either to control another company or in the anticipation of earning a return from them.

Intangible assets include goodwill (which was described briefly earlier in this chapter), patents, copyrights, leases, licenses, franchises, and similar valuable, but nonphysical, things owned by the business. Items included in this category have a longer life span than items included in the current asset, prepaid expenses.

Liabilities

Liabilities are the claims of outsiders against the business or, to put it another way, the amounts that the business owes to persons other than the owners. It should be noted that all the liabilities shown on the balance sheet are claims against all the assets; ordinarily they are not claims against any *specific* asset or group of assets. Thus, accounts payable may arise through the purchase of material for inventory, but accounts payable are claims against all the assets, not merely against inventories.

Even if a liability is a claim against a specific asset, it is shown separately on the right-hand side of the balance sheet, rather than as a deduction from the asset amount to which it relates.

EXAMPLE: If land is purchased for $100,000, and a $70,000 mortgage is given, secured by the land, the balance sheet reports land at $100,000 on the asset side, and the mortgage payable of $70,000 on the equities side, *not*—

$$
\begin{array}{lr}
\text{Land} \dots\dots\dots\dots\dots\dots\dots\dots & \$100,000 \\
\text{Less: Mortgage} \dots\dots\dots\dots\dots\dots & \underline{70,000} \\
\text{Net Amount} \dots\dots\dots\dots\dots\dots & \$30,000 \\
\end{array}
$$

Current Liabilities

In brief, current liabilities are obligations which become due in the near future, usually within the next year, except for those obligations which are expected to be met by the incurrence of a noncurrent liability (as in the case of a maturing bond issue which is to be refunded). The Accounting Principles Board gives a more detailed definition, as follows:

The term *current liabilities* is used principally to designate obligations whose liquidation is reasonably expected to require the use of existing resources properly classifiable as current assets, or the creation of other current liabilities. As a balance-sheet category, the classification is intended to include obligations for items which have entered into the operating cycle, such as payables incurred in the acquisition of materials and supplies to be used in the production of goods or in providing services to be offered for sale; collections received in advance of the delivery of goods or performance of services; and debts which arise from operations directly related to the operating cycle, such as accruals for wages, salaries, commissions, rentals, royalties, and income and other taxes. Other liabilities whose regular and ordinary liquidation is expected to occur within a relatively short period of time, usually 12 months, are also intended for inclusion, such as short-term debts arising from the acquisition of capital assets, serial maturities of long-term obligations, amounts required to be expended within one year under sinking fund provisions, and agency obligations arising from the collection or acceptance of cash or other assets for the account of third persons.[7]

Accounts payable represent the claims of vendors and others. Usually these claims are unsecured. If the claim was evidenced by a note or some other written acknowledgment of debt, the item would be called *notes payable, bank drafts payable,* or some other term that describes the nature of the obligation.

Estimated tax liability is the amount owed the government for taxes. It is shown separately from other obligations both because of its size and because the amount owed is not precisely known as of the date of the balance sheet. Often, the liability for federal and state income taxes is shown separately from other tax liabilities.

---

[7] *Ibid.,* p. 21.

Accrued expenses are the converse of prepaid expenses. They represent certain obligations, which are indeed valid claims against the assets but which are "intangible" in the sense that they are not evidenced by an invoice or other document submitted by the person to whom the money is owed. An example is the wages and salaries owed to employees for work they have performed but for which they have not been reimbursed.

Deferred income represents the liability that arises because the company has received advance payment for a service it has agreed to render in the future. An example is precollected rent, which represents rental payments received in advance for which the company agrees to permit the tenant to use a specified building (or other property) during some future period.

Other Liabilities

Other liabilities are claims of outsiders that do not fall due within one year. Evidently the mortgage bonds of the Garsden Corporation do not mature within the next year, nor do any fraction of them; otherwise all or part of this liability would appear as a current liability (unless, as stated above, it is planned to refund them).

Owners' Equity

The *owners' equity* section of the balance sheet shows the claims of the owners, in this case the stockholders. The terminology used in this section of the balance sheet varies with different forms of organization. In a corporation, which the Garsden Corporation is, the claims of the owners are evidenced by documents called *stock certificates.* The first item in the stockholders' equity section of the Garsden Corporation balance sheet is the "stated value" of this stock. This may be the par value of the stock, or the price at which it was sold, or some other figure fixed by the board of directors. In the interest of consistency, once the basis of stating each share of stock has been determined, it is rarely changed.

The owners' equity increases through *earnings* (i.e., the results of profitable operations) and decreases when earnings are paid out in the form of dividends. The difference between the total earnings to date and the total amount of dividends to date is *retained earnings;* that is, that part of the total earnings which have been retained for use in the business.[8] If the difference is negative, the item is labeled *deficit.*

---

[8] Stockholders' equity is also affected by events other than the accumulation of earnings and the withdrawal of these earnings. Examples are the sale of stock at a premium or a discount, the revaluation of stock, and the creation of special reserves. Some of these events will be discussed in Chapter 8.

The term "surplus" was formerly used instead of "retained earnings," and is still used by some companies. The word "surplus" is apt to be misleading since to the uninitiated "surplus" represents something tangible, something "left over." There is, in fact, nothing tangible about retained earnings. All the tangible things owned by the business appear on the assets side of the balance sheet. It is because of this misleading connotation that use of this word is no longer recommended. The word "surplus" is sometimes used with appropriate modifiers (capital surplus, paid-in surplus, etc.) for certain special items that will be described in Chapter 8.

In unincorporated businesses, different terminology is used in the owners' equity section. In a *proprietorship,* which is a business owned by one person, it is customary to show the owner's equity as a single figure, with a title such as "John Jones, capital," rather than making a distinction between the owner's initial investment and the accumulated earnings retained in the business.

In a *partnership,* which is an unincorporated business owned jointly by several persons, there is a capital account for each partner, thus:

James Smith, capital......................$15,432
John Smith, capital....................... 15,432
    Total Partners' Equity................$30,864

In addition to these basic owners' equity items, a proprietorship or a partnership may, for convenience, use a temporary item called a *drawing account* in which amounts withdrawn from the business by the owner(s) are recorded. Periodically, the total accumulated in the drawing account is subtracted from the capital item, leaving the net equity of the owner(s). For example, a balance sheet might show the following:

John Jones, capital.............$25,000
Less: Drawings............... 2,400
    Net Proprietorship Equity.... $22,600

After the two items have been combined, the balance sheet would read simply:

John Jones, capital.............$22,600

The student may have heard of the terms "partnership accounting" and "corporation accounting," and from these he may have formed the impression that different accounting systems are used for different forms of business organization. As a matter of fact, the treatment of assets and liabilities is generally the same in all forms of organization; differences occur principally in the owners' equity section as noted above.

BALANCE SHEET CHANGES

At the moment a business starts, its financial status can be recorded on a balance sheet. From that time on, events occur that change the figures on this first balance sheet, and the accountant records these changes in accordance with the concepts given above. Full-fledged accounting systems provide a means of accumulating and summarizing these changes and of preparing new balance sheets at prescribed intervals.

In learning the accounting process, however, it is useful to consider the changes one by one. This makes it possible to study the effect of individual events without getting entangled with the mechanisms used in practice to record these events. The technical name given to an event that affects an accounting figure is *transaction*. An example of the effect of a few transactions on the balance sheet will now be given. For simplicity, they are assumed to occur on successive days.

Jan. 1. John Smith starts a business, called Glendale Market, by depositing $10,000 of his own funds in a bank account which he has opened in the name of the store. The balance sheet of Glendale Market will then be as follows:

GLENDALE MARKET

Balance Sheet as of January 1

ASSETS		EQUITIES	
Cash.....................$10,000		John Smith, capital........$10,000	

Jan. 2. The business borrows $5,000 from a bank giving a note therefor. This transaction increases the asset, cash, and the business incurs a liability to the bank. The balance sheet after this transaction will appear as follows:

GLENDALE MARKET

Balance Sheet as of January 2

ASSETS		EQUITIES	
Cash.....................$15,000		Notes payable, bank........$ 5,000	
		John Smith, capital	10,000
Total.................$15,000		Total.................$15,000	

Jan. 3. The business buys inventory in the amount of $2,000, paying cash. The balance sheet is as follows:

GLENDALE MARKET

Balance Sheet as of January 3

ASSETS		EQUITIES	
Cash	$13,000	Notes payable, bank	$ 5,000
Inventory	2,000	John Smith, capital	10,000
Total	$15,000	Total	$15,000

Jan. 4. The store sells for $300 cash, merchandise that cost $200. The effect of this transaction is that inventory has been decreased by $200, cash has been increased by $300, and John Smith's own equity has been increased by the difference, or $100. The $100 is the profit on this sale. The balance sheet will then look like this:

GLENDALE MARKET

Balance Sheet as of January 4

ASSETS		EQUITIES	
Cash	$13,300	Notes payable, bank	$ 5,000
Inventory	1,800	John Smith, capital	10,100
Total	$15,100	Total	$15,100

These illustrations could be extended indefinitely; some additional transactions are given in Case 2–2. As we delve more deeply into the mechanics of accounting, it is worth remembering that every accounting transaction can be recorded in terms of its effect on the balance sheet.

AN OVERALL VIEW OF THE BALANCE SHEET

We have described the balance sheet as a list of assets and of claims against those assets. This is a useful way of thinking about it, especially when trying to decide how to record the effect of a specific transaction. In trying to understand the picture of a business that the balance sheet provides, it is often useful to use a different, but equally correct, description, as given in the following paragraphs.

The right-hand side of the balance sheet may be viewed as a description of the sources from which the business has obtained the capital with which it operates, and the left-hand side as a description of the form in which that capital is invested on a specified date. On the right-hand side of the balance sheet, the several liability items describe how much capital was obtained from trade creditors (accounts payable), from banks (notes payable), from bondholders (bonds payable), and other outside parties. The owners' equity section shows the capital supplied by the stockholders. If the business is a corporation, the stockholders' contribution consists of two principal parts: capital directly supplied (capital stock) and capital which the stockholders provided by permitting earnings to remain in the business (retained earnings).

Capital obtained from various sources has been invested according to the management's best judgment of the optimum mix, or combination, of assets for the business. A certain fraction is invested in buildings, another fraction in inventory, another fraction is retained as cash for current needs of the business, and so on. The asset side of the balance sheet therefore shows the result of these management judgments as of the date of the balance sheet.

When the balance sheet is viewed in this way, some of the apparent inconsistencies in accounting principles and definitions described above may be resolved. Considering assets as items in which capital has been invested makes it reasonable to record assets at their cost rather than at market value, for the cost basis shows the amount of capital tied up in each asset category. Furthermore, a description of retained earnings as one source of capital—the accumulated earnings of past periods not paid out as dividends—is probably easier to understand than a description of retained earnings as someone's "claim" against the business; it is difficult to see how earnings can be a "claim" against anything.

In any event, either one of these approaches to the balance sheet is at best only a brief introduction to the balance sheet idea. Real comprehension comes through constructing and using balance sheets in cases or practical business situations.

SUGGESTIONS FOR FURTHER READING ON ACCOUNTING PRINCIPLES

(For Chapters 2–10)

1. There are several excellent textbooks, any of which may be useful either for additional information or to obtain a different viewpoint on topics discussed here. Some are listed on pp. 55 and 56.

2. Eric L. Kohler, *A Dictionary for Accountants* (3d ed.; Englewood Cliffs, N.J.: Prentice-Hall, Inc., 1963), is much more than a dictionary. It contains a good discussion of many terms and concepts, and because of its dictionary format provides a quick way of locating desired information.

3. Rufus Wixon (ed.), *Accountants' Handbook* (New York: The Ronald Press Co., 1960), is a standard source for detailed information.

4. Norman J. Lenhart and Philip L. Defliese, *Montgomery's Auditing* (8th ed.; New York: The Ronald Press Co., 1957), contains accounting principles arranged so they are easy to find.

5. Publications of the AICPA, American Accounting Association, and U.S. Securities and Exchange Commission, referred to in the text, are important sources of the latest information on what constitutes "generally accepted accounting principles."

CASES

CASE 2–1.   PROBLEM IN BALANCE SHEET CONSTRUCTION

As of December 31, 1963, the accounts of the Fintley Corporation showed the following balances (000 omitted):

Accounts payable	$ 131
Accounts receivable	526
Accrued expenses	243
Accumulated depreciation on plant and equipment	840
Bank notes payable	5
Bonds payable	300
Capital stock	438
Cash	69
Deferred income (progress payments from customers)	229
Dividends payable	43
Estimated tax liability	254
Inventories	610
Investments in other companies	157
Marketable securities	409
Other assets	169
Other liabilities	131
Plant and equipment (at original cost)	1,553
Retained earnings	879

Question

Prepare a balance sheet as of this date, in proper form.

CASE 2–2.   PROBLEM IN BALANCE SHEET CHANGES

On a sheet of paper, set up in pencil the balance sheet of Glendale Market as it appears after the last transaction described in the text, page 51, leaving considerable space between each item. Record the effects, if any, of the following happenings on the balance sheet, either by revising existing figures (cross out, rather than erase) or by adding new items as necessary. At least one of these happenings does not affect the balance sheet. The basic equation, Assets = Equities, must be preserved at all times. Errors will be minimized if you make a separate list of the balance sheet items affected by each transaction and the amount (+ or −) by which each is to be changed.

After you have finished recording these happenings, prepare a balance sheet in proper form.

1. The store purchased and received merchandise for $2,000, agreeing to pay within 30 days.
2. Merchandise costing $500 was sold for $800, which was received in cash.

3. Merchandise costing $600 was sold for $900, the customer agreeing to pay $900 within 30 days.
4. The store purchased a three-year fire insurance policy for $200, paying cash.
5. The store purchased two lots of land of equal size for a total of $10,000. It paid $2,000 in cash and gave a ten-year mortgage for $8,000.
6. The store sold one of the two lots of land for $5,000. It received $1,000 cash, and in addition, the buyer assumed $4,000 of the mortgage; that is, Glendale Market became no longer responsible for this half.
7. Smith received a bona fide offer of $15,000 for the business, and although his equity was then only $10,700, he rejected the offer. It was evident that the store had already acquired goodwill of $4,300.
8. Smith withdrew $500 cash from the store's bank account for his personal use.
9. Smith took merchandise costing $400 from the store's inventory for his personal use.
10. Smith learned that the man who purchased the land (No. 6 above) subsequently sold it for $8,000. The lot still owned by Glendale Market was identical in value with this other plot.
11. The store paid off $2,000 of its bank loan (disregard interest).
12. Glendale Market was changed to a corporation, Glendale Market, Inc. Smith received common stock with a par value of $9,800 in exchange for his equity in the store. (Disregard costs of organizing the corporation. Note that this event changes the title of the balance sheet.)
13. Smith sold one fourth of the stock he owned in Glendale Market, Inc., for $3,000 cash.

CASE 2–3. PROBLEMS ON THE DEFINITION OF "CASH"

The consolidated balance sheets of General Motors Corporation as of December 31, 1962, and 1961 are reproduced as Exhibit 1. Your attention is invited to the item which reads:

	December 31, 1962	December 31, 1961
Cash	$377,460,248	$404,759,560

The Company's auditors stated that these statements "fairly present the financial position of the company . . . in conformity with generally accepted accounting procedures consistently applied."

Definition of Cash

"Cash" is defined in certain widely used references and texts as follows:

Finney and Miller: "Cash consists of legal tender, checks, bank drafts, money orders, and demand deposits in banks. In general, nothing

Exhibit 1

GENERAL MOTORS CORPORATION

Condensed Balance Sheets as of December 31

ASSETS	1962	1961
Current Assets:		
Cash....................................	$ 377,460,248	$ 404,759,560
U.S. government securities...............	1,705,322,442	1,291,290,584
Accounts and notes receivable...........	1,069,578,481	987,295,501
Inventories............................	2,006,492,551	1,800,142,041
Total Current Assets.................	$5,158,853,722	$4,483,487,686
Investments (including treasury stock)....	657,565,638	624,072,212
Fixed Assets:		
Plant and equipment....................$7,510,111,293		
Less: Accumulated depreciation......... 4,302,965,024	3,207,146,269	3,028,866,377*
Other Assets:		
Prepaid expenses.......................	82,045,521	72,727,439
Goodwill, patents......................	63,442,466	63,442,466
Total Assets.....................	$9,169,053,616	$8,272,596,180
LIABILITIES, RESERVES, AND CAPITAL		
Current Liabilities:		
Estimated tax liability..................	$ 78,124,215	$ 88,383,687
Accounts payable......................	657,143,664	564,145,920
Accrued expenses......................	892,323,789	769,148,942
Dividends payable......................	3,232,072	3,232,073
Total Current Liabilities............	$1,630,823,740	$1,424,910,622
Debentures............................	200,491,000	221,322,000
Other liabilities.......................	468,589,961	385,132,704
Reserves..............................	218,177,294	215,575,837
Capital stock and capital surplus........	1,438,969,718	1,409,337,149
Reinvested earnings...................	5,212,001,903	4,616,317,868
Total Liabilities and Capital......	$9,169,053,616	$8,272,596,180

* Plant and equipment......................$7,004,849.133
  Less: Accumulated depreciation......... 3,975,982,756
  $3,028,866,377

should be considered unrestricted cash unless it is available to the management for disbursements of any nature."[9]

Kohler: "Money, negotiable money orders and checks, and balances on deposit with banks after deducting outstanding checks. As an unqualified balance-sheet caption under *current assets,* cash may be assumed to be available for any ordinary use within the enterprise. . . ."[10]

[9] Harry A. Finney and Herbert E. Miller, *Principles of Accounting, Intermediate* (5th ed.; Englewood Cliffs, N.J.: Prentice-Hall, Inc., 1958), p. 186.

[10] Eric L. Kohler, *A Dictionary for Accountants* (3d ed.; Englewood Cliffs, N.J.: Prentice-Hall, Inc., 1963), p. 88.

Montgomery's Auditing: "Cash on Hand and on Deposit. This caption on a balance sheet should include only cash on hand and demand deposits in banks at the close of business on the balance sheet date.

"The practice of including cash received after the close of the period and reducing accounts receivable correspondingly is not in accordance with the foregoing rule although it has been defended on the ground that such receipts were forwarded by debtors before the close of the period and represented cash in transit. Checks drawn prior to the balance sheet date, but held for later delivery to creditors, and checks drawn after, but dated prior to, the balance sheet date should not be treated as outstanding checks; they should be restored to the cash balance and to liabilities."[11]

Noble and Niswonger: "Cash includes bank deposits, currency, checks, bank drafts, and money orders. Any medium of exchange that a bank will accept at face value on deposit is usually shown on the balance sheet as cash. Most of the cash may be on deposit at the bank; some of it may be in the cash drawer or safe."[12]

Paton and Dixon: "Cash is a very important business asset, but although coin and paper currency can be inspected and handled the major part of the 'cash' of most enterprises is in the form of bank checking accounts, which represent claims to money rather than tangible property."[13]

Pyle and White: "The cash of a business consists of money or any media of exchange that a bank will accept at face value for deposit."[14]

Problems

In preparing its consolidated balance sheet, the company's accountants were faced with the problem of determining the amount to be included as "cash." Some items which may or may not have been included are listed below; these items are illustrative only, and do not necessarily reflect the items or amounts which were actually considered by General Motors. You are asked to suggest which of these items should be included as cash and how the amounts to be included should be determined, giving the reasons for your choice.

---

[11] Norman J. Lenhart and Philip L. Defliese, *Montgomery's Auditing* (8th ed.; New York: The Ronald Press Co., 1957), p. 122.

[12] Howard S. Noble and C. Rollin Niswonger, *Accounting Principles* (8th ed.; Cincinnati: South-Western Publishing Co., 1961), p. 25.

[13] William A. Paton and Robert L. Dixon, *Essentials of Accounting* (New York: Macmillan Co., 1958), p. 16.

[14] William W. Pyle and John Arch White, *Fundamental Accounting Principles* (3d ed.; Homewood, Ill.: Richard D. Irwin, Inc., 1963), p. 24.

1. At the close of business on December 31, each of the company's financial offices had on hand a part of the day's receipts from customers. Since the banks had already closed their accounts for the day, these receipts would not be deposited in time to appear on the December bank statements.

2. The company maintained checking accounts in various banks throughout the United States. Assume that on December 31, 1962, these banks reported a total of $389,967,519 on deposit from the company, but the company had written and mailed checks of, say, $10,615,731 which had not yet been cashed by the banks on which they had been written.

3. In addition to the $10,615,731 of uncashed checks, there were probably uncashed dividend checks of several thousand dollars. Dividend checks were mailed to the last-known address of stockholders, but sometimes stockholders moved without notifying the company of their new address. Some of these uncashed checks dated back for years.

4. The company paid many of its employees out of special payroll checking accounts. At the time their checks were written, the exact amount of cash to pay the checks was transferred from regular checking accounts to payroll accounts. On December 31, there were cash balances in many of these special checking accounts.

5. The company owned 100 per cent of the stock of General Motors Acceptance Corporation, a finance company, which it listed as an investment on its balance sheet. On December 31, 1962, General Motors Acceptance Corporation listed on *its* balance sheet cash in the amount of $184,811,701.

6. Perhaps some of the company's funds were deposited in savings banks. The savings banks could require notice of 30 to 90 days before these funds could be withdrawn. Generally, however, this requirement was waived.

7. Frequently cash was advanced to company officers or salesmen for travel expenses. After these individuals completed their trip, they made an accounting of what they had spent and returned any unused cash. Most likely some of these individuals were holding unused cash on December 31.

8. Some of the company's customers had paid their bills by checks written and dated December 30 and 31. Many of these checks were received in the mail on January 2, 1963, or later.

9. Frequently the company itself wished to transfer funds from one of its bank accounts to another. Suppose that on December 31 a check for $80,000 was written on a bank in Denver and mailed to New York, where it was received and deposited on January 2.

CASE 2–4.   HENRY MERCER

After a slow start, Henry Mercer's business grew to the point where the simple records on which he had been relying for information became inadequate. He therefore sought help in devising and installing a set of accounting records that would provide the information he needed to manage his company.

Mr. Mercer got the idea for his business while he was serving as a pharmacists mate in the Navy. In his off-duty hours he liked to carry on experiments in the pharmaceutical laboratory on his ship, and although he had only a high school education in chemistry, he developed several chemical compounds that seemed to have commercial possibilities. Of these, the most promising seemed to him to be a liquid which, when sprayed into the air, tended to neutralize unpleasant odors.

After his discharge from the Navy, he obtained a job in a drugstore and continued his experiments in his spare time. In order to test the commercial potentiality of his spray, he bottled a small quantity under the trade name AirNu and attempted to find customers. Several competing products were on the market, and at first he had great difficulty in convincing anyone that AirNu was in any way superior to them. Some of his prospects, principally hospitals, jails, and other city and state institutions, agreed to try AirNu, however, and several of these trials resulted in sales. From this beginning business increased to the point where, two years after he left the Navy, Mr. Mercer gave up his job in the drugstore to devote full time to his venture, which he named the Mercer Chemical Company.

At first he carried on the business alone, with some assistance from his wife on the paper work. Mrs. Mercer had studied bookkeeping in the local business college. The records consisted of a checkbook, a file of unpaid bills, another file of paid bills, and a memorandum record of sales to and amounts owed by customers. Funds of the Mercer Chemical Company were kept in a separate bank account, and each week Mrs. Mercer drew a check for $100 on this account and deposited it in the Mercer family account. The original capital of the business had been furnished by Mr. Mercer from savings accumulated during his Navy days. It totaled about $500.

At the end of another year, Mr. Mercer decided to hire a man part time to help with the manufacture of AirNu and also to hire a full-time salesman who would visit drugstores and supermarkets in an attempt to break into the consumer market.

The manufacture of AirNu was a simple process. Water was added to a prepared base of several commercially available ingredients, the mixture was shaken, and then bottled in either gallon or eight-ounce containers. A spray nozzle was inserted in the top of the container, and a label was pasted on. The eight-ounce containers were packed in cartons, each of which held six bottles. Cartons, bottles, labels, and spray nozzles were purchased as required. Operations were carried on in the basement of the Mercer home, although storage space there was becoming so crowded that Mr. Mercer thought he soon would have to move the business into its own quarters.

At about the time he decided to hire the new men, Mr. Mercer became concerned about the adequacy of his records. He talked the matter over one evening with Mr. James Finnerty, controller of a large chemical company, who was a friend of Mr. Mercer's father.

Mr. Finnerty listened to the story of the Mercer Chemical Company's birth and growth with considerable interest and with some surprise and then made the following observations:

The favorable response of tough-minded industrial buyers to AirNu should be gratifying to you and indicates that your product has merit. A successful business requires more than a good product, however; it also requires good management. In order to manage the business, you need, among other things, records. The records for your business do not need to be as elaborate as those used in the large company I work for; in fact, I doubt that a study of our system would help you very much in setting up a system for the Mercer Chemical Company.

The need for adequate records is particularly important in view of your recent decision to add people to your payroll. Furthermore, as your business grows, you probably will need to borrow money from the bank, and the bank will certainly want to study the facts about your progress and your status before granting you a loan. If, as you indicate, you plan to introduce other products, records showing cost and profit by products will become increasingly important. As a matter of fact, good figures on your experience with AirNu might turn up some valuable information that will help you make your company more profitable.

Questions

1. Describe, as completely as you can, the types of information that you think Mr. Mercer needs to have in order to manage his business.

2. How would you go about constructing a balance sheet for the Mercer Chemical Company? What items would probably be shown on such a balance sheet, and how would you obtain the dollar amount to put opposite each item?

CASE 2–5.   SMOKY VALLEY CAFE[15]

On August 12, 1946, three people, who had previously been employed to wait on tables in one of the cafes in Baxter, Oregon, formed a partnership. The eldest of the three was Mrs. Bevan, a middle-aged widow. The other two were Mr. and Mrs. Elmer Maywood. The partnership lasted for slightly more than four months, and in connection with its dissolution the preparation of a balance sheet became necessary.

Each of the partners contributed $2,000 cash, a total of $6,000. On

---

[15] Based on a case argued before the Supreme Court of the State of Oregon, March 28, 1950. See 216 P2d 1005.

August 12, the partnership purchased the Smoky Valley Cafe for $16,000. The purchase price included land valued at $2,500, improvements to land at $2,000, buildings at $10,500, and cafe equipment at $1,000. The partnership made a down payment of $4,500 (from its $6,000 cash) and signed a mortgage for the balance of the $16,000. The doors of the cafe were opened for business shortly after August 12.

One of the things that made this particular piece of property attractive to them was the fact that the building contained suitable living accommodations. One of these rooms was occupied by Mrs. Bevan, another by the Maywoods.

The Maywoods and Mrs. Bevan agreed that Mrs. Bevan would operate the kitchen, Mrs. Maywood would have charge of the dining room, and that Mr. Maywood would attend the bar. Mrs. Bevan agreed to keep the accounting records. She was willing to perform this task because she was vitally interested in making the business a success. She had invested the proceeds from the sale of her modest home and from her husband's insurance policy in the venture. If it failed, the major part of her financial resources would be lost.

A beer license was granted by the state authorities. On August 15, the partnership sent a check for $35 to the distributor who supplied beer. This $35 constituted a deposit on bottles and kegs necessary for the operation of the bar and would be returned to the Smoky Valley Cafe after all bottles and kegs had been returned to the beer distributor.

In October, the partners decided that to continue to offer their patrons quality food, they would have to add to their equipment. This new equipment cost $415.95, and because the supplier of the equipment was unimpressed with the firm's credit rating, the equipment was paid for in cash.

The month of November did not improve the cash position of the business. In fact, the cash balance became so low that Mrs. Bevan contributed additional cash in the amount of $400 to the business. She had hopes, however, that the future would prove to be more profitable.

The Smoky Valley Cafe was located on a major highway, and a great deal of business was obtained from truck drivers. One of these truck driver patrons, Fred Mead, became a frequent customer. He soon gained the friendship of Mrs. Maywood. On the night of December 12, Fred Mead stopped in the cafe. Shortly after he left, Mrs. Maywood retired to her room. A few hours later, Mr. Maywood came in and asked for her, and after a brief search discovered that she had departed through a window. Her absence led him to the conclusion that she had departed with Fred Mead, and he thereupon set out in pursuit of the pair.

On December 16, Mrs. Bevan decided that the partnership was dissolved because she had not heard any word from either of the Maywoods. (The courts subsequently affirmed that the partnership was dissolved as of December 16, 1946.) Although she had no intention of ceasing operations, she realized that an accounting would have to be made as of December 16. She called in Mr. Bailey, a local accountant, for this purpose.

Mrs. Bevan told Mr. Bailey that they had been able to pay $700 on the mortgage while the partnership was operating. Cash on hand amounted to $65.35, but the bank balance was only $9.78. Mr. Bailey found bills owed by the cafe totaling $92.01. Mrs. Bevan said that her best estimate was that there was $100 worth of food on hand.

Mr. Bailey estimated that a reasonable allowance for depreciation on the fixed assets was as follows:

Assets	Depreciation Allowance
Land improvements	$ 44.45
Buildings	233.45
Cafe equipment	44.19

Questions

1. Draw up a balance sheet for the Smoky Valley Cafe as of August 12, 1946, taking into account the events described in the first two paragraphs of the case.

2. Draw up a balance sheet as of December 16, 1946.

3. What were the equities of the Maywoods and Mrs. Bevan, respectively? (In partnership law, the partners share equally in profits and losses unless there is a specific provision to the contrary. Each partner in the Smoky Valley Cafe, therefore, would have an equity in one third of the profits, or his equity would be decreased by one third of the losses.)

4. Do you suppose that the partners received these amounts? Why?

Chapter 3

INTRODUCTION TO THE MEASUREMENT OF INCOME

LET US REFER back to the January 4 transaction of Glendale Market (p. 51). On that day, merchandise costing $200 was sold for $300 cash. Looking first at the affect of this transaction on assets, we note that although inventory decreased by $200, cash increased by $300, so that the total assets increased by the difference, $100. From the dual-aspect concept, which states that the total of the assets must always equal the total of the equities, we know that the equities side of the balance sheet must also have increased by $100. Since no liabilities were affected, the increase must have occurred in the owner's equity item. In summary, because assets were sold for more than was paid for them, the owner's equity increased. Such increases in owner's equity are called *profit* or *income.*

Because of the importance to the success of the business of the transactions affecting profit, a separate accounting report is prepared to summarize all such transactions occurring over a specified period of time. This report is called the income statement.

This chapter discusses the income statement and two accounting concepts which govern its preparation, the accrual concept and the realization concept.

THE ACCRUAL CONCEPT

The essence of the accrual concept is that income arises from operating events that increase owner's equity, and only from such events. The sale of merchandise at a profit, as described above, is one such event. In understanding how this profit came about, it is useful to consider two aspects of this event separately: the $300 received from the sale, and the $200 decrease in inventory. If we look only at the $300, we see that it is an increase in the asset, and a corresponding *increase* in owner's equity. The $200, taken by itself, is a decrease in the asset, inventory, and a corresponding *decrease* in owner's equity. These two aspects illustrate the only two ways in which business operations can affect owner's equity: they can increase it, or they can decrease it.

62

Any increase in owner's equity resulting from the operation of the business is called a *revenue*. Any decrease is called an *expense*. Income is the excess of revenues over expenses.[1] (If expenses exceed revenue, the difference is called a *loss*.) Restating the transactions described above in these terms, there was revenue of $300, expense of $200, and income of $100.

It is extremely important to recognize that income is associated with changes in owner's equity, and has no necessary relation to changes in cash. Income connotes "well-offness." Roughly speaking the bigger the income, the better off are the owners. An increase in cash, however, does not necessarily mean that the owners are any better off—that their equity has increased. The increase in cash may merely be offset by a decrease in some other asset or an increase in a liability, with no affect on owner's equity at all.

Again, reference to the transactions of Glendale Market may help clarify this point. When Glendale Market borrowed $5,000 from the bank on January 2 (p. 50), its cash was increased, but this was exactly matched by an increase in the liability to the bank. There was no change in owner's equity since Mr. Smith, the owner, had no greater claim on the assets. No income resulted from this transaction; the $5,000 was not revenue. Similarly, the purchase of inventory for $2,000 cash on January 3 (p. 51) resulted in a decrease in cash but there was an exactly corresponding increase in another asset, inventory, and therefore owner's equity was not changed.

As we have already seen, the sale for $300 of inventory costing $200 did result in income, but it should be noted that the income was $100, whereas cash increased by $300, so even here the income is different from the amount by which the cash changed. In short, although the typical person measures his personal income by the amount of money he receives, he must be careful *not* to use a similar line of reasoning when thinking about the income of a business.

The Accounting Period

Considering the whole life of the business, net income is simply the excess of the amount the owners get out of the business over what they

---

[1] Some years ago, the terms, "income" or "gross income" were also used to refer to the concept here defined as revenue, which obviously led to much confusion. Some people still use *income* in this obsolete sense. The student is urged to think of *income* as always referring to a *difference,* but to be aware of the fact that not everyone follows this practice. (For example, the Income Tax Form 1040 still uses the phrases "dividend income," "interest income," and "pension and annuity income," for items that actually are *revenues,* according to the modern definition; the government is not always quick to change its ways.)

put into it, an amount that can easily be determined. Businessmen cannot wait until the business has ended for information on how much income has been earned, however. They need to know at frequent intervals "how things are going." Therefore, accountants choose some convenient segment of time, such as a year, and they collect, summarize, and report all the material changes in owners' equity that have occurred during that time. The time interval chosen is called the *accounting period*.

For the purpose of reporting to outsiders, the year is the usual accounting period. Pacioli, the first author of an accounting text, wrote in 1494: "Books should be closed each year, especially in a partnership, because frequent accounting makes for long friendship."[2] Most corporate bylaws require an annual report to the stockholders, and income tax reporting is also on an annual basis.

Formerly, the accounting year, or *fiscal* year, corresponded to the calendar year, but an increasing number of businesses are finding that there are advantages in using the *natural business year* instead of the calendar year. For example, nearly all department stores end their fiscal year on January 31, after the Christmas rush and its repercussions in the form of returns and clearance sales.

Management invariably needs information oftener than once a year, and reports for management are therefore prepared more frequently. The most common period is a month, but the period may be as short as a week or even a day. These reports are called *interim* reports to distinguish them from the annual reports.

Businesses are living, continuing organisms. The act of chopping the stream of business events into time periods is therefore somewhat arbitrary since business activities do not stop or change measurably as one accounting period ends and another begins. It is this fact that makes the problem of measuring expense and revenue in an accounting period the most difficult problem in accounting.

The diagram in Illustration 3–1 shows a portion of the life of a

Illustration 3–1

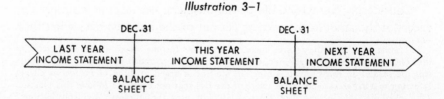

<hr />

[2] Lucas Pacioli, *Summa de Arithmetica Geometria Proportioni et Proportionalita* from the translation by John B. Geijsbeck.

business that has been divided into annual accounting periods. For each of these accounting periods an income statement is prepared, and for each point between periods (i.e., the close of business December 31) there is a balance sheet. In the next sections the measurement of expenses in "this year" will be discussed.

Measurement of Expense

Expenses are the costs incurred in connection with the earning of revenue. The term "expense" connotes "sacrifices made," "the cost of services or benefits received," or "resources consumed" during an accounting period. The term "cost" is not synonymous with "expense." As just explained, "expense" means a decrease in owners' equity that arises from the operation of a business during a specified accounting period, whereas "cost" means any monetary sacrifice, whether or not the sacrifice affects owners' equity during a given accounting period.

The American Accounting Association Committee gives the following definition:

> Expense is the expired cost, directly or indirectly related to a given fiscal period, of the flow of goods or services into the market and of related operations. . . . Recognition of cost expiration is based either on a complete or partial decline in the usefulness of assets, or on the appearance of a liability without a corresponding increase in assets.[3]

Expenses and Expenditures. An *expenditure* takes place when an asset or service is acquired. The expenditure may be made by cash, by the exchange of another asset, or by incurring a liability. Over the entire life of a business most expenditures made by a business become expenses, and there are no expenses that are not represented by an expenditure. In any time segment *shorter* than the life of a business, however, there is no necessary correspondence between expense and expenditure.

> EXAMPLE: In 1963, $1,000 of fuel oil was purchased for cash. This was an *expenditure* of $1,000, the exchange of one asset for another. If none of this fuel oil was consumed in 1963, there was no *expense* in 1963. If the fuel oil was consumed in 1964, there was an *expense* of $1,000 in 1964.

The American Accounting Association Committee describes the recognition of expenses as follows:

> Expense is given recognition in the period in which there is (a) a direct identification or association with the revenue of the period, as in the case of merchandise delivered to customers; (b) an indirect association with the revenue

---

[3] "Accounting and Reporting Standards for Corporate Financial Statements," 1957 Revision, *The Accounting Review,* October 1957, p. 541

of the period, as in the case of office salaries or rent; or (c) a measurable expiration of asset costs even though not associated with the production of revenue for the current period, as in the case of losses from flood or fire.[4]

The expenses of "this year" therefore include the cost of the products *sold* during the year, even though these products were purchased or manufactured in a prior year; the wages and salaries *earned* by employees who sold these products, whether or not they were paid during the year; and the supplies, telephone, electricity, and other assets or services *consumed* or *used* during the year in connection with the production of this revenue.

Four types of events need to be considered in distinguishing between amounts that are properly considered as expenses of a given accounting period and the expenditures or cash payments made in connection with these items. Focusing on "this year" in the diagram in Illustration 3–1, these are as follows:

1. Expenditures this year that are also expenses of this year.
2. Expenditures made prior to this year that become expenses during this year. These appeared as assets on the balance sheet at the beginning of this year.
3. Expenditures made this year that will become expenses in subsequent years. These will appear as assets on the balance sheet at the end of this year.
4. Expenses of this year that will be paid for in a subsequent year. On the balance sheet at the end of this year, these appear as liabilities.

Expenditures That Are Also Expenses. This is the simplest type of event, and the least troublesome to account for. If an item is acquired during the year, it is an expenditure; if it is consumed during the same year, it is also an expense of the year.

Assets That Become Expenses. On January 1, the balance sheet shows certain assets. During "this year" some of these assets are used up and hence are transformed into expenses. The three principal types of such assets are described below.

First, there are *inventories* of products; these become expenses when the products are sold.

Second, there are *prepaid expenses* and *deferred charges*. These represent services or other assets purchased prior to "this year" but not yet used up when the year begins. They become expenses in the year in which the services are used or the assets are consumed. *Insurance protection* is one such item; the premium on most types of insurance policies is paid in advance, and the insurance protection bought with this

---

[4] *Ibid.,* p. 341.

premium is an asset until the accounting period in which the insurance protection is received, at which time it becomes an expense. Prepaid rent follows the same pattern, with the expense being associated with the year in which the company receives the benefit of occupying the rented premises.

> EXAMPLE: A company purchased three-year insurance protection on December 31, 1963. The $900 appears as an asset on the balance sheet of December 31, 1963. In 1964, $300 becomes an expense and $600 remains as an asset on the balance sheet of December 31, 1964. In 1965, $300 more becomes an expense, and so on.

> EXAMPLE: A company paid $10,000 to its landlord on July 1, 1963, representing an advance payment of one year's rent. Of this amount $5,000 is rent expense of 1963. On the balance sheet of December 31, 1963, $5,000 appears as an asset, and this amount becomes an expense in 1964.

Another, and somewhat different, type of prepaid expense is *prepaid taxes.* Certain taxes are paid for in advance of the accounting period to which they apply, and although it is farfetched to say that this accounting period "benefits" from the taxes, it is reasonable to charge these taxes as an expense in the accounting period, or periods, for which the tax is levied.

The third category of assets that will become expenses is *long-lived* assets. Most fixed assets (with the exception of land) have a limited useful life. They are purchased with the expectation that they will be used in the operation of the business in future periods, and they will become expenses in these future periods. The principle is exactly the same as that of the insurance policy previously mentioned, which also was purchased for the benefit of future periods. An important difference between a fixed asset, such as a building, and an insurance policy is that the life of a building is usually difficult to estimate, whereas the life of an insurance policy is known precisely. It follows that estimating the portion of a building's cost that is an expense in a given accounting period is a more difficult task than that of determining the insurance expense of a period. The mechanism used to convert the cost of fixed assets to expense is called "depreciation" and is described in Chapter 6.

Expenditures That Are Not Yet Expenses. As the preceding examples show, some expenditures made to acquire assets "this year" are not expenses of "this year" because the assets have not yet been used up. These include not only the purchase of assets as such but also expenditures incurred in connection with the *manufacture* of products that are to be sold in some future year. Thus, wages and salaries earned by production personnel and all other costs associated with manufacturing become part of the cost of the product manufactured and remain as an asset, inventory, until the product is sold. The distinction between manufacturing costs, which initially are added to inventory amounts and other costs, which are expenses of the current period, will be discussed in more detail in Chapter 7.

Expenses Not Yet Paid. Some expenses which were incurred "this year" are not paid for by the end of the year. The parties who furnished these goods or services have a claim against the business for the amounts owed them, and these amounts are therefore liabilities of the company as of December 31. The liability for wages earned but not paid for is an example that has already been mentioned. Several other types of obligations have the same characteristic; namely, that although services were rendered in an accounting period prior to that for which the balance sheet is prepared, these services have not yet been paid for. The *incurrence* of these expenses reduces owners' equity; the subsequent *payment* of the obligation does not affect owners' equity.

For all obligations of this type, the transaction involved is essentially the same: the expense is shown in the period in which the services were used, and the obligation that results from these services is shown on the liability section of the balance sheet as of the end of the period.

> EXAMPLE: In 1962 an employee earned $50 that was not paid him. This is an expense of $50 in 1962, and there is a corresponding liability of $50 (called accrued wages) on the balance sheet as of December 31, 1962. In 1963, when the employee is paid, the liability disappears, and there is a corresponding reduction in cash.

Note that in these examples, the basic equality, Assets = Equities, is always maintained. The earning of wages resulted in an expense of $50, which was a decrease in owners' equity, and there was an equal increase in the liability, accrued wages, so the total of the equities was unchanged. The payment of the $50 resulted in a decrease in cash and a decrease in the liability, accrued wages; that is, both assets and equities were reduced by $50.

Another common item of this type is *interest*. Interest is the cost of borrowing money, and it is an expense of the period during which the money was borrowed. Interest rates are usually stated on an annual basis. The treatment is different depending on whether the interest is paid when the loan *matures* (i.e., falls due) or whether it is paid in advance. The latter practice is called *discounting* and is customary for short-term bank loans. An example of each will be given.

EXAMPLE: On December 1, 1963, the company borrowed $1,000 for four months at 6 per cent interest, the interest and principal to be paid on March 31. The loan itself results in an increase of cash, $1,000, and creates a liability, loans payable, of $1,000. The total interest cost is $1,000 × 4/12 × 0.06 = $20. One fourth of this interest, $5, is an expense of 1963. Since it has not been paid, $5 also appears as a liability item, interest payable, on the December 31, 1963, balance sheet. The remaining $15 interest is an expense of 1964. When the loan is repaid on March 31, cash is reduced by $1,020, and this is balanced by the decrease in loans payable of $1,000, the decrease in interest payable of $5, and the interest expense of $15.

EXAMPLE: On December 1, 1963, the company borrowed $1,000 for four months at 6 per cent discounted. The company receives $980. Interest expense for 1963 is $5, as in the preceding example, but now there is an asset, prepaid interest, of $15 on the December 31, 1963, balance sheet, representing the interest cost that will not become an expense until 1964. Thus, the following items are affected by this transaction in 1963: Cash has increased by $980; there is an asset, prepaid interest, of $15; owners' equity has decreased by the applicable $5 of interest expense; and there is a liability, notes payable, of $1,000. Note that, as always, the change in assets ($980 + $15) equals the change in equities ($1,000 − $5).

Measurement of Revenue

Revenues are also measured in accordance with the accrual concept; that is, revenue accrues in the accounting period in which it is earned, which is not necessarily the same as the period in which the cash is received.

As was the case with expenses and expenditures, a careful distinction must be made between revenues and cash receipts. Referring back to our diagram in Illustration 3–1, the balance sheet at the end of "last year" may show, as liabilities, some items that become revenues in "this year." On that balance sheet these are called *deferred revenues* or *precollected revenues*. They represent an advance payment which creates a liability to render a service in some future period. The owner of a building who receives rent in advance, the insurance company which receives insurance premiums in advance, and the magazine publisher who receives subscription revenue in advance will have such liabilities on their books.

Conversely, revenue may be earned "this year" even though payment is not received until "next year." In this case, the balance sheet as of the end of "this year" will show the asset "accounts receivable" representing amounts owed to the business on account of sales made "this year" for which payment has not yet been received. The year-end balance sheet may also show the asset, *accrued revenue* (or a more descriptive term such as accrued *interest* revenue). representing amounts due the business for services rendered during the accounting period that have not been actually invoiced to the recipient. For example, interest on funds loaned by the business is revenue for the period during which the loan is outstanding, and recognition of this revenue results in corresponding recognition of the amount of interest receivable from the borrower; the latter amount is an asset.

The difference between revenue and receipts is illustrated in the following tabulation that shows various types of sales transactions and classifies the effect of each on cash receipts and sales revenue for "this year":

	Amount	This Year	
		Cash Receipts	Sales Revenue
1. Cash sales made this year...........	$200	$200	$200
2. Credit sales made last year; cash received this year.................	300	300	0
3. Credit sales made this year; cash received this year.................	400	400	400
4. Credit sales made this year; cash received next year................	100	0	100
Total........................		$900	$700

Note that in the above illustration the total cash receipts does not equal the total sales revenue for the period. The totals would be equal in a given accounting period only (1) if the company made all its sales for cash, or (2) if the amount of cash collected from credit customers in an accounting period happened to equal the amount of credit sales made during that period.

THE REALIZATION CONCEPT

We have referred to the "earning" of revenues. A basic accounting concept is that revenue is considered as being earned on the date at which it is *realized;* that is, on the date when goods or services are furnished to the customer in exchange for cash or some other valuable consideration. For services, revenue is recognized in the period in which the service is rendered. For tangible products, revenue is recognized not when a sales order is received, not when a contract is signed, not when the goods are manufactured, but rather when the product is shipped or delivered to the customer.

There are many fine points concerning the exact date on which legal title, or ownership, of the goods passes from one party to the other. In general, the accountant uses the date the product was shipped or the date shown on the invoice to the customer, whichever is later.

There is a difference here between accounting and economics. In economics (and in fact), the manufacturing process is regarded as creating value, but in financial accounting only the *costs* of manufacture are recognized as adding to the value of the product during the manufacturing cycle; all the profit (i.e., the increase in owners' equity) is recorded at the time of sale.

This difference between accounting and economics is explained by the importance of the criterion of objectivity in accounting. There is no objective way of measuring how much profit is created during the manufacturing process. The outcome of the whole process is known with reasonable certainty only when the buyer and seller have agreed on a price and the goods have been delivered. Also, at this time there is usually an invoice, a cash register record, or some other tangible evidence as to the revenue arising from the transaction—evidence that permits the facts to be verified by some outside party. This "test of the marketplace," or "arm's-length agreement," as it is called, provides an objective measure of the revenue, and this is the essential reason for the realization concept.

In cases where revenue can be objectively measured earlier than the date of exchange between buyer and seller, it is often recognized on this earlier date. In gold mining, for example, revenue is recognized in the accounting period in which the gold is mined, rather than the period in which it is sold, because gold always has a specified value, and a market exchange is not necessary to establish this value.

Conversely, revenue may not be recognized in the period in which the goods are delivered if there is considerable doubt as to the amount of cash that is actually going to be received from the customer. In certain types of installment selling, for example, a sizable fraction of the customers default on their contracts; and in view of the uncertainty of realizing the full amount of the sale, the seller may decide to recognize revenue only as the installment payments are received.

The general rule that realization occurs on the date when goods are shipped or services rendered implies a reasonable certainty, but not an absolute certainty, that revenue has been earned on that date. The customer may not pay his bill, or he may return the goods, or he may, perhaps several months later, ask to have repairs made under the terms of a warranty agreement. These subsequent events, which make the actual income less than it was thought to be on the date of realization, are recognized in the accounts if reasonable estimates can be made of their impact. The method of doing this is described in Chapter 5.

> EXAMPLE: A company manufactures a machine in March, ships and bills it to a customer in April, and receives payment in May. The machine carries a guarantee which provides for free repairs over the next five years. The revenue from this transaction is realized not in March, the month of manufacture, nor in May, the month in which cash is received, but in April, the month in which the exchange takes place. The fact that there may be future costs associated with this transaction is recognized by setting up, also in April, a provision for the estimated future repair cost. This is an expense account.

Matching

The accrual concept is often described as the "matching" concept. It is important that the expenses recognized in an accounting period be *matched* with (i.e., be measured in a manner consistent with) the revenues recognized in that period. This means that under the usual practice of recognizing revenue at the time of shipment, the total cost of the products shipped is an expense of this same period. In other words, the "cost of products sold" item and the "sales" item on an income statement should refer to the same physical products.

Expenses incurred in producing revenue are also matched against the revenue produced. For example, if "this year" a salesman received an advance commission for selling a product that is to be shipped and recognized as revenue "next year," the commission is an expense of "next year" rather than of "this year." This distinction is not always easily made in practice, however; and in accordance with the doctrine of materiality, it is sometimes disregarded.

If expenses cannot be traced to specific items of revenue, they are charged to the year in which they are incurred. Salary earned by a salesman whether or not he makes sales, as contrasted with a commission paid on a specific sale, is an example. Such salary is an expense of the period in which the salesman earned it.

THE INCOME STATEMENT

The accounting report that summarizes the revenue items, the expense items, and the difference between them (net income) for an accounting period is called the *income statement* (or the "profit and loss statement," "statement of earnings," or "statement of operations"). In a technical sense the income statement is subordinate to the balance sheet in that it shows in some detail the items that together account for the change in one balance sheet item, retained earnings, during an accounting period. Nevertheless, the information on the income statement is usually much more important than information on the balance sheet since the income statement reports the results of operations and indicates reasons for the business's profitability or lack thereof. The importance of the income statement is illustrated by the fact that in situations where accountants in recording an event must choose between a procedure which distorts the balance sheet or one which distorts the income statement (a choice which is unfortunately necessary on occasions), they usually choose the former.

Like any accounting report, the income statement should be prepared in the form most useful to those who read it. No specific format is prescribed. The following categories are found, in the order given, on many income statements of merchandising companies:

1. *Sales* (and other revenue from operations).
2. *Cost of sales* (or "cost of goods sold").
3. *Gross profit* (or "gross margin," or "gross income"), the difference between sales and cost of sales.
4. *Operating expenses,* which are frequently broken down into selling expenses, administrative expenses, and general expenses, with the significant items of expense reported separately under each category.
5. *Operating profit,* the difference between gross profit and operating expenses.
6. *Nonoperating revenue* (or "other revenue"), including interest, rent, and the like (unless the company's principal business is loaning money or renting property).
7. *Nonoperating expenses,* including financial costs and other expenses not directly related to the conduct of the principal activity of the business during the accounting period.
8. *Profit before income taxes,* Item 5, plus Item 6, less Item 7.
9. *Provision for income taxes.*
10. *Net income* (or net profit, or net loss), Item 8, less Item 9.

Instead of the format outlined above, some companies use a *single-step* income statement. This format shows sales and other revenue as the first item, followed by a list of all expenses one after the other; the total of these expenses is subtracted from revenue to give net income. An example is shown in Illustration 3–2. It should be noted that when the statement is presented in this manner, the reader cannot ascertain the gross profit. In some industries (e.g., certain service industries), the gross profit figure has little if any significance, but in other situations the single-step statement hides what may well be an important piece of information.

The "sales" and "cost of goods sold" item on the income statement are discussed in more detail below.

Illustration 3–2

SINGLE-STEP INCOME STATEMENT

United States Steel Corporation

	1963	1962
Products and services sold..........	$3,637,173,138	$3,500,955,567
Costs		
Employment costs		
Wages and salaries..............	$1,390,262,471	$1,395,308,906
Employe benefits................	221,214,016	213,012,241
	$1,611,476,487	$1,608,321,147
Products and services bought.........	1,210,924,632	1,192,422,092
Wear and exhaustion of facilities......	307,828,526	265,875,921
Interest and other costs on long-term		
debt.........................	35,580,838	37,471,879
State, local and miscellaneous taxes....	102,813,317	101,184,711
Estimated United States and foreign		
taxes on income.................	165,000,000	132,000,000
Total......................	$3,433,623,800	$3,337,275,750
Income...........................	$ 203,549,338	$ 163,679,817
Dividends declared		
On cumulative preferred stock ($7 per		
share).........................	$ 25,219,677	$ 25,219,677
On common stock ($2.00 per share		
1963, $2.50 per share 1962)........	108,231,284	135,286,105
Income reinvested in business.......	$ 70,098,377	$ 3,174,035

Sales

An income statement often shows several separate items in the revenue section, the net of which is the *net sales* figure. For example:

Gross sales....................		$15,400
Less: Returns and allowances...$450		
Sales discounts.......... 350		800
Net sales....................		$14,600

Gross sales is the total invoice price of the goods shipped (or services rendered) plus the cash sales made during the period. It does not ordinarily include *sales taxes* or *excise taxes* that may be charged the customer. Such taxes are not revenue but rather represent collections which the business makes on behalf of the government. They are a liability to the government until paid. Similarly, postage, freight, or other items billed to the customer at cost are not revenue; they appear not in the sales figure but as an offset to the costs the company incurs for these items. Exceptions are made to these rules when it is not feasible to disentangle the revenue and nonrevenue portions of the transaction.

Sales returns and allowances represent the sales value of goods that were returned by the customer or on which he was given a credit because they were not as specified or for some other reason. The amount could have been subtracted from the sales figure directly, without showing it as a separate item on the income statement, but it is often considered as being important enough information to management to warrant reporting it.

Sales discount is the amount of *cash* discounts taken by customers for prompt payment. For example, if the business sells merchandise for $1,000 on terms 2/10, n/30 (2 per cent off if payment is made in 10 days, and the net, or total, amount due in 30 days), and the customer takes advantage of the discount by paying within 10 days, the business receives only $980 cash, and records the other $20 as a sales discount. On some income statements, sales discounts are listed as an operating expense rather than a deduction from sales; but showing them as an adjustment to the billed price, as above, is probably more common and is more indicative of their character. *Trade discounts,* which are formulas used in figuring the actual selling price from published catalogues or price lists (e.g., "list less 40 per cent"), do not appear in the accounting records at all.

Cost of Goods Sold

At the identical moment that income is increased by the sales value of a product sold, it is also decreased by the cost of that product. Indeed, were it not for the fact that the separate figures for sales revenue and the cost of products sold are useful to management, a record could be made only of the net increase in owners' equity that results from a sale; this is the gross profit—the difference between cost and selling price.

Some businesses, especially those that sell high unit value merchandise in small quantities (such as automobile dealers), keep a record of the cost of each individual item sold. In these businesses, the total cost of the goods sold in an accounting period can be determined simply by adding up the costs recorded for the individual transactions. This same cost is also subtracted from the asset, inventory, so that at all times the asset item shows the cost of merchandise still on hand. This method is referred to as the *perpetual inventory* method.

If the business does not have such a direct method for ascertaining the cost of the products sold during an accounting period, it must deduce the cost by indirect means. The procedure for doing this is described in Chapter 5. The measurement of cost of sales in a manufacturing business involves special problems that are discussed in Chapter 7.

OTHER CHANGES IN OWNERS' EQUITY

If the logic of the accrual concept were considered narrowly, only those expenses that relate to operations of the current period would be shown on the income statement for that period. There are a number of events, however, that although not strictly conforming to this concept are nevertheless reported as expenses of the period in which they are recognized.

An example that happens frequently is the transaction required to correct an error made in a *prior* accounting period. Suppose that in 1964 a company receives a bill for services performed for it by a lawyer in 1963, but the cost of these services had been overlooked when the 1963 financial statements were prepared. This cost is not properly an expense of 1964, and the logical procedure, therefore, would be to make the deduction in owners' equity directly rather than to report it on the income statement for 1964 as an expense of that year. Such a procedure is followed by some companies. Many other companies, however, follow the doctrine of the "clean surplus," or the "all-inclusive income statement," and report *all* (or almost all) increases and decreases in owners' equity, other than dividend payments and changes in capital structure, on the current year's income statement.

The Accounting Principles Board has gone on record in favor of this practice, as follows:

> . . . there should be a general presumption that all items of profit and loss recognized during the period are to be used in determining the figure reported as net income. The only possible exception to this presumption relates to items which in the aggregate are material in relation to the company's net income and are clearly not identifiable with or do not result from the usual or typical business operations of the period. Thus, only extraordinary items such as the following may be excluded from the determination of net income for the year, and they

should be excluded when their inclusion would impair the significance of net income so that misleading inferences might be drawn therefrom:

(a) Material charges or credits (other than ordinary adjustments of a recurring nature) specifically related to operations of prior years and adjustments of income taxes for prior years;

(b) Material charges or credits resulting from unusual sales of assets not acquired for resale and not of the type in which the company usually deals;

(c) Material losses of a type not usually insured against, such as those resulting from wars, riots, earthquakes, and similar calamities or catastrophes except where such losses are a recurrent hazard of the business;

(d) The write-off of a material amount of intangibles;

(e) The write-off of material amounts of unamortized bond discount or premium and bond issue expenses at the time of the retirement or refunding of the debt before maturity.[5]

The import of this statement is that items not relating to current operations should nevertheless appear on the current income statement unless they are material in relation to net income and unless their inclusion would be likely to lead to "misleading inferences" about net income for the period. This preference for the all-inclusive income idea leaves considerable latitude for judgment in specific situations, and income statements and changes in owners' equity not reflected in the income statement need to be examined carefully so as to determine what the practice has been in the company studied.

Statement of Retained Earnings

Sometimes, all changes in the retained earnings item are reported in what is called a "statement of retained earnings" (also called "surplus reconciliation statement"). This statement shows the balance of the retained earnings item at the beginning of an accounting period; the changes that have occurred during the period arising from net income, dividends, and the items listed in the preceding section; and the balance at the end of the period. Such a statement links the income statement to the balance sheet. It is often shown at the bottom of an income statement.

The Report Package

A moment's reflection will show that the two types of accounting reports, the balance sheet and the income statement, can be combined into a package that discloses important information about the events of an accounting period. Such a package would consist of (1) a balance sheet as of the beginning of the period, (2) an income statement for the period, and (3) a balance sheet as of the end of the period. In

---

[5] AICPA, *Accounting Research Bulletin No. 43*, p. 63.

addition, there may be a statement of retained earnings. A much condensed version of such a package, presented so as to show the relationships among the various components, is shown in Illustration 3–3. (The same December 31, 1963, balance sheet is shown in more detail in Illustration 2–1.)

A Reminder: The Dual-Aspect Concept

Each of the statements and examples given in the foregoing discussion is consistent with the dual-aspect concept. Going back to the fuel oil example on page 65, the purchase of fuel oil for cash is reflected on the balance sheet by a decrease in the asset, cash, and a corresponding increase in the asset, fuel oil inventory; the consumption of fuel oil is represented by a decrease in the asset, fuel oil inventory, and an equal decrease in owners' equity. The recognition of revenue, which increases owners' equity, is accompanied by an equal increase in cash or some other asset. Every other event described in this chapter can be analyzed in terms of its dual effect on balance sheet items, so that at all times the basic equation, Assets = Equities, is preserved. Expense and revenue items represent no more than decreases and increases in owners' equity during an accounting period. For purposes of management analysis, it is important to collect and report these items in some detail, but insofar as their effect on the balance sheet goes, they can all be expressed directly in terms of their effect on owners' equity.

Another Reminder: Materiality

The doctrine of *materiality* is important in the process of determining the expenses and revenue for a given accounting period. Many of the expense items that are recorded for a given accounting period are necessarily estimates, and in some cases they are not very close estimates. There is a point beyond which it is not worthwhile to attempt to refine these estimates. Telephone expense is a familiar example. Telephone bills, although rendered monthly, often do not coincide with a calendar month. It would be possible to analyze each bill and classify all the toll calls according to the month in which they were made. This would be following the accrual concept precisely. Few companies bother to do this, however. They simply consider the telephone bill as an expense of the month in which the bill is received, on the grounds that a system that would ascertain the real expense would not be justified by the accuracy gained. Since in many businesses the amount of the bill is likely to be relatively stable from one month to another, no significant error may be involved in this practice. Similarly, very few businesses attempt to match

Illustration 3-3

A "PACKAGE" OF ACCOUNTING REPORTS

Balance Sheet
As of December 31, 1962

ASSETS

Current assets	$23,839,904
Fixed assets	14,255,720
Other assets	180,535
Total Assets	$38,276,159

EQUITIES

Current liabilities	$12,891,570
Other liabilities	3,000,000
Common stock	15,000,000
Retained earnings	7,384,589
Total Equities	$38,276,159

Income Statement
For the Year 1963

Net sales		$75,478,221
Less: Cost of sales		52,227,004
Gross profit		$23,251,217
Less: Operating expenses		10,784,830
Operating profit		$12,466,387
Provision for income taxes		6,344,000
Net Income		$ 6,122,387

Statement of Retained Earnings

Retained earnings, 12/31/62		$ 7,384,589
Add: Net income, 1963		6,122,387
		$13,506,976
Less: Dividends		4,390,000
Retained Earnings, 12/31/63		$ 9,116,976

Balance Sheet
As of December 31, 1963

ASSETS

Current assets	$22,651,072
Fixed assets	13,411,779
Other assets	173,214
Total Assets	$36,236,065

EQUITIES

Current liabilities	$ 9,119,089
Other liabilities	3,000,000
Common stock	15,000,000
Retained earnings	9,116,976
Total Equities	$36,236,065

the expenses of making telephone calls to the specific revenues that might have been produced by those calls.

TAX ACCOUNTING VERSUS BUSINESS ACCOUNTING

In figuring its income tax, a business must determine its net taxable income. The amounts of revenue and expense used to determine federal taxable income are usually similar to, but not identical with, amounts measured in accordance with the principles of financial accounting. The differences are such that it is unwise to rely on income tax regulations as a basis for solving business accounting problems.

Unless tax rates applicable to the business are expected to increase in the future, a business usually reports the minimum possible amount of taxable income in the current year, thus postponing tax payments as much as possible to future years. It does this generally by recognizing expenses as soon as legally possible, but postponing recognition of revenue for as long as possible. Note that this is a process of shifting revenue and expense from one period to another; over the long run in most businesses, there is little difference between the total expenses and revenues computed for tax purposes and the total expenses and revenues computed for financial accounting. The objective of minimizing current taxes is, as the Supreme Court has pointed out, a perfectly legal and ethical one, provided it is done consistently with the tax regulations. It is also legal and proper under most circumstances to figure income one way for tax purposes and another way for accounting purposes.

The objective of minimizing current taxes is not by any means the same as the objective of financial accounting, which is to inform management and others as to the income earned. Therefore, the two measurements of income may well be different. For example, in order to encourage research, the tax regulations permit most research costs to be counted as expenses in the year in which the research is done; whereas if the research results in products that will produce revenue in future years, it is consistent with the accrual concept to spread these costs over the years in which the revenue from the new products is earned.

As a practical matter, many businesses choose to pattern their accounting practices after the tax regulations. This policy is convenient in that it reduces somewhat the number of separate records that must be maintained. However, if it is carried to the point of complete subservience to the tax regulations, serious distortions in accounting reports can result. In constructing a business income statement, the accountant should not use the authority of a tax regulation as a substitute for careful thinking about the best way of measuring income in accordance with accounting principles.

Although tax regulations are not described in detail in this book, references are made to accounting practices which are or are not consistent with them. The businessman learns early the importance of becoming thoroughly familiar with the principal tax rules that affect his operations and the importance of consulting an expert when unusual situations arise.

SUMMARY

Management is especially interested in how the operations of the business change the owners' equity, that is, in revenues and expenses and the difference between them, net income. In measuring net income, the continuing life stream of the business is divided into accounting periods, and an income statement is prepared for each period. Revenues and expenses are measured in accordance with the accrual concept; that is, the measurements are of the revenues earned and the expenses incurred during an accounting period, as distinguished from the cash received and expenditures made during the period. Revenues are generally recognized in the accounting period in which they are realized; that is, at the time goods or services are exchanged for cash or some other valuable consideration. To the extent feasible, expenses shown for a period should match the revenues shown for the same period; that is, expenses should be those associated with the production and sale of the same goods and services that give rise to revenues in the period.

CASES

CASE 3–1.   ELMER KUPPER

In 1960, Elmer Kupper opened his own retail store. At the end of 1961, his first full year of operation, he thought he had done moderately well, and he was therefore somewhat chagrined when the trade association to which he belonged sent him figures which indicated that he had operated at a loss.

Mr. Kupper had been employed as manager of the local unit of a chain store for several years. In 1960 he had received an inheritance, and this, together with his savings, provided him with enough funds to buy a small store building on the main street of his town for $30,000, in which he opened his store.

He joined the trade association to which several thousand independent retailers in the same line of business belonged. One of the services furnished by this association was the annual compilation of typical operating figures of member firms. These figures were prepared by Hartje & Mees, a large public accounting firm. Early in 1962, Hartje & Mees sent Mr. Kupper a standard form and requested that he report his revenue and expenses on this form and return it so that his figures could be averaged in with those of other member stores. Exhibit 1 shows the figures which, with some difficulty, Mr. Kupper entered on this form.

Exhibit 1

ELMER KUPPER

Income Statement for 1961, as Prepared by Mr. Kupper

Gross sales		$65,927
Less: Returns and allowances to customers		2,426
Net sales		$63,501
Cost of merchandise sold		43,086
Gross margin		$20,415
Expenses:		
Salaries and wages	$7,232	
Advertising	1,182	
Supplies and postage	793	
Taxes, insurance, repairs, and depreciation on building	1,347	
Heat, light, and power	426	
Business and social security taxes	992	
Insurance	472	
Depreciation on equipment	375	
Interest expense	240	
Miscellaneous expense	1,827	
Income taxes	1,220	16,106
Net Profit		$ 4,309

Subsequently, he received a request from Hartje & Mees for information on his salary and on the rental value of his building. Mr. Kupper answered substantially as follows:

I own my own business, so there is no point in my charging myself a salary. I drew $6,000 from the business in 1961 for my personal use. My annual salary as manager of a Mogell store in recent years was $5,000, although I don't see what bearing this has on the figures for my own store.

I thought I made it clear in my original submission that I own my own building. It would cost me $3,500 a year to rent a similar building, and you can see from the figures that I save a considerable amount of money by not being forced to rent.

On the basis of the information in this letter, Hartje & Mees revised Mr. Kupper's figures and sent him the income statement shown in Exhibit 2. Mr. Kupper was considerably upset by this revised statement.

Exhibit 2

ELMER KUPPER

Income Statement for 1961, as Revised by Hartje & Mees

Gross sales...		$65,927
Less: Returns and allowances to customers.....................		2,426
Net sales..		$63,501
Cost of merchandise sold.................................		43,086
Gross margin...		$20,415
Expenses:		
Salaries and wages.......................................$12,232		
Advertising...	1,182	
Supplies and postage.....................................	793	
Rent..	3,500	
Heat, light, and power..................................	426	
Business and social security taxes........................	992	
Insurance..	472	
Depreciation on equipment..............................	375	
Interest expense.......................................	240	
Miscellaneous expense...................................	1,827	22,039
Net Loss...		$ 1,624

He showed it to a friend and said:

These fancy accountants have gotten my figures all mixed up. I want to know the profit I have made by operating my own business rather than by working for somebody else. They have turned my profit into a loss by calling part of it salary and part of it rent. This is merely shifting money from one pocket to another. On the other hand, they won't even let me show my income tax as an expense. I realize that the tax is levied on me as an individual rather than on the business as such, but my only source of income is my store, and I therefore think the tax is a legitimate expense of my store.

Questions

1. How much profit did Mr. Kupper's store earn in 1961? How do you explain the difference between the profit shown on Exhibit 1 and the loss shown on Exhibit 2? What, if any, accounting principles are violated in either statement?

2. Should Mr. Kupper continue to operate his own store? Has he been successful?

3. Does the income statement that would be most useful to Mr. Kupper differ from the income statement that would be most useful in compiling average figures for use by the trade association membership?

CASE 3–2.   VITAR ELECTRONICS, INC.

After six months of operation, Victor Peterson and Harold Corning met to decide what to do next with their "baby," Vitar Electronics, Inc. The company seemed to be off to a profitable start, and they were intrigued by the possibility of changing it from a part-time to a full-time venture.

Mr. Peterson, 29, was a production engineer for the Davis Machine Company, a large manufacturer; Mr. Corning, 32, was on the sales promotion staff of the same company. Each earned a salary of $7,000 per year. They were neighbors and close friends. Mr. Peterson had an inventive bent, and among his ideas was a new type of stepping switch. A stepping switch is a device which activates a number of electrical circuits in sequence automatically, one after the other. One of its uses is in product inspection and testing.[6] On his own time, Mr. Peterson developed a working model and applied for a patent. He interested the Davis quality control department in his stepping switch, and after tests and negotiation, the Davis Company, on May 1, 1959, agreed to purchase 20 units at $375 each.

Messrs. Peterson and Corning thereupon formed Vitar Electronics, Inc. Each took 200 shares of stock in exchange for $2,000 cash, a sizable fraction of their savings. Mr. Peterson also assigned his rights in the invention to the corporation in exchange for a noninterest-bearing ten-year note in the amount of $5,000.

The manufacture of the stepping switch involved principally assembly and wiring. The two men did this themselves in Mr. Corning's basement, working evenings and weekends. The 20 units were completed, and payment received, by September 1959.

Meanwhile, Mr. Corning wrote and placed free "product announcements" and a small amount of paid advertising in trade publications. These resulted in inquiries that led to orders for additional units from other companies. The owners were thereby encouraged to seek sales more vigorously, so in September they placed larger advertisements costing a total of approximately $1,000. In order to be able to fill promptly the orders expected to result from this advertising, they continued to assemble stepping switches in September and October, and by the end of October had six completed units on hand. They also had on hand a supply of printed circuits and other component parts, most of which were made to Vitar's specifications by outside companies.

During the entire six-month period from May 1 to October 31,

---

[6] A more complete description is: The Vitar Stepping Switch M-1 consists of 20 single-pole switching positions and can be wired through a plug board to perform any programing of switching forward, backward, or in any preselected pattern, up to 200 impulses per second. It can be wired to advance one position on each successive impulse fed into it or can be timed to complete the entire switching cycle automatically. There are no moving parts except for vacuum-sealed mercury whetted magnet operated relays—each guaranteed to perform 4,000,000 times. The controlling circuit is transistor powered and can operate at a speed of 7,000 impulses per second.

Messrs. Peterson and Corning each worked about ten hours a week making stepping switches, plus some additional time in preparing promotional material, answering inquiries, talking with prospective customers, and handling other Vitar problems. During this time they had paid themselves no salary, since Vitar's available cash was needed to buy components and to pay for equipment, most of which was built to

Exhibit 1

VITAR ELECTRONICS, INC.

Financial Statements as of October 31, 1959

Balance Sheet

ASSETS

Current Assets:

Cash..	$ 288.76	
Accounts receivable.............................	750.00	
Inventory of parts and components.................	2,361.90	
Completed stepping switches.....................	1,187.62	
Total Current Assets........................		$ 4,588.28
Equipment (at cost)..............................$2,879.42		
Patent rights.................................... 5,000.00		7,879.42
Total Assets.............................		$12,467.70

EQUITIES

Liabilities:

Accounts payable................................	$ 987.22
Notes payable...................................	5,000.00
Total Liabilities............................	$ 5,987.22

Capital:

Capital stock....................................$4,000.00	
Retained earnings............................... 2,480.48	
Total Capital.............................	6,480.48
Total Equities.............................	$12,467.70

Income Statement for Six Months

Sales...		$ 9,375.00
Cost of sales...................................		4,862.21
Gross profit....................................		$ 4,512.79
Advertising.....................................$1,462.10		
Other expenses................................. 570.21		2,032.31
Net Profit.....................................		$ 2,480.48

their design in a local machine shop. They decided that the time had come to think about devoting full time to Vitar. As part of their appraisal of where they stood, Mr. Corning prepared the financial statements shown in Exhibit 1. In addition to the component parts shown on the balance sheet, Vitar had also ordered $1,820.70 of printed circuits and other components, with delivery expected some time in November.

Mr. Peterson, upon seeing these statements, remarked: "Not bad for a starter. Even with our organization costs and advertising expenses deducted, we show an excellent profit, and a very gratifying return on our investment."

Questions

1. Comment on the performance of Vitar Electronics, Inc., and its status on October 31.

2. What additional information, if any, would you need before recommending a course of action for Messrs. Peterson and Corning?

CASE 3–3.   JOHN BARTLETT

John Bartlett was the inventor of a hose-clamp for automobile hose connections. Having confidence in its commercial value, but possessing no excess funds of his own, he sought among his friends and acquaintances for the necessary capital to put the hose-clamp on the market. The proposition which he placed before possible associates was that a corporation, Bartlett Manufacturing Company, should be formed with capital stock of $25,000 par value.

The project looked attractive to a number of the individuals to whom the inventor presented it, but the most promising among them—a retired manufacturer—said he would be unwilling to invest his capital without knowing what uses were intended for the cash to be received from the proposed sale of stock. He suggested that the inventor determine the probable costs of experimentation and of special machinery, and prepare for him a statement of the estimated assets and liabilities of the proposed company when ready to begin actual operation. He also asked for a statement of the estimated transactions for the first year of operations, to be based on studies the inventor had made of probable markets and costs of labor and materials. This information Mr. Bartlett consented to supply to the best of his ability.

After consulting the engineer who had aided him in constructing his patent models, Mr. Bartlett drew up the following list of data relating to the transactions of the proposed corporation during its period of organization and development:

1. The retired manufacturer would pay the corporation $10,000 cash for which he would receive stock with a par value of $10,000. The remaining stock (par value, $15,000) would be given to Mr. Bartlett in exchange for the patent on the hose-clamp.
2. Probable cost of incorporation and organization, including estimated officers' salaries during developmental period, $825.

3. Probable cost of developing special machinery, $5,000. This sum includes the cost of expert services, materials, rent of a small shop, and the cost of power, light, and miscellaneous expenditures.
4. Probable cost of raw materials: $500, of which $300 is to be used in experimental production.

On the basis of the above information, Mr. Bartlett prepared the estimated balance sheet shown in Exhibit 1.

Exhibit 1

BARTLETT MANUFACTURING COMPANY

Estimated Balance Sheet as of Date Company Begins Operations

ASSETS		EQUITIES	
Cash......................	$ 3,675	Stockholders' equity........	$25,000
Inventory.................	200		
Machinery................	5,000		
Organization costs.........	825		
Experimental costs.........	300		
Patent....................	15,000		
Total Assets...........	$25,000	Total Equities.........	$25,000

Mr. Bartlett then set down the following estimates as a beginning step in furnishing the rest of the information desired:

1. Expected sales, all to be received in cash by the end of the first year of operation, $28,000.
2. Expected additional purchases of raw materials and supplies during the course of this operating year, all paid for in cash by end of year, $9,000
3. Expected borrowing from the bank during year but loans to be repaid before close of year, $2,000. Interest on these loans, $50.
4. Expected payroll and other cash expenses and manufacturing costs for the operating year: $11,000 of manufacturing costs plus $3,000 for selling and administrative expenses, a total of $14,000.
5. New machinery and equipment to be purchased for cash, $1,000.
6. Expected inventory of raw materials and supplies at close of period, at cost, $1,800.
7. No inventory of unsold hose-clamps expected as of the end of the period. All products to be manufactured on the basis of firm orders received; none to be produced for inventory.
8. All experimental and organization costs, previously capitalized, to be charged against income of the operating year.
9. Estimated depreciation of machinery, $600.
10. Dividends paid in cash, $3,000.

It should be noted that the transactions summarized above would not necessarily take place in the sequence indicated. In practice, a considerable number of separate events, or transactions, would occur throughout the year, and many of them were dependent on one another. For example, operations were begun with an initial cash balance and inventory of raw materials, products were manufactured, and sales of these products provided funds for financing subsequent operations. Then, in turn, sales of the product subsequently manufactured yielded more funds.

Questions

1. Trace the effect on the balance sheet of each of the projected events appearing in Mr. Bartlett's list. Thus, Item 1, taken alone, would mean that cash would be increased by $28,000 and that (subject to reductions for various costs covered in later items) stockholders' equity would be increased by $28,000. Notice that in this question you are asked to consider all items in terms of their effect on the balance sheet.

2. Prepare an income statement covering the first year of planned operations and a balance sheet as of the end of that year.

3. *Assume* that the retired manufacturer received capital stock with a par value of $8,000 for the $10,000 cash he paid to the corporation, John Bartlett still receiving stock with a par value of $15,000 in exchange for his patent. Under these circumstances, how would the balance sheet in Exhibit 1 appear?

4. *Assume* that the management is interested in what the results would be if no products were sold during the first year, even though production continued at the level indicated in the original plans. The following changes would be made in the 10 items listed above: Items 1, 6, 7, and 10 are to be disregarded. Instead of Item 3, assume that a loan of $29,000 is obtained, that the loan is not repaid, but that interest thereon of $1,050 is paid during the year. Prepare an income statement for the year and a balance sheet as of the end of the year. Contrast these financial statements with those prepared in Question 2.

CASE 3–4.   AURORA MOTOR COURTS

Mr. and Mrs. Gilbert Kennard had purchased the Aurora Motor Courts in 1958 with their life savings supplemented by a loan from a close personal friend. The motor courts consisted of 15 units (i.e., rentable rooms) in a favorable location near a sizable city. They had entered the motor court business because Mr. Kennard had long wanted to run a business of his own.

Both Mr. and Mrs. Kennard felt that they had been successful. Each year saw a growth in revenue from room rentals. Furthermore, their bank balance had increased. They noted that many of their tourist and business customers returned year after year. This was attributed to their location and effort to provide consistently clean rooms and up-to-date furnishings. Fortunately no significant competition had arisen along the route on which the Aurora Motor Courts was situated.

Mr. Kennard had no formal business training, but he felt his experience since acquiring the motor courts had alerted him to the management problems involved. Both Mr. and Mrs. Kennard devoted their full time to operating the motor courts. In addition, they hired part-time help for cleaning and chambermaid work during peak seasons. They had no dining facilities but had installed coffee, cigarette, and

Exhibit 1

OPERATING DATA FOR TOURIST COURT OF 11–20 UNITS,*
1961
(Expressed as Percentages of Total Income)

Income:

Room rentals	94.31%
Other income	5.69
Total Income	100.00%

Operating Expenses:

Salaries and wages	11.48%
Executive salaries	2.46
Laundry	4.50
Linen, chinaware, glassware	1.07
Advertising, printing, stationery	3.04
Payroll, taxes, insurance	1.46
Heat, light, and power	7.45
Repairs and maintenance	4.45
Cleaning and other supplies	1.48
Telephone and telegraph	2.31
Other operating expenses	2.62
Total Operating Expenses	42.32%
Gross operating profit	57.68%

Capital Expenses:

Real estate and property taxes	4.37%
Insurance	1.65
Interest	8.35
Rent	1.11
Depreciation	17.47
Total Capital Expenses	32.95%
Net Profit	24.73%

* Copyright July 1962 issue of *Tourist Court Journal*, Temple, Texas. Further reproduction in part or in whole prohibited unless written permission obtained from the copyright owner.

candy vending machines to supplement room rentals. The vending machines posed no inventory or maintenance problem as the vending machine company provided servicing and maintenance.

A frequent guest at Aurora Motor Courts was Mr. George Austen, assistant controller of a large company. Mr. Austen visited a company branch plant in the nearby city several times a year. As he stayed at the motor courts during these trips, he became acquainted with the Kennards.

In August 1962, Mr. Kennard showed Mr. Austen the July issue of the *Tourist Court Journal,* a trade journal which contained operating percentages of motor courts for the calendar year 1961. Data were given for motor courts of various size groups. Exhibit 1 shows the percentages for motor courts with 11–20 units. Mr. Kennard commented: "These figures show a profit of 25 per cent. Our profit last year was $10,459 on sales of $20,670, or over 50 per cent. We think 1961 was our best year to date, but we can't make our figures jibe with those in the magazine, and we wonder if we really are 25 per cent ahead of the industry average. Can you help us?"

Mr. Austen was interested and willing to help. He told Mr. Kennard

Exhibit 2

CASH REGISTER AND CHECKBOOK SUMMARY DURING 1961

Receipts		*Checks Drawn*	
From rooms	$19,680	Owners' drawings	$ 6,600
From vending machines	990	Salaries and wages	1,540
		Paid to laundry	1,025
		Replacement of linen, glass, and china	314
		Advertising	786
		Payroll taxes and insurance	335
		Fuel for heating	890
		Repairs and maintenance	967
		Cleaning and other supplies	350
		Telephone and telegraph	242
		Light bill	872
		Real estate and property taxes	628
		Insurance	894
		Interest	1,368
Total	$20,670	Total	$16,811

to get the available figures for 1961 so that he could look them over that evening. The principal records Mr. Kennard kept to reflect the motor court financial transactions were a record of receipts, taken from the cash register, and a checkbook describing cash paid out. In addition, certain rough notations of other expenses incurred were available.

That evening Mr. Kennard showed Mr. Austen the cash summary for the year 1961 as given in Exhibit 2. Mr. Austen immediately noted that the difference between receipts and expenditures was $3,859, and asked Mr. Kennard to explain why he had stated the profit was $10,459. Mr. Kennard replied, "Oh, that's easy. Our drawings aren't expenses; after all, we are the owners. My wife and I have consistently taken only $6,600 a year out because we want the rest of the profits to accumulate in the business. As I said, our bank balance has steadily risen. Furthermore, I have a local accountant make out the annual income tax statements so I don't have to worry about them. That income tax business is so complicated that I avoid it."

Mr. Austen worked with the cash summary (Exhibit 2) and the *Tourist Court Journal* figures (Exhibit 1) that evening and quickly found he needed more information. He told Mr. Kennard that he was returning to the home office the next morning but would be back in two weeks for another visit to the branch plant. Meanwhile, he wanted Mr. Kennard to get together some additional information. Mr. Austen suggested to Mr. Kennard that an important noncash expense was depreciation. Mr. Austen also wanted to know about expenses that had been incurred in 1960 but not paid until 1961. He told Mr. Kennard to check up on wages and salaries, insurance, advertising, taxes, and any other items paid in 1961 but applicable to 1960.

In addition, Mr. Austen instructed Mr. Kennard to try to find items of expense properly chargeable to 1961 but not paid by December 31, 1961. He told Mr. Austen the same types of expense were involved, that is, wages and salaries, insurance, advertising, taxes, etc. Also Mr. Austen inquired about income from room rentals. He asked if any of the cash

Exhibit 3

ADDITIONAL INFORMATION ABOUT THE BUSINESS

Chargeable in 1960, but paid in January, 1961:

Wages and salaries	$123
Advertising	103
Fuel for heating	55
Telephone and telegraph	22
Light bill	65
Real estate and property taxes	181
Insurance	447
Interest	110
Payroll taxes and insurance	8

Chargeable in 1961, but not paid by December 31, 1961:

Wages and salaries	429
Advertising	213
Fuel for heating	140
Cleaning and other supplies	18
Telephone and telegraph	24
Light bill	160
Real estate and property taxes	210
Interest	100
Payroll taxes and insurance	26

Also depreciation charges of $3,878.

Also 1961 cash receipts included a $225 payment from a company which had rented several units during December 1960 for a convention in the nearby city. There were no such uncollected rentals as of December 31, 1961.

receipts during 1961 related to rentals during 1960 and if there were any rentals during 1961 that had not been collected.

During the two weeks Mr. Austen was back at the home office, Mr. Kennard checked his records and compiled the additional information requested by Mr. Austen. The evening Mr. Austen returned to the Aurora Motor Courts, Mr. Kennard gave him a summary of the information he had gathered (Exhibit 3). With all the additional information, Mr. Austen constructed an operating statement that matched in form the one appearing in the *Tourist Court Journal*. He calculated both the dollar amounts and percentage composition of each expense for more accurate comparison with the *Journal* figures.

Questions

1. Prepare an operating statement such as Mr. Austen prepared.

2. As Mr. Austen, what comments would you make to the Kennards regarding their progress to date?

Chapter 4

ACCOUNTING RECORDS AND SYSTEMS

UP TO this point, the effect on the financial statements of each individual transaction has been described separately. Thus, starting with a balance sheet that contained the item "Cash, $10,000," a transaction involving an increase in cash of $5,000 would be recorded by, in effect, erasing the $10,000 and putting in the new figure, $15,000. This procedure was appropriate as an explanatory device in view of the small number of transactions with which we have been dealing. Clearly, however, such a technique is not a practical way of handling the large volume of transactions that occur in actual business operations. This chapter describes some of the bookkeeping procedures that are used in practice. It should be emphasized that *no new accounting concepts are introduced;* the devices described here are no more than the mechanical means of increasing the facility with which transactions can be recorded and summarized.

Some of the considerations that are important in designing and operating accounting systems are also described.

BOOKKEEPING

In this study of accounting, we are not concerned with bookkeeping procedures per se, that is, for the purpose of training bookkeepers. Some knowledge of accounting mechanics is useful, however, for at least two reasons. First, as is the case with many subjects, accounting is something that is best learned by doing—by the actual solution of problems—and although any accounting problem can theoretically be solved without the aid of the tools discussed in this chapter, their use will often speed up considerably the problem-solving process. Secondly, the debit-and-credit mechanism, which is the principal technique discussed here, provides a framework for analysis with much the same purpose, and the same advantages, as the symbols and equations that are studied in elementary algebra. This mechanism can often be used to reduce an apparently complex, perhaps almost incomprehensible, statement of facts to a simple, specific set of relationships. Thus, the debit-and-credit mecha-

93

nism provides a useful way of thinking about many types of business problems—not only strictly accounting problems but also problems of other types.

The Account

Consider again a balance sheet on which the item "Cash, $10,000" appears. Subsequent cash transactions can affect this amount in only one of two ways: they can increase it, or they can decrease it. Instead of increasing or decreasing the item by erasing the old amount and entering the new amount for each transaction, considerable effort could be saved by collecting all the increases together and all the decreases together and then periodically figuring, in a single arithmetic operation, the net change resulting from all of them. This could be done by adding the sum of the increases to the amount of cash shown at the beginning and then subtracting the sum of the decreases. The difference would be the new cash *balance*, reflecting the net effect of all the separate increases and decreases.

In accounting, the device called an *account* is used for just this purpose. The simplest form of account, called a *T-account*, looks like this:

Cash

(Increases)		(Decreases)	
Beginning balance	10,000		2,000
	5,000		600
	4,000		400
	100		1,000
	2,700		
	800		
	22,600		4,000
New balance	18,600		

All increases are listed on one side, and all decreases are listed on the other. The saving in effort can be seen even from this brief illustration. If the balance were changed for each of the nine transactions listed, five additions and four subtractions would be required. By using the account device, the new balance is obtained by only two additions (to find the 22,600 and 4,000) and one subtraction (22,600 − 4,000).

Note that the dollar sign ($) is omitted; this is the usual practice in most accounting procedures.

In actual accounting systems, the account form is set up so that other useful information, in addition to the amount of each increase or decrease, can be recorded. A common arrangement of the columns is the following:

CASH

Date	Explanation	(R)	Amount	Date	Explanation	(R)	Amount

The above headings are self-explanatory except that of "R" (standing for "reference") under which is entered a simple code showing the source of the information recorded. This is useful if it is necessary to check back on the source of the entry at some future time.

Debit and Credit

The left-hand side of any account is arbitrarily called the *debit* side, and the right-hand side is called the *credit* side. Amounts entered, or to be entered, on the left-hand side are called "debits," and amounts on the right-hand side, "credits." The verb "to debit" means "to make an entry in the left-hand side of an account,"[1] and the verb "to credit" means "to make an entry in the right-hand side of an account." *The words "debit" and "credit" have no other meaning in accounting.* The preceding sentence is emphasized because in ordinary usage these words do have other meanings. The student may be tempted to carry over into his study of accounting the impression that "credit" has a favorable connotation (such as: "he is a credit to his country") and that debit has an unfavorable connotation (from the term "debtor"). Such is not the case in the accounting usage of these words. "Debit" and "credit" are usually abbreviated to "Dr." and "Cr."

If an account were considered by itself, without regard to its relationship with other accounts, it would make no difference whether increases were recorded on the debit side or on the credit side. In the fifteenth century a Franciscan Monk, Lucas Pacioli, described a method of arranging accounts in such a way that the dual aspect that is present in every accounting transaction would be expressed by a debit amount and an equal and offsetting credit amount. This made possible the rule, *to which there are absolutely no exceptions,* that for each transaction the debit amount (or the sum of all the debit amounts, if there are more than one) must equal the credit amount (or the sum of all the credit amounts). This is why accounting is called *double-entry* accounting. It

---

[1] The verb "to charge" is often used as a synonym for "to debit."

follows that the recording of a transaction in which debits do not equal credits is incorrect. It also follows that, for all the accounts combined, the sum of the debit balances must equal the sum of the credit balances; otherwise, something has been done incorrectly. Thus the debit and credit arrangement used in accounting provides a useful means of checking the accuracy with which the work has been done.

The student could reason out such an arrangement for himself from the simple equation: Assets = Liabilities + Owners' Equity, taking into account also the fact that expenses and revenue accounts are subdivisions of owners' equity, since the rules of debit and credit are merely an expansion of the algebraic relationships that follow from this equation. He may find it easier, however, to memorize the following five rules:

1. Increases in *assets* are debits; decreases are credits.
2. Increases in *liabilities* are credits; decreases are debits.
3. Increases in *owners' equity* are credits; decreases are debits.
4. Increases in *expense* are debits; decreases are credits.
5. Increases in *revenue* are credits; decreases are debits.

Rule No. 4 follows from the fact that expense items represent decreases in owners' equity, and Rule No. 5 follows from the fact that revenue items represent increases in owners' equity.

Note that assets, which are a "good" thing, and expenses, which are a "bad" thing, both increase on the debit side, and that liability and revenue accounts both increase on the credit side. This is another illustration of the fact that "debit" and "credit" are neutral terms; they do not connote value judgments.

These rules are illustrated in the diagram shown in Illustration 4–1.

Debits and credits to certain special accounts are not covered by these rules, but they can be deduced from them. As an example, consider the account, Sales Discount, which is a deduction from sales revenue. We know that Sales is a revenue account and that increases are therefore recorded on the credit side. Since Sales Discount is a deduction from Sales, it must be treated in the opposite way from Sales. Sales Discount, therefore, increases on the debit side.

The Ledger

A ledger is a group of accounts. The student has probably seen a bound book with the word "ledger" printed on the cover. All the accounts of a small business could be maintained in such a book. Or, the business might have an "Accounts Receivable Ledger," an "Accounts

Illustration 4–1

RULES OF DEBIT AND CREDIT

| ASSETS | = | EQUITIES |

ASSETS = **EQUITIES**

Asset Accounts (Example: Cash)		Liability Accounts (Example: Accounts Payable)	
Dr.	Cr.	Dr.	Cr.
Increases (+)	Decreases (−)	Decreases (−)	Increases (+)

Owners' Equity Accounts
(Example: Retained Earnings)

Dr.	Cr.
Decreases (−)	Increases (+)

TEMPORARY SUBDIVISIONS OF RETAINED
EARNINGS

Expense Accounts (Example: Wage Expense)		Revenue Accounts (Example: Sales)	
Dr.	Cr.	Dr.	Cr.
Increases (+)	Decreases (−)	Decreases (−)	Increases (+)

Payable Ledger," and a "General Ledger," each containing the group of accounts suggested by the title. The ledger is not necessarily a bound book; it may consist of a set of loose-leaf pages, a set of punched cards, or, with the advent of electronic computers, a set of coded dots on a reel of magnetic tape. No matter what its form may be, the essential character of the account and the rules for making entries to it remain exactly as stated above.

The ledger will contain at least as many separate accounts as there are items on the balance sheet and income statement. Usually there are many more accounts than this minimum number so that information can be collected in more detail than is reported on the financial statements. The number of accounts is governed by management's need for information. For example, although the single item "accounts receivable" ordinarily appears on the balance sheet, there are obvious advantages in maintaining in the ledger a separate account for each customer.

There is no limit, other than the cost of record keeping, to the proliferation of accounts that may be found in practice. Take, for example, transactions concerned with the inflow and outflow of merchandise in a store. In the simplest set of books, all such transactions could be recorded as debits or credits to a Merchandise Inventory account. Or, additional information could be obtained by setting up a Purchases account, in which all purchases of merchandise during the accounting period are recorded, or there could be several Purchases accounts, one for each type of merchandise. Carrying the detail further, the Purchases account (or accounts) could be further subdivided so as to record in separate accounts (1) the invoice cost of merchandise purchased, (2) inward freight, (3) discounts allowed on purchases, and (4) merchandise returned to vendors (i.e., purchase returns). The inward freight item could be subdivided according to the several means

Illustration 4–2

JOURNAL

1960		Transactions	LF	Debit	Credit
Jan.	2	Cash...	1	120.50	
		Sales.....................................	41		120.50
	2	Accounts Receivable...........................	2	676.32	
		Sales.....................................	41		650.00
		Sales Tax Liability.........................	15		19.50
		Postage...................................	32		6.82
	2	Cash...	1	196.00	
		Sales Discount.................................	43	4.00	
		Accounts Receivable........................	2		200.00
	3	Sales Returns and Allowances....................		47.00	
		Accounts Receivable........................			47.00

of transportation used, or into an account for the freight bills themselves and another account for transportation taxes, and so on.

The Journal

A journal is a chronological record of accounting transactions showing the names of accounts that are to be debited or credited, the amounts of the debits and credits, and any useful supplementary information about the transaction. A simple form of the journal is shown in Illustration 4–2. The entries shown relate to the sales transactions described on pages 74–75. It helps in understanding these transactions if the student reasons out for himself the events that gave rise to each of them.

With respect to format, note that the debit entry is listed first, that the debit amounts appear in the first of the two money columns, that the account to be credited appears below the debit entry and is indented, and that credit amounts appear in the second money column. "LF" is an abbreviation for "ledger folio," that is, the page reference to the ledger account where the entry is to be made; these references are inserted at the time the entry is recorded in the account, and their presence indicates that the entry has been recorded. (In the illustration, the first nine items have been recorded in the accounts, and the remaining two have not yet been recorded.) In some businesses, a brief explanation of each entry is written beneath it.

The journal contains explicit instructions as to the changes that are to be made to the balances in the accounts. The process of making these changes is called *posting*. No account balance is ever changed except on the basis of a journal entry. (The balance in the account is periodically computed and recorded, as explained on page 94, but this process does not in any way *change* the balance in the account.)

Thus, the ledger is a device for *reclassifying* and *summarizing,* by accounts, information originally listed in chronological order in the journal.

THE ADJUSTING AND CLOSING PROCESS

Adjusting Entries

Most of the entries that are to be made in accounts come to the accountant's attention easily and obviously. When checks are drawn against the company's bank account, it is obvious that an entry must be made crediting Cash and debiting some other account. When invoices are sent out, a credit to Sales and a debit to Accounts Receivable is obviously generated. Entries of this type are called *original entries* or *spot entries* and constitute the bulk of the entries made in the typical business.

Some events that affect the accounts are not evidenced by such obvious documents. The effects of these events are recorded at the end of the accounting period by means of what are called *adjusting entries.* The purpose of the adjusting entries is to modify account balances so that they will reflect fairly the situation as of the end of the period.

Continuous Transactions. Most adjusting entries are made in connection with events that are, in effect, continuous transactions. Consider a tank of fuel oil purchased for $1,000. On the day of delivery, the $1,000 of fuel oil was an asset, but each day thereafter some fuel oil was consumed in the furnace, whereupon part of the $1,000 became an expense. Rather than record this consumption daily, a single adjusting entry is made at the end of the accounting period to show how much of the fuel oil is still an asset at that time and how much has become expense during the period. There are two ways of handling these events, both of which come out to the same result. Under one method, the fuel oil is originally recorded as an asset, and at the end of the accounting period the asset account is adjusted by subtracting the cost of fuel oil consumed, thus:

```
*dr.  Fuel Expense.................................................600
   cr.  Fuel Oil Inventory...........................................   600
```

* As a reminder to the student, the notations "dr." and "cr." are used in Chapters 4 and 5 to designate the debit and credit portions of each journal entry. These notations are not used in practice since the accountant understands from the order and indentation of the accounts what is meant.

Under the other method, the $1,000 expenditure for fuel oil is originally recorded in an expense account, and the fuel oil remaining at the end of the period is subtracted and shown as an asset, thus:

```
dr.  Fuel Oil Inventory...........................................400
   cr.  Fuel Expense.................................................   400
```

Although neither method reflects the correct facts _within_ the period (with the trivial exception that the first method does reflect the facts on the first day), both reflect a correct statement of the facts as of the _end_ of the accounting period, namely, that the fuel oil inventory is $400 and that fuel oil expense for the period was $600. Since accounting focuses on deriving the proper amounts for the statements that are prepared at the end of the accounting period, and since both methods result in the correct final amounts, the choice between these methods depends solely on which is more convenient.

Several other types of events that require adjusting entries were described in the sections of Chapter 3 that dealt with the distinction between expense and expenditure (pp. 64–69) and between revenue and receipts (pp. 69–72). The following list gives the form of the adjusting entries for several such events:

	Dr.	Cr.

1. For insurance protection, originally recorded as an asset, Prepaid Insurance, $300 of which becomes an expense in the current period:

```
dr.  Insurance Expense...........................................  300
   cr.  Prepaid Insurance...........................................       300
```

2. For a rent paid in advance and originally recorded as an expense, $5,000 of which is an asset at the end of the period since it covers rental for the next period:

```
dr.  Prepaid Rent.....................................5,000
     cr.  Rent Expense........................................        5,000
```

3. For $200 of supplies consumed in the period:

```
dr.  Supplies Expense.................................. 200
     cr.  Supplies Inventory...................................        200
```

4. For $50 of wages earned by an employee during the period but not yet paid to him:

```
dr.  Wages Expense..................................... 50
     cr.  Accrued Wages Payable...............................        50
```

5. For interest expense of $5 which has not yet been paid:

```
dr.  Interest Expense.................................. 5
     cr.  Accrued Interest Payable.............................        5
```

6. For interest (i.e., discount) deducted from a loan in advance and originally recorded as an asset, Prepaid Interest, $5 of which becomes an expense of the current period:

```
dr.  Interest Expense.................................. 5
     cr.  Prepaid Interest....................................        5
```

7. For $20 of interest earned by the business during the period which has not yet been received:

```
dr.  Accrued Interest Receivable...................... 20
     cr.  Interest Revenue....................................        20
```

Depreciation.   Most fixed assets are continuously being converted to an expense, just like fuel oil, prepaid insurance, and supplies. This expense is called depreciation. Instead of subtracting the amount of expense for the period directly from the asset amount, however, a separate account, *Accumulated Depreciation,* is used. This account shows the total of such subtractions to date and is subtracted from the cost of fixed assets on the balance sheet, thus:

```
Equipment (at cost)..................................................$1,000
     Less: Accumulated depreciation....................................   400
          Net Book Value.............................................   $600
```

The adjusting entry to record the depreciation expense for a period is therefore of the following form:

```
dr.  Depreciation Expense.............................200
     cr.  Accumulated Depreciation...............................        200
```

This process is described in more detail in Chapter 6.

Other Adjustments. The accountant may make a variety of other adjusting entries in his attempt to make the accounts reflect fairly the results of operations and the status of the business. An example, discussed in more detail in Chapter 5, is that for *bad debt expense,* an adjustment made in order to recognize the likelihood that not all credit customers will pay their bills and that therefore the Accounts Receivable account may overstate the collectible amount of the company's claims against its customers. An adjusting entry that records the estimated amount of bad debts is as follows:

```
dr.  Bad Debt Expense..............................................300
     cr.  Allowance for Doubtful Accounts.............................         300
```

On the balance sheet, Allowance for Doubtful Accounts is subtracted from Accounts Receivable, thus:

```
Accounts receivable (gross).....................................$1,000
Less: Allowance for doubtful accounts..........................    50
     Net Accounts Receivable...................................         $950
```

A Caution. When the student is given a problem involving the preparation of accounting statements, he must be told the precise nature of the original entries since he has no way of finding them out for himself. He will not necessarily be told about the adjusting entries, however; and he, like any accountant, is expected to be on the lookout for situations that require adjustment. For example, if the balance sheet at the beginning of a period shows the asset, prepaid insurance, the accountant knows that he must make an adjusting entry at the end of the period to show the expired cost, even though no routine document tells him to do so.

Closing Entries

Revenue accounts and expense accounts are called *temporary* (or "nominal") accounts, as distinguished from asset, liability, and owners' equity accounts which are called *permanent* (or "real") accounts. The temporary accounts are actually subdivisions of owners' equity. They are a means of classifying the various revenue and expense transactions that occur during an accounting period so as to provide the information needed to prepare the income statement for the period. The temporary accounts are periodically *closed* to owners' equity in order to determine the net effect (i.e., the profit or the loss) of all the revenue and expense transactions.

Closing procedures differ from company to company. Under all closing methods, however, revenue and expense accounts are ultimately closed to an account called *Profit and Loss* or *Loss and Gain* or *Expense and Revenue Summary,* which reflects the net income or loss for a given accounting period. Loss and Gain is a temporary account which in turn is closed to some owners' equity account, such as Retained Earnings, to complete the closing process. In many businesses, the revenue and expense accounts are not closed directly to Loss and Gain. Instead, one or more additional temporary or *clearing* accounts are set up, such as Cost of Goods Sold and Trading (an account which shows the gross profit for the period), and successive closings are made to these accounts. The purpose of these intermediate clearing accounts is to show separately some or all of the elements comprising Loss and Gain (e.g., cost of goods sold and gross profit). The ultimate effect, however, is the same as direct closing to Loss and Gain.

The closing process consists of transferring the balance of each temporary account to the same side of a clearing account. This is done by making a journal entry debiting the account to be closed if it has a credit balance (or crediting it if it has a debit balance) in an amount equal to the balance. This has the effect of reducing the balance in the account to zero, thereby closing it. Note that each entry is made on the opposite side from the side with the balance. The other half of this entry is made to Loss and Gain or to one of the intermediate clearing accounts.

> EXAMPLE: If the credit balance in the Sales account at the end of an accounting period is $174,000, the account is closed by the following entry:
>
> dr. Sales...174,000
>   cr. Loss and Gain.................................   174,000
>
> EXAMPLE: If the Salaries and Wages expense account has a debit balance of $21,000, it is closed by the following entry:
>
> dr. Loss and Gain.................................. 21,000
>   cr. Salaries and Wages...........................   21,000

At the completion of the closing process, all temporary accounts have zero balances; the only accounts remaining open are the permanent accounts—the asset, liability, and owners' equity accounts.

Ruling and Balancing Accounts

At the end of the accounting period, each account is ruled and balanced so that it is in a convenient form for the preparation of financial statements and ready to begin accumulating entries for the coming period. A frequently followed procedure is as follows: First, a balancing amount is written in the appropriate column so as to make equal totals in both columns. The totals are then shown and double ruled to indicate the end of the accounting period sequence. Finally, the new balance is "brought down" on the opposite side from that in which it was first written, as the initial figure for the new period.

The Trial Balance

The trial balance is simply a list of the account names and the balances in each account as of a given moment of time, with debit balances in one column and credit balances in another column. The preparation of the trial balance serves two principal purposes: (1) it shows whether the equality of debits and credits has been maintained, and (2) it provides a convenient transcript of the ledger record as a basis for making adjusting and closing entries or in the preparation of financial statements.

To maintain the relationship "Total Assets = Total Liabilities + Owners' Equity," debits and credits must be kept in balance. Although the fact that totals on a trial balance are equal does indicate that the integrity of the accounting equation has been maintained, it does not prove that errors have not been made. Entries may have been omitted entirely; they may have been posted to the wrong account; counter-balancing errors may have been made; or the transaction may have been analyzed incorrectly. For example, when a debit for the purchase of a truck is made incorrectly to an expense account rather than correctly to a fixed asset account, the totals of the trial balance are not affected. Nevertheless, errors that result in unequal debits and credits are common, and the fact that such errors exist is evident when a trial balance does not balance; that is, when the debit column does not add to the same total as the credit column.

A trial balance may be prepared at any time after all journal entries have been posted. A *pre-adjustment* trial balance is one prepared after the original entries for the period have been posted, but prior to the adjusting and closing process. A *post-closing* trial balance is prepared after the closing process.

The Work Sheet

The work sheet is a preliminary compilation of figures that facilitates recording or analysis. A work sheet is often used as a preliminary to the formal journalizing and posting of the adjusting and closing process. Its use permits the accountant to make a "dry run" of the whole process. Since a pencil is ordinarily used, any errors detected on the work sheet can be easily corrected, whereas alterations to the formal records are to be avoided wherever possible. The work sheet also classifies account balances according to the financial statements in which they are to be used.

The form of the adjusting-and-closing work sheet varies depending upon the procedure followed in closing the books, the form of the statements to be prepared, and the preference of the accountant. The work sheet consists of several pairs of columns, the first column in each pair is used for debits and the second column for credits. On most adjusting-and-closing work sheets the first pair of columns contains the pre-adjustment trial balance. The next pair of columns is used for the adjustments for the period. These are followed by pairs of columns for each financial statement, and in some cases for principal subdivisions of the income statement, such as the cost of goods sold section.

A work sheet is often used *in lieu of,* rather than as a preliminary to, the process of adjusting and closing the accounts. Many companies close their books only once a year, but nevertheless prepare monthly financial statements. These interim statements are prepared from a work sheet on which are listed the account balances at the end of the month together with the adjustments necessary to reflect revenue and expense in that month. Statements are prepared from the adjusted account balances that are developed on this work sheet. The income statement figures on such a work sheet would be cumulative for the year to date. An income statement for the current month can be derived from the cumulative figures simply by subtracting the corresponding figures on the work sheet for the preceding month.

A sample work sheet for a merchandising company is shown in Illustration 4–3. The five adjustments shown thereon reflect:

a) Cost of merchandise sold, $121,300 (dr. Cost of Goods Sold, cr. Inventory). During the period all purchases of merchandise had been debited to inventory, but no entries had been made to show the movement of merchandise out of inventory.

b) Expired insurance of $300 (dr. Insurance Expense, cr. Prepaid Insurance).

c) Accrued interest expense of $100 (dr. Interest Expense, cr. Accrued Interest Payable).

d) Accrued wages of $1,000 (dr. Salaries and Wages, cr. Wages Payable).

e) Accrued employer's tax on wages of $30 (dr. Social Security Tax Expense, cr. Withholding and Social Security Taxes Payable).

f) Estimated income tax for the year of $5,400 (dr. Income Tax Expense, cr. Income Tax Liability).

Note that additional accounts are added as needed at the bottom of the work sheet.

Illustration 4-3

ILLUSTRATIVE WORK SHEET

(In Round Numbers to Facilitate Study)

	Trial Balance, December 31		Adjustments		Income Statement		Balance Sheet	
	Dr.	Cr.	Dr.	Cr.	Dr.	Cr.	Dr.	Cr.
Cash	18,600						18,600	
Inventory	156,300			121,300(a)			35,000	
Prepaid insurance	900			300(b)			600	
Accounts payable		8,700						8,700
Withholding and social security taxes payable		570		30(e)				600
Notes payable		4,000						4,000
Capital stock		20,000						20,000
Retained earnings		1,300						1,300
Sales		174,000				174,000		
Rental and other space costs	8,300				8,300			
Salaries and wages	20,000		1,000(d)		21,000			
Social security tax expense	670		30(e)		700			
Advertising expense	2,100				2,100			
Miscellaneous expenses	1,900				1,900			
Nonoperating revenue		400				400		
Interest expense	200		100(c)		300			
	208,970	208,970						
Cost of goods sold			121,300(a)		121,300			
Insurance expense			300(b)		300			
Accrued interest payable				100(c)				100
Wages payable				1,000(d)				1,000
Income tax expense			5,400(f)		5,400			
Income tax liability				5,400(f)				5,400
Net Income to Retained Earnings					13,100			13,100
			128,130	128,130	174,400	174,400	54,200	54,200

The last item, $13,100, is the net income for the period. It is found by subtracting the sum of the other debits to "Income Statement" from the sum of the credits to "Income Statement." Showing the same amount in the credit column of "Balance Sheet" has the effect of closing the net income to retained earnings. After this amount is entered, each column of a pair should add to the same total, which is a check on the arithmetic accuracy of the whole closing process.

So that the connection between the adjusting and closing process and the financial statements will be clear, financial statements prepared from Illustration 4–3 are shown in Illustration 4–4. All figures used are condensed and rounded in order to make the process easier to follow. These statements therefore do not indicate the amount of detailed work that is involved in an actual business situation.

Illustration 4–4

FINANCIAL STATEMENTS PREPARED FROM DATA SHOWN IN ILLUSTRATION 4–3

Balance Sheet as of December 31, 19XX

ASSETS		EQUITIES	
Cash	$18,600	Accounts payable	$ 8,700
Inventory	35,000	Withholding and social security	
Prepaid insurance	600	taxes payable	600
		Wages payable	1,000
		Notes payable	4,000
		Accrued interest payable	100
		Income tax liability	5,400
		Total Liabilities	$19,800
		Capital stock	20,000
		Retained earnings	14,400
Total Assets	$54,200	Total Equities	$54,200

Income Statement for the Year 19XX

Sales		$174,000
Less: Cost of goods sold		121,300
Gross profit		$ 52,700
Operating expenses:		
Rental and other space costs	$ 8,300	
Salaries and wages	21,000	
Social security tax expense	700	
Advertising expense	2,100	
Insurance expense	300	
Miscellaneous expense	1,900	34,300
Operating profit		$ 18,400
Less: Interest expense		300
		$ 18,100
Plus: Nonoperating revenue		400
Profit before income taxes		$ 18,500
Provision for income taxes		5,400
Net Income		$ 13,100

Reversing Entries

Under some conditions, it is desirable to *reverse* the adjusting entries made to record accruals. This is done by making an entry, subsequent to the closing entries, which is the reverse of the adjusting entry. Consider the adjustment that recognizes $5 of interest expense accrued on transactions related to borrowing $1,000 for four months, one of which is in one accounting period and the other three are in the next period, the total interest cost of $20 to be paid when the loan is repaid (see p. 69). The adjusting entry at the end of the first period, which recognizes the interest expense of that period, is as follows:

```
dr.  Interest Expense...........................................  5
     cr.  Accrued Interest Payable.................................       5
```

Now what happens in the next period when the loan and interest thereon is paid? A natural entry to make is the following:

```
dr.  Notes Payable..............................................1,000
dr.  Interest Expense...........................................  20
     cr.  Cash.................................................       1,020
```

But this overstates interest expense for the next period, which is in fact only $15, and also leaves the liability, accrued interest payable, outstanding on the books even though it no longer exists. Such an error is avoided if the adjusting entry is reversed before the accounting for the next period starts, thus:

```
dr.  Accrued Interest Payable....................................  5
     cr.  Interest Expense.......................................       5
```

The credit to Interest Expense is made to offset a part of the debit entry that will be made in the normal course of bookkeeping in the next period. After this entry has been made, as above, the accounts will show the correct amount of interest expense for the period ($20 — $5 = $15). The following T-account summarizes these entries for the two periods:

Interest Expense			
Dec. 31 (Adjusting)	5	Dec. 31 (Closing)	5
Mar. 31 (Payment)	20	Jan. 1 (Reversing)	5
		Dec. 31 (Closing)	15
	20		20

The same result can be attained by omitting the reversing entry and recording the repayment of the loan as follows:

```
dr.  Notes Payable..................................................1,000
dr.  Interest Expense..............................................   15
dr.  Accrued Interest Payable.....................................    5
     cr.  Cash.......................................................      1,020
```

This entry requires, however, that the bookkeeper remember the fact that part of the interest was an expense of the prior period.

Summary of the Accounting Process

1. The first, and by far the most important, part of the accounting process is the *analysis of transactions;* that is, the process of deciding which account or accounts should be debited, which should be credited, and in what amounts, in order to reflect events in the accounting records. This requires judgment.

2. Next comes the purely mechanical step of *journalizing original entries,* that is, recording the result of the analysis.

3. *Posting* is the process of recording changes in the ledger accounts, exactly as specified by the journal entry. This is another purely mechanical step.

4. At the ending of the accounting period, judgment is involved in deciding on the *adjusting entries,* and these are journalized and posted in the same way as are original entries.

5. The *closing entries* are journalized and posted. *Reversing entries,* if any, are also journalized and posted. These are purely mechanical steps.

6. *Financial statements* are prepared. This requires judgment as to the best arrangement and terminology, but the figures that are used result from the judgments made in Steps No. 1 and No. 4.

ACCOUNTING SYSTEMS

The simple journals, ledgers, and work sheets, together with the rules for using them, described in the preceding pages, constitute *an* accounting system, but such a system would not usually be the *best* system for an actual business. The best system is that which best achieves the following objectives:

1. To process the information efficiently, that is, at low cost;
2. To obtain reports quickly;
3. To insure a high degree of accuracy; and
4. To minimize the possibility of theft, fraud, or misrepresentation.

Designing a good accounting system is a specialized job requiring a high degree of skill, and is largely outside the scope of this book. Only a few of the principles and techniques are noted here.

Special Journals

The journal form illustrated on page 98 is called a *general journal*. This form requires that the title of each account affected by each entry be written down. If there are a large number of entries made to a single account, time can be saved, both in journalizing and in posting, by using a *special journal* or *register*. In the special journal there are several columns, each headed with the name of an account that is to be debited or credited plus, usually, a "miscellaneous" column in which entries to other accounts may be recorded. Entries to the accounts indicated by column headings are made simply by entering the proper amount in these columns. At the end of the accounting period, all the amounts in

Illustration 4–5

CHECK REGISTER

Date	To Whom Drawn	Cash Cr.	Accounts Payable Dr.	Miscellaneous Dr.	
				Account	Amount

each column are added, and the total is posted as one figure to the appropriate account. Entries in the "miscellaneous" column are posted individually. Illustration 4–5 is an example of a check register, which is a special journal used to record credits to Cash and debits to various accounts. Columns are provided for the accounts in which entries are likely to be made frequently (here, Cash and Accounts Payable), and a miscellaneous column is provided for other debits.

The special-journal device illustrates one of the important considerations in systems design: to keep to a minimum the amount of *manual copying* of information from one document to another. Copying not only requires effort, and hence costs money, but it also increases the possibility of making errors. In the simple check register shown, the amount of copying required is reduced, as compared with the general journal, in that all the credits to Cash and all the debits to Accounts Payable are posted to the ledger as single totals. The special journal also reduces the amount of writing effort since the name of the account at the head of the column does not have to be written for each entry.

The same idea can be extended further by the use of bookkeeping machines. In recording sales on credit, for example, the use of a machine makes it possible to make the journal entry and post the debit to the customer's ledger account in the same operation: the operator positions the journal form and the ledger account form properly in the machine, and the amounts are entered on both forms simultaneously by the use of carbon paper. Carrying the anticopying idea one step further, once information has been recorded on punched cards, magnetic tape, or in some other form that can be handled by automatic machines, it can be manipulated and recorded thereafter without any human intervention whatsoever.

Control Accounts and Subsidiary Ledgers

Most businesses use one or more *subsidiary ledgers,* which are groups of related accounts taken out of the general ledger. For example, all the separate accounts for individual customers may be kept in an accounts receivable ledger. One advantage of this practice is that several book-keepers can be working on the ledger accounts simultaneously. More-over, it facilitates the process of localizing errors, since each ledger can be made the responsibility of a specific individual. If there are three bookkeepers working on accounts receivable, for example, there can be three accounts receivable ledgers.

In order to keep the general ledger in balance, a *control account* takes the place of the individual accounts removed to the subsidiary ledgers. A control account shows in summary form debits and credits that are shown in detail in a subsidiary ledger. When subsidiary ledgers are used, each amount is in effect posted twice: it is posted, often daily, to the proper account in the subsidiary ledger, and it also becomes a part of the total which is posted at the end of the period to the control account in the general ledger. In a large business, most if not all of the general ledger accounts are control accounts.

The use of various *ledgerless bookkeeping* devices should also be noted. The accounts receivable "accounts," for example, may consist not of actual ledger records but rather of copies of the invoices themselves. Or, bills for vendors may be kept in an "accounts payable" file, with the accounting entry made when the bill is paid rather than when it is received. The total of bills in the file at the end of the accounting period constitutes the accounts payable liability for the balance sheet and is recorded by an adjusting entry, crediting Accounts Payable and debiting various expense and asset accounts. In the latter situation, work is saved, but the possibility of verifying the accounts against the invoices is sacrificed.

Imprest Funds

The imprest fund is another device for saving work. An imprest fund consists of cash advanced to a responsible person and periodically replenished by additional cash that equals the amounts expended by this person.

The operation of an imprest fund may be illustrated by its most common version, the *petty cash* fund. The fund is established by drawing a check on the regular bank account. The person responsible for the fund cashes the check and puts the money in a separate place, a petty cash box. This transaction is recorded by the following entry:

```
dr.  Petty Cash.....................................................50
     cr.  Cash......................................................      50
```

The petty cash is used to pay small bills until it is nearly exhausted. At that time, these bills are summarized, and a check is drawn for the amount they total. The journal entry for this check debits the various expense or asset accounts represented by the bills, for example:

```
dr.  Office Supplies...............................................21
dr.  Miscellaneous Expense.........................................25
     cr.  Cash......................................................      46
```

Note that the credit is to the regular Cash account. Once established, the Petty Cash account is not touched unless the size of the fund is changed.

This procedure saves the effort involved in drawing checks and making separate journal entries for small bills. It also provides a safeguard, since the petty cash box should at all times contain cash and receipted bills which together total $50.

The imprest device is by no means limited to petty cash. Many government disbursing agencies operate on the same principle, but in amounts that run into millions of dollars. These agencies are advanced funds from the central treasury, they disburse these funds to pay properly authorized bills, and they submit these bills to the treasury as a basis for replenishing the fund. The accounting entries are the same as those given above for petty cash.

Internal Control

Two of the objectives of an accounting system stated above—accuracy and protection against theft, fraud, or misrepresentation—cannot be attained absolutely without conflicting with the other two—speed and economy. A system that "can't be beaten" would be prohibitively expensive and time consuming. A basic principle of internal control therefore is that the system should make it *as difficult as is practical* for people to be dishonest or careless. This is significantly different from making the system absolutely foolproof. Such a principle is based not on a cynical view of people in general but rather on the realistic assumption that a small fraction of people will be dishonest or careless if it is easy for them to do so.

Some of the devices used to insure reasonable accuracy have been touched on—the idea of verifying one set of figures against another, for example. The idea of divided responsibility is another important one. Whenever feasible, no one person should be responsible for recording all aspects of a transaction, nor should the *custodian* of assets (e.g., the storekeeper or the cashier) be permitted to do the *accounting* for the assets. Thus, one person's work is a check on another's, and although this does not eliminate the possibility that two people will steal through collusion, the likelihood of dishonesty is greatly reduced.

The *voucher system* is another commonly used internal control device. Under this system, every incoming bill is inserted in a voucher, or folder, which contains spaces in which authorized people write their initials to signify their approval of the appropriateness of the charge and the accounting entries made. Under this system, all bills, even those that are paid immediately in cash, are credited to Accounts Payable (or to "Vouchers Payable") and debited to the appropriate asset or expense account. For cash payments, putting the bill through Accounts Payable involves additional work, but this is often warranted in the interest of having a single, uniform procedure through which all bills must pass and a prescribed set of approvals to assure that the business makes only proper payments.

These brief comments indicate only the nature of the problem of internal control, which is a big subject. Furthermore, a study that focuses on accounting principles, as this one does, leads to incorrect impressions of the complexities involved in operating accounting *systems*. Cash transactions, for example, are very easy to analyze, whereas *Montgomery's Auditing* contains a 16-page list of questions that should be considered in connection with the internal control of the single item, cash.

Auditing

All companies whose securities are listed on an organized stock exchange, nearly every company that sells its securities to the public, most other corporations, and a great many unincorporated businesses have their financial statements and the accounting records from which they are produced, examined by independent, outside public accountants called auditors. Usually, these are Certified Public Accountants, who meet prescribed professional standards and who have received a certificate or license to practice from the state in which they do business.

In their *opinion,* or written report of this examination, the auditors state that they followed generally accepted auditing standards (such standards are spelled out in publications of the AICPA), and that the financial statements are fairly presented and conform to generally accepted accounting principles consistent with the principles followed in the preceding year. If any of these statements cannot be made, the auditors explain the discrepancy in what is called an *exception.* Note, incidentally, that the auditors state that the statements are *fairly presented* not that they are *accurate.* As explained in the preceding chapters, there are many transactions which two equally well-informed and well-intentioned accountants would treat differently, and this fact prohibits anyone from stating that the final statements are precisely accurate.

In making their examination, auditors no longer rely primarily on a detailed rechecking of the analysis, journalizing, and posting of each transaction; rather, they satisfy themselves that the accounting system is designed to insure that the data are processed properly. This reliance on the internal control system is relatively new. As late as 1949, the U.S. General Accounting Office received a copy of every one of the millions of accounting documents generated annually in the federal government and, theoretically at least, checked each of them for propriety and accuracy. When the General Accounting Office changed its emphasis to a reliance on properly designed accounting systems, it not only was able to release several *thousand* employees but also was able to do a better auditing job by concentrating its efforts on checking the reliability of accounting systems and by examining the relatively few important or unusual transactions which previously had tended to be buried in the detail.

In addition to the examination of the adequacy of the accounting system, the auditors make test checks of how well it is working, they verify the existence of assets (for example, they usually are present at the taking of physical inventory, they ask a sample of customers to *confirm* or verify the accuracy of the accounts receivable shown for each of them, they check bank balances, and so on), and they make sure that especially important or nonroutine transactions are recorded in conformity with generally accepted accounting principles. The observation of inventories and the confirmation of receivables is regarded as being so important that auditing standards require that the omission of either of them be specifically mentioned in the auditor's opinion.

SIGNIFICANT BOOKKEEPING IDEAS

At least two significant ideas should emerge from this description of the bookkeeping process.

The first is the idea of debit and credit equality—"every debit must have an equal credit." This idea is much more than a mechanical requirement of bookkeeping. It is a way of thinking that is extremely useful in analyzing what is going on in a business. There is a natural human tendency to think only about part of the consequences of a decision and to overlook some equally important part. For example, although a growing cash balance superficially looks good, this is only half of the story. It makes considerable difference whether the credits offsetting these debits to cash reflect income from profitable operations or whether they reflect emergency bank loans.

The second significant idea is that of *balancing,* the notion that one total should always equal some other total. Three balancing techniques have been described: (1) the fundamental debit-credit structure; (2) the control-subsidiary relationship, in which the total of the subsidiary items must always equal a control total; and (3) the imprest technique, in which the sum of cash and paid bills must always equal a predetermined total. As noted above, these devices provide a check on arithmetic accuracy, they lessen the risk of loss through dishonesty, and they lessen the chance that some part of a transaction will be overlooked.

These balancing techniques have a much wider applicability than in business accounting. In recent years economists have come to use the debit-credit idea to construct national income accounts which show, in balanced form, the impact of the main economic forces at work in a nation. Electronic computers are designed with built-in checks on accuracy which are derived from the control-subsidiary idea. Figures derived from a system that does *not* contain some balancing mechanism should be regarded skeptically; the likelihood of errors or omissions is great.

APPENDIX

Locating Errors Revealed by the Trial Balance

Following are four suggested aids in detecting errors revealed by differences in the totals of the trial balance:

1. If the difference between the totals is 1, 0.01, 1.00, 100, 1,000, etc., the error is probably in addition. Such an error is usually detected by re-adding the columns of the trial balance, or, if necessary, the columns in the ledger accounts.

2. When the discrepancy is an even number, the error may be the result of making a debit entry in a credit column, or vice versa. Divide the difference in totals by 2, and look, first, through the trial balance and, then, the ledger accounts for an amount corresponding to the quotient secured. The difference is divided by 2 because an item placed in the wrong column results in a difference of twice its amount.

3. If the difference is divisible by 9, the error is probably either a transposition or a transplacement, and the search can be narrowed down to numbers where these errors might have been made. A *transposition* occurs when 79 is written for 97, 318 for 813, and so on. A *transplacement* or *slide* occurs when the digits of the number are moved to the left or right, as when $6,328.00 is written as $632.80 or $63.28.

4. When the source of error is not readily discernible, it is advisable to check the trial balance against the ledger to determine whether all the account balances have been copied properly. This check may reveal that certain accounts have been omitted. As a last resort, it may be necessary to check all of the figures in the ledger with the journal and to check all additions and subtractions in the several accounts.

Care in making the entries, such as writing legibly, double checking additions and subtractions as journalizing and posting proceeds, and making sure all entries are entered properly, will save much time otherwise spent in hunting for errors.

SUGGESTIONS FOR FURTHER READING ON SYSTEMS AND AUDITING

HOLMES, ARTHUR W. *Auditing: Principles and Procedures.* 5th ed. Homewood, Ill.: Richard D. Irwin, Inc., 1959.

LENHART, NORMAN J., AND DEFLIESE, PHILIP L. *Montgomery's Auditing.* 8th ed. New York: The Ronald Press Co., 1957.

NEUSCHEL, RICHARD F. *Management by System.* New York: McGraw-Hill Book Co., Inc., 1960.

CASES

CASE 4–1.   GROVES' GIFT CORNER

Groves' Gift Corner was a small shop that specialized in the sale of gifts for the home. The owner, George Groves, invested his savings of $15,000 in this new business venture. He found a suitable location in a popular year-round resort town, and after installing the necessary furniture and fixtures in his new shop and purchasing a carefully selected stock of gifts, Groves opened the Gift Corner for business on May 1.

Groves had never been in business for himself and therefore was not familiar with accounting procedures. Hence, at the end of May he engaged a local accountant to set up a simple bookkeeping system. The accountant suggested double-entry records consisting of a general journal and ledger accounts. He initiated the accounting records by himself making the journal entries for certain May transactions. Many of these transactions were recorded in summary form. Groves intended

Exhibit 1

GENERAL JOURNAL

Entry Number	Account	Amount Dr.	Amount Cr.
(1)	Cash..........	15,000	
	Groves' Capital..........		15,000
(2)	Furniture and Fixtures..........	950	
	Cash..........		950
(3)	Merchandise Inventory..........	5,313	
	Accounts Payable..........		5,313
(4)	Rent Expense..........	300	
	Cash..........		300
(5)	Miscellaneous Expenses..........	148	
	Cash..........		148
(6)	Advertising Expense..........	35	
	Cash..........		35
(7)	Prepaid Insurance..........	416	
	Cash..........		416
(8)	Salaries Expense..........	585	
	Cash..........		585
(9)	Wages Expense..........	235	
	Cash..........		235

to prepare the May statements from these records under the accountant's guidance and thereafter to take charge of all the accounting himself.

Exhibit 1, taken from the general journal, shows the first nine entries for May that the accountant made.

Following are the remainder of the transactions that are to be journalized and posted:

10. Cash sales for the month were $1,836.
11. Credit sales for the month were $1,092.

12. Mr. Groves paid bills (i.e., accounts payable) in the amount of $4,289.
13. Cash was received from credit customers in the amount of $430.
14. Wages earned but unpaid at the end of May amounted to $113. (Note: For the purpose of this case, social security taxes and withholding taxes are to be ignored.)
15. Insurance protection had expired during the month in the amount of $25.
16. Depreciation expense on furniture and fixtures amounted to $29.
17. Mr. Groves had received a bill from the public utilities company for $72.
18. Mr. Groves ascertained that the cost of the merchandise he sold during the month was $1,890.

Questions

1. Be prepared to explain the events that gave rise to journal entries No. 1 through No. 9.

2. Set up a ledger account (in T-account form) for each account named in the general journal. Post entries No. 1 through No. 9 to these accounts, using the entry numbers as a cross-reference.

3. Analyze the facts listed as No. 10 through No. 18, resolving them into their debit and credit elements. Prepare journal entries and post to the ledger accounts. (Do not prepare closing entries.)

4. Prepare an income statement for May and a balance sheet as of May 31.

CASE 4–2.   CORBY COMPANY

The account balances in the ledger of the Corby Company on December 31, before adjustments, were as follows:

Debit Balances		*Credit Balances*	
Cash	$ 11,600	Accumulated depreciation on	
		store equipment	$ 7,800
Accounts receivable	39,620	Notes payable	25,000
Merchandise inventory	225,950	Accounts payable	35,410
Store equipment	26,760	Common stock	40,000
Supplies inventory	5,200	Retained earnings	15,940
Prepaid insurance	3,600	Sales	220,000
Selling expenses	3,500		
Sales salaries	15,500		
Miscellaneous general expenses	9,230		
Sales discounts	980		
Interest expense	1,620		
Social security tax expense	590		
Total	$344,150	Total	$344,150

The data for the adjustments are:

Cost of merchandise sold, $163,300.
Depreciation on store equipment, $2,670.

Supplies inventory, December 31, $1,400. (Purchases of supplies during the year were debited to the Supplies Inventory account.)
Expired insurance, $2,500.
Interest accrued on notes payable, $185.
Sales salaries earned but not paid to employees, $550.
Interest earned on Savings account, but not recorded, $300.

Questions

1. Set up T-accounts with the balances given above.

2. Journalize and post adjusting entries, adding other T-accounts as necessary.

3. Journalize and post closing entries.

4. Prepare an income statement and balance sheet.

CASE 4–3. WESTERN HILLS PHARMACY

Sam Parker was the owner of the Western Hills Pharmacy. His general ledger contained the following proprietorship, revenue, and expense accounts, which before adjustments had balances as shown below for the month ending August 31. (Asset and liability accounts are not shown.)

Sam Parker, capital	$ 5,000	Miscellaneous selling expenses	$420
Sam Parker, withdrawals		Rent expense	200
(debit balance)	500	Bad debt expense	0
Sales	12,400	Miscellaneous general expenses	150
Cost of goods sold	8,460	Rent income	360
Sales salaries	800	Purchase discounts	100
Advertising expense	250	Interest income	20
Store supplies used	0	Interest expense	48
Expired insurance	0	Loss and gain	0

Adjusting entries based on the following information are required in order to determine the net income or loss for the month of August:

1. Rent income of $360 represents three months' rent received in advance on August 1 for the subletting of the fountain and newspaper and magazine concession.

2. Allowance for bad debts, $50.

3. Interest has accrued for one month on a $1,000, 6 per cent note received on August 1 from former concessionnaire for unpaid rent.

4. Sales salaries unpaid, $120.

5. Store supplies used, $90.

6. Interest expense of $48 represents amount deducted from a 90-day note payable for $3,200 discounted at 6 per cent by the bank, August 16 (count as half a month).

7. Insurance coverage expiring during the month, $25.

8. An examination of the unpaid bills file revealed a statement from the utility company in the amount of $40 and an invoice for store supplies purchased the preceding week amounting to $30.

Questions

1. Set up T-accounts with the balances given above.
2. Journalize and post adjusting-entries.
3. Prepare an income statement for August.

CASE 4–4.   MASTERS FUEL OIL COMPANY

On the morning of January 14, 1959, Mr. Leonard Masters appeared at the office of his accountant, Wallace Stone. Masters was troubled, and explained his concern to Stone in the following words: "When you started handling my accounts last May you said that my books seemed to be in pretty good shape. Since then we've been doing about the same volume of business as last year—maybe a little more, but not very much. I've been thinking about the informal reports you've been giving me on how we're doing and from what you say it looks like we've doubled last year's profit. I can't see how that can be right. Don't you think we ought to check this out before you make up our 1958 reports?"

Mr. Masters, with his son-in-law, Louis Webster, operated Masters Fuel Oil Company. The principal activity of this company was delivery of heating fuel to residential customers; it had been registered as a partnership on July 1, 1956, after having been operated as a sole proprietorship by Leonard Masters for 17 years. The company was operated from the Masters home. Mrs. Masters and her daughter kept the records of deliveries (sales), receipts, and disbursements; Mrs. Masters billed all customers monthly. In addition to these members of the family, the company had recently taken on one full-time and two part-time workers to handle residential service work and to operate the company's second truck, acquired December 1, 1958. Louis' younger brother was frequently paid for performing such tasks as washing the trucks or answering the telephone.

Prior to the formation of the partnership and the hiring of driver-servicemen, the needs of the firm for formal records and accounting information were limited largely to billing and tax requirements. The changes, however, brought about a need for determining the partners' share of profits and for reporting payroll information to state and federal offices. Louis Webster was also somewhat more businesslike than his father-in-law and pressed for more formal handling of the company's records. For these reasons Masters and Webster decided that they would no longer depend on a "friend of the family" to figure their annual profit and income tax. Wallace Stone was contacted and was engaged to review the records of transactions monthly, to post to a set of accounts in a general ledger, to prepare quarterly statements and payroll reports, and to prepare the annual tax returns.

When Mr. Stone first visited the Masters home he was given the income statement and balance sheet for the company's last full business year which ended December 31, 1957 (see Exhibits 1 and 2). He discussed the operations of the firm at some length with the principals

Exhibit 1

MASTERS FUEL OIL COMPANY

Balance Sheet, December 31, 1957

ASSETS

Current Assets:			
Cash in bank			$13,993
Accounts receivable			12,486
Inventory of parts			5,490
Deposits on commercial bids			900
Total Current Assets			$32,869
Fixed Assets:			
Furniture and fixtures	$ 1,481		
Less: Depreciation allowance	566	$ 915	
Delivery and service equipment	$23,786		
Less: Depreciation allowance	9,787	13,999	
Building	$21,699		
Less: Depreciation allowance	7,364	14,335	
Land		6,000	
Total Fixed Assets			35,249
Total Assets			$68,118

LIABILITIES AND CAPITAL

Liabilities:			
Accounts payable		$ 4,382	
Other liabilities		256	
Total Liabilities		$ 4,638	
Capital:			
Leonard Masters, capital, January 1	$28,970		
Less: Drawings for the year	10,364		
	$18,606		
Add: Half share of profit for year	12,689		
Leonard Masters, capital, December 31		31,295	
Louis Webster, capital, January 1	$29,860		
Less: Drawings for the year	10,365		
	$19,495		
Add: Half share of profit for year	12,690		
Louis Webster, capital, December 31		32,185	
Total Liabilities and Capital			$68,118

Exhibit 2

MASTERS FUEL OIL COMPANY

Income Statement For the Year Ended December 31, 1957

Revenue from sales and services:

Fuel oil, nonbudget accounts		$ 97,587
Budget plan income		80,896
Burner service and repairs		14,876
Installations		10,980
Total Revenue		$204,338

Cost of sales and services:

Fuel oil delivered	$143,367	
Burner parts and supplies	3,877	
Installation costs	5,219	
Subcontractor charges	1,472	
Total Cost of Sales		153,935
Gross profit on sales		$ 50,403

Operating expenses:

Depreciation expense	$ 5,602	
Wages	6,751	
Vehicle expense	2,496	
Telephone	219	
Advertising	3,423	
Office and printing	1,019	
Utilities	437	
Taxes (other than payroll)	912	
Professional fees	1,480	
Payroll taxes	335	
Uniform rental expense	386	
Supplies	198	
Miscellaneous expense	1,766	
Total Operating Expense		25,024
Net Profit from Operations		$ 25,379

and was reasonably well satisfied that the affairs of the company were fairly presented in the statements.

On the basis of his initial interview, and his monthly visits, Stone observed the general manner in which the records were maintained. Briefly stated, his observations follow:

Cash Receipts: A record of all receipts, entered chronologically by the name of the payer, was maintained by Mrs. Masters.

Cash Disbursements: A record of all checks issued was maintained by Mrs. Webster. She reconciled the cash balance each month with the bank statement and noted any errors or discrepancies.

Cash Records: The receipts and disbursements journals (above) were completely transcribed, totaled, and balanced each month prior to Mr. Stone's visit.

Payroll Records: A record of hours worked by each employee was maintained by Louis Webster. This record was the basis for issuance of payroll checks and preparation of payroll reports.

Sales: Although customers were billed monthly on the basis of metered delivery tickets, no entry in the sales accounts was made to reflect either the delivery or the billing. Instead, all cash receipts were recorded as sales when Mrs. Masters entered them in the cash receipts journal. She also prepared a list of accounts receivable on December 31 of each year; this list was used as the basis for year-end adjustment of the sales and receivables accounts.

Budget Accounts: Approximately half of the annual gallonage was sold to customers participating in the company's Budget Account Plan. Each of these customers made equal monthly payments for nine months of the year (September through May) and in June balanced the account. If the customer's account showed a credit balance in June, he could choose either to receive a refund check at that time, or to apply the credit against the next following payment.

Budget Plan customers paid neither a service charge nor a carrying charge. They were required, however, to purchase an annual service contract for which a $25 charge was the initial entry against their account. The contract covered cleaning and inspection of heating apparatus once during the year, usually in the July or August preceding the budget period, and expired each year at the end of the budget period. It also guaranteed free service and parts according to terms and conditions specified in the agreement.

Mr. Masters' experience was that it was virtually impossible to tell when he would have to provide repair service. The dollar cost had not varied greatly, however, for several years. Cleaning service, on the other hand, was much simpler to plan for; it involved a fixed commitment which could be scheduled conveniently and discharged under predictable conditions of cost and time.

Mr. Masters was particularly enthusiastic about the cleaning portion of the service contracts. Except for incidental costs of replacing filters, labor time was his only real cost. Masters maintained that the cleaning work done under the Budget Plan Service Contract was at least as good as the work billed to noncontract customers. These customers were charged $15 for cleaning and inspection. Although relatively few noncontract accounts called for cleaning service, Masters denied that his rate was established to induce customers to enroll in the Budget Group. Competing firms offered similar cleaning services for $10 to $12.

The foregoing is a reasonably complete summation of Wallace Stone's knowledge of the Masters company up to the time of Mr. Masters' visit to his office. He did, of course, have a complete file of data on the 1958 operations (see Exhibit 3) and was about to prepare the annual statements for the partners. Now that Masters had questioned the profit figures, Stone felt obliged to spend a little more time before releasing any statements.

Stone discussed the matter briefly with Masters and then agreed to meet with him and the other members of the family the following evening at Masters' home. At the meeting, attention soon centered on the marked difference in accounts receivable at the end of the two years in question. Mrs. Masters recalled, then, that there was some problem in setting up the balance of receivables at the end of last year. The friend

Exhibit 3

MASTERS FUEL OIL COMPANY

Operating Data 1958

Cash Receipts Journal:

Received from regular customers	$106,478
Received from budget plan customers	97,798
Received for burner service and repairs	12,714
Received for installation work	4,460
Received deposit refunds	750
Total Receipts	$222,200

Cash Payments Journal:

Paid 1957 accounts payable	$ 4,382
Withdrawn by L. Masters	12,650
Withdrawn by L. Webster	15,000
Paid for fuel purchases	146,260
Paid for burner parts	5,905
Paid for installations	2,111
Paid to subcontractors	314
Paid for utilities	424
Paid for supplies	277
Paid for new truck	12,133
Paid for telephone	231
Paid for advertising	2,627
Paid property taxes	972
Paid office and printing costs	1,119
Paid fees for professional services	1,520
Paid 1957 other liabilities	256
Paid payroll taxes (1958)	212
Paid for rental of uniforms	512
Paid for vehicle operation	2,312
Paid wages*	9,816
Paid miscellaneous expenses	1,949
Total Disbursements	$220,982

Accounts payable, 12/31/58:

For fuel oil purchases	$ 3,962
For utility bills	36
For burner parts	438
For advertising	159

Other liabilities, 12/31/58:

Employers payroll taxes unpaid	278

Accounts receivable, 12/31/58:

Regular accounts	18,640
Budget accounts	12,172

Depreciation for 1958:

Furniture and fixtures—straight-line at 10 per cent of asset cost.
Delivery and service equipment—straight-line at 20 per cent of asset cost.
Building—straight-line at 5 per cent of asset cost.

Inventory of burner parts, 12/31/58	$ 8,250

* Withholding taxes not to be considered.

who had been helping with the books had completed preparation of the tax returns before Mrs. Masters had totaled all of the accounts. Explaining to Stone, Mrs. Masters said, "He had only the tape on the budget accounts.[2] When I called him and told him that I had the tape on all the other accounts, he said that he'd already finished the work and that it would all balance out." Mrs. Masters searched her desk and found the listing of accounts receivable that had not been recorded on December 31, 1957. The adding machine tape showed a total of $14,377.

Questions

1. Using the data that Stone had prior to Masters' visit on January 14, prepare the income statement and balance sheet for Masters Fuel Oil Company.

2. How shall Mr. Stone explain the situation to the Masters and Websters? Will it "all balance out"? Why?

3. What accounts, if any, were misstated on December 31, 1957? December 31, 1958?

4. What corrections, if any, would you make in the two sets of statements?

5. Do you have any recommendations for the handling of the record of customers' accounts in the future?

6. How should Stone reflect Masters' year-end liability on service contracts?

---

[2] Under the system used by this company, receipts on budget accounts had been recorded as budget plan income when received. The excess of delivery values over budget receipts had not been formally recorded. It was these amounts that Mrs. Masters calculated so that they could be added to budget plan income for the year.

Chapter 5

FURTHER ASPECTS OF INCOME MEASUREMENT

IN CHAPTERS 2 and 3 the basic concepts governing the measurement of income were described, and some of the problems involved in applying these concepts were outlined. As noted there, this class of problems is by far the most difficult in accounting. Also, it is the area in which there is the greatest disagreement among accountants.

Additional aspects of the income measurement problem are discussed in Chapters 5 through 9. Those treated in Chapter 5 include the following: deducing cost of goods sold; accounts receivable and bad debts; other problems of revenue measurement; wages, salaries, and related costs; income tax allocations; and losses. The techniques and conventions described are basically derived from the concepts already given; that is, they are an application of these concepts, rather than new concepts.

DEDUCING COST OF GOODS SOLD

When a company's accounting system contains a record of the cost of each item it sells, the amount to be recorded as cost of goods sold can be determined simply by adding up these costs for all items sold in the accounting period. In many businesses, notably in retail stores, it is not practicable to keep track of the cost of each individual item that is sold, however. One can easily visualize the delay, and indeed the embarrassment, that would result in a supermarket if the cashiers attempted to record the cost, as well as the sales value, of each item the customer brought to the check-out station. In such situations, the cost of goods sold during an accounting period is determined by the process of *deduction*. This process requires that a physical inventory, or count, be taken of the merchandise on hand and available for sale at the beginning of each accounting period and another at the end of the period. (The cost of merchandise on hand at the end of one period is of course identical with the figure for the beginning of the next period.) The dollar value of these inventories appears as an asset on the appropriate balance sheets.

Having determined the value of inventory, the cost of goods sold during a period is determined by the following reasoning process: The total amount of inventory available for sale during a period is what was on hand at the beginning of the period plus what was added (through purchasing additional merchandise) during the period; the difference between the total amount available for sale and the amount remaining at the end of the period is assumed to have been sold. Thus:

Beginning inventory	$ 4,000
Plus: Purchases	7,400
Equals: Goods available for sale	$11,400
Less: Ending inventory	2,000
Cost of Goods Sold	$ 9,400

Some companies show such a calculation in the cost of goods sold section of the income statement itself. Others, although deducing cost of goods sold by the method shown above, do not present the details.

The amount of detail shown can be carried even further. For example, the cost of a product includes not only its invoice price but also the cost of delivering it to the premises, and the amount of this "freight-in" might be shown separately. Also, a separate record might be kept of purchased items that were subsequently returned. A calculation giving this detail follows:

Beginning inventory		$ 4,000
Plus: Purchases, gross	$7,000	
Plus: Freight-in	600	
	$7,600	
Less: Purchase returns	200	
Net purchases		7,400
Goods available for sale		$11,400
Less: Ending inventory		2,000
Cost of Goods Sold		$ 9,400

Accounts

When the cost of goods sold is deduced by the calculation described above, a separate account is established for each element in the calculation. Thus, a Purchases account is established, and the invoice cost of merchandise purchased is debited to this account, rather than directly to inventory. Accounts are also established for Freight-In, Purchase Returns, and any other items involved in the calculation.

Rules for debiting and crediting these accounts can be deduced from their relationship to other accounts. Since Purchases shows additions to the asset account, Inventory, it increases on the debit side. Purchase Returns is a reduction in Purchases and hence must have the opposite rule; it increases on the credit side. Freight-In adds to the cost of purchases and therefore increases on the debit side. (The rules can also be deduced by thinking of the offsetting part of the transaction. Whenever possible, it is simplest to assume that the other account is Cash. Thus, a cash purchase involves a decrease in Cash, which is a credit; therefore, the entry to Purchases must be a debit.)

Adjusting and Closing

The accounts described above are temporary accounts which must be closed at the end of each accounting period. Furthermore, when these accounts are used, no entries are made during the accounting period to the Inventory account; therefore the amount shown in Inventory when the adjusting process begins will be the amount of *beginning* inventory. The Inventory account must be adjusted to show the proper inventory amount as of the end of the period. These adjusting and closing entries are customarily made in a certain order, which is more in the nature of a ritual than something of fundamental significance. It is as follows:

(1) Transfer the beginning inventory to Cost of Goods Sold.

(2) Close Freight-In, Purchase Returns, and similar accounts to Purchases, thereby showing the amount of net purchases in the Purchases account.

(3) Close Purchases to Cost of Goods Sold.

(4) Enter the ending inventory by debiting Inventory and crediting Cost of Goods Sold.

(5) Close Cost of Goods Sold to Loss and Gain.

EXAMPLE: Using the figures given above, these entries would be as follows:

(1)
```
dr.  Cost of Goods Sold..................................4,000
     cr.  Inventory....................................        4,000
```

(2)
```
dr.  Purchases........................................  600
     cr.  Freight-In...................................        600

dr.  Purchase Returns.................................  200
     cr.  Purchases ...................................        200*
```

(3)
```
dr.  Cost of Goods Sold..............................7,400
     cr.  Purchases....................................        7,400
```

(4)
```
dr.  Inventory.......................................2,000
     cr.  Cost of Goods Sold..........................        2,000
```

(5)
```
dr.  Loss and Gain...................................9,400
     cr.  Cost of Goods Sold..........................        9,400
```

* The entry is shown in this form for clarity. In practice, the two parts of this entry would be combined, thus saving some work, as follows:
```
dr.  Purchases.......................................................400
     Purchase Returns................................................200
cr.  Freight-In......................................        600
```

If a work sheet is used, there might be a separate pair of columns labeled Cost of Goods Sold, and amounts corresponding to the above would be entered in these columns.

Limitation of the Deduction Process

Note that the validity of the reasoning behind the calculations described above rests on the *assumption* that if the merchandise is not found to be on hand at the end of the period, it must have been sold. This assumption is not necessarily correct; some of the goods may have been lost, or stolen, or thrown away, or overlooked when the physical inventory was taken. Usually, but not always, safeguards are set up to detect or avoid most of the shrinkages resulting from these causes. Nevertheless, in this system the physical inventory count must be used to determine the cost of goods sold, whereas in the perpetual inventory system an actual count of the goods on hand can be used as a check on the accuracy of the inventory records.

Service Businesses

The cost of the services from which a service business derives its revenue is not as easily identifiable as the cost of the physical products sold by a retail store. Many service businesses do not attempt to measure the cost of the services they sell and hence do not develop a gross profit figure, since gross profit is the difference between sales revenue and cost of sales. Others do calculate a cost of sales, counting wages and salaries and other direct costs as their "cost of services."

> EXAMPLE: A plumbing business might show the wages of plumbers and the cost of pipes, fittings, and other material as its cost of sales, and list as operating expenses, below the gross profit figure, its management salaries, office costs, and other expenses.

ACCOUNTS RECEIVABLE AND BAD DEBTS

The main source of revenue in many businesses is the sale of merchandise to customers for credit, that is, "on account." This type of transaction gives rise to the asset, accounts receivable, and to an increase in sales revenue and hence in owners' equity. Let us assume that the Essel Company began operations in 1962 and that during the year the company made sales of $262,250, all on credit. In the interest of simplicity, let us further assume that none of the customers had paid their bills by the end of 1962. The record made of these transactions would show accounts receivable in the amount of $262,250 and sales of

$262,250. It would be correct to report $262,250 as an asset on the balance sheet as of the end of 1962 and $262,250 as sales on the income statement for 1962 if, *but only if,* it is believed that the customers eventually will pay their obligations to the Essel Company. The unfortunate fact is, however, that some of these customers may never pay their bills; that is, their accounts will become *bad debts.*

Consider the extreme case: the person who purchases merchandise with no intention of paying for it and who in fact does not pay for it. In this case, the company has not actually made a sale at all. Although the fact was not known at the time, no revenue was actually earned and nothing valuable was added to the asset, accounts receivable, as a result of this transaction. If this event is recorded as an increase in Sales and as an increase in Accounts Receivable, both these accounts will be overstated.

In the more usual bad debt situation, the customer fully intends to pay his bill, but for one reason or another he never actually does make payment. The effect is the same as that in the extreme case. Such a sale would also be recorded initially by debiting Accounts Receivable and crediting Sales at the sales value of the merchandise. In this situation, a subsequent entry must be made to show that the amount debited to Accounts Receivable does not represent a valid asset and that owners' equity has not in fact increased by the amount of the sale.

Accounting Recognition of Bad Debts

When the company made the sale, the fact that the customer would never pay his bill was not known; otherwise the sale probably would not have been made. Even at the end of the accounting period, the company probably does not know which of the obligations carried as accounts receivable will never be collected. An estimate of the amount of bad debts can nevertheless be made, and it is customary to adjust the accounting records at the end of each accounting period to reflect this estimate.

One method of making this adjustment is by a *direct write-off.* Accounts that are believed to be uncollectible are simply eliminated from the records by subtracting the amount of the bad debt from Accounts Receivable and showing the same amount as an expense item on the income statement. The entry to accomplish this would be as follows:

```
dr.  Bad Debt Expense.................................................200
     cr.  Accounts Receivable.........................................     200
```

The direct write-off method, however, requires that the specific uncollectible accounts be detected, whereas this usually is not possible.

An alternative procedure, therefore, is to estimate the *total* amount of uncollectible accounts and to show this estimated amount as a deduction from accounts receivable on the balance sheet and as an expense on the income statement. Instead of reducing the accounts receivable figure directly, the estimate is often shown as a separate figure on the balance sheet, so that the reader can observe both the total amount owed by customers and that portion of the amount which the company believes will not be collected.

An account used to record deductions in the amount shown in some other account is called a *contra* account. The balance sheet contra account for accounts receivable is often labeled *allowance for doubtful accounts* or *allowance for uncollectible accounts.* It may also be labeled "reserve for bad debts," but this is likely to cause confusion since the word "reserve" connotes to many people that a sum of money has been set aside, and such is not the case. The allowance for doubtful accounts is in the nature of a suspended credit to accounts receivable for specific, but as yet unknown, customers.

The corresponding item on the income statement is called *bad debt expense* or *loss on bad debts.* Ordinarily, this item appears as one of the miscellaneous operating expenses listed below the gross profit, on the grounds that this is an item that is an almost inevitable cost in any business that extends credit to its customers. Some companies show it as a subtraction from gross sales, reflecting the belief that bad debts represent sales that never actually resulted in revenue; still others show it as a nonoperating expense. This possible difference in treatment should be kept in mind when comparing the income statements for two companies in which bad debts are a significant item since the gross profit of one may reflect the recognition of bad debt expense, while that of the other may not.

Methods of Making the Estimate. Any one of several methods may be used to estimate the amount of bad debt expense in an accounting period. One method is to examine each of the customer accounts and to set up an amount that is large enough to equal those accounts that seem to be uncollectible. In companies with hundreds, or thousands, of customer accounts, an analysis of each individual account may not be feasible. A common practice, therefore, is to rely on some overall formula developed on the basis of experience over a period of years. Some of the methods commonly used are as follows:

1. Estimate bad debt expense as a *percentage of total sales* for the period. This method can logically be used only when cash sales are either negligible or a constant proportion of total sales, for bad debt expense is not, of course, related to cash sales.

2. Estimate bad debt expense as a *percentage of credit sales.*
3. Adjust the Allowance for Doubtful Accounts so that it equals a prescribed *percentage of accounts receivable* outstanding at the end of the period.

The percentage used in each case depends on what the records show as to experience in the past and on management's judgment as to the extent to which past experience reflects the current situation.

   Aging Accounts Receivable.   Sometimes different percentages are applied to accounts outstanding for various lengths of time. This requires the preparation of an aging schedule, which is also a useful device for analyzing the quality of the asset, accounts receivable. An example is shown in Illustration 5–1.

Illustration 5–1

AGING SCHEDULE FOR ESTIMATING BAD DEBTS

Status	Amount Outstanding	Estimated % Uncollectible	Allowance for Doubtful Accounts
Current....................	$207,605	1	$2,076
Overdue:			
Less than 1 month........	26,003	1	260
1 up to 2 months..........	10,228	5	511
2 up to 3 months.........	7,685	10	768
3 up to 4 months..........	3,876	20	775
Over 4 months............	6,853	40	2,741
Total...............	$262,250		$7,131

The Adjusting Entry.   Once the amount has been determined, it is recorded as one of the adjusting entries made at the end of the accounting period. If Essel Company management estimated the Allowance for Doubtful Accounts on the basis of the above aging schedule, the entry would be as shown below:

dr. Bad Debt Expense..7,131
    cr. Allowance for Doubtful Accounts...........................   7,131

The accounts receivable section of the December 31, 1962, balance sheet would then appear as follows:

Accounts receivable...$262,250
    Less: Allowance for doubtful accounts.....................   7,131
        Accounts Receivable, Net...............................$255,119

The income statement for 1962 would show bad debt expense in the amount of $7,131.

For reasons to be described, the Allowance for Doubtful Accounts usually will have a balance even before the adjusting entry is made. In these circumstances the amount reported as bad debt expense on the income statement will be different from the amount reported as allowance for doubtful accounts on the balance sheet. (In the Essel Company example just given, this did not occur because the company was organized in 1962, and the above entry was the first one made to Allowance for Doubtful Accounts.)

When the Allowance for Doubtful Accounts has a balance, care must be taken in applying the formulas listed above. Formulas No. 1 and No. 2, which are related to sales, give the amount of bad debt *expense* for the period; this same amount is credited to whatever balance existed in Allowance for Doubtful Accounts prior to the entry. Formula No. 3, which is related to accounts receivable, gives the amount that is to appear as the Allowance for Doubtful Accounts; the journal entry is made in an amount that brings the Allowance for Doubtful Accounts *up to* the desired balance.

> EXAMPLE: If at the end of 1963, in the Essel Company, Allowance for Doubtful Accounts had a credit balance of $1,000, and if it was decided that the allowance should be 2 per cent of accounts receivable, which at that time amounted to $300,000, the balance must be increased *to* $6,000, an increase of $5,000. The journal entry would therefore be the following:
>
> ```
> dr.  Bad Debt Expense.....................................5,000
>     cr.  Allowance for Doubtful Accounts......................     5,000
> ```
>
> The balance sheet as of December 31, 1963, would then show—
>
> ```
> Accounts receivable...........................................$300,000
>   Less: Allowance for doubtful accounts........................   6,000
>   Accounts Receivable, Net.....................................$294,000
> ```

Write-off of an Uncollectible Account

When the company decides that a specific customer is never going to pay his bill, Accounts Receivable is reduced by the amount he owes and a corresponding reduction is made in the Allowance for Doubtful Accounts. This entry is made whenever it is recognized that a specific account is bad, which may be either during the accounting period or at the end of the period. This event has *no* effect on Bad Debt Expense.

> EXAMPLE: If sometime in 1964 the Essel Company decided that John Jones was never going to pay his bill of $200, the following entry would be made:
>
> ```
> dr.  Allowance for Doubtful Account.............................200
>     cr.  Accounts Receivable.................................     200
> ```

A balance sheet prepared immediately after this transaction had been recorded (assuming no other changes since December 31) would appear as follows:

Accounts receivable..$299,800
Less: Allowance for doubtful accounts........................ 5,800
Accounts Receivable, Net..............................$294,000

Note that the *net* amount of accounts receivable is unchanged by this entry.

Collection of a Bad Debt Written Off

If, by some unexpected stroke of good fortune, John Jones should subsequently pay all or part of his bill, cash would be increased (i.e., debited) and a corresponding credit would be recorded to have one of the following effects:

1. Increase retained earnings on the balance sheet.
2. Add the amount back to allowance for doubtful accounts on the balance sheet.
3. Show as bad debts recovered, a separate item of revenue on the income statement.
4. Decrease bad debt expense on the income statement.

The first method ordinarily is not used since it goes counter to the "clean surplus" doctrine. The second method has the effect of reversing the previous entry, and it is often used. The third method is rarely used because the amount involved is ordinarily too small to warrant reporting it as a separate item. The fourth method is not entirely logical but is often used in practice since it provides a convenient way of handling the transaction.

Still another common procedure is, first, to reverse the entry by which the account was written off (i.e., debit Accounts Receivable and credit Allowance for Doubtful Accounts) and, then, to treat the collection just like any other payment on account (i.e., debit Cash and credit Accounts Receivable). This has the advantage of showing a complete record of the transaction in the account for the customer.

The allowance for doubtful accounts should be sufficient at all times to absorb the accounts that prove to be uncollectible. Because the amount so established is an *average* based on past experience, and because business conditions fluctuate, the amount will turn out to be too large in some periods and too small in others. In practice, because of the doctrine of conservatism, it is common to find that the allowance is too large rather than too small. On the other hand, there have been some cases where the allowance for doubtful accounts turned out to be woefully inadequate.

Summary

Let us summarize the handling of events described above by showing the effect of hypothetical transactions in 1964 on the Essel Company accounts:

1. *Write-off of $5,000 more of bad debts during the year:*

    dr. Allowance for Doubtful Accounts............................5,000
        cr. Accounts Receivable..   5,000
        The balance in Allowance for Doubtful Accounts becomes $800.

2. *Recovery of $500 previously written off:*

    dr. Cash...   500
        cr. Allowance for Doubtful Accounts*.........................   500
        The balance in Allowance for Doubtful Accounts becomes $1,300.
        * As mentioned, this is only one of several possible treatments.

3. *Adjustments at end of 1964*, assuming allowance is to be maintained at 2 per cent of accounts receivable, which are $400,000 as of December 31, 1964:

    dr. Bad Debt Expense..6,700
        cr. Allowance for Doubtful Accounts..........................   6,700
        This brings the allowance up to $8,000, which is 2 per cent of accounts receivable.

OTHER PROBLEMS OF REVENUE RECOGNITION

The rationale of the bad debt adjustment is that expense should be matched with revenue, regardless of the time of *discovery* that accounts are uncollectible. The same rationale applies to sales discounts, sales returns and allowances, and similar items. If the amounts involved are material, similar adjustments should be made for these items; for example, the amount of sales discounts that will be taken in future periods on sales counted as revenue in the current period should be estimated, and the sales discount expense adjusted accordingly. However, although the procedure of estimating bad debt expense on a reasonable basis is acceptable for income tax purposes, such a procedure is not acceptable with respect to sales discounts and similar items. For tax purposes, most types of sales discounts can be deducted only if the customer actually took the discount during the period in question.

For other reasons, the amount specified in the sales contract may not be the best estimate of the revenue that actually will be realized from the transaction. The possibility that the company might incur repair costs or make replacements in order to discharge its obligations under a warranty agreement, mentioned in Chapter 3, is an example. When such amounts are significant, the matching principle requires that these future costs be estimated and set up as deductions from the current period's revenue. The mechanics of doing this are similar to those described above for bad debts.

Long-Term Contracts

When, under a firm contract, a business works for several accounting periods on a single product, a portion of the revenue is often recognized in each of these periods rather than solely in the final period in which the product is completed and shipped. Shipbuilding and major construction projects are examples of situations in which this *percentage-of-completion* method is used. The revenue recognized for a period can easily be estimated when the product is constructed under a straight *cost-plus* contract, since the revenue is a specified percentage of the costs incurred in the period. In the case of fixed-price contracts or contracts with a fixed dollar amount of profit (cost plus fixed fee, or CPFF), the total amount of profit, and hence the amount applicable to each period, cannot be known exactly until the total costs have been determined at the completion of the job. In these situations, an estimated revenue may nevertheless be assigned to each of the accounting periods in the same proportion to the cost of the period that total revenue is expected to be of total cost, the proportion being estimated conservatively so as to avoid overstatement of interim profits.

In accordance with the matching principle, when revenue is measured by the percentage-of-completion basis, the expenses for the period are the costs associated with the revenue.

Installment Sales

Consumers who pay for their purchases on installments (so much a month or so much a week) are, as a class, not exceptionally good credit risks; a significant number of them do not complete their payments, and the seller accordingly repossesses, or tries to repossess, the merchandise. When this happens, the face amount of the installment contract overstates the amount of revenue that actually is earned on the transaction. One way of allowing for these defaults is to use the estimated bad debt mechanism already described. Another method used by many businesses is to recognize the revenue only as the installment payments are received, rather than when the sale is made. Either method is acceptable for income tax purposes. If the installment method is used in measuring revenue, the relevant expense is that fraction of the product's cost that corresponds to the fraction of installment payments received during the period.

Cash Basis

Despite the realization concept, a number of businesses, particularly small ones, recognize revenue only when cash is received. Many doctors and other professional people use this so-called *cash basis* rather than recording revenue as of the period when they render the service. This practice is conservative and is permitted under certain circumstances for income tax purposes, but it is not in accordance with generally accepted accounting principles. A business that uses the cash basis cannot measure its net income in the accounting sense of this term.

Consignments

Shipments on *consignment* are not sales.[1] The consignor, that is, the manufacturer, retains title to consignment merchandise, and the sale is not consummated until the consignee, who is usually a retailer, resells to the final customer. A consignment shipment therefore represents only the movement of the asset, inventory, from one place to another. In order to show the amount of merchandise out on consignment, it may be desirable to reflect this movement by a journal entry, at cost:

```
dr.  Inventory on Consignment......................................100
     cr.  Merchandise Inventory......................................        100
```

In the period in which the goods are sold, the effect on the accounts would be as in the following entries (although these amounts would probably be recorded in practice as a part of other summary entries for revenues and expense):

```
dr.  Cost of Goods Sold.............................................100
     cr.  Inventory on Consignment...................................        100
     To record the cost of consigned goods sold.

dr.  Accounts Receivable............................................150
     cr.  Sales......................................................        150
     To record the sales value.
```

WAGES, SALARIES, AND RELATED COSTS

As a matter of custom, the word "wages" usually refers to the compensation of employees who are on a piece-rate, hourly, daily, or

---

[1] Nevertheless, some businesses treat consignment shipments as if they were sales on the grounds that they have learned through experience that the consigned merchandise ordinarily is not returned, and that the sale for all practical purposes is therefore consummated at the time of shipment.

weekly basis; while the word "salaries" usually refers to compensation expressed in monthly, or longer, terms. The effect on the accounting records of earning and paying wages and salaries is more complicated than merely increasing costs or expenses and decreasing cash, for when wages and salaries are earned or paid, certain other transactions occur almost automatically.

An employee is rarely paid the gross amount of wages or salary he earns since from his gross earnings there must be deducted—

1. An amount representing his contribution under the Federal Insurance Contribution Act (F.I.C.A.), which currently (1964) is 3.625 per cent of the first $4,800 of wages earned each year.
2. The withholding deduction, which is an amount withheld from gross earnings to apply toward his income tax.
3. Deductions for pension contributions, savings plans, health insurance, union dues, and a variety of other items.

None of these deductions represents an expense to the business. In the case of the tax deductions, the business is acting as a collection agent for the government; the withholding of these amounts and their subsequent transfer to the government does not affect owners' equity. Similarly, the business is acting as a collection agent in the case of the other deductions. The employee is paid the net amount after these deductions have been taken.

When wages and salaries are earned, other expenses are automatically created. The employer must pay a tax equal in amount to the employee's F.I.C.A. tax, and the employer must pay an additional percentage of the employee's pay (the rate varies in different states) for the *unemployment insurance tax.* (Collectively, F.I.C.A. and unemployment insurance are called *social security taxes.*) The *employer's* share of these taxes *is* an expense of the business.

Thus, if an employee with three dependents earns $100 for his work in a given week in 1964, there would be deducted from his pay $3.62 for his F.I.C.A. tax contribution and $9.00 for withholding tax, and he would receive the balance, $87.38. This is his "take-home pay." (Other possible deductions are omitted for purposes of simplification.) The *business* would incur an expense of $3.62 for F.I.C.A. tax and an additional expense of, say, $2.50 for the unemployment insurance tax, or a total of $6.12 for the two social security taxes.

The journal entries for these transactions are as follows:

1. *When wages are earned; wages expense:*

    dr. Wages Expense. 100.00
       cr. Wages Payable. 100.00

2. *When wages are earned; business tax expense:*[2]

   dr. Social Security Tax Expense.............................. 6.12
      cr. F.I.C.A. Taxes Payable............................ ....   3.62
           Unemployment Taxes Payable.......................   2.50

3. *When the employee is paid:*

   dr. Wages Payable...100.00
      cr. Cash...   87.38
           F.I.C.A. Taxes Payable...........................   3.62
           Withholding Taxes Payable........................   9.00

4. *When the government is paid:*

   dr. F.I.C.A. Taxes Payable.................................... 7.24
          Unemployment Taxes Payable............................. 2.50
          Withholding Taxes Payable.............................. 9.00
      cr. Cash..   18.74

In practice, the above entries would be made for all employees as a group rather than separately for each person. The government does require, however, that a record be kept for the amount of F.I.C.A. tax and withholding tax accumulated for each employee, and that he be furnished a copy of this record.

The above transactions, although complicated, involve no new problem in the application of accounting principles. One matter related to wages does involve a very difficult problem. This is the liability and related expense for pensions.

Pensions

About 20,000,000 Americans work for companies that agree to pay them pensions when they retire. All or part of the cost of these pensions is borne by the company; the remainder, if any, comes from contributions made by employees. Accounting for the company's cost for pensions is a particularly difficult matter because the expense is incurred during the years in which the employee works for the company, but the payments to him are made at some distant future time, and the total amount of the payment is uncertain, depending on how long he lives, on his final wage or salary, and possibly on other considerations.

The pension plans of many companies are *funded;* that is, an estimate is made of the amount that will be necessary to meet the future pension payments arising out of the employees' earnings in the current year, and this amount is either set aside in a trust fund or paid to an outside agency that guarantees to make the future pension payments.

---

[2] This entry matches the tax expense with wages *earned* in the period, which is in principle the correct treatment. Some businesses compute the tax as of the period in which the wages are *paid,* on the grounds that this involves a much simpler calculation and that there is no material difference between the results of the two methods.

The amount paid into such a fund is a deductible expense for income tax purposes, provided certain other conditions are met, and is usually treated as an expense of the current year for accounting purposes. If the company retains the fund, the following entries are required each year:

```
dr.  Pension Expense.................................................xxxx
    cr.  Pension Liability.........................................        xxxx
    To establish the expense and related liability.

dr.  Pension Fund (a noncurrent asset)..............................xxxx
    cr.  Cash.....................................................        xxxx
    To transfer cash to the fund.
```

When the pension is paid to the retired employee, the entry is as follows;

```
dr.  Pension Liability..............................................xxxx
    cr.  Pension Fund.............................................        xxxx
```

If the plan is not funded, only the amount actually paid to retired employees is deductible for tax purposes. Many companies record this same amount as an expense in the year the payment is made, even though it relates to work done in prior years rather than to the current year and thus is not matched with the correct revenue. They argue that an estimate of the expense actually created by work done in the current year is so uncertain as to be meaningless. Note that the balance sheets of companies following this practice would show no liability for future pension payments despite the fact that an obligation to make such payments clearly exists.

When a pension plan is first adopted, an especially difficult problem arises: What shall be done about the liability created for employees who are entitled to benefits because of the years they have worked for the company up to the time of adoption of the plan? Although this liability arises as a result of work done in prior years, for income tax purposes the estimated amount thereof may be treated as a tax deduction over the next 10 or 12 *future* years. The Accounting Principles Board recommends that the estimated cost of these *past-service benefits* be charged as expenses of present and future periods (but not necessarily 10 or 12 years) and opposes the practice of debiting this cost directly to retained earnings.[3]

Even a careful estimate of the future liability under a pension plan may turn out to be wrong, partly because such factors as whether the employee will stay with the company until retirement and his length of life after retirement are quite uncertain, and also because there is a

---

[3] AICPA, *Accounting Research Bulletin No. 47.*

tendency to liberalize benefits as time goes on. Consequently, the actual amount of expense attributable to the work done in a given year cannot be known for many years later.

INCOME TAX ALLOCATIONS

In accordance with the matching concept, the income tax reported as an expense for a year should be related to the income reported for the year; that is, if the company reports an income of $1,000,000 before taxes, and the tax rate is approximately 52 per cent, the income tax expense should be approximately $520,000. If companies figured their taxable income exactly the same way they figured their net income on the income statement, there would be no matching problem. Many companies use different rules for tax purposes than they use for financial accounting purposes, however, and the income tax calculated for a given year will therefore be based on a different amount of income from that reported on the income statement. Under these circumstances, the income tax as calculated will not match the reported income. When there is a difference between net income measured in accordance with accounting principles and net *taxable* income calculated in accordance with tax regulations, a problem arises.

> EXAMPLE: Assume that in 1963 a company spends $400,000 on research and development which results in a successful new product; that it decides for accounting purposes to charge this cost as an expense over the next five years, during which time the new product is expected to be producing revenue; but for tax purposes it deducts the $400,000 in the year of expenditure, thus postponing the payment of a corresponding amount of taxes. If its net income prior to considering the research and development item is $1,000,000 for both tax purposes and accounting purposes, its income subject to tax will be $600,000, and its income tax will be approximately 52 per cent[4] of this, or $312,000. If the company regarded this $312,000 as its income tax *expense* for 1963, then its net income for accounting purposes would be $1,000,000 − $312,-000 = $688,000. This, however, would be incorrect, for the $312,000 tax matches, or relates to, an income of $600,000, not of $1,000,000. The tax applicable to the $1,000,000 is $520,000, and the net income should be reported as $1,000,000 − $520,000 = $480,000.
>
> The opposite situation will arise in the next five years, for in each of them the company will charge $80,000 as research and development expense for accounting purposes, but it cannot deduct this amount

---

[4] In 1963, federal income taxes on ordinary corporations were 30 per cent of the first $25,000 of taxable income and 52 per cent of income in excess of $25,000. In 1964, the tax rate drops to 50 per cent, and in 1965, it drops to 48 per cent. Many states also impose corporate income taxes.

again for tax purposes, so its accounting income will be lower than its taxable income. By the end of the fifth following year, 1968, the difference between taxable income and accounting income will have washed out.

When such differences between accounting income and taxable income in a year are material, the AICPA recommends that the income tax actually calculated for the year be adjusted so that it equals the income tax that would have been paid had the accounting income been taxable in that year. The offsetting entry is made to an appropriate asset or liability account.

EXAMPLE: Carrying on the above illustration, the estimated amount of income tax actually payable for 1963 is recorded by this entry:

```
dr.  Income Tax Expense...............................312,000
   cr.  Income Tax Liability..........................          312,000
```

A second entry is then made to bring the income tax up to the amount applicable to the accounting income, which is $520,000. Of the several acceptable ways in which this could be done, a common one follows:

```
dr.  Income Tax Expense...............................208,000
   cr.  Deferred Income Tax Liability..................          208,000
```

Deferred Income Tax Liability appears on the balance sheet and is written off in each of the next five years by this entry:

```
dr.  Deferred Income Tax..............................  41,600
   cr.  Income Tax Expense............................           41,600
```

In this way, the income tax expense figure is made to match the income as measured by accounting principles.

It should be noted that the American Accounting Association Committee disagrees with the AICPA Accounting Principles Board on the treatment of income taxes. The American Accounting Association Committee recommends that no adjustment of the income tax expense be made, on the grounds that "the possible figure offsets are often subject to unusual uncertainties; and treatment on an accrual basis is in many cases unduly complicated." The Committee states that the adjustment may be "more confusing than enlightening."[5]

LOSSES

A distinction is often made between an *expense,* which is made to benefit the operations of a period, and a *loss,* which is an expenditure

---

[5] American Accounting Association, 1957 Revision, *Accounting Review,* October 1957, p. 542.

that does not benefit anything. The destruction of an uninsured building by fire, or the theft of some asset, results in a loss. Since both expenses and losses are ordinarily charged to the accounting period to which they relate, there is no great need to draw a fine line between them. Losses are often shown in the nonoperating section of the income statement. An extraordinary loss that has a material effect on income may be charged directly to retained earnings rather than to the income statement of the current year, as noted on page 76.

CONCLUSION

As additional problems are discussed, it should become increasingly apparent that the goal of matching revenue and expense in an accounting period can never be exactly attained. This fact could easily lead to a sense of frustration, were it not for the doctrine of materiality. In this doctrine we have the practical solution: one does the best he can with the information and in the time available, realizing that despite his best efforts, a perfect matching is not likely to result. The doctrine of materiality should of course be used sparingly in classroom discussions or examinations. When the emphasis is on the proper interpretation of principles, materiality should not be invoked as a substitute for sound reasoning.

CASES

CASE 5–1.   PALMER CORPORATION (A)

On December 31, 1963, before the yearly financial statements were prepared, the controller of the Palmer Corporation reviewed certain transactions that affected accounts receivable and the allowance for doubtful accounts. The controller first examined the December 31, 1962, balance sheet, Exhibit 1 (p. 144). His subsequent review of the year's transactions applicable to accounts receivable revealed the items listed below:

1. Sales on account during 1963 amounted to $4,799,621.
2. Payment received on accounts receivable during 1963 totaled $4,786,797.
3. During the year accounts receivable totaling $8,847 were deemed uncollectible and were written off.
4. Two accounts which had been written off as uncollectible in 1962 were collected in 1963. One account for $916 was paid in full. A partial payment of $600 was made by the King Company on another account which originally had amounted to $1,185. The Palmer Corporation was reasonably sure this account would be paid in full because reliable reports were circulating that the trustee in bankruptcy for the King Company would pay all obligations 100 cents on the dollar.

Exhibit 1

PALMER CORPORATION

Balance Sheet as of December 31, 1962

ASSETS

Current Assets:

Cash		$ 371,261
Accounts receivable	$ 399,329	
Less: Allowance for doubtful accounts	11,979	387,350
U.S. Treasury securities at cost		139,466
Inventories		945,013
Total Current Assets		$1,843,090
Investments		$ 206,681

Fixed Assets:

Land		$ 76,534
Building	$1,080,572	
Less: Accumulated depreciation	333,802	746,770
Factory machinery	$1,799,176	
Less: Accumulated depreciation	848,121	951,055
Furniture and fixtures	$ 26,962	
Less: Accumulated depreciation	16,796	10,166
Automotive equipment	$ 28,676	
Less: Accumulated depreciation	16,654	12,022
Office machines	$ 20,895	
Less: Accumulated depreciation	13,141	7,754
Tools		30,418
Patent		35,000
Total Fixed Assets		$1,869,719
Prepaid expenses		56,963
Total Assets		$3,976,453

LIABILITIES AND CAPITAL

Current Liabilities:

Accounts payable	$ 234,589
Unpaid taxes	380,323
Accrued salaries, wages, and interest	75,960
Long-term debt, due within one year	36,455
Total Current Liabilities	$ 727,327

Fixed Liabilities:

Long-term debt	$ 524,680

Contingent Liabilities:

Current operating reserves	$ 65,951

Capital:

Common stock	$1,337,810
Retained earnings	1,320,685
Total Capital	$2,658,495
Total Liabilities and Capital	$3,976,453

5. The allowance for bad debts was adjusted to equal 3 per cent of the balance in accounts receivable at the end of the year.

Questions

1. Analyze the effect of each of these transactions in terms of their effect on accounts receivable, the allowance for doubtful accounts, and any other accounts that may be involved, and prepare necessary journal entries.

2. Give the correct totals for accounts receivable and the allowance for doubtful accounts, as of December 31, 1963, after the transactions affecting them had been recorded.

CASE 5–2. SENECA MEMORIAL HOSPITAL

Roy Sanders, a senior accountant on the staff of Young and Mitchell, was in charge of the examination of the financial statements of the Seneca Memorial Hospital for the year ended June 30, 1962. The hospital served the people in Seneca and those from the rural areas within a radius of about 50 miles. Its operating revenues were derived primarily from charges to patients, but operations were further supported by income from endowment funds and by contributions from the state. The hospital building and much of its equipment had resulted from fund-raising campaigns and special gifts over the past 20 years.

The affairs of the hospital were directed by a self-perpetuating board of 20 trustees, all of whom were leading figures in the Seneca area. Robert R. Samuelson, an attorney, was president of the board, having served in that capacity for 17 years and as a member of the board for 30 years. Director of the hospital was Leroy Johnson, who was assisted in the areas with which we are concerned by Andrew Wiley, controller, and Frank Abbot, credit manager.

Mr. Sanders felt that the present year's examination was progressing smoothly and that the work was well along. At the moment, he was reflecting on accounts receivable—the stickiest part of his entire examination. He recalled that in a supplementary report by his firm to the board of trustees made in connection with the 1961 examination, the following statement had been included:

It is estimated that accounts receivable amounting to over $160,000 are more than one year old. This is the result of a failure to charge off old and uncollectible accounts, to an apparent lack of a standard, routine follow-up, and to many instances when patients are discharged without an effective attempt to realize a collection of the balance due. Procedures and form letters are in use for credit follow-up, but our observation was that they are applied on a selective, individual basis instead of in a regular routine.

The accounts have never been completely aged to determine the status and trend of collections. As a result, we found no person who could accurately evaluate the status of the accounts.

Mr. Sanders also remembered a public statement made by Mr. Samuelson following a recent board of trustees meeting: "An examination of the status of our accounts receivable indicates that there is need of more arduous efforts in collecting accounts from those who can afford to pay, should pay, but are willing to evade a just debt where possible. Those responsible for many of these accounts have ignored our request for payment, and your board of trustees is instituting for the next fiscal year a more stringent collection policy. In a charitable institution it is always difficult to know when the debtor should be considered a worthy recipient of beneficence and when he should be made to pay through the medium of all legal collection forces available to the institution. While the trustees, if they err, would err in favor of benevolence where needed, yet it is only fair to remind those who owe the hospital and can afford to pay that they may expect payment to be enforced."

The problems implicit in the above statement were quite apparent to Mr. Sanders. The hospital's own figures for the year under examination showed that, including endowment fund income of $46,000, the excess of revenues over expenses was only $20,000 on total billed charges of $1,420,000 and that there was an accumulated deficit from past operations of $162,000. The continued operation of the hospital was thus dependent on the recovery of the major portion of the operating expenses from the hospital's patients; nevertheless, a "hard" attitude on rates and collections would be inconsistent with the continued need for gifts which were secured largely on the strength of the beneficent activities of the hospital.

Frank Abbot, the credit manager, was in the middle of this conflict in objectives. In discussing the current year's results with Mr. Abbot, Mr. Sanders learned that about six months ago Mr. Abbot had requested permission to press for collections on a number of accounts of people in Seneca who were clearly able to pay, but that he had been dissuaded by the hospital director. The director had stated that his desire to refrain from taking action was based on repercussions that might result from one group of board members. As a result of this incident, Abbot had concluded that there was no point in pressing anyone for collection. Since then, his clerical assistants had practically discontinued the mailing of follow-up letters which had been used in an effort to obtain collection after two statements had been mailed to the responsible party.

Among the voluminous details in the working papers prepared by his staff, Mr. Sanders gave particular attention to the data in Exhibits 1 and 2. (Amounts in these exhibits have been rounded for ease in analysis.)

Exhibit 1

SENECA MEMORIAL HOSPITAL

Preliminary Balance Sheet as of June 30, 1962

Assets:

Cash	$ 14,000
Accounts receivable (net)	497,000
Inventories	112,000
Property and equipment (net)	677,000
Other assets	43,000
	$1,343,000
Current liabilities	47,000
Net Assets	$1,296,000

Fund Capital:

Expendable principal	$1,458,000
Accumulated deficit	162,000
Net Expendable Principal	$1,296,000

Preliminary Summary of Hospital Operations

Year Ended June 30, 1962

Earnings from patients—gross	$1,420,000
Less: Provision for uncollectible accounts, charity allowances, loss on state aid, etc.	121,000
Net earnings	$1,299,000
Operating expenses	1,325,000
Excess of expenses over net earnings	$ 26,000
Endowment income	46,000
Net Income	$ 20,000

Exhibit 2

SENECA MEMORIAL HOSPITAL

Selected Balance Sheet and Operating Figures

	Amount at June 30, or for Year Ended June 30		
	1960	1961	1962 (Prelim.)
Gross earnings from patients	$1,174,000	$1,254,000	$1,420,000
Allowance for:			
Free treatment (Note 1)	80,000	101,000	66,000
Uncollectible accounts (Note 2)	39,000	48,000	55,000
Accounts receivable (per general ledger)	625,000	742,000	698,000
Uncollectible accounts charged off (Note 3)	106,000	68,000	274,000
Balance, reserve for bad debts	273,000	354,000	201,000

Exhibit 2 (Continued)

Analysis of Accounts Receivable at June 30, 1962, Together with Hospital
Estimate of Reserve Necessary to Provide for Uncollectible Accounts

	Amount Receivable	Estimated Loss
In-patient accounts, loss estimated by Mr. Abbot:		
New account cards (Note 4):		
Free treatment balances....................................	$104,000	$104,000
Regular accounts..	322,000	20,000
Total New Account Cards (4,281 Accounts).................	$426,000	$124,000
Employee free treatment balances.............................	17,000	17,000
Old account cards (1,038 accounts; should be able to collect 50% if turned over to collection agency, less 30% fee—per Mr. Abbot)	91,000	59,000
Patients still in hospital or recently discharged..................	49,000	6,000
Due from Blue Cross or from state............................	30,000	
Out-patient accounts (9,266 accounts; 40% loss estimate used last year deemed "not unrealistic" by Mr. Wiley).....................	97,000	39,000
Total (Note 5)..	$710,000	$245,000

Notes

1. An account receivable is established for every person treated by the hospital, and all services rendered are charged to the account at the regularly established rates. Free treatment represents the estimated loss on state-aid cases, certain Blue Cross cases (low-income families), and services to hospital employees (for whom all charges are waived). The estimated loss is based on the accounts charged, less collections from the state and Blue Cross. The state increased the state-aid stipend to hospitals July 1, 1961, and as a result a total of $108,000 was received from the state during the current year, as against $87,000 in the preceding year. The state-aid stipend has been deducted in arriving at the amounts shown in Exhibit 2.

2. The hospital has regularly followed the policy of providing for uncollectible accounts on the basis of 4 per cent of in-patient charges and 10 per cent of out-patient charges (exclusive of charges on state aid or other welfare cases). Out-patient charges in the year ended June 30, 1962, amounted to $66,-000.

3. Mr. Abbot prepares each year a list of all accounts which he deems to be uncollectible (including remaining balances on state aid and other welfare cases), which Mr. Johnson presents to the board of trustees for their approval. His list for 1962 included the following:

1,206 state-aid account balances....................................	$126,000
2,091 other in-patient accounts.....................................	129,000
2,642 out-patient accounts..	19,000
Total............	$274,000

Mr. Abbot was unable to write off all the out-patient accounts that he believed to be uncollectible, because the hospital director had stated that the trustees did not want more than $25,000 charged off in any one year.

4. A new bookkeeping machine was installed on July 1, 1961, and a new form of ledger card was used on all accounts receivables beginning on that date; hence, any account on a new card was no more than one year old, with the exception of accounts which had been billed prior to July 1, 1961, but on which collections were received after that date. In such instances the balance due was transferred to a new ledger card so that the cash collected could be posted on the new machine. Cash collections were received by the cashier department under Mr. Wiley, and postings were made to the ledger from copies of the receipt forms prepared by the cashiers.

5. The hospital made no effort to balance the detailed accounts receivable cards against the general ledger control account. The only listing of the ledger cards was made by the auditor as a part of his examination, and the total shown was derived from such a listing. The total of the ledger cards at June 30, 1961, was $751,000, including out-patient balances of $88,000. No effort had been made to locate the difference between this figure and the general ledger amount of $742,000.

A special "aging" study was made of the accounts receivable "new" ledger cards for patients A through Cz. The ledger cards involved represented $97,000 of the total of $426,000 on new ledger cards. Of these, 28 accounts had a balance of $600 or more, and these 28 cards totaled $31,000.

Balances were aged according to the date of discharge, and the amounts of these balances were distributed as follows:

Discharged—June, 1962	7.2%	November, 1961	3.8%
May, 1962	18.0	October, 1961	4.3
April, 1962	10.7	September, 1961	4.6
March, 1962	6.4	August, 1961	5.8
February, 1962	5.4	July, 1961	3.6
January, 1962	5.4	Prior to 7/1/61	19.4
December, 1961	5.4		
		Total	100.0%

Question

What amounts should be shown for gross accounts receivable and for provision for uncollectible accounts on the balance sheet as of June 30, 1962?

CASE 5–3.   BRADFORD PRESS

In the 1930's, Bradford Press had acquired a tract of land on the outskirts of Craneville, a large city, with the intention eventually of constructing a branch warehouse thereon. Over the years, however, the company's marketing practices had changed, and by 1959 the management concluded that a warehouse would never be needed at Craneville. Consequently, the company sought to dispose of this land.

Bradford Press had paid $3,000 for the land and had made permanent improvements on it at a cost of $1,600, so it was carried on the accounts of Bradford Press at $4,600. The best cash offer that could be found in 1959 was $35,000. Since an independent appraiser, hired by Bradford Press, had appraised the land at $44,000, the management was unwilling to accept this offer.

As it happened, the Craneville land was located adjacent to a warehouse owned by the Birch Paper Company, one of Bradford's four regular suppliers of paper. Birch expressed an interest in acquiring the property so that it could later expand its own facilities. Birch was unwilling to pay cash but offered instead to exchange 3,000 cwt. (hundredweight) of 70-pound machine coated paper, to be delivered at the rate of 600 cwt. per month for the five months. In addition, Bradford was to pay the freight on this paper, in accordance with usual practice. The going market price for this grade of paper was at that time $17 per cwt., plus freight.

Bradford Press typically used more than 600 cwt. of 70-pound machine coated paper per month in the manufacture of booklets, brochures, and similar items, but Bradford Press placed orders for delivery not more than two months in the future, unless it had firm contracts from its own customers that required such paper. It had no such contracts in the fall of 1959. After considerable discussion among Bradford executives as to the risk involved in the unusually large commitment for paper, the Bradford management finally decided to accept Birch's offer.

The contract was signed on September 21, 1959, and as of that date the following journal entry was made by Bradford's accountant, recording the paper at its market price, and showing the difference between this amount and the book value of the land as profit:

Inventory Due from Supplier	51,000	
Craneville Land		4,600
Profit on Sale of Land		46,400

During the last three months of 1959, 1,800 cwt. of the paper was received from Birch as promised, and in the aggregate the entries made to record this receipt had the following effect:

Paper Inventory	31,140	
Inventory Due from Supplier		30,600
Cash (for freight charges)		540

When he was examining the accounts of Bradford Press for 1959, the company's auditor raised questions about this transaction. He pointed out that the net effect of the above entries was that the entire profit on the transaction was shown in 1959, despite the fact that only 1,800 cwt. of paper had actually been delivered, and of this only about

1,200 cwt. had actually been used in the manufacture of products. (The physical inventory as of December 31 showed 600 cwt. of this paper as still on hand.)

A suggested alternative treatment was to split the profit into two parts. One part, $30,400, was the difference between the book value of the land and the best cash offer; this was to be called "Profit on price level changes" and shown on the 1959 income statement. The remainder, $16,000, was to be called "Profit on sale of land" and divided two fifths to 1959 and three fifths to 1960, representing the fraction of the total paper consumed in each year. The auditor stated that such a separation was not usually made, but neither was this an ordinary transaction.

Bradford Press management disliked the implication in the above treatment that they had not made the $46,400 profit in 1959, especially since the price of 70-pound machine coated paper had risen to $18 per cwt. as of December 31, 1959.

Questions

1. How do you think this transaction should be handled?
2. How would you answer the arguments of those who think it should be handled differently?
3. Would your answer be different if the market price had decreased to $16 as of the end of 1959?

CASE 5–4.   PRENTISS DRESS SHOP

For over 20 years, Mr. Murray Prentiss had owned and operated a women's specialty shop in a suburban town. Early in 1962 Mr. Milton Wilcox, a representative of Dynamic Stores Inc., discussed with Mr. Prentiss the possibility of selling his business to Burroughs Stores, which owned 16 specialty shops in the same metropolitan area. Over the past several years, several other chains had approached Mr. Prentiss with similar propositions, but the Dynamic proposal was the first one that he seriously considered.

After a series of conversations, Mr. Prentiss told Mr. Wilcox that he would consider selling his business provided they could agree on a fair price and provided Dynamic would agree to employ him as store manager. Mr. Wilcox assured him that Dynamic would certainly be happy to have Mr. Prentiss continue as manager of the store, and the discussion then turned to the problem of deciding the selling price.

Mr. Wilcox asked what financial information was available, and Mr. Prentiss replied:

The only formal statements I have are balance sheets and my income tax returns, which I have a tax man prepare for me. I expect him to work up the returns for 1961 within the next month. I know what is going on in the business well enough so that I don't need other statements. Of course, I have a checkbook, a file of charge slips showing what customers owe me, and a file of unpaid invoices from suppliers. On New Year's day, or the preceding afternoon, I take a physical inventory and determine the purchase cost of goods on hand.

I have two women salespersons helping me, but I am at the store most of the time, and I try to keep a close tab on everything that takes place. There are two cash registers which everyone uses regardless of the kind of merchandise sold. None of us specializes in the sale of any particular kind of goods.

Mr. Wilcox replied that the lack of financial statements for 1961 probably would not prove to be any great obstacle to the conclusion of negotiations. All that was necessary was permission from Mr. Prentiss to

Exhibit 1

PRENTISS DRESS SHOP

Balance Sheet as of December 31, 1960

ASSETS			EQUITIES		
Current Assets:			*Current Liabilities:*		
Cash	$12,919		Salaries payable	$ 820	
Notes receivable	2,000		Notes payable	7,600	
Accounts receivable	8,562		Accounts payable	4,188	
Merchandise inventory	22,601		Total Current Liabilities	$12,608	
Total Current Assets	$46,082				
			Owner's Equity:		
Fixed Assets:			M. W. Prentiss, prop	16,500	
Furniture and fixtures	$6,870		Retained earnings	19,931	
Less: Accumulated depreciation	3,913	2,957			
Office equipment	$1,920				
Less: Accumulated depreciation	1,920	0			
Total Assets	$49,039		Total Equities	$49,039	

examine whatever records were available, from which it was highly probable that Dynamic could ascertain all the operating facts about the business that were needed. Mr. Prentiss agreed with this arrangement.

Mr. Wilcox was able to gather the data presented in Exhibits 1 and 2. In going over this information with Mr. Prentiss, Mr. Wilcox commented: "If Dynamic takes over this store, even if you stay on as manager, we will need more figures than you have been gathering for yourself."

Exhibit 2

INFORMATION COLLECTED BY MR. WILCOX

Cash Record for 1961

Receipts:

Cash sales...................	$ 59,762
Collection of accounts receivable.....................	32,118
Total Receipts.........$ 91,880	

Expenditures:

Payroll....................	$ 23,489
Rent......................	3,300
Advertising.................	2,432
Taxes.....................	1,241
Supplies...................	3,890
Travel.....................	310
Telephone.................	412
Repairs to building.........	210
Insurance..................	450
Miscellaneous expenses.......	978
Paid on accounts payable for merchandise...............	63,291
Total Expenditures.....$100,003	

Plus cash balance, December 31, 1960....................	12,919
Total...............$104,799	

Plus cash balance, December 31, 1961....................	4,796
Total...............$104,799	

Other Information

The expenditures for payroll includes Mr. Prentiss' salary of $14,000. Social security and withholding taxes may be disregarded since the expense portion was included in the payroll figure and amounts due to the government were immediately deposited in a separate bank account that does not appear on the financial statements.

Wages payable (including taxes thereon) as of December 31, 1961..............	$ 1,248

Accounts payable represented only invoices for merchandise purchased on credit.

As of December 31, 1961, these unpaid invoices amounted to................	8,696
Amounts due from customers on December 31, 1961, totaled..................	15,110
Merchandise inventory, December 31, 1961................................	32,936

The note receivable carried a 4 per cent rate of interest. The note payable carried a 5 per cent rate of interest. The note receivable was not collected in 1961, nor was the note payable paid in 1961.

Miscellaneous expenses included $600 paid to Ajax Truck Rental for a three-month lease on a delivery truck entered into on December 1, 1961.

Depreciation on furniture and fixtures was computed at 10 per cent of cost.

Questions

1. From the information given in Exhibits 1 and 2, determine (*a*) sales, (*b*) the cost of merchandise sold, and (*c*) the expenses for the year.

2. Prepare an income statement for 1961 and a balance sheet as of December 31, 1961.

3. Why should more figures apparently be justifiable under chain responsibility than when the store owned by Mr. Prentiss?

4. How should the parties proceed to decide on a fair selling price for the business?

Chapter 6

FIXED ASSETS AND DEPRECIATION

THIS CHAPTER discusses principles and procedures involved in recording the acquisition of fixed assets and in the subsequent amortization of their cost as expenses of the periods benefited.

ACQUISITION OF FIXED ASSETS

In accordance with the cost concept, fixed assets are initially recorded on the books at their cost to the company. When an expenditure is recorded in the accounts as a fixed asset (rather than as an expense or a current asset), it is said to be *capitalized*. The amount to be capitalized is usually regarded as the total of all costs involved in acquiring the asset, installing it, and making it ready to provide service. Often, this cost can be determined easily. The cost of a truck purchased for cash, for example, is simply the price shown on the invoice. In other cases, the amount to be capitalized includes a number of elements in addition to the purchase price. In the case of the purchase of a piece of land, the capitalized cost includes the purchase price of the land, broker's commission, legal fees, and even the cost of tearing down unwanted existing structures so as to make the land ready for its intended use. In the case of machinery and equipment, transportation costs and installation costs are usually included as part of the cost of the asset.

Nevertheless, many companies do not capitalize all items which in principle are costs of getting the equipment ready to provide service, both on the grounds of conservatism and to minimize income and property taxes. (Although there is no statutory requirement that fixed asset records for accounting purposes match those used in calculating taxes, questions may be raised if there is a difference between the two.)

When the company constructs a machine or a building with its own personnel, the amount to be capitalized includes all the costs incurred in construction. If the actual cost of building a machine is unreasonably high (as would be the case if the machine was an experimental model and required a considerable amount of development work), the doctrine of conservatism dictates that the asset be "booked" (i.e., recorded in the accounts) at an amount not greater than the purchase price of a similar machine from an outside vendor or not greater than what the cost of building a duplicate machine would be if the "trial-and-error" cost involved in building the original machine could be avoided.

Occasionally a company acquires a fixed asset that turns out to be worth significantly more than the amount paid for it, as, for example, when valuable minerals are discovered on land that was acquired at low cost. These are called *fortunate acquisitions*. Under such circumstances, an exception is often made to the principle that assets are carried on the books at an amount not in excess of their cost, and the asset is recorded at its estimated current value. The difference between this recorded value and actual cost is credited directly to a special category of owners' equity called capital surplus.

Trade-ins

When a new fixed asset is acquired in exchange for another, the old asset is part of the consideration given; therefore its value is part of the cost of the new asset. If the stated "trade-in allowance" differs from the actual value of the old asset, as is often the case with automobiles for example, then this artificial price should not be used in valuing the new asset; under these circumstances, the value is arrived at indirectly, often by estimating what the new asset would have cost if it had been purchased for cash. An offer to sell a new automobile for $800 cash plus a used automobile on which the dealer says he will make an allowance of $1,700 does not necessarily mean that the new automobile is worth $2,500. Upon further inquiry, it may be discovered that the new automobile can actually be purchased for $2,300 cash; if so, its cost is $2,300.

Betterments and Replacements versus Maintenance

Repair and maintenance is work done to keep the asset in good operating condition or to bring it back to good operating condition if it has broken down. Repair and maintenance costs are ordinarily expenses of the accounting period in which the work is done; they are *not* added to the cost of the fixed asset.

A betterment *is* added to the cost of the asset. The distinction between maintenance expenses and betterments is simple to state: maintenance work keeps the machine in good condition, but in no better condition than when it was purchased; a betterment makes the machine better than it was when it was purchased. In practice, the line between the two is difficult to draw. A new accessory designed to make the machine operate more efficiently or perform new functions is a betterment; an overhaul during which worn-out parts are replaced with new ones is maintenance. In the interests of conservatism some work which strictly speaking should be considered as a betterment is charged as an expense of the current period.

Replacements may be either assets or expenses, depending on how the asset unit is defined. The replacement of an entire asset results in the writing off of the old asset and the booking of the new. The replacement of a component part of an asset is maintenance expense. Thus, if one company treats a complete airplane as a single asset unit and another company treats the airframe as one unit and the engine as another, then the replacement of an engine results in a maintenance charge in the first company and in a new asset in the second. In general, the broader the definition of the asset unit, the greater will be the amount of costs charged as "maintenance" and hence expensed in the year of acquisition.

DEPRECIATION

With the exception of land, most fixed assets have a limited useful life; that is, they will be of use to the company over a finite number of future accounting periods. The cost of the asset is properly chargeable as an expense in the accounting periods in which the asset is used by the company. The accounting process for this gradual conversion of fixed assets into expense is called *depreciation*. It is described as follows by the Accounting Principles Board:

> The cost of a productive facility is one of the costs of the service it renders during its useful economic life. Generally accepted accounting principles require that this cost be spread over the expected useful life of the facility in such a way as to allocate it as equitably as possible to the periods during which services are obtained from the use of the facility. This procedure is known as depreciation accounting, a system of accounting which aims to distribute the cost or other basic value of tangible capital assets, less salvage (if any), over the estimated useful life of the unit (which may be a group of assets) in a systematic and rational manner. It is a process of allocation, not of valuation.[1]

The question is sometimes asked: Why is depreciation an expense? The answer is that *all* goods and services consumed by a business during an accounting period are expenses. The cost of insurance protection provided in a year is an expense of that year even though the insurance premium was paid two or three years previously. Depreciation expense is like insurance expense except that the fraction of total cost of a fixed

---

[1] AICPA, *Accounting Research Bulletin No. 43*, p. 76.

asset that is an expense in a given year is difficult to estimate, whereas the fraction of the total cost of an insurance policy that is an expense in a given year can be easily calculated. This difference does not change the fundamental fact that both insurance policies and fixed assets provide service to the company over a *finite* number of accounting periods and must therefore be charged as expenses of each of these periods.

The useful life of an asset is limited for one of two reasons: *deterioration,* which is the physical process of wearing out; and *obsolescence,* which refers to loss of usefulness because of the development of improved equipment or processes, changes in style, or other causes not related to the physical condition of the asset. No distinction need be made between the two since depreciation relates to both of them. The word "depreciation" is sometimes used as referring only to physical wear and tear; this usage is incorrect.

Judgments Required

In order to determine the depreciation expense for an accounting period, three judgments or estimates must be made for each fixed asset:

1. The *service life* of the asset; that is, over what period of time will it be useful to the company?

2. *Salvage or resale value* at the end of its life. The net cost of the asset to the company is its original cost less any amount eventually recovered through sale or salvage, and it is this net cost that should be charged as an expense over the asset's life. In a great many situations, however, the estimated salvage or resale value is so small and uncertain that it is disregarded.

3. *The method of depreciation;* that is, the method that will be used to allocate a fraction of the net cost to each of the accounting periods in which the asset is expected to be used.

Businessmen, not being clairvoyant, cannot *know* in advance how long the asset will last or what its salvage value will be; and they usually have no scientific or strictly logical way of deciding the best depreciation method. The figure of depreciation expense that results from all these judgments is therefore an estimate, and often it is only a rough estimate.

Service Life

The most widely used basis for estimating the service life of assets is the *Depreciation Guidelines,* published by the Internal Revenue Service.[2]

---

[2] *Depreciation Guidelines and Rules,* Internal Revenue Service publication No. 456 (Washington, D.C.: U.S. Government Printing Office, 1962).

This publication contains estimates for the service lives of machinery and equipment used in all types of industries. Some examples are: petroleum drilling, 6 years; aerospace industry and electrical manufacturing industry, 8 years; shoe manufacturing and printing and publishing, 11 years; cement making, 20 years. The booklet also gives estimates for other assets without regard to industry: for office equipment, the guideline is 10 years; and for factory and office buildings, it is 45 years.

It should be emphasized that these figures are only *guidelines*. If a company has reason to believe that some other estimate is better, it should by all means use the better estimate.

Depreciation Methods

Consider a machine purchased for $1,000 with an estimated life of ten years and estimated salvage value of zero. The problem of depreciation accounting is to charge this $1,000 as an expense over the ten-year period. How much should be charged as an expense each year?

This question cannot be answered by observing the amount of asset value physically consumed in a given year, for physically the machine continues to be a machine; usually, there is no observable indication of its decline in usefulness. Nor can the question be answered in terms of changes in the machine's market value during the year, for accounting is concerned with the amortization of cost, not with changes in market values. An indirect approach must therefore be used. Three conceptual ways of looking at the depreciation process are described below, together with the methods that follow from each.

Straight-Line Method. One concept views a fixed asset as existing to provide service over its life, with its readiness to provide this service being equal in each year of life, just as a three-year insurance policy provides equal protection in each of the three years. This concept leads to the straight-line method, which is to charge an equal fraction of the cost each year. For a machine costing $1,000 with an estimated service life of ten years, $\frac{1}{10}$ of $1,000 is the depreciation expense of the first year, another $\frac{1}{10}$ is the depreciation expense of the second year, and so on. Expressed another way, the machine is said to have a *depreciation rate* of 10 per cent per year, the rate being the reciprocal of the estimated useful life.

Accelerated Methods. A second concept takes what is perhaps a broader view of the asset since it relates to the *amount* of service provided each year. Many fixed assets are more valuable in their youth than in their old age—because their mechanical efficiency tends to decline with age, because maintenance costs tend to increase with age, and because of the increasing likelihood that better equipment will become available and make them obsolete. It is argued, therefore, that when an asset was purchased the probability that the earlier periods would benefit more than the later periods was taken into account, and that the depreciation method should reflect this. Such a line of reasoning leads to a method which charges a larger fraction of the cost as an expense of the early years than of the later years. This is called an *accelerated* method.[3]

Accelerated methods have been widely adopted since their use was permitted for income tax purposes beginning in 1954. A 1960 survey of 994 companies, including 850 manufacturing companies, made by the Financial Executives Institute, showed that 22 per cent of the respondents used the straight-line method for both financial statements and for income tax purposes, 56 per cent used accelerated depreciation for both purposes, 19 per cent used accelerated depreciation for tax purposes and straight-line for their financial statements, and 3 per cent used some other method.

The two methods specifically mentioned in the 1954 tax law, the double declining-balance method and sum-of-years'-digits (or simply "years'-digits") method, are described below. The effect of either of these methods is to write off approximately two thirds of the cost in the first half of the asset's estimated life, as contrasted with the straight-line method under which, of course, half the cost is written off in each half of the asset's estimated life. Thus, if an accelerated method is used, depreciation expense is greater in the early years and less in the later years as compared with the straight-line method.

In the *double declining-balance method,* the depreciation for each year is found by applying a rate to the book value of the asset at the beginning of that year rather than to the original cost of the asset. *Book value* is cost less total depreciation accumulated up to that time. If the declining-balance method is used, the tax law permits the company to take *double* the rate allowed under the straight-line method, hence the name, double declining balance.

In the *years'-digits method,* the numbers 1, 2, 3 . . . n are added, where n is the estimated years of useful life. The depreciation rate each year is a fraction in which the denominator is the sum of these digits and

---

[3] An argument can also be made for an opposite approach, that is, charging a smaller fraction of the cost to the early years and a larger fraction to the later years. This leads to an *annuity method,* which is not discussed here since it is relatively uncommon.

the numerator is for the first year, $n;$ for the second year, $n - 1$; for the third year $n - 2$; and so on. Assume, for example, a machine with an estimated life of ten years. The sum of the numbers 1, 2, 3 . . . 10 is 55. Depreciation in the first year would be $^{10}\!/_{55}$ of the cost; in the second year, $^{9}\!/_{55}$; in the third year, $^{8}\!/_{55}$; and so on.

Illustration 6–1 is an example of the way these three methods work out for a machine costing $1,000 with an estimated life of ten years and no salvage value.

Illustration 6–1

Year	Straight-Line (10% Rate)		Declining-Balance (20% Rate)			Years'-Digits		
	Book Value, 12/31	Annual Depreciation	Book Value, 12/31	Annual Depreciation	Rate	Book Value, 12/31	Annual Depreciation
0....................	$1,000	$ ...	$1,000.00	$	....	$1,000.00	$ ....
First................	900	100	800.00	200.00	10/55	818.18	181.82
Second..............	800	100	640.00	160.00	9/55	654.54	163.64
Third...............	700	100	512.00	128.00	8/55	509.09	145.45
Fourth..............	600	100	409.60	102.40	7/55	381.82	127.27
Fifth................	500	100	327.68	81.92	6/55	272.73	109.09
Sixth................	400	100	262.14	65.54	5/55	181.82	90.91
Seventh.............	300	100	209.71	52.43	4/55	109.09	72.73
Eighth..............	200	100	167.77	41.94	3/55	54.54	54.55
Ninth...............	100	100	134.22	33.55	2/55	18.18	36.36
Tenth...............	0	100	107.38	26.84	1/55	0	18.18
Eleventh............	....	...	85.90	21.48	....	....	....
Twelfth.............	....	...	68.72*	17.18	....	....	....
		$1,000		$931.28*			$1,000.00

* Under the strict declining-balance method, depreciation continues until the asset is disposed of or until the book value declines to salvage value. Many companies, however, switch from the declining-balance method to the straight-line method in the later years of life, and thus write off the entire cost in a specified number of years. This is permitted for tax purposes.

As a further acceleration for tax purposes, a 1958 statute permits the deduction in the year of acquisition of 20 per cent of the cost, in addition to regular depreciation. The deduction is limited to a total of $2,000 per year and is allowed only for tangible personal property (not buildings) with an estimated useful life of at least six years.

Units-of-Production Method. A third concept of depreciation views the asset as consisting of a bundle of service units, the cost of each being the total cost of the asset divided by the number of such units, and the depreciation charge for a period therefore being related to the number of units consumed in the period. This leads to the units-of-production method. If a truck has an estimated net cost of $12,000 and is expected to give service for 300,000 miles, depreciation would be charged at a rate of $0.04 per mile, the depreciation expense in a year in which the truck traveled 50,000 miles being $2,000.[4]

Choice of a Method

In deciding on the best depreciation method, tax considerations should be kept separate from financial accounting considerations. For tax purposes, the best method is that which minimizes the effect of taxes. Unless tax rates applicable to the business are expected to increase, this is usually one of the accelerated methods.

With respect to financial accounting, each of the concepts described above has its advocates. Many businesses still use the straight-line method on the practical grounds of its simplicity both in record keeping and in understanding, but the number using one of the other methods continues to grow. It should be emphasized that in a single business different methods can be used for different types of assets; for example, straight-line for buildings, accelerated for certain types of machinery and equipment, and units-of-production for other types. An essential requirement also is that there *be* a method. The former practice of charging "whatever the income statement can stand" is indefensible.

If a company uses one depreciation method for income tax purposes and a different method for financial accounting, its taxable income will not match the income as measured by financial accounting. Under these circumstances, it must adjust its reported income tax expense, as explained on page 141.

Accounting for Depreciation

Assume that the Trantor Company purchased on December 31, 1952, for $90,000 a building with an estimated useful life of 45 years and zero salvage value and that it has decided to depreciate this building on a straight-line basis, that is, $2,000 per year. Let us now consider how to record this depreciation on the accounting records.

It would be possible to reduce the asset value by $2,000 a year and to show on the balance sheet only the remaining amount, which at the end of 1953 would be $88,000; but this is *not* ordinarily done. Instead, a separate contra account is shown on the balance sheet for the accumulated amount of depreciation. This item is usually called *accumulated depreciation,* or it may have some other name such as "allowance for depreciation," "reserve for depreciation," and so on. (The last term is

---

[4] An alternative method is to charge a decreasing rate as the number of miles increases, as in the accelerated methods.

another example of a misleading use of the word "reserve"; the depreciation process does not "reserve" money or anything else.) Both the original cost and the accumulated depreciation figures appear on the balance sheet. The figures as of December 31, 1953, would look like this:

```
Building.................................................$90,000
    Less: Accumulated depreciation................................  2,000
        Net.................................................$88,000
```

As of December 31, 1954, another year's depreciation would be added, and the balance sheet would then show:

```
Building.................................................$90,000
    Less: Accumulated depreciation................................  4,000
        Net.................................................$86,000
```

The foregoing figures can be interpreted as follows:

```
Original cost of the building.....................................$90,000
That portion of the cost charged to operations for all periods to date....  4,000
That portion of the cost remaining to be charged to operations of future
    periods.................................................$86,000
```

A few companies report accumulated depreciation on the right-hand, or equities, side of the balance sheet rather than as a subtraction from the appropriate asset account, but this practice is obsolete.

On the income statement, the expense item is usually labeled *depreciation expense.* In the income statement for 1953, this item for the Trantor Company would be $2,000 (disregarding depreciation on assets other than the building we are considering), and $2,000 would also appear in the income statement for 1954, 1955, and following years until either the building was disposed of or it was fully depreciated. Usually, the Depreciation Expense account includes depreciation for all types of fixed assets, but there must be a separate accumulated depreciation account for each category of fixed assets (building, machinery, office equipment, etc.) shown separately on the balance sheet, except for the category, land, since land does not depreciate.

The annual journal entry, which is one of the adjusting entries, would therefore be as follows:

```
Depreciation Expense.................................................2,000
    Accumulated Depreciation, Building...........................          2,000
```

If the Trantor Company should use its building for more than 45 years, depreciation would cease to be accumulated at the end of the forty-fifth year, since by then the total cost of the building would have been charged to expense. (If the fact that its life will be longer than 45 years became apparent earlier, the depreciation rate should be decreased so as to spread the remaining book value over the longer period.) Until the asset is disposed of, it is customary to continue to show the asset on the balance sheet. Thus, from December 31, 1992, onward, the balance sheet would show the following:

Building	$90,000
Less: Accumulated depreciation	90,000
Net	$ 0

Often, half a year's depreciation is recorded in the year of acquisition and half in the year of disposal no matter what the actual date of acquisition or disposal is, on the grounds that depreciation is a rough estimate and there is no point in attempting to figure it to exact fractions of a year. This practice, if followed consistently, is permitted for tax purposes. Similarly, if accounts are kept on a monthly basis, half a month's depreciation may be recorded the first month.

The Investment Credit

In order to encourage purchases of machinery and equipment, Congress included an "investment credit" provision in the Revenue Act of 1962. Under this statute purchasers of long-lived assets (with certain exceptions, notably buildings) are allowed a credit of up to 7 per cent of the cost of the asset. This credit is used to reduce the amount of current income taxes they must pay. It is a direct reduction of taxes; that is, if a company acquires $100,000 of equipment during the year, it can subtract $7,000 from the taxes it would otherwise pay. The 1962 Act permitted only 93 per cent of the cost of the asset to be depreciated for tax purposes, but this was changed by the Revenue Act of 1964 which permits 100 per cent of the cost of the asset to be depreciated.

The AICPA Accounting Principles Board approves either of two methods of handling the investment credit for accounting purposes.[5] The first method, called the *cost-reduction* method, is to spread the effect of the investment credit over the useful life of the asset by making a reduction in the depreciation expense of each year of the useful life. The second method, called the *flow-through* method, reduces income tax expense, and hence increases net income, in the year in which the credit is taken.

The Accounting Principles Board prefers the first method on the grounds that the investment credit "should be reflected in net income over the productive life of acquired property and not in the year in which it is placed in service." The flow-through method has the strange

---

[5] See AICPA Accounting Principles Board, *Opinion No. 4*, March, 1964.

effect of creating income by the act of *acquiring* assets rather than by *using* them. Nevertheless, a number of companies use this method. The fact that either method is acceptable is another illustration of the latitude that is permissible with the framework of generally accepted accounting principles.

The accounting entries involved in both methods are shown in the following example:

> EXAMPLE: Assume that in December 1963 a company purchases $100,000 of machinery that qualify for the investment credit, that the service life of these assets is ten years and that (for simplicity) straight-line depreciation is to be used. The investment credit is $7,000, and this $7,000 is subtracted from the income tax liability in 1963.
>
> Under the cost-reduction method, the investment credit would be recorded, in effect, as:

```
Income Tax Liability......................................7,000
    Machinery..........................................         7,000
```

(Many companies make the credit entry to a separate contra account rather than directly to the asset account, but the ultimate effect is the same.)

Note that net income for 1963 is unaffected by this entry. In 1964 and subsequent years depreciation expense would be calculated on a net cost of $93,000, rather than $100,000, and would therefore be $9,300 per year. This has the effect of increasing net income $700 in each of the next ten years, as compared with what the net income would have been had the depreciation expense been $10,000 per year.

Under the flow-through method, the investment credit would be recorded as:

```
Income Tax Liability............................7,000
    Income Tax Expense..........................         7,000
```

This has the effect of increasing 1963 income by $7,000.

DISPOSAL OF FIXED ASSETS

Suppose that at the end of ten years the Trantor Company sells its building. At that time, $10/45$ of the original cost, or $20,000, will have been built up in the Accumulated Depreciation account, and the net book value of the building will be $70,000. If the building is sold for $70,000 cash, the accounts are changed, as follows: Cash is increased by $70,000; the Building account is decreased by $90,000, and Accumulated Depreciation is decreased by $20,000, which is the amount of depreciation accumulated up to that time. The entry is as follows:

```
Cash...............................................70,000
Accumulated Depreciation...........................20,000
    Building.......................................         90,000
```

This has the effect of eliminating from the accounts both the original cost of the building and the accumulated depreciation thereon.

If the building were sold for less than $70,000, say $60,000, the transaction would be recorded as follows: Cash is increased by $60,000, the Building account is decreased by $90,000, Accumulated Depreciation is decreased by $20,000, and an account, Loss on the Sale of Fixed Assets, or some similar title, is set up, as in the following entry:

```
Cash..................................................................60,000
Accumulated Depreciation.........................................20,000
Loss on Sale of Fixed Assets.....................................10,000
     Building.....................................................                90,000
```

Note that the effect on the Building and Accumulated Depreciation accounts is identical with that in the previous illustration: the amounts relating to this building disappear. The loss is a decrease in owners' equity, reflecting the fact that the total depreciation expense recorded for the preceding ten years was less than what we now know to have been the actual net cost of the building over that period of time. The actual net cost turns out to have been $30,000, whereas the total depreciation expense charged has amounted to only $20,000.

Since the depreciation expense as originally recorded turns out to have been incorrect, the Retained Earnings account which reflects the net of all revenue and expenses is also incorrect, and there is therefore some logic in closing the Loss on Sale of Fixed Assets account directly to Retained Earnings, thus correcting the error contained therein. Nevertheless, the "clean surplus" doctrine requires that unless the loss is both material and unusual, it be shown as an expense on the income statement of the current period. The item usually appears in the "nonoperating expense" portion of the statement.

If an asset is sold for more than its book value, the entries correspond to those described above. The account, Gain on the Sale of Fixed Assets, is usually classified as nonoperating revenue on the income statement.

A trade-in involves the disposal of an asset, and the asset traded in is treated in the accounting records exactly like the sale of the building described above; that is, both its cost and its accumulated depreciation are removed from the books. As mentioned in a preceding section, a problem may arise in determining the proper "sales" value to use in recording this transaction. For income tax purposes, however, a trade-in is treated quite differently. When one asset is exchanged for another of "like kind," no gain or loss is ordinarily recognized for tax purposes. The definition of "like kind" and the circumstances under which this principle is applicable are intricate, and expert tax advice is needed on all except the most routine fixed asset exchanges.

Debits to Accumulated Depreciation

If a machine is given an unusual major overhaul which makes it "as good as new," the cost of this overhaul is sometimes debited to Accumulated Depreciation rather than to Maintenance Expense on the grounds that the overhaul has actually canceled or offset some of the accumulated depreciation. Or, it can be argued that the overhaul has extended the useful life of the machine, and that the depreciation accumulated up to the time of overhaul is therefore excessive. In theory, if the estimated useful life has changed, the depreciation rate should be recalculated and the accounts changed to reflect the new estimate of useful life; but in practice, charging the overhaul to Accumulated Depreciation may have approximately the same effect.

GROUP AND COMPOSITE DEPRECIATION

The procedure described above related to a single fixed asset, one building. To find the total depreciation expense for a whole category of assets, this procedure could be repeated for each single asset, and the total depreciation for all the assets in the category would then be recorded by one journal entry. This is the procedure used in many businesses.

An alternative procedure is to treat several assets together rather than making the calculation for each one separately. If similar assets with approximately the same useful life, such as all typewriters or all general-purpose lathes, are treated together, the process is called *group* depreciation. If dissimilar assets are treated together, the process is called *composite* depreciation. The depreciation rate in composite depreciation is a weighted-average rate, the weights being the dollar amounts of assets in each of the useful-life categories. All the production equipment in a plant, for example, might be included in a single composite account, even though the useful lives of the various items of equipment were not the same. The *Depreciation Guidelines* referred to above give a single depreciation rate for all the machinery and equipment in most types of manufacturing plants (e.g., 11 years for the machinery and equipment in a chemical plant). These are composite rates, and the publication in 1962 of the *Depreciation Guidelines* has therefore resulted in a considerable increase in the use of composite depreciation.

The annual depreciation expense under group or composite depreciation is computed in a manner similar to that described above for an individual asset. If the straight-line method is used, for example, the depreciation rate is applied to the total cost of the whole group of assets.

The accumulation of depreciation does not stop when one item in the group reaches its estimated useful life, however, but continues indefinitely unless it becomes apparent that the accumulation is too large or too small for the whole group of assets. In this case, the depreciation rate is changed. For tax purposes, the Internal Revenue Service has established a set of maximum "reserve ratios" for various asset categories, and companies are penalized if they exceed these ratios. A reserve ratio is the ratio of accumulated depreciation to the cost of the assets in the group.

If a group or composite method is used, no gain or loss is recognized when an individual asset is sold or otherwise disposed of. The asset account is credited for the cost, and the difference between cost and the sales proceeds is simply debited to Accumulated Depreciation. This procedure assumes that gains on some sales are offset by losses on others.

SIGNIFICANCE OF DEPRECIATION

The amount shown as accumulated depreciation on the balance sheet does not represent the "accumulation" of any tangible thing; it is merely that portion of the assets' original cost that has been already charged off against income.

Occasionally a company does set aside money for the specific purpose of purchasing new assets, and this process is sometimes called "funding depreciation." This transaction is completely separate from the depreciation mechanism described above. If depreciation is funded, cash or securities are physically segregated; that is, they are set aside in such a way that they cannot be used in the regular operation of the business (for example, a special bank account may be created). This fact is reflected on the balance sheet by an asset titled "new building fund," or some similar name, the offsetting entry being a credit to Cash. This practice is not common and is mentioned here only to emphasize, by contrast, the point that the depreciation process itself is *not* a means of automatically creating a fund for the replacement of assets.

There is a widespread belief that, in some mysterious way, depreciation does represent money, specifically, money that can be used to purchase new assets. Depreciation is *not* money; the money that the business has is shown by the balance in its Cash account.

EXAMPLE: This quotation is from a well-known publication: "Most large companies draw much of the cash flow they employ for expanding and modernizing their operations from their depreciation reserves." This statement is not true in anything remotely approaching a literal sense. Possibly the author intended some figurative, rather than literal, meaning, but it is difficult to imagine how the statement could be true in even a figurative sense.

There is also a widespread belief that the book value of assets is related to their real value, and this is equally erroneous.

EXAMPLE: An auditor's report included the following statement: "Our inspection of insurance policies in force at the close of the year disclosed that the plant assets, on the basis of book values, were amply protected against fire." Such a statement has little if any significance. What the management wants to know is whether the insurance policies equal the *actual cash value* of the assets, and this is unlikely to correspond to their *book value*.

Concluding Comment

The key to a practical understanding of depreciation is a sentence from the AICPA statement quoted earlier: *Depreciation is a process of allocation, not of valuation.* Depreciation expense does *not* represent the shrinkage in real value during an accounting period; physically, the machine may be as useful and as valuable at the end of the period as it was at the beginning. Neither does the net book value represent the market value of the assets on hand. Depreciation expense is a write-off of a portion of the *cost* of the asset, and it follows that the net book value of fixed assets reported on the balance sheet represents only that porition of the original cost of the fixed asset which has *not yet* been charged to expense.

No one really knows how long an asset will last or what its residual value will be at the end of its life. Without this knowledge, the depreciation figure is necessarily an estimate.

OTHER ASPECTS OF TANGIBLE ASSETS

Depletion

Natural resources such as coal, oil, other minerals, and timber are called *wasting assets.* The process of writing off the cost of these fixed assets to expenses in the accounting periods benefited is called *depletion.* The objective is the same as that for depreciation: to amortize the cost in some systematic manner over the asset's useful life. The unit-of-production method is ordinarily used. For example, if an oil property cost $500,000 and is estimated to contain 1,000,000 barrels of oil, the depletion rate is 50 cents per barrel; the total depletion for a year in which 80,000 barrels of oil were produced would be $40,000.

For income tax purposes, however, the depletion allowance usually bears no relation to cost; rather, it is a percentage of revenue. The permitted percentage (as of 1964) varies from 5 per cent on clay, gravel, and other common materials to 27½ per cent on oil and gas. This is perhaps the most clear-cut example of an income tax provision that is inconsistent with generally accepted accounting principles. This provision in the tax law is designed to stimulate exploration for and development of new supplies of natural resources.

Accretion and Appreciation

Accretion is the increase in value of timberland, cattle, and other agricultural products that arises through the natural process of growth. Since accretion does not represent realized revenue, it is ordinarily not recognized in the accounts, although the *costs* incurred in the growing process may be added to the asset value, just as is done in the case of costs incurred in manufacturing products.

Appreciation is also an increase of value and is therefore *not* the opposite of depreciation, which is a write-off of *cost*. Appreciation is recognized in the accounts only under highly unusual circumstances; for example, if new management took over a business and an appraisal disclosed that the current market value of fixed assets is substantially above their book value, it is conceivable that the asset values would be written up to their current value. Even under these circumstances, appreciation is not usually recognized, however, and the point is mentioned simply as another illustration of the principle that an increase in value is ordinarily recognized in the accounts only when revenue is realized, whereas expiration of cost is recognized when it occurs.

INTANGIBLE ASSETS

Intangible long-lived assets, such as goodwill, organization cost (i.e., cost incurred to get a business started), trade-marks, and patents are usually converted to expenses over a number of accounting periods. The periodic write-off is specifically called *amortization,* although the word "amortization" is also used in the broad sense of any write-off of a cost. The amortization of intangible assets is essentially the same process as the depreciation of tangible assets. Amortization is ordinarily recorded as a credit directly to the asset account, not to a separate account analogous to Accumulated Depreciation.

The Accounting Principles Board suggests that these intangibles be classified into two categories:

(a) Those having a term of existence limited by law, regulation, or agreement, or by their nature (such as patents, copyrights, leases, licenses, franchises for a fixed term, and goodwill as to which there is evidence of limited duration);

(b) Those having no such limited term of existence and as to which there is, at the time of acquisition, no indication of limited life (such as goodwill generally, going value, trade names, secret processes, subscription lists, perpetual franchises, and organization costs.)[6]

The treatment recommended for each category is as follows:

The cost of the type (a) intangibles should be amortized by systematic charges in the income statement over the period benefited, as in the case of other assets having a limited period of usefulness. . . .

When it becomes reasonably evident that the term of existence of a type (b) intangible has become limited and that it has therefore become a type (a) intangible, its cost should be amortized by systematic charges in the income statement over the estimated remaining period of usefulness.[7]

Although the above statement does not sanction such a treatment, many companies *do* write off "type (b)" intangibles (those that do not have a definitely limited life) over one or more accounting periods. Organization cost is frequently handled in this manner, for although the "benefit" of organizing a company may be said, in a sense, to extend over the whole life of the company, it would be a considerable bother, with little offsetting benefit to anyone, to hold this cost as an asset on the balance sheet year after year. There is, by definition, no logical way of determining over how many periods such assets should be written off. In some cases, they are written off as an expense in the year of acquisition. Other companies choose to write them off over some fairly short period, such as five or ten years, with the choice of the time period depending on the amount that safely can be charged without having a material effect on income.

These practices have been heavily influenced by the doctrine of conservatism, although custom has a great deal to do with them also. Customarily, for example, advertising expenditures are not capitalized even though it may be quite clear that these expenditures benefit future rather than current periods. Often, these practices are justified on the grounds that the future benefits are so uncertain that an attempt to estimate them is unwarranted. With respect to the argument for conservatism, it should be pointed out that a practice that understates

---

[6] AICPA, *Accounting Research Bulletin No. 43*, p. 37.
[7] *Ibid.*, p. 38.

asset values and current income inevitably overstates future income.

Incidentally, some companies exphasize their conservatism by showing intangible assets at a nominal amount on the balance sheet, thus:

Goodwill, patents, and other intangibles. $1.00

This practice stems from the pre-1930's when some companies *watered* their assets by capitalizing a wide variety of intangibles of dubious value and hiding these values in with other asset items. Companies that followed the more conservative practice of writing off intangibles as acquired indicated this fact to the reader of the balance sheet by the above wording. Since current practice requires that intangibles be reported as a separate item if they are material in amount, the absence of any such item means that no material amount of intangibles is being carried as an asset, and the above method of presentation is not as necessary as formerly.

The *useful* life of a "type (a)" intangible may be shorter than its legal life; if so, the cost of the asset is written off over the shorter period. For example, although a patent is legally valid for 17 years, the company may decide that technological change or other forces may make it obsolete within a shorter period of time; if such is the case, the patent may be written off over 15 years, 10 years, or even less.

Leasehold improvements are the costs incurred by the lessee to improve leased property. Since, as a matter of law, any remaining value of these improvements reverts to the owner when the leased property is given up, the benefits to the lessee automatically end when he gives up the leased property, and the cost must therefore be written off over the time he expects to have the use of the property.

SUMMARY

Fixed assets are originally recorded at their acquisition cost, including costs involved in making them ready to provide service. This cost is charged off as depreciation expense in some systematic manner over the periods in which the asset is expected to be useful. The method selected may charge an equal amount each year, a larger amount in early years than in late years, or an amount that depends on usage. A corresponding reduction is made in the asset value. Upon disposition, both the cost and the accumulated depreciation are removed from the accounts, and any gain or loss is reported separately, usually on the income statement.

Intangible assets are amortized by a similar process. Although the write-off of intangibles that have no limited life is not officially approved, many companies do amortize such assets on the grounds of conservatism.

CASES

CASE 6–1. PALMER CORPORATION (B)

After the controller of the Palmer Corporation had ascertained the changes in accounts receivable and the allowance for doubtful accounts in 1963, he made a similar analysis of fixed assets and accumulated depreciation. Again he examined the December 31, 1962, balance sheet (Exhibit 1 in Palmer Corporation [A], p. 144). He also reviewed the following transactions which he found to be applicable to these accounts:

1. On January 2, 1963, one of the factory machines was sold for its book value, $1,964. This machine was recorded on the books at $15,865 with accumulated depreciation of $13,901.

2. Tools were carried on the books at cost, and at the end of each year a physical inventory was taken to determine what tools still remained. The account was written down to the extent of the decrease in tools as ascertained by the year-end inventory. At the end of 1963, it was determined that there had been a decrease in the tool inventory amounting to $3,117.

3. On March 1, 1963, the company sold for $831 cash, an automobile which was recorded on the books at a cost of $2,820 and had an accumulated depreciation of $1,739 as of January 1, 1963. In this and other cases of sale of fixed assets during the year, the accumulated depreciation and depreciation expense items were both increased by an amount which reflected the depreciation chargeable for the months in 1963 in which the asset was held prior to the sale, at rates listed in Item 7 below.

4. The patent listed on the balance sheet had been purchased by the Palmer Corporation on December 31, 1957, for $52,500. This patent had been granted on December 31, 1955. The cost of the patent was to be written off as an expense over the remainder of its legal life. (The total life of a patent is 17 years from the date granted.)

5. On July 1, 1963, a typewriter which had cost $191 and had been fully depreciated on December 31, 1962, was sold for $20.

6. On October 1, the company sold a desk for $40. This piece of furniture was recorded on the books at a cost of $216 with an accumulated depreciation of $171 as of January 1, 1963.

7. Depreciation on fixed assets was figured as follows:

Buildings... 2%
Factory machinery...10*
Furniture and fixtures...10
Automotive equipment..20
Office machines...10

* Included in the factory machinery cost of $1,799,176 was a machine costing $41,602 which had been fully depreciated on December 31, 1962, and which was still in use.

Questions

1. Analyze the effect of each of these transactions upon the fixed asset accounts, accumulated depreciation, and any other accounts which may be involved in a manner similar to that used in Palmer Corporation (A), and prepare journal entries.

2. Give the correct totals for the fixed assets and the amount of accumulated depreciation as of December 31, 1963, after the transactions affecting them had been recorded.

CASE 6–2. MASSASOIT TRUST COMPANY

The Massasoit Trust Company conducted a commercial banking business in a city of approximately 100,000. The company did not own its banking quarters but operated under a lease which still had six years to run in 1959. While the lease contained no renewal provisions, the bank had occupied the building since 1905 under successive ten-year leases. Relations with the owner of the building, who was also the operator of a nearby department store, continued to be cordial. The lease provided, however, that the owner could cancel the lease on two years' notice if he required the property for his own business.

In the spring of 1959, the directors of the bank were considering a proposal to remodel and air-condition the bank quarters. The bank had received firm bids from contractors on the work to be done, and these totaled approximately $63,000.

In the course of the discussion, a debate arose over the way in which the expenditure would be carried in the bank's books. One of the directors favored carrying the improvement as an asset and depreciating it over its physical life, which he estimated at about 25 years.

Several directors objected to this procedure. Under the so-called "rule of fixtures," which was a well-established legal principle, permanent improvements to leased property were generally considered to be the property of the owner of the real estate. Since the bank did not own the property, these directors did not think the improvements should be considered as an asset. They favored charging the entire cost of the improvements as an expense in the current year, which had been the procedure with minor renovation expenses in the past.

Other directors felt that capitalizing the expenditure would be acceptable, but they did not think it wise to adopt a depreciation period longer than the life of the lease. They also wondered what consideration should be given to the two-year cancellation provision.

The first director was not convinced by either of these approaches. He said he would not favor the remodeling project were he not convinced that the lease would be renewed as it had been in the past. He was also disturbed about the effect that a rapid write-off might have on the bank's earnings.

Section 178 (c) of the Internal Revenue Code provides that for income tax purposes, as a general rule, improvements made to leased assets should be amortized over either the remaining life of the lease or the life of the improvement, whichever is shorter. If, however, upon completion of the improvement, the remaining life of the lease is less than 60 per cent of the useful life of the improvement, it is ordinarily presumed that the lease will be renewed, and this longer life will determine the amortization period.

Exhibit 1

MASSASOIT TRUST COMPANY

Statement of Condition, December 31, 1958
(Thousands of Dollars)

RESOURCES

Cash on hand and in banks	$ 2,464
U.S. government securities	6,886
Other securities	275
Loans and discounts	2,587
Other assets	42
	$12,254

LIABILITIES

Commercial deposits		$ 8,667
Savings deposits		2,402
Total Deposits		$11,069
Reserve for taxes, etc.		61
Capital stock	$350	
Surplus	774	1,124
		$12,254

In 1958, the Massasoit Trust Company had a gross revenue of $285,000, including $205,000 in income from loans, discounts, and investments in securities. After operating expenses but before income taxes, earnings were approximately $70,000. Federal income taxes amounted to about $20,000. The operating expenses were largely of a fixed nature.

The bank's statement of condition as of December 31, 1958, is given in Exhibit 1. According to the state banking law, trust companies could accept deposits of up to ten times the amount of their capital and surplus. The law also required 15 per cent of deposits to be maintained as a liquid reserve; the balance could be used for loans, discounts, and investments in United States government and other securities. The bank was not permitted to loan an amount greater than 20 per cent of its capital stock and surplus to any one individual or firm.

Questions

1. Why should the directors be concerned about this problem?
2. What action do you recommend?

CASE 6–3. BRAZOS PRINTING COMPANY

The Brazos Printing Company was founded in 1940 as a one-man job printing firm in a small southwestern town. Shortly after its founding, the owner decided to concentrate on one specialty line of printing. Because of a high degree of technical proficiency, the company experienced a rapid growth.

Exhibit 1

BRAZOS PRINTING COMPANY

Condensed Balance Sheet as of March 31, 1962

ASSETS			EQUITIES	
Current Assets:			Current liabilities........$ 40,016	
Cash.....................	$102,612		Common stock.......... 110,000	
Other current assets........	76,816		Retained earnings....... 88,933	
Total Current Assets....	$179,428			
Fixed Assets:				
Land....................		7,000		
Buildings................$72,000				
Less: Accumulated deprecia-				
tion................... 41,000		31,000		
Equipment...............$66,212				
Less: Accumulated deprecia-				
tion................... 44,691	21,521			
Total Assets...........	$238,949		Total Equities....$238,949	

However, the company suffered from a competitive disadvantage in that the major market for its specialized output was in a metropolitan area over 300 miles away from the company's plant. For this reason, the owner, in 1962, decided to move nearer his primary market. He also decided to expand and modernize his facilities at the time of the move. After some investigation, an attractive site was found in a suburb of his primary market, and the move was made.

A balance sheet prepared prior to the move is shown in Exhibit 1. The transactions that arose from this move are described in the following paragraphs:

1. The land at the old site together with the building thereon was sold for $36,000. The land had originally cost $7,000. The building appeared on the company's books at a cost of $72,000, and a depreciation allowance of $41,000 had been accumulated on it.

2. Certain equipment was sold for $5,000 cash. This equipment appeared on the books at a cost of $18,200 less accumulated depreciation of $10,200.

3. A new printing press was purchased. The invoice cost of this equipment was $20,000. A 2 per cent cash discount was taken by the Brazos Company, so that only $19,600 was actually paid to the seller. The Brazos Company also paid $80 to a trucker to have this equipment delivered. Installation of this equipment was made by Brazos workmen who worked a total of 60 hours. These men received $2.50 per hour in wages, but their time was ordinarily charged to printing jobs at $5.00 per hour, the difference representing an allowance for overhead ($2.00) and profit ($0.50).

4. The city to which the company moved furnished the land on which the new plant was built as a gift. The land had an appraised value of $25,000. The appraisal had been made recently by a qualified appraiser. The company would pay property taxes on its assessed value, which was $16,000.

5. The Brazos Company paid $3,800 to have an old building on the gift plot of land torn down. (The value of this building was not included in the appraised or assessed values named above.) In addition, the company paid $2,400 to have permanent drainage facilities installed on the new land.

6. A new strip caster with an invoice cost of $5,000 was purchased. The company paid $3,200 cash and received a trade-in allowance of $1,800 on a used strip caster. The used strip caster could have been sold outright for not more than $1,500. It had cost $3,000 new, and accumulated depreciation on it was $1,300.

7. The company erected a building at the new site for $100,000. Of this amount, $75,000 was borrowed on a mortgage.

8. After the equipment had been moved to the new plant, but before operations began there, extensive repairs and replacements of parts were made on a large paper cutter. The cost of this work was $1,000. Prior to this time, no more than $100 had been spent in any one year on the maintenance of this paper cutter.

9. Trucking and other costs associated with moving equipment to the new location and installing it were $1,500. In addition, Brazos Company employees worked an estimated 125 hours on that part of the move that related to equipment.

10. During the moving operation, a piece of equipment costing $2,500 was dropped and damaged; $500 was spent to repair it. The management believed, however, that the salvage value of this equipment had been reduced to $250. Up until that time, the equipment was being depreciated at $200 per year, representing a 10 per cent rate after deduction of estimated salvage of $500. Accumulated depreciation was $800.

Question

Analyze the effect of these transactions on the items in the balance sheet and income statement. For transactions that affect owners' equity, distinguish between those that affect the net income of the current year and those that do not. In most cases, the results of your analysis can be set forth most clearly in the form of journal entries.

CASE 6–4. SHERATON CORPORATION OF AMERICA[8]

Recent guest at the prandial delights of the New York Society of Security Analysts was self-assured president Ernest "Mr. Sheraton" Henderson of giant hotel chain Sheraton Corp. of America. His theme: how a hotel chain can show remarkable revenue growth without improvement in earnings—and why this is a good thing for its stockholders.

No doubt about it, Sheraton gross income has risen 600% since World War II. Profits have not. They came to $3,100,000 or 60¢ a share in the fiscal year ended April 30. This was off from $3,916,000 or 71¢ a year earlier and substantially below the high of $8,870,000 or $1.95 in 1954.

To save his audience the trouble Ernest Henderson asked himself this question: "How can a company like Sheraton which shows infinitesimal earnings have such a growth record?" His answers centered around two words: debt management and depreciation.

Now the operator of 56 hotels with 27,000 rooms and 22,000 employees, Sheraton is willing to go into debt at the rate of 50% of the fair market value of its hotels. In many cases such as with the Philadelphia Sheraton, Ernest Henderson says "we have been able to borrow" from local bankers at especially low rates "amounting to a subsidy" to build or improve a downtown hotel to attract more people to the area. He adds: "That's why downtown hotels have in many cases been more interesting for us than motels."

Equally important to Sheraton has been depreciation. With accelerated depreciation, which deliberately keeps earnings at a minimum, Sheraton had avoided high income or capital gains taxes and has been able to plough more money back into improvements. The improvements (air conditioning, new banquet halls, etc.) generate more earnings, which are in turn reinvested.

---

[8] This case is quoted from *Investor's Reader,* published by Merrill Lynch, Pierce, Fenner and Smith, Inc., August 3, 1960, issue, pp. 5, 6.

Says Ernest Henderson: "Five or six years ago when Sheraton was half its present size and when the value of depreciation was not as well understood as it is now, we had $4,500,000 of depreciation charges and reported $3,500,000 in tax-paid earnings. Today, with our size doubled, depreciation would be $9,000,000 if calculated at the normal rate. By using accelerated methods it is actually $17,500,000. We invest this money in projects which in turn improve the earnings capacity of our hotels."

He adds: "Last year we completed $21,000,000 in improvements. As far as we can tell, they have added $30,000,000 to our net worth." It would have been $10,000,000 more were it not for the "competitive havoc played on our Penn Sheraton (the old William Penn) in Pittsburgh by the new Hilton hotel there. So while reported earnings for the year are only around $3,000,000 we increased our net worth ten times that."

*   *   *   *   *

This growth emphasis has apparently won great favor with stock-holders—and not merely a group of sophisticated insiders—for there are 15,600 holders of Sheraton common.

As recently as 1950 the 5,200,000 shares sold at 2; they reached a high of 24¼ on the Big Board in 1959, now trade around 18. . . .

For Ernest Henderson, who adorns the cover of his autobiography "The World of Mr. Sheraton," there has been considerable satisfaction in doing what he calls "creating results without reporting earnings."

Question

Comment on the extent to which the company's depreciation policy was responsible for the company's growth record and the extent to which the practices described are "a good thing for its stockholders."

Chapter 7

INCOME MEASUREMENT IN MANUFACTURING COMPANIES

MANUFACTURING companies perform different functions from those performed by merchandise trading companies (e.g., retail stores, wholesalers, distributors), and there is a corresponding difference between methods of accounting for the cost of goods sold in the two types of companies. A manufacturing company has as a major function the conversion of raw materials into finished goods. In any company, cost of goods sold is the total of the purchase price plus conversion costs, if any, of the products that are sold. The manufacturer, therefore, includes in cost of goods sold the cost of raw material used, the cost of labor, and other costs incurred in the manufacture of the goods that are sold. The difference between accounting for the cost of sales in a merchandising company and in a manufacturing company arises because the merchandising company usually has no conversion costs; thus, its cost of sales is practically the same as the price that the company paid for the products that it sells.

Both manufacturing and merchandising companies usually have general and administrative expenses. Generally, the manufacturer is also a merchandiser and incurs selling expenses in disposing of his goods. These selling expenses, along with general and administrative and financial costs, appear on the income statement of a manufacturing company in the same manner as in a merchandising firm, that is, below the gross profit figure.

FLOW OF COSTS

Elements of Cost

Illustration 7–1 shows elements of cost that are frequently considered in determining the total cost of a manufactured product. These are described below.

Raw Materials. Raw materials (sometimes called "stores") are those materials which actually enter into and become part of the finished product. They are to be distinguished from *supplies,* which are materials used in the operation of the business but not directly in the product itself.

179

Raw material costs include the cost of inward freight, and many companies also include storage and handling costs. Purchase discounts are often deducted from the invoice price of goods purchased.

Direct Labor. A second element of manufacturing cost is direct labor, which is labor applied to convert raw material into the finished

Illustration 7–1

ELEMENT OF COST

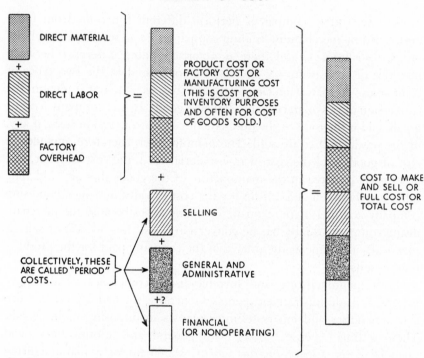

Variations:

1. The sum of direct material and direct labor is sometimes called "prime cost."
2. Factory overhead is also called "overhead," "burden," "indirect cost," or "manufacturing expense."
3. In "direct cost" systems, only part of the factory cost is included in inventory and in cost of goods sold.
4. Financial costs are more often than not excluded from product costs entirely.
5. Cost of goods sold is sometimes taken to mean manufacturing costs plus all or a portion of general and administrative costs.

product. Direct labor costs are those which can be specifically identified with a product or which vary so closely with the number of products produced that a direct relationship is presumed to be present. The wages and related costs of workers who assemble parts into a finished product, or who operate machines in the process of production, or who work on the product with tools would be considered as direct labor cost.

Manufacturing Overhead. The third category of manufacturing costs is manufacturing overhead, sometimes termed "burden," or, simply, "overhead." Manufacturing overhead includes all costs other than raw materials and direct labor which are associated with the manufacture of the product. One overhead element is indirect labor, which represents wages and salaries earned by employees who do not work directly on the product itself but whose services are related to the process of production, such as foremen, truckmen, and janitors. Manufacturing overhead also includes such costs as heat, light, power, maintenance, supplies, and depreciation, taxes, and insurance on the assets used in the manufacturing process.

Selling costs or *distribution costs* are those incurred in an effort to make sales and costs incurred in storing the completed product and in transferring it to the customer. These costs incurred "beyond the factory door" include warehousing costs, billing costs, and transportation costs.

General and administrative costs is a catchall classification to cover items not included in the above categories. Such items are as follows: costs incurred in the general and executive offices; research, development, and engineering costs (which may be wholly or partly included in factory overhead); public relations costs (often included in selling); donations; and miscellaneous items.

Financial costs include interest and other costs incurred in connection with borrowed capital. Sometimes these costs are included in general and administrative costs, although they are often collected separately and treated as nonoperating expenses.

As Illustration 7–1 indicates, the cost figure which is used for inventory valuation and cost of goods sold is typically the factory cost, that is, the sum of direct material, direct labor, and factory overhead costs.

Product Costs and Period Costs

Elements of cost that are included in the cost of a product are called *product* costs; other elements are called *period* costs. There is considerable disagreement among accountants as to where the line between these two types of costs should be drawn.

At one extreme there are those who view a business as performing only two functions, production and distribution; they assign all costs to one of these functions, and thus assign a large fraction of general and administrative costs to product costs. Selling costs are never included in product costs.

The great majority of companies define product costs as the sum of direct labor, direct material, and factory overhead, excluding general and administrative costs. Among these companies there are differences in the treatment of specific items. Some companies include the cost of such functions as manufacturing administration, personnel and industrial relations, plant protection and accounting in manufacturing overhead and hence in product costs; other companies include part of the cost of some or all of these functions; and still others exclude all of them.

At the other extreme are the advocates of "direct costing," a procedure in which fixed overhead costs are excluded from product costs. However, although a direct cost system may provide useful information for management, it is not an accepted procedure for financial accounting.[1]

The way in which a manufacturing company classifies its costs into period costs and product costs can have an important effect on its reported net income. Period costs are expenses in the accounting period in which they are incurred, whereas product costs add to the cost of the product and do not have an impact on net income until the product has been sold, which may well be a later accounting period than the period in which the costs were incurred. Further discussion of this point is deferred to Chapter 15.

Inventory Accounts

A manufacturing company typically has three types of inventory accounts: raw materials, goods in process, and finished goods. *Raw Materials Inventory* shows the cost of the raw materials on hand. *Goods in Process* (or *Work in Process*) *Inventory* shows the costs accumulated for those products on which production has been started but not yet completed as of the end of the accounting period. This includes the direct material, direct labor, and manufacturing overhead assigned to such products. *Finished Goods Inventory* shows the cost of products that have been manufactured but not yet sold. This account is comparable to the Merchandise Inventory account in a trading company.

The Account Flow Chart

The flow of costs through the inventory accounts, ending with their appearance on the income statement as cost of goods sold, is described in the next section. As an aid in understanding this flow, the concept of the

---

[1] AICPA, *Accounting Research Bulletin No. 43*, p. 29, states: ". . . the exclusion of all overheads from inventory costs does not constitute an accepted accounting procedure." American Accounting Association, 1957 Revision, *Accounting Review*, October 1957, p. 536, states: "The omission of any element of manufacturing costs [from product cost] is not acceptable."

account flow chart is first introduced. Such a flow chart consists of the accounts used in the system, shown in "T-account" form, with lines indicating the flow of figures from one account to another.

Most of the accounts associated with the manufacturing process are either asset accounts (principally inventory accounts) or expense accounts. (For some purposes, the general term "cost account" is useful, but a cost account is always classifiable either as an asset, if the cost will benefit a future period, or as an expense, if the benefit has expired.) A characteristic of both asset and expense accounts is that increases are shown on the debit side and decreases are shown on the credit side. Since a line on a flow chart indicating a transfer "from" one account "to" another account signifies that the first account is being decreased and the second account is being increased, it follows that the typical line on a flow chart of the manufacturing process leads from the credit side of one account to the debit side of another. In addition to the lines designating "flow," other lines indicate debit and credit entries that are generated in the production process; an example is the entry for the acquisition of raw material, which is a debit to Raw Materials Inventory and a credit to Accounts Payable.

Flow of Costs

Illustration 7–2 illustrates the flow-chart concept and shows the essential cost flows in a manufacturing company. This flow chart contains a hypothetical set of figures for a month's operation in a small company manufacturing smoking pipes. The cycle of operations shown therein may be explained as follows:

1. During the month, $3,000 of raw material was purchased on open account, $4,200 of other assets were purchased, and $15,000 of accounts payable were paid.
2. During the month, raw material costing $4,000 (principally briar wood, hard rubber blanks for stems, and filters) was withdrawn from inventory and sent to the shop to be worked on. This decreased Raw Materials Inventory and increased Goods in Process.
3. During the month, men worked on this material and fashioned it into pipes. The amount which they earned, $2,500, was added to the value of the Goods in Process, and the resulting liability was credited to Wages Payable.
4. The men were paid $2,700. This decreased the liability account, Wages Payable, and also decreased Cash. (The payment of wages also involved social security taxes, withholding taxes, and certain other complications; these matters have been omitted from this introductory diagram.)
5. Factory overhead costs were incurred during the month in the amount of $2,000. Of the total, $1,200 was ascertained from current invoices for

Illustration 7–2

FLOW CHART OF A PIPE COMPANY

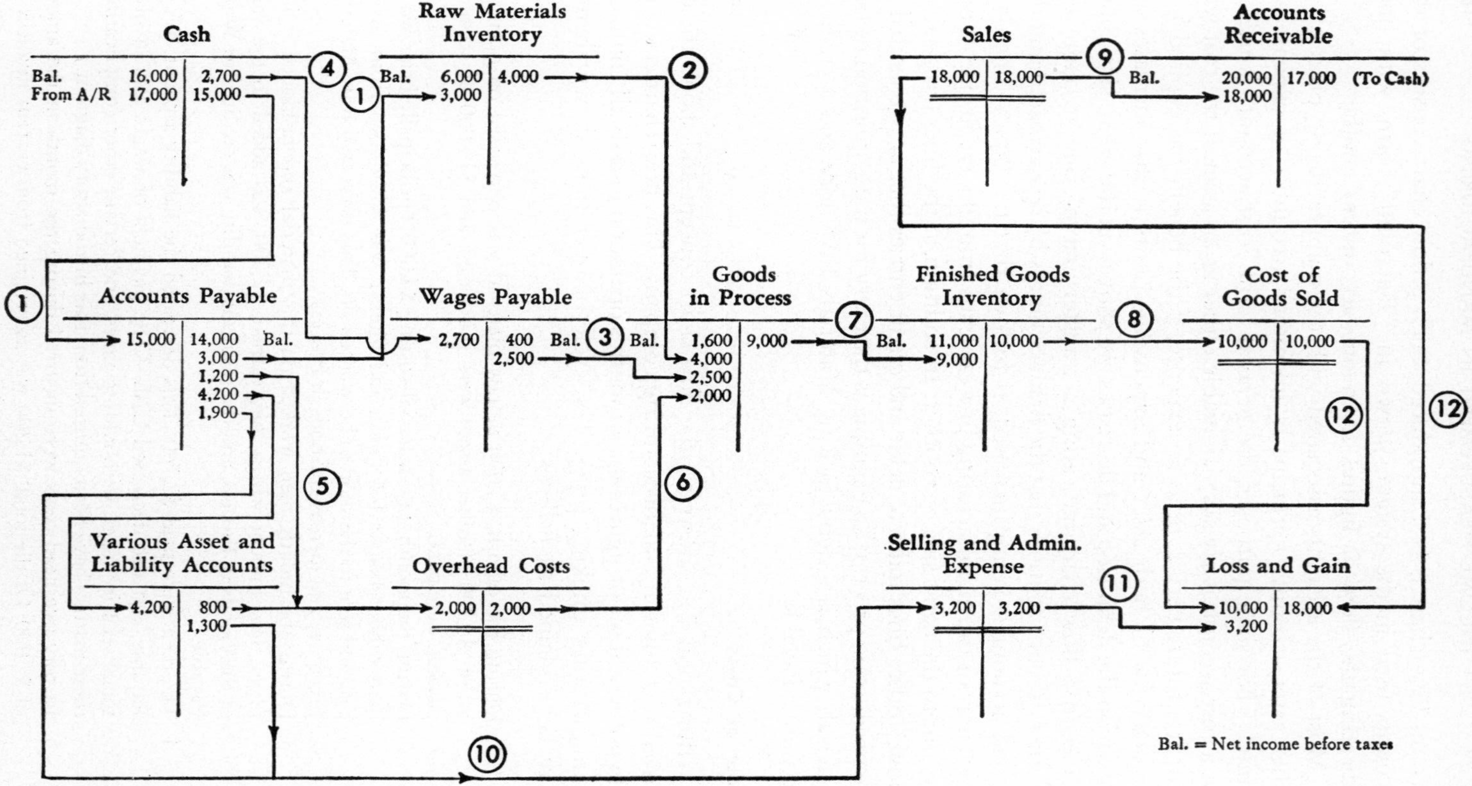

Note: Circled numbers refer to events described in the text.

such things as electricity and telephone bills, or current earnings of indirect labor and supervisors. The remaining $800 represented depreciation, the charge-off of prepaid expenses, and other credits to asset accounts or obligations credited to liabilities other than Accounts Payable. All of these items are here summed up in the general account, Overhead Costs, but in practice they are usually shown in separate overhead cost accounts, one for each type of cost.

6. Since the overhead cost is a part of the cost of the pipes that were worked on during the month, the total overhead incurred was transferred to Goods in Process.

7. Pipes whose total cost was $9,000 were completed during the month and were transferred to Finished Goods Inventory. This resulted in a decrease in Goods in Process and an increase in Finished Goods Inventory.

8. Pipes with a cost of $10,000 were sold during the month. Physically, these pipes were removed from inventory and shipped to the customer. On the accounting records, this was reflected by a credit to Finished Goods Inventory and a debit to Cost of Goods Sold.

9. At the same time, and for the same products, sales revenue of $18,000 was created, and this was shown on the books by a credit to Sales and a debit to Accounts Receivable. Later on, these receivables were paid, thus resulting in a debit to Cash and completing the accounting cycle. It should be particularly noted that the Sales transaction described here and the Cost of Goods Sold transaction described in Item 8 related to the same physical products. The difference between the balances in Sales and Cost of Goods Sold, $8,000, therefore represented the gross margin earned on products sold during the month.

10. During the month $3,200 selling and administrative expenses were incurred, $1,900 of which represented credits to Accounts Payable and $1,300 credits to various asset and liability accounts.

11. Since these were expenses applicable to the current period, Selling and Administrative Expense was closed to Loss and Gain.

12. The balances in Sales and Cost of Goods Sold were also closed to Loss and Gain, and Loss and Gain then showed the net profit for the period. This is a somewhat oversimplified statement, for income taxes and certain nonoperating and financial items which would appear in many income statements have not been considered.

ACCOUNTING FOR THE COST OF GOODS SOLD

The Deduction Process

Many manufacturing companies have a *cost accounting* system that collects the data required to make each of the entries listed above and illustrated on the flow chart. Since cost accounting data are used for many purposes other than the preparation of financial statements, however, a discussion of cost accounting is deferred to Chapter 15. In the absence of this direct means of finding cost of goods sold, we must find it by a process of deduction. This is essentially similar to, but more complicated than, the deduction process used to find cost of goods sold in a merchandising company. The increased complexity can readily be seen by comparing the income statement for a merchandising company in Illustration 7–3 with the income statement for a manufacturing company in Illustration 7–4. (Many manufacturing companies break such an income statement into two parts, as in the Marrett Manufacturing Company case, pp. 194–97.)

Illustration 7–3

MALONE STORES, INCORPORATED

Income Statement, 1963

Net sales...			$666,720
Cost of goods sold:			
Beginning inventory, January 1.................		$184,350	
Merchandise purchases.........................$454,920			
Freight and express............................	30,210	485,130	
Cost of goods available for sale.................		$669,480	
Less: Ending inventory, December 31..........		193,710	
Cost of goods sold............................			475,770
Gross profit......................................			$190,950
Selling, administrative, and general expenses:			
Salaries and wages............................		$ 88,170	
Employment taxes and benefits.................		4,623	
Rent...		24,390	
Light, heat, and power........................		8,840	
State and local taxes and licenses..............		5,130	
Depreciation.................................		4,140	
Repairs......................................		2,110	
Other expenses...............................		16,677	154,080
Profit from operations...........................			$ 36,870
Other revenue...................................			5,810
Net income before taxes..........................			$ 42,680
Provision for income tax.........................			15,120
Net Income.....................................			$ 27,560

In order to deduce cost of goods sold, the amounts for each inventory account as of the end of the period must be determined on the basis of a physical inventory. In the description that follows, these amounts are merely stated. In practice, however, the problem of assigning a reasonable value to the partially completed items in Goods in Process Inventory and to the completed items in Finished Goods Inventory without a cost accounting system can be formidable.

In order to find the cost of goods sold by the deduction process, two other costs must be deduced first—the cost of raw materials used and the cost of goods manufactured. A set of journal entries for finding these costs are given and explained below. They relate to the income

Illustration 7–4

ALFMAN MANUFACTURING COMPANY

Income Statement, 1963

Net sales...............................			$669,100
Cost of goods sold:			
Raw materials cost:			
Raw materials inventory, January 1........		$154,300	
Purchases............................$263,520			
Plus: Freight-in........................ 9,400			
Total Purchases......................		272,920	
Total Inventory and Purchases........		$427,220	
Less: Raw materials inventory, December 31		163,120	
Cost of materials used................		$264,100	
Direct labor cost.........................		150,650	
Manufacturing overhead cost:			
Indirect labor...........................	$ 23,750		
Factory heat, light, and power...........	89,500		
Factory supplies used....................	22,100		
Insurance and taxes......................	8,100		
Depreciation—plant and equipment........	35,300		
Total Manufacturing Overhead Cost.....		178,750	
Total Manufacturing Costs............		$593,500	
Add: Goods in process inventory, January 1...		18,800	
Total.............................		$612,300	
Less: Goods in process inventory, December 31.		42,600	
Cost of goods manufactured................		$569,700	
Add: Finished goods inventory, January 1....		69,200	
Cost of goods available for sale.............		$638,900	
Less: Finished goods inventory, December 31...		66,400	
Cost of goods sold...........................			572,500
Gross profit................................			$ 96,600
Selling and administrative expenses:			
Selling expense...........................		$ 38,500	
Depreciation—selling.....................		3,200	
Administrative expense....................		32,200	73,900
Net operating profit.........................			$ 22,700
Other revenue..............................			15,300
Net income before taxes.....................			$ 38,000
Provision for income tax.....................			12,640
Net Income................................			$ 25,360

statement in Illustration 7–4 and are diagrammed in a flow chart,
Illustration 7–5.

Raw Materials Used

In determining the cost of raw materials used, the assumption is
made that the amount of raw materials used is the difference between the
materials available for use during the period (which is the total of the
beginning inventory and the net purchases) and the ending inventory.
This assumption does not take into account any waste or spoilage of

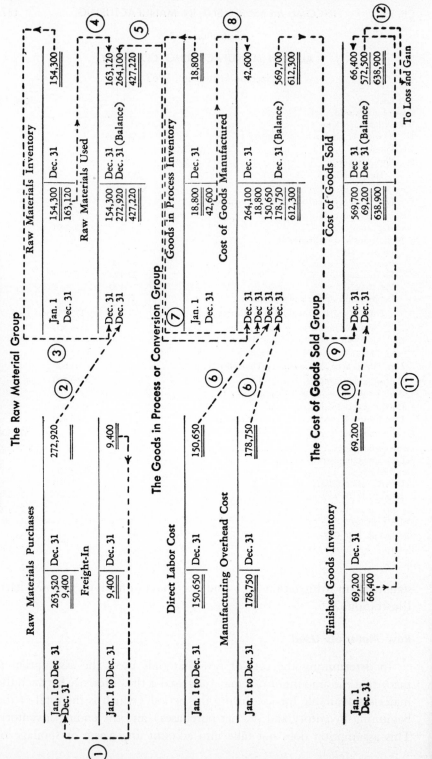

Illustration 7-5

FLOW OF FIGURES THROUGH THE ACCOUNTS

material that might have occurred. In practice, waste and spoilage is either disregarded or is collected separately and removed from material costs by crediting Raw Materials Inventory and debiting a manufacturing cost account.

This calculation can be made in a temporary account, Raw Materials Used. The journal entries that bring the necessary data to this account are as follows:

(1)

Raw Materials Purchases	9,400	
Freight-In		9,400
To find net purchases.		

(2)

Raw Materials Used	272,920	
Raw Materials Purchases		272,920
To transfer net purchases.		

(3)

Raw Materials Used	154,300	
Raw Materials Inventory		154,300
To add the beginning inventory.		

(4)

Raw Materials Inventory	163,120	
Raw Materials Used		163,120
To deduct ending inventory.		

Cost of Goods Manufactured

The sum of raw materials used, direct labor, and manufacturing overhead, together comprise the total amount of cost added to Goods in Process Inventory during the period. Given the amount in Goods in Process Inventory at the beginning of the period and the amount remaining at the end of the period, the *cost of goods manufactured,* that is, the goods completed and transferred to Finished Goods Inventory, can be deduced. Again, the assumption is made that if the goods are no longer in Goods in Process Inventory, they must have been completed and transferred to Finished Goods Inventory. To apply this line of reasoning, another temporary account, Cost of Goods Manufactured, is created, and the following journal entries are made:

(5)

Cost of Goods Manufactured	264,100	
Raw Materials Used		264,100
To transfer raw materials used.		

(6)

Cost of Goods Manufactured	329,400	
Direct Labor Cost		150,650
Indirect Labor		23,750

Factory Heat, Light, and Power.   89,500
Factory Supplies Used.   22,100
Insurance and Taxes.   8,100
Depreciation—Plant and Equipment.   35,300
To add direct labor and manufacturing overhead.

(7)

Cost of Goods Manufactured. 18,800
   Goods in Process Inventory.   18,800
To add the beginning inventory.

(8)

Goods in Process Inventory. 42,600
   Cost of Goods Manufactured.   42,600
To deduct the ending inventory.

Cost of Goods Sold

Having determined the cost of goods manufactured, the cost of goods sold is found by adding this to the beginning Finished Goods Inventory so as to find the total amount available for sale, and then subtracting the ending Finished Goods Inventory. As with a merchandising company, the assumption is that if the merchandise is not in inventory, it has been sold. The following journal entries are made:

(9)

Cost of Goods Sold. 569,700
   Cost of Goods Manufactured.   569,700
To transfer goods completed.

(10)

Cost of Goods Sold. 69,200
   Finished Goods Inventory.   69,200
To add the beginning inventory.

(11)

Finished Goods Inventory. 66,400
   Cost of Goods Sold.   66,400
To deduct the ending inventory.

The balance in the Cost of Goods Sold account is the cost of goods sold during the year, and this is now closed to Loss and Gain:

(12)

Loss and Gain. 572,500
   Cost of Goods Sold.   572,500

Condensed Closing Process

The form of closing process that has just been described in detail was chosen so as to make it possible to relate the accounting entries to the actual events that occur in a manufacturing company: the acquisition of raw material, the conversion of this material into a manufactured product, the temporary storage of this finished product, and its eventual shipment to customers. The identical end result would be achieved if all the separate entries described were compressed into three entries which (1) closed all beginning inventory balances; (2) set up new inventory balances; and (3) closed purchases, direct labor, and manufacturing overhead accounts. The three entries would be as follows:

(1)

Cost of Goods Sold	242,300	
Raw Materials Inventory		154,300
Goods in Process Inventory		18,800
Finished Goods Inventory		69,200
To close beginning inventories.		

(2)

Raw Materials Inventory	163,120	
Goods in Process Inventory	42,600	
Finished Goods Inventory	66,400	
Cost of Goods Sold		272,120
To enter ending inventories.		

(3)

Cost of Goods Sold	602,320	
Purchases		263,520
Freight-In		9,400
Direct Labor		150,650
Indirect Labor		23,750
Factory Heat, Light, and Power		89,500
Factory Supplies Used		22,100
Insurance and Taxes		8,100
Depreciation—Plant and Equipment		35,300
To close costs.		

The transfer of the Cost of Goods Sold to Loss and Gain would be made exactly as before:

Loss and Gain	572,500	
Cost of Goods Sold		572,500

Alternative Income Statement Format

The income statement given in Illustration 7–4 is useful in showing the steps involved in calculating the cost of goods sold. It is, however, a cumbersome and complicated looking document. Illustration 7–6 recasts this information in a form that is both shorter and better suited for analysis. Instead of showing separately the figures for beginning and ending inventories, this statement shows only the *changes* in inventory. These changes account for the difference between the costs incurred in manufacturing and the cost of goods sold. It is suggested that the student think out for himself the reason why inventory increases are subtracted and why inventory decreases are added.

Illustration 7–6

ALFMAN MANUFACTURING COMPANY

Income Statement, 1963
(Alternative Format)

Net sales			$669,100
Manufacturing costs:			
Raw material costs:			
Purchases	$272,920		
Increase in raw materials inventory	8,820		
Cost of materials used		$264,100	
Direct labor cost		150,650	
Manufacturing overhead cost:			
Indirect labor	$23,750		
Factory heat, light, and power	89,500		
Factory supplies used	22,100		
Insurance and taxes	8,100		
Depreciation—plant and equipment	35,300		
Total Manufacturing Overhead Cost.		178,750	
Total Manufacturing Costs		$593,500	
Changes in inventory:			
Increase in goods in process	$23,800		
Decrease in finished goods	2,800		
Net Increase in Inventory		21,000	
Cost of goods sold			572,500
Gross profit			$ 96,600
Selling and administrative expenses:			
Selling expense		$ 38,500	
Depreciation—selling		3,200	
Administrative expense		32,200	73,900
Net operating profit			$ 22,700
Other revenue			15,300
Net income before taxes			$ 38,000
Provision for income tax			12,640
Net Income			$ 25,360

Entries with a Cost Accounting System

Since in a cost accounting system the cost of raw materials used, the cost of goods manufactured, and the cost of goods sold are found directly rather than by the roundabout process of deduction, the entries required under this system are even fewer than above. They would be:

(1)

Raw Materials Inventory	272,920	
Accounts Payable		272,920
To record inventory purchased.		

(2)

Goods in Process Inventory	593,500	
Raw Materials Inventory		264,100
Direct Labor		150,650
Manufacturing Overhead		178,750
To show material, labor, and overhead costs put into process.		

(3)

Finished Goods Inventory......................................569,700
    Goods in Process Inventory...............................   569,700
    To transfer completed products to finished goods inventory.

(4)

Cost of Goods Sold...572,500
    Finished Goods Inventory................................   572,500
    To record cost of goods sold and reduce inventory.

SIGNIFICANCE OF THE PROCESS

For the objective of this book, there is no particular reason why the student should memorize the details of the procedures described in this chapter; he can easily refer back to them as needed. He should, however, understand thoroughly the nature of the process, for without such an understanding, events that are reflected on the income statement of a manufacturing company can easily be misinterpreted.

A fundamental difference between a manufacturing company and a merchandising company is illustrated by the procedures described. In a merchandising company, costs of labor, supplies, depreciation, and so on affect net income *in the accounting period in which these costs are incurred.* In a manufacturing company, on the other hand, those labor and other costs that are associated with the manufacturing process affect, initially, the value of inventory; they affect net income only in the *accounting period in which the products containing these costs are sold.* This may be a later accounting period than that in which the product was manufactured. The larger the inventory in relation to sales, the longer the time interval that elapses between the incurrence of a cost and its impact on net income.

Consider, for example, a wage increase amounting to $50,000 per year. In a merchandising company, net income would be reduced $50,000 in the year in which the increase becomes effective, other things being equal. In a manufacturing company, however, that part of the increase paid to manufacturing employees would first go to increase the inventory value of the products they worked on, and net income would receive the full impact of the increase only when these products were sold. You may find it interesting to explore this phenomenon by tracing through the impact of a $50,000 increase in wages on the two companies whose statements are shown in Illustrations 7-3 and 7-4, assuming (so that the effect of the wage increase can be isolated) that selling prices are not changed.

CASES

CASE 7–1.   PROBLEM IN INCOME STATEMENT PREPARATION

Listed below in alphabetical order are certain accounts of the Exco Manufacturing Company with balances for the year ended December 31. You are asked to prepare a detailed income statement on the basis of this information:

Administrative expense	$ 35,000
Customer returns and allowances	54,400
Depreciation—plant and equipment	38,800
Depreciation—selling	3,400
Direct labor cost	186,500
Dividends	10,000
Factory heat, light, and power	84,300
Factory supplies expense	24,100
Finished goods inventory, 1/1	71,500
Finished goods inventory, 12/31	74,400
Freight-in	7,800
Goods in process inventory, 1/1	28,000
Goods in process inventory, 12/31	47,200
Indirect labor	25,750
Insurance and taxes (factory)	12,600
Interest expenses	8,500
Loss on disposal of machinery	11,500
Provision for income tax	5,500
Purchases	275,500
Raw materials inventory, 1/1	169,290
Raw materials inventory, 12/31	148,300
Sales	829,300
Selling expense	41,500

CASE 7–2.   MARRETT MANUFACTURING COMPANY (A)

The management of the Marrett Manufacturing Company prepared annually a budget of expected financial operations for the ensuing calendar year. The completed budget provided information on all aspects of the coming year's operations. It included an estimated balance sheet as of the end of the year and an estimated income statement.

The final preparation of statements was accomplished only after careful integration of detailed computations submitted by each department. This was done to insure that the operation of all departments were in balance with one another. For example, the finance department needed to base its schedules of loan operations and of collections and disbursements on figures that were dependent upon manufacturing, purchasing, and selling expectations. The level of production activity would be geared to the forecasts of the sales department, and purchasing would be geared to the proposed manufacturing schedule. In short, it was necessary to integrate the estimates of each department and to revise them in terms of the overall effect on operations to arrive at a well-formulated and profitable plan of operations for the coming year. The budget statements ultimately derived from the adjusted estimated transactions would then serve the company as a reliable guide and measure of the coming year's operations.

At the time the 1964 budget was being prepared in November of 1963, estimated 1963 financial statements were compiled for use as a comparison with the budgeted figures. These 1963 statements were based on nine months' actual and three months' estimated transactions. They appear as Exhibits 1, 2, and 3.

Below is the summary of expected operations for the budget year 1964 as finally accepted:

1. *Sales* (all on credit), $407,000; sales returns and allowances, $3,000; sales discounts taken by customers, $8,000. (The sales figure is net of expected bad debts.)
2. *Purchases of goods and services:*
   a) New assets:
      Purchased for cash: manufacturing plant and equipment, $15,000; prepaid manufacturing taxes and insurance, $6,000.
      Purchased on accounts payable: raw materials, $117,000; supplies, $13,000.
   b) Services used to convert raw materials into goods in process,[2] all purchased for cash: direct manufacturing labor, $70,000; indirect manufacturing labor, $29,000; social security taxes on labor, $3,400; power, heat, and light, $22,200. (Accrued payroll was ignored in these estimates.)
   c) Sales and administrative service, purchased for cash: $67,000.
3. *Conversion of assets into goods in process:* This appears as an increase in the "value" of goods in process and a decrease in the appropriate asset accounts.
   Depreciation of building and equipment, $13,400; expiration of prepaid taxes and insurance, $5,000; supplies used in manufacturing, $15,000; raw materials put into process, $131,000.
4. *Transfer of goods in process into finished goods.* This appears as an increase in finished goods and a decrease in goods in process.
   Total cost accumulated on goods that have been completed and transferred to finished goods inventory, $275,000.
5. *Cost of finished goods sold to customers, $253,000.*

---

[2] In a manufacturing company, inventory is assumed to increase in value by the amounts spent to convert raw material into salable products. These amounts include the items listed in 2 (b) plus the items listed in (3) below.

6. *Financial transactions:*
   a) $77,000, borrowed on notes payable to bank.
   b) Bank loans paid off (i.e., retired), $100,000.
   c) Cash payment to bank of $1,200 for interest on loans.
7. *Cash receipts from customers* on accounts receivable, $404,300.
8. *Cash payments of liabilities:*
   a) Payment of accounts payable, $139,800.
   b) Payment of 1963 income tax, $5,000.
9. *Estimated federal income tax* on 1964 income, $29,600, of which $15,000 is estimated to be unpaid as of December 31, 1964.
10. *Dividends* declared for year and paid in cash, $21,000.

This summary presents the complete cycle of the Marrett Manufacturing Company's budgeted yearly operations from the purchases of goods and services through their various stages of conversion to completion of the finished product to the sale of this product. All costs and cash receipts and disbursements involved in this cycle are presented, including the provision for federal income tax and the payment of dividends.

Exhibit 1

MARRETT MANUFACTURING COMPANY

Estimated Balance Sheet, December 31, 1963

ASSETS

Current Assets:

Cash			$ 25,500
Accounts receivable (net of allowance for doubtful accounts).			60,500
Inventories:			
Raw materials		$ 55,000	
Goods in process		24,200	
Finished goods		14,300	
Supplies		16,500	110,000
Prepaid taxes and insurance			5,700
Total Current Assets			$201,700
Fixed Assets:			
Manufacturing plant		$320,000	
Less: Accumulated depreciation		100,000	220,000
			$421,700

LIABILITIES AND CAPITAL

Current Liabilities:			
Notes payable			$ 33,000
Accounts payable			25,500
Unpaid estimated federal income taxes			5,000
Total Current Liabilities			$ 63,500
Capital:			
Capital stock		$330,000	
Retained earnings		28,200	358,200
			$421,700

Exhibit 2

MARRETT MANUFACTURING COMPANY

Estimated Statement of Cost of Goods Sold, 1963

Finished goods inventory, 1/1/63			$ 84,000
Goods in process inventory, 1/1/63		$ 26,000	
Raw materials used		90,000	
Plus: Factory expenses:			
Direct manufacturing labor		49,000	
Factory overhead:			
Indirect manufacturing labor	$19,000		
Power, heat, and light	14,000		
Depreciation of plant	12,800		
Social security taxes	2,500		
Taxes and insurance, factory	5,000		
Supplies	7,900	61,200	
		$226,200	
Less: Goods in process inventory, 12/31/63		24,200	
Cost of goods manufactured (i.e., completed)			202,000
			$286,000
Less: Finished goods inventory, 12/31/63			14,300
Cost of Goods Sold			$271,700

Exhibit 3

MARRETT MANUFACTURING COMPANY

Estimated Income Statement, 1963

Sales		$364,000
Less: Sales returns and allowances	$2,800	
Sales discounts allowed	7,100	9,900
Net sales		$354,100
Less: Cost of goods sold (per schedule)		271,700
Gross profit margin		$ 82,400
Less: Sales and administrative expense		60,000
Net operating profit		$ 22,400
Less: Interest expense		1,200
Net profit before federal income tax		$ 21,200
Less: Estimated income tax		10,500
Net Profit after Federal Income Tax		$ 10,700

Questions

1. Journalize each of the estimated transactions. Set up T-accounts with balances as shown on the balance sheet for December 31, 1963, and post the journal entries to these accounts.

2. Prepare an estimated statement of cost of goods sold for 1964, an estimated income statement for 1964, and an estimated balance sheet as of December 31, 1964.

3. Describe the principal differences between the 1964 estimates and the 1963 figures as shown on Exhibits 1, 2, and 3. In what respects is 1964 performance expected to be better than 1963 performance, and in what respects is it expected to be poorer?

Chapter 8 | LONG-TERM EQUITIES

THE TREASURER and other executives who are responsible for financial affairs in a company need a considerable store of technical knowledge regarding the various means of raising money, the legal and tax rules relating to financing, and so on. Other members of management should have some understanding of these matters, even though they scarcely can be expected to be conversant with all the details. All members of management need to know how the principal types of financing transactions affect the financial statements; otherwise, certain items reported on the equities side of the balance sheet and certain income statement items will be either incomprehensible or misunderstood.

This chapter discusses the accounting aspects of these financial matters at the broad level that is adequate for the nonfinancial manager. To cover the subject at the detailed level appropriate for the specialist would require 100 pages or so; books giving such a coverage are listed in the suggestions for further reading at the end of this chapter. The topics all relate to items listed on the equities side of the balance sheet: bonds and other long-term liabilities, the capital stock and surplus of corporations, and the owners' equity of unincorporated businesses. The principles underlying the preparation of consolidated financial statements are described briefly.

NATURE OF LIABILITIES

In Chapter 2, a liability was defined as a claim against assets by an outside party, as distinguished from a claim by the owners. This definition is approximately correct; however, not all legal obligations to outside parties are liabilities in the accounting meaning of this word, nor are all liabilities legally enforceable claims.

As an example of a claim that is not a liability, consider the case of an employee who has a written contract guaranteeing him employment at a stated salary for the next two years (e.g., professional athletes, coaches, executives). Such a contract is a legally enforceable claim against the business, but it is *not* a liability; in fact, this transaction is not recorded in the accounts at all until the man actually performs the work.

What distinguishes such a contract from those that do give rise to liabilities? Essentially, the distinction is determined by whether or not there is an asset or expense debit to offset the liability credit. When an employee works, the offsetting debit to the liability Accrued Wages Payable is Wages Expense. But when a contract is signed covering *future* employment, no expense account in the current period is affected, nor is an asset created.

For the same reason, a lease agreement, even though it may be just as binding and cover just as long a time period as a first-mortgage bond, is not a liability because the leased property is not owned by the lessee and hence is not an asset.[1] As a general rule, this indirect method of distinguishing between liabilities and nonliabilities in terms of whether or not there is an offsetting debit is a better way of solving borderline problems than the alternative of attempting to construct a direct definition of "obligation" or "claim" that will apply to all situations.

An estimated allowance for future costs under a warranty agreement mentioned in Chapter 3 is an example of a liability that is not a definite obligation at the time it is set up. Liabilities of this type arise out of attempts to match revenue and costs. As explained in Chapter 3, revenue is ordinarily recognized when products are shipped; but when a warranty agreement applies, some of the costs associated with the transaction will not be incurred until later on when customers obtain repairs or replacement of products that turn out to be defective. The liability account is set up in the period in which the revenue is recognized, the offsetting debit being to an expense account of that period, such as Estimated Warranty Expense.

Contingent Liabilities

A contingent liability is one that although not now an obligation may become one in the future if certain possible, but not probable, events happen. An unfavorable verdict in a lawsuit in which the company is a defendant is an example; retroactive wage payments arising from current negotiations with a labor union is another. Contingent liabilities are not recorded on the balance sheet. Although not shown as a liability on the balance sheet itself, the existence of material amounts

---

[1] However, in its Opinion No. 5 (September, 1964), the Accounting Principles Board states that long-term noncancelable leases give rise to assets and liabilities if the lease results "in the creation of a material equity in the property."

of contingent liabilities is disclosed in footnotes or explanations which accompany the balance sheet.

Distinction between Liabilities and Owners' Equity

The exact dividing line between liabilities and owners' equities is a difficult one to draw. Although a distinction based on whether the claim is that of an owner or that of an outside creditor is satisfactory for most situations, in borderline cases fine-spun philosophical arguments can often be made for either solution. A more practical approach is to ask whether the claim involves a definite promise to pay; if so, the claim is a liability. If, on the other hand, the business does not incur a firm obligation to pay—firm in the sense that failure to make payment would be grounds for legal action by the creditor—the item is part of owners' equity. The problem has become more acute in recent years because interest on a liability is a tax-deductible expense, whereas a dividend paid to owners is not; therefore companies have an incentive to make agreements that are sufficiently like liabilities to qualify for tax purposes but which impose as slight an obligation as possible.

BONDS

The most common form of long-term liability is a bond, which is a certificate, usually negotiable, promising to pay the holder a specified sum of money, usually $1,000, plus interest at a stated rate. Bonds may be sold to the general public through investment bankers, or they may be sold directly to an insurance company or other financial institution.

Recording the Issue

To illustrate the entries typically made to record the sale of an issue of bonds, assume the Mason Corporation sells an issue of 100 bonds, each with a face or *par* value of $1,000, with an interest rate of 4 per cent, payable in 20 years, and secured by a first mortgage on certain Mason Corporation assets. (Such a bond would be called a "4 per cent, 20-year, first-mortgage bond.") If the corporation receives $1,000 each for the sale of these bonds, the following entry would be made:

```
Cash.................................................................100,000
    Bonds Payable...........................................             100,000
```

Frequently bonds are sold for less than their par value, that is, at a *discount,* or for more than their par value, that is, at a *premium.* The words "discount" and "premium" carry no connotation of "bad" or "good." They reflect simply a difference between the stated interest rate for the issue and the going rate of interest at the time of issuance. The stated rate may be made intentionally different from the going market rate in the belief that this makes the bonds more attractive. Thus, with a market rate of 4 per cent and neglecting issuance costs, $100,000 of capital can be secured either by the sale of $100,000 face amount of 4 per cent bonds sold at par, by the sale of less than $100,000 face amount of 5 per cent bonds sold at a premium, or by the sale of more than $100,000 face amount of 3.5 per cent bonds sold at a discount. If the Mason Corporation received only $950 for each $1,000 bond, the following entry would be made:

```
Cash.......................................................  95,000
Bond Discount..............................................   5,000
    Bonds Payable.........................................           100,000
```

If the bonds are sold at a premium, this entry would be made:

```
Cash......................................................  105,000
    Bond Premium..........................................             5,000
    Bonds Payable.........................................           100,000
```

The sale of a bond issue is usually undertaken by an investment banking firm which charges a fee for this service. Determination of bond premium or discount is based on the net amount the corporation receives after this fee has been deducted, not on the price at which the bonds are sold to the public. In addition to this fee, the corporation also incurs printing, legal, and accounting costs in connection with a bond issue. These issue costs are usually taken into account when determining the net amount of discount or premium, but in some cases they are set up separately as an asset and amortized over the life of the issue.

If bonds are sold after the bond contract date (i.e., the date on which interest starts to be earned), the purchaser pays both the price of the bond itself and the interest that has accrued up to the date of the transaction. This is done because the corporation, for reasons of convenience, will pay to all bondholders the interest earned for the full period (usually six months) beginning with the contract date, and the purchaser is clearly not entitled to interest for the period prior to the time he purchased the bonds. If, for example, these 4 per cent Mason Corporation bonds were sold three months after the contract date, at a price that netted their par value to the corporation, the following entry would be made:

```
Cash......................................................  101,000
    Bonds Payable.........................................           100,000
    Bonds Interest Payable................................             1,000
```

In this case, when the semiannual interest payment is recorded, $1,000 of it will be debited to Bond Interest Payable, and the remainder to Bond Interest Expense; thus Bond Interest Expense will reflect the net interest expense of the period.

Balance Sheet Presentation

Bonds payable are shown in the long-term liabilities section of the balance sheet until one year before they mature, when ordinarily they become current liabilities. The description should give the principal facts about the issue, e.g., "4 per cent first-mortgage bonds of 1983." When a bond issue is to be refunded, however, it is not shown as a current liability in the year of maturity since it then will not require the use of current assets. If the bonds are to be retired in installments (as with *serial bonds*), that portion to be retired within a year is shown in the current liabilities section.

Bond discount is preferably shown on the balance sheet as a deduction from, and bond premium as an addition to, the face amount of bonds payable so as to reflect the net amount of the liability.

Bond Interest

An accounting entry is made to record the semiannual interest payments to bondholders and at the same time to amortize a portion of the bond premium or discount. The effect of this entry is that the *net* debit to Interest Expense reflects not the stated amount of interest actually paid to bondholders (unless the bonds are sold at par); rather, it reflects the effective rate of interest, which is larger or smaller than the stated rate according to whether the bonds were sold at a discount or at a premium. The existence of bond discount in effect increases the interest expense, while the existence of bond premium decreases it.

Bond discount or premium may be amortized in one or two ways: by the straight-line method, in which the discount is debited (or the premium is credited) to Interest Expense in equal installments over the life of the issue; or by the compound interest method in which the discount or premium is written off in such a way that the net interest expense bears a constant ratio to the book value of the bonds over the whole life of the issue. This ratio is the effective interest cost of the borrowed funds.

The following entry records the semiannual bond interest payment and amortization of discount on a straight-line basis for the Mason Corporation bonds that were assumed to have been sold at $950 each:

Interest Expense...2,125		
Bond Discount...	125	
Cash...		2,000

Although the cash paid out as interest is $2,000, interest expense for the period is $2,125 because of the amortization of bond discount.

If the interest payment date does not coincide with the closing of the company's books, an adjusting entry is made to record accrued interest expense and the amortization of discount or premium. Assuming that the Mason Corporation bonds are sold at $950 each on September 30, that the interest dates are September 30 and March 31, and that the fiscal year ends on December 31, the following entries would be made:

1. *Adjustment on December 31:*

Bond Interest Expense..1,062.50		
Bond Discount...	62.50	
Accrued Interest Payable..................................	1,000.00	

2. *Payment of semiannual interest on March 31:*

Bond Interest Expense..1,062.50		
Accrued Interest Payable.....................................1,000.00		
Bond Discount...	62.50	
Cash...	2,000.00	

3. *Payment of semiannual interest on the following September 30:*

Bond Interest Expense..2,125.00		
Bond Discount...	125.00	
Cash...	2,000.00	

Bond issue costs are likewise amortized by debits to Interest Expense over the life of the issue.

Retirement of Bonds

Bonds may be retired in total, or they may be retired in installments over a period of years. In either case the retirement is recorded by a debit to Bonds Payable and a credit to Cash, or to a sinking fund which has been set up for this purpose. The bond discount or premium will have been completely amortized by the maturity date, so no additional entry is required for discount or premium at that time.

Bonds are sometimes retired at maturity out of a sinking fund which has been created in installments over the life of the issue. Bond sinking funds may be controlled by the originating corporation, or they may be controlled by a trustee under specified contractual arrangements. In either case, such funds usually appear in the investment section of the assets side of the balance sheet.

The company may decide to retire bonds earlier than the date originally specified. If such bonds were sold at a discount (or premium), an unamortized discount (or premium) will exist as of the date of early retirement because the schedule of amortization was originally set up so as to charge off the discount (or premium) over the specified life of the issue. The unamortized balance is accordingly charged against retained earnings. It may, or may not, be shown as an expense of the current accounting period, depending on whether or not the "clean surplus" doctrine is followed. An illustrative entry, showing the retirement of Mason Corporation bonds at the end of ten years (i.e., half their scheduled life), assuming no sinking fund (and neglecting for the moment the call premium to be discussed in the next paragraph), would be as follows:

```
Bonds Payable..............................................100,000
Retained Earnings..........................................  2,500
    Cash...................................................           100,000
    Bond Discount.........................................             2,500
```

Refunding a Bond Issue

The terms of some bond issues state that the bonds can be called, or retired before maturity, by paying for them at a premium, that is, by paying more than the par value. In this case, a schedule of *call prices* is included in the terms of the issue. In periods when interest rates have declined, a company may consider it advantageous to *refund* a bond issue, that is, to call the old issue, and float a new one with a lower rate of interest. Problems then arise in accounting for the call premium (the difference between the call price and par value) and any unamortized issue costs and discount (or premium) on the old bonds.

The preferred treatment is to write off these costs over the remaining life of the issue being retired. Since for tax purposes these costs are a deductible expense in the year of refunding, thereby decreasing income taxes in that year, it is appropriate to report a fraction of the unamortized costs, equal to the income taxes saved, as an expense of the year of refunding and to spread only the remainder of the cost over the future years. This is consistent with the treatment of income taxes discussed on page 141.

It is also in accordance with accounting principles to write off all the unamortized costs and the call premium in the year of refunding, either as an expense on the income statement or as a debit directly to retained earnings. If the debit is made to retained earnings, part of the costs should nevertheless be shown on the income statement as an offset to the income taxes that are saved so that the income tax expense will be related to the revenue and expenses reported.

The alternative of writing off the unamortized costs and call premium over the life of the *new* bond issue is *not* in accordance with generally accepted accounting principles.

Generally, if the alternative of amortizing over the remaining years of the old bond issue is chosen, the balances of all accounts which refer to the refunded issue, such as call premium, unamortized premium or discount, and issue costs, are closed into a single account, for example, "Unamortized Charges on 4 Per Cent Series A Mortgage Bonds." This single account is carried on the books and amortized over the remaining years of the old bond issue.

CAPITAL STOCK

Capital stock may be either *common* or *preferred*. Preferred stock has preference, or priority, over common as to the receipt of dividends, as to assets in the event of liquidation, or in other specified matters. There is no substantial difference in the accounting treatment of these two types of stock, however, so no distinction is here made between them.

Stock may be either *par value* or *no-par value*. Par value stock appears in the accounts at a fixed amount per share (often $10 or $100), which is specified in the corporation's charter or bylaws. Except by coincidence, the par value of the stock in a going concern has no relation either to the stock's market value or to its book value. *Market value* is what people will pay for the stock. *Book value* is the stockholders' equity as reported on the balance sheet, that is, the sum of capital stock plus surplus (or, stated another way, assets minus liabilities).

No-par value stock has a *stated value,* which is either specified in the corporation's charter or bylaws or fixed by the board of directors. The stated value governs the amounts to be entered in the Capital Stock account just as if it were a par value. The difference between par value and no-par value stock is therefore of little practical significance.

Recording the Issue

To illustrate the issuance of stock, let us consider the Mason Corporation, which received a charter from the state authorizing the issuance of 10,000 shares of $10 par value common stock. If 1,000 shares of this stock are issued at par ($10) and immediately paid for, the following entry would be made:

```
Cash..................................................................10,000
    Common Stock..........................................................        10,000
```

Stock is often sold for more than its par or stated value; that is, it is sold at a *premium*. In such situations the Common Stock account still reflects the par or stated value, and the premium is shown separately, usually in the account, Paid-In Surplus (or Capital Surplus). If 1,000 shares of Mason Corporation $10 common stock were sold at $12 a share, the following entry would be made:

```
Cash..................................................................12,000
    Common Stock..........................................................        10,000
    Paid-In Surplus........................................................         2,000
```

Unlike bonds, stock is almost never sold at a discount. In most states and under most circumstances, this is illegal. Even where sale at a discount is permitted, individual stockholders would be required to contribute the amount of the discount in cash if the company should go bankrupt, and such a possibility makes discount stock unattractive to investors. Corporations therefore set the par value or stated value low enough so that the stock can be sold at a premium.

The sale of an issue of stock is often handled by an investment banking firm which receives a fee or "spread" for this service. Logically, the corporation should record only the net amount received from the investment banker, that is, the price paid by the public less the banker's spread, since this is the only amount that the corporate entity receives. Many companies, however, record the stock at the price paid by the public, and show the banker's spread as an expense. When this is done, the ultimate effect on owners' equity is the same as if only the net amount were recorded since the expense item winds up as a decrease in owners' equity. The practice of recording the spread separately provides a useful piece of information, namely, the size of the spread, which is not revealed in the alternative treatment.

In connection with the issuance of stock, the corporation itself incurs issue costs over and above the banker's spread. These amounts may also be deducted from the amount received from the issue. The facts are perhaps more clearly recorded, however, if these costs are recorded separately either as an expense of the current period or, if they are material, as an asset, such as organization cost.

The following example illustrates the handling of the banker's spread and the issue costs. Suppose the Mason Corporation issues 10,000 shares of $10 par value common stock and the public buys these shares at $13. Suppose also that the investment banker's spread is $2 per share and that the issue costs incurred by the Mason Corporation total $4,000. The entries below would be made:

1. *Entry for issue costs:*

Stock Issue Costs.	4,000	
Cash (or Accounts Payable).		4,000

2. *Entry when payment is received from investment bankers:*

Cash.	110,000	
Common Stock.		100,000
Paid-In Surplus.		10,000

3. *Possible entry closing stock issue costs:*[2]

Paid-In Surplus.	4,000	
Stock Issue Costs.		4,000

Note that the $130,000 actually paid by the public does not appear in the company's accounts. Note also that these transactions are between the company and its stockholders. When one stockholder sells his stock to another stockholder, the amounts in the company's accounts are not affected in any way; only the detailed record showing the identity of stockholders is changed.

Treasury Stock

Treasury stock is a corporation's own stock that has been issued and subsequently reacquired by purchase or donation but not canceled. Although a few corporations show treasury stock as an asset on their balance sheet, this practice is not generally accepted since treasury stock is clearly not a "valuable thing or property right owned by the business"; a business can't own a claim against itself. The preferable practice is to treat treasury stock as a reduction in stockholders' equity, that is, as a reduction in the number and value of the shares outstanding, which is what it is.

In many companies, treasury stock purchased is debited to the Treasury Stock account at its cost, regardless of its par or stated value. It continues to be shown at cost until it is canceled or reissued, at which time adjustments are made in stockholders' equity to dispose of any differences between this cost, the paid-in value (i.e., the net proceeds at the time the stock was originally issued), and, in the event of reissuance, the amount then received.

Any excess of selling price above cost is credited to a surplus account

---

[2] This entry not made if stock issue costs are capitalized or charged to expense.

(such as Capital Surplus from Treasury Stock Transactions), which may be shown as a separate item in the capital surplus section of the balance sheet. If treasury stock is sold at a price below cost, the loss may be deducted from the related surplus account if such an account already exists from prior transactions; otherwise the loss is debited to Retained Earnings.

If the capital stock was originally issued over a period of time at varying prices, there may be no way of determining the amount originally received from the issuance of the specific shares later reacquired as treasury stock. In this situation the "average paid-in value" becomes the base against which the costs of reacquisition are compared. The average paid-in value is determined by dividing the total number of shares outstanding at the time of the treasury stock transaction into total stated value less discounts or plus premiums.

None of these transactions enter into the determination of net income, nor are gains or losses from such transactions recognized for tax purposes.

Balance Sheet Presentation

The capital stock item in the stockholders' equity section of a balance sheet usually states the *number* of authorized shares, and the *number* of issued shares, although the *dollar amount* pertains only to the shares issued. If there are several classes of stock, each class is shown separately. Paid-in surplus is shown as a separate item, immediately beneath the capital stock item. The term "paid-in surplus" may be replaced by a more descriptive phrase, such as "capital contribution in excess of stated value." However labeled, the amounts for paid-in surplus and for earned surplus (i.e., retained earnings) are not added

Illustration 8–1

MASON CORPORATION

Portion of Balance Sheet as of December 31

Assets	*Liabilities*	$ 21,200
	Stockholders' Equity:	
	Preferred stock, par value $10, authorized and issued 2,900 shares	$ 29,000
(Details omitted)	Common stock, $10, authorized 100,000 shares; issued 10,000 shares	100,000
	Add: Paid-in surplus	4,000
	Contributed Capital	$133,000
	Retained earnings	10,000
		$143,000
	Less: 100 common shares in treasury at cost	1,200
	Total Stockholders' Equity	$141,800
Total Assets $163,000	Total Equities	$163,000

together to give a "total surplus," since the two items are of a quite dissimilar nature.

Treasury stock is ordinarily shown on the balance sheet as the last item of the stockholders' equity section. It is a deduction from the whole of the stockholders' equity, not from the capital stock item alone.

Illustration 8–1 illustrates the treatment of capital stock accounts in the balance sheet.

SURPLUS

Although the term "retained earnings" has replaced the former term "earned surplus" so as to avoid giving an erroneous connotation about the nature of the item, the word "surplus" still persists as a general term for all items of stockholders' equity other than the stated value of the stock. Surplus consists of two categories: (1) retained earnings and (2) capital surplus. (The "paid-in surplus" referred to above is one type of capital surplus.) The term "deficit" means a negative surplus and ordinarily arises from losses from operation (i.e., "minus" retained earnings).

Events and accounting entries that affect *retained earnings* have been described in earlier chapters. In general, retained earnings is increased by net income, is decreased by the declaration of dividends, and is also increased or decreased by certain adjustments in owners' equity that are not shown on the income statement, such as material and unusual corrections to the reported income of prior years. It should be emphasized that these adjustments and other losses of the type described in Chapter 5 are debited or credited to retained earnings, *not* to capital surplus.

Dividends are debited to retained earnings in the period in which they are declared, that is, voted, by the board of directors, even though payment is made at a later date. For example, if the Mason Corporation declared a $5,000 dividend on December 15 to be paid on January 15, the entries would be as follows:

Dec. 15

Dividends...	5,000	
Dividends Payable.....................................		5,000

Dec. 31

Retained Earnings......................................	5,000	
Dividends..		5,000
A closing entry.		

Jan. 15

Dividends Payable......................................	5,000	
Cash..		5,000

The *capital surplus* item is usually subdivided into items indicating source, and a brief list of some of these will be used to indicate the nature of the category. As described in the preceding section, *paid-in surplus* arises when the proceeds from the sale of stock exceeds its par value or stated value. *Donated surplus* arises from gifts made to the corporation. *Appraisal surplus* arises when the book value of assets is increased as the result of an appraisal; that is done only under highly unusual circumstances.

Increasingly, the practice is not to classify the stockholders' equity section of the balance sheet into (1) stated value of capital stock and (2) surplus, but rather into (1) *contributed capital,* consisting of the stated value of stock plus capital surplus, and (2) retained earnings. This new grouping is more indicative of the real significance of the items than is the traditional one.

Significance of Surplus

A study of the stockholders' equity section may provide some clues as to the methods used to obtain capital, as to transactions involving the purchase or sale of treasury stock, or as to the occurrence of unusual events not reflected in the income statement that result in changes in the stockholders' equity. An analysis of the growth in retained earnings in relation to net income may indicate the extent to which the company has obtained capital by "plowing back" its earnings.

In most states, dividend payments are limited to the amounts reported as surplus. In some states, dividend payments cannot exceed the amount shown on the books as retained earnings, while other state laws allow dividend payments to equal retained earnings plus certain types of capital surplus. In still other states, however, dividend payments can be made if there are earnings in the current year, even though a deficit is shown in the surplus section of the balance sheet. Banks or other lenders may impose other restrictions on the amounts that can be paid as dividends.

Whatever the legal restriction on dividend payments may be, factors other than the amount reported as retained earnings or surplus are likely to have a much more important bearing on dividend decisions in the ordinary situation. These factors include the amount of cash available, the funds required for expansion, the anticipated effect of dividends on stock prices and on the sale of new securities, the desire to maintain an unbroken record of dividend payments, a sense of fairness to stockholders, and so on.

Some accountants advocate that stockholders' equity be reported as a single figure rather than showing separate amounts for stock and for various types of surplus. Although this is not in accordance with generally accepted accounting principles, the suggestion does emphasize the difficulty of obtaining useful information from the separate figures that appear in the stockholders' equity section of the balance sheet.

Stock Dividends and Stock Splits

Some stockholders, in the mistaken belief that the amount reported as surplus is "their money," put pressure on the directors to authorize cash dividends equal to, or almost equal to, the amount of surplus. Clearly, surplus is not money at all, and for any of a number of reasons, cash may not be available for dividend payments even though the balance sheet shows a large surplus. These same stockholders may be quite satisfied with a *stock dividend,* which actually does not change their equity in the corporation since it results in nothing more than a decrease in surplus and an exactly equal increase in the dollar amount of stock outstanding. The amount transferred from retained earnings to capital stock is usually calculated on the basis of the current market price of the stock.

> EXAMPLE: Suppose that the Mason Corporation directors voted a 5 per cent stock dividend shortly after the date of the balance sheet in Illustration 8–1. Each stockholder would receive $\frac{1}{20}$ of a share of new stock for every share he then held. If the stock currently had a market price of $12 a share, the common stock item on the balance sheet would increase by $6,000 (500 shares at $12 per share), and retained earnings would decrease by $6,000, but the *total* stockholders' equity would remain exactly as before.

As a matter of custom, a stock dividend is ordinarily not more than 20 per cent or 25 per cent of the number of shares issued and usually is 5 per cent or 10 per cent.

A stock dividend has the effect of "capitalizing surplus," that is, of changing surplus to capital stock. Such a change can also be accomplished in other ways, for example, simply by a vote of the board of directors.

The legal effect of such a change is that the amounts so capitalized become part of the capital stock item, and the limit on the maximum amount of dividends that can be paid is correspondingly reduced. By capitalizing surplus, the directors signal their intention that the amount so capitalized will be permanently invested in the corporation. Failure to capitalize surplus is by no means an indication that the surplus will be distributed as dividends, however.

A stock dividend is therefore one way of advising the stockholders of the company's intention to hold retained earnings permanently in the business. Also, a stockholder may realize cash by selling his dividend stock while preserving the number of his owned shares intact; but if he does this, he is in fact selling a fraction of his equity in the business.

A *stock split* merely increases the number of shares of stock outstanding, with no change in the total stated value of the stock and no change in surplus. As with a stock dividend, it has no effect on owners' equity; indeed, the effect of both is solely to repackage the evidence of ownership in smaller units. A stock split automatically reduces the market price of a share of stock. Often, however, the reduction is not quite proportional to the split since stock with a fairly low market price per share tends to be more attractive than stock with a high market price per share. Thus, if a stock selling at $150 is split "3-for-1," the new shares often will sell for somewhat more than $50 each.

The stock referred to in the preceding paragraphs is the company's own stock. If the company distributes to its shareholders the shares of some other corporation's stock which it owns, this distribution is similar to a regular cash dividend, and is recorded in the same manner except that the credit is to the Investments account rather than to Cash. Such a transaction is called a *spin off.*

Surplus Reserves

In an attempt to explain to stockholders why they do not receive dividends that are equal to the amount shown as surplus, a corporation may show on its balance sheet an appropriation, or reserve, as a separate item that is subtracted from surplus. Some of the terms used to describe the reasons for such an appropriation are as follows: *reserve for bond sinking fund,* which indicates a restriction on dividends in accordance with agreements made to bondholders; *reserve for contingencies,* indicating management's belief that funds may be required for an unusual purpose or to meet a possible obligation that does not yet have the status of a liability (such as settlement of a pending lawsuit, or a retroactive wage increase); *reserve for future inventory price decline,* indicating the possibility that inventory may be sold at a price less than the value reported on the balance sheet; and *reserve for expansion,* indicating an intention to use funds for the acquisition of new assets.

None of these reserves represent money, or anything tangible; the assets of a business are reported on the assets side of the balance sheet, not in the stockholders' equity section. The accounting entry creating the reserve involves a debit to Retained Earnings (or some other surplus account) and a credit to the reserve. This entry obviously does not affect any asset account, nor does the reserve represent anything more than a segregated portion of surplus.

Other Types of Reserves

In addition to its use in the situations described above, the word "reserve" is also used in two other quite different connections in accounting: as asset contra accounts and as liability accounts. Because of the confusion that naturally arises when the same word has three different meanings, its use in these other two senses is becoming obsolete. Reserve for bad debts and reserve for depreciation are examples of contra accounts; terms such as "allowance for bad debts" or "accumulated depreciation" are now preferred. A *liability reserve* refers to an obligation whose existence is definite but whose amount is uncertain at the time the balance sheet is prepared. Reserve for income taxes is an example. This title is being superseded in practice by terms such as "estimated income tax liability" or "provision for income taxes."

UNINCORPORATED BUSINESSES

Not much more need be said about the owner's equity accounts in a single proprietorship than the brief comments made in Chapter 2. There may be a single account in which all entries affecting the owner's equity are recorded, or a separate "drawing" account may be set up to handle periodic withdrawals made by the owner. If the latter, the drawing account may either be closed into the capital account at the end of the accounting period, or it may be kept separate so as to show the owner's original contribution of capital separate from the effect on his equity of subsequent events. As far as the ultimate effect is concerned, it is immaterial whether the owner regards his withdrawals as salary or as a return of profit, but if he wishes to compare his income statement with that of a corporation, he will undoubtedly treat a certain part of his withdrawals as salary (although in a corporation that is managed by its owners, the distinction between salary and dividends may also be quite fuzzy in practice).

A partnership has the problem of showing in the accounts the equity of the individual partners, and this varies depending on the terms of the partnership agreement. The accounts are set up to facilitate the computation of each partner's equity, in accordance with whatever the agreement may be. In the absence of a specific agreement, the law assumes that net income is to be divided equally among the partners, and this is also common in written partnership agreements. If such is the case, in a three-man partnership the capital account, or the drawing account, of each partner is credited with one third of net income and debited with the actual amount of his withdrawals.

If the agreement is that profits are to be divided in proportion to the capital originally contributed by each partner, then the capital account is maintained to show the amount of that contribution, and other transactions affecting the partners' equity are debited or credited to separate drawings or personal accounts. If one of the partners made a temporary loan to the partnership, it would be shown in a liability account (but separate from loans made by outside parties) rather than in the partner's equity account.

Partnership agreements may also provide that the partners receive stated salaries and a stated share of residual profits after salaries, or a stated percentage of interest on the capital they invested and a stated share of residual profits, or a combination of salary and interest. The accounting required in connection with such arrangements depends on the specific terms of the agreement.

Whatever the partnership arrangement, the law does not regard salaries or interest payments to the partners as being different from any other type of withdrawal since the partnership is not an entity legally separate from the individual partners. Neither does the partnership as such ordinarily pay a federal income tax; the income of the partnership, regardless of whether it has been withdrawn, is taxable income to the individual partners. A partnership can, however, elect to be taxed as if it were a corporation, and certain small corporations can elect to be taxed as partnerships; special rules apply in these cases.

CONSOLIDATED FINANCIAL STATEMENTS

A "company," as it is thought of by its management, its employees, its competitors, and the general public, may actually consist of a number of different corporations, created for various legal, tax, and financial reasons. The existence of a family of corporations is by no means peculiar to "big business." A fairly small enterprise may consist of one corporation that owns the real estate and buildings, another that primarily handles production, another for marketing activities, and over them all a *parent* corporation which is the locus of management and control. Each of these corporations is a legal entity, and each therefore has its own financial statements. The "company" itself may not be a separate legal entity, but it is an important *business* entity, and a set of financial statements for the whole business enterprise may be more useful than the statements of the separate corporations of which it consists.

Such statements are called *consolidated financial statements.* They are prepared by first adjusting and then combining the financial statements of the separate corporations; usually, no separate journals or ledgers are kept for the consolidated entity.

Basis for Consolidation

The legal tie that binds the other corporations, or *subsidiaries,* to the parent is the ownership of their stock. Although the parent can control a subsidiary with less than 50 per cent ownership if the other owners do not act in concert, as a matter of practice a subsidiary is not consolidated unless more than 50 per cent of its common stock is owned by the parent; some companies use an even higher percentage as the criterion.

Even though it is 100 per cent owned by the parent, a subsidiary may not be consolidated if its business is so different from that of the other companies in the family that including it in the consolidation would result in financial statements that do not well describe the family as a whole. General Motors Corporation does not consolidate the statements of General Motors Acceptance Corporation with those of its other corporations because GMAC is a huge financial corporation dealing principally in installment payments on automobiles, and its assets and liabilities are quite unlike those of an industrial company. Many companies do not consolidate their foreign subsidiaries.

Consolidation Procedure

Illustration 8–2 shows the consolidation process in the simplest possible situation, consisting of the parent company and one subsidiary company, named "Parent" and "Subsidiary," respectively. Parent owns 100 per cent of Subsidiary's stock; this is an asset which is shown on its balance sheet as Investment in Subsidiary. The investment is recorded at cost, and it is assumed here that Parent purchased Subsidiary's stock at its book value as of the time of acquisition.

In the illustration, the separate balance sheets of Parent and Subsidiary are given in the first two columns. The "combined" balance sheet in the third column is simply the sum of the figures in the first two columns. This combined balance sheet contains some items which, so far as the consolidated entity is concerned, are counted twice, and the effect of this double counting is eliminated by the adjustments made in the next two columns and explained below. Essentially, these adjustments eliminate the effect of transactions that have occurred between the two

Illustration 8–2

CONSOLIDATION WORK SHEET

| | Separate Statements | | Com-bined | Eliminations | | Consoli-dated Balance Sheet |
	Parent	Sub-sidiary		Dr.	Cr.	
Debit Balances						
Accounts receivable......	40,000	11,000	51,000		(1) 5,000	46,000
Inventory...............	30,000	15,000	45,000		(2) 1,000	44,000
Other current assets......	45,000	12,000	57,000			57,000
Fixed assets, gross.......	405,000	65,000	470,000			470,000
Investment in Subsidiary	55,000		55,000		(3) 55,000	
	575,000	103,000	678,000			617,000
Credit Balances						
Accumulated depreciation	160,000	20,000	180,000			180,000
Accounts payable........	20,000	13,000	33,000	(1) 5,000		28,000
Other current liabilities	25,000	9,000	34,000			34,000
Long-term liabilities.....	100,000		100,000			100,000
Capital stock...........	100,000	40,000	140,000	(3) 40,000		100,000
Retained earnings........	170,000	21,000	191,000	(2) 1,000		175,000
				(3) 15,000		
	575,000	103,000	678,000			617,000

corporations as separate legal entities. Since the consolidated financial statements should report only assets owned by the consolidated entity and the equities of parties *outside* the consolidated entity, these internal transactions must be eliminated. The consolidated balance sheet that results from these adjustments appears in the last column. The adjustments are as follows:

1. *Intercompany Financial Transactions.* The consolidated balance sheet must show as accounts receivable and accounts payable only amounts owed by and owed to parties outside the consolidated business; therefore, amounts that the companies owe to one another must be eliminated. Assuming that Parent owes Subsidiary $5,000, this amount is eliminated from Accounts Payable and Accounts Receivable. The effect is as in the following journal entry (although it should be remembered that no journal entries actually are made in the books of either corporation):

Accounts Payable...5,000
     Accounts Receivable..   5,000

Interest on intercompany loans would also be eliminated in a similar manner.

The payment of dividends by the subsidiary to the parent is a financial transaction that has no effect on the consolidated entity. In the separate statements, this was recorded on Parent's books as a credit to Other Income (which was closed to Parent's Retained Earnings), and on Subsidiary's books as a debit to Dividends (which was closed to Subsidiary's Retained Earnings). Since this transaction affected only the two retained earnings accounts, overstating one and understating the other, the act of combining the two of them automatically eliminated its effect; therefore, no further adjustment is necessary.

2. *Intercompany Profit.* In accordance with the realization principle, the consolidated company does not earn revenue until sales are made to the outside world. The revenue, the related costs, and the resulting profit for sales made between companies in the consolidated entity must therefore be eliminated from the consolidated accounts.

The sales and cost of sales on intercompany transactions are subtracted from the total sales and cost of sales figures on the consolidated income statement; if this were not done, the figures would overstate the volume of business done by the consolidated entity with the outside world. In order to do this, records must be kept that show both the sales revenue and the cost of sales of shipments made within the family.

On the balance sheet, these intercompany transactions may affect the Inventory account of the company receiving the goods and the Retained Earnings account of the company selling them, and adjustments to these accounts are required. Assume that during 1963 Subsidiary shipped products with a sales value of $60,000 to Parent. During the year, Parent sold three fourths of these products to outside customers, and the other one fourth remains in Parent's inventory at the end of the year at its cost to Parent of $15,000. The products sold to the outside world present no problem since they have disappeared from inventory and since the revenue has been realized. If these products were sold by Parent for more than $45,000, the excess will wind up in Parent's Retained Earnings as profit. When Parent's Retained Earnings is added to Subsidiary's Retained Earnings, the total profit on this part of the transaction will be included, and properly so.

The $15,000 remaining in Parent's inventory, however, is regarded by Subsidiary as a sale, the profit on which appears in Subsidiary's Retained Earnings. This portion of the profit must be eliminated from the consolidated balance sheet. This is done by reducing Retained Earnings and Inventory by the amount of the profit, assumed to be $1,000 as in the following entry:

```
Retained Earnings.................................................1,000
    Inventory....................................................        1,000
```

3. *Elimination of the Investment.* The Parent company's investment in the Subsidiary's stock is strictly an intrafamily matter and must therefore be eliminated from the consolidated balance sheet. Since it is assumed here that the stock was purchased at book value, the $55,000 cost shown on Parent's books must have equaled Subsidiary's Capital Stock plus Retained Earnings at the time of purchase. We know that Capital Stock is $40,000, and the difference, $15,000, must therefore equal the balance of Retained Earnings at that time. The additional amount of retained earnings now shown on Subsidiary's books has been created subsequent to the acquisition by Parent. To eliminate the investment, therefore, the entry in effect is as follows:

```
Capital Stock...................................................40,000
Retained Earnings..............................................15,000
      Investment in Subsidiary.....................................        55,000
```

The necessary eliminations having been recorded, the figures for the consolidated balance sheet can now be obtained by carrying each line across the page.

In the preceding example, two of the most difficult problems in preparing consolidated statements did not arise because of simplifying assumptions that were made. These problems are described below.

Asset Valuation

In the example, it was assumed that Parent purchased Subsidiary's stock at its book value. Quite often, a subsidiary's stock is purchased at a figure other than its book value. Under these circumstances, the first step is to examine the value of Subsidiary's underlying assets; if their fair value differs from the amount at which they appear in Subsidiary's accounts, the accounts are adjusted to show the fair value, but not to exceed the purchase price. If after this revaluation, book value is still less than the price paid for the stock, the difference appears on the consolidated statement as Goodwill.[3] In the above illustration, if Parent had paid $65,000, rather than $55,000, for Subsidiary's stock, and if Subsidiary's assets were found to be recorded at their fair value, there would be goodwill of $10,000, and the adjustment marked (3) above would have been:

```
Goodwill.......................................................10,000
Capital Stock...................................................40,000
Retained Earnings..............................................15,000
      Investment in Subsidiary.....................................        65,000
```

---

[3] The accounts are adjusted in this manner if one company purchases the stock of another in a true parent-subsidiary relationship. If, however, there is a *pooling of interests*, in which two companies of roughly equal importance merge forces, the assets of the two companies are carried to the new entity at their book value without adjustment.

Minority Interest

In the illustration above, it was assumed that Parent owned 100 per cent of the stock of Subsidiary. If, instead, it owned less than 100 per cent, the *minority interest,* which is the equity of the other owners in Subsidiary's assets, would appear as an equity item on the consolidated balance sheet. In measuring this equity, the matter of intercompany profits discussed in the second entry above raises a problem to which there is no completely satisfactory answer. From the standpoint of the minority stockholders of Subsidiary, products sold to Parent result in realized income, while from the standpoint of the consolidated entity these same products result in income only when they are sold to an outside party. This problem is often solved by eliminating the intercompany profit from the minority interest. In other words, the adjustment to inventory described in the item marked (2) above would still be $1,000. Such a solution results in some understatement of the equity of the minority owners, but an attempt to show their equity correctly would inevitably result in an offsetting distortion of either the inventory or the retained earnings items on the consolidated balance sheet.

If in the above illustration, Parent purchased only 80 per cent of Subsidiary's stock at book value of $44,000, adjustment (3) to eliminate the investment would be 80 per cent of the figures given above, or—

Capital Stock	32,000	
Retained Earnings	12,000	
Investment in Subsidiary		44,000

The remaining 20 per cent of Subsidiary's Capital Stock plus 20 per cent of Subsidiary's Retained Earnings after the elimination of intercompany profits would be set up as the equity of the minority interest on the consolidated statement, as follows:

Capital Stock	8,000	
Retained Earnings	4,000	
Minority Interest		12,000

Retained Earnings on the consolidated balance sheet would then be $174,000. The minority interest, $12,000, would appear just above the owners' equity section.

Concluding Comment

The preceding brief discussion of consolidated statements is by no means adequate as a basis for actually preparing consolidated financial statements. A great many problems in addition to those discussed above arise in practice. The illustration given does, however, indicate the main types of problems and the principles applied in solving them, and thus should help the user, as distinguished from the preparer, in understanding how the figures on a consolidated statement were derived.

SUMMARY

Long-term equities consist, in general, of bonds and owners' equity.

The liability arising from the sale of bonds is shown at its face amount, and the difference between this amount and the net proceeds received is recorded as bond premium or discount. Premium or discount is amortized over the life of the issue. This amortization is combined with the periodic interest payments to give the effective interest expense of each period.

In a corporation, owners' equity is represented by capital stock and surplus, the latter in turn consisting of retained earnings and capital surplus. Capital stock is shown on the balance sheet at the stated value of the shares outstanding, and differences between this amount and the net proceeds received from shareholders appears as capital surplus. In unincorporated businesses, the distinction between the original contribution of capital and subsequent changes in owners' equity may or may not be set forth on the balance sheet.

A business may consist of more than one corporation. If so, consolidated financial statements are prepared for the whole enterprise as a single entity. This is done by eliminating the effect of intercompany transactions from the accounts of the separate corporations and then combining them.

SUGGESTIONS FOR FURTHER READING

BACKER, MORTON (ed.). *Handbook of Modern Accounting Theory,* chaps. xiii, xiv, xv. New York: Prentice-Hall, Inc., 1955.

PATON, WILLIAM A., AND PATON, WILLIAM A. JR. *Corporation Accounts and Statements.* New York: The Macmillan Co., 1955.

WELSCH, GLENN A.; ZLATKOVICH, CHARLES T.; AND WHITE, JOHN ARCH. *Intermediate Accounting,* chaps. xv and xvi. Homewood, Ill.: Richard D. Irwin, Inc., 1963.

WIXON, RUFUS (ed.). *Accountants Handbook.* New York: The Ronald Press Co., 1960.

CASE

CASE 8–1. RICHARD D. BREW AND COMPANY, INCORPORATED[4]

In order to retire funded debt and to provide funds for additional plant, equipment, working capital, and research, Richard D. Brew and Company, Incorporated, offered for sale 70,000 shares of $1 par value common stock in July 1959. The offering price to the public was $9.00 a share, from which an underwriting discount of $0.90 a share would be deducted, leaving $8.10 a share as proceeds to the company. Expenses in connection with the offering estimated at $16,900 also were to be borne by the company. Financial statements are shown in Exhibits 1 and 2.

The Brew Company started operations in 1946. It was engaged in research, design, development, and manufacture in the general area of applying advanced physics to military and civilian needs. Among its products were high-precision delay lines, used in missiles, in radar, and in electronic computers; and high-vacuum, ultra-high temperature electric furnaces used for processing certain rare metals used in missiles.

The balance sheet of May 31, 1959, reported 9,300 shares of no-par value common stock outstanding with a stated value of $112,664. Of this amount, $12,664 resulted from owners' equity transactions occurring prior to 1958. During the year 1958 the company transferred $100,000 from retained earnings to capital stock. In 1958 also, the company split the 310 shares of stock then outstanding on the basis of 30 for 1 and increased its authorized capital from 1,000 to 10,000 shares.

In 1959, concurrently with the sale of stock, the company again changed its capitalization. The common stock was changed from no-par to $1 par value, the number of authorized shares was increased to 500,000, and the number of shares outstanding (not counting the sale of additional stock) was increased from 9,300 to 310,000 by means of a 33⅓ for 1 split.

In its prospectus the company stated that it planned to use the proceeds of the stock issue as follows:

Of the net proceeds (estimated at approximately $550,000 after the deduction of expenses) from the sales by the Company of 70,000 shares of its Common Stock to the Underwriters, approximately $106,000 will be used to discharge the Company's outstanding short term Bank Notes, Second and Third Mortgage

---

[4] Information in this case was obtained from the company's prospectus.

Exhibit 1

RICHARD D. BREW AND COMPANY, INCORPORATED

Condensed Balance Sheet, May 31, 1959

ASSETS

Current Assets:

Cash...		$ 24,580
Accounts receivable, net................................		78,150
Inventories, at lower of cost or market:		
Raw materials and supplies............................	$ 13,107	
Work in process.....................................	289,168	302,275
Prepaid expenses......................................		2,223
Total Current Assets...............................		$407,228
Property, plant, and equipment, at cost......................	$366,531	
Less: Accumulated depreciation.........................	123,493	243,038
Other assets..		3,468
Total Assets.....................................		$653,734

LIABILITIES AND STOCKHOLDERS' EQUITY

Current Liabilities:

Notes payable—banks.................................		$ 66,000
Current maturities of long-term debt......................		5,994
Accounts payable......................................		205,671
Accrued liabilities....................................		22,133
Federal income taxes..................................		17,600
Total Current Liabilities..........................		$317,398

Long-Term Debt:

4½% first-mortgage note, payable monthly to May 1974........	$100,000	
6% second-mortgage note, payable monthly to December 1969...	15,046	
6% third-mortgage note, payable monthly to May 1974.........	18,411	
5% land mortgage.....................................	6,525	
	$139,982	
Less: Principal payments due within one year..............	5,994	133,988

Stockholders' Equity:

Common stock, no-par value, authorized 10,000 shares, issued and outstanding 9,300 shares................................	$112,664	
Retained earnings (exclusive of amounts transferred to capital)...	89,684	202,348
Total Liabilities and Stockholders' Equity..............		$653,734

Notes and Land Mortgage. The borrowings evidenced by the Bank Notes were made to reimburse the Company's treasury for part of the funds spent for additions to the Company's plant facilities, substantially completed as of June 1, 1959, and for additional machinery and equipment related thereto, and to provide working capital.

It is presently contemplated that out of the balance of such proceeds approximately $25,000 will be expended for further equipment in connection with current expansion and for costs of rearrangement and moving of machinery and equipment.

It is likewise contemplated that an amount not yet definite (but currently estimated at not less than $75,000) will be applied to defray the cost of additional plant and equipment for expansion of the Company's Vacuum Furnace Division.

Exhibit 2

RICHARD D. BREW AND COMPANY, INCORPORATED
Summary of Earnings and Retained Earnings

	Year Ended December 31					Five Months Ended May 31	
	1954	1955	1956	1957	1958	1958	1959
Net sales.............	$375,697	$412,416	$443,538	$969,883	$1,178,897	$465,152	$367,900
Operating costs and expenses:							
Cost of sales.........	$250,499	$282,095	$344,206	$658,931	$ 836,042	$289,299	$323,567
Selling, administrative, and general..	46,115	65,755	116,426	181,351	221,387	90,876	106,474
Interest expense, principally on long-term debt.........	1,802	4,025	5,506	7,362	5,900	2,122	3,455
Income (loss) before federal income taxes...	$ 77,281	$ 60,541	$(22,600)	$122,239	$ 115,568	$ 82,855	$(65,596)
Provision for federal income taxes.........	32,646	26,275	(11,476)	58,691	55,000	41,100	(34,100)
Net income (loss)......	$ 44,635	$ 34,266	$(11,124)	$ 63,548	$ 60,568	$ 41,755	$(31,496)
Retained earnings at beginning of period...	29,287	73,922	108,188	97,064	160,612	160,612	121,180
	$ 73,922	$108,188	$ 97,064	$160,612	$ 221,180	$202,367	$ 89,684
Transferred to capital stock.............					100,000		
Retained Earnings at Close of Period.....	$ 73,922	$108,188	$ 97,064	$160,612	$ 121,180	$202,367	$ 89,684

It is the intention of the Company to use $64,000 of the remainder to pay off the entire amount of short term bank borrowings made since June 15, 1959, for working capital requirements, approximately $36,000 of the remainder for current working capital requirements and the balance for an expanded program of research in delay lines, vacuum furnaces and related new products.

The additional common stock was offered to the public on July 28, 1959, and the issue was oversubscribed before that day was over.

Questions

1. Prepare journal entries to record the effect of the changes in capitalization made in 1958.

2. Prepare journal entries to record the effect of the change of capitalization and the sale of additional stock in 1959, including the entries (if any) for (a) the increase in the number of shares authorized, (b) the stock split, (c) the

change in capitalization from no-par to $1 par value, (*d*) the incurrence of $16,900 expenses, (*e*) the sale of the additional stock, and (*f*) the disposition of the $16,900 expenses.

3. Assuming that the proceeds were utilized as described in the prospectus, prepare journal entries to reflect (*a*) the retirement of debt, and (*b*) the acquisition of equipment and plant. Explain, without making journal entries, how the use of the proceeds for "an expanded program of research" will affect the financial statements.

4. What do you suppose was the reasoning behind these changes in the company's capital structure?

5. Assuming that the entire book value of the stock prior to 1958 represented cash contributions of the original stockholders (which is in fact not the case), how much would an original stockholder have gained if, on July 28, 1959, he sold the equivalent of one of his original shares?

Chapter 9

THE PRICE LEVEL PROBLEM

THE ACCOUNTANT measures the goods and services that enter into his calculation of net income essentially at their acquisition cost, that is, at the prices paid when these goods and services were originally acquired by the company. The economist, however, often measures cost not in terms of the price originally paid for the goods and services but rather in terms of "real prices"; that is, he adjusts acquisition prices to allow for changes in purchasing power or in the economic significance of the specific good or service. In periods when there are substantial changes in prices, such as the downward movement in the early 1930's or the inflationary movement which began in the 1940's, the difference between the accounting concept of income and the economist's concept of income can be substantial. In short, although accounting facts are measured in monetary terms, money is not a uniform measuring stick of value in periods of changing prices.

Several proposals have been advanced for changing the accounting basis of measuring costs, and three are described in this chapter. One of these, the Lifo method of inventory measurement, has become a generally accepted accounting principle and is also allowed for tax purposes. The second, depreciation on replacement cost, is not a generally accepted accounting principle in the United States. The third, price level adjustments, involves the preparation of supplementary financial statements rather than a change in the principles underlying the regular balance sheet and income statement. All are important to know about, partly because they are widely discussed, but primarily because they demonstrate, by contrast, some limitations of the figures developed under conventional principles.

THE LIFO METHOD

Lifo, which stands for "last-in, first-out," is a method of measuring inventory. In this method, inventory is costed *as if* the units most recently added to inventory (last-in) were the first units sold (first-out) *even though this is in fact not the case.* Ending inventory is therefore assumed to consist of the older units and is measured at the cost of these older units. If the number of physical units in inventory remains constant from period to period, the accounting measurement of the inventory will also remain constant, regardless of what happens to the market replacement price of the inventory items. It follows that under the Lifo method, cost of goods sold tends to reflect the cost of the items most recently purchased.

The Lifo inventory method normally does not reflect the physical flow of material, nor do its advocates claim that it has any relation to physical flow. Physically, material would be expected to move out of inventory on approximately a Fifo, or first-in, first-out, basis; that is, the oldest stocks would normally be used up first. Advocates of Lifo contend, however, that in certain industries Lifo does match the *economic* flow of values since, they claim, the profit margin that actually influences business pricing decisions is the margin between sales prices and *current* costs, not the margin between sales prices and cost levels that existed at the time inventory was purchased. If this contention is correct, the conventional Fifo system results in the reporting of false "inventory profits" during periods of rising cost prices since during these periods goods are sold at sales prices commensurate with current costs, while cost of goods sold reflects earlier, lower costs rather than current costs. (Lifo only *approximates* current costs since it shows the cost of *most recent* purchases, and this is not necessarily the same as current cost.)

A frequently used example of what is meant by this economic flow is the following excerpt from the Report of the Special Committee on Inventories of the AICPA (1936), a report which had much to do with the adoption of Lifo as a generally accepted principle:

> A wagon maker has a wagon in stock which cost him $50, the selling price of which is $65 to yield him his desired profit of $15 per wagon. Before he sells the wagon he learns from the concern supplying him with his material of a price increase, the result of which is to make the reproduction cost of his wagon $60. By reason of this knowledge the wagon maker "marks up" his wagon to $75, at which figure he sells it for cash and builds a new wagon costing him $60. The net change resulting from the whole transaction is that his till shows $15 more cash than he had before.
>
> Now the advocate of "reproduction cost of sales" says to the wagon maker:
>
> The profit you made is $15, and the proper inventory price for the present wagon you have in stock is $50. That is the number of dollars of your capital invested in your stock-in-trade; the only change that you have effectively realized in that investment is the substitution of one wagon for another exactly like it —the same wagon, in fact, except only as regards physical identity.
>
> On the other hand, the advocate of "first-in, first-out" says to the wagon maker: Your profit is $25, although you may have only $15 more in cash to show

for it. The other $10 is contained in the increased cost and value of the new wagon—$60 as against the old one at $50. You must not fail to recognize and to give effect to the price level change.

Considering the other side of the problem, let us assume that after the above transaction the price level reverted to its original status, thus consummating the economic cycle; accordingly the wagon at present in stock, which actually had cost $60 to build (but was inventoried at either $50 or $60, according to the procedure followed) is sold for $65 and replaced in stock by one which cost $50 to build. Now, under either procedure the latest wagon will be inventoried at $50. The profit on the second transaction, however, will have been $15 according to the "reproduction cost of sales" advocate, or $5 according to the "first-in, first-out" advocate. The aggregate profit on the two transactions, of course, will be the same in either case, but the periodic distribution will differ.

The "false profit" argument implies that an underlying objective of Lifo is to postpone the recognition of income until the cost factors used have been replaced; that is, one virtue of the Lifo method is its tendency to limit the amount of reported net profits to an amount which might be made available to stockholders without impairing the scope and intensity of the operations of a going concern. Advocates also argue that such restrictions in reported income serve to conserve funds by reducing income taxes.

Opponents of Lifo, while recognizing that it is not good management policy to regard funds needed to maintain the level of operations as representing disposable income, attack the Lifo argument on the grounds that it confuses two distinct processes, the measurement of income, and the utilization of income. They argue that income may be realized and valid even though such income is to be subsequently invested in inventories or other assets. They also point out that the Lifo method falls short of achieving the underlying objective in that costs of only the most recent acquisitions are charged against revenue rather than the total cost of replacing all the items sold.

No one argues that Lifo is applicable to every company; rather it is recommended only when there is a definite relationship between selling price and *current* cost. For example, if a retailer sets his selling price by adding a fixed markup to the invoice cost of specific units of merchandise, and if he usually can sell the merchandise at this price, his profit is based not on replacement cost but rather on his invoice cost, and he should not use the Lifo system. If, on the other hand, he finds it necessary or possible to change his retail prices as soon as, or shortly after, a change in wholesale prices occurs, his cost may be considered to be the replacement or Lifo cost.

A close correspondence between changes in selling prices and changes in current costs may reflect a general change in the value of money in the economy. If this is the case, it is argued that it makes little sense to state the revenue component of profit at the current value of the dollar while stating the principal expense component, cost of goods sold, in terms of a different kind of dollar. On the other hand, if the facts are that in a particular company the profit margin has really changed, for reasons having nothing to do with fluctuations in price levels, the use of Lifo may conceal such changes.

In addition to companies whose selling prices are related to invoice costs rather than to current costs, Lifo is also not appropriate for companies which eliminate inventory profits by the practice called "hedging," nor for companies which are in the business of speculating on price changes, as are certain companies that trade in grain and other commodities.

The relative importance of inventory profits varies among companies, and Lifo has a more important influence on profits when—

1. Material cost constitutes a relatively large part of total cost.
2. The inventory is relatively large.
3. The manufacturing process is relatively long (which is a variation of No. 2 because a long manufacturing process means a large work in process inventory).

Example

Illustration 9–1 illustrates the effect of the Lifo method on profit and on inventory valuation, as contrasted with the Fifo method. The situation illustrated is the simplest possible, namely, where—

1. Selling price is immediately and exactly adjusted for changes in material cost.
2. There is no change in inventory quantity, that is, as soon as a unit is sold, it is replaced in inventory by another unit.
3. Sales *volume* each year is constant (at 1,000 units), hence purchases are also constant.
4. One hundred per cent of the product cost is material cost.
5. Inventory turnover is 1; that is, inventory consists of 1,000 units.

In the example prices are assumed to go through a complete cycle; that is, they rise and then fall back to the starting point. The following points can be noted from these calculations: (1) There is no difference in total profits under Lifo and under Fifo over the complete cycle. (2) Under the conventional Fifo method profits are high in years of high prices and low in years of low prices, even though the quantity sold and the margin between selling price and current material cost remains constant; also inventory values fluctuate widely, and inventory is at its

Illustration 9–1

GROSS PROFIT CALCULATION UNDER FIFO AND LIFO

	(1) Inventory, January 1	(2) Purchases	(3) Inventory, December 31	(4) Cost of Sales*	(5) Sales†	(6) Gross Profit
		UNDER FIFO				
19X1.............	1,000 at $1.00	1,000 at $1.00	1,000 at $1.00	$1,000	$2,000	$1,000
19X2.............	1,000 at 1.00	1,000 at 1.50	1,000 at 1.50	1,000	2,500	1,500
19X3.............	1,000 at 1.50	1,000 at 2.00	1,000 at 2.00	1,500	3,000	1,500
19X4.............	1,000 at 2.00	1,000 at 0.50	1,000 at 0.50	2,000	1,500	(500)
19X5.............	1,000 at 0.50	1,000 at 1.00	1,000 at 1.00	500	2,000	1,500
				Total Five-Year Profit		$5,000
		UNDER LIFO				
19X1.............	1,000 at $1.00	1,000 at $1.00	1,000 at $1.00	$1,000	$2,000	$1,000
19X2.............	1,000 at 1.00	1,000 at 1.50	1,000 at 1.00	1,500	2,500	1,000
19X3.............	1,000 at 1.00	1,000 at 2.00	1,000 at 1.00	2,000	3,000	1,000
19X4.............	1,000 at 1.00	1,000 at 0.50	1,000 at 1.00	500	1,500	1,000
19X5.............	1,000 at 1.00	1,000 at 1.00	1,000 at 1.00	1,000	2,000	1,000
				Total Five-Year Profit		$5,000

* Beginning inventory, plus purchases, less ending inventory, each being assumed in this example to be 1,000 units. With an inventory turnover of 1, cost of sales under Fifo will equal the value of the beginning inventory, since it is assumed that the units sold were the oldest units on hand and equal in units to purchases. Under Lifo, cost of sales will equal the value of purchases, since it is assumed that the units sold were the units most recently purchased.
† 1,000 units times sales price per unit, which is assumed to be the current purchase price +$1.

highest price at the very top of the cycle. (3) Under the Lifo method, profit and inventory values are the same in each year; in one year 19X4, inventory was valued at more than "market."

Basic Arguments

A more generalized argument in favor of Lifo goes beyond the limitation of exact agreement of cost and selling price, as was presumed in the example given above. The real issue, from this point of view, is whether or not the company has properly counted its current costs against its current revenue in figuring profit. In periods of rising prices the company does have increased costs in maintaining its inventory position, and current sales should be charged with a cost of goods sold that reflects these current costs. To do otherwise, this argument runs, is to count a cost as a profit and to pay stiff taxes on the amounts so reported.

This broader view of Lifo looks on inventory as a necessary stock in trade, just as essential to operations as are plant or facilities. Accordingly, such an investment ought *not* to be revalued on the balance sheet with every cyclical swing of prices any more than plant is revalued. As

Illustration 9–1 demonstrates, the Lifo method tends to stabilize both profits and the reported value of inventory as prices change.

Opponents of Lifo argue that one of management's primary responsibilities is effective utilization of the economic resources at its disposal. They admit that over sustained periods of price level changes, conventional accounting fails to reflect the economic values of such resources as plant and inventory, but they claim that Lifo confuses, rather than clarifies, the picture. Under Lifo, inventory is valued forever in terms of whatever the price level happened to be at the time Lifo was introduced. As time goes on and price levels change, the inventory figure under Lifo departs further and further from reality, becoming neither a reflection of actual purchase costs nor of current costs. Thus Lifo may make the inventory figure on the balance sheet of dubious usefulness to management or to others who attempt to appraise the financial status of the business.

Advocates of Lifo are thinking primarily of its effect on the income statement and are willing to accept the fact that the usefulness of the balance sheet inventory figure may be impaired. Opponents of Lifo emphasize its effect on the balance sheet; they admit that the conventional Fifo income statement may not reflect the flow of economic values, although they do not grant that this is necessarily bad.

Dollar Value Method

Originally, Lifo was used only by companies whose inventory consisted of fungible products, such as wheat, each unit of which is physically like every other unit. Other companies, however, argued that this was unfair to them, and Lifo may now be used for almost any kind of inventory. It is applied to an inventory of physically unlike items by the so-called *Lifo dollar value method.* In this method, items whose prices tend to move together are grouped into an *inventory pool.* A pool may consist of all the items in the hardware department of a department store, for example, or it may consist of a company's entire inventory. The dollar amount invested in such a pool is treated as a unit in figuring the Lifo inventory value and cost of goods sold, and changes in the value of the dollar during the accounting period are allowed for by the application of index numbers of price changes.

As an illustration, assume that the beginning inventory in a pool had an actual invoice cost of $780,000, and that the inventory at the end of the year had an actual invoice cost of $880,000. Without additional information, we do not know how much of the $100,000 increase in the amount of inventory represents an increase in the *physical size* of the inventory and how much results from the same quantity being valued at a higher price because of inflation. By the use of an index number of price changes, the change associated with size can be separated from the change associated with price movements. Thus, if an appropriate price index increased from 100 at the beginning of the year to 110 at the end of the year, the year-end inventory can be *deflated* to the beginning price level by multiplying it by the ratio of the index change, or $100/110$. The value of the ending inventory expressed in beginning prices is therefore $100/110$ of $880,000, or $800,000. Since $800,000 exceeds the beginning inventory of $780,000 by $20,000, we estimate that the physical size of the inventory has increased by $20,000 during the year. This $20,000 is expressed in beginning prices, however, and under the Lifo method it must be added to inventory at the most recent prices, so it is *reinflated* by multiplying by the ratio $110/100$, to give $22,-000. The ending inventory thus is valued at the beginning inventory, $780,000, plus the increase in physical inventory, $22,000, a total of $802,000. Cost of goods sold is then found by the deduction formula —beginning inventory, plus purchases, less ending inventory—which results in a difference of $78,000 between the invoice cost and the Lifo cost of ending inventory going into cost of goods sold.

In applying the dollar value method, department stores use price indexes especially computed for this purpose by the government. Other companies compute their own index from the movement of prices of all, or a sample of, items in inventory.

Decreases in Inventory

When the physical size of the inventory increases, in a Lifo system the inventory account is increased by the current cost of the units added. During a period of growth, the inventory account will therefore consist of a number of *layers,* a new layer being added each year. If subsequently the physical inventory should decrease in size, these layers in effect are stripped off, taking the most recently added layer first, in accordance with the basic Lifo rule. This process can have a peculiar effect on the income statement. If, for example, inventory is decreased even below its original size when the Lifo system started, inventory items will be moving into cost of goods sold at costs established several years previously; and if there has been constant inflation during the interim, such a shrinkage in inventory can result in a significant increase in reported income. Some people assert that in the recession year of 1958 some companies deliberately ate into their Lifo inventories in order to increase reported income in a lean year.

Variations

In applying the general idea of Lifo to a particular situation, several alternatives are possible:

1. Lifo may be applied to all inventories, or only to the raw materials inventory, or only to certain items in inventory.
2. Products may be run through the cost accounting mechanism at Lifo values, or the detailed cost records may show Fifo or specific invoice values, with an adjustment to Lifo being made only at the end of the accounting period.
3. Inventory changes may be calculated annually, or monthly, or even daily.

Usually the differences in results between the several methods of applying Lifo are small compared with the basic difference between Lifo and Fifo, but the fact that these differences in the application of Lifo exist is one reason why Lifo is criticized. Opponents argue that Lifo itself violates the fundamental doctrine of "consistency," since it makes it difficult to compare the earnings of a company that uses Lifo with the earnings of a company that uses Fifo; variations within the general Lifo idea make "confusion worse confounded."

Tax Considerations

A company that wishes to use Lifo for income tax purposes must make application to do so, and once having been granted permission, it must continue to use Lifo thereafter unless it receives special permission to change again; such permission is not easily obtained.

If the company uses Lifo for tax purposes, it must also use Lifo in its annual financial statements (although not necessarily in monthly or quarterly statements). Incidentally, this is the only instance of a statutory requirement that the same method be used for financial accounting purposes as is used for tax purposes.

A company using Lifo cannot use the "lower of cost or market" rule for tax purposes; that is, it cannot write down its inventory to market if market values are below Lifo cost. On its financial statements, however, the company is permitted to show a write-down to market.

Although it is easy to calculate whether or not tax savings will result in the year in which Lifo is adopted, it is impossible to determine whether the net effect over a number of years will be a savings or not. The existence and amount of any future tax savings depends largely upon future price movements, fluctuations in tax rates applicable to the business, and variations in the amounts and kinds of physical inventories held at the end of each taxable year. Although over a period of years total income computed under either the Lifo or Fifo method may be the same, it does not follow that total income taxes will also be the same. Generally, total income taxes tend to be greater under Fifo than under Lifo if the following conditions exist: if income is taxed progressively, if undistributed profits or excess profits taxes exist, if income tax rates are higher in years of rising prices than in years of falling prices, or if there is no provision for carry-back of losses. There is a permanent deferment of taxes, of course, if prices continue upward indefinitely; that is, if inflation is always with us. Although tax savings under Lifo are likely in periods of rising prices, they are by no means certain if prices are near their peak when the change to Lifo is made, for tax losses after prices begin to fall may be greater than the initial tax savings when prices were rising.

Base Stock Method

Another method of recognizing the impact of price changes on inventory, the *base stock method,* actually antedates Lifo in practice. It accomplishes approximately the same result as the Lifo method and indeed reflects current costs more closely than Lifo, but since its use is not permitted for tax purposes, it has not become widely adopted.

DEPRECIATION ON REPLACEMENT COST

Since the fixed assets of a company may have been purchased at various times extending many years into the past, price fluctuations cause the expense and asset balances associated with these items to deviate even farther from current cost than is the case with inventory. The American Appraisal Company index of construction costs has almost quadrupled in the period from 1940 to 1963, and it doubled in the period from 1946 to 1963. This means that a dollar spent on construction in 1963 would buy only about half as many physical units of assets as a dollar spent in 1946, or that a 1963 dollar is a "50-cent dollar" in terms of its 1946 purchasing power.

Conventional accounting does not differentiate between 50-cent dollars and 100-cent dollars. If a company, for example, purchased a 80,000 square-foot factory building for $500,000 in 1946, this building, exclusive of accumulated depreciation, would appear on the balance sheet at $500,000; and if the building was replaced with a physically identical 80,000 square-foot factory building for $1,000,000 in 1963, this would appear at $1,000,000. Although the balance sheet figure for the new building is double that of the old, the company actually has the same amount of factory space as it had before.

Moreover, the annual depreciation charge for fixed assets, being based on the actual cost of the asset, is not expressed in the same kind of dollars as the revenue item on the income statement. In periods of inflation, depreciation expressed in past dollars of relatively high purchasing power is matched against revenue expressed in current dollars of relatively low purchasing power.

Although the depreciation mechanism charges off the cost of the asset over its useful life, it does not, and is not designed to, provide for the replacement of the asset. Suppose, for example, that a company actually set aside a cash fund equal to its depreciation charge, paying out all its net income as dividends. Some might believe that a company could operate indefinitely on such a plan, using this fund to buy new assets as the old assets required replacement. If prices were steady this would be possible, but in periods of inflation the replacement fund could not purchase the same quantity of assets as those discarded, and the company would gradually shrink and eventually disappear.

The impact of income taxes increases the severity of the replacement problem. If the company recognizes the inadequacy of depreciation as a replacement medium and tries to earn additional income to add to its "replacement fund," it must earn $2.00 of income before taxes for every $1.00 it wishes to put into a fund; at a 50 per cent rate the other $1.00 will be siphoned off in taxes.

Replacement Cost Proposal

In view of these problems, some people argue that depreciation should be calculated on the estimated replacement cost of an asset rather than on its original cost. The most famous attempt to do this is that of the United States Steel Corporation in the 1940's, described in Case 9–3. This attempt did not succeed in obtaining either a change in accounting principles or a change in income tax regulations. The discussion has by no means ended, however. In a 1958 Survey by the AICPA, it was reported that 74 per cent of the respondents favored changes in accounting practices so as to reflect current dollar costs for depreciation when reporting to stockholders, compared with only 34 per cent favoring such a change in 1948. At every session of Congress, numerous proposals are made for a similar change in the income tax rules.

A change to a replacement cost basis of figuring depreciation would imply an extremely fundamental change in the concepts of accounting since it would represent a breaking away from the basic idea that balance sheet and expense amounts are based on monetary cost, and not on purchasing power or economic values. Even the Lifo inventory method uses monetary costs as obtained from actual transactions. The advantages of the cost basis of measurement—certainty, uniformity of interpretation, objectivity—have been discussed in earlier chapters. The question is whether an accounting system based on the attempt to measure the existence and flow of economic values has additional advantages that more than offset these.

A further question is whether assets should in fact be replaced by funds generated by current operations. Should selling prices be high enough so that net income will provide for both an adequate profit and the replacement of assets? Or should selling prices only provide for profits plus recovery of the costs actually incurred? Stated another way: Who should pay for the future machines, the current customers or the future customers who buy products made on the future machines? If operations do not generate enough funds for replacement, it is argued, the difference can and should be raised through borrowing or issuing new stock.

A more complete statement of the arguments for and against depreciation based on replacement cost will be found in the United States Steel Corporation case.

Calculating depreciation on replacement cost is to be distinguished from *accelerated depreciation,* such as the double declining-balance or sum-of-years'-digits methods. Accelerated depreciation does mitigate somewhat the income tax problem discussed above since it permits depreciation to be written off faster than under the straight-line method, but accelerated depreciation is nevertheless restricted to actual cost. A replacement cost mechanism would, in periods of inflation, write off as expense *more than* the actual monetary cost of the asset.

PRICE LEVEL ADJUSTMENTS

In studies sponsored by the AICPA, by the American Accounting Association, and by a few university groups, procedures have been devised for expressing each item on the balance sheet and the income statement in dollars that have the same purchasing power.[1] Usually, these procedures are advocated as a supplement to, not a replacement of, the conventional procedures. In other words, the conventional statements would continue to be the "official" reports, and the adjusted statements would be given separately.

The process of making such adjustments is a fairly long and

---

[1] The pioneering effort is that of H. W. Sweeney, *Stabilized Accounting* (New York: Harper & Bros., 1936).

complicated one, and it requires information as to the approximate date on which each asset was acquired, which usually involves considerable searching of old records. Essentially, an index number of prices is selected and each item is converted to current prices by multiplying its original cost by the ratio of the current price index to the index value at date of acquisition. (The best index for this purpose is probably the "Gross National Product Implicit Price Deflator," prepared by the U.S. Department of Commerce.) Thus, if an asset were purchased when the index was 100, and currently the index is 200, the dollar amount of the asset value would be doubled. If this were a depreciable asset, depreciation would be recalculated on the basis of the doubled amount.

In a period of inflation, the effect of these adjustments is to increase the book value of the assets and to decrease the reported income for the year. The decrease in income results primarily from the increased depreciation charge but also from upward adjustments in other expense items. The Reece Corporation has for several years reported the difference between net income computed on a "historical dollars" or conventional basis and on a "uniform dollars" basis. In its 1957 annual report, management pointed out that although on the conventional basis net income for 1956 was the largest ever reported in the company's 76 years of existence, on a uniform dollars basis 1956 net income was actually less than that of 1955. Its 1961 annual report showed net income as 225 per cent of that in 1943 when reported on a conventional basis, but only 130 per cent of 1943 on a uniform dollar basis.

Advocates of the price level adjustment process point to this shrinkage of income as a measure of how much the company may be fooling itself by relying on conventional accounting as a measure of economic progress. Those who do not prepare these adjusted statements say that they are not in fact misled; they can recognize the approximate impact of price level changes without going through all the calculations. In any event, only a very few companies actually recast their statements along these lines.

Instead of adjusting all items, some accountants advocate that only depreciation expense be adjusted for changes in prices. Such a procedure would not give the same end result as the calculation of depreciation based on replacement costs since the underlying procedures are different. In both cases, however, the adjustment grows out of a desire to recognize the effect of inflationary forces on the accounts.

The AICPA Study

In April 1961 the Accounting Principles Board of AICPA took the action summarized in the following excerpt from its minutes:

. . . the Board . . . agreed that the assumption in accounting that fluctuations in the value of the dollar may be ignored is unrealistic, and that therefore the Director of Accounting Research should be instructed to set up a research project to study the problem and to prepare a report in which recommendations are made for the disclosure of the effect of price-level changes upon the financial statements. In this study, special attention should be paid to the use of supplementary statements as a means of disclosure.

The report on this research project, published in October 1963, is an excellent presentation of all facets of the problem.[2] Some of the "highlights" of this study are quoted below:

1. [There is] clear evidence of the widespread concern of businessmen and accountants with the need for changes in financial reporting to reflect the effects of inflation and deflation.

2. The examples quoted from financial statements around the world are sufficient to demonstrate that recognition of price-level changes in financial statements is practical, and not misleading or dangerous to investors.

3. The study of the index number problem indicates that at least one index of the general price level is available in the United States and is reliable enough for use in financial statements.

4. The effects of price-level changes should be disclosed as a supplement to the conventional statements. This disclosure may take the form of physically separate statements, or of parallel columns in a combined statement, or of detailed supporting schedules (including charts and graphs), or some combination of these.

5. In the supplementary data, all elements of the financial statements (e.g., balance sheet, income statement, analysis of retained earnings) should be re-stated by means of a single index of the general price level as of the balance-sheet date so that all the financial data will be expressed in terms of dollars of the same purchasing power.

It should be emphasized that publication of this Research Study does not constitute approval of the recommendations by the Accounting Principles Board. Currently (early 1964) the Board has this topic under consideration, but no action has yet been taken.

CONCLUSION

Of the techniques discussed in this chapter only Lifo is currently (1964) in accordance with generally accepted accounting principles. In fact, *either* Lifo or Fifo is acceptable, although they are completely

---

[2] AICPA Accounting Research Division, *Reporting the Financial Effects of Price-Level Changes* (Accounting Research Study No. 6) (New York, 1963). For earlier studies, see Ralph C. Jones, *Price Level Changes and Financial Statements* (American Accounting Association, 1955); Perry Mason, *Price-Level Changes and Financial Statements* (American Accounting Association, 1956).

inconsistent with one another. Depreciation on replacement costs may become accepted either as in accordance with accounting principles, as a basis of income taxation, or both, although acceptance seems less likely now than was the case in the 1950's. The overall adjustment of all financial statement items to current prices is likely to remain as a supplementary report rather than as a substitute for figures based on historical cost.

The brief description of the techniques and proposals given in this chapter is inadequate as a basis for reaching a sound judgment as to whether they should be generally adopted. In order to make such a decision, many more arguments and analyses need to be considered. The objective here is to point out the existence of these proposals so that the reader of accounting statements will recognize that conventional statements do not give recognition to the changing value of the monetary measuring stick, and so that he can have some appreciation of the significance of this fact on the information presented in the statements.

CASES

CASE 9–1.   R. J. REYNOLDS TOBACCO COMPANY[3]

In 1957 the R. J. Reynolds Tobacco Company adopted the Lifo basis of inventory valuation, with results as indicated by the following quotation from its annual report:

> During 1956 and prior years, inventories were valued on the average cost method. Effective for 1957, however, the Company adopted the last-in, first-out (LIFO) method of inventory valuation. By this method, the current costs of replacing materials used are more nearly reflected in determining earnings. In 1957, acquisitions of leaf tobacco were made at prices considerably higher than the average cost of tobacco in inventories at the beginning of the year. The effect of LIFO and related adjustments was to reduce earnings before income taxes by $26,897,049 and net earnings by $12,342,049. The resultant income tax saving for the year amounted to $14,555,000. Inventories at the year end were carried at $28,312,684 less than they would have been under the previous method.[4]

The reaction of investors to this change is indicated by the following quotation from the *Wall Street Journal* for February 3, 1958:

> Last week saw a brief wave of selling in the hitherto strong tobacco shares. It apparently grew out of the change by R. J. Reynolds Tobacco Co. to the "last-

---

[3] This case is based on published information.

[4] Note that the $26,897,049 was only 95 per cent of the $28,312,684 reduction in inventories. This is because 5 per cent of operating income in excess of a stated amount is set aside in a profit-sharing plan. The amount so set aside was reduced by $1,415,635 because of the reduction in operating income resulting from the shift to Lifo.

in-first-out" method of valuing inventories. Although this reduced reported earnings below what they would have been under the old system of accounting, it did not in any way cut Reynolds' real earnings or the company's ability to pay dividends. On the contrary, the change saved the company $14 million, or $1.40 a share, in cash by cutting the Federal income tax that much. Because of increased prices, the tobacco bought by Reynolds in 1957 cost $28 million more than the average cost of its three-year inventory, such as every tobacco company must maintain. Under the LIFO system, that extra cost was charged into the income account, reducing the pre-tax profit by that much. After taxes, it cut profit by $14 million, but it also cut the tax itself, at the 52% rate, by about the same amount. The LIFO system is expected to be put into force by the other tobacco companies. After the brief selling, the Street evidently saw it was unwarranted, because tobacco share prices recovered.

The 1958 Annual Report of Reynolds contains the following statement:

> During the second year of the Company's use of the LIFO method of inventory valuation, first adopted in 1957, acquisitions of both flue-cured and Burley tobaccos were made at prices higher than were paid in the previous year. The resulting LIFO adjustment enabled the Company to effect a further saving in income taxes estimated at $8,500,000. Thus, during the two years under LIFO, the Company has been able to conserve about $23,000,000 that otherwise would have been required for taxes. Inventories at the close of the year were carried at $45,031,770 less than they would have been under the previously used average cost method of inventory valuation.

In its 1959 report, the company reported that inventories at the end of 1959 were carried at $64,399,895 less than they would have been under the average cost method used prior to 1957.

Financial statements of R. J. Reynolds Tobacco Company are given in Exhibit 1. Financial statements of two of its principal competitors are given in Exhibits 2 and 3; these companies continued to use average cost in valuing inventories. These statements have been condensed and rearranged from those presented in the annual reports. Of total operating costs, approximately 50 per cent consists of excise taxes paid on finished products, approximately 25 per cent is tobacco, and approximately 25 per cent is all other manufacturing, selling, and administrative costs.

Inventory Values

Leaf tobacco is the most important element of cost in the manufacture of cigarettes and also the most volatile. Rising tobacco costs normally can be offset by higher prices, particularly since the average inventory method used results in only a gradual increase in tobacco costs charged to any one year's production.

Tobacco has to be aged before it is used in cigarettes, and the quality tends to vary from year to year. Hence, large inventories are needed.

Exhibit 1

R. J. REYNOLDS TOBACCO COMPANY

Financial Statements (000 Omitted)

Condensed Position Statements as of December 31

	1959	1958	1957	1956
ASSETS				
Current Assets:				
Cash	$ 27,109	$ 29,646	$ 26,142	$ 23,697
Accounts receivable, customers	44,530	36,990	33,910	30,155
Inventories (Note A)	684,507	594,905	586,540	557,247
Total Current Assets	$756,147	$661,542	$646,593	$611,100
Fixed and other assets	97,205	81,791	66,505	48,294
Total Assets	$853,352	$743,333	$713,097	$659,394
EQUITIES				
Current Liabilities:				
Notes and accounts payable	$179,656	$121,196	$106,460	$ 68,131
Federal and state taxes	87,619	75,002	63,744	71,202
Other current	10,470	9,984	9,780	8,231
Total Current Liabilities	$277,744	$206,182	$179,985	$147,564
Funded debt	92,000	98,000	104,000	110,000
Capital stock	136,640	139,260	168,040	169,542
Retained earnings	346,968	299,891	261,073	232,288
Total Equities	$853,352	$743,333	$713,097	$659,394

Statements of Earnings for Years Ended December 31

	1959	1958	1957	1956
Net sales	$1,286,856	$1,146,559	$1,053,326	$957,367
Cost of sales and other expenses	1,082,700	969,712	907,914	815,323
Operating profit	$ 204,156	$ 176,847	$ 145,412	$142,044
Other income and deductions, net	− 6,386	− 4,863	− 6,805	− 4,942
Income, before taxes	$ 197,770	$ 171,984	$ 138,607	$137,102
Taxes on income	107,412	93,658	74,446	75,190
Net earnings	$ 90,358	$ 78,326	$ 64,160	$ 61,913
Dividends*	43,280	39,248	35,375	33,470
Additions to Retained Earnings	$ 47,078	$ 39,078	$ 28,785	$ 28,443
Earnings per common share	$5.37	$4.68	$3.72	$3.76

Note A: Inventories at average cost in 1956 and Lifo thereafter.
* Includes preferred dividends of $1,281,000 in 1959, $2,282,000 in 1958, $2,657,000 in 1957, and $2,763,000 in 1956.
Details may not add to totals because of rounding.
Source: Annual reports.

Exhibit 2

THE AMERICAN TOBACCO COMPANY

Consolidated Financial Statements (000 Omitted)

Condensed Balance Sheets as of December 31

	1959	1958	1957	1956
ASSETS				
Current Assets:				
Cash..............................	$ 17,740	$ 20,696	$ 22,972	$ 23,418
Accounts receivable, customers..........	51,911	46,943	45,180	44,752
Leaf tobacco, at average cost..........	586,605	578,305	612,315⎫	655,116
Other inventories, at average cost.......	70,075	70,005	59,066⎭	
Other current assets..................	1,697	1,318	950	1,137
Total Current Assets..............	$728,028	$717,268	$740,483	$724,423
Fixed and other assets................	78,498	79,264	74,724	69,981
Total Assets...................	$806,526	$796,532	$815,207	$794,404
EQUITIES				
Current Liabilities:				
Notes and accounts payable............	$ 71,760	$ 81,211	$105,779	$ 93,984
Accrued taxes.......................	53,817	50,655	52,132	51,512
Other current.......................	14,826	11,313	13,227	12,347
Total Current Liabilities..........	$140,403	$143,179	$171,138	$157,842
Funded debt........................	150,653	165,402	179,330	193,188
Capital stock.......................	260,561	260,561	260,561	260,561
Retained earnings...................	254,908	227,390	204,178	182,813
Total Equities.................	$806,526	$796,532	$815,207	$794,404

Income Statements for Years Ended December 31

	1959	1958	1957	1956
Net sales..............................	$1,161,377	$1,105,176	$1,098,093	$1,091,206
Cost of sales and operating expenses.......	1,019,129	971,132	969,805	971,168
Operating profit.......................	$ 142,248	$ 134,044	$ 128,288	$ 120,039
Other income and deductions, net........	− 6,177	− 9,050	− 9,683	− 8,687
Income, before taxes....................	$ 136,071	$ 124,994	$ 118,605	$ 111,352
Taxes on income......................	72,823	66,138	61,510	59,663
Net income...........................	$ 63,248	$ 58,856	$ 57,095	$ 51,689
Dividends*............................	35,730	35,730	35,730	35,730
Additions to Retained Earnings...........	$ 27,518	$ 23,126	$ 21,365	$ 15,959
Earnings per common share..............	$9.23	$8.55	$8.28	$7.45

* Includes preferred dividends of $3,167,000 each year.
Details may not add to totals because of rounding.
Source: Annual reports.

Exhibit 3

LIGGETT & MYERS TOBACCO COMPANY

Consolidated Financial Statements (000 Omitted)

Condensed Balance Sheets as of December 31

	1959	1958	1957	1956
ASSETS				
Current Assets:				
Cash and government securities...............	$ 12,321	$ 4,459	$ 12,263	$ 11,635
Accounts receivable, customers...............	21,190	23,095	23,090	22,579
Leaf tobacco, at average cost.................	292,005	306,965	346,472	372,484
Other inventories, at average cost............	38,388	34,353	34,558	36,587
Other current assets........................	1,160	1,102	1,030	1,408
Total Current Assets.....................	$365,064	$369,974	$417,412	$444,693
Fixed and other assets......................	39,327	39,128	39,028	36,978
Total Assets..........................	$404,391	$409,103	$456,440	$481,671
EQUITIES				
Current Liabilities:				
Notes and accounts payable..................	$ 3,296	$ 7,576	$ 57,119	$ 82,469
Accrued taxes..............................	22,794	23,764	24,992	26,325
Other current liabilities.....................	6,817	5,581	6,930	6,977
Total Current Liabilities.................	$ 32,907	$ 36,921	$ 89,041	$115,771
Funded debt...............................	84,250	90,000	95,750	101,500
Capital stock..............................	138,066	138,453	138,111	138,111
Retained earnings..........................	149,169	143,729	133,538	126,290
Total Equities........................	$404,391	$409,103	$456,440	$481,671

Income Statements for Years Ended December 31

	1959	1958	1957	1956
Net sales.....................................	$554,936	$556,046	$570,385	$564,966
Cost of sales and operating expenses..............	488,216	485,935	506,027	503,923
Operating profit..............................	$ 66,720	$ 70,111	$ 64,358	$ 61,043
Other income and deductions, net...............	− 1,645	− 2,198	− 2,463	− 2,676
Income, before taxes...........................	$ 65,075	$ 67,913	$ 61,895	$ 58,367
Income and franchise taxes.....................	35,036	36,689	33,621	31,916
Net income...................................	$ 30,039	$ 31,223	$ 28,274	$ 26,451
Dividends*...................................	24,015	21,032	21,025	21,023
Additions to Retained Income..................	$ 6,024	$ 10,191	$ 7,249	$ 5,428
Earnings per common share....................	$7.28	$7.60	$6.85	$6.39

* Includes preferred stock dividends of $1,430,000 in 1959, $1,461,000 in 1958, 1957, and 1956.
Details may not add to totals because of rounding.
Source: Annual reports.

The low point of the year's inventory cycle falls in June or July, when the companies have on hand supplies sufficient for 14 to 18 months' production. Tobacco markets open around the end of July in Georgia, followed by a succession of market openings moving north through the following February. Based on estimates made in June, when the inventory is low, the companies purchase according to plan their estimated needs for the succeeding 30 months. The peak of inventory holdings is reached in February.

As the tobacco is purchased at the auctions, the cost for each grade is estimated, adjusting for the loss of weight in drying, stemming, and regrading. The inventory cost for each grade is adjusted to average in new purchases as made. When all purchases for a crop year are completed, costs are reviewed in the light of experience in loss of weight and regrading, and average inventory costs are established for the season for each grade.

It will be seen that the costs of new purchases have an immediate effect on inventory costs of leaf used in manufacture. But it is to be noted that a large factor in that average is the previously established costs of the tobacco in inventory at the start of the buying season, which in turn had been determined by a process of averaging with costs established in former years. Hence, while changing prices of leaf are reflected quickly in costs, the changes in costs are not fully commensurate with the changes in prices paid. In fact, the process of averaging from year-to-year permits the prices in any one year to influence costs over a long period.[5]

Questions

1. Recast the R. J. Reynolds financial statements for 1957 and 1958 to show how they would have appeared if the company had not shifted to Lifo.

2. As well as you can, compare the performance of the three companies in 1957, 1958, and 1959.

3. Do you agree with R. J. Reynolds' decision to adopt Lifo? Do you think its competitors should also adopt Lifo?

CASE 9–2.   THE MILLION DOLLAR LATHE[6]

Thompson Products, for the 18th year, has continued its custom of furnishing its employees with a simple concise report of its financial operations, showing how much money the company took in and what happened to it. The income for 1956 totaled $306,508,120. Expenses, not including wages, salaries or dividends, were $175,535,061, leaving $130,973,059 to be divided among employees and stockholders. Of this, $117,960,454 went for payrolls, $4,183,904 was paid out in dividends and $8,828,701 was plowed back into the business.

---

[5] Standard and Poor's Trade and Securities, *Tobacco*, Vol. CXXVII, No. 53, Sec. 1 (December 31, 1959), pp. 63–64.

[6] This case consists of a quotation taken from a report prepared by the management of a company for the information of its employees.

Why was it necessary to plow that much back into the business? The tale of the million-dollar turret lathe, included in the report, explains that. It seems that in 1942 the company bought a lathe for $12,000. Under federal tax laws, it was permitted to depreciate the cost of the lathe over a 14-year period. So, last year, when the lathe became obsolete, the company had $12,000 to buy a new one, plus $1,000, which was the resale value of the old one. But the replacement cost in 1956 was $35,000 for a lathe that would perform the same functions as the old model, or $67,000 for a new one with attachments to meet today's more exacting needs.

The company had only $13,000 to do a $67,000 job. The difference of $54,000 had to come out of profits, and in order to get that amount in 1956 the company had to earn a profit of more than $112,500 before taxes, because $54,000 was all there was left after the government took its corporate profit tax of 52%. And to earn that amount of profit, the company had to sell more than a million and a quarter dollars worth of products to customers. It took more than $1,250,000 of sales to buy just one machine!

Thus, while $112,500 sounds like a lot of profit, in this case, the stockholders got none of it. The government took more than half, and the rest went to replace a machine. This story is duplicated hundreds of times each year throughout the company in the case of machines, large and small. This is why only a relatively small amount of profit is paid to stockholders in dividends, and why a large portion must be retained to finance expansion and replacement so the company can continue to operate and employees can continue working.

Question

Comment on this statement. Is it the truth, the whole truth, and nothing but the truth?

CASE 9–3.   UNITED STATES STEEL CORPORATION[7]

For several years prior to 1946 the management of United States Steel Corporation had been concerned with the effects upon the company's capital replacement program of the steady rise in the general price level since the late 1930's. This concern, shared by a major segment of American business management, arose chiefly from the realization that the amounts being deducted from earnings to cover the depreciation and amortization of plant and equipment were not sufficient

---

[7] This case was developed primarily from published material.

to provide for the replacement of such facilities when they were worn out or became obsolete. The inadequacy of the amounts set aside could be traced directly to the fact that the costs of replacing capital goods had risen, along with the general price level, while the company's allowances for depreciation were still being made on the basis of the original cost of plant and equipment which had been acquired when the price level was markedly lower. Executives of U.S. Steel believed that if they failed to take action on this problem, they were not discharging one of the major responsibilities placed upon them by the company's stockholders—the responsibility for the preservation of the capital of the corporation.

The inadequacy of the depreciation allowance could have two main consequences: (1) it could lead to selling prices that were not high enough to permit the recovery, through the sales of its goods and services, of the real costs of wear and exhaustion of facilities used to provide those goods and services simply by making too small an allowance for, or completely omitting, that element in arriving at the true costs of its products; and (2) it could result in a misleading net profit figure which could be used as an argument for higher wages or dividend payments than actually were warranted by the company's condition. The management believed that unless price, wage, and dividend policies were predicated upon a full recognition of the need to replace worn-out plant and equipment, the company would be dissipating its capital in the course of its normal operations.

The 1947 Change

The abrupt upturn of prices following the relaxation of most government price controls in late 1946 and early 1947 brought into sharper focus than ever before the problem of providing for the replacement of worn-out facilities. The following table, based on virtually identical facilities acquired by U.S. Steel in 1940 and 1947, gives some indication of how costs had increased for specific items of equipment and types of construction during that seven-year period:

	Percentage Increase 1947 over 1940
Wire drawing machine	91
Standard electric crane	105
Reheating furnace	108
Blast furnace	105
By-product coke ovens	150
Mine locomotive	44
Large electric motor	50
Continuous rolling mill	84
Concrete construction	124
Brick construction	250

As a step toward stating depreciation in an amount which would recover in current dollars of diminished buying power the same purchasing power represented by the original plant expenditure, the company therefore deducted, in arriving at net income for 1947, an amount of $26,300,000 over and above its regular depreciation charge. Although the federal tax authorities would not allow the extra depreciation as a deduction in arriving at taxable income for that year, the company's executives considered it essential that they recognize this element of cost in arriving at a measure of income to be used in other matters of company management.

In its 1947 annual report the management stated that "while awaiting accounting and tax acceptance, U.S. Steel believed that it was prudent for it to give some recognition to increased replacement costs rather than to sit idly by and witness the unwitting liquidation of its business should inadequate recording of costs result in insufficient resources to supply the tools required for sustained production."

The additional depreciation charge was shown in the company's income statement as a separate item in the section under "Wear and Exhaustion of Facilities" and labeled, "Added to Cover Replacement Cost"; it was shown in the balance sheet, on the liability side, as "Reserve for Replacement of Properties." The sum of $26,300,000, which amounted to approximately 30 per cent of the regular depreciation based on original cost, was arrived at partly on the basis of cost increases actually experienced by the company and partly through study of construction cost index numbers (notably the *Engineering News-Record Index*). The management pointed out that, although the amount was actually much less than that which could be substantiated by actual cost increases, it was all that was deemed appropriate in view of the newness of the application of such a method of computing depreciation.

Reaction to the Change

The company's independent auditors took exception to this practice. They stated in their report to the stockholders for 1947 that the corporation had included in costs additional depreciation of $26,300,000 "in excess of the amount determined in accordance with the generally accepted accounting principle heretofore followed of making provision for depreciation on the original cost of facilities."

Opinion among professional economists and accountants on depreciation during an extended period of rising prices was divided. U.S. Steel drew support for its position from economist Sumner H. Slichter:

An enterprise which expects to continue in business must obviously replace its plant and equipment as they wear out. If it distributes in the form of dividends, higher wages, or lower prices, income needed to replace plant and equipment, the enterprise is, in effect, living off its capital, because it will have to bring in new capital to maintain its productive capacity. In other words, only after management has set aside enough of current income to maintain the productive capacity of the enterprise, does it have funds which may be properly regarded as available for dividends, higher wages, or lower prices.[8]

Carman G. Blough, director of research, AICPA, recognized the need for consideration of the problem of plant replacement by management, but he disagreed as to the accounting treatment that should be prescribed:

There can be no argument but that a going concern must be able to replace its productive assets as they are used up if it is to continue to do business. It is also important for management to understand that the difference between cost and estimated replacement value may be significant in determining production and pricing policies. It does not follow, however, that the excess of the cost of replacement over the cost of existing assets should be accounted for as current charges to income. All who have dealt with appraisal values know how very difficult it is just to determine current replacement costs, but the most striking difficulty in this respect is the impossibility of predicting what will be the eventual cost of replacing a productive asset. How many men are prepared to state what the price level will be two years from today, to say nothing of trying to guess what it will be five or ten years hence when many of these assets are to be replaced?[9]

The AICPA Committee on Accounting Procedure issued, in late 1947, *Accounting Research Bulletin No. 33*, in which it stated that it disapproved "immediate write downs of plant cost by charges against current income in amounts believed to represent excessive or abnormal costs occasioned by current price levels." (See Appendix A for a fuller statement of the committee's view.)

The Securities and Exchange Commission, in its 1949 *Annual Report*, formally stated the position which it had already indicated informally that it would take on the question of depreciation during periods of rising prices:

The conclusion reached was that depreciation charges in financial statements filed with the Commission should continue to be based upon cost. Revisions of financial statements on file have been made in accordance with this conclusion. In some cases accounting recognition had been given to the high rates of production enjoyed in postwar years by accelerating depreciation charges in periods

---

[8] From testimony presented before the Joint Committee on the Economic Report of the President, Washington, D.C., December 6, 1948.

[9] "Replacement and Excess Construction Costs," *The Journal of Accountancy*, Vol. LXXXIV (October 1947), p. 335.

during which productive capacity was used in excess of normal average production over a representative period of years. Similarly, the amortization of plant costs incurred to capture a temporarily expanded demand was deemed to comply with the generally applicable accounting principle of matching cost with revenues. In such cases a clear explanation of the circumstances justifying the early amortization of costs has been obtained.

The 1948 Retreat

United States Steel Corporation continued through the first three quarters of 1948 its practice of charging additional depreciation to cover higher costs of replacing worn-out facilities, and in view of the continued increase in the cost of facilities during 1948, advanced the additional charge from 30 per cent to 60 per cent of the depreciation based on original cost.

In the release of its quarterly statements for the third quarter of 1948, however, the company stated that, in view of the position taken by the AICPA and the discussions between the corporation and the Securities and Exchange Commission, further study was being made in an effort to agree upon principles satisfactory to the commission for "determining and reflecting additional wear and exhaustion cost."

In its annual report for 1948 U.S. Steel announced that it was abandoning the policy adopted in 1947 of charging to costs an amount over and above the regular depreciation on original cost and was substituting in its place a method of charging "accelerated depreciation on cost." The following quotation from the notes to the financial statements in the 1948 annual report provides a brief description of the formula to be used in determining the amount of annual charge for accelerated depreciation:

> The accelerated depreciation is applicable to the cost of postwar facilities in the first few years of their lives when economic usefulness is greatest. The amount thereof is related to the excess of current operating rates over U.S. Steel's long-term peacetime average rate of 70% of capacity. The annual accelerated amount is 10% of the cost of facilities in the year in which the expenditures are made and 10% in the succeeding year, except that this amount is reduced ratably as the operating rate may drop, no acceleration being made at 70% or lower operations. The accelerated depreciation is an addition to the normal depreciation on such facilities, but the total depreciation over their expected lives will not exceed the cost of the facilities.

This method was made retroactive to January 1, 1947, and there was included, in the $55,335,444 deducted for accelerated wear and exhaustion of facilities for 1948, an amount of $2,675,094 to cover a deficiency in the $26,300,000 sum reported in 1947 as "depreciation added to cover replacement cost." In other words, the new method when applied to the 1947 situation resulted in a deduction that exceeded the figure actually reported in 1947. It was again pointed out at this time that the accelerated depreciation was not "presently deductible for federal income tax purposes."

Reactions to the 1948 Change

The company's independent auditors apparently interpreted the concept of accelerated depreciation as being within the AICPA standards as a "systematic basis related to economic usefulness" (see Appendix A); for they stated in their report to the stockholders for 1948 that they "approved" the new policy.

The management's convictions on the change in policy were, however, clearly set forth by the chairman of the board of directors in the following quotation from the company's annual report for 1948:

> U.S. Steel believes that the principle which it adopted in 1947 and continued in 1948, is a proper recording of the wear and exhaustion of its facilities in terms of current dollars as distinguished from the dollars which it originally expended for those facilities. However, in view of the disagreement existing among accountants, both public and private, and the stated position of the American Institute of [Certified Public] Accountants, which is supported by the Securities and Exchange Commission, that the only accepted accounting principle for determining depreciation is that which is related to the actual number of dollars spent for facilities, regardless of when or of what buying power, U.S. Steel has adopted a method of accelerated depreciation based on cost instead of one based on purchasing power recovery.

Subsequent Developments

United States Steel Corporation continued its policy of charging accelerated depreciation through 1952. Deductions for accelerated depreciation for 1947 through 1952 totaled slightly more than $201 million; none of this sum, however, had been allowed in computing taxable income during that period.

In its annual report for 1952 the company commented that "so long as depreciation that is deductible for tax purposes is measured by the relatively smaller number of dollars of greater buying power expended in an earlier period, it will be inadequate to recover the original purchasing power invested in the facilities consumed in production. Real wear and exhaustion costs are thus understated, real profits are overstated, and there results an erosion of capital through taxation."

Subsequent to 1952, the corporation apparently did not charge depreciation expense in its accounts in excess of that allowed for tax purposes. Sizable amounts of "Certificate of Necessity" amortization, which is a type of rapid write-off permitted for tax purposes on new assets essential for National Defense, gave an equivalent type of deduction.

The company's 1960 Annual Report contains the following comment:

> . . . Past and prospective dollar debasement is now a continuing—and often overriding—concern of business and government. It intrudes upon, complicates and warps all business, saving, investing, wage and tax decisions. It has introduced immeasurable injustice.

*   *   *   *   *

> Illustrative of the seriousness of these matters are the facts of U.S. Steel. For the post-war years, 1946–1960, U.S. Steel's recorded wear and exhaustion— sometimes called depreciation—aggregated $2,872 million. Of this amount, $2,671 million was deductible in determining taxable income. If, each year, depreciation had been sufficient to recover the appropriate *buying* power—not just the number—of dollars originally expended, the total would have been $4,276 million. The deficiency from this amount needed to stay even was $1,605 million, on which taxes were levied as though it were income. Tax destruction to the flow of dollars that maintains the nation's tools of production in their status quo not only darkens the prospect that new jobs will be created by productive investment; it threatens continuation of existing jobs. It directly handicaps all corporations heavily invested in long-life facilities. It indirectly handicaps all other enterprises who do business with them as their capabilities as customer or supplier are undermined.
>
> In former times when the tax rate on corporate income was smaller and inflation was not a big factor, these same injustices and impediments to growth were present but not of as great moment. But with the enormous increases in the tax rate until it is now over 50 per cent—some *three* times the pre-war rates— they are indeed worthy of most serious consideration and correction if we are to have economic growth.[10]

In 1962 the company adopted the new life guideline procedure set forth by the Internal Revenue Service in Procedure 62–21. This added $44 million to the wear and exhaustion amount as previously determined. The use of the investment credit provision in 1962 also resulted in a reduction in federal income tax of $8.2 million. The company's comment with respect to the effect of these provisions on depreciation allowances was:

> The guideline procedure and the investment credit against federal income tax are recognitions of the vital depreciation problem that exists. They serve currently to lift total wear and exhaustion to an amount more nearly approaching true depreciation based on current dollars. However, they fall short in dealing

[10] U.S. Steel Annual Report, 1960, pp. 27, 28, 29.

with the fundamental facility replacement problem arising from inflation since total depreciation over the lives of the facilities is still limited to original cost.[11]

Income tax provisions relating to depreciation are described briefly in Appendix B.

Questions

1. Do you agree with the corporation's handling of depreciation in its 1947 report? Should a company be prohibited from using such a method if in its own best judgment this is the best method?

2. The depreciation charge under the accelerated depreciation method adopted in 1948 actually exceeded the depreciation charge under the 1947 method. Why then should not the corporation prefer the 1948 method?

3. Should companies generally be either permitted or required to take depreciation on replacement cost in their financial statements?

APPENDIX A

Excerpt from Accounting Research Bulletin No. 43

*   *   *   *   *

3. Accounting Research Bulletin No. 33 read as follows:

4. "The American Institute of Accountants committee on accounting procedure has given extensive consideration to the problem of making adequate provision for the replacement of plant facilities in view of recent sharp increases in the price level. The problem requires consideration of charges against current income for depreciation of facilities acquired at lower price levels.

5. "The committee recognizes that business management has the responsibility of providing for replacement of plant and machinery. It also recognizes that, in reporting profits today, the cost of material and labor is reflected in terms of 'inflated' dollars while the cost of productive facilities in which capital was invested at a lower price level is reflected in terms of dollars whose purchasing power was much greater. There is no doubt that in considering depreciation in connection with product costs, prices, and business policies, management must take into consideration the probability that plant and machinery will have to be replaced at costs much greater than those of the facilities now in use.

6. "When there are gross discrepancies between the cost and current values of productive facilities, the committee believes that it is entirely proper for management to make annual appropriations of net income or surplus in contemplation of replacement of such facilities at higher price levels.

7. "It has been suggested in some quarters that the problem be met by increasing depreciation charges against current income. The committee does not believe that this is a satisfactory solution at this time. It believes that accounting and financial reporting for general use will best serve their purposes by adhering to the generally accepted concept of depreciation on cost, at least until the dollar is stabilized at some level. An attempt to recognize current prices in providing

---

[11] *Ibid.*, p. 5.

depreciation, to be consistent, would require the serious step of formally recording appraised current values for all properties, and continuous and consistent
depreciation charges based on the new values. Without such formal steps, there
would be no objective standard by which to judge the propriety of the amounts
of depreciation charges against current income, and the significance of recorded
amounts of profit might be seriously impaired.

8. "It would not increase the usefulness of reported corporate income figures if some companies charged depreciation on appraised values while others
adhered to cost. The committee believes, therefore, that consideration of radical
changes in accepted accounting procedure should not be undertaken, at least until a stable price level would make it practicable for business as a whole to make
the change at the same time.

9. "The committee disapproves immediate write-downs of plant cost by
charges against current income in amounts believed to represent excessive or
abnormal costs occasioned by current price levels. However, the committee calls
attention to the fact that plants expected to have less than normal useful life can
properly be depreciated on a systematic basis related to economic usefulness."

10. The letter of October 14, 1948, was addressed to the members of the
Institute and read as follows:

11. "The committee on accounting procedure has reached the conclusion
that no basic change in the accounting treatment of depreciation of plant and
equipment is practicable or desirable under present conditions to meet the problem created by the decline in the purchasing power of the dollar.

12. "The committee has given intensive study to this problem and has examined and discussed various suggestions which have been made to meet it. It
has solicited and considered hundreds of opinions on this subject expressed by
businessmen, bankers, economists, labor leaders, and others. While there are
differences of opinion, the prevailing sentiment in these groups is against any
basic change in present accounting procedures. The committee believes that such
a change would confuse readers of financial statements and nullify many of the
gains that have been made toward clearer presentation of corporate finances.

13. "Should inflation proceed so far that original dollar costs lose their practical significance, it might become necessary to restate all assets in terms of the
depreciated currency, as has been done in some countries. But it does not seem
to the committee that such action should be recommended now if financial statements are to have maximum usefulness to the greatest number of users.

14. "The committee, therefore, reaffirms the opinion it expressed in Accounting Research Bulletin No. 33, December, 1947.

15. "Any basic change in the accounting treatment of depreciation should
await further study of the nature and concept of business income.

16. "The immediate problem can and should be met by financial management. The committee recognizes that the common forms of financial statements
may permit misunderstanding as to the amount which a corporation has available
for distribution in the form of dividends, higher wages, or lower prices for the
company's products. When prices have risen appreciably since original investments in plant and facilities were made, a substantial proportion of net income
as currently reported must be reinvested in the business in order to maintain
assets at the same level of productivity at the end of a year as at the beginning.

17. "Stockholders, employees, and the general public should be informed that

a business must be able to retain out of profits amounts sufficient to replace productive facilities at current prices if it is to stay in business. The committee therefore gives its full support to the use of supplementary financial schedules, explanations or footnotes by which management may explain the need for retention of earnings."

Six members of the committee, Messrs. Andrews, Peloubet, Peoples, Smith, Wellington, and Williams, dissented to adoption of section (a) of chapter 9.

The six dissenting members object to the reprinting, in this section, of Bulletin No. 33 of December, 1947, and the reaffirming letter of October 14, 1948. That bulletin was issued to check the extention of certain then-emerging practices and it was successful in that purpose. However, Bulletin No. 33 contains assertions which are not now appropriate and should be eliminated, notably:

(a) "An attempt to recognize current prices in providing depreciation . . . would require the serious step of formally recording appraised current values . . . and consistent depreciation charges based on the new values" (par. 7 of this section).

Those dissenting believe this is not the only method which may be followed—a conclusion also reached by the Study Group on Business Income (see page 61 of its report).*

(b) ". . . consideration of radical changes in accepted accounting procedure should not be undertaken, at least until a stable price level would make it practicable for business as a whole to make the change at the same time" (par. 8).

This statement virtually precludes changes in accounting practice in so far as the monetary unit is concerned and is inconsistent with the paragraphs on Accounting and the Corporate System in the introduction to this volume.

(c) The warnings (in paragraphs 5, 6, 16 and 17) to management as to the use of profits.

Such warnings are irrelevant; it is no part of the accountant's function to tell management what it may or may not properly do with income after it has been determined.

Those dissenting believe that acceptable accounting practices should comprehend financial statements to stockholders, employees, and the public designed to reflect those concepts of cost and net income which are recommended in paragraph 5 to management in determining product costs, prices, and business policies. They question whether net income can properly be so designated if appropriations therefrom, as suggested in paragraph 6, are needed to preserve capital invested in plant.

They believe that plant may continue to be carried in the balance sheet at historical cost with deduction for depreciation based thereon. In addition to historical depreciation, a supplementary annual charge to income should be permitted with corresponding credit to an account for property replacements and

---

* Study Group on Business Inome, *Changing Concepts of Business Income*, New York: The Macmillan Co., 1952. 160 pp.

substitutions, to be classified with the stockholders' equity. This supplementary charge should be in such amount as to make the total charge for depreciation express in current dollars the exhaustion of plant allocable to the period. The supplementary charge would be calculated by use of a generally accepted price index applied to the expenditures in the years when the plant was acquired. The last sentence of paragraph 7 would then be no longer valid; the usefulness of financial statements would be enhanced without sacrifice of presently existing comparability.

APPENDIX B

Excerpts from 1954 Internal Revenue Code[12]

Sec. 167. Depreciation

(a) *General Rule.*—There shall be allowed as a depreciation deduction a reasonable allowance for the exhaustion, wear and tear (including a reasonable allowance for obsolescence)—

(1) of property used in the trade or business, or

(2) of property held for the production of income.

(b) *Use of Certain Methods and Rates.*—For taxable years ending after December 31, 1953, the term "reasonable allowance" as used in subsection (a) shall include (but shall not be limited to) an allowance computed in accordance with regulations prescribed by the Secretary or his delegate, under any of the following methods:

(1) the straight line method,

(2) the declining balance method, using a rate not exceeding twice the rate which would have been used had the annual allowance been computed under the method described in paragraph (1).

(3) the sum of the years-digits method, and

(4) any other consistent method productive of an annual allowance which, when added to all allowances for the period commencing with the taxpayer's use of the property and including the taxable year, does not, during the first two-thirds of the useful life of the property, exceed the total of such allowances which would have been used had such allowances been computed under the method described in paragraph (2).

Nothing in this subsection shall be construed to limit or reduce an allowance otherwise allowable under subsection (a).

(c) *Limitations on Use of Certain Methods and Rates.*—Paragraphs (2), (3), and (4) of subsection (b) shall apply only in the case of property (other than intangible property) described in subsection (a) with a useful life of 3 years or more—

(1) the construction, reconstruction or erection of which is completed after December 31, 1953, and then only to that portion of the basis which is properly attributable to such construction, reconstruction, or erection after December 31, 1953, or

(2) acquired after December 31, 1953, if the original use of such property commences with the taxpayer and commences after such date.

---

[12] These excerpts were not changed by the Revenue Act of 1964.

(d) *Agreement as to Useful Life on Which Depreciation Rate Is Based.*— Where, under regulations prescribed by the Secretary or his delegate, the taxpayer and the Secretary or his delegate have, after the date of enactment of this title, entered into an agreement in writing specifically dealing with the useful life and rate of depreciation of any property, the rate so agreed upon shall be binding on both the taxpayer and the Secretary in the absence of facts or circumstances not taken into consideration in the adoption of such agreement. The responsibility of establishing the existence of such facts and circumstances shall rest with the party initiating the modification. Any change in the agreed rate and useful life specified in the agreement shall not be effective for taxable years before the taxable year in which notice in writing by registered mail is served by the party to the agreement initiating such change.

(e) *Change in Method.*—In the absence of an agreement under subsection (d) containing a provision to the contrary, a taxpayer may at any time elect in accordance with regulations prescribed by the Secretary or his delegate to change from the method of depreciation described in subsection (b) (2) to the method described in subsection (b) (1).

*   *   *   *   *

Note: Sec. 167(f), 1011, and 1012 provide that depreciation is to be based on the "cost of such property."

CASE 9–4.   R. L. BOGGS

According to the terms of his grandfather's will, R. L. Boggs received a bequest of $50,000. At the time of his grandfather's death, the general index of prices was 100. It rose rapidly while the estate was being settled, however, and had reached 120 when Boggs actually received the money. Since he felt that the inflationary rise in prices was likely to continue, he borrowed $30,000 for one year at 6 per cent with the intention of keeping most of the $80,000 fund invested in common stocks. His transactions during the ensuing year were as follows:

1. He bought common stocks for $75,000 when the price index was 125.
2. Later when the index was 133⅓, he sold for $30,000 stocks which had originally cost $25,000.
3. While the index was 133⅓, he received dividends of $6,000.
4. He bought additional common stocks for $40,000 when the price index was 150.
5. Near the end of the year the price index rose to 180 and remained steady for several weeks. Strong anti-inflationary measures were being prepared by the government, and some steps to curb the rapidly rising price level had already been taken. Because of this, Boggs sold his entire portfolio of common stocks for $100,000, paid off the $30,000 note with interest, and invested the entire fund (except the amount required to pay the income tax) in tax-exempt state bonds purchased to yield 3 per cent per annum.

Questions

1. Mr. Boggs asks you to analyze the results of his financial and investment policies in order to determine the net gains and losses in terms of purchasing power during the settlement of the estate and during the full year between the receipt of the cash and the purchase of the state bonds. Assume, for simplicity. that Mr. Boggs is subject to a flat 25 per cent tax on all income and capital gains. He is particularly anxious to learn where and why the real gains and losses occurred. It is suggested that the end-of-year dollar (price index 180) be taken as the basic unit of measurement.

2. Mr. Boggs also asks you to show how the results of a second year will compare with those of the first in terms of purchasing power if the price index falls to 150 within six months and remains there for the rest of the year. All this, of course, is entirely prospective, but he wants to know, nevertheless, how the book and real gains and losses on the state bonds under the assumed conditions would compare with the results obtained by investing in common stocks during the year just ended.

Chapter 10

THE SIGNIFICANCE OF ACCOUNTING PRINCIPLES

OUR DESCRIPTION of the basic concepts, principles, conventions, and procedures of accounting having been completed, the student will find it useful at this point to think back over the material discussed, both in the text and in the cases, and to decide for himself what it all adds up to. The material in the present chapter is intended to facilitate such a review.

THE BASIC CONCEPTS

All the basic concepts of accounting were listed in Chapters 2 and 3. In the succeeding chapters, many conventions and procedures were described, but these are amplifications and applications of, rather than additions to, the basic concepts. As a matter of convention, for example, accumulated depreciation is shown in a separate account rather than being credited directly to the asset account, but the basic idea of depreciation accounting is nevertheless in accordance with the concepts that assets are recorded at cost and costs are matched against revenue in the period benefited.

Any conceivable transaction, provided that it is clearly described, can be analyzed in terms of its effect on the assets and equities of the business in accordance with the basic accounting concepts. An extremely large fraction of the transactions are simple: debit Cash and credit Sales; debit Accounts Receivable and credit Cash; and so on. For the minority of complicated or difficult transactions, the student has perhaps worked out his own method of attack. One useful approach is to relate the transaction wherever possible to Cash. Does part of the transaction involve a cash receipt or disbursement or an analagous change in some other asset? If so, the debit or credit portion is obvious, and the remaining problem is to find other accounts which are affected and to arrange the figures so that debits equal credits.

Misconceptions about Concepts

Some of the basic concepts are intuitively sensible: for example, the idea that accounting data are expressed in monetary terms. Certain

257

concepts, however, are rather different from the impression that the typical layman has about them. As Professor Walter F. Frese puts it:

> . . . Generally, the character of accounting is not fully understood either by the people who use it as a means of communicating the results of operations for which they are responsible (business managers) or by people to whom such results are communicated (stockholders, investors, labor, general management and others). Those at both ends of this communication process often believe that somewhere in the middle the accountant, through application of mysterious specialized techniques, can translate the facts and judgments underlying business transactions into quantitative terms, predigest them, and come out at the end of the process with figures which precisely measure the results of business operations.[1]

Undoubtedly the greatest misconception on the part of laymen relates to the cost concept. To the layman, it seems only reasonable that the accountant should report the *value* of assets, what they are really worth, rather than merely to trace the flow of costs. The layman finds it difficult to believe that the balance sheet is not, even approximately, a statement showing what the business is worth, especially when he sees on many balance sheets an item labeled "net worth." And even if he eventually recognizes that the balance sheet does not in fact report values, he criticizes accounting and accountants for adhering to such a concept.

The root of the layman's difficulty is his failure to appreciate the importance of the criteria of objectivity and feasibility. A balance sheet that set forth the real value of the assets would of course be more useful to the reader than a balance sheet based on cost. But there simply is no objective and feasible way of ascertaining true values under most circumstances. A reasonable estimate of the value of the assets could be made only by the management, but the financial statements are supposed to be reports of management's stewardship. To base them on management's own estimates would be equivalent to letting the batter call his own balls and strikes. The accountant traces the acquisition and expiration of assets in terms of cost, which can be done with reasonable objectivity; he does not attempt to guess at fluctuations in real values.

A related misconception is the layman's failure to appreciate the significance of the going-concern concept. If one accepts the idea that the productive assets are held not for sale but rather for their future usefulness, then one sees that there is no necessity for determining the current sales value of these assets.

The layman also finds the accrual concept—the matching of costs

---

[1] Walter F. Frese, in the Foreword to *Contemporary Accounting Problems* by Leonard Morrissey (Englewood Cliffs, N.J.: Prentice-Hall, Inc., 1963).

and revenues—a difficult one to comprehend. In his personal life, he knows that when he makes an expenditure to the grocer, to the service station, and so on, he is that much "out of pocket." He has difficulty in understanding the fact that many business expenditures are merely the exchange of one asset for another, with the business getting as much as it gives up. Expenses occur in the time period when costs expire—when they are used up—and this time period is not necessarily the same as the time period in which the expenditure is made.

Those who do understand the basic concepts do not necessarily agree with all of them. The accounting profession is constantly involved in debates over one or another of the currently accepted principles. Since they are not laws of nature, they are subject to a change, and occasionally they are changed. At the same time, the *user* of accounting information must do the best he can with the situation as it exists. He may wish that the principles were different, but as he reads an accounting report he needs to know how it *was* prepared, not how it might have been prepared.

LIMITATIONS OF ACCOUNTING

Although the person who understands the basic concepts of accounting can make an acceptable record of any accounting transaction, this knowledge does not, unfortunately, equip him fully to understand the financial statements prepared by others. The rules governing the preparation of financial statements vary considerably from one company to another, for at least three reasons: (1) there is no general agreement as to what the principles are; (2) not everyone applies even those principles which are generally agreed to; and (3) principles are not applied uniformly.

Absence of a Complete Set of Principles

The most authoritative source of accounting principles is the Accounting Principles Board of the American Institute of Certified Public Accountants. Its pronouncements have been relied on heavily in the preceding chapters. (The Securities and Exchange Commission also makes authoritative pronouncements, but these usually follow, or are at least consistent with, those of the Accounting Principles Board.) Although not generally known, it is a fact that these pronouncements do not comprise a complete, consistent body of principles. Instead, they are statements on specific topics, usually topics about which a controversy arose at some time in the past.

The Accounting Principles Board is currently (1964) attempting to formulate a complete set of principles. Until it has done so, accountants (and authors) must make their own judgment as to what the principles are in some important areas.

Lack of Agreement on Principles

The pronouncements of the Accounting Principles Board are not binding, even on the members of the AICPA. An auditor can and does, in good conscience, state that a certain practice is "in accordance with generally accepted accounting principles" if he knows of a number of reputable companies that follow the practice, even though the practice is not consistent with pronouncements of the Accounting Principles Board. For example, in 1963 the APB recommended that the "investment credit" allowed under the 1962 Revenue Act be treated as affecting income in the years over which a fixed asset is depreciated, rather than the year in which the asset is acquired. Nevertheless, three of the eight largest accounting firms certified financial statements which followed the opposite practice. (As noted in Chapter 6, the APB now permits either practice.)

Moreover, certain groups of companies are required to adhere to principles that are not necessarily consistent with those recommended by AICPA. Railroads and other common carriers follow rules prescribed by the Interstate Commerce Commission; public utilities, by the Federal Power Commission; banks and insurance companies, by state regulatory agencies. Government agencies, colleges and universities, hospitals, and other not-for-profit organizations follow practices that in important respects are inconsistent with AICPA recommendations. In certifying the financial statements of such bodies, the auditor does not state that the statements are prepared in accordance with "generally accepted principles"—rather, he says they are "consistent with practice followed in the industry," or words to that effect.

Income Tax Principles. We should note at this point that the principles governing the calculation of income for federal income tax purposes are basically the same as the principles of financial accounting; that is, in general, taxable income is the difference between realized revenue and expired cost. There are, however, some important differences, which are as follows:

First, taxpayers may, if they wish, disregard the accrual concept and elect to be taxed on the difference between cash receipts and cash expenditures. Many small businesses do this.

Second, the depletion allowance computed for tax purposes bears no relation to the principles of financial accounting (see p. 169).

Third, in taxation, a distinction is made between ordinary income and capital gains, with the latter being taxed less heavily than the former. In financial accounting, the distinction, although present, is not so important since both ordinary income and capital gains usually enter into the measurement of net income.

Finally, as already pointed out, although the principles are basically the same, a company usually applies them differently in its tax accounting and its financial accounting, respectively. It does this primarily by changing the *timing,* rather than the *amount,* of revenues and expenses. Thus, for tax purposes, a company usually reports costs as early as it legitimately can and defers revenue until as late as it legitimately can. For accounting purposes, it tends to report costs in later time periods and revenues in earlier time periods.

Differences in the Application of Principles

The Chief Accountant of the Securities and Exchange Commission has listed the following areas of accounting where alternative practices could produce materially different results under generally accepted accounting principles: valuation of inventories, depreciation and depletion, income tax allocation, pensions, research and development costs, goodwill, time of recognizing income, "all inclusive" versus "current operating performance" income statement, intercorporate investments, long-term leases, principles of consolidation, business combinations, income measurement in finance and small loan companies, and intangible costs in the oil and gas industries. Even this list is set forth as "illustrative" rather than complete. Note that the topics mentioned affect the income statement and practically every balance sheet asset item except cash.[3]

Even within the boundaries of a single principle, there is considerable latitude in applying the principle. Examples that have been mentioned in earlier chapters are as follows: inventory can be recorded at Lifo, at Fifo, or some parts of inventory may be handled one way and some the other; inventory cost may or may not include inward transportation, storage costs, handling costs, or cash discounts on purchases; research and development costs, organization costs, goodwill, advertising costs, and the like may be charged to expense as incurred or they may be capitalized as an asset; if capitalized, they may or may not be written off over future periods; and if written off, the number

---

[3] Testimony before the Subcommittee on Commerce and Finance of the Committee on Interstate and Foreign Commerce, House of Representatives, February 19, 1964.

of periods over which they are written off and the proportion written off each period may vary from company to company.

In part, these differences reflect differences in personal judgment as to what is or is not *material* and as to the importance that should be attached to the *conservatism* convention. In attempting to describe a complex situation, such differences are inevitable. In part, the differences reflect customs that have grown up in particular companies or industries.

Mr. Leonard Spacek, managing partner of Arthur Andersen and Company, illustrates this point with the following comparison between the reported earnings of two hypothetical companies, with the same revenue, and the same physical operations.[2] Company A reports a net profit of $480,000, and Company B reports a net profit of $1,076,000. The difference of $596,000 is explained entirely by differences in accounting practices, as follows:

1. Company B uses Fifo in pricing inventory; Company A uses Lifo.........$192,000
2. Company B uses accelerated depreciation; Company A uses straight-line.... 48,000
3. Company B capitalizes research costs and amortizes over five years; Company A expenses on incurrence.. 38,000
4. Company B charges the present value of pensions vested; Company A expenses actual current pension costs................................... 72,000
5. Company B grants stock options to executives, which are not an expense; Company A pays a cash bonus...................................... 96,000
6. Company B credits capital gains to income; Company A credits them directly to retained earnings.. 150,000

Total..$596,000

Example: Nudoll Company

A company, here called the Nudoll Company, spent three years and some $90,000 developing a new product. By the end of 1954 the product was ready for market and seemed to have a promising future. Of the funds used up to that point, $30,000 had been contributed by the management, in exchange for common stock, and $60,000 had been loaned by a friend of the principal owner, payable on demand. The balance sheet at that time, in round numbers, was as shown in Illustration 10–1. According to this balance sheet, current assets were about one-ninth current liabilities and the company had a substantial deficit.

The Nudoll Company needed additional capital, which the management planned to raise by selling stock. An advisor pointed out that the balance sheet shown in Illustration 10–1 would look unattractive to

---

[2] Quoted in Myles L. Mace and George G. Montgomery, Jr., *Management Problems of Corporate Acquisitions* (Boston: Division of Research, Harvard Business School, 1962), pp. 178–80.

prospective investors. Two steps were therefore taken: (1) the person who had loaned the $60,000 agreed to sign a five-year note, with the informal understanding that he would be repaid as soon as funds were available (this understanding was the same as his understanding when he made the loan, even though technically the original note was payable

Illustration 10–1

NUDOLL COMPANY

Balance Sheet as of October 31, 1954

(As Originally Prepared)

ASSETS		EQUITIES		
Cash	$1,000	Accounts payable		$ 2,000
Inventory	6,000	Notes payable		60,000
Total Current Assets	$7,000	Total Current Liabilities		$62,000
		Capital stock	$30,000	
		Less: Deficit	−85,000	−55,000
Total Assets	$7,000	Total Equities		$ 7,000

on demand); and (2) the expenditures to develop the new product were set up as an asset on the grounds that these costs were incurred in order to benefit future periods. These changes produced the balance sheet shown in Illustration 10–2. According to this revised balance sheet, current assets were 3.5 times current liabilities, total assets were 14 times

Illustration 10–2

NUDOLL COMPANY

Balance Sheet as of October 31, 1954

(As Adjusted)

ASSETS		EQUITIES		
Cash	$ 1,000	Accounts payable		$ 2,000
Inventory	6,000	Total Current Lia-		
Total Current Assets	$ 7,000	bilities		$ 2,000
Unamortized development costs	90,000	Long-term debt		60,000
		Capital stock	$30,000	
		Retained earnings	5,000	35,000
Total Assets	$97,000	Total Equities		$97,000

as large as those shown on the first balance sheet, and the company had retained earnings (which resulted from the profitable sale of trial lots of the new product).

Arguments can be made to support the view that both these balance sheets were prepared in accordance with generally accepted accounting principles. Each statement shows certain useful information: that the company has some cash and a little inventory, that it is probably going to have difficulty meeting its bills unless it obtains more cash quickly, and that it owes someone $60,000. Neither one describes the overall status of this company, for its status depends almost entirely on the excellence of the new product, and this will not be known until the product is marketed.

Implications of These Differences

No one can state reliably what the "general practice" is or how the majority of companies handle any specific problem. There are at least 4,000,000 accounting entities in the United States, of which about 1,000,000 are corporations. No report on the accounting practices of these companies exists. The largest survey is probably that published by the U.S. Office of Price Administration in 1946,[4] summarizing a few of the practices of 187,370 companies. *Accounting Trends and Techniques,* an annual publication of the AICPA, reports the practices of approximately 600 of the largest corporations. A person who has a personal knowledge of the detailed procedures of as many as 100 companies has an unusually broad experience. Thus, generalizations about what "the majority of companies" do with respect to detailed accounting matters should not be taken too seriously.

It follows that a detailed comparison of the items reported in the financial statements of two companies is a difficult problem. Useful comparisons can often be made in terms of rough approximations, but precise statements are rarely possible.

The existence of diversity in accounting practice should not be considered as a reason for criticizing accountants or accounting. The fundamental fact is that a business is a complex organism. There is no conceivable way of prescribing a uniform set of rules by means of which the significant facts about that organism can be reduced to a few pages of figures, any more than there is any way of formulating a standard set of rules for biographers. Standard procedures for listing physical characteristics, birth dates, marital status, and certain other information about a person can easily be specified, but these details do not really describe the person completely. The accuracy and usefulness of the "picture" of a person that emerges from a biography depends on the author's skill and judgment in the collection, analysis, and presentation of information about his subject. So it is with financial statements.

Nor should the existence of diversity lead to frustration on the part of the user. The doctrine of *consistency* prevents diversity from becoming

---

[4] Accounting Department, U.S. Office of Price Administration, *A Report on Cost Accounting in Industry,* June 30, 1946.

chaos. Although Company A may follow practices that differ from those of other companies, Company A ordinarily follows the same practices year after year, or if it changes, the doctrine of consistency requires that it disclose the change. Thus its statements are likely to be comparable with one another from year to year. Also, although railroads use rules that are different from those used by industrial companies, railroad A is likely to use the same rules as railroad B, and thus the two can be compared (with some notable exceptions).

Inherent Limitations

In addition to the points noted above, it is important to remember that accounting has inherent limitations. A business is such a complex organism that no one should expect that accounting, or any device, can record a complete and accurate picture of its activities. The two most important limitations—limitations which no foreseeable change in accounting can overcome—are (1) accounting reports are necessarily monetary and (2) they are necessarily influenced by estimates of future events.

Accounting reports are limited to information that can be expressed in monetary terms. Nothing in the accounts explicitly describes personalities, the impact of outside forces, or other nondollar information that is vital to the complete understanding of a business.

Some accounting figures are influenced by future events which cannot conceivably be foreseen; these figures are necessarily estimates. The depreciation expense of the current period, for example, depends partly on how long the assets will be used in the future. The real significance of accounts receivable and the related item of sales revenue cannot be assessed until the number of credit customers who will not pay their bills is known. The actual value of inventory depends on what the merchandise can be sold for in the future. The possible impacts of contingent future events, such as the results of pending or threatened litigation, retroactive agreements on wage rates, and redetermination of profits on contracts, are not shown in the financial statements, although if material they should appear in a footnote. Incidentally, the very fact that footnotes, which may be numerous, are labeled as being an "integral part of the financial statements" is an indication of the limitation of the statements themselves.

Attempts to Reduce Diversity

The AICPA Accounting Principles Board is working vigorously to reduce the diversity in accounting practice. It is discussing a number of proposals to resolve currently controversial accounting issues, and it is also preparing a statement of accounting principles that is expected to be issued in 1964 or 1965. Furthermore, in May 1964, the governing body of the AICPA adopted a resolution stating that auditor's certificates on financial statements "should disclose material departures from opinions of the Accounting Principles Board." When and if this resolution is implemented, there should be a reduction in the number of instances in which financial statements are prepared in a manner contrary to the opinions of the APB.

If these efforts of the APB do not bear fruit, it is quite possible that the government will promulgate accounting principles, as is done in several European countries, since many people regard the vagueness of the existing principles as intolerable. The Securities and Exchange Commission has the statutory authority to do this under the Securities Act of 1933, the Securities Exchange Act of 1934, the Public Utility Holding Company Act of 1935, and the Investment Company Act of 1940, but to date the SEC has been most cautious about exercising this authority.

SIGNIFICANCE OF THE FINANCIAL STATEMENTS

The limitations mentioned above must be taken into account when one tries to understand a set of financial statements. The existence of these limitations should not, of course, lead to a complete rejection of accounting. After all, accounting does provide a way of summarizing numerous, complicated, and heterogeneous events into two brief documents, the balance sheet and the income statement. This is a remarkable achievement.

It is therefore useful at this point to balance the limitations with the virtues, and attempt to describe their net effect in terms of the principal categories on the financial statements.

The Balance Sheet

It is neither necessary nor possible to define the whole balance sheet in anything other than vague terms. The AICPA definition of the balance sheet as a "list of balances in the asset, liability, or net worth accounts" is like the statement that "a rose is a rose"; it is accurate but not meaningful. A more meaningful statement is the following: the balance sheet shows the sources from which funds currently used to operate the business have been obtained (i.e., liabilities and owners' equity) and the types of property and property rights in which these funds are currently locked up (i.e., assets). This statement regards the balance sheet as essentially a report of management's *stewardship;* that is, what management has done with the funds entrusted to it. The concept of the flow of funds through a business is more fully described in Chapter 12.

Although a meaningful, overall definition is difficult to formulate, an attempt to describe the various sections of the balance sheet separately is much easier and more useful.

Current assets and current liabilities (the difference between which constitutes *working capital or circulating capital*) show the funds that are circulating through the business reasonably rapidly. They reflect the recurring, circular flow: inventory → accounts receivable → cash → payables → inventory. The essential characteristic that distinguishes the current items from other balance sheet items is their flexibility; that is, management has more frequent opportunities to make decisions on the recommitment of funds in the case of current items than in the case of noncurrent items.

Current assets are measured in two somewhat different ways. One group, consisting of cash, temporary investments held in lieu of cash, and accounts receivable, is measured essentially at market or realizable value. (For receivables, this statement implies that the company can make a reasonable estimate of its bad debt losses.) The other group, consisting of inventories and prepaid assets, is measured essentially at cost. Items in this group are held for the benefit of operations in future periods, and their value to the business is that their existence reduces the necessity for making outlays for similar goods and services in future periods. Except for the difference in their life, items in this latter group are essentially similar to fixed assets.

The *fixed asset* section of the balance sheet is a statement of unexpired costs; that is, it shows costs that have not yet been charged against operations. Ordinarily, the amounts listed bear no relation to market value, and no inference as to such value should be attempted solely on the basis of balance sheet information.

Interpretation of the *liabilities* section involves a subtle point. The items included there are indeed "claims against the assets," but they are only those claims which are recorded with an offsetting debit to an asset or another equity account, and these are not necessarily all the obligations which the company knows it must pay. For example, if an automobile is purchased on December 31 for $2,000 and if the business signs a note agreeing to pay the $2,000 at the rate of $50 per month for 40 months, the note appears as a liability (notes payable) on the December 31 balance sheet, and the automobile appears as an asset. On the other hand, if, instead, the business *rents* an automobile on December 31 and signs an agreement to pay $50 a month rent for 40 months, no record of this obligation appears as a liability (although it may be indicated in a footnote to the balance sheet).

One important point about the liabilities section is that the amounts are usually definite, more so than the amounts in any other section. The amount shown as accounts payable *is* the amount owed to creditors; and the amounts shown as notes payable or bonds payable *are* the amounts owed to banks and to the bondholders. Even the tax liability and the other accruals, although estimated, are likely to be close estimates.

The *owners' equity* section gives some useful bits and pieces of information, such as the number of outstanding shares of stock of various types, clues as to dividend policy, and so on. Dividends may be limited to the amount shown as surplus, although considerations other than this accounting relationship are usually more important. In the event of liquidation or other crises, the amounts recorded as capital and surplus are important in determining the relative claims of the stock-holders, and especially of each class of stockholders if there are several classes. In the usual situation, however, the amount shown as owners' equity in no way indicates the actual "worth" of the stockholders' equity, except in those rare instances where a company's assets consist entirely of cash or readily marketable assets.

The Income Statement

What is the meaning of "net income," the final item on an income statement? It is correct to say that net income is the difference between revenues and expenses, but this statement begs the question because there is no general agreement on the precise definitions of "revenue" and "expense" or on the method of measuring each of them. In the absence of such an agreement, there is room for considerable differences of opinion about the real meaning of net income.

How reliable is the estimate of the net income for an accounting period? Reliability depends primarily on (1) the length of the accounting period chosen, (2) the extent to which events relating to the current period are separated from events affecting prior or future periods, (3) the amount of long-lived assets owned by the company, and (4) the stability of prices. Estimates of net income for a day or a month are likely to be much less reliable than estimates for a year, and estimates for a year less reliable than estimates covering a longer period.

Although the expenses assigned to a period are supposed to relate to the revenues realized in that period, it usually is not practicable to attempt a precise matching. For example, advertising is typically "bread cast upon the waters" in the hope of stimulating sales in future periods, yet advertising is usually charged as an expense in the period in which the advertising is done. The difficulty of estimating the portion of the cost of a long-lived asset applicable to a given accounting period has already been described. The manner in which fluctuations in prices influence the income statement was discussed in Chapter 9.

For all these reasons, the net income reported on the income statement is unlikely to correspond exactly to the true increase in the owners' equity during an accounting period. The true *monetary* income of an enterprise can be known only after the enterprise has been completely terminated and its assets disposed of. The nonmonetary "income"—personal satisfaction, service rendered to society, and so on—are not determined from accounting reports even then. Any attempt to measure income for a shorter interval of time is necessarily inexact.

Nevertheless, certain of the individual items on an income statement may be highly reliable. The sales revenue figure is usually a close approximation to actual sales revenue, and the amounts for many expense items, such as wages, supplies, light, and power, are close approximations to actual expenses. Depreciation, on the other hand, is usually only a rough approximation, while some special adjustments reported as nonoperating expenses may be little more than informed guesses.

THE EXPERT ACCOUNTANT

Some of the knowledge that the expert accountant has acquired through study and experience, beyond the material in this introductory treatment, is listed below:

1. The expert accountant knows the procedures for recording accounting transactions quickly, efficiently, accurately, and in a way that minimizes the opportunity for fraud or theft. Only a few of the techniques and mechanical or electronic aids for facilitating the bookkeeping process have been mentioned here.

2. The expert accountant knows techniques for summarizing, arranging, and presenting information so that it meets the needs of various types of users of the information.

3. The expert accountant knows the legal requirements that govern or influence certain types of transactions. These are especially important in transactions affecting owners' equity items. Only a small fraction of

these requirements have been described in the chapter on owners' equity.

4. The expert accountant knows, or knows how to find out, tax laws and regulations. Although tax requirements should not govern financial accounting, tax considerations do play a major part in many business decisions.

5. The expert accountant knows, or can find by referring to accounting texts or handbooks, generally accepted ways of handling many specialized types of transactions that have not been mentioned here, or that have been touched on only briefly. For example, whole books have been written on the preparation of consolidated financial statements, on methods of valuing inventory, and even on the question "What is a sale?"

6. The expert accountant has acquired knowledge about terminology and procedures that are customarily used by companies in the same industry as his company. Many industries tend to develop a more or less common pattern for handling certain types of transactions, and in some industries these common practices are set forth in industry accounting manuals.

7. The expert accountant knows a great deal about his own company, the type of information that management and others have found useful, the way in which recurring transactions have been handled—in short, all the matters that are connoted by the word "experience," for which no book or classroom is a satisfactory substitute.

MANAGEMENT ACCOUNTING

The discussion in the present chapter, and indeed in Chapters 2 through 9, has been focused on *financial* accounting—the accounting that produces financial statements that convey information to investors, banks, and other interested outside parties. Since the book itself is principally concerned with *management* accounting, an introductory comparison of the two types is appropriate at this point.

Management accounting is the accounting that is useful to management in the operation of the company. An essential difference between management accounting and financial accounting is that the former need not be governed by the "generally accepted principles" that are so important in the latter. Investors, who usually have no choice but to accept the information the company furnishes, need assurance that all the reports they read are prepared according to some known set of ground rules, and are based on reasonably objective information.

Otherwise, they could not make sense out of the figures. Management can make and enforce its own ground rules; it need not, for internal purposes, adhere to those prescribed by AICPA or SEC, if other rules are more useful.

The criteria for management accounting are the same as those for financial accounting—usefulness, objectivity, and feasibility—but these criteria may lead to different principles in the two types of accounting. As an example, consider the question of imputed rent, which came up in the Elmer Kupper case (Case 3–1). In this situation, a trade association collected income statements from its members so that useful statistics could be developed. The trade association asked the members to report as rent expense an amount equivalent to what rental costs would have been, even though they owned their buildings and did not actually pay rent. It did this so as to put owners and rentors on a comparable basis. Such a practice would not be permitted in financial accounting; in accordance with the cost concept, only the actual costs incurred in occupying the building could be shown.

The difference is readily explainable in terms of the objectivity criterion. If financial accounting permitted imputed rents to be reported, the door would be open to all sorts of manipulation of the rent figure. The trade association, by contrast, need not be concerned about a deliberate attempt to bias the figures and can therefore relax the objectivity criterion in order to gain usefulness in the form of increased comparability.

Similarly, the accounting rules followed within a single company can depart from generally accepted principles if there is a gain in usefulness without too great an offsetting sacrifice of objectivity or feasibility. Thus, for internal purposes, some companies value their fixed assets at appraisal value, or they omit overhead costs from inventory, or they record orders when booked, or they estimate profit from manufacturing as contrasted with sales realization, even though none of these practices is in accordance with the generally accepted principles of financial accounting.

Although these differences do exist, most elements of financial accounting are also found in management accounting. There are two reasons for this. First, the same considerations that make these principles sensible for the purposes of financial accounting are likely to be relevant for purposes of management accounting. For example, management cannot base its reporting system on unverifiable, subjective estimates of profits submitted by lower echelons, which is the same reason that financial accounting adheres to the cost and realization concepts. Second, the internal accounting system must furnish the information used in preparing the financial statements. There is a presumption, therefore, that the basic data will be collected in accordance with generally accepted financial accounting principles, for to do otherwise would require two separate systems.

Further discussion of management accounting is deferred until Chapter 13.

CONCLUSION

Perhaps the best way to summarize the intent of the discussion in this chapter is to point out that in accounting, one refers to the *measurement* of income rather than to the *determination* of income. To determine is "to fix conclusively and authoritatively"; accounting cannot do this. A measurement, on the other hand, is an approximation, according to some agreed-upon measuring stick, and this is what accounting sets out to do.

A person can and should find out about the particular rules that govern the accounting for the company in which he works. He usually cannot do this for other companies, and when he is using financial statements prepared in these companies, he must recognize, even though he cannot allow precisely for, the probable existence of differences in the preparation of these statements.

CASES

CASE 10–1. CIRCLE LUNCH

Early in 1959 Mr. and Mrs. Elmer Symington decided to go into the restaurant business. Mr. Symington was dissatisfied with his job as cook in a restaurant, where he earned $2 an hour.

During July 1959, the Symingtons found a business which seemed to be what they wanted. This was the Circle Lunch, a lunch counter located in the Acme Department Store, in a working-class section of Jersey City. The Circle Lunch was operated under a lease with the department store; only the equipment was actually the property of the operator of the lunchroom. The equipment was old, but Mr. Symington thought that it was in fairly good condition.

They opened negotiations with the operator and quickly reached an agreement to take over the lease and equipment on September 1, and to pay the operator a price of $2,000. Of this price, Mr. Symington estimated that $900 represented the fair value of the equipment. The lease expired on August 31, 1960, and was renewable for three years if Acme consented. Under the terms of the lease, Acme furnished space, heat, light, and water, and the operators (i.e., the Symingtons) paid Acme 15 per cent of gross receipts as rent.

The Symingtons paid the $2,000 from their personal savings account and also transferred $1,000 to a checking account which they opened in the name of Circle Lunch.

Shortly after they started operations, the cooking range broke down. The Symingtons thereupon sold the range for $80 (which was approximately its estimated value, as a part of the $900) and purchased a new range for $800. It was installed immediately, and they paid $120 for its installation.

The coffee urn also broke down, but Mr. Symington was able to repair it himself by working 16 hours one Sunday.

Early in 1960, the Symingtons called in a firm which specialized in making out reports for small businesses, and requested financial statements for Circle Lunch for the period ended December 31, 1959. From their cash register and checkbook, they had the following figures:

Cash Receipts:

Cash receipts from customers.................................	$6,420
Sale of cooking range......................................	80
Total Cash Receipts.................................	$6,500

Cash Disbursements:

Food and supplies..	$2,763
City restaurant license, valid September 1, 1959, to September 1, 1960...	45
15 per cent rent paid to Acme for September, October, and November...	670
New cooking range..	800
Installation of cooking range................................	120
Other operating expenses..................................	18
Withdrawals for personal use................................	750
Total Cash Disbursements................................	$5,166

Before going home on December 31, the Symingtons had estimated the value of food and supplies then on hand to be about $146 at cost.

Early in January, they paid two bills, the December meat bill of $173 and the bill for the December rent of $293.

The Symingtons also explained to the accountant that the cash receipts of $6,420 included $620 received from the sale of 124 "coupon books" at $5 each. Each book contained coupons with a face value of $5.50, which could be used to pay for meals. As of December 31, coupons with a face value of $430 had been used to pay for meals; therefore coupons with a face value of $252 were still outstanding.

Questions

1. Prepare a balance sheet as of December 31, 1959, and an income statement for the four-month period ending December 31, 1959. Explain briefly your treatment of the coupon books and of anything else you believe needs comment.

2. Comment briefly on the significant information revealed by your financial statements.

CASE 10–2   FREDERICK MEARS

On March 15, 1963, Mr. Frederick Mears signed a lease agreement to operate a gasoline service station which was owned by the Octane Oil Company. Mr. Mears had contacted the regional sales manager of the Octane Oil Company in response to an advertisement which solicited applicants "with $2,500 to invest" to lease and operate a newly erected Octane Oil Company gasoline service station in a large eastern city. Mr. Mears had been able to accumulate approximately $3,000 for investment purposes as a result of a $2,000 inheritance and small savings on the salary of $100 per week which he earned as manager of a service station operated as a separate department of an automobile agency. Most of this $3,000 was held in government bonds.

The regional sales manager for the Octane Oil Company was impressed with Mr. Mears' personal and financial qualifications, and after several interviews, a lease agreement was signed. During one of these meetings, the sales manager informed Mr. Mears that the new porcelain-exterior service station would be completed and ready for occupancy on May 1 at a total investment cost of $60,000. Of this amount, $15,000 had already been paid for land and a total of $45,000 would be spent for a building which would be "good for about 40 years." In discussing profit potentiality, the sales manager pointed out that the national advertising program of the Octane Oil Company and the consumer appeal generated by the attractive station "will be worth at least $3,000 a year to you in consumer goodwill."

The lease agreement stipulated that Mr. Mears pay a rental of $110 per month for the station plus $0.01 for each gallon of gasoline delivered to the station by the Octane Oil Company.[5] A separate

---

[5] The lease, which covered a period of one year beginning May 1, was automatically renewable unless notice of cancellation was given by either party at least 30 days prior to an anniversary date. The regional sales manager of the Octane Oil Company estimated that approximately 150,000 gallons of gasoline would be delivered to Mr. Mears' service station during the first 12 months of operation. Subsequently, Mr. Mears' records revealed that 27,000 gallons were actually delivered during the first two months of operation.

agreement was also signed whereby the Octane Oil Company agreed to sell and Mr. Mears agreed to buy certain minimum quantities of gasoline and other products for the service station operation.

As both an evidence of good faith and as a prepayment on certain obligations which he would shortly incur to the Octane Oil Company, Mr. Mears was required to deposit $2,500 with the Octane Oil Company at the time the lease was signed. Mr. Mears raised the cash for this deposit by liquidating government bonds. The Octane Oil Company used most of this money to defray certain obligations incurred by Mr. Mears to the oil company prior to the opening of the new station. The deductions from the $2,500 deposit were applied as follows:

1. Opening inventories of gasoline, oil, grease, tires, batteries, and accessories $1,525
2. Rental fee ($110 flat rental for the month of May and $45 figured at $0.01 per gallon on the gasoline delivered in the opening inventory) . . .   155
3. Down payment (on Mears' behalf) on equipment costing $720   170
$1,850

The equipment, including floor and hydraulic jacks, a battery charger, tune-up sets, and oil and grease guns, became the property of Mr. Mears. A representative of the oil company stated that this equipment would last about five years. The unpaid, noninterest-bearing balance of $550 due for equipment to the Octane Oil Company was to be paid in five semiannual installments of $110 each. The first such payment was due October 30, 1963. The $650 remaining from the $2,500 originally deposited with the Octane Oil Company was returned to Mr. Mears on April 30. He deposited this money in a special checking account he had set up for his service station venture.

Prior to May 1, Mr. Mears wrote the following checks: $150 for office furniture which had an expected life of ten years and $65 for a fire and casualty insurance policy extending coverage for a one-year period beginning May 1. On April 30, Mr. Mears transferred $50 from the service station checking account to the cash drawer at the service station. It was Mr. Mears' intention to deposit in the bank all but $50 of the cash on hand at the close of each business day. The balance in the service station checking account at the start of business was, therefore, $385. In addition, Mr. Mears had $450 in his personal savings account.

On May 1, the service station was opened for business. In his effort to build up a clientele, Mr. Mears worked approximately 60 hours per week compared with 40 in his previous job. In addition, three other men were employed on either a full- or part-time basis. Mr. Mears was reasonably well satisfied with the patronage he was able to build up during the first two months the station was open. At the end of June, however, he felt it would be desirable to take a more careful look at how he was making out in his new business venture. Mr. Mears felt that he should record his progress and present position in a form which would be useful not only at the present time but also for comparative purposes in the future, perhaps at six-month intervals ending on June 30 and December 31.

Mr. Mears maintained a simple record-keeping system in which cash receipts and cash payments were itemized daily in a loose-leaf notebook. During the months of May and June, the following cash receipts and payments had been recorded:

Cash Receipts (May and June, 1963):

Sales of gasoline, motor oils, tires, batteries, accessories, revenue from lubrications, washing and polishing, and miscellaneous sales and services...$9,621

Rental from parking area on service station land......................   90

$9,711

Cash Payments (May and June, 1963):

Purchases (includes gasoline, motor oils, lubes, greases, new tires, batteries, and accessories)...$5,064

Rent (does not include $155 deductions from $2,500 deposit).............. 315

Payroll (does not include any payment to Mr. Mears)..................1,386

Utilities...   72

Advertising...   43

Miscellaneous...   33

Withdrawals by Mr. Mears (June 1 and June 19).................... 700

$7,613

The $90 listed in cash receipts as rental from parking area had been received from an adjacent business establishment that used one portion of the service station site as a parking space for certain of its employees. The rental received covered a period extending from May 15 to July 15, 1963.

In addition to the record of cash receipts and payments, a detailed listing was kept of the amounts of money which were due from or owed to other individuals or companies. An analysis of these records revealed that $38 was due the business for gas, oil, and car servicing from a wealthy widow friend of the Mears family who preferred to deal on a credit basis. Also, on the evening of June 30, one of the employees completed the waxing of a car for a regular customer who was out of town and would be unable to call for his car until July 3. Mr. Mears had quoted a price of $15 for this job. Mr. Mears recalled that when he was working at the automobile agency, he had heard that setting up a reserve for bad debts equal to 2 per cent of all outstanding accounts was a good idea.

Mr. Mears had also jotted down the fact that he and his family had used gas and oil from the service station worth $24 at retail prices, for which no payment had been made. Approximately $18 had been paid to the Octane Oil Company for this merchandise.

A further summary of his records revealed the following unpaid bills resulting from operations in June:

Octane Oil Company for merchandise	$416
Rent payable (figured at $0.01 per gallon on most recent delivery of gasoline)	20
Utilities for the month of June	65
	$501

The employees had last been paid on June 28 for services rendered through that date. Wages earned but unpaid for June 29 and 30 would amount to $43. Mr. Mears had deducted $240 from employees' earnings for federal income and social security taxes through the last payday; this amount would have to be remitted to the government in July. In addition, he would be required to pay $59 as the employer's social security taxes on wages earned in May and June.

Mr. Mears took a physical inventory on the evening of June 30, and he found gasoline, motor oils, lubes, greases, tires, batteries, and accessories on hand which had cost $1,142. While Mr. Mears was figuring his inventory position, he compared his recorded gallonage sales of gasoline from daily readings of the pump meters plus the volume of gasoline on hand at the end of the period against the volume of gasoline in the beginning inventory plus deliveries. In this manner, Mr. Mears ascertained that shrinkage due to evaporation, temperature changes, waste, and other causes amounted to 302 gallons of gasoline which he estimated had cost $59.

Late in June, Mr. Mears' married son realized that he would be unable, because of a prolonged illness, to make a payment of $48 for interest expense and $400 for principal repayment on a $1,200 bank loan. Mr. Mears, who had acted as cosigner on the 4 per cent note, would be obliged to meet this payment on July 1, 1963.

Questions

1. Prepare a May 1 and a June 30 balance sheet for Mr. Mears' service station and an income statement for the intervening period.

2. Be prepared to discuss, in particular, your treatment of the following events:

a) Mr. Mears' withdrawals of $700. (Should this be treated as a reduction in owner's equity or as a wage expense? If the latter, should recognition be made of Mr. Mears' previous salary of $100 per week, and/or his earnings from June 19 to June 30?)

b) Accounts receivable. (How much, if anything, should be provided for bad debts?)

c) The merchandise used by Mr. Mears and his family. (Does the business make a profit on such a transaction?)

d) The $59 shrinkage of gasoline. (Should this be taken into account at all? If taken into account, should it be shown as a part of the cost of sales calculation or as an expense, or both?)

CASE 10–3. VITREOMETALS, INC.

In May 1959, C. R. Newton, president of Vitreometals, Inc., was discussing with W. P. Mason, vice president and treasurer, some problems encountered in their efforts to secure funds for working capital and other purposes. A tentative loan agreement had been worked out a short time previously with financial institutions by which $720,000 in mortgage money and $480,000 from sale of prior preferred stock was to have been secured. When the agreements were submitted to counsel for the lending institutions to work out the details, several questions arose over terms and conditions to be written into the loan and stock purchase agreements.

Company History

Vitreometals, Inc., was organized in the early 1920's to produce porcelain enamel products for one principal customer. It had not been singularly successful but had managed to remain on the business scene until after World War II. In 1946, Newton, a recent business school graduate, stumbled onto the company while looking about for a good postwar business in which he could try out some of his ideas on management and product development. He was impressed with the favorable qualities of porcelain enamel on metal as a durable product with strength, beauty, and general flexibility in use. Many areas, he felt, had not been tapped in the market for such a product and, in general, companies manufacturing and marketing such products were unimaginative and lacking in managerial know-how.

Newton acquired a 50 per cent interest in Vitreometals, Inc., and became vice president in 1946. In 1947 he was able to arrange a plan by which the company acquired the remaining outstanding stock, thus removing outside ownership and giving him a free hand to carry out his long-range plans.

Seasoned and skilled men, who shared Newton's philosophy of how a small company ought to be managed, joined the organization. These top executives set about selecting and training younger men to provide the organizational strength needed. Once the management group was formed, brainstorming for ideas was carried on continually.

A timetable was set for achieving selected goals. From 1947 to 1952, all possible effort was to be devoted to product development. From 1952 to 1957, emphasis was to shift to the kind of plant or plants that would eventually be needed for the growing company. By 1958, it was expected that a modern plant would be ready to turn out a wide range of products for a rapidly expanding domestic and world market.

From 1952 to 1958, two companies were acquired as subsidiaries, while a third was brought under voting control in a foreign country. Connections with some minor companies were also made during this period. Penetration of foreign markets had been effected principally through licensing agreements under which Vitreometals furnished technical and production know-how.

Initially, one main product with one principal customer characterized the company. Newton and his associates realized that a growing dynamic company would require a product line offering diversification, flexibility, and market depth. Every conceivable use for ceramic-coated metals was examined. Research and development costs mounted to more than $3,000,000 by the end of the ten-year period, and in 1957 more than 90 per cent of sales were accounted for by products that were not in the line in 1947.

Financing

"In a small growing company engaged simultaneously in product research and development and standard production, there is always an acute problem of working capital shortage. Research and development costs overbalance the nominal income from limited product sales, hence reinvestment is inadequate as a source of funds," Newton noted. "Such a situation places a strain on the credit position of a company." Vitreometals chose to obtain needed funds through the public sale of stock rather than borrowing. Newton wanted to establish a public market for its shares to be in a better position for meeting future needs. A modest offering of common stock in 1949 was absorbed by the public with good distribution. A second offering of common stock with warrants for purchase of additional common was successfully distributed in 1952. Almost all of the warrants had been exercised before the expiration date in 1955.

During 1958 the company incurred heavy moving and start-up costs as operations were transferred to a modern new building held on a long-term lease. Working capital was again reduced to an unsatisfactory level, so additional common stock was publicly distributed. Outstanding convertible debentures in the amount of $420,000 were also converted into common stock.

These moves furnished the base for the next major financing. This was undertaken early in 1959 to provide $720,000 through a first-mortgage note, and $480,000 through sale of prior cumulative preferred (callable) stock. Common stock warrants were attached to each covenant giving holders the right to purchase common stock during the next 15 years.

Originally, Vitreometals and the lending institutions had tentatively agreed that net assets were to be maintained at a minimum of $2 million. For this purpose net assets were defined as being equal to total net worth, less appraisal surplus and goodwill. However, when counsel for the lending institutions worked out the customary loan and purchase covenants, it was proposed that in addition to appraisal surplus and goodwill, other assets including deferred research and development costs, plant move and start-up costs, and blueprints and drawings related to a package building plan also be deleted in arriving at "net tangible assets" to be maintained. As a result of these deletions, it was apparent that Vitreometals might find it difficult to maintain net tangible assets at the minimum level specified.

Newton and Mason both felt that the tentative commitment definition should be honored, proposing that these values be established: the package building plan, $48,000; plant-move and start-up expense, $144,000; and deferred research and development costs, $564,180. They further proposed that if these amounts were accepted, no further additions would be made to these accounts. Also, these accounts were to be reduced by applicable amortizations and write-offs in the future.

Newton said to Mason: "Bill, I don't think these lawyers, or the professional accountants, understand some of the problems a small growing company like ours is up against. Those drawings of the package building plan are just as hard assets as the machinery in our plant and ought to be included in determining the minimum net tangible assets requirement. As a matter of fact, you know that those plans and engineering drawings are the main assets we acquired from the Builtwell Company. The other assets were insignificant, yet those boys want to throw out the best assets we acquired as if they have no value at all. Sometimes I think public accountants and lawyers hinder a growing business more than they help."

"And while we are on the subject," continued Newton, "I have often wondered why the accounting profession has never developed some way to show on the balance sheet the value of such intangibles as our licensing agreements with Foreco, Ltd., of Canada; Sollingen-Stahlblechbau of Germany; Emailleries-Girondaux of Belgium; Ceramic Enamel Corporation of South Africa; Lesperes Reunies of France; Smalterie Lombardi, S. A. of Italy; and the others. These licensing and royalty agreements represent tremendous asset values in terms of future income to the company, yet they are hidden away in an obscure footnote to the balance sheet, if they are mentioned at all. They ought to be quantified in monetary terms on the balance sheet. That would give a truer picture of the sound going-concern value of a company like ours than present accounting and legal practices permit."

Mason replied: "Yes, I know what you say is largely true, Bob. The accountants and the lawyers have developed a lot of so-called generally accepted principles and conventions that are applied to financial statements in a rather indiscriminate manner. It grows out of practices of the past that have largely disappeared from the business scene, but the attitude of accountants toward these soft assets is still prevalent. The bulletins of the American Institute of Certified Public Accountants have a great deal of weight and influence in such matter, in fact, perhaps too much."

Information drawn from financial statements is given in Exhibits 1–5.

Exhibit 1

Year	Sales	Net Income after Tax
1945	$ 131,600	$ 30,160 loss
1946	325,610	18,120
1947	465,440	11,760
1948	689,520	15,490
1949	726,850	25,790 loss
1950	891,320	5,400
1951	1,267,140	23,330
1952	1,458,440	24,240
1953	2,382,220	50,290
1954	2,409,020	51,470
1955	2,435,700	140,230 loss (strike)
1956	3,473,590	104,490

Exhibit 2

VITREOMETALS, INC.

Consolidated Balance Sheets, December 31, 1958 and 1957

ASSETS

	1958	1957
Current Assets:		
Cash..	$ 201,480	$ 201,240
Accounts and notes receivable (Note 1).................	796,980	769,620
Inventories at lower of cost or market....................	685,140	749,760
Claim for refund of prior years' federal income taxes.......	14,340	1,860
Prepaid expenses (Note 1)............................	41,520	50,760
Total Current Assets..............................	$1,739,460	$1,773,240
Investment in affiliated companies, at Cost (Market December 31, 1958, $84,000) (Notes 1–2)........................	27,420	27,420
Plant and Equipment (Notes 3–4):		
Land, buildings, machinery, equipment..................	$2,107,920	$1,648,080
Less: Accumulated depreciation.......................	443,880	533,760
Net Plant and Equipment.........................	$1,664,040	$1,114,320
Goodwill from acquisition of subsidiary...................	152,640	152,640
Package building plan acquisition........................	48,000	48,000
Other Assets:		
Cash Surrender value of life insurance (Note 4)............$	25,980	$ 22,620
New plant start-up expense............................	144,000	..
Deferred charges—research and development expense.......	564,180	413,280
Total Other Assets...............................$	734,160	$ 435,900
Total Assets.............................	$4,365,720	$3,551,520

LIABILITIES AND STOCKHOLDERS' EQUITY

	1958	1957
Current Liabilities:		
Notes and mortgages payable, current portion (Notes 1–4).$	694,920	$ 368,640
Accounts payable and accrued liabilities..................	925,080	702,900
Federal income taxes payable..........................	8,040	8,040
Total Current Liabilities...........................	$1,628,040	$1,079,580
Long-term notes and mortgages payable, less current portion above (Notes 1–4).................................	408,960	338,050
Convertible subordinated debentures, 5–¾%, due 1971.......		420,000
Minority Interest:		
5% cumulative preferred stock (Note 5)	33,600	33,600
Stockholders' Equity:		
Capital stock, par value $1.00 per share authorized 600,000, issued and outstanding 476,470 (1958), 306,360 (1957) (Note 6)...$	476,470	$ 306,360
Capital in excess of par value of common shares—Exhibit 3..	1,316,480	736,880
Appraisal surplus—Exhibit 3...........................	364,820	457,650
Retained earnings—Exhibit 3...........................	137,350	179,400
Total Stockholders' Equity.......................	$2,295,120	$1,680,290
Total Liabilities and Stockholders' Equity..........	$4,365,720	$3,551,520

Exhibit 3

VITREOMETALS, INC.

Statement of Changes in Stockholders' Equity for the Year Ended December 31, 1958

	Common Stock, Par $1	Capital in Excess of Par Value	Appraisal Surplus	Retained Earnings
Balance, January 1, 1958	$306,360	$736,880	$457,650	$179,400
Consolidated net income for year ended December 31, 1958, per Exhibit 4				8,600
Amortization and write-off of appraisal (Note 3)			(92,830)	(8,120)
Dividends paid on subsidiary preferred stock				(1,680)
Amortization of bond discount on conversion to stock				(40,850)
Proceeds of issue of 170,110 shares of common stock	170,110	579,600		
Balance, December 31, 1958, Exhibit 2	$476,470	$1,316,480	$364,820	$137,350

Exhibit 4

VITREOMETALS, INC.

Statement of Consolidated Income for the Years Ended December 31, 1958 and 1957

	1958	1957
Total revenues	$2,886,580	$3,387,110
Cost of goods sold	2,412,710	2,810,270
Gross profit	$ 473,870	$ 576,840
Selling and administrative expenses	440,740	396,350
Income from operations	$ 33,130	$ 180,490
Other income (charges) net	(37,010)	(66,480)
Net income (loss) before federal income taxes	$ (3,880)	$ 114,000
Federal income taxes		7,800
Net income (loss) after provision for federal income taxes	$ (3,880)	$ 106,210
Refund of federal income taxes due to net operating loss carrybacks	12,480	1,870
Consolidated Net Income, Exhibit 3	$ 8,600	$ 108,080

Exhibit 5

NOTES ACCOMPANYING FINANCIAL STATEMENTS
DECEMBER 31, 1958

NOTE 1: Accounts receivable of $401,040 are assigned as security for notes payable-bank in the amount of $328,740. 24,000 shares of Foreco, Ltd. common stock are assigned as security for notes payable in the amount of $60,000. Unexpired insurance premiums of $11,600 are pledged against notes payable of $60,000. Unexpired insurance premiums of $11,600 are pledged against notes payable of $11,900.

NOTE 2: Investment in affiliated companies of $27,420 is as follows:

Company	Investment	% Owned
Foreco, Ltd.	$24,300	23
A	3,000	33
B	120	49
C	..	10
	$27,420	

NOTE 3: As a result of independent appraisals the fixed assets are shown at cost plus an appraisal increment of $416,300 (net of amortization). Depreciation on the amount of appreciation has been charged in the amount of $8,120 to consolidated retained earnings and in the amount of $25,990 to consolidated appraisal surplus. In addition the balance of the appraisal increment on the A-Plant which was disposed of in 1958 was written off, in the amount of $666,840.

NOTE 4: Plant and equipment having a book value of $1,664,070 together with cash surrender value of life insurance amounting to $25,990 are pledged to secure notes and mortgages of $471,220.

NOTE 5: Dividends on the 5% cumulative preferred stock of subsidiary E have been paid to and including December 1, 1958.

NOTE 6: Of the 123,530 shares of Vitreometals, Inc. common stock unissued at December 31, 1958, 17,140 shares are held for the redemption of warrants which expire September 1, 1962.

AUDITOR'S OPINION

To the Board of Directors
Vitreometals, Inc.
Alton, Connecticut

We have examined the balance sheet of Vitreometals, Inc. and its subsidiaries, Company D and Company E, as of December 31, 1958, and the related statements of income and changes in stockholders' equity for the year then ended. Our examination was made in accordance with generally accepted auditing standards and accordingly included such tests of the accounting records and such other auditing procedures as we considered necessary in the circumstances, except for inventories of Company D. Inventories of Company D which amounted to $173,090 were taken by responsible employees of the company and priced at the lower of cost or market. We did not verify the condition or quantities of merchandise at December 31, 1958 of Company D, such quantities and values being stated at company figures. However, a responsible officer of the company did certify to the quantities, condition and valuation of the inventory.

Subject to the foregoing, in our opinion, the accompanying consolidated balance sheet and statements of consolidated income and statement of changes in stockholders' equity present fairly the consolidated financial position of Vitreometals, Inc., and its subsidiaries, Company D and Company E at December 31, 1958, and the results of consolidated operations for the year then ended, in conformity with generally accepted accounting principles applied on a basis consistent with that of the preceding year.

ALFRED D. SESSIONS,
Certified Public Accountant

Questions

1. How should the problems discussed in the case be handled in accordance with generally accepted accounting principles?

2. Do you think that a departure from accounting principles will be desirable in this situation?

CASE 10–4. MOREHOUSE CONTAINER CORPORATION

Arthur L. Morehouse was the operator of a moderately successful box and crate manufacturing company. The business had been started in 1947 when Morehouse, unemployed, applied for a job at a local aircraft plant. Unable to secure employment, Morehouse left the plant and took a shortcut home through the company dump. As he was walking, Morehouse noticed that a truck crew was dumping and piling a load of damaged, but obviously repairable, wooden crates. On inquiring, Morehouse was told that the crates would, as usual, be burned when a sufficient number had accumulated.

By the time that he reached home Morehouse had decided that the crates stacked up in the dump could be turned into a profit. In rapid order, he obtained permission from the aircraft company to remove (free of charge) all damaged crates from the dump, to repair and recondition the crates, and to resell them (at negotiated prices) to the company.[6]

On the strength of the verbal commitments from the purchasing agent of the aircraft firm, Morehouse withdrew $350 from his fast-dwindling savings account and purchased a used truck. On the advice of a friend he purchased a parcel of land about a mile from the aircraft plant. The land, which was acquired for $915 in back taxes, was occupied by a weather-beaten, barn-type structure which was suitable for a shop or garage operation. Thus, although Arthur Morehouse was unable to secure employment with the aircraft manufacturer, his visit to that firm led to the establishment of the Morehouse Container Corporation.

By the end of 1957 the container company had grown in size and was considered to be one of the outstanding examples of personal success in the community. The Morehouse company employed 14 full-time and four part-time workers; it manufactured crates, packing boxes, structural forms, and many types of wooden shipping containers; and it supplied

---

[6] Morehouse had to agree to continue to cart away all crates that were taken to the dump; failure to satisfy this requirement would cause him to lose his privilege.

the needs of a large number of firms in the local area. Although the aircraft manufacturer was still Morehouse's primary customer, the "dump-clearing" arrangement had, by 1957, long since been terminated. Morehouse's lumber needs had grown to the point where it was necessary for him to purchase board lumber directly through agents dealing in New England and Canadian growth.

Exhibit 1

MOREHOUSE CONTAINER CORPORATION

Record of Revenue and Expenses, 1957

Revenue:

Sales of boxes, crates, etc.		$137,910
Sale of lumber scraps		480
Rental of packing boxes		3,260
Deposits on packing boxes		850
Miscellaneous income		116
		$142,616

Expenses:

Wages to employees		$ 52,680
Wages to Arthur Morehouse		10,200
Supplies used		3,880
Truck repairs—regular		320
Machinery repairs		620
Loss from bad accounts		125
Delivery expense		11,095
Depreciation expense		3,896
Utilities and operating		2,504
Installment on truck note		900
		$ 86,220

Use of inventory:

Last year's inventory	$ 9,876	
Purchase payments in 1957	31,420	
	$41,296	
This year's inventory	6,640	34,656
Total Costs		$120,876
Profit		$ 21,740

Early in 1958, Morehouse was considering several opportunities for expanding his business. He felt that bank borrowing was generally better suited for his purposes than attempting to secure additional invested capital, and accordingly he contacted John Thurman, loan officer at his business bank, for information. At Thurman's request, Morehouse forwarded his tabulation of income and expense for 1957, and his balance sheet for the end of that year. (See Exhibits 1 and 2 for these statements as they were prepared by Morehouse.)

Within a few days, Thurman called and suggested that he and Morehouse meet to discuss matters in more detail. At the bank the next day, Thurman explained that his primary purpose was to make sure that the loan committee received the most useful information that was available. The two men spent several hours discussing the operation of the business and the methods by which Morehouse kept his records; Thurman expressed satisfaction with the meeting and, after securing from Morehouse a folder of papers which contained information in

Exhibit 2

MOREHOUSE CONTAINER CORPORATION

Balance Sheet, December 31, 1957

ASSETS		LIABILITIES	
Cash in checking account.............$11,383		Owed to suppliers..................$ 846	
Petty cash at office.................. 162		Wages not picked up................ 22	
Accounts receivable—good.......... 8,740		Note on truck (due in 1958)......... 1,800	
Accounts receivable—disputed....... 482*		Charged for bad accounts............ 500	
Accounts receivable—bad........... 66†		Total........................$ 3,168	
Lumber inventory.................. 6,640			
Miscellaneous supplies.............. 320			
Boxes on consignment.............. 1,296‡			
Inventory of rental boxes........... 1,540			
Total.......................$30,629			
Machinery....................... 8,960		Depreciation—machinery............ 8,064	
Trucks........................... 12,200		Depreciation—trucks................ 9,760	
Land and building................ 12,000		Depreciation—land and building.... 4,400	
Storage sheds..................... 4,800		Depreciation—storage sheds......... 1,120	
Total....................... $68,589		Total........................$26,512	

OWNER'S INTERESTS

Balance of owners' interests last year............................$28,737	
Deduct: Dividends paid in 1957................................. 8,400	
	$20,337
Add: Profit earned in 1957..................................... 21,740	
Balance of owners' interests this year...........................$42,077	

* Amount in dispute on a September 1956 shipment to aircraft plant. Morehouse cannot locate receipted delivery ticket, and customer has no record of receiving the shipment. No word on matter in last six months; last prior word was that payment could not be made without proof of delivery.
    † Due from firm declared bankrupt on May 16, 1957.
    ‡ A local lumber supply house carried six dozen packing boxes on a "subject to sale" (or consignment) basis. They pay for boxes only as boxes are sold and retain a 10 per cent commission for their services. The boxes were similar to rental boxes, cost about the same to manufacture, and were priced to sell for $20.

support of the statements, promised that he would contact Morehouse shortly. On the basis of the statements, the papers in the folder, and his meeting with Morehouse, John Thurman accumulated the information that follows:

Land and Buildings: As was previously mentioned, the land and original building were acquired in 1947 for payment of back property taxes. Arthur Morehouse was well aware that his payment was an extremely poor reflection of the real value of the property. For that reason, he had carried the property on his records, from the time that he acquired it, at a conservative appraised value. In 1950, to reflect a general increase in property values in the vicinity, Morehouse decided to adjust his books. He discussed the value of the property with a local realtor, and then revised his balance sheet to show the property valued at $12,000.

In 1951, Morehouse received a bid of $4,800 for construction of a row of concrete sheds in which to store lumber so that it would be protected from the weather. Prior to approving a contract for the work, he was able to acquire a substantial portion of the necessary materials at extraordinary savings. As a result of his acquisition of building materials that cost him $950, Morehouse secured a reduction of the bid amount to $2,800. He nevertheless carried the improvement in his records at the original bid figure. Unquestionably, he maintained, the lesser total cost[7] did not fairly reflect the real value of the addition under normal conditions.

Factory Equipment: The principal pieces of equipment in the factory were the power saw and the nailing machine. Both pieces of equipment were purchased new in 1949 and had an expected useful life of 15 years. (Morehouse traded in some useless pieces of machinery when he purchased the two new units. The pieces traded in were in the building when he took possession, were valued at $600 for trade-in credit, and resulted in a net cash outlay of $8,360 at the time of purchase. Morehouse figured that the machinery which he traded in would have been worth about $250 if he had tried to sell it.)

Morehouse considered such things as small hand tools to be temporary in nature and, thus, an immediate item of expense. He estimated that he had $350 worth of small hand tools in the shop at the end of 1957.

Delivery Equipment: In addition to the truck that he purchased in 1947, Morehouse operated another vehicle that he purchased new in 1954. The old truck had, of course, been fully depreciated and no longer showed in the records. In March, Morehouse paid $2,680 to have the old truck completely reconditioned. The cost of reconditioning was included in the amount that Morehouse figured for delivery expense for 1957. In Morehouse's estimation, the reconditioning work was the sole factor that would make it possible for him to use the truck for another three or four years.

Bad Debts: The debt loss experience of the company had been next to nothing for several years. Morehouse understood, however, that the tax law allowed him a bad debt deduction each year and, accordingly, he

---

[7] The total cost to Morehouse was $3,750; that is, the bid amount of $2,800 was paid to the contractor; in addition, Morehouse provided the materials worth $950.

charged a flat $125 annually as expense. In 1957 his only loss was $66; this amount was due from a small local concern that was legally adjudged bankrupt.

Depreciation: Morehouse figured depreciation on his property at the following rates:

Land and buildings.....................30 years
Machinery and equipment...............10 years
Trucks............................... 5 years

Other Information: The inventory figure for December 31, 1957, included $1,980 which was the agreed purchase price, plus freight, of an order of Canadian pine which was due for delivery in early January. Morehouse usually received notice approximately a week before the shipment would reach his yard; he would take title on delivery and would pay the shipper at that time.

In addition to selling boxes and crates outright, Morehouse had developed a sideline in a box-rental service. While the gains from his rental service were not significant, Morehouse was interested in the possibility of further developing that type of business. Essentially, Morehouse constructed a packing or storage box in one standard size at a cost of approximately $15.40. Then, he rented the boxes to local moving and storage companies at a charge of one dollar a month plus an initial five-dollar deposit. At the end of 1957 there were about 300 of the boxes out in use, and there were 100 in the storage sheds. As best he could tell, Morehouse figured that the boxes would last anywhere from one to five years depending upon the type of use to which they were put. As a rule of thumb, he allowed an average of two years for the normal life of a rental packing box. (Experience indicated, also, that about 20 per cent of the boxes that were rented out were never returned. Normally, Morehouse would receive rental on these boxes for a year, more or less, and then the user would discontinue making rental payments.) Very rarely did any of the users request that their deposits be returned; whenever, of course, a box was returned (regardless of condition), Morehouse was obliged to return the deposit. Morehouse made no distinction between the rental receipts and the deposits, but rather took both into income as they were received.

Question

As analyst for the bank's loan officer, prepare an income statement for 1957, and a year-end balance sheet. Prepare these statements in a form that you feel will be helpful to the bank's loan committee. If you find it necessary to adopt one method of handling in preference to another method, explain briefly how you chose between alternate methods.

Part

II

USING INFORMATION
IN FINANCIAL STATEMENTS

Chapter 11

FINANCIAL STATEMENT ANALYSIS

THE PURPOSE of Part I was to provide an understanding of the fundamental concepts of accounting and the construction of financial statements. We turn now to the *use* of accounting information. In the present chapter and the next chapter, we discuss how the information contained in the financial statements can be used. We begin with the financial statements, both because the information on these statements is familiar from the preceding discussion and because the financial statements give the "big picture," the overall results of detailed actions to be discussed in subsequent chapters.

BUSINESS OBJECTIVES

All analyses of accounting data involve comparisons. An absolute statement, such as "X Company earned $1,000,000 profit" is, by itself, not useful. It becomes useful only when the $1,000,000 is compared with something else. The comparison may be quite imprecise and intuitive. For example, if we know that X Company is an industrial giant with tens of thousands of employees, we know intuitively that $1,000,000 profit is a poor showing because we have built up in our minds the impression that such companies should earn much more than $1,000,000. Or, the comparison may be much more formal, explicit, and precise, as is the case when the $1,000,000 profit this year is compared with last year's profit. In either case, it is the process of comparison that makes the figure meaningful.

In general terms, the process of analysis can be described as one of comparing what actually happened with a *standard. A standard is a measure of what should have happened under the circumstances prevailing.*

In order to decide the types of comparisons that are useful, we need first to consider what business is all about—what its objectives are—for the comparisons are essentially intended to shed light on how well business is achieving its objectives. As a generalization, it may be said that *insofar as it can be measured quantitatively, the overall objective of a business is to earn a satisfactory return on the funds invested in it, consistent with maintaining a sound financial position.*[1] It should be noted that this statement is limited to facts that can be expressed numerically. Personal satisfaction, public responsibility, ethical considerations, and other nonmeasurable objectives may be important and must be taken into account wherever relevant in appraising the overall success of the enterprise.

The foregoing statement of objectives has two aspects: (1) earning a satisfactory return on its investment and (2) maintaining a sound financial position. Each aspect is discussed briefly below.

Return on Investment

The fact that return on investment is the broadest measure of overall performance can be seen from Illustration 11–1, which shows how return on investment is calculated and relates it to the main categories of items appearing on the balance sheet and income statement. The assets side of a balance sheet shows the categories to which investors' funds are committed. A portion of the current assets is offset by current liabilities, and investors must furnish only the remainder, which is called *working capital.*[2] They must also furnish the funds for noncurrent assets. The return-on-investment measure is used in two senses: (1) the return on stockholders' investment, which is assets less liabilities; and (2) the return on total investment, which includes both the stockholders' investment and that of bondholders and other long-term creditors.

Investors who commit their funds to an enterprise do so because they expect to earn a return on these funds. The diagram shows how a change in any single category affects this return. Thus, an increase in gross profit, or a decrease in expenses, or a decrease in income taxes increases net income and hence increases return on investment IF these changes are not accompanied by an offsetting change in some other category. On the other hand, if an increase in gross profit is accompanied by a corresponding increase in working capital (as can happen, for example, when a growth in sales volume is accompanied by a corresponding increase in inventories and accounts receivable), there will be no change in the

---

[1] This statement is not consistent with the *profit maximization* assumption often made in economics. The techniques in this chapter are equally applicable under a profit maximization assumption, however, so there is no point in arguing here whether the profit maximization assumption is valid and useful. Discussion of this point is deferred to Chapter 17.

[2] Occasionally, "working capital" is taken to mean total current assets. This is of course confusing and is unnecessary since "total current assets" is a perfectly good term. In order to avoid any possibility of confusion, the term "net working capital" is sometimes used for the difference between current assets and current liabilities.

Illustration 11–1

FACTORS AFFECTING RETURN ON INVESTMENT

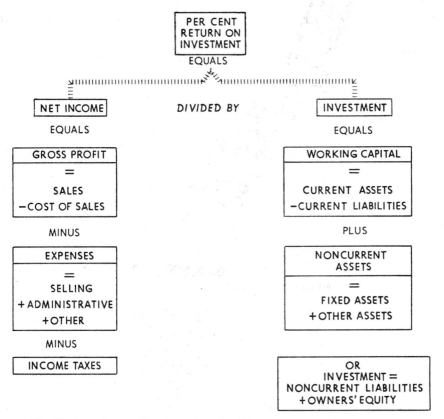

Note: The above refers to total investment. Stockholders' investment equals total investment less noncurrent liabilities.

overall per cent return. It is therefore important that the relationships among the various categories be studied; this is done by the use of ratios as described in the next section. Illustration 11–2 shows the average return on net assets (which corresponds to the definition of investment implicit in Illustration 11–1) for various industry classes.

Sound Financial Position

In addition to desiring a satisfactory return, the investor expects that his capital will be protected from more than a normal amount of risk. The return on the *stockholders'* investment could be increased if a larger proportion of the investment came from long-term liabilities and net income remained unchanged. This move, however, would increase the stockholders' risk of losing their investment, since the interest charges

Illustration 11-2

1962 RETURN ON NET ASSETS

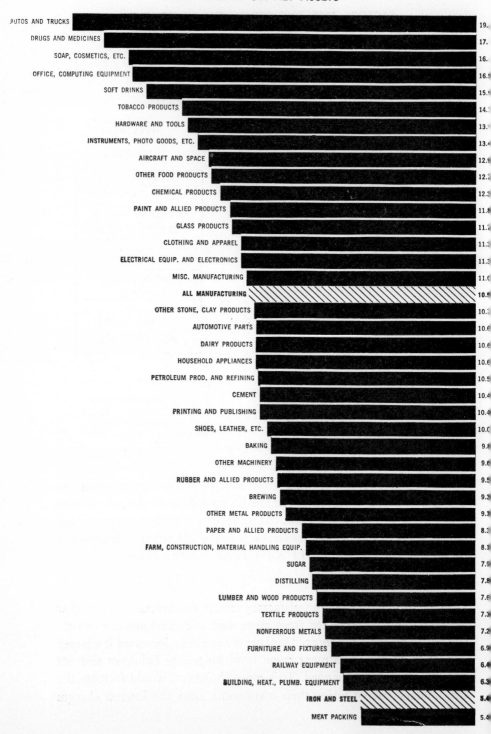

AUTOS AND TRUCKS	19.
DRUGS AND MEDICINES	17.
SOAP, COSMETICS, ETC.	16.
OFFICE, COMPUTING EQUIPMENT	16.9
SOFT DRINKS	15.4
TOBACCO PRODUCTS	14.1
HARDWARE AND TOOLS	13.
INSTRUMENTS, PHOTO GOODS, ETC.	13.4
AIRCRAFT AND SPACE	12.9
OTHER FOOD PRODUCTS	12.7
CHEMICAL PRODUCTS	12.3
PAINT AND ALLIED PRODUCTS	11.8
GLASS PRODUCTS	11.7
CLOTHING AND APPAREL	11.3
ELECTRICAL EQUIP. AND ELECTRONICS	11.3
MISC. MANUFACTURING	11.0
ALL MANUFACTURING	10.9
OTHER STONE, CLAY PRODUCTS	10.7
AUTOMOTIVE PARTS	10.6
DAIRY PRODUCTS	10.6
HOUSEHOLD APPLIANCES	10.6
PETROLEUM PROD. AND REFINING	10.5
CEMENT	10.4
PRINTING AND PUBLISHING	10.4
SHOES, LEATHER, ETC.	10.0
BAKING	9.8
OTHER MACHINERY	9.6
RUBBER AND ALLIED PRODUCTS	9.5
BREWING	9.3
OTHER METAL PRODUCTS	9.1
PAPER AND ALLIED PRODUCTS	8.3
FARM, CONSTRUCTION, MATERIAL HANDLING EQUIP.	8.1
SUGAR	7.9
DISTILLING	7.8
LUMBER AND WOOD PRODUCTS	7.6
TEXTILE PRODUCTS	7.3
NONFERROUS METALS	7.2
FURNITURE AND FIXTURES	6.9
RAILWAY EQUIPMENT	6.4
BUILDING, HEAT., PLUMB. EQUIPMENT	6.3
IRON AND STEEL	5.4
MEAT PACKING	5.4

*First National City Bank of New York

and principal repayments on the long-term liabilities are fixed obligations, and failure to make these payments when due could throw the company into bankruptcy. The degree of risk in a situation can be measured in part by the relative amounts of various types of liabilities and of the funds available to discharge them, and this also involves the use of ratios.

SOME COMMON RATIOS

A *ratio* is simply one number expressed in terms of another. It is found by dividing one number, the base, into the other. A *percentage* is one kind of ratio, in which the base is taken as equaling 100 and the quotient is expressed as "per hundred" of the base.

Conceivably, dozens of ratios could be computed from a single set of financial statements, but usually only a few are helpful in a given situation. Thus, although many frequently used ratios are described below, the best analytical procedure is not to compute all of them mechanically but rather to decide first which ratios might be relevant in the particular type of investigation being made and then to compute these, and only these, ratios.

Financial ratios can be grouped loosely into these categories: (*a*) tests of profitability, (*b*) tests of liquidity, (*c*) tests of solvency, and (*d*) overall ratios. The ratios listed under each category are illustrated by figures drawn from Illustrations 11–3 and 11–4 which show a simplified balance sheet and income statement for a hypothetical company.

Since the balance sheet figures refer to one instant of time while the income statement figures refer to events over a period of time, care must be taken in calculating ratios that use amounts from both statements. For many purposes, the income statement figure is best compared to the *average* of the balance sheet figures. In the examples below, such an average is necessarily computed as one half the sum of the amounts on the beginning and ending balance sheets. When other information is available, a more representative average is often preferable, such as the average of the twelve monthly balance sheet figures.

Tests of Profitability

Illustration 11–4 shows each of the items on the income statement expressed as a percentage of sales, which is a commonly used method of examining them. Usually, net sales is taken as 100 per cent, as in the illustration. Of the percentages shown, gross profit (40 per cent), the operating profit (14 per cent), and net income, either before taxes

Illustration 11–3

ARLEN COMPANY

Balance Sheets

(In Thousands of Dollars)

	December 31 1964	1963
ASSETS		
Current Assets:		
Cash	30	30
Accounts receivable	42	32
Less: Allowance for bad debts	2	2
Accounts receivable, net	40	30
Merchandise inventory	60	50
Prepaid expenses	10	10
Total Current Assets	140	120
Fixed Assets:		
Land	30	30
Buildings and equipment	120	120
Less: Accumulated depreciation	70	60
Net buildings and equipment	50	60
Total Fixed Assets	80	90
Other Assets:		
Goodwill and patents	10	0
Total Assets	230	210
EQUITIES		
Current Liabilities:		
Accounts payable	30	25
Accrued wages and taxes	10	10
Estimated income taxes payable	20	15
Total Current Liabilities	60	50
Fixed Liabilities:		
Mortgage bonds, 4 per cent	40	40
Total Liabilities	100	90
Stockholders' Equity:		
Common stock (5,000 shares outstanding)	60	60
Retained earnings	70	60
Total Stockholders' Equity	130	120
Total Equities	230	210

(13.3 per cent) or after taxes (6.7 per cent), are perhaps the most important.

The *gross profit percentage* indicates the average markon or margin obtained on products sold. Since it is an average, it does not necessarily represent the markon on individual products, and these may differ widely from the average.

The *net income percentage* is a measure of overall profitability. Some regard it as the most important single measure of a company's performance, but, as pointed out above, this is not so, since the net income

Illustration 11–4

ARLEN COMPANY

Condensed Income Statement, 1964

(In Thousands of Dollars)

	Dollars	*Percentage*
Gross sales..................................	303	101.0
Less: Returns and allowances....................	3	1.0
Net sales..................................	300	100.0
Less: Cost of sales............................	180	60.0
Gross profit................................	120	40.0
Operating expenses............................	78	26.0
Operating profit............................	42	14.0
Interest....................................	2	0.7
Income before taxes...........................	40	13.3
Provision for income taxes......................	20	6.7
Net Income................................	20	6.7

percentage does not reflect the amount of investment utilized in earning the income.

EXAMPLE: Company A operates a supermarket, and Company B operates a department store. Operating results of each are summarized below:

	A *Super-* *market*	*B* *Department* *Store*
Sales............................	$10,000,000	$10,000,000
Profit...........................	100,000	1,000,000
Total investment..................	1,500,000	5,000,000
Return on sales...................	1%	10%
Return on investment..............	20%	20%

Supermarkets typically operate on a low gross margin, and therefore have a small profit on each dollar of sales, but they also have a much smaller investment per dollar of sales than do department stores. Thus an investor in Company A earns just as high a return on each dollar of his investment as an investor in Company B, even though Company A has a much smaller profit per dollar of sales.

Tests of Liquidity

Liquidity refers to the company's ability to meet its current obligations. The liquidity ratios therefore have to do with the size and relationships of current liabilities, which are the obligations soon coming due, and current assets, which presumably provide the source from which these obligations will be met. A company's financial position is not sound unless it has adequate liquidity. The ratios listed below help to answer the question: "Will the business probably be able to meet its obligations when they become due?"

Current Ratio.

$$\frac{\text{Current assets}}{\text{Current liabilities}} = \frac{\$140,000}{\$60,000} = 2.3 \text{ times, or 2.3 to 1.}$$

In other words, current assets are 2.3 times current liabilities.

The current ratio is the most commonly used of all balance sheet ratios. It is not only a measure of the company's liquidity but also is a measure of the margin of safety that management maintains in order to allow for the inevitable unevenness in the flow of funds through the current asset and liability accounts. If this flow were absolutely smooth and uniform each day (so that, for example, money coming in from customers exactly equaled maturing obligations), the requirements for such a safety margin would be small. Since a company rarely can count on such an even flow, it needs a supply of liquid funds to be assured of being able to pay its bills when they come due. The current ratio indicates the size of this buffer.

The current assets will ordinarily not be used to liquidate the current liabilities, that is, to reduce them to zero, since as some liabilities are paid off others are being created.

In interpreting the current ratio, consideration of the proportion of various types of current assets is important. A company with a high percentage of its current assets in cash is more liquid than one with a high percentage in inventory, even though the companies have the same current ratio.

Acid-Test Ratio.

$$\frac{\text{Quick assets}}{\text{Current liabilities}} = \frac{\$70,000}{\$60,000} = 1.2 \text{ times, or 1.2 to 1.}$$

Quick assets include cash, temporary investments held in lieu of cash, and current accounts and notes receivable. Presumably, these items can be converted into cash quickly and at approximately their stated amounts, unlike inventory which is the principal current asset excluded. The acid test ratio, or *quick ratio,* is therefore a measure of the extent to which liquid resources are immediately available to meet current obligations.

Receivables to Sales.

$$\frac{\text{Receivables (net)}}{\text{Net sales}} = \frac{\$40,000}{\$300,000} = 13.3 \text{ per cent.}$$

If available, the base should be net *credit* sales, which is of course more closely related to accounts receivable than is total sales. Sometimes *average* accounts receivable ($35,000) is used as the numerator, but attention is more properly focused on the year-end figure. Receivables include trade accounts receivable plus trade notes receivable.

Average Collection Period. This is derived from the preceding ratio:

$$\text{RECEIVABLES TO SALES} \times \text{DAYS IN THE PERIOD} = \text{COLLECTION PERIOD.}$$
$$13.3\% \qquad \times \qquad 365 \qquad = \qquad 49 \text{ days.}$$

The collection period can be related roughly to the credit terms offered by the company. A rule of thumb is that the collection period should not exceed $1\frac{1}{3}$ times the regular payment period; that is, if the company's typical terms call for payment in 30 days, it is said that the average collection period should not exceed 40 days. Like all rules of thumb, this one has a great many exceptions. Changes in the ratio indicate changes in the company's credit policy or changes in its ability to collect its receivables.

Inventory Turnover.

$$\frac{\text{Cost of sales}}{\text{Average inventory}} = \frac{\$180,000}{\$55,000} = 3.3 \text{ times.}$$

Inventory turnover is an indication of the velocity with which merchandise moves through the business. An increase in the absolute size of inventory, for example, may represent the additional stocks required by an expanding business, or it may represent an accumulation of merchandise because sales have dropped off. In the latter case, the inventory turnover will decrease. A decrease in the inventory turnover ratio may therefore be a significant danger signal.

If the cost of sales figure is not available, a turnover ratio may be computed using the sales figure instead. Such a ratio does not then show literally how many times the inventory turned over during the year, but if profit margins remain roughly constant, a comparison of this ratio for several years may nevertheless be useful.

Tests of Solvency

As liquidity refers to current obligations, *solvency* refers to a company's ability to meet the interest costs and repayment schedules associated with its long-term obligations.

Equity Ratios. The division of equities among current liabilities, long-term liabilities, and owners' equity and the size of these categories in relation to assets have an important bearing on solvency. These relationships are shown in the following condensed 1964 balance sheet of Arlen Company, derived from Illustration 11–3.

ASSETS		EQUITIES	
	Per Cent		Per Cent
Current assets..............	61	Current liabilities.........	26
Fixed assets...............	35	Long-term liabilities.......	17
Other assets..............	4	Equity capital.............	57
Total Assets........	100	Total Equities......	100

Of the ratios apparent in the above tabulation, the most important are those showing the relationship between *debt capital* and *equity capital*. Debt capital is another name for liabilities. From the point of view of the company, debt capital is risky because if bondholders and other creditors are not paid promptly, they can take legal action to obtain payment which can, in extreme cases, force the company into bankruptcy. Equity capital is much less risky to the company because stockholders receive dividends only at the discretion of the directors.[3] Because the stockholders have less certainty of receiving dividends than the bondholders have of receiving interest, stockholders usually are unwilling to invest in a company unless they see a reasonable expectation of making a higher return than they could obtain as bondholders; that is, they would be unwilling to give up the relatively certain prospect of receiving 5 per cent or 6 per cent interest on bonds, unless the probable, but less certain, return on an equity investment were considerably higher, say 10 per cent or more.

From the company's standpoint, the greater the proportion of its capital that is obtained from stockholders, the less worry the company has in meeting its fixed obligations, but in return for this lessened worry, the company must expect to pay a higher overall cost of obtaining its capital. Conversely, the more funds that are obtained from bonds, the more the company can *trade on the equity;* that is, it can use funds obtained at relatively low interest rates in the hopes of earning more on these funds for the stockholders. The equity ratio shows the balance that the management of a particular company has struck between these forces.

Unfortunately, the equity ratio (often called the *debt/equity ratio* or the *capital/equity ratio*) is defined in two quite different ways; the user

---

[3] Note that "risk" is here viewed from the standpoint of the company. From the standpoint of investors, the opposite view prevails. Thus bondholders have a relatively low risk of receiving their payments, and stockholders have a relatively high risk. From this latter standpoint, equity capital is called "risk capital."

must be always careful to ascertain which meaning is intended in a given situation. One definition includes the current liabilities, and the other excludes them. Including current liabilities, the debt/equity ratio for Arlen Company is 43 to 57, or, expressed the other way around as is often done, 57 to 43, or 1.3 to 1. Excluding current liabilities, the corresponding figures are 17 to 57, or, reversed, 3.4 to 1. This difference in meaning is confusing in general, but in particular situations it is less so because a company or an industry usually settles on one meaning or the other, and those who use the ratios then have a common basis of understanding.

Times Interest Earned.

$$\frac{\text{Operating profit}}{\text{Bond interest}} = \frac{\$42,000}{\$1,600} = 26 \text{ times.}$$

The numerator of this ratio is the amount of earnings available to meet the fixed obligation of bond interest. In the example, interest requirements are said to be *covered* 26 times. This ratio is a measure of the level to which income can decline without impairing the company's ability to meet interest payments on its fixed liabilities. Income is taken before income taxes because if income declined, income taxes would decline proportionately. The ratio implies that net income is equivalent to additional cash, which is not necessarily the case, of course.

If preferred stock is outstanding, a similar coverage ratio can be computed for the preferred stock dividends, but here the numerator is income after taxes and after interest charges ($20,000).

A company may have fixed obligations in addition to its interest payments, as, for example, when it has rental commitments on leased property. In such a case coverage is properly computed by adding these other obligations to the amount of interest. The ratio is then labeled "Times Fixed Charges Earned."

Overall Measures

Return on Investment. This is the grand, overall measure described earlier in this chapter. It can be expressed in several ways. From the viewpoint of the stockholders, it is the *return on stockholders' investment:*

$$\frac{\text{Net income}}{\text{Average stockholders' equity}} = \frac{\$20,000}{\$125,000} = 16 \text{ per cent.}$$

In computing the average stockholders' equity, a simple average of the beginning and ending figures should not be used if additional equity funds were obtained and put to use at other than at the middle of the year. New funds obtained near the end of the year, for example, might well be excluded from the denominator of the fraction because the income in the numerator did not arise from the use of these funds.

A variation of the above, called the return on *tangible net worth,* eliminates intangible assets from the stockholders' equity, thus:

$$\frac{\text{Net income}}{\text{Avg. net worth} - \text{Avg. intangibles}} = \frac{\$20,000}{\$125,000 - \$5,000} = 16.7 \text{ per cent.}$$

Return on total investment looks at income in relation to the total of the permanent funds invested in the enterprise. These permanent funds consist of stockholders' equity plus noncurrent liabilities; or the same figure may be found by subtracting current liabilities from total assets. The earnings on these funds are usually taken as net income before income taxes, plus interest on noncurrent liabilities. The ratio is as follows:

$$\frac{\text{Pretax operating profit}}{\text{Equity capital} + \text{Fixed liabilities}} = \frac{\$42,000}{\$125,000 + \$40,000} = 25.5 \text{ per cent.}$$

If the interest figure on the income statement included interest on current borrowings as well as bond interest, the interest on current liabilities would be subtracted from operating profit. Sometimes an after-tax figure is used.

The return-on-total-investment ratio is a measure of how well management has used all the permanent funds entrusted to the business. Or, put another way, this ratio is intended to measure the earning power of the net assets (net working capital plus other assets) of the business.

For many purposes, especially for comparing one division of a company with another division, return on investment is best figured on the basis of *gross assets,* which means working capital plus fixed assets at cost but with no deduction for accumulated depreciation. The rationale for such a computation is discussed in Chapter 15.

Return on investment can be calculated in another manner which, although it is longer and gives the same result, is often more illuminating. Two subsidiary ratios, *investment turnover* and *operating profit on sales,* are calculated first. Investment turnover is as follows:

$$\frac{\text{Sales}}{\text{Equity capital} + \text{Fixed liabilities}} = \frac{\$300,000}{\$125,000 + \$40,000} = 1.82 \text{ times.}$$

The operating profit ratio, 14.0 per cent, is given on Illustration 11–4. Then:

INVESTMENT TURNOVER $\times$ OP. PROFIT RATIO = RETURN ON INVESTMENT.

     1.82 times $\times$ 14.0 per cent   =   25.5 per cent.

Many consider this to be the most useful way of looking at the overall performance of a business. It shows that performance can be improved either by generating more sales volume per dollar of capital employed or by increasing the profit margin on each sales dollar generated. It shows that a supermarket earning 1 per cent on sales may be doing as good a job for its investors as a department store earning 10 per cent when the supermarket has an investment turnover of twenty and the department store a turnover of two.

Market Tests. Persons who study the financial statements of companies as a basis for deciding where to invest their funds may use any of a number of other ratios in addition to those already listed. Some of these are mentioned below.

Earnings per share:

$$\frac{\text{Net income}}{\text{Shares outstanding}} = \frac{\$20,000}{5,000} = \$4 \text{ per share.}$$

If there is preferred stock, its claim to earnings (usually its dividend) is deducted from net income in order to find the amount earned on the common stock. Earnings per share is of considerable importance in estimating the value, and hence the proper market price, of a share of stock.

The *price-earnings ratio* is based on the average market price of the stock. Assuming the market price for Arlen Company's stock is $36, the ratio is as follows:

$$\frac{\text{Market price per share}}{\text{Earnings per share}} = \frac{\$36}{\$4} = 9 \text{ to } 1.$$

Turning this ratio upside down gives the *capitalization rate,* the rate at which the stock market is apparently capitalizing the value of current earnings:

$$\frac{\text{Earnings per share}}{\text{Market price per share}} = \frac{\$4}{\$36} = 11 \text{ per cent.}$$

Finally, the *yield,* or more properly the *dividend yield,* is based on dividends declared during the year. Assuming the Arlen Company declares a $2 dividend, the ratio is as follows:

$$\frac{\text{Dividends per share}}{\text{Price per share}} = \frac{\$2}{\$36} = 5.6 \text{ per cent.}$$

DIFFICULTIES IN MAKING COMPARISONS

Reasonably accurate reports of actual performance often can be obtained (although the problems involved in obtaining them may be by no means trivial). Finding an adequate standard, however, is in business always a perplexing and difficult matter.

Some of the problems are described below. Financial statement analysis is used as an example, but the same problems arise in analyzing other types of quantitative data. When a person says that performance is "good" or "poor," "better" or "worse," he is, either implicitly or explicitly, comparing actual performance to some standard that he believes is relevant.

1. Deciding on the Proper Basis for Comparison

Subject only to minor qualifications, a boy who runs a mile in six minutes (or, expressed as a ratio, ten miles per hour) is a better miler than a boy who runs a mile in seven minutes. In business, there are many situations in which one cannot tell whether a higher number represents better performance than a lower number.

A high current ratio is by no means necessarily better than a low current ratio. The current ratio for the Arlen Company on December 31, 1964, was 2.3 to 1. Suppose that $40,000 of the current liabilities came due the very next day and that the company in fact paid these liabilities, using every dollar of its available cash and liquidating other current assets as well. A balance sheet prepared subsequent to this transaction would show $100,000 of current assets and $20,000 of current liabilities, and the current ratio would accordingly be 5.0 to 1, more than double the ratio of the previous day. Yet one could scarcely say that a company that had used up all its cash was in an improved financial condition. Or, conversely, consider what happens when a company expands, as illustrated by the Arlen Company balance sheet at the end of 1964 compared with its balance sheet for the end of 1963. Current assets have increased by $20,000, and current liabilities have increased by only $10,000; yet the current ratio has dropped from 2.4 : 1 to 2.3 : 1. The decrease may indicate no worsening of the company's liquid position at all; rather, it may reflect the result of a well-carried-out expansion program.

In some comparisons the direction of change that represents "good" or "better" is reasonably apparent. Generally, a high net profit percentage is better than a low one, and a high return on investment is better than a low one. Even these statements have many qualifications, however.

Many standards can usefully be thought of as a *quality range* rather than as a single number. When actual performance is within this rage, it may be regarded as satisfactory. When it begins to go outside the range, *in either direction,* there is an indication of an unsatisfactory situation. For a certain company, the current ratio may be considered satisfactory if it is within the range 2.0–3.0. Below 2.0, there is the danger of being unable to meet maturing obligations. Above 3.0, there is an indication that funds are being left idle rather than being efficiently employed. As another example, a too-high profit ratio may indicate that the company is only "skimming the cream" off the market; a deeper penetration may increase sales and total return on investment even if the ratio of profit to sales is reduced.

2. Differences in the Situations Being Compared

No reasonable person would expect a nine-year-old boy to run as fast as a nineteen-year-old athlete; in judging the boy's performance, we attempt to compare his speed with that of other boys of the same age and with similar training. Differences in the factors that affect one company's performance this year as compared with those that affect the same company's performance last year, or the performance of another company, are complex and difficult to evaluate. Nevertheless, some attempt must be made to allow for these differences. In general, this task is least difficult when all the figures being compared pertain to the same company (although even here changes in size, in the functions performed by the company, in outside influences, and so on may make comparisons of tenuous validity). The task is more difficult when attempting to compare one company with another, even if they are both of the same size and in the same industry, and it becomes exceedingly difficult if the two companies are in different industries or if they are of substantially different size.

3. Changes in the Dollar Measuring Stick

Accounting figures are expressed in historical dollars. A change in the value of a dollar, that is, a change in price levels, may therefore seriously lessen the validity of comparisons of ratios computed for different time periods. Also, a ratio whose numerator and denominator are expressed in different kinds of dollars may have no useful meaning.

The fact that asset amounts are stated as unexpired historical dollar costs causes particular difficulty in making comparisons of ratios calculated from such amounts. Two companies, for example, might have facilities that were physically identical in all respects except age, and they might operate exactly the same way and earn exactly the same net income. If, however, the buildings and equipment of one company had been purchased at a time when prices were low or if they had been almost fully depreciated, and if the buildings and equipment of the other company had been purchased at a time of higher prices or if they were relatively new, then the return-on-investment ratio for the company that carried its assets at a low book value would be much higher than the ratio for the other company.

4. Differences in Definition

The terms "one mile" and "six minutes" used to measure the runner are precisely defined and easily measured, but such terms as "current assets" and "current liabilities" are by no means precisely defined, and there is considerable diversity in practice as to how they should be measured. Some of the many differences have been described in earlier chapters.

Similar differences affect the standards against which actual performance is compared. For example, the following are estimates of the "Profits as a per cent of sales of U.S. Manufacturing Companies in 1960" as reported by various agencies:[4]

	Per Cent
First National City Bank	5.5
Federal Trade Commission—SEC	4.5
Department of Commerce	3.3
Internal Revenue Service	2.7

The highest figure is twice as high as the lowest. The differences result both from differences in the way "profits" are defined and from differences in the data collected.

5. Hidden Short-Run Changes

A balance sheet may not reflect the average or typical situation. A balance sheet is prepared as of one moment of time, and it tells nothing about short-term fluctuations in assets and equities that have occurred

---

[4] Estimated from charts in *First National City Bank Letter*, January 1963, which gives some explanation of the differences.

within the period bounded by the two balance sheet dates. Many department stores, for example, end their fiscal year and publish annual balance sheets as of January 31. By that date, Christmas inventories have been sold out and many of the Christmas receivables have been paid, but Easter merchandise has not started to arrive and payables for this merchandise have not yet been generated. Current assets (other than cash) and current liabilities as reported on the January 31 balance sheet are therefore likely to be lower than at other times of the year, and as a result ratios such as merchandise turnover and the average collection period may be distorted, and other ratios may not be representative of the situation at other seasons. A company that is analyzing its own data can study the seasonal movements by using monthly, rather than annual, balance sheets, but these are ordinarily not available to the outsider.

The analyst should also recognize that companies have been known to take deliberate steps to "clean up" their balance sheets. They may, for example, pay off loans just before the end of the year, which inevitably increases the current ratio, and then borrow again early in the next year. Such transactions, which are called *window dressing,* may not be discernible on the balance sheet.

6. The Past as an Indication of the Future

Financial statements are historical documents, and financial ratios show relationships that have existed in the past. The analyst is, of course, interested in what is happening now and what is likely to happen in the future rather than what did happen in the past. Often the analyst has no choice but to rely on past data as an indication of the current situation, but he should not be misled into believing that the historical ratios necessarily reflect current conditions.

POSSIBLE BASES FOR COMPARISON

There are three types of standards against which an actual figure can be compared: (1) a goal; (2) a historical figure; and (3) an external figure, that is, a figure for performance in another company, or other companies.

Goals

Many companies prepare *budgets,* which show *what performance is expected to be under the circumstances prevailing.* If actual performance corresponds with budgeted performance, there is a reasonable inference that the performance is good. There are two important qualifications that affect this inference, however. First, the budgeted figures may not have been set very carefully in the first instance, and the comparison can of course be no more valid than the goal figures themselves. Secondly, the goals were necessarily set on the basis of certain assumptions as to the conditions that would be prevailing during the period, and if these assumptions turn out to be incorrect, the goal figures are also incorrect as a measure of results "under the circumstances prevailing." If, because of a recession or other economic phenomenon outside the control of management, profits are lower than the amount budgeted, it cannot fairly be said that the difference between actual and budgeted profit indicates "poor" performance. Nevertheless, the budget is a type of standard that has fewer inherent difficulties than either the historical standards or the external standards.

Historical Standards

A comparison of current performance with past figures for the same company usually does not run into the problem of differences in accounting practice. If practices have changed, the change is presumably known to the analyst. Moreover, the analyst can also recollect, or find out from supplementary data, some of the circumstances that have changed between the two periods and thus allow for these changes in making his comparison. At best, however, a comparison between a current figure and a historical figure in the same company can show only that the current period is "better" or "worse" than the past. In many cases this does not provide a sound basis for judgment, for the historical figure may not have represented an acceptable standard. If a company increases its return on investment from 1 per cent to 2 per cent, it has improved, but it still is not doing very well.

External Standards

When one company is compared with another, the environmental and accounting differences affecting the two sets of figures may raise serious problems of comparability. If, however, the analyst is able to allow for these differences, even approximately, he obtains an outside check on performance that has the advantage, over a standard derived from internal sources, of being independently arrived at. Moreover, the two companies may well have been affected by the same set of economic conditions, so this important cause of noncomparability may not be operating.

Corporations whose stock is traded on organized security exchanges file annual reports with the U.S. Securities and Exchange Commission, and these "Form 10-K" reports are likely to be more useful for comparisons than the annual reports sent to stockholders, both because the SEC prescribes a uniform format and terminology and because the 10-K reports usually contain more detailed information than reports to stockholders.

Many sources contain *average ratios* for groups of companies in the same industry or of similar size. Perhaps the best known are those published by Dun & Bradstreet, Inc., in the magazine *Modern Industry* and in separate booklets. For each of seventy industry groups, the following ratios are published (starred items have been described above; the derivation of the others should be apparent):

*Current ratio
*Net profit as a percentage of net sales
*Return on tangible net worth
 Net profit as a percentage of net working capital
*Net sales as a percentage of tangible net worth
 Net sales as a percentage of net working capital
*Average collection period
*Ratio of net sales to inventory
 Ratio of fixed assets to tangible net worth
 Ratio of current debt to tangible net worth
*Equity ratio
 Ratio of inventory to net working capital
 Ratio of current liabilities to inventory
 Ratio of funded debt to net working capital.

Ratios prepared by another organization, Robert Morris Associates, are given in Case 11–2. A variety of ratios will also be found in *Moody's Manual of Investments, Standard and Poor's Corporation Records,* and other publications prepared for investors.

Use of these industry-wide ratios involves all the difficulties of using ratios derived from one other company plus the special problems that arise when the figures for several companies are thrown together into a single average. Nevertheless, they may give some worthwhile impressions about the average situation in an industry.

Many trade associations and other groups collect and publish figures for the companies in an industry. In some instances, the association prescribes in detail the accounting definitions and concepts to be used in reporting these figures, and the resulting figures are therefore much more comparable than those compiled by the sources mentioned above, who must use the basic data in whatever form the company chooses to report it.

USE OF COMPARISONS

The principal value of an analysis of financial statement information is that it suggests questions that need to be answered; such an analysis rarely provides the answers. An unfavorable difference between actual performance and whatever standard is used, if it is large, indicates that something *may be* wrong, and this leads to an investigation. Even when the analysis indicates strongly that something *is* wrong (as when one company's profits have declined while those of comparable companies have increased), the analysis rarely shows what the *cause* of the difficulty is. Nevertheless, the ability to pick from the thousands of questions that *might* be asked those few that are really worth answering is an important one.

In analyzing financial statements, the experienced person usually does not rely completely on any one of the standards discussed above. He tempers the numerical comparisons with his personal "feel" for what is right in a given set of circumstances. He cannot explain exactly how he does it, but judgment based on experience is certainly superior to the mere mechanical application of ratios.

It is well to keep in mind the basic relationships shown in Illustration 11–1, or some variation of these applicable to the situation being analyzed. The only number that encompasses all these relationships is a return-on-investment ratio. A change in any less inclusive ratio may be misleading as an indication of better or worse performance unless possible compensating changes in factors not covered by the ratio are taken into account. An increase in net profits indicates improved performance only if there was no offsetting increase in the investment required. An increase in the net profit ratio indicates improved performance only if there was no offsetting decrease in sales volume or increase in investment. An increase in the gross profit percentage indicates improved performance only if there was no offsetting decrease in sales volume, increase in investment, or increase in expenses.

In short, any ratio other than return on investment, taken by itself, implies that all other things are equal. This *ceteris paribus* condition ordinarily does not prevail, and the validity of comparisons is lessened to the extent that it does not. Yet the return-on-investment ratio is so broad that it does not give a clue as to which of the underlying factors may be responsible for changes in it. It is to find these factors, which if unfavorable indicate possible trouble areas, that the subsidiary ratios of profitability are used. Furthermore, the return-on-investment ratio tells nothing about the financial condition of the company; liquidity and solvency ratios are necessary for this purpose.

In addition to, or in place of, the simple ratio of one number to another, many businessmen develop a more complicated set of interrelationships that they find useful in isolating the key factors that affect good performance. An automobile dealer may say: "If the gross profit on service and parts sales is large enough to cover total general and administrative expenses, and if we break even on used car sales, then we will earn an adequate profit for the whole business from the gross margin less selling costs on new car sales." Usually, there is no way of demonstrating that these relationships are logically correct,—there is no logical reason why gross profit on one part of the automobile dealer's business should just equal general and administrative costs for the whole business—but the fact is that they do work out.

SUMMARY

The figures on financial statements are usually useful for analytical purposes only when they are expressed in relative terms in the form of ratios and percentages. Although a great many ratios can be calculated, only a few are ordinarily necessary in connection with a given problem.

The essential task is to find a standard or norm with which actual performance can be compared. In general, there are three types of standards: (1) goals, or budgets, set in advance of the period under review; (2) historical figures, showing performance of the same company in the past; and (3) the performance of other companies, as shown by their financial statements, or by averages compiled from the financial statements of a number of companies. None of these is perfect, but a rough allowance for the factors that cause noncomparability often can be made.

The comparison may then suggest important questions that need to be investigated; it rarely indicates answers to the questions.

APPENDIX

Comparisons Involving Percentages

Two of the technical matters involved in making a comparison of percentage figures are discussed below: (1) the choice of a base, and (2) averaging.

Choice of a Base

Suppose that sales in a company were $1.5 million in 1959 and $1.8 million in 1960. The change can be expressed in any one of four ways: (1)

sales in 1960 were 120 per cent of sales in 1959 (1.8/1.5 [100] = 120); (2) sales in 1960 were 20 per cent higher than 1959 sales (120 − 100 = 20); (3) sales in 1959 were 83 per cent of 1960 sales (1.5/1.8 [100] = 83); and (4) sales in 1959 were 17 per cent lower than 1960 sales (83 − 100 = −17). All these statements are true, but the first two statements imply the use of the 1959 sales figure as a base while the third and fourth refer to 1960 sales as a base. So long as the particular base chosen is clearly indicated, either base may be used. When statements about the percentage choice do not clearly indicate what figure is used as the base, misunderstandings can easily be created. In order to lessen these misunderstandings, it has become conventional when comparing one time period with another to *use the earlier period as the base.* This practice should be followed as a matter of course, unless there is a compelling reason to make an exception to it. In the example above, then, the better choices would be "1960 sales were 120 per cent of 1959," or "1960 sales were 20 per cent higher than 1959 sales."

Another convention customarily followed is the one for expressing "markon," which is a relationship between cost and selling price. Markon is ordinarily expressed as a percentage of selling price, *not* as a percentage of cost. Thus, if an article has a cost of $0.60 and a selling price of $1.00, its markon is said to be 40 per cent, not 66⅔ per cent.

Incidentally, note the following type of difficulty that arises when the base is unconsciously shifted: Suppose the number of employees in a company is reduced 50 per cent, that subsequently it is increased 30 per cent, and still later it is increased 20 per cent. Is the number of employees now the same as at the beginning? Not if each change is figured from the base existing at the time of the change, for a quick calculation will show that the two increases have brought the labor force back to only 78 per cent of its original size. This illustrates the general point that if a number is decreased by a certain percentage, the resulting number must be increased by a larger percentage to get back to the original number. For example, if the number 10 is decreased by 40 per cent, the result, 6, must be increased by 66⅔ per cent (rather than 40 per cent) to get back to the original number, 10.

Another problem in using the correct base arises when percentages are compared with one another. If the net profit on Product A is 2 per cent of sales and on Product B, 3 per cent, B's profit ratio is 50 per cent, *not* 1 per cent, higher than A's, since 3 is 150 per cent of 2. It is, however, a common and correct practice to describe B's profit as one *percentage point* higher than A's.

Averaging Percentages

Suppose that the divisional income statements of a company with three divisions show the following percentages of net profit to sales:

Division	Profit Percentage
A	3
B	7
C	5

Can it be said that the average profit for all divisions is 5 per cent (i.e., 3 per cent + 7 per cent + 5 per cent, divided by 3)? Unless the divisions are the same size, the answer is "no." A simple average is valid only when the separate percentages have the same relative importance. If the percentages are of varying importance, either the overall percentage must be computed from the totals for the three divisions or a *weighted* average must be used. Assume the following performance of the three divisions:

Division	Sales (Thousands of Dollars)	Profit (Thousands of Dollars)	Profit Percentage
A	1,000	30	3
B	300	21	7
C	700	35	5
Total	2,000	86	

One way of finding the profit percentage of the company is to divide total profit (86) by total sales (2,000), giving an overall profit percentage of 4.3 per cent. This procedure is simple if sales and profit data are available for the three divisions, but there are situations where the aggregates cannot be determined from the available data. In these situations, an overall percentage may be found by taking a *weighted average* of the individual percentages. Weights may be expressed either in *absolute* terms (e.g., sales dollars) or in *relative* terms (e.g., the proportion of each plant's sales to the whole). Both methods are shown below. Although the weighting procedure is not actually necessary in this case, since the answer has already been found from the aggregates, the figures illustrate the method:

Division	A. Absolute Weights			B. Relative Weights		
	Weight (Sales in Thousands of Dollars)	Profit Percentage	Weighted Percentage	Weight (Sales Relative)	Profit Percentage	Weighted Percentage
A	1,000	3	3,000	50	3	150
B	300	7	2,100	15	7	105
C	700	5	3,500	35	5	175
	2,000		8,600	100		430

$$\text{Average} = \frac{8,600}{2,000} = 4.3 \qquad \text{Average} = \frac{430}{100} = 4.3$$

Note that the sum of the weighted values is divided by the sum of the weights, not by the number of items being averaged.

Rounding

Rounding is dropping some of the digits at the right-hand portion of a number. Thus, on highway sign posts 22.16 miles would be reported as 22, and we often say an automobile cost $2,800, even though its exact price was, perhaps, $2,793.55.

The customary rules for rounding are as follows:

1. In rounding numbers, a digit *less than 5* or a *fraction less than one half* is discarded; a digit *greater than 5* or a *fraction more than one half* adds 1 to the digit next to the left. For example, 12.7 is rounded to 13; 12.4 to 12; and 12,501 to 13,000.

2. When an *even 5* or the *fraction* ½ is to be dropped, the digit to the left, if *even,* is unchanged; if *odd,* it is raised by one. Under this rule, all numbers which have been rounded by dropping an even 5 or the fraction ½ will be reported as even numbers: thus 11½ is rounded to 12; 12½ to 12; 13½ to 14; 87½ to 88; and 12,500 to 12,000. Some people follow the practice of raising all numbers ending in 5 or ½ by one. This rule introduces a slight upward bias in the rounding process, and its use as a general rule of rounding is therefore not recommended.

Rounding is a process which can be of great help in the use and interpretation of figures. Most people find it difficult to think in terms of large numbers. For example, a speaker may state that a certain expenditure was two billion, one hundred ninety-one million, four hundred thirteen thousand, two hundred seventy-six dollars and twenty-three cents. By the time he has finished, the strongest impression remaining with his audience is "23 cents," the least important part of the entire figure. It is much more effective to report such a figure as "2 billion dollars" or "2.2 billion dollars."

In other circumstances, limits of accuracy call for rounding. Where digits included in a number are not known to be correct, they should be dropped and the remaining figures which are known to be correct should be rounded, as described below.

Significant Digits

The significant digits in a number are the digits known to be correct (although the digit farthest to the right may often be only an approximation). In considering the problem of determining how many significant digits should be reported, it is helpful to remember that there are two kinds of numbers: (1) those which represent a *count,* and (2) those which represent a *measurement* or estimate. Examples of the first type are "three children," "1,067 students," "twelve months." These numbers are said to be discontinuous or discrete; that is, there is a gap or space between each number (e.g., there cannot be "three and a fraction" children; the next number has to be four). Counts, or discrete numbers, are completely significant; that is, every digit has significance.

On the other hand, many of the numbers used in accounting are *measurements,* and all measurements are approximations. Their significance is limited by the accuracy of the measuring rod or of the observer. When a man views a tower from a distance and judges its height to be 500 feet, he may mean that in his opinion the tower is closer to 500 than to either 400 or 600 feet. When this is the intended meaning, the number 500 has only one significant digit, 5; the zeros were inserted merely to locate the decimal point.

A second man might estimate the tower's height as 520 feet, by which he means that it is closer to 520 than to either 510 or 530 feet. The degree of reported uncertainty has been considerably reduced in this estimate, and this is shown by the fact that the number now has two significant digits, 5 and 2. The zero once again does not represent a measurement but is used only to locate the decimal point. If the second man is in fact a keener observer than the first, his measurement is more precise; it has more significant digits. The use of even better observers and more refined measuring instruments can increase the accuracy in successive stages, for example: 500, 520, 523, 522.8, 522.81. The number of significant digits thus increases from 1 to 5. However, there is always some limit to accuracy; even radar, which measures the timing of electrical waves in terms of millionths of a second, is not precisely accurate.

The following rules are helpful in counting the significant digits in a number, subject to the qualification explained in the next paragraph:

1. All digits other than *zeros* are significant.
2. Zeros are not significant when—
   a) They are at the extreme left of a number (0.0019); or
   b) They are at the extreme right of a number *and* at the left of the decimal point (19,000).

Thus, the number 0.0019 and the number 19,000 each have two significant digits. The number 4,203 has four, and 500.00 has five significant digits. Note that a zero to the right of the decimal point, as above, indicates that all digits to the left are significant. Zeros at the left of a whole number (e.g., 0019) are meaningless and should be omitted.

These rules are not sufficient for all cases. A person might give a measurement as 500 feet and really mean "closer to 500 than to 499 or 501." In this context, 500 has three significant digits. In situations of this kind, the significance can be inferred only from the context and not solely from the number and location of zeros.

Rules for Significant Digits

The following rules for treatment of significant digits are worth noting:

1. In *multiplication and division* the number of significant digits in a product or quotient is not more than the number of significant digits in the less precise of the two numbers entering into the calculation. That figure is less precise which has the smaller number of significant digits and not the number of decimal places (i.e., digits beyond the decimal point). For example, 91,100 tons per year is equal to 7,590 tons per month since 91,100 (with three significant digits) divided by the whole number 12 gives an answer with three significant digits. Although 91,100 divided by 12 equals 7,591.66666⅔, the final figure should not be reported as more significant than 7,590. Note that in the above example, 91,100 is the less significant of the two figures since the other number, 12, is significant to an infinite number of places. (There are exactly 12.000 . . . months in a year.)

2. In *addition and subtraction* the answer contains no more correct decimal places than those in the least precise of the numbers. Thus, in addition and subtraction it is the number of significant digits with reference to the decimal place that governs. For example, $25,000 plus $1,000 (both estimates) equals $26,000; and $25,000 (an estimate) plus $1,312.21 (six significant digits) equals $26,000.

Following these rules will still not guarantee the same degree of accuracy as a scientist would require; however, they are adequate for most business purposes.[5]

Use of the Rules

Application of these rules does not require that digits without significance always be dropped, especially in intermediate stages of the calculation. It is usually desirable to retain one and perhaps two digits beyond the number that is significant. At each stage of the work, however, all digits that have no influence on the final result should be rejected. In the final answer all digits that are not significant should be eliminated by the process of rounding.

In the application of the above rules, some sticky problems arise. Fortunately, most of these are of academic, rather than practical, importance. In a practical situation, reporting one digit more or less than those that actually are significant makes little real difference. The important thing is to recognize that no amount of calculating can make a number more precise than it was to begin with.

SUGGESTIONS FOR FURTHER READING

FOULKE, ROY A. *Practical Financial Statement Analysis.* 5th ed. New York: McGraw-Hill Book Co., Inc., 1961.

GRAHAM, BENJAMIN; DODD, DAVID L.; AND COTTLE, SIDNEY. *Security Analysis: Principles and Technique.* 4th ed. New York: McGraw-Hill Book Co., Inc., 1963.

KENNEDY, RALPH DALE, AND MCMULLEN, STEWART YARDWOOD. *Financial Statements: Form, Analysis, and Interpretation.* 4th ed. Homewood, Ill.: Richard D. Irwin, Inc., 1962.

MYER, JOHN N. *Financial Statement Analysis: Principles and Technique:* 3d ed. New York: Prentice-Hall, Inc., 1961.

CASES

CASE 11–1.   SWIFT AND COMPANY

Exhibits 1 and 2 show financial statements for Swift and Company. Exhibit 3 gives financial ratios for this company and three other meat-packers.

---

[5] For some purposes, the significance of an answer is determined by using the maximum *percentage* of error in each figure in the calculation. This is a more precise statement of the rule than that given here, but it is also more complicated to apply. Considering zeros as insignificant, as is done here, will usually give satisfactory results.

Exhibit 1

SWIFT AND COMPANY

Balance Sheets

	Oct. 28, 1961		Oct. 27, 1962	
ASSETS				
Current Assets:				
Cash..............................	$ 16,747,536	3%	$ 22,429,471	4%
Marketable securities................	....	..	4,894,167	1
Accounts receivable.................	117,332,517	20	117,250,307	20
Inventories........................	172,048,699	29	171,697,113	29
Prepaid items......................	3,075,736	1	3,048,285	0
Total Current Assets..............	$309,204,488	53%	$319,319,343	54%
Investments and other long-term assets...	$ 28,430,336	5%	$ 31,351,813	5%
Fixed Assets:				
Property, plant, and equipment........	$498,416,218	86%	$500,679,410	84%
Less: Accumulated depreciation......	(253,701,197)	(44)	(257,953,858)	(43)
Net Fixed Assets................	$244,715,021	42%	$242,725,552	41%
Total Assets...................	$582,349,845	100%	$593,396,708	100%
LIABILITIES				
Current Liabilities:				
Accounts payable and accrued liabilities.	$ 69,274,567	12%	$ 72,015,239	12%
Income taxes for current and prior years.	3,628,386	1	5,042,499	1
Provision for replacement of basic Lifo				
inventory.........................	695,168	0	558,675	0
Current portion of long-term debt.....	262,500	0	393,750	0
Total Current Liabilities..........	$ 73,860,621	13%	$ 78,010,163	13%
Long-term debt......................	$112,390,500	19%	$111,140,750	19%
Reserve for costs of closing plants........	$ 10,384,175	2%	$ 8,138,486	1%
Deferred income taxes..................	$ 5,252,645	1%	$ 5,697,030	2%
Stockholders' Equities:				
Capital stock......................	$150,000,000	26%	$150,000,000	25%
Accumulated earnings................	230,715,052	39	237,432,931	40
Less: Treasury stock...............	(253,148)	0	(22,652)	0
Total Stockholders' Equities......	$380,461,904	65%	$387,410,279	65%
Total Liabilities..............	$582,349,845	100%	$593,396,708	100%

Exhibit 2

SWIFT AND COMPANY

Income Statements

	1961		1962	
Sales and service revenues......	$2,488,980,885	100.00%	$2,494,552,800	100.00%
Cost of goods sold............	2,280,825,135	91.64	2,275,395,745	91.21
Gross profit....................	$ 208,155,750	8.36%	$ 219,157,055	8.79%
Operating expenses:				
Depreciation...............	$ 21,999,806	0.88%	$ 21,566,157	0.87%
Selling and administration....	142,740,096	5.74	138,852,645	5.57
Other charges..............	24,758,063	0.99	26,760,353	1.07
Total Operating Expenses..	$ 189,497,965	7.61%	$ 187,179,155	7.51%
Operating profit..............	$ 18,657,785	0.75%	$ 31,977,900	1.28%
Other income.................	6,236,795	0.25	3,811,620	0.15
Total Income..............	$ 24,894,580	1.00%	$ 35,789,520	1.43%
Interest charges..............	4,652,154	0.19	5,046,549	0.20
Net income before taxes........	$ 20,242,426	0.81%	$ 30,742,971	1.23%
Taxes on income..............	8,192,738	0.33	14,429,044	0.58
Net Income after Taxes.........	$ 12,049,688	0.48%	$ 16,313,927	0.65%

ADDITIONAL INFORMATION FOR 1962

Average capital stock outstanding.....................5,995,204 shares
Price range of stock............................... 49⅜–31½
Dividends declared................................. $1.60

Exhibit 3

COMPARATIVE RATIOS IN THE MEAT-PACKING INDUSTRY

	1952	1960	1961	1962
Gross Profit as a % of Sales:				
Swift...........................	7.9	9.2	8.4	....
Armour..........................	7.0	10.3	9.8	10.3
Cudahy..........................	3.5	6.2	5.8	6.2
Wilson..........................	9.7	8.7	9.5	9.4
Net Income as a % of Sales:				
Swift...........................	0.84	0.75	0.48	....
Armour..........................	0.33	0.93	0.75	0.80
Cudahy..........................	(0.12)	0.24	(0.11)	(0.27)
Wilson..........................	0.45	0.34	1.11	1.07
Current Ratio:				
Swift...........................	2.52	3.44	4.18	....
Armour..........................	2.30	4.45	4.28	3.90
Cudahy..........................	1.84	2.17	1.92	1.81
Wilson..........................	1.97	4.12	3.51	3.51
Acid-Test Ratio:				
Swift...........................	1.03	1.48	1.86	....
Armour..........................	0.86	2.51	2.40	2.12
Cudahy..........................	0.76	0.94	0.87	0.77
Wilson..........................	0.75	1.83	1.81	1.72
Receivables as a % of Sales:				
Swift...........................	3.71	4.34	4.71	....
Armour..........................	3.84	5.02	5.27	5.70
Cudahy..........................	2.51	2.94	3.36	3.52
Wilson..........................	3.83	4.43	4.16	4.47
Average Collection Period in Days:				
Swift...........................	13.5	15.8	17.2	....
Armour..........................	14.0	18.3	19.2	20.8
Cudahy..........................	9.2	10.7	12.3	12.8
Wilson..........................	14.0	16.2	15.2	16.3
Inventory Turnover (Based upon Sales):				
Swift...........................	15.3	14.9	14.3	....
Armour..........................	11.6	15.1	15.7	16.0
Cudahy..........................	13.9	15.5	15.5	15.0
Wilson..........................	10.9	12.5	14.9	15.3
Equity as a % of Total Assets:				
Swift...........................	66.8	68.3	65.3	....
Armour..........................	53.7	55.1	53.0	55.7
Cudahy..........................	46.1	58.2	55.8	55.6
Wilson..........................	56.6	68.6	66.7	66.4
Number of Times the Fixed Charges Were Earned:				
Swift...........................	14.5	6.4	5.4	...
Armour..........................	4.1	6.1	5.3	5.1
Cudahy..........................	(11.0)	3.8	(1.8)	0.29
Wilson..........................	3.0	3.7	15.5	15.6

Exhibit 3—Continued

	1952	1960	1961	1962
Return on Investment:				
Swift............................	6.4	4.7	3.1	....
Armour..........................	3.1	8.8	9.2	7.4
Cudahy..........................	DEF	2.1	DEF	DEF
Wilson..........................	3.9	2.1	8.1	7.7
Return on Total Assets:				
Swift............................	4.2	3.2	2.1	....
Armour..........................	1.4	4.1	3.0	3.4
Cudahy..........................	DEF	1.2	DEF	DEF
Wilson..........................	2.4	1.5	5.3	5.1
Investment Turnover:				
Swift............................	6.6	5.1	4.9	....
Armour..........................	5.9	5.1	4.7	5.1
Cudahy..........................	10.1	6.8	7.1	7.2
Wilson..........................	7.9	5.0	5.8	5.8
Earnings per Share:				
Swift............................	$3.66	$3.09	$2.01	....
Armour..........................	1.02	3.10	2.45	$2.75
Cudahy..........................	(4.77)	0.24	(0.54)	(0.84)
Wilson..........................	1.28	0.53	3.08	2.98
*Price Earnings Ratio:**				
Swift............................	9.0	14.7	22.0	....
Armour..........................	10.4	11.5	18.6	16.2
Cudahy..........................	Nil	47.0	Nil	Nil
Wilson..........................	8.5	73.3	15.3	15.2
*Capitalization Rate:**				
Swift............................	11.1	6.8	4.5	....
Armour..........................	9.6	8.7	5.4	6.2
Cudahy..........................	Nil	2.1	Nil	Nil
Wilson..........................	11.8	1.4	6.5	6.6
*Dividend Yields:**				
Swift............................	6.1	4.1	4.2	....
Armour..........................	Nil	3.4	3.1	3.1
Cudahy..........................	Nil	Nil	Nil	Nil
Wilson..........................	6.9	4.1	3.4	3.5

* In these ratios the market price was calculated as the average of the year's high and low prices.

Questions

1. Compute and fill in the 1962 ratios for Swift and Company.

2. What significant information about Swift can be learned from those data?

CASE 11–2.   SECOND NATIONAL BANK

Mr. Fred Guthart, the president of Housewares, Inc., had recently discussed with Mr. John Irving, a loan officer of the Second National Bank, the possibility of establishing a relationship with the bank. Mr. Guthart hoped that in the future his company could borrow money from the bank. From his discussion on December 15, 1959, with Mr. Guthart and from subsequent credit investigations, Mr. Irving had obtained the information about Housewares, Inc., given in the following paragraphs.

The company manufactured injection molded plastic products with 90 per cent of its volume in housewares, such as refrigerator ice trays, cups, and mixing bowls, and the remaining 10 per cent in custom molded components for industry. Manufacturers' representatives distributed the products nationally to jobbers, department stores, and rack jobbers who installed and maintained display racks in supermarkets.

The company was originally chartered in 1945. In 1949 the late Thomas Starr acquired a controlling interest in Housewares, Inc., which passed to his wife when he died in 1952. After Mr. Starr's death, Mr. Guthart (age 44) was elected president and began to devote full time to company management. Previously he had been Mrs. Starr's attorney. Mrs. Starr, though officially a vice president, was not active in the business. Mr. Small (age 42) was elected vice president and plant manager. He had served in the same capacity with a small manufacturing company in Indiana.

The manufacturing operations were conducted in a one-story building recently purchased by the company in northwest Detroit. The buildings and grounds were well maintained, and the plant had adequate transportation facilities. The plant was selected because it provided ample space for manufacturing plus storage of both raw materials and finished goods inventory. Housewares' old plant was sold for $70,000, late in 1959, and the buyer paid $27,500 in cash and the remainder in a three-month note.

Housewares' sales figures showed two definite peaks and two slack periods. The peak sales periods directly follow the trade shows in January and June. Sales reach their low points in May and December just before these shows. Housewares' sales were made primarily to many small companies; however, loss experience on receivables was very low, 0.2 per cent of sales in 1957, and 0.4 per cent of sales in 1958.

Mr. Irving learned that Housewares had maintained a satisfactory deposit account at another bank with balances averaging about $25,000.

From time to time this bank had extended loans in amounts up to $75,000. In February 1959, this bank had loaned Housewares $100,000 for 20 months in order to finance the acquisition of the new $110,000 plant. This note was personally endorsed by Mrs. Starr and Mr. Guthart. By December 1959, $50,000 of this loan had been repaid. Mr. Guthart's reason for seeking a new banking connection was the other bank's reluctance to continue fulfilling Housewares' aggressive credit demands.

Exhibit 1

HOUSEWARES, INC.

Balance Sheets

	Dec. 31, 1957	Dec. 31, 1958	Nov. 30, 1959
ASSETS			
Current Assets:			
Cash	$ 50,650	$ 47,356	$ 38,429
Accounts receivable	100,990	123,723	310,549
Inventory	112,169	160,605	197,359
Total Current Assets	$263,809	$331,684	$ 546,337
Investments	27,237	27,237	27,237
Fixed assets	208,675	223,728	377,162
Prepaid items	4,602	13,875	37,925
Patents	34,836	31,215	28,198
Total Assets	$539,159	$627,739	$1,016,859
EQUITIES			
Current Liabilities:			
Notes payable	.....	.....	......
Current debt maturity	$ 9,000	$ 9,000	$ 79,800
Accounts payable	41,451	56,600	212,073
Accruals	52,813	69,642	115,278
Equipment rental payable	9,940	10,940	17,940
Income tax accruals	30,342	45,972	42,228
Total Current Liabilities	$143,546	$192,154	$ 467,319
Mortgage payable	19,510	12,017	76,601
Subordinated debentures	51,388	51,388	130,000
Long-term notes	82,070	82,070	1,740
Total Debt	$296,514	$337,629	$ 675,660
Capital:			
Capital stock	$132,816	$132,816	$ 132,816
Capital surplus	24,504	24,504	24,504
Earned surplus	85,325	132,790	183,879
Total Capital	$242,645	$290,110	$ 341,199
Total Equities	$539,159	$627,739	$1,016,859

As part of his analysis of Housewares, Inc., Mr. Irving developed some ratios from the balance sheets and income statements, Exhibits 1 and 2. Exhibit 3 is a comparison of Housewares' ratios for 1957 and 1958 with corresponding ratios representing, for our purposes here, the plastic products industry as a whole. (These industry ratios were taken

Exhibit 2

HOUSEWARES, INC.

Income Statements

Item	1957	1958
Sales.......................................	$1,532,800	$1,873,500
Cost of sales.............................	1,135,100	1,428,400
Gross profit..............................	$ 397,700	$ 445,100
Operating expenses.......................	297,400	343,700
Operating profit..........................	$ 100,300	$ 101,400
Other expenses...........................	31,400	15,100
Profit before taxes.......................	$ 68,900	$ 86,300
Income taxes.............................	30,300	39,400
Net Profit................................	$ 38,600	$ 46,900

from, and are typical of, the ones calculated annually by Robert Morris Associates, for over 170 separate industry groups. Robert Morris Associates is the national association of bank loan officers and credit men. The 1958 ratios were computed from 13,934 financial statements submitted by more than 500 member banks.)

Exhibit 3

COMPARISON OF HOUSEWARES, INC., AND PLASTICS INDUSTRY

A. Balance Sheet Items, Expressed as Percentages

	1957		1958	
	Housewares	Industry*	Housewares	Industry*
ASSETS				
Current Assets:				
Cash............................	9.4%	8.3%	7.5%	7.9%
Accounts receivable.................	18.8	25.0	19.7	20.8
Inventory........................	20.8	21.0	25.6	22.1
Other current assets.................	....	2.3	....	5.8
Total Current Assets.............	49.0%	56.6%	52.8%	56.6%
Fixed assets.......................	38.7	40.1	35.6	36.5
Prepaid items.....................	12.3	3.3	11.6	6.9
Total Assets..................	100.0%	100.0%	100.0%	100.0%
EQUITIES				
Current Liabilities:				
Notes to bank (includes current debt maturity).......................	1.7%	10.5%	1.4%	8.8%
Accounts payable...................	7.7	20.6	8.9	16.8
Income taxes due..................	5.7	2.4	7.3	3.6
Accruals and other sources...........	11.5	7.0	12.8	10.2
Total Current Liabilities..........	26.6%	40.5%	30.4%	39.4%
Long-term debt.....................	28.4	11.8	23.3	13.3
Total Debt...................	55.0%	52.3%	53.7%	52.7%
Net worth.........................	45.0	47.7	46.3	47.3
Total Liabilities...............	100.0%	100.0%	100.0%	100.0%

* Extracted from the industry classification "Miscellaneous Plastics Products" in the *1958 Statement Studies*, an annual copyrighted publication of Robert Morris Associates. These particular figures represent, for 1957, 14 companies with from $250,000 to less than $1,000,000 total assets, and for 1958, 29 companies in the same asset size category. Used by permission of Robert Morris Associates.

Exhibit 3—Continued

B. Income Statement Percentages

Item	1957		1958	
	Housewares	Industry	Housewares	Industry
Net sales............................	100.0%	100.0%	100.0%	100.0%
Cost of sales........................	74.1	79.6	76.2	81.4
Gross profit.........................	25.9%	20.4%	23.8%	18.6%
Other expenses......................	21.4	19.0	19.2	16.1
Operating profit.....................	4.5%	1.4%	4.6%	2.5%
Income taxes........................	2.0	0.6	2.1	1.4
Income after Taxes..................	2.5%	0.8%	2.5%	1.1%

C. Financial Ratios

	1957		1958	
	Housewares	Industry	Housewares	Industry
Current ratio........................	1.83	1.40	1.73	1.44
Net worth/fixed assets...............	1.15	1.19	1.30	1.30
Net worth/total debt.................	0.82	0.91	0.84	0.90
Sales/receivables....................	15.2	9.06	15.1	10.43
Cost sales/inventory.................	10.1	8.55	8.9	8.00
Sales/inventory.....................	13.7	10.75	11.7	9.84
Sales/fixed assets...................	7.3	5.63	8.4	5.95
Sales/net worth.....................	6.3	4.74	6.4	4.59
Per cent profits/net worth............	16.0	3.61	16.0	5.22
Sales/total assets...................	2.8	2.26	2.9	2.17
Per cent profit/total assets...........	7.2	1.73	7.4	2.47

Questions

1. Comment on the facts given in the case that are particularly important to Mr. Irving in deciding whether to grant credit to Housewares, Inc.

2. Do you recommend that credit be granted?

Chapter	FUNDS FLOW
12	STATEMENTS

THE INCOME statement summarizes revenues realized and expenses incurred in an accounting period. Another accounting statement, the *funds flow statement,* summarizes the events of the period from another standpoint; it describes the sources from which additional funds were derived and the uses to which these funds were put. This statement is also called "statement of sources and applications of funds," "where got—where gone statement," "analysis of working capital changes," "funds statements" and a variety of other names.

The funds flow statement is essentially derived from an analysis of changes that have occurred in asset and equities items between two balance sheet dates. It is *not* prepared directly from the accounts, as is the balance sheet itself. Many of the accounting transactions that produced these balance sheet changes were recorded in accordance with the accrual concept. Since the funds flow concept is different from the accrual concept, these transactions must be recast.

THE CONCEPT OF FUNDS FLOW

In Chapter 10, reference was made to the more-or-less continuous flow that occurs among the current asset and current liability accounts. When goods are purchased or manufactured, inventory is increased; when goods are sold, inventory is decreased, accounts receivables are increased, and income is earned; when the receivables are collected, cash is increased; and the cycle is completed with the use of cash to pay off the payables created when purchases were made or costs incurred. Because this cycle occurs over and over again in the course of normal operations, current assets and current liabilities are often referred to collectively as *circulating capital.*

Part of the funds tied up in current assets is supplied by vendors (accounts payable) and other short-term creditors. The remainder, which is the difference between current assets and current liabilities, and which is called working capital, must come from other, more permanent sources. These other sources must also supply the funds that are tied up in buildings, equipment, and other noncurrent assets. Funds supplied for these purposes are called *permanent capital.*

Changes in the sources of permanent capital and the uses to which it is put are likely to be of more than ordinary interest both to management and to outsiders since they reflect the results of the important financial decisions that have significant long-run consequences. The funds flow statement shows these changes. In order to focus on this "big picture," the funds flow statement disregards the recurring circulation of funds among the individual current asset and current liability accounts. It does this by lumping all these accounts into a single item, working capital. The funds flow statement therefore shows changes in the total amount of working capital, but not fluctuations in the individual items comprising working capital, much like national population statistics show births, deaths, immigration, and emigration for the country as a whole rather than complicating the picture by showing the continual movement of people from one house to another within the country.

But just as it is important for some purposes to study detailed population movements within a country, so it is also important for some purposes to look at the detailed flow of funds among the individual working capital accounts. This is done by a variation of the funds flow statement, called the *cash flow statement,* which will be described subsequently.

Basic Relationships

Illustration 12–1 shows the total flow of funds for American industrial and commercial companies for an average year in the 1950's. Collectively, American companies generated $34.0 billion of funds from operations (that is, from the excess of operating revenue over operating expenditures); they obtained $6.1 billion of new permanent capital from the sale of stocks and bonds to investors; and they obtained $2.2 billion from other long-term creditors, a total of $42.3 billion. They used this $42.3 billion to acquire $23.7 billion of new plant and equipment, to increase working capital by $10.0 billion, and to pay $8.6 billion in dividends.

Our present task is to construct a similar picture for an individual company. We can do this by working with the information shown on its balance sheets.

A balance sheet shows the net effect of all the funds transactions from the beginning of the business to the balance sheet date. The equities side shows the sources from which funds have been obtained, and the assets side shows the way in which these funds have been used.

Illustration 12–1

FLOW OF FUNDS IN NONFINANCIAL BUSINESS FIRMS

Average Year in 1950's

(Billions of Dollars)

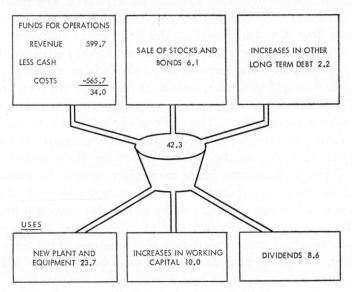

SOURCES

FUNDS FOR OPERATIONS		SALE OF STOCKS AND BONDS 6.1	INCREASES IN OTHER LONG TERM DEBT 2.2
REVENUE	599.7		
LESS CASH			
COSTS	−565.7		
	34.0		

42.3

USES

NEW PLANT AND EQUIPMENT 23.7	INCREASES IN WORKING CAPITAL 10.0	DIVIDENDS 8.6

Source: Adapted from Claude Robinson, *Understanding Profits* (Princeton, N.J.: D. Van Nostrand Co., Inc., 1961), p. 137.

The balance sheet in Illustration 12–2 shows that as of the end of 1962, long-term creditors have furnished $145,000 of capital, and stockholders have furnished $394,000. Of the latter, $211,000 represents their original contribution and $183,000 represents earnings that they have permitted the company to retain in the business. The total amount of funds provided is therefore $539,000, of which $125,000 is used for working capital and $414,000 is in fixed assets.

If all earnings were paid out in dividends and if replacements of

Illustration 12–2

Condensed Balance Sheet

December 31, 1962

ASSETS		EQUITIES	
Working capital	$125,000	Long-term debt	$145,000
Fixed assets	414,000	Capital stock	211,000
		Retained earnings	183,000
Total Assets	$539,000	Total Equities	$539,000

fixed assets exactly equaled the annual depreciation charge, the amounts shown on Illustration 12–2 could remain unchanged year after year. Although there would be numerous changes in the several current asset and current liability accounts, these could offset one another so that the total working capital could remain constant. Under these circumstances, the business would not need additional financing. But of course the balance sheet items do change; additional funds are provided; and these are put to use.

From this simple balance sheet, we can see the possible ways in which the company can obtain additional funds. If it wished to buy a new plant, for example: (1) it could borrow, thus increasing long-term debt; (2) it could sell more stock, thus increasing the Capital Stock account; (3) it could wait until operations had generated funds, which would show up as an increase in Retained Earnings; (4) it could use available cash, thus decreasing Working Capital; or (5) it could sell some of its existing fixed assets, thus decreasing Fixed Assets. The first, second, and third possibilities would show up as an increase in equities; the fourth and fifth would show up as a decrease in assets. We can therefore generalize as follows: *sources of funds are indicated by increases in equities and decreases in assets.*

Looking at the other side of the coin, what uses could the company make of additional funds that it acquired? The possible uses are as follows: (1) it could add new fixed assets; (2) it could add to working capital; (3) it could pay off existing debt; (4) it could pay dividends to the stockholders, which decreases Retained Earnings; or (5) it could repay capital to the stockholders.

The first three possibilities would show up as an increase in assets, and the fourth and fifth as a decrease in equities. We can therefore generalize as follows: *uses of funds are indicated by increases in assets and decreases in equities.*

In accordance with the dual-aspect concept, total sources of funds must equal total uses of funds. The following relationships therefore exist:

1. SOURCES = USES
2. INCREASES IN EQUITIES + DECREASES IN ASSETS =
   INCREASES IN ASSETS + DECREASES IN EQUITIES

These same relationships can be explained in terms of debit and credit. Increases in equities and decreases in assets are both credits; increases in assets and decreases in equities are both debits. Thus, the above equation follows from the fact that changes in debits must equal changes in credits.

CONSTRUCTING THE FUNDS FLOW STATEMENT

Comparative Balance Sheets

A first approximation of the flow of funds during a period can be obtained by finding the changes in the balance sheet amounts between the beginning and end of the period. This is done in Illustration 12–3, where *comparative balance sheets* for the beginning and end of the year 1963 are given, and the differences between amounts on the two balance

Illustration 12–3

CONDENSED BALANCE SHEET

(000 Omitted)

	December 31		Change in 1963	
	1963	1962	Use	Source
ASSETS				
Working capital.................	$150	$125	25	
Fixed assets....................	435	414	21	
Total Assets.................	$585	$539		
EQUITIES				
Long-term debt..................	$171	$145		26
Capital stock....................	211	211		
Retained earnings................	203	183		20
Total Equities...............	$585	$539		
Total.....................			46	46

sheets are classified as either "uses" or "sources" according to the rules given above.

This comparison indicates that during the year funds were obtained from an increase in long-term debt, $26,000, and in retained earnings, $20,000, and that these funds were used to finance additional fixed assets, $21,000, and working capital, $25,000.

These changes are only *indications* of the flow of funds, however, for they show only the net effect of transactions, rather than the transactions themselves. The change in retained earnings, for example, is the net effect of two quite different types of transactions: (1) the earning of income, which is a source of funds; and (2) the payment of dividends, which is a use of funds. Also, balance sheet items may be changed by transactions which do not have anything to do with the flow of funds; the declaration of a stock dividend decreases retained earnings and increases capital stock, but does not represent any funds coming into or going out of the business.

Reconstructing Transactions

In order to find the actual sources and uses of funds during the period, we must therefore reconstruct the transactions whose net effect is shown on the comparative balance sheet. We seek to answer the questions: (1) from what sources were additional funds obtained? and (2) to what uses were these new funds put? The analysis is facilitated if the word "funds" is thought of as being synonymous with "working capital," and each transaction is considered separately in terms of its effect on working capital. The key questions then become: (1) Did this transaction, taken by itself, result in an increase in working capital? (If so, it was a source of funds.) (2) Did this transaction, taken by itself, result in a decrease in working capital? (If so, it was a use of funds.) (3) Did this transaction have no effect on working capital? (If so, it was neither a source nor a use of funds.)

Of the several methods of reconstructing transactions, the one developed by Professor William J. Vatter is perhaps the most straightforward and is the basis for the procedure described below:[1]

1. A T-account is set up for each noncurrent item on the balance sheet including net working capital, and the *change* in each item as obtained from the comparative balance sheets is entered in the account. It is entered on the debit side if it is a debit change, that is, an increase in an asset item or a decrease in an equities item; it is entered on the credit side if it is a credit change, that is, a decrease in an asset item or an increase in an equities item. A single line is then drawn under these amounts.

Two additional T-accounts are established, one headed Operations Summary and the other headed Funds Flow Summary.

2. From various sources, information about transactions affecting these accounts is obtained, and a summary total of each different transaction is recorded in the same way the transactions were recorded originally, except that (*a*) all revenue and expense items are credited or debited to Operating Summary and (*b*) all current asset and current

---

[1] Some prefer to use a work sheet for this purpose. Others make the calculation on scratch paper, which is the fastest method of all if the relationships can be visualized mentally. In any event, it is the end result that is important, not the method used to arrive at it.

liability items are debited or credited to Funds Flow Summary. The change in working capital is transferred from the Working Capital Account to the Funds Flow Summary. These transactions explain the balance sheet changes recorded in Step No. 1.

3. Operating Summary is closed to Funds Flow Summary. After these entries have been made, each account except Funds Flow Summary will contain entries that in total equal the amount originally recorded in Step No. 1, and this is a proof that all transactions have been located and recorded. Funds Flow Summary will contain an itemized list of the sources and uses of funds.

4. A funds flow statement is prepared from the information collected in Funds Flow Summary.

Illustration of the Procedure

This procedure will be applied to the situation shown in Illustration 12–3, starting with the balance sheet changes shown there, except that the fixed asset item, shown on the balance sheet as a single amount, is given in the more customary expanded form: gross plant and equipment, accumulated depreciation, and intangible assets. The amounts are assumed to be as follows:

	December 31		Change	
	1963	1962	Use	Source
Plant and equipment (cost)........	648	601	47	
Accumulated depreciation.........	(227)	(204)		23
Intangible assets................	14	17		3

(Since Accumulated Depreciation is a contra asset account, its changes are recorded opposite to the rule for asset changes; therefore the increase is recorded as a Source.)

The first step is to set up T-accounts and record balance sheet changes, as in Illustration 12–4. The changes are the amounts above the single lines. The amounts below the single lines are described in the following paragraphs.

Next, we shall search for the transactions that together resulted in these changes. Many of them are reflected on the income statement, which is shown in Illustration 12–5. Each of the transactions is explained below with letters corresponding to those in Illustration 12–4.

Illustration 12–4

T-ACCOUNTS FOR FUNDS FLOW ANALYSIS
(Thousands of Dollars)

Working Capital			Accumulated Depreciation		
Change	25			Change	23
(a)	25		(f) 6	(e)	29

Plant and Equipment			Long-Term Debt		
Change	47			Change	26
(b)	61	(f) 14		(g)	26

Intangible Assets			Retained Earnings		
	Change	3		Change	20
	(d)	3	(c) 22	(b)	42

Operating Summary

(b) Income	42	(f) Gain on disposal	2
(d) Goodwill	3	(i) To close	72
(e) Depreciation	29		
	74		74

Funds Flow Summary

(Sources)		(Uses)	
(f) Disposal of fixed assets	10	(a) Working capital increase	25
(g) Additional borrowing	26	(c) Dividends	22
(i) Funds from operations	72	(b) New fixed assets	61
	108		108

Working Capital Change. The net change in working capital is transferred to Funds Flow Summary:

(a)

Working Capital.	25,000	
Funds Flow Summary		25,000

This entry summarizes the many changes in current asset and current liability items during the year, the net effect of which is a $25,000

Illustration 12–5

INCOME STATEMENT, 1963
(000 Omitted)

Sales..		$1,080
Costs and expenses:		
Cost of goods sold.......................	$890	
Selling and administrative...............	68	
Depreciation............................	29	
Amortization of goodwill...............	3	
Interest................................	7	997
Operating income.........................		$ 83
Gain on disposal of fixed assets.............		2
Income before taxes.......................		$ 85
Income taxes.............................		43
Net income..............................		$ 42
Dividends................................		22
Added to Retained Earnings...............		$ 20

increase in working capital. Thus, of the new funds coming into the business, $25,000 has gone to increase working capital; it has been *used* to build up inventories, to reduce the level of current liabilities, or in similar ways which we are not tracing in detail because our emphasis is on working capital as a whole.

Net Income. We note that the net income of the period was $42,000. This was originally recorded as a closing entry, debiting Loss and Gain (the net of all revenue and expense accounts) and crediting Retained Earnings. We shall record the same entry, except that Operating Summary will be used instead of Loss and Gain:

(b)

Operating Summary..	42,000	
Retained Earnings...		42,000

Dividends. Dividends in the amount of $22,000 were declared. The entry was a debit to Retained Earnings and a credit to Cash or Dividends Payable, in any event to a working capital account. Therefore it involved a use of funds. The entry is as follows:

(c)

Retained Earnings..	20,000	
Funds Flow Summary.......................................		20,000

Note that at this point, we have already accounted for the change in Retained Earnings, as evidenced by the fact that the entries below the line equal the amount of the net change ($42 - 22 = 20$).

Amortization of Intangibles. The income statement shows $3,000 as amortization of goodwill, and the balance sheet shows an equal decrease in Intangible Assets, which indicates the following entry:

(d)

Operating Summary	3,000	
Intangible Assets		3,000

This is an example of a transaction that involved no flow of funds in the current period, but only the amortization of a cost incurred in a previous period. The fact that Funds Flow Summary was not affected by this entry also shows that no funds were involved.

Depreciation. The income statement shows $29,000 of depreciation expense. This represents the annual depreciation charge, and we know that the credit part of this entry is always to Accumulated Depreciation. Therefore, we record the following:

(e)

Operating Summary	29,000	
Accumulated Depreciation		29,000

As is the case with the amortization of Goodwill, this entry does not involve a flow of funds. At the time when the assets were purchased, funds were used; but the subsequent write-off of this cost through the depreciation mechanism does not affect the flow of funds.

Disposal of Fixed Assets. The income statement item, gain on disposal of fixed assets, shows that assets were sold for $2,000 more than their book value. To find the facts about this transaction, the underlying records (e.g., the general journal) must be consulted. Assume that these reveal that an asset with an original cost of $14,000 on which accumulated depreciation amounted to $6,000 was sold for $10,000. The gain of $2,000 therefore is the difference between the book value of $8,000 and the proceeds of $10,000. The entry recording this transaction writes off the cost and accumulated depreciation and shows the cash proceeds and the gain, as follows:

(f)

Funds Flow Summary	10,000	
Accumulated Depreciation	6,000	
Plant and Equipment		14,000
Operating Summary		2,000

The funds arising out of this transaction clearly are the $10,000 proceeds from the sale, not the $2,000 gain appearing on the income statement.

Additional Borrowing. The Long-Term Debt account shows an increase of $26,000 which undoubtedly represents the borrowing of additional capital, which was recorded as a debit to Cash and a credit to the noncurrent liability account. Assuming that the underlying records confirm this supposition, the following entry is made:

(g)

```
Funds Flow Summary.............................................26,000
    Long-Term Debt.......................................          26,000
```

Acquisition of Fixed Assets.   After entry *(g)* above, the entries made to each T-account equal the net change in the account, with the single exception of Plant and Equipment, which appears as follows:

Plant and Equipment

Change	47		
		(f)	14

This account started out with a net *increase* of $47,000. The disposition of the asset recorded in entry *(f)* would have resulted in a net *decrease* of $14,000. Some other entry must have increased Plant and Equipment by the algebraic sum of these two amounts, or $61,000. The most likely transaction having such a result is the acquisition of new fixed assets, with a debit to Plant and Equipment and a credit to Cash or a current liability. Assuming the underlying records show that in fact this happened, the following entry is made:

(h)

```
Plant and Equipment...........................................61,000
    Funds Flow Summary....................................          61,000
```

All the changes have now been accounted for, which is proved by the fact that each account, excluding the summary accounts, contain entries that equal the total change.

Funds from Operations.   The $72,000 balance that has been built up in the Operating Summary account represents the total amount of funds generated from operations of the period, and this is transferred to Funds Flow Summary, as follows:

(i)

```
Funds Flow Summary.............................................72,000
    Operating Summary....................................          72,000
```

The completeness and arithmetic accuracy of the work can now be verified by checking the equality of the totals of the two sides of the Funds Flow Summary account.

Preparation of the Statement.   The Funds Flow Summary account is used as the basis for preparing the funds flow statement, which is given in Illustration 12–6.

Illustration 12–6

FUNDS FLOW STATEMENT, 1963

Sources of Funds:

Funds provided by operations	$ 72,000
Proceeds from sale of fixed assets	10,000
Additional long-term debt	26,000
Total	$108,000

Uses of Funds:

New plant and equipment	$ 61,000
Dividends	22,000
Increase in working capital	25,000
Total	$108,000

Summary of Transactions

The preceding description has included a number of the common transactions that are encountered in funds flow analysis. These, together with some others not illustrated, are summarized below:

Nature of Item	Debit	Credit
1. Change in working capital (increase)	Working Capital	Funds Flow Summary
2. Change in working capital (decrease)	Funds Flow Summary	Working Capital
3. Net income (vice versa for net loss)	Operating Summary	Retained Earnings
4. Dividend declaration	Retained Earnings	Funds Flow Summary
5. Amortization of intangibles	Operating Summary	Intangible Assets
6. Annual depreciation change	Operating Summary	Accumulated Depreciation
7. Removal of fixed asset, fully depreciated	Accumulated Depreciation	Fixed Asset
8. Sale of fixed asset at book value	Funds Flow Summary and Accumulated Depreciation	Fixed Asset
9. Sale of fixed asset above book value	Funds Flow Summary and Accumulated Depreciation	Fixed Asset and Operating Summary
10. Acquisition of fixed assets	Fixed Asset	Funds Flow Summary
11. Noncurrent borrowing	Funds Flow Summary	Long-Term Debt
12. Paying off noncurrent debt	Long-Term Debt	Funds Flow Summary
13. Amortization of bond discount	Operating Summary	Bond Discount
14. Stock dividend	Retained Earnings	Capital Stock
15. Addition to surplus reserve	Retained Earnings	Reserve Account

Note that if neither the debit nor the credit is to Funds Flow Summary, no flow of funds is involved in the transaction. The last three items above are examples, in addition to those already given, of such nonfund transactions.

In the following paragraphs some matters that were passed over quickly in order to give an overall view of the whole procedure are discussed in more detail.

Hidden Transactions

The foregoing description assumed that the analyst had access to the detailed accounting records of the company, for in several places the procedure required him to consult these records. An outside analyst may wish to construct a funds flow statement, even though he has only the information contained in the company's annual report, principally the balance sheet and income statement. (For example, he may be interested in a competitor's funds flow, but only a minority of companies publish funds flow statements.) He often can do a reasonably good job of deducing what transactions *probably* caused the change in balance sheet items. In the description already given, the inference that the increase in Long-Term Debt resulted from additional borrowing is a highly reasonable one, for example.

In other cases, the exact nature of the transaction cannot be deduced, but an approximation can be derived that is better than nothing. The fixed asset transactions discussed above will be used as an example of what can be done. After the depreciation entry had been recorded, the relevant T-accounts were as follows:

Plant and Equipment		Accumulated Depreciation	
Change 47			Change 23
			(*e*) Depreciation 29

The item on the income statement, gain on disposal of fixed assets, shows that assets have been disposed of and that this transaction resulted in an inflow of funds. Further, the fact that the depreciation charge is greater than the change in Accumulated Depreciation shows that there is a missing debit to this account, and the most likely transaction that debits Accumulated Depreciation is that which removes the depreciation accumulated on an asset disposed of.

These facts lead to the conclusion that part of the entry must have been—

```
Cash.............................................    ?
Accumulated Depreciation........................  6,000
    Plant and Equipment.........................         ?
    Gain on Disposal............................       2,000
```

Since there are two missing terms, we cannot complete the entry without more information. We do know, however, that the fixed asset credit must have been *at least* $6,000, since accumulated depreciation never exceeds cost. If we accept this minimum, then the entry becomes—

Cash..2,000		
Accumulated Depreciation...6,000		
Plant and Equipment..	6,000	
Gain on Disposal..	2,000	

Reference back to transaction (f) shows that this understates the situation by $8,000, but we have no way of knowing this without reference to the underlying records.

We can go one step further. After the above entry has been posted, the Plant and Equipment account will look like this:

Plant and Equipment

Change	47		
		Disposal	6

A debit of $53,000 is necessary to explain the net change of $47,000, and we can therefore conclude that new assets costing *at least* $53,000 were acquired. Again, this is an understatement that can be corrected only by access to the underlying records, but it is closer to reality than the impression given by the balance sheet change, which implies an addition of only $47,000.

Compound Transactions

A single transaction may involve the simultaneous source and use of funds. If so, it is usually more informative if the source is separated from the use. For example, if a $100,000 building was purchased and a mortgage loan of $80,000 was made for part of it, one could argue that the funds required for this transaction were only $20,000. Regardless of the theoretical merit of this argument, the reader of a funds flow statement undoubtedly wants to know about the two separate facts, the acquisition of the building and the incurrence of an additional liability. Such a transaction should therefore be recorded in the T-accounts as two separate items, a use of $100,000 for the building and a source of $80,000 from the mortgage loan.

Even in the case of a bond refunding, which involves only the exchange of one liability for another, it may be helpful to show separately the retirement of the old issue as a use of funds and the sale of the new issue as a source of funds.

Funds Provided by Operations

The $72,000 "funds from operations" that was developed from our analysis of funds flow differs considerably from the net income figure on the income statement, which was only $42,000. Reference back to the Operating Summary account shows that the $72,000 was arrived at by adding to net income the nonfund transactions involved in the net income calculation, principally the depreciation charge; that is,

Net income......................................$42,000
Plus depreciation and other nonfund items.......... 30,000
Equals funds provided by operations..............$72,000

Many funds flow statements in fact show such a breakdown of "funds provided by operations," or "internally generated funds," which means the same thing.

Exactly the same result could have been obtained by subtracting expense items requiring the use of funds from revenue items that were a source of funds. Illustration 12–5 shows these expense items as cost of goods sold, selling and administrative expense, interest expense, and income taxes. Each of these items is associated with either a decrease in a current asset (cash, inventory, prepaid expenses) or an increase in a current liability (accounts payable, taxes payable, accrued liabilities), both of which are decreases in working capital. The revenue item, Sales, is associated with an increase in cash or accounts receivable and hence with an increase in working capital. Operations generate funds to the extent that revenue which brings in funds exceeds expenses which require the use of funds, or—

Sales revenue.........................$1,080,000
Less expenses using funds.............. 1,008,000
Equals funds provided by operations.....$ 72,000

This calculation shows more clearly how the funds were actually generated than the method of adding back depreciation and other nonfund items to net income. The funds from operation section of some funds flow statements are prepared in this way.

The choice of methods is relatively unimportant; they give identical results. It is important, however, to appreciate the fact that *depreciation is not a source of funds.* In the first method, depreciation is added to net income to find the funds provided by operations, but it is operations, not depreciation, that provides the funds. Depreciation is neither a source nor a use of funds.

The Funds Flow Statement

There is no prescribed format for the funds flow statement. The items are arranged and described in whatever way seems most clearly to show the important financial events of the period. Minor items should be combined in order to emphasize the major changes.

Incidentally, as mentioned above, reporting working capital as a source or use of funds may seem to involve a contradiction of terms. How can we regard uses of funds as "events that result in a decrease in working capital" and at the same time treat an increase in working capital itself as a use of funds? Actually, there is no contradiction if it is recalled that all transactions have two aspects. In a funds flow statement, increases in assets and decreases in equities are uses of funds, and the other aspect of each such change is a decrease in working capital; working capital *used* for the items stated is not available for other purposes. An increase in the working capital item itself represents management's decision to *use* this additional amount in the various working capital items rather than for some other purpose, such as paying it out as dividends.

In any event, the possible confusion can easily be avoided by treating the change in working capital as a residual item. This is done by arranging the funds flow statement in the following form:

Source — Uses = Working Capital Change

The funds flow statements for the Ford Motor Company in Illustration 12–7 have such an arrangement. Note, also, that in these statements

Illustration 12–7

FORD MOTOR COMPANY

Funds Flow Statements

	1957 (In Millions)	1958 (In Millions)
Increase in Net Working Capital:		
Net income for the year........................	$282.8	$ 95.7
Less: Dividends paid...........................	130.7	109.4
Retained earnings.............................	$152.1	$(13.7)
Noncash charges against income:		
Depreciation................................	177.1	187.3
Amortization of commercial special tools.........	208.8	215.9
Other, net.................................	(37.8)	(11.7)
Issuance of additional shares of capital stock........	9.9	5.8
Proceeds from 4% promissory notes..............	191.4	. . .
Total Increases...........................	$701.5	$383.6
Decreases in Net Working Capital:		
Gross additions to property, plant and equipment (including commercial special tools), less proceeds from property dispositions..............	$542.1	$234.2
Increases in investments and noncurrent receivables..	8.4	14.0
Total Decreases...........................	$550.5	$248.2
Increase in Net Working Capital...................	$151.0	$135.4

dividends are netted against net income, and the proceeds from the sale of fixed assets are not disclosed.

The Ford statement shows dramatically the difference between the concept of net income and the concept of funds flow. In 1957, Ford reported one of the highest net incomes in its history up to that time, but it nevertheless had to borrow $191,400,000 of new funds to finance plant expansion. In 1958, its net income did not even equal dividends, but the funds provided from operations were adequate to finance the entire fixed asset acquisition program without the necessity for additional outside borrowing.

CASH FLOW STATEMENTS

Instead of lumping all current assets and current liabilities together as working capital, it may be desirable to consider changes in some or all of these items separately. A statement that has such a purpose is technically called a *cash flow statement*. Except that changes in individual current asset and liability items are treated separately, the procedures for analyzing the transactions are the same as those described above. Increases in assets and decreases in equities indicate uses. Transactions that do not involve a flow of cash are eliminated.

Some people use the word "funds" as synonymous with "cash," as in statements such as "we borrowed funds to increase our inventory," or "we obtained funds by speeding up the collection of receivables." The cash flow statement is called by them a funds flow statement. This difference in terminology is unimportant since the content of the statement will indicate which concept is used. Illustration 12–8 diagrams the flow of cash or its equivalent through a typical business.

Illustration 12–9 shows a cash flow statement. This particular statement describes the effects of an expansion program, and since the expansion involved an increase in inventory and receivables as well as additional fixed assets, it was informative to show these current items on the statement rather than combine them into the single item, working capital. The unimportant changes, principally prepaid expenses and accrued liabilities, are lumped together as "miscellaneous changes."

Another cash flow statement, using a format suggested by Professor Almand R. Coleman of the University of Virginia, is shown in Illustration 12–10.

Although not usually contained in published financial reports, a cash flow statement is essential to management in examining short-run financial movements. It is frequently prepared for monthly or weekly

Illustration 12–8

DIAGRAMMATIC REPRESENTATION OF CASH FLOW

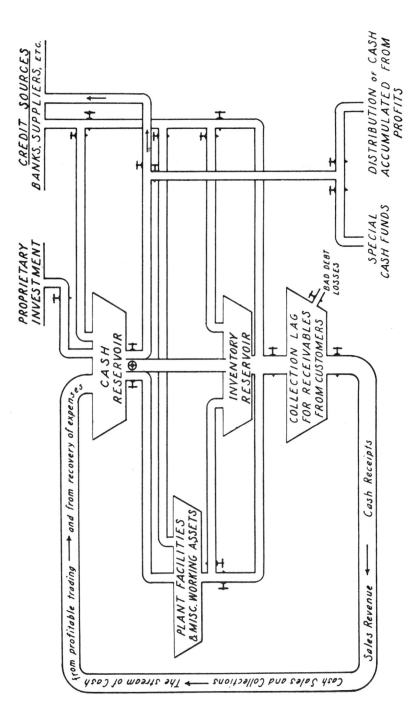

Illustration 12–9

BALDWIN MARKET COMPANY
Cash Flow Statement for the Year 1959

What We Did		*How We Financed It*		
Expanded:		Reduced cash		$ 2,453
Accounts receivable	$ 67,477	Sold security holdings		100,000
Inventories	61,586	Borrowed:		
Acquired new fixed assets	255,861	Accounts payable		43,185
Paid dividends	78,315	Bank loan		26,000
Miscellaneous changes	1,653	Mortgage		175,000
		Obtained funds from operations:		
		Net income	$95,679	
		Depreciation	22,575	118,254
	$464,892			$464,892

Illustration 12–10

ALTERNATIVE FORM OF CASH FLOW STATEMENT
(In Millions of Dollars)

In 1963, sales revenue amounted to		$150.6
Whereas cost of goods sold and operating "cash" expenses (exclusive of $7.2 depreciation) was		128.8
So net income before noncash charges was		$ 21.8
And there would have been a net inflow of cash of this amount from operations, except that—		
A. The company collected less from customers than it billed	$(14.1)	
B. The company bought and manufactured more than the cost of goods it shipped	(2.9)	
C. The company paid out less cash than the costs it incurred	0.8	
The net effect of these items being		(16.2)
So that operating activities resulted in an "internally generated" cash inflow of		$ 5.6
There were inflows from—		
Sale of common stock	$ 12.6	
Increase in short-term loans	5.0	
Increase in long-term debt	2.4	20.0
		$ 25.6
Outgo of cash was required for—		
Dividends	$ 3.0	
Property, plant, and equipment acquired in excess of dispositions	30.8	
Increase in investments and other assets	2.0	35.8
So that the net decrease in cash during 1963 was		$(10.2)

time intervals. The amount of cash required to finance peak seasonal needs is obscured in an annual statement.

A *cash budget* is a cash flow statement—the only difference between it and the type illustrated above being that the changes are those anticipated in the future rather than those actually recorded in the past. One way to prepare such a budget is to list all the estimated uses of cash and all the sources other than from additional financing. The difference between these totals is the amount that must be obtained by borrowing or selling additional stock if the planned program is to be carried out. If it is believed that this amount cannot be raised, the indication is that the estimated uses of cash must be cut back. In other respects, the technique is the same as that already described.

MISUSES OF THE FUNDS FLOW STATEMENT

In recent years, the number of companies publishing funds flow or cash flow statements has increased rapidly. As is often the case with a newly popular idea, a great deal of misunderstanding, and hence misuse, is prevalent. Basically, the misunderstanding results from a tendency to think that sources of funds are synonymous with increases in owners' equity. This is not so. For reasons examined in detail in Part I of this book, increases in owners' equity must be measured in accordance with the accrual concept; there is not necessarily a correspondence between the earning of net income and changes in working capital. The using up of fixed assets is a real cost, a real decrease in owners' equity, even though no change in funds flow is involved.

The Accounting Principles Board of the AICPA, alarmed at the misunderstandings, has published a useful clarification, part of which is quoted below:[2]

Accountants have long prepared statements of source and application of funds for management, which are in fact reports on the flow of funds in individual companies. These statements have often been presented in annual reports. The concept of "funds" used in these statements has varied somewhat in practice, and variations in the concept have resulted in variations in the nature of the statements. For example, "funds" has sometimes been interpreted to mean cash or its equivalent; in such cases the resulting statement of source and application of funds is a statement of cash receipts and disbursements. The most common concept of "funds" has, however, been that of working capital, i.e., current assets less current liabilities. If the definition is applied literally, the resulting statement includes only those transactions which affect the current assets or the current liabilities. A broader interpretation identifies "funds" as all financial resources arising from transactions with parties external to the business enterprise.

In recent years a new concept (or more correctly, an old concept with a new name) has become increasingly important in the analysis of the flow of funds. The term "cash flow" has been used to refer to a variety of concepts, but its most common meaning in financial literature, and to a lesser extent in accounting

---

[2] Accounting Principles Board, AICPA, Opinion No. 3, *The Statement of Source and Application of Funds*, October 1963, paragraphs 2, 6, and 7.

literature, is the same as "funds derived from operations" in a statement of source and application of funds. It is often defined as "net income plus depreciation," or "net income before deducting depreciation, depletion, amortization, etc." Synonyms which are sometimes used include "cash earnings," "cash income," and "cash throw-off."

Many of the comments made in connection with "cash flow" analysis leave the reader with the erroneous impression that "cash flow" or "cash earnings" is superior to net income as a measure of a company's real earning power. Calculations of the Price/Cash Flow ratio are sometimes made and presented as a substitute for or supplement to the Price/Earnings ratio in evaluating a company's stock. The amount of "cash flow" or the "cash flow per share" has often been presented in the president's letter, the financial review, or the statistical section of the annual report of a corporation apart from or in the absence of a complete statement of source and application of funds in the report. In other words, there has been a growing tendency on the part of some people to single out one of the items on the statement of source and application of funds, thereby implying that this figure is more important than other information regarding the flow of funds and often carrying the implication that "net income plus depreciation" is the best measure of the company's profitability. There is a strong implication running through the comments in the literature, including those in the annual reports of some corporations, that the total "cash flow" can be considered available for the payment of dividends.

Misconceptions about Depreciation

Most of the difficulty referred to above stems from the misconception that depreciation is a source of funds; for example, the following quotations:[3]

"Most people pay too little attention to depreciation reserves as a contributor to corporate health. In some years depreciation actually exceeds net profit."

"Company X shifted to accelerated depreciation last year, thus increasing its depreciation charge and its cash flow earnings by $6 million."

"Depreciation money is cash. In your bank account, depreciation dollars and profit dollars look alike."

The most charitable thing that can be said about such quotations is that they are half truths. Some are in no sense true; the statement that an increase in depreciation results in an increase in "cash flow earnings," overlooks the fact that such an increase in depreciation is exactly offset by a decrease in net income. As Gaa has put it: "Depreciation should be sued for nonsupport; it does *not* provide funds or any other

---

[3] Adapted from quotations collected by William J. Vatter and reported by him in "Operating Confusion in Accounting," *Journal of Business,* University of Chicago, July 1963, pp. 290–301.

assets for the replacement of property."[4] And Robert C. Tyson, chairman of the Finance Committee of U.S. Steel, puts it this way:[5]

> . . . For the security analyst the sum of profits plus depreciation may provide a measure of management discretion to choose between paying dividends, paying off debt or spending money to replace depreciated facilities. But as a measure of corporate success it is just as fallacious to add these two items as it is to add back taxes to profits.

The misuse of this type of measurement may be partly attributable to the vocabulary quirks in which the financial fraternity indulges when speaking of depreciation as a source of funds. If those supposed to know of what they speak say that depreciation is a source of funds, then those less well-informed can say, "The bigger the source, the better." So perhaps we had "better mind our language," as mothers used to admonish. The fact is, of course, that the only continuing source of cash that any firm has out of which to cover all its costs is its sales receipts from customers. Among those costs are the prepaid expenditures for facilities. It takes a long time to get them covered. Depreciation is the record of their cost slowly being covered. To hold that big depreciation cost in the guise of big cash flow is good for a company is the same as saying that the bigger its costs the better off it is. And that is plain nonsense! Here, then, is another area in which clarification of public understanding is necessary for establishment of prudent public policy.

Finally, from the opinion of the Accounting Principles Board of AICPA:[6]

> The amount of funds derived from operations cannot be considered as a substitute for or an improvement upon properly determined net income as a measure of results of operations and the consequent effect on financial position. Misleading implications can result from isolated statistics in annual reports of "cash flow" which are not placed in proper perspective to net income figures and to a complete analysis of source and application of funds. "Cash flow" and related terms should not be used in annual reports in such a way that the significance of net income is impaired, and "cash earnings" or other terms with a similar connotation should be avoided. The Board regards computations of "cash flow per share" as misleading since they ignore the impact of cash expenditures for renewal and replacement of facilities and tend to downgrade the significant economic statistic of "earnings per share."

SUMMARY

A funds flow statement shows the sources from which funds were provided and the uses to which these funds were put during an

---

[4] Charles J. Gaa, "Depreciation—the Good Provider?", *Business Topics,* Michigan State University, Winter 1962.

[5] Speech before the Eastern Area Conference of the Financial Executives Institute, June 14, 1963.

[6] *Op. cit.,* paragraph 15.

accounting period. The term "funds" is equivalent to "working capital." The net effects of funds flows are indicated by changes in noncurrent asset and equities accounts between the beginning and ending balance sheets of the periods. Increases in assets and decreases in equities indicate uses of funds; decreases in assets and increases in equities indicate sources.

The actual flows are found by reconstructing the transactions that resulted in these changes. In this process, transactions which affected balance sheet items but which did not involve a flow of funds are eliminated. When the analyst has access to the company's accounting records, all transactions can easily be identified. Even when he has only the incomplete information obtainable in published statements, he often can make a good approximation to the funds flows by deducing what transactions probably caused the balance sheet changes.

The amount of funds provided by operations of the period is by no means the same as the reported net income of the period. In a sense, funds provided by operations is net income adjusted for depreciation and other nonfund expenses and revenues, but this adjustment should not lead to the inference that depreciation is itself a source of funds.

A cash flow statement is the same as a funds flow statement except that important current asset and current liability changes are identified separately rather than combined in the single item, working capital.

In recent years, there has been a widespread tendency to use "cash flow earnings" as an indicator of corporate health that is equal to or superior to the indication provided by the net income figure. This is erroneous.

CASES

CASE 12–1.   THE ABC COMPANY[7]

Mr. Jones of the ABC Company started the year in fine shape. His company made widgets—just what the customer wanted. He made them for $0.75 each, sold them for $1.00. He kept a 30-day supply in inventory, paid his bills promptly, and billed his customers 30-day net. The sales manager predicted a steady increase of 500 widgets each month. It looked like his lucky year, and it began this way:

January 1	Cash, $875; receivables, $1,000; inventory, $750.
January	In January, he sold 1,000 widgets; shipped them at a cost of $750; collected his receivables—winding up with a tidy $250 profit and books like this:

---

[7] Adapted from an article in *Business Week*.

February 1   Cash, $1,125; receivables, $1,000; inventory, $750.

                 This month's sales jumped, as predicted, to 1,500. With a cor-
                 responding step-up in production to maintain his 30-day inven-
February   tory, he made 2,000 units at a cost of $1,500. All receivables from
                 January sales were collected. Profit so far, $625. Now his books
                 looked like this:

March 1   Cash, $625; receivables, $1,500; inventory, $1,125.

                 March sales were even better: 2,000 units. Collections: On time.
March   Production, to adhere to his inventory policy: 2,500 units. Operat-
                 ing results for the month, $500 profit. Profit to date: $1,125. His
                 books:

April 1   Cash, $250; receivables, $2,000; inventory, $1,500.

                 In April, sales jumped another 500 units to 2,500, and Jones
                 patted his sales manager on the back. His customers were paying
                 right on time. Production was pushed to 3,000 units, and the
April   month's business netted him $625 for a profit to date of $1,750.
                 He took off for Florida before he saw the accountant's report.
                 Suddenly he got a phone call from his treasurer: "Come home!
                 We need money!" His books had caught up with him:

May 1   Cash, $000; receivables, $2,500; inventory, $1,875.

Questions

1. Why did the ABC Company need money?

2. Assume that business keeps growing at 500 widgets per month. How much cash will the company need, month by month, through December?

CASE 12-2.   MARRETT MANUFACTURING COMPANY (B)

Refer to the situation described in Marrett Manufacturing Company (A) (p. 194). Prepare an estimated funds flow statement for the year 1964.

CASE 12-3.   GRETLIN CORPORATION

Balance sheets as of December 31, 1958, and December 31, 1959, for the Gretlin Corporation are shown in Exhibit 1.

Sales for the year 1959 were $210,000. Net income after taxes was $7,000. In arriving at net profit, items deducted from sales included, among others: cost of goods sold, $165,000; depreciation, $5,000; wages and salaries, $20,000; and a gain of $1,000 on the sale of a truck. The truck had cost $6,000, depreciation of $4,000 had been accumulated for it, and it was sold for $3,000. This was the only asset written off during the year. The company declared and paid $6,000 in dividends during the year.

Exhibit 1

GRETLIN CORPORATION

Comparative Balance Sheets

	Dec. 31, 1958		Dec. 31, 1959		Increase or Decrease*
ASSETS					
Cash...............................		$ 5,000		$ 6,000	$ 1,000
Accounts receivable (net)............		14,000		14,000	
Inventory..........................		22,000		8,000	14,000*
Prepaid insurance...................		200		250	50
Prepaid rent.......................		150		100	50*
Prepaid property taxes..............		300		400	100
Land..............................		4,000		8,000	4,000
Building and equipment.............	$30,000		$48,000		
Less: Accumulated depreciation......	10,000	20,000	11,000	37,000	17,000
Total Assets....................		$65,650		$73,750	$ 8,100
EQUITIES					
Accounts payable...................		$20,000		$18,000	$ 2,000*
Accrued expenses...................		2,000		4,000	2,000
Income tax payable.................		1,000		1,100	100
Capital stock.......................		30,000		37,000	7,000
Retained earnings..................		12,650		13,650	1,000
Total Equities..................		$65,650		$73,750	$ 8,100

Questions

1. Prepare a funds flow statement for the Gretlin Corporation for the year 1959.

2. Without redoing the detailed work, convert this to a cash flow statement.

3. Describe the most significant development revealed by this statement.

CASE 12–4.   MANOMET ELECTRONICS, INC.

Balance sheets for Manomet Electronics, Inc., as of December 31, 1962, and December 31, 1963, are shown in Exhibit 1, and a statement of income and reconciliation of earnings for 1963 appears in Exhibit 2.

The only item in the Buildings and Equipment account sold during the year was a specialized machine that originally cost $15,000. The accumulated depreciation on this machine at the time of sale was $8,000. The machine was sold for $6,000, and full payment was received in cash.

Exhibit 1

MANOMET ELECTRONICS, INC.

Comparative Balance Sheets

	Dec. 31, 1962	Dec. 31, 1963	Increase or Decrease*
ASSETS			
Cash...	$ 74,000	$ 37,000	$ 37,000*
Accounts receivable.........................	54,000	47,000	7,000*
Inventories..................................	312,000	277,000	35,000*
Prepaid expenses...........................	6,000	4,000	2,000*
Land.......................................	60,000	60,000	.....
Patents....................................	55,000	65,000	10,000
Buildings and equipment....................	420,000	480,000	60,000
Less: Accumulated depreciation buildings and equipment...............	(105,000)	(120,000)	(15,000)
Total Assets.........................	$876,000	$850,000	$ 26,000*
LIABILITIES AND CAPITAL			
Accounts payable...........................	$ 58,000	$ 94,000	$ 36,000
Notes payable..............................	28,000	8,000	20,000*
Estimated real estate, excise and income tax.....	86,000	12,000	74,000*
Social security taxes accrued.................	3,000	5,000	2,000
Bonds payable.............................	220,000	60,000	160,000*
Capital stock..............................	250,000	460,000	210,000
Retained earnings.........................	231,000	211,000	20,000*
Total Liabilities and Capital...........	$876,000	$850,000	$ 26,000*

Exhibit 2

MANOMET ELECTRONICS, INC.
Statement of Income and Reconciliation of Earnings for 1963

Net sales...		$1,970,000
Less: Cost of goods sold..................................		1,480,000
Gross profit...		$ 490,000
Less: Operating expenses (includes depreciation on buildings and equipment of $23,000; patent amortization of $6,000)...		500,000
Net loss from operations..................................		$ 10,000
Less: Other revenue......................................		7,000
Net loss...		$ 3,000
Add: Retained earnings, December 31, 1962..................		231,000
		$ 228,000
Less: Dividend paid.......................................	$16,000	
Nonrecurring loss on sale of asset.....................	1,000	17,000
Retained Earnings, December 31, 1963		$ 211,000

Question

Prepare a funds flow statement.

CASE 12–5.   BLAINE CORPORATION

The Blaine Corporation, a medium-size industrial firm, was considering an expansion of its plant and manufacturing facilities in order to keep abreast of growth in the industry. In formulating future plans the financial analyst of the Blaine Corporation, Mr. Sloan, made an analysis of the Chapman Corporation, a strong competitor, which had recently engaged in a large expansion program. This expansion program involved not only the addition of new plant and manufacturing and transportation facilities but also the disposal of old worn-out equipment and buildings.

As part of his research, Mr. Sloan planned to make a detailed analysis of the Chapman Corporation's expansion program, the way in which it was financed, and the consequent effect on the assets and liabilities and capital structure. He planned to draw up a funds flow statement as an aid in making this analysis.

Exhibit 1 presents a comparative balance sheet for the years 1951–52; Exhibit 2, the income statement for 1952; and Exhibit 3, the statement of reconciliation of retained earnings for 1952. These exhibits were condensed slightly from financial statements published in the annual report of the Chapman Corporation.

An analysis of the increases and decreases in asset and liability accounts as indicated on the comparative balance sheet gave some insight into the magnitude of expansion, how funds were provided, and to what use they were applied. The income statement and reconciliation of retained earnings provided additional information with respect to sources and applications of funds.

Mr. Sloan obtained certain other information from the description of the year's operations in the Chapman Corporation's annual report. He learned from this source that assets with the gross book values (i.e., before deduction for depreciation) shown below were disposed of during 1952:

Land...$ 12,000
Plant and manufacturing properties............................ 462,000
Transportation properties.................................... 88,000

Depreciation on these assets had been accumulated in the following amounts:

Plant and manufacturing properties...........................$410,000
Transportation properties.................................... 78,000

Exhibit 1

CHAPMAN CORPORATION

Comparative Balance Sheet, December 31, 1951, and 1952
(000 Omitted)

	Dec. 31, 1952	Dec. 31, 1951	Increase or (Decrease)
ASSETS			
Current Assets:			
Cash	$ 2,149	$ 2,334	$ (185)
Receivables, less estimated bad debts	2,637	2,528	109
U.S. government securities, at cost	1,064	3,267	(2,203)
Inventories	4,247	3,998	249
Prepaid expenses	781	748	33
Total	$10,878	$12,875	($1,997)
Investments:			
Miscellaneous investments	$ 210	$ 197	$ 13
U.S. government securities set aside, at cost:			
For property additions and replacements	200	2,500	(2,300)
For expenditures arising out of war	80	120	(40)
Total	$ 490	$ 2,817	($2,327)
Fixed Assets:			
Land	$ 774	$ 777	$ (3)
Plant and manufacturing properties	$32,535	$28,811	$3,724
Less: Accumulated depreciation	18,242	17,024	1,218
Net	$14,293	$11,787	$2,506
Transportation properties	$ 5,838	$ 5,429	$ 409
Less: Accumulated depreciation	2,389	2,280	109
Net	$ 3,449	$ 3,149	$ 300
Total	$18,516	$15,713	$2,803
Total Assets	$29,884	$31,405	($1,521)
LIABILITIES AND CAPITAL			
Current Liabilities:			
Accounts payable	$ 3,753	$ 3,397	$ 356
Unpaid taxes	2,750	5,097	(2,347)
Dividends payable	259	259	....
Long-term debt due within one year	31	24	7
Total	$ 6,793	$ 8,777	($1,984)
Fixed Liabilities:			
Long-term debt	$ 610	$ 549	$ 61
Capital:			
Preferred stock—7% cumulative, par value $100	$ 3,603	$ 3,603	$....
Common stock—stated capital $33⅓ per share	8,703	8,703	....
Retained earnings	10,175	9,773	402
Total	$22,481	$22,079	$ 402
Total Liabilities and Capital	$29,884	$31,405	($1,521)

Exhibit 2

CHAPMAN CORPORATION

Income Statement For the Year Ended December 31, 1952

(000 Omitted)

Sales..		$31,373
Less: Cost of sales*....................................		22,891
Gross profit...		$ 8,482
Less: Expenses		
Selling, general, and administrative expenses*...........	$5,220	
Interest...	19	
State, local, and miscellaneous taxes....................	682	5,921
Net operating profit before income taxes.................		$ 2,561
Add profit from sale of fixed assets......................		46
Net income before income taxes.........................		$ 2,607
Less: Estimated federal income taxes...................		1,170
Net Income...		$ 1,437

* Includes depreciation expense for the year totaling $1,815,000.

Exhibit 3

CHAPMAN CORPORATION

Reconcilation of Retained Earnings

For the Year Ended December 31, 1952

(000 Omitted)

Retained earnings, January 1, 1952.......................		$ 9,773
Add: Net income for year..............................		1,437
Total..		$11,210
Deduct: Dividends:		
Preferred ($7.00 per share).............................	$252	
Common ($3.00 per share).............................	783	
		1,035
Retained Earnings, December 31, 1952.....................		$10,175

The land was sold for its book value of $12,000. The sale and salvage of the other fixed assets resulted in additional proceeds of $108,000; this was $46,000 more than their book value.

Fixed assets totaling $4,692,000 were acquired during the year, but the report did not state how this total was broken down among the three categories of fixed assets.

Questions

1. Prepare a statement, such as Mr. Sloan would prepare upon completion of his computations, which lists (*a*) all the sources of funds for the Chapman Corporation during the year, and (*b*) all the applications of these funds both as a result of normal manufacturing operations and any other transactions the company made.

2. What conclusions can you draw regarding the method of financing the expansion program?

Part

ACCOUNTING IN
MANAGEMENT CONTROL

Chapter 13 | BASIC CONCEPTS OF MANAGEMENT CONTROL

THE TECHNIQUES for analyzing financial statements that were discussed in Part II are useful both to outside parties and to the management of the company. From here on, we shall focus exclusively on the use of accounting information by management. This is the subject matter of management accounting.

MANAGEMENT ACCOUNTING AND FINANCIAL ACCOUNTING

Whereas financial accounting has been written about for over 400 years, management accounting is a much newer subject, about which little was written until well into the twentieth century. The actual practice of management accounting goes back much further; many of the techniques to be described here were used by Josiah Wedgwood and Sons, Ltd., in the eighteenth century. And the need for a type of accounting that was not aimed exclusively at the preparation of financial statements is well set forth in this 1875 memorandum by Thomas Sutherland, a British business executive:[1]

The present system of bookkeeping in the Accountant's Department is admirably suited for the end it has in view, viz., that of ascertaining once a year or oftener the profits upon the company's transactions; but it is evident that in a business of this kind much detailed information is necessary regarding the working of the Company, and this information should be obtainable in such a practical form, as to enable the Directors to see readily and clearly the causes at work in favor of or against the success of the Company's operations. To this end Supplementary Books are necessary and the question is what kind of Supplementary Books are most suited for the purpose. It appears to me that the Supplementary Books formerly kept in the Accountant's Department were ill qualified for any practical use . . . .

Some differences between financial accounting and management accounting were noted on pages 270–72. Most important is the difference in viewpoint. The governing objective of financial accounting

---

[1] This memorandum was called to my attention by Professor Lyle E. Jacobsen, who saw it reprinted in the London *Economist* in 1960.

is to furnish information to outsiders in order to report on stewardship, while the objective of management accounting is to be helpful to insiders. Outsiders have a right to expect that the information they receive is prepared according to generally agreed upon definitions and principles; otherwise, the information will be unintelligible. Management, on the other hand, can make whatever rules and definitions it finds most useful for its own needs, without worrying whether these conform to some outside standard.

The principles of financial accounting are therefore not necessarily governing in management accounting, although the fact that some of the accounting information used by management will also be used in the financial statements must of course be kept in mind. Management may, for example, be interested in information on the amount of sales orders received, which is not a part of financial accounting since unfilled sales orders do not represent realized revenue. Management may be interested in the number of hours worked, the pounds of product scrapped, or other nonmonetary information. It may be interested in replacement costs or estimates of future costs rather than historical costs. It may be interested in information outside the debit-credit structure. Thus, the basic question in management accounting is the pragmatic one: "Is the information useful?"—not "Does it conform to generally accepted principles?"

There are other important differences. First, financial accounting focuses on the *whole* of the business, while management accounting is more interested in the *parts*. The financial statements report on the overall status and performance of the enterprise, but most management accounting reports have to do with departments, products, types of inventory, or other subdivisions of the business entity. Second, financial accounting *must be done,* while management accounting is *optional.* Enough effort must be expended to collect financial accounting data in acceptable form, but any piece of management information is justified only if its value exceeds the effort required to collect it. Third, in management accounting there is more emphasis on furnishing information *quickly* than in financial accounting; up-to-date information is essential as a basis for management action. Fourth, there is *less emphasis on precision* in management accounting; approximations are often as useful as, or even more useful than, figures worked out to the last penny. Finally, whereas financial accounting is exclusively concerned with historical information—what *has* happened—management accounting is concerned both with historical information and with estimates of what *will* happen in the future.

MANAGEMENT CONTROL

Management accounting is closely associated with the process called *management control,* which is the process of assuring that resources are obtained and used effectively and efficiently in the accomplishment of an organization's objectives. This process has to do with the ongoing operation of a business; it is a recurring process with no definable beginning or end. For purposes of describing management control and showing how accounting information is useful in connection with it, however, the process may be divided into three parts: (1) planning, (2) operating, and (3) measuring and analyzing performance.

Planning is the process of deciding what the organization is going to do. The principal formal device for making business plans is the *budget,* which is a statement of plans in financial terms, and hence incorporates accounting data. The preparation of budgets is described in Chapter 14.

In the actual conduct of operations, accounting data are used to communicate plans and other information and to guide the organization in the direction in which management wants it to go. Some concepts governing the accounting data used for this purpose are discussed in the present chapter.

As operations proceed, accounting data are used in the measurement of performance and in analyzing performance for the purpose of making better plans the next time around. Thus, this last step leads directly into another planning cycle. The collection and use of accounting data for this purpose are discussed in Chapters 15, 16, and 17.

As pointed out in Chapter 1, accounting is by no means the sole source of the information used in the management control process, nor are the collection and use of quantitative information the most important parts of the process. Accounting reports are not a substitute for informal person-to-person communication or for the creation and maintenance of a good "control atmosphere."

MOTIVATION

An obvious and fundamental fact about organizations is that they are made up of human beings. The management control process in part consists of inducing the people in an organization to do certain things and to refrain from doing others. Although for some purposes an accumulation of the costs of manufacturing a product is useful, management literally cannot "control" a product, or the costs of making a product. What management does—or at least what it attempts to do—is control the actions of the people who are responsible for incurring these costs.

The effectiveness of a control technique can be judged in two ways: by the *direction* and by the *strength* of its motivation.

Direction of Motivation

It is reasonable to expect that a person will act according to what he perceives his own best interests to be. Essentially, therefore, the control system should be designed so that actions that it leads people to take in accordance with their perceived self-interest are actions that are also in the best interests of the company. In the language of social psychology, the system should encourage *goal congruence;* that is, it should be structured so that the goals of people in the organization are, so far as feasible, consistent with the goals of the organization as a whole.

Perfect congruence between individual goals and organizational goals does not exist, but as a minimum the system should not *encourage* the individual to act *against* the best interests of the company. For example, if the system signals that the emphasis should be only on reducing costs, and if the individual responds by reducing costs at the expense of adequate quality, or by reducing costs in his own department by measures that cause a more than offsetting increase in some other department, he has been motivated, but in the wrong direction. It is therefore important to ask two separate questions about a control technique: (1) What will it motivate people to do in their own selfish interests? and (2) Is this action in the best interests of the company?

An Example: Maintenance Costs

As an illustration of this point, let us consider the problem of the control of maintenance costs in a factory that has a separate maintenance department. The maintenance function is that of insuring that the buildings and equipment are in good operating condition. This is partly the responsibility of the maintenance department, which incurs costs when it makes repairs or does other maintenance work; and it is partly the responsibility of the operating department foreman, who can influence the amount of required maintenance work by how well he takes care of his equipment. In addition, some maintenance work, such as outside painting, is required simply because of the uncontrollable forces of nature.

There are at least a dozen ways in which the costs of the maintenance department can be charged to the several operating departments, and each gives a different "message" to the foremen as to how they should view their responsibility for maintenance. Here are a few of the possibilities and the implications that each is likely to convey:

Method No. 1: Do not charge any maintenance costs to the operating departments.

> *Message:* The operating foreman has no responsibility for maintenance costs. He requests the maintenance department to do the work that he thinks should be done, and the maintenance department has the responsibility for doing it. (Note that this system does not motivate the foreman to curb unnecessary requests for maintenance work.)

Method No. 2: Prorate total maintenance costs to the operating departments on the basis of the volume of activity in the department.

> *Message:* Maintenance costs in total are expected to vary proportionately with plant activity. However, the foreman of each department has no direct responsibility for maintenance work, and the maintenance department, as in the first method, has full responsibility. The operating foreman is told what is his "fair share" of total maintenance costs incurred.

Method No. 3: Charge departments for each maintenance job at a prescribed amount for each type of job.

> *Message:* The operating foreman is responsible for situations that create the need for maintenance work, such as machine breakdowns. The maintenance department is responsible for the cost of doing a given maintenance job. The foreman therefore need not be concerned with the efficiency with which maintenance men work, once he has requested that the job be done, since he will be charged a prescribed amount no matter how much is actually spent in doing the job.

Method No. 4: Charge each department for maintenance work at a prescribed hourly rate for each hour that a maintenance man works in the department.

> *Message:* The operating foreman is responsible both for situations that create the need for maintenance work and for the time taken by the maintenance people to do the work. Presumably, he has some control over the work of the maintenance men. In some situations, he may even be

authorized to hire outside maintenance people if he believes that they will do the work less expensively than
the rates charged by the maintenance department.

None of the above methods is necessarily better than the others.
Each of them tends to motivate the foreman differently. The best
method is the one that motivates the foreman to act most nearly as
management wants him to act. Depending on what management
wishes to accomplish, any one of these methods, or other methods not
listed, or some combination of them, may be best for a given company.

Strength of Motivation

Motivation is in the subject area of psychology, but an adequate
discussion of psychological principles is outside both the scope of this
book and the competence of its author. Furthermore, social psychologists
regard the currently accepted principles of the behavior of individuals in
groups as extremely tentative, since the evidence from which they are
derived is (except for that based on the unflattering assumption that
humans behave like chimpanzees or white rats) both inconclusive and
often contradictory. There are, however, generalizations relevant to the
design of a management control system on which many psychologists
agree. Some of these are as follows:

1. An individual strives to satisfy his needs. Among these needs are
the following:

   a) Physiological considerations, such as food, bodily comfort, and
   sex;

   b) Realistic recognition of his abilities and achievements by his
   colleagues and superiors;

   c) Status and social acceptance as a member of a group;

   d) Self-esteem, a sense of personal worth;

   e) Security, including an understanding of what is expected of him
   and a belief that his performance will be judged fairly;

   f) Autonomy, the freedom to exercise discretion;

   g) The opportunity for aesthetic experiences (for some persons);
   and

   h) The opportunity to be creative (for some persons).[2]

---

[2] Many social psychologists, following Maslow, believe that these needs are arranged
in a "need hierarchy," running from (a) through (h), and that a higher need has little
or no force until all lower needs have been satisfied. For example, recognition of ability is
unimportant until the purely physiological needs have been satisfied. See A. H. Maslow,
Motivation and Personality (New York: Harper & Bros., 1954).

2. *Reward* is the satisfaction of a need, and *punishment* is the deprivation of satisfaction. Individuals tend to be more strongly motivated by reward, or expectation of reward, than by punishment, or fear of punishment.

3. Monetary compensation is an important means of satisfying certain needs, but beyond the subsistence level the amount of pay is not necessarily so important as nonmonetary rewards. Nevertheless, pay is often important indirectly as an indication of how achievement and ability are regarded. (A man earning $50,000 a year may be unhappy if a colleague of equal ability receives $51,000 a year.)

4. The effectiveness of reward or punishment diminishes quickly the longer the time between an action and the reward or punishment administered for it.

5. Needs may be unconscious, or they may be expressed as aspirations or goals. Motivation is weakest when the individual perceives a goal as either unattainable or too easily attainable. Motivation is strong when the goal can be attained with some effort and when the individual regards its attainment as important.

6. An individual tends to accept evidence of his performance more willingly and to use it more constructively when it is presented in a manner that he regards as objective, that is, without personal bias.

7. Individuals are receptive to learning better ways of doing things only when they personally recognize the inadequacies of their present behavior.

8. Beyond a certain point, pressure for improved performance accomplishes nothing. This optimum point is far below the maximum amount of pressure that conceivably could be exerted. (When the coach says, "Don't press; don't try too hard," he is applying this principle.)

9. Individuals differ greatly in the importance they attach to various need satisfactions. Their attitude also changes with time and circumstances and is heavily influenced by the attitudes of their colleagues and superiors.

In view of the differences among individuals mentioned in the ninth point above, precise rules for designing control systems could not be constructed even if the above list of generalizations were fully substantiated by experiment. They nevertheless seem to be sufficiently valid so that useful concepts for control can be derived from them. Some of these are described in the next section.

SOME MANAGEMENT CONTROL CONCEPTS

Management Sponsorship

A control system will probably be ineffective unless the organization is convinced that management considers the system to be important. Some systems are installed with no more management backing than the directive, "Let's have a good control system," and with no subsequent interest or action by managements. Such a system, instead of being a part of the management process, becomes a paper shuffling routine whose principal virtue is that it provides employment for a great many clerks. In a talk describing the remarkable reorganization of Ford Motor Company, Mr. Ernest R. Breech gave an excellent illustration of the importance of this point:[3]

In the course of reorganizing Ford Motor Company, by 1948 we had set up a modern cost control system and a supplemental compensation plan. Having done so, we were startled to find that nothing in particular happened. We had built, or so we thought, a log fire under the company. But we had not, up to that point, applied the torch of internal competition.

In the fall of 1948 we called together several hundred of our top management men. We analyzed and compared the profit performance of each key operation, and showed how performance was reflected in the supplemental compensation fund. It was quite a show, and each man went out of that meeting determined to put his own house in order. Each man in turn set up similar meetings of his own supervisors and the process continued on down the line. These meetings were held, and still are, at regular intervals. The results were almost unbelievable.

Our direct labor costs were reduced from an off-standard of 65% in July of 1948 to only 6% off-standard in 1951, and manufacturing overhead improved 48 percentage points during the same period. We never could have achieved that performance without a real incentive system and internal competition that reached deep into our management structure.

Action is a sure signal, probably the only effective signal, that management is interested in the control system. Basically, this action involves praise or other reward for good performance, criticism of or removal of the causes for poor performance, or questions leading to these actions. If, in contrast, reports on performance disappear into executive offices and are never heard from again, the organization has reason to assume that management is not paying attention to them. And if management does not pay attention to them, why should anyone else?

---

[3] Ernest R. Breech, "Planning the Basic Strategy of a Large Business," *Harvard Business School Bulletin,* Summer 1955, pp. 28, 29. Mr. Breech was at that time chairman of the board.

Responsibility Centers

A *responsibility center* is simply an organization unit headed by a responsible person. The center is responsible for performing some function, which is its *output,* and for using resources, or *inputs,* as efficiently as possible in performing this function. For a production or selling responsibility center, output can be measured in terms of value of products produced or sold, and for some other responsibility centers output can be measured in terms of the services performed. Inputs can be measured in terms of cost incurred.

Within a business there is a whole hierarchy of responsibility centers. At the top, there is the president or chief executive officer, who is held responsible by the owners for the overall profitability of the enterprise. Beneath him, the several operating and staff departments are each responsibility centers, and at still lower levels, responsibility centers may consist of sections, subsections, or even individuals. The delineation of responsibility centers is in practice a difficult task, and the installation of a control system often uncovers instances of overlapping responsibility which need to be corrected. If the company's organization chart reflected the actual lines of responsibility, this difficulty would not exist, but for various reasons the chart may not do this.

In thinking about the kind of accounting data that are useful for management control, we find it convenient to recognize three types of responsibility centers: (1) expense centers, (2) profit centers, and (3) investment centers.

Expense Centers.   If the control system measures the expenses incurred by an organization unit, but does not measure the monetary value of its output, the unit is an expense center. Although every organization unit *has* an output (i.e., it does something), in many cases it is neither feasible nor necessary to measure this output in monetary terms. It would be extremely difficult to measure the monetary value that the accounting department contributes to the whole business, for example, and although it would be relatively easy to measure the monetary value of the output of an individual production department, there is no reason for doing so if the responsibility of the factory foreman is simply to produce a stated *quantity* of output at the lowest feasible cost.

Thus most individual production departments and most staff units are expense centers. For these, the accounting system records expenses incurred, but not revenue earned.

Profit Centers.   Revenue is a monetary measure of output, and expense is a monetary measure of inputs, or resources consumed. Profit is the difference between revenue and expense. Thus if performance in a responsibility center is measured in terms of both the revenue it earns and the cost it incurs, it is called a *profit center*.

Although in financial accounting, revenue is considered as being earned only when it is realized, in management accounting it is quite all right to define revenue as the value of the output of the center, whether realized or not. Thus, the factory may be a profit center, "selling" its production to the sales department; or service departments, such as the maintenance department, may "sell" their services to the departments receiving them.

Since the value of products or services sold within the company is not established by a market transaction, a *transfer price* must be established. If a market price exists for comparable products or services, this may be used as the transfer price. In the absence of a market price, the transfer price often is built up on the basis of cost plus an allowance for profit. In this case, there is usually some mechanism for *negotiating* the price between the two departments involved; otherwise, the producing department could simply pass its inefficiencies along to the receiving department in the form of higher costs.

The profit center concept is a powerful one. If properly operated, it has the effect of "putting the supervisor in business for himself," a business in which he can earn a profit. The development of this concept is one of the factors that has made possible the recent tendency for large companies to decentralize.

Investment Centers. The ultimate extension of the responsibility center idea is the investment center, in which the supervisor is responsible not only for profit but also for the assets that he uses. The investment center idea is not yet widely adopted and is usually restricted to large units, such as the several product divisions of a company making a variety of types of products.

Controllability

The control system should provide a way of separating the cost and revenue items that are controllable by the head of the responsibility center from the items which he cannot control. As a practical matter, this separation usually cannot be achieved perfectly. Only in rare cases does one individual have complete control over *all* the factors that influence a given cost element. The influence of the foreman of a manufacturing department over labor costs may actually be quite limited, since wage rates may be established by the personnel department or by union negotiations; the amount of labor required for a unit of product may be largely determined by the engineers who designed the product and who specified how it was to be manufactured; and the number of units produced, and hence total labor costs, may be influenced by the output of some other department, by the ability of the purchasing department to obtain materials, or by a variety of other factors. Nevertheless, the foreman usually has a significant influence on the amount of direct labor cost incurred. He has some control over the amount of idle time in his department, the speed and efficiency with which work is done, and other factors which to some extent affect labor costs.

Although the head of a responsibility center may never have the *sole* responsibility for any element of cost, if he has a *significant influence* on the amount of costs incurred, such elements are properly considered "controllable."

The use of a *standard cost* is one way of distinguishing between those parts of a cost element for which a person is responsible and those for which he is not. A standard labor cost, for example, presumably states what the cost should be, considering the influence of wage rates, product design, and other factors over which the foreman has no control. Ideally, the difference between standard cost and actual cost incurred represents the effect of actions by the foreman, and it is this difference for which the foreman is held responsible. As explained in Chapter 17, there are many reasons why this concept does not work out precisely in practice, but it nevertheless may work well enough to provide an acceptable basis for control.

Some people argue that the *separation* of controllable from non-controllable costs is not enough; they insist that noncontrollable costs should not even be recorded in a management accounting system. Actually, there may be good reasons for charging all, or certain types of, noncontrollable costs to responsibility centers.

One reason is that management may want the supervisor to be concerned about such costs, the expectation being that his concern may indirectly lead to better cost control. For example, an operating unit may be charged with part of the costs of the personnel department, even though the foreman of the unit has no direct responsibility for that department. Such a charge can be justified either on the grounds that the foreman will be careful about making unnecessary requests of the personnel department if he is made to feel some responsibility for personnel department costs or on the grounds that the foreman may in various ways influence the head of the personnel department to exercise good cost control in his own department.

Another reason for charging all costs is that the collection of all costs in responsibility centers may facilitate the calculation of selling prices, a topic to be discussed in Chapter 18. A third reason is that if the supervisor is made aware of the total amount of costs that are incurred in the operation of his unit, he may have a better understanding of how much the company contributes to the operation. Such a practice may boomerang, however, for the supervisor may conclude that his controllable costs are so small, relative to the costs that he cannot control, that they are not worth worrying about.

In any event, when noncontrollable costs are charged to responsibility centers, it is important that they be clearly separated from the cost elements that the supervisor is expected to control.

Incidentally, the term "controllable costs" refers to the costs controllable by the particular responsibility center; *all* costs are controllable by someone.

Basis of Measurement

The performance of a responsibility center is judged in terms of its output and its input. Since output is often usefully divided into *quality* of output and *quantity* of output, three key questions need to be considered simultaneously: (1) How much was accomplished? (2) How good was it? and (3) How much did it cost? The second question is often answered on a "go, no-go" basis; that is, quality was either satisfactory or it was not satisfactory. Actual results are always compared with some standard showing what is expected under the circumstances, as described more fully in Chapter 17. The importance of giving due consideration to all three aspects of performance should be mentioned, since there is sometimes a tendency to concentrate on one and neglect the others. In some cases, this is justifiable; for example, if the supervisor has no control over the volume of production and if any quality defects are reflected in the form of increased rework costs, he may be judged primarily on cost performance. In other cases, it is not. In Russian industry, until recently, the control system emphasized the quantity of output, with substantial bonuses being paid to supervisors for output that exceeded quotas. Although there may have been some justification for this on the basis that "shoddy shoes are preferable to going barefoot," it did lead to poor quality and inadequate attention to costs.[4]

Performance is not always best measured in terms of revenue or cost.

[4] See Joseph S. Berliner, *Factory and Manager in the U.S.S.R.* (Cambridge, Mass.: Harvard University Press, 1957), especially chaps. iii–ix.

In the case of a purchasing officer who is responsible for having the right quantity and quality of material on hand, the dollar cost of material purchased is much less important than factors such as the investment in inventory as measured by inventory turnover, or the frequency with which items are unavailable when they are needed.

Ideally, there should be a single measure encompassing all aspects of performance. In practice, such a measure can rarely be constructed, and different measures must be used for different aspects. This creates the difficult problem of deciding the relative importance of each measure, especially when performance is good according to one measure and poor according to another.

Costs should be collected and measured only to the extent that they are *significant*. Reporting a long list of cost elements, many of which have only minor amounts, tends to obscure the few really significant ones. This can happen when the report is a standard form containing a long list of cost items that are reported uniformly for each responsibility center. Preferably, the control system is tailor-made to the situation in each responsibility center, having in mind also the probable uses of the information for purposes other than control.

Participation and Understanding

Whatever standard of good performance is adopted, it is likely to be effective as a means of control only if the person being judged agrees that it is an equitable standard. If he does not agree, he is likely to pay no attention to comparisons between his performance and the standard; and he is likely to resent, and if possible reject, an attempt by anyone else to make such a comparison.

The best way to assure this agreement is to ask the person whose performance is to be measured to participate in the process of setting the standard. This was not the usual practice some years ago. The earliest budgets were "imposed budgets"; that is, they were edicts promulgated by management, which said, in effect, to the organization: "Thou shalt do such and such." The results obtained from these imposed budgets were frequently unsatisfactory because the organization tended to resent and disregard them. The more recent trend is in the direction of permitting the person who is being held responsible for performance to have a considerable voice in the preparation of the budget. This trend is a manifestation of the general tendency to decentralize decision making to lower echelons in the organization.

Although the responsible supervisor participates in the budgeting process, he is not solely responsible for deciding on the budget allowances. Rather, the supervisor and his superior discuss the matter until they *jointly* agree.

In order to participate intelligently, the supervisor needs to understand clearly what the control system is, what he is expected to do, what basis he is going to be judged on, and so on. As illustrated by the remarks of Mr. Breech quoted above, such an understanding probably cannot be achieved by written communication. Frequent meetings of supervisors for discussion and explanation are required.

The process of educating the individuals involved in the system is necessarily a continuous one. Not uncommonly, a system is introduced with a loud fanfare, works well for a time, and then gradually withers away in effectiveness as the initial stimulus disappears.

The Time Interval of Control

The proper control period is the shortest period of time in which management can usefully intervene and in which significant changes in performance are likely. The period is different for different responsibility centers and for different items within responsibility centers. Spoilage rates in a production operation may be measured hourly, or oftener. The key cost elements of the center may be measured daily. Reports on overall performance, particularly those going to top levels of management, are often on a monthly basis, and sometimes for quarterly or longer intervals, since top management does not have either the time or the inclination to explore local, temporary problems. Also, performance for a short period of time is influenced by random factors that tend to average out over longer periods; a system with a short time interval costs more to operate and consumes more time of the participants at all levels than a system with longer intervals; and frequent reports may be associated with unduly restrictive supervision. These considerations may be offset, of course, by the necessity for detecting serious trouble quickly: a change in the behavior of a continuous chemical processing operation must be known as soon as it occurs, or there may be an explosion.

Comparing Performance with Standards

It seems obvious that control is not possible unless actual performance and the standard against which it is being measured are comparable; yet instances of complete noncomparability do occur. This often happens when a management accounting system is separated from the financial accounting system, perhaps being operated by different staff organizations. An extreme case is that of the federal government, notably the Defense Department. For cost control purposes, an operating manager in the Defense Department should be judged on the basis of the costs *incurred* in doing his job. Nevertheless, until recently and despite the recommendations of two Hoover Commissions, the Congress attempted to exercise control through a limitation on obligations, which are essentially the cost of goods and services *purchased.* Since purchases are made by different persons from those who actually use the goods and services, and since they are made in different time periods from the time of consumption, this basis of control did not permit a matching of the control standard, the obligation, against the desired basis of control—costs incurred in responsibility centers. Although the practice is currently being corrected in the federal government, similar situations continue to exist in some businesses.

Inconsistencies between the standard desired by management and the standard as perceived by the organization also arise when aspects of performance are being measured in separate control systems. If a supervisor's performance as to quality is being measured in one system, his performance as to cost control in another, and his performance as to volume in a third, he may be uncertain as to the relative weights that he should attach to these three aspects of performance. He will tend to regard one of these aspects as more important than the others, but his choice may be different from what management actually intends.

Management by Exception

The use of a formal standard as a basis for comparison makes possible the practice of "management by exception." A management control system operated on the exception principle is one in which management's attention is focused on the relatively small number of items in which actual performance is significantly different from the standard; when this is done, little or no attention need be given to the relatively large number of situations where performance is satisfactory.

No control system makes a perfect distinction between the situations that warrant management attention and those that do not. For example, it is the usual practice to "red flag" those items for which actual spending significantly *exceeds* the budgeted amount, but an investigation of these items may reveal that a difference between actual and budgeted spending was entirely warranted. On the other hand, even though actual spending for an item exactly matches the budget allowance, an unsatisfactory situation may exist. The exception principle is thus tricky to apply in practice. It is nevertheless a useful starting point for indicating the significance of what would otherwise be a bewildering mass of data, provided that the need for some examination of the superficially unexceptional situations is not overlooked. Conforming precisely to the budget is not necessarily good, and departing from the budget is not necessarily bad.

The distinction between significant and insignificant results is usually a matter of judgment. Attempts are being made to define "significant" in statistical terms, and these new techniques will probably have applications to business problems in the future.

Individual Differences

As pointed out above, individuals differ in their needs and in their reactions to rewards and punishments of various types. An important function of the manager, at each level, is to adapt the system to the personalities of the individuals whom he supervises. Thus, the impersonal system can never be a substitute for personal management; rather, the system is a framework that is adapted by management to fit individual situations.

Incentives

Many management control systems rely for the strength of their motivation on the attitude and actions that management takes in response to reported performance. Some tie the supervisor's compensation to his performance. In view of the importance which people attach to monetary compensation, this is a strong motivation indeed. In some cases it may be too strong, for unless the standards are very carefully worked out, incessant arguments can be created about the justice and equity of the reported results. If the system is being used only for praise or blame, inequities in the figures can be allowed for in interpreting the results, but this is not possible when a bonus is computed mechanically on the basis of reported performance. Thus, a bonus plan is most successful when there is general agreement that the basis of measurement is fair.

Control of the Management Control System

Like a fruit tree, a management control system can become both unsightly and unproductive unless it is pruned periodically. What happens is that a new technique, usually in the form of a new report, is worked out to meet a particular problem, the problem is solved, but the report continues. To avoid this result, companies either have a periodic overhaul of their control structure to eliminate such reports, or they have a person whose job is to ascertain that proposed new reports are likely to be worth the cost of preparing and using them and that existing reports continue to fill a real need.

Reports

Examples of control reports are given in cases that accompany this and the next two chapters, and in the C. F. Church Company case, Case 21–1. A few general comments about these reports are in order. They should be *objective;* that is, they should report what actually happened without bias. They should be *timely;* if they are to be the basis of action, they must be received before the time for effective action has passed. They should be *clear and easily understood,* although clarity should not be achieved by oversimplifying an inherently complicated situation. They should indicate, if possible, the *reasons why,* not only the facts about performance itself.

Control reports, in the literal sense, are intended as a basis for action. Copies of the same reports together with other data on performance may be used for *information,* even though the person receiving them is not expected to take action.

Function of the Controller

There is a tendency to regard the controller as the person who is primarily responsible for exercising control. Such an inference is natural because of the similarity between the two words, but it is erroneous. Generally, the controller is responsible for the design and operation of the *system* by means of which control information is collected and reported, but the *use* of this information in actual control is the responsibility of line management. The controller is something more than an accountant and something less than a chief executive. In addition to his responsibility for collecting figures, the controller may also be responsible for analyzing figures, for pointing out their significance to management, and for making recommendations as to what should be done. Moreover, he may police the adherence to limitations on spending laid down by the chief executive. He controls the integrity of the accounting system and is responsible for safeguarding assets from theft and fraud. In recent years the controllership function has become increasingly important in companies generally. The controller does *not,* however (unless *de facto* he *is* the chief executive), make or enforce management decisions. The responsibility for control runs from the president down through the line organization, not through the controller, who is a staff officer.

APPRAISAL OF PERFORMANCE

Control devices are usually thought of as providing a means of appraising a person's performance—of indicating whether or not he has done a good job—and this is indeed one of their important functions. The appraisal of performance involves a paradox, however. A man's performance can be measured only *after* he has performed, but at that time the work has already been done, and nothing management does later can change what was done. Of what value, therefore, are techniques for judging performance?

There seem to be two valid answers to this question. First, if a person knows in advance that his performance is going to be judged, he tends to act differently from the way he will if he believes no one is going to check up on him. (Anyone who receives grades in school should appreciate the importance of this point.) Secondly, even though it is literally impossible to change an event that has already happened, an appraisal of how well a person has performed in the past may indicate, both to the person and to his superior, ways of obtaining better performance in the future. Corrective action taken by the person himself is important; the system should "help the man to help himself." Action by the superior is also necessary, and such action ranges from the extremes of firing or promoting the person, to giving criticism or praise or suggesting specific means of improving future performance.

The Search for a Standard

As described in Chapter 11, the task is, essentially, to compare what a person *actually did* with what he *should have done* under the circumstances. In many cases, actual performance can be ascertained without difficulty. The trick is to find a *standard,* or basis of comparison, that states what performance should have been under the conditions existing at the time.

The task of judging performance in business is complicated because results are affected by a complex set of factors, and the net influence of all these factors is never identical at two different times or on two different jobs done at the same time. A man who runs the mile in 4:04 minutes has done an excellent job, but what can we say about a foreman who spent $404 on supplies? First of all, we are not even sure of the *direction* that represents good performance. Offhand, one might conclude that spending $404 is "better" than spending $504, but there are many situations in which such a conclusion would be incorrect. If the foreman had spent another $100, for example, the department might have been able to turn out a much larger quantity of products, or the quality of the products might have been better, or safety conditions might have been improved, or other results worth more than $100 might have been achieved. Secondly, the actual spending of $404 may have been occasioned by any of a large number of factors over which the foreman has no control—company policies, an accident, orders from a superior, and a long list of others. Unless we recognize these factors and measure their impact, we cannot obtain an exact measurement of the phenomenon we are trying to measure: the performance of the foreman himself.

Despite these difficulties, judgments about performance must be made, and some kind of standard, imperfect though it may be, is used as a guide in making such judgments. The three possible types of standards have been described in Chapter 11 in connection with the specific problem of analyzing financial statements, and are repeated in more general terms below. They can be used either separately or jointly.

1. *Predetermined Standards or Budgets.* These are statements of expected performance under an assumed set of circumstances. Although actual events will never exactly match the assumed conditions, the standard may nevertheless be an adequate approximation to what should have been done. The use of such standards is discussed in more detail in Chapter 17.

2. *Performance of Others in Comparable Jobs.* Department A may be compared with Department B, and if conditions in the two departments are reasonably similar, the comparison may provide a useful basis for judging performance.

3. *Performance in the Past.* Results this month may be compared with results last month, or with results in the same month a year ago. In addition to the need to allow for circumstances that may have changed between the two periods, this comparison has the weakness that when a man is measured against his own record, there may be no way of knowing whether the prior period's performance was acceptable to start with. A foreman whose spoilage cost is $100 a week, week after week, is consistent, but we do not know, without other evidence, whether he is consistently good or consistently poor.

Attacking an Appraisal Problem

The cases accompanying this chapter raise the problem of attempting to judge performance on the basis of some sort of standard. A characteristic of all these cases is that they contain less information than ideally would be desired as the basis for reaching a judgment. This fact, however, is a characteristic of similar problems in real life; rarely is it possible to obtain as much information as one would like. Everyone would agree that both the Union and Confederate leaders made mistakes at the battle of Gettysburg; but despite volumes of analysis by military experts and historians, there is not unanimous agreement, even today, as to what these mistakes were or who was responsible for them. Nevertheless, the field commanders at the time, without the benefit of any historical research, had to make judgments on the performance of those participating in this battle and to take action on the basis of these judgments.

In view of the inevitable incompleteness of the data, the following guides may suggest a useful way of attacking a problem that involves the appraisal of performance:

1. From the information available or obtainable, decide on the best possible standard or basis of comparison.

2. Define the factors that are not included in the standard, attempt to estimate the importance of these factors, and either modify the standard to take them into account or reduce the degree of certainty attached to the comparison of actual against standard.

3. Find, and attempt to estimate the importance of, nonquantitative considerations that cannot be included in a standard (e.g., morale, quality, intangible future benefits).

4. Make a judgment and be prepared to act on it. (One possible judgment is that no action should be taken until more information is available. This judgment should be made only if one is reasonably confident that it is both feasible and necessary to obtain additional facts.)

SUMMARY

In the design of a management control system, principles of psychology, imperfect though they are, are much more important than generally accepted accounting principles. The system should motivate the organization, as strongly as feasible, to work toward the company's objectives. The direction and strength of motivation are likely to be optimum when the following conditions exist:

1. The system has the active backing of management and is regarded by the organization as a part of the management process.
2. The locus of control is the responsibility center, an organization unit headed by a responsible person.
3. The costs used in measuring performance are, to some significant degree, controllable by the head of the responsibility center.
4. The basis of measuring desired performance reflects those aspects of output and input that are important under the circumstances.
5. The responsible supervisor participates in the process of setting standards and understands the basis on which he is being judged.
6. The control period is short enough so that management can intervene quickly before trouble becomes serious, but not so short that the system becomes too restrictive, too expensive to operate, or too much subject to insignificant, random fluctuations.
7. The results of actual performance are collected according to the same definitions and concepts used in setting the standards of desired performance.
8. In reports of performance, attention is focused on exceptional items; that is, those in which actual performance is significantly different from standard.
9. Management adjusts the system to differences in individual personalities.
10. If financial incentives are used, there is general agreement that the basis of measurement is fair.
11. Unnecessary reports are not permitted to creep into the system, and reports that become unnecessary are eliminated.
12. Reports are objective, timely, clear, and easily understood, and if feasible show the reasons why.

There are successful management control systems that violate some or all of the above statements. For example, a chief executive with an extremely strong personality can be as effective as an entire formal system of controls. Such situations are unusual, however, and do not destroy the usefulness of these comments as generalizations.

In the measurement of performance, the essential task is to compare what actually happened with what should have happened under the circumstances. The standard, or measurement of what should have happened, can rarely be determined with precision. Yet judgments must be made, and they can be made with some assurance that they are correct if the best possible use is made of the available information.

SUGGESTIONS FOR FURTHER READING

BARNARD, CHESTER I. *The Functions of the Executive.* Cambridge, Mass.: Harvard University Press, 1938.

BEYER, ROBERT. *Profitability Accounting for Planning and Control.* New York: The Ronald Press Co., 1963.

JEROME, WILLIAM TRAVERS. *Executive Control; The Catalyst.* New York: John Wiley & Sons, Inc., 1961.

LEWIS, RALPH F. *Management Uses of Accounting; Planning and Control for Profits.* New York: Harper & Bros., 1961.

MARCH, JAMES G., AND SIMON, HERBERT A. *Organizations.* New York: John Wiley & Sons, Inc., 1958.

CASES

CASE 13–1. GILLETTE SAFETY RAZOR COMPANY

On the morning of March 5, Miss Ruth Fillipetti, an employee of the Gillette Safety Razor Company, reported for work in the buffing room of the South Boston plant. At the stock cage she picked up a tray containing handles for one of the current models of the Gillette safety razor. These stamped copper handles had been sent to the buffing department for smoothing and polishing. After being polished, the handles went to the plating department for the final stage in their manufacture.

Miss Fillipetti's job was to smooth and polish the end of the razor handle. In this work she used a power-drive buffer wheel, against which she held the handle. The operation was not a difficult one, but it was not automatic; that is, she was required to place the end of the handle against the buffer wheel manually. For certain models, an automatic machine could be used that required only that the handles be placed on a moving belt of spindles. This belt carried the handles automatically across a buffer wheel. Miss Fillipetti spent the full day of March 5 buffing razor handle ends and by 5 o'clock had completed the smoothing and polishing of 2,100 pieces.

A close check was kept on the amount of work given to Miss Fillipetti and also on the amount of time she spent doing it. Although none of the employees of the Gillette Safety Razor Company was paid on a piece-rate basis, a daily comparison was made of the actual and standard times required to do the work assigned. On the morning of March 6 the timecard for Miss Fillipetti, together with timecards of other employees in the buffing room, was sent upstairs to the accounting department, where work and time requirements were posted and compared with previously established standard times. By 4 o'clock that afternoon—that is, the afternoon of March 6—the complete record of gains and losses with reference to standard times for work done on March 5 was reported back to the foreman in the buffing room. A procedure similar to that used for the buffing department was followed for each of the production departments of the razor division. In some departments the reports were referred to by the foreman when talking privately with operators, but in other departments the reports were posted daily. A portion of the March 5 report for the buffing department is reproduced as Exhibit 1.

The time standard set up for the operation of buffing the ends of the razor handles was 375 handles an hour.[5] The normal time to produce 2,100 units at the rate of 375 an hour was 5 hours and 36 minutes. The time records were kept in 5-minute units; and, therefore, the expected time for the work done by Miss Fillipetti on March 5 was listed on the report as $5\frac{7}{12}$ hours. Her day's work actually took $7\frac{10}{12}$ hours, so that a loss of $2\frac{3}{12}$ hours in standard time was indicated. When actual time exceeded standard allowable time, the amount lost was reported on the daily record sheet in red pencil; when actual time was under standard time, the gain was shown in black. A summary for the whole department was shown at the top of each report form.

Once a week the daily summary reports were combined into a weekly report that was furnished each of the foremen and the plant superintendent. From these weekly reports a continuous tabulation was maintained by the plant superintendent. The departmental labor control record for the buffing room shown in Exhibit 2 contains data for the three-month period beginning with the week ending December 23, through and including the week ending March 16.

The first column of the departmental labor control record (Exhibit 2) gives the normal or standard allowable hours for the volume of work done. Normal hours were the daily average of the "expected" hours shown on the daily report. Columns 2 and 3 of Exhibit 2 show the average daily hours lost and gained. Column 4 gives the daily average of actual hours required to do the same work for which the normal operating time is given in column 1. It will be noted that column 1 plus column 2 minus column 3 equals column 4. The entries in column 5, "General Ledger," refer to hours spent on special work ordered by the general office and therefore not part of the normal production flow. Column 6 gives the number of hours' work that was not measured and for which no normal times were available for comparison. Columns 7 and 8 relate to nonproductive time devoted to the work of maintenance

---

[5] This operation was coded as 195 D 20; the "195" refers to the model, the "D" to the handle of the razor, and the "20" to the operation. A similar code number was given every other operation. The letter "B" was used to refer to the cap of the razor, "C" to the guard, and "A" to the complete razor. The operation on which Miss Fillipetti was engaged, 195 D 20, was known as "cut down and color."

Exhibit 1

DAILY REPORT OF PRODUCTION BY OPERATORS

GILLETTE SAFETY RAZOR COMPANY
DAILY REPORT OF PRODUCTION BY OPERATORS

DATE March 5   490 BUFFING DEPARTMENT

Summary

	Hours
Total Expected Hours	181 9/—
" Productive Hours Not Measured	48 6/—
Lost Hours	13 3/—
Gained Hours	5
Nonproductive Hours Charged to This Dept.	50 4/—
" " Not Charged to This Dept.	2
Loaned Hours	48
Total Actual Hours Worked incl. Loaned	343 10/—

Production Detail

No.	Name	Operation Number	Acct.	Total Actual	Expected per Hour	Expected (Hrs)	Actual (Hrs)	Diff. Red-Loss R	Diff. Bl.-Gain B
4126	MOORE, STELLA	195 D 20	502	2800	375	7	8	6/—	
4126	MOORE, STELLA								
4127	MACCAREY, ELEANOR	1001 DG 25	502	2800	-		7		
4127	MACCAREY, ELEANOR	195 DG 25	502	400	400	1	1		
4128	MURPHY, ELLEN	1005 R 200	502	200		1	1	9/—	
4128	MURPHY, ELLEN	1005 RG 26	502	100			6/—		
4129	LEIGH, VIRGINIA	139 B 204	502	20000	2250	8	8		11/—
4129	LEIGH, VIRGINIA								
4130	FILLIPETTI, RUTH	195 D 20	502	2100	375	5	7	10/—	2 3/—
4130	FILLIPETTI, RUTH								
4131	LURRELLO, HELEN	139 B 24	502	14000	1750	8	8		
4131	LURRELLO, HELEN								

Production Detail (continued)

No.	Name	Operation Number	Acct.	Total Actual	Expected per Hour	Expected (Hrs)	Actual (Hrs)	Diff. Red-Loss R	Diff. Bl.-Gain B
4128	MURPHY, ELLEN	195 D 20	502	450	375	1	2 1/—	6 1/—	4 1/—
4128	MURPHY, ELLEN	194 H 20	522	600	300	2	3 1/—	3 1/—	1 3/—

	Name										
4132	CONRAD, HORTENSE	Loaned						8			
4132	CONRAD, HORTENSE										
4133	O'LEARY, KATHARINE	1005 AG 210	502	76				3			
4133	O'LEARY, KATHARINE	195 D 20	502	2275	375	6	1	7	9	8 1	
4134	WOODROW, ESTHER	139 B 206	502	20000	2250	8	11	8			11
4134	WOODROW, ESTHER										
4135	ROVETA, MILDRED	195 C 24	502	12000	1750	6	10	8		2 1	
4135	ROVETA, MILDRED										
4136	CAPRA, JOSEPHINE	1004 A 20	522	500				3	5		
4136	CAPRA, JOSEPHINE	195 D 20	502	1600	375	4	3	4	7	4 1	
4137	CASSIDY, ELINOR	195 D 20	502	2400	375	6	5	8		7 1	
4137	CASSIDY, ELINOR										
4138	LOVITT, MARION	Group									
4138	LOVITT, MARION										
4139	LESLIE, ALTHEA	1004 A 20	522	1100				8			
4139	LESLIE, ALTHEA										
4140	SMITH, MARY	139 B 29	502	14000	1750	8		8			
4140	SMITH, MARY										
4141	GRADY, ANNE	Loaned									
4141	GRADY, ANNE										
4142	LAMB, ELIZABETH	1001 D 211	502	23000	3500	6	7	8		5 1	
4142	LAMB, ELIZABETH										

Exhibit 2

DEPARTMENTAL LABOR CONTROL, DEPARTMENT 490—BUFFING
AVERAGE DAILY HOURS

Week Ending	Normal Hours	Hours Lost	Hours Gained	Actual Measured Hours	General Ledger	Productive Hours Not Measured	Nonproductive		Total Hours
							Hours	Ratio to Normal Hours	
	(1)	(2)	(3)	(4)	(5)	(6)	(7)	(8)	(9)
December 9...	212.9	8.0	8.1	212.8	6.4	30.1	50.8	23.86	300.1
16...	183.8	10.5	5.6	188.7	12.7	23.4	51.3	27.91	276.1
23...	192.0	5.5	5.2	192.3	11.9	22.7	51.4	26.77	278.3
January 6...	174.7	9.2	5.0	178.9	2.0	39.8	57.6	32.97	278.3
13...	196.4	24.4	4.9	215.9	1.5	28.2	54.2	27.60	299.8
20...	194.9	14.6	6.1	203.4	4.0	54.5	50.3	25.80	312.2
27...	194.7	11.3	7.5	198.5	8.0	63.0	54.8	28.15	324.3
February 3...	160.8	10.5	4.5	166.8	6.0	106.9	56.7	35.26	336.4
10...	153.8	14.5	3.4	164.9	5.8	86.1	41.7	27.11	298.5
17...	168.4	19.7	5.4	182.7	3.6	72.7	50.9	30.23	309.9
24...	177.1	13.2	3.7	186.6	2.5	72.7	57.5	32.47	319.3
March 2...	192.5	10.6	3.5	199.6	1.8	68.3	54.8	28.47	324.5
9...	201.1	13.2	3.2	211.1	0.4	46.7	54.1	26.90	312.3
16...	169.6	5.4	4.8	170.2	...	17.7	56.3	33.20	244.2

and similar work not directly resulting in produced goods. The final column gives the total number of hours worked in the department.

A report similar to that shown in Exhibit 2 was prepared weekly for each of the departments engaged in manufacturing razors. Exhibit 3

Exhibit 3

EXCERPTS FROM PRODUCTION CONTROL REPORT, SELECTED DEPARTMENTS
AVERAGE DAILY HOURS

Department	Hours Lost		Measured Hours		Total Hours	
	Week Ending March 9	Week Ending March 16	Week Ending March 9	Week Ending March 16	Week Ending March 9	Week Ending March 16
Cap and guard........	0.3	0.7	167.9	208.5	297.2	279.2
Buffing..............	13.2	5.4	211.1	170.2	312.3	244.2
Handle inspection.....	6.0	2.8	143.2	135.7	157.4	146.2
Wire and plating......	0.1	...	79.3	86.3	181.7	188.1
Handle packing.......	34.5	50.9	440.2	546.5	535.9	683.4
Auto-strop and probak department........	13.2	7.9	64.4	60.4	186.4	156.1

shows for the weeks ending March 9 and March 16 the hours lost in each of six departments. The exhibit also shows the total number of hours reported for the departments and the number of measured hours for which losses were computed.

The daily report comparing actual and normal times by operators was prepared for the department foremen. The personnel department did not receive copies of the daily report and, therefore, could not make the operator's performance a formal part of his personnel record. It was estimated that the time of two clerks was required to prepare the daily and weekly reports for the entire razor division.

Questions

1. What is the source, so far as you can judge, of the entries in each of the columns of Exhibit 1? If you were handed this report, what would you look for first? Should the plant superintendent request that the daily production report be put on his desk?

2. If Miss Fillipetti's record on operation 195 D 20 continued to be poor, should the department manager refer the matter to the personnel department? Before taking such action, what should the department manager consider?

3. Rank, from best to poorest, the performance of Stella Moore, Ellen Murphy, Ruth Fillipetti, and Esther Woodrow.

4. What purpose could be served by the operating report illustrated in Exhibit 1? Is it worth the cost? Should the cost be shared by other reports, perhaps not shown in the case?

5. What is Exhibit 2? Why is this type of report called a comparative report? Why are the figures in Exhibit 2 in terms of daily averages instead of weekly totals?

6. Look at Exhibit 2, *not Exhibit 3,* and decide what items you would select to be included in a summary report comparing performance in various departments in the factory.

7. What do Exhibits 2 and 3 tell other than the number of hours put in by employees? Doesn't management really want to know whether any work was done during those hours?

8. If you were receiving these control reports, what standards would you develop?

CASE 13–2. CANTON COMPANY

The Canton Company, a manufacturer of office supplies, sold to wholesalers and retailers. The company wished to establish standards by which the efficiency of the packers in the shipping room could be judged each week. If the standards proved satisfactory, the company expected to put packing on a piecework basis.

The company carried about 5,000 items in its warehouse. Items

Exhibit 1

Canton Company

Diagram of Conveyor Used in Packing Room

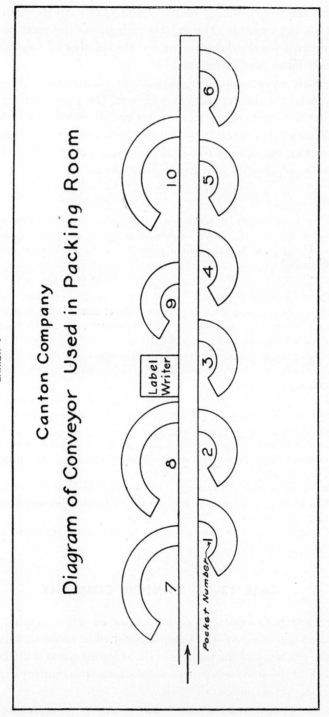

TABLE 2

PERCENTAGE OF EFFICIENCY ATTAINED BY PACKERS IN SHIPPING ROOM

Week Ending	A Pocket	A Per-centage	B Pocket	B Per-centage	C Pocket	C Per-centage	D Pocket	D Per-centage	E Pocket	E Per-centage	F Pocket	F Per-centage	G Pocket	G Per-centage
July 5	2	72	6	70	9	69	8	119	5	91	...	...	1	80
12	1	70	5	76	...	...	9	102	4	83	...	...	7	108
19	7	75	4	75	6	67	10	91	3	76	...	...	8	79
26	8	63	3	82	5	66	6	74	2	77	...	...	9	67
Aug. 2	9	56	2	92	4	74	5	80	1	85	8	95	...	...
9	10	68	1	95	3	81	4	96	7	89	9	76	6	46
16	6	57	7	120	2	79	3	103	...	...	10	90	5	64
23	5	71	8	81	1	90	2	90	9	63	6	76	4	72
30	4	69	9	65	7	106	1	115	10	74	5	80	3	73
Sept. 6	3	71	10	81	8	68	7	121	6	64	4	88	2	74
13	2	77	6	71	9	75	8	113	5	83	3	98	1	91
20	1	79	5	79	10	66	...	...	4	90	2	91	7	94
27	7	86	4	85	6	66	10	90	3	90	1	104	8	61
Oct. 4	8	74	3	93	5	71	6	79	2	84	7	119	9	62
11	9	70	2	99	4	75	5	86	1	101	8	106	10	60
18	10	74	1	122	3	71	4	94	7	110	9	98	6	70
25	6	61	7	115	2	80	3	101	8	92	10	93	5	68
Nov. 1	5	66	8	103	1	86	2	103	9	88	6	85	4	71
8	4	80	9	88	7	107	1	114	10	75	5	90	3	72
15	3	91	10	78	8	86	7	120	6	84	4	104	2	84
22	2	89	6	83	9	73	8	103	5	81	3	103	1	83
29	1	98	5	81	10	68	9	98	4	92	2	96	7	107
Total		1,617		1,934		1,624		2,092		1,772		1,692		1,586
No. of Weeks		22		22		21		21		21		18		21
Average		73.5		87.9		77.2		99.6		84.4		94.0		75.5

ordered were picked from the warehouse shelves, assembled in metal containers, and sent by gravity conveyors to the shipping room. There the goods were transferred to another gravity conveyor that ran between two lines of packers. Each packer was located next to a side track leading off from the main conveyor. The space occupied by a packer was called a "pocket." There were six pockets on one side of the conveyor and four pockets on the other side, as shown in Exhibit 1. The manager rotated the men from pocket to pocket so that a man occupied each pocket one week and usually did not occupy the same pocket again until he had occupied every other pocket. The men usually occupied the pockets in the following order: 6, 5, 4, 3, 2, 1, 7, 8, 9, 10.

As the metal containers of merchandise to be packed came slowly down the conveyor, the packers pulled them onto the side tables that formed their pockets. There they packed the merchandise in corrugated cardboard cartons, and shipping labels were affixed. Within limits, the management found it possible to adjust the number of packers to the amount of work to be done. Ordinarily there was work for ten packers; if not, one of the packers was temporarily withdrawn.

The time-study department worked out a method for giving a standard time allowance quickly for packing each shipment. This standard time varied according to the number of packages going into each carton and the numbers of cartons per order. This method of assigning standards necessarily was rough, but it was felt that since an average man packed about 18 cartons an hour, each man would get the same chance at the various types of packing in the course of a week. Before putting into effect a system of piecework based on such standards, however, the company decided to test it by trial. The manager of the packing department kept a record showing, for each man, the percentage of standard time to actual time. He called this the percentage of efficiency. The packers were told that they would be judged according to this percentage of efficiency.

Exhibit 2 summarizes the percentages of efficiency for seven of the packers, called A, B, C, D, E, F, G, by weeks, for a five months' period. The average performance ratings ranged from 73.5 for Packer A to 99.6 for Packer D. The position of the label writer was believed to have no effect upon efficiency in any pocket.

Questions

1. What are the facts of the situation learned from a close examination of Exhibits 1 and 2? Make a list of the various points discovered and note their significance to management.

2. What possible explanations can you find for these facts?
3. What would you do if the responsibility for action were yours?

CASE 13–3.   BENTLEY CORPORATION

The management of the Bentley Corporation, manufacturers of corrugated paper, was aware that the company would soon face intense competition. For several years, its mills had been operating at capacity, but demand appeared to be slackening. Consequently, the management started an intensive program to find means of reducing costs.

As one of the first steps in the economy program, the main office cut costs by eliminating unnecessary personnel in the staff departments, dropping unused reports, and tightening controls on administrative expenses. At the same time top management and the various plant managers had conferences on the need for cost reduction at the factory level.

The company operated seven mills scattered throughout the northern part of the United States. In each mill, there were four processing departments, with the product moving in succession through Departments 1, 2, 3, and then 4. Up to this time, the managers of the seven mills had been given monthly reports that compared costs of the different processing departments in the seven mills. The costs were compiled according to a uniform accounting system. It was recognized that mill costs differed because of size, technology, local cost situations, current volume of output, and so forth. Nevertheless, top management believed that all factors affecting a plant's costs were controllable by someone, either plant management or top management.

In an attempt to dramatize the cost differences among mills and the opportunities for cost reductions, the controller's office held several conferences on the subject with plant managers. As a follow-up on such discussions, a new report, based on the old comparative cost reports, was prepared and sent to the plant managers. An accompanying letter, signed by the controller, closed with a request for comments or suggestions on the report.

A copy of the new report is given in Exhibit 1. It shows unit products costs in each of the four departments, with a separate tabulation of the cost of waste in the whole mill.

Exhibit 1

COMPARATIVE COST REPORT, JUNE

	Department 1			Department 2			Department 3	
Mill	Unit Cost	Loss over Best	Mill	Unit Cost	Loss over Best	Mill	Unit Cost	Loss over Best
A	$0.655	$ 0	D	$3.89	$ 0	C	$6.74	$ 0
B	0.772	2,210	C	4.09	235	F	7.15	176
C	0.781	2,146	A	4.26	502	G	7.42	391
D	0.855	3,785	E	4.95	3,160	B	7.54	712
E	0.965	10,001	F	5.80	1,755	A	8.01	775
F	1.129	4,100	B	5.85	2,885	E	8.39	2,724
G	1.220	9,790	G	5.96	2,849	D	14.39	2,360

	Department 4			Total Waste			Cost Standing	
Mill	Unit Cost	Loss over Best	Mill	Percentage	Loss over Best	Mill	Total Loss over Best	
G	$ 5.00	$ 0	F	7.4	$ 0	F	$ 6,499	
B	6.71	525	B	8.4	1,985	B	8,317	
F	6.86	468	E	8.8	6,420	C	9,527	
D	7.32	3,798	D	9.0	4,070	A	9,558	
C	7.65	995	C	10.5	6,151	D	14,013	
A	8.41	1,881	A	11.0	6,400	E	30,155	
E	10.51	7,850	G	14.8	18,510	G	31,540	

Questions

1. Comment on the strong and weak points of the comparative cost report.
2. What would you do next to examine and reduce costs?

CASE 13–4.   DAY COMPANY

The president of the Day department store has received the facts tabulated in Exhibit 1 from one of the operating executives. He has asked you to comment on the significant points revealed by these data.

The data relate to the operating results of Department A, which handles gloves and ladies' hosiery. The president is interested in the results of your analysis because the department adopted a higher markup percentage in pricing goods sold in this department beginning in 1956. The effect of this policy may be noted clearly in the percentage gross margin figures.

Exhibit 1

COMPARATIVE OPERATING STATISTICS FOR DEPARTMENT A AND SIMILAR
DEPARTMENTS OF COMPARABLE STORES

	1954	1955	1956	1957	1958
Department A:					
Sales...........................	$100,000	$104,400	$109,600	$98,800	$100,600
Gross margin......................	$ 25,900	$ 28,814	$ 38,250	$35,469	$ 36,517
Direct expenses....................	$ 8,264	$ 8,601	$ 9,024	$ 8,861	$ 8,980
Indirect expenses..................	20,000	20,880	21,920	24,700	25,150
Total Expenses..................	$ 28,264	$ 29,481	$ 30,944	$33,561	$ 34,130
Net Profit (Loss)................	$ (2,364)	$ (667)	$ 7,306	$ 1,908	$ 2,387
Percentages, Department A:					
Sales (1954 = 100)................	100%	104.4%	109.6%	98.8%	100.6%
Gross margin.....................	25.9	27.6	34.9	35.9	36.3
Transactions (1956 = 100)..........	96	98	100	95	96
Percentages, Similar Departments of Other Stores:					
Sales (1954 = 100)................	100%	106.1%	111.3%	112.7%	114.2%
Gross margin.....................	25.1	27.2	29.4	30.1	34.6
Transactions (1956 = 100)..........	....	....	100	97	98
Published index of retail prices of products sold in Department A (1956 = 100)...........................			100	102	103

Chapter 14 | BUDGETING

ALL MANAGEMENTS make plans. One cannot conceive of an organization of any kind whose leaders were not giving some thought to what the organization's objectives should be and to the best way of reaching those objectives. A group of people not operating under some sort of plan is merely an incoherent, directionless mob, not an organization.

Although all managements plan, there are considerable differences in the way in which they plan. Some people do their planning entirely in their heads, others make notes and rough estimates on the backs of old envelopes, and still others express their plans in quantitative terms and commit these to paper in some orderly, systematic fashion. The process engaged in by the latter group is called "budgeting," for a *budget* is merely a plan expressed in quantitative terms. We are here primarily concerned with budgets that are expressed in monetary terms, although some budgets are expressed in units of product, number of employees, units of time, or other nonmonetary quantities. In addition to its use in planning, the budget is also used for control and for coordination.

Types of Budgets

There is a considerable diversity of practice in budgeting, much greater than the diversity in accounting practice. Most companies except the smallest have some sort of budget, but a great many do not have a truly comprehensive budgeting system. Such a system consists of three types of budgets: an *operating* budget, showing planned operations for the forthcoming period; a *cash* budget, showing the anticipated sources and uses of cash; and a *capital* budget, showing planned changes in fixed assets.

THE OPERATING BUDGET

An operating budget usually consists of two parts, a "program" budget and a "responsibility" budget. These represent two ways of depicting the overall operating plan for the business, two different methods of slicing the pie; therefore, both arrive at the same figure for projected net income and return on investment.

The *program budget* describes the major "programs" the company plans to undertake. Such a budget might be arranged, for example, by products lines and show the anticipated revenue and costs associated with each product. This type of budget is useful to an executive examining the overall balance among the various programs of the business. It helps to answer such questions as these: Is the profit margin on each product line satisfactory? Is production capacity in balance with the size and capability of the sales organization? Can we afford to spend so much for research? Are adequate funds available? And so on. A negative answer to any of these questions indicates the necessity for revising the plan.

The *responsibility budget* sets forth plans in terms of the persons responsible for carrying them out. It is therefore primarily a control device, since it is a statement of expected or standard performance against which actual performance can later be compared. In the factory, for example, there may be a responsibility budget for each department, showing the costs that are controllable by the foreman of the department. There may also be a budget showing costs for each product, including both direct costs and allocated costs. The figures on both sets of budgets add up to total factory costs, but the product-cost budget would not be useful for control purposes, since the costs shown on it could not ordinarily be related to the responsibility of specific individuals.

Since it is likely that actual volume during a period will be different from expected or budgeted volume, and since costs vary significantly with volume, a budget may be prepared, showing the expected behavior of costs at various volume levels. This is called a *variable budget.*[1] Techniques for preparing it will be discussed in Chapter 16. The figure used in an estimate of the overall income for the company is one figure in the variable budget, namely, the cost at the planned level of activity.

Principles of Budgeting

The general principles relevant to the management control process apply to the budgeting process. Those given in Chapter 13 are therefore repeated here, with specific references to budgeting.

The budget should be *sponsored by management.* The organization must regard it as primarily a tool of management, not as primarily an accounting device.

---

[1] Logically, this should be called a *semivariable* budget, since the costs are partly variable and partly nonvariable.

The responsibility budget should be built up by *responsibility centers* and should show separately the *controllable costs* in each responsibility center.

Responsible supervisors should *participate* in the process of setting the budget figures, and should agree that the budget goals are reasonable. If they do agree, their attitude during the budget period is likely to be, "I said I could meet this goal, and I will do my best to live up to this promise." If they are not consulted, their attitude toward the budget is likely to be one of indifference or resentment.

Responsible supervisors must have a thorough understanding of the budget process, and this requires a program of *continuous education.* To a limited extent, this can be accomplished through written manuals or memoranda, but the main reliance must be placed on meetings, both to discuss the preparation of the budget and to discuss actual results achieved.

The *time period* covered by one budget should be related to the necessity for and the possibility of effective management action.

The planned figures in the responsibility budget should *match* in definition the accounting figures that report actual performance. If "direct labor" in the budget includes vacation pay, social security costs, retirement allowance, and other fringe benefits, so should "direct labor" in the control accounting system.

The budget figures should represent *reasonably attainable goals,* not so high as to be frustrating, yet not so low as to encourage complacency.

In a comparison of actual performance with budgeted performance, attention should be focused on *significant exceptions*—figures that are significantly different from those expected.

The budget system should not cost more to operate than it is worth. Since no one can calculate exactly what a budget system is worth, this statement is necessarily vague. It implies, however, a caution against adding expensive refinements unless their value clearly justifies them.

The *staff* function of facilitating the budget process should not be confused with the *line* function, which is to make the plans. Line management makes the decisions; the budget organization assists the line organization.

The *review* of budget estimates by successively higher levels of management should be thorough. Perfunctory review is a signal that management is really not much interested in the budget process.

Final *approval* of the budget should be specific, and this approval should be communicated to the organization. An attempt to operate on the doctrine "silence gives consent" inevitably leads to misunderstanding.

The Budget Process

The preparation of a budget can be studied both as an accounting process and as a management process. From an accounting standpoint, the procedures are essentially the same as those described in Part I, and the end result of the recording and summarizing operations is a set of financial statements—a balance sheet and income statement—identical in format with those resulting from the process of recording historical events. The only difference is that the budget figures are estimates of what will happen in the future rather than historical data on what has happened in the past. Some of the cases in Part I of this book dealt with future rather than with past events, and the balance sheets and income statements prepared in connection with these cases were budgets.

From a management standpoint, the budgeting process is so closely associated with the operation of the business that a complete description of the factors and considerations involved would take us far beyond the scope of this book. Rather than attempt such a description, we shall merely indicate some of the important general considerations in the budget process.

Choice of Time Periods

A useful time period for a budget is one year. Probably the majority of companies prepare budgets once a year, but some companies follow the practice of preparing a new budget every quarter. Each quarter, the quarter just completed is dropped, the figures for the three quarters originally covered in the previous budget are revised if necessary, and a new budget for the fourth quarter is added. This is called a *rolling budget.*

Within the year, the budget may be broken down by months; that is, the month usually constitutes the basic time period for comparison of actual results with the budget. In many companies, only the data for the next three months or the next six months are shown in detail, and totals are given by quarters for the remainder of the year.

For the purpose of showing the general direction in which the company plans to move, and the long-run implications of management policies as to expansion, new products, new facilities, and so on, a useful tool is a *long-range budget,* covering a period of three, five, or even more, years ahead. This is not prepared in so much detail as the annual budget, and it is usually prepared entirely at headquarters without the participation of operating personnel. Such a budget is especially useful in preparation of plans for obtaining new, permanent capital.

Organization for Preparation of Budgets

A *budget committee,* consisting of several members of the top-management group, may oversee the work of preparing the budget. This committee will set the general guidelines that the organization is to follow, coordinate the separate budgets prepared by the various organizational units and resolve differences among them, and submit the final budget to the president and also to the board of directors for approval. In a small company, this work is done by the president himself, or by his immediate line subordinate. Instructions go down through the regular chain of command, and the budget comes back up for successive reviews and approvals through the same channels. The essential point is that decisions about the budget are made by the line organization, and the final approval is given by the head of that organization, the president or the board.

The line organization usually is assisted in its preparation of the budget by a staff unit headed by the *budget director,* preferably reporting to the controller. If he reports to the president, as is sometimes the case, he is likely to be performing the functions described above for the budget committee and therefore acting in a line, rather than a staff, capacity.

As a staff man, his functions are to disseminate instructions about the mechanics of budget preparation (the forms and how to fill them out), to provide data on past performance that are useful in preparation of the budget, to make computations on the basis of decisions reached by the line organization, to assemble the budget figures, and to see that everyone submits his figures on time. Thus, the budget organization may do a very large fraction of the budget work; it is not the crucial part, however, for the significant decisions are always made by the line organization. Once the members of the line organization have reached an agreement on labor productivity and wage rates, for example, the budget man can calculate all the detailed figures for labor costs by products and by responsibility centers; this is a considerable job of computation, but it is entirely based on the judgments of the line supervisors.

The budget organization is like a telephone company, operating an important communication system; it is responsible for the speed, accuracy, and clarity with which messages flow through the system, but not for the content of the messages themselves.

Preparation of Estimates

In almost all companies, the most difficult estimate to make is that of sales revenue. There are in general two ways of proceeding: to make a *statistical* forecast on the basis of an analysis of general business conditions, market conditions, product growth curves, and the like; or to make an *internal* forecast, by collecting the opinions of executives and salesmen. In some companies salesmen are asked to estimate the sales of each product made to each of their customers; in others, they estimate total sales in their territory; in still others, salesmen do not participate in the estimating process. There are advantages and weaknesses in both the statistical and the internal methods; both are often used together, but neither can be guaranteed to yield an even reasonably close estimate in view of the inevitable uncertainties of the future.

The sales budget is more than a sales *forecast.* A forecast is merely passive, while a budget should reflect the positive actions that management plans to take in order to influence future events. For example, this may be the sales forecast: "With the present amount of sales effort, we expect sales to run at about the same level as currently." By contrast, the sales *budget* may show a substantial planned increase in sales, reflecting management's intention to add salesmen, increase advertising and sales promotion, or redesign the product.

Whenever feasible, estimates for quantities and for unit prices should be shown separately in order to facilitate the subsequent analysis of performance. If the sales estimate is shown only as a total dollar amount, one cannot know whether a difference between actual and expected sales is the result of a difference in volume or a difference in selling price. This separation of quantity and unit price applies throughout the system: material cost is preferably shown as number of pounds times cents per pound, labor costs as hours times the hourly wage rate, and so on. The basic reason for doing this is that different factors, and often different people, are responsible for changes in the quantity component and the price component, respectively. The purchasing officer is responsible for the cost per pound of material, but the factory foreman is responsible for the quantity used, for example. For similar reasons, the estimates are broken down by product lines, by significant items of cost, and in other ways that will facilitate subsequent analysis of actual performance.

The Budget Timetable

"The" budget for a manufacturing company consists of several parts: the sales budget, the sales expense budget, the inventory and purchases budget, the factory budget (which may consist of separate parts for direct materials, direct labor, and factory overhead), the general and administrative budget, the research and development budget, the budgeted financial statements, and the cash budget. Some of these depend on others. All are affected by the estimate of sales; the factory budget depends on estimated sales volume and inventory levels, the purchases budget depends on estimated production volume and inventory levels, and so on. Thus, there has to be a timetable specifying the order in which the budgets are to be prepared and the time when each must be completed. In general the steps in the budget process, in chronological order, are these: setting guidelines, preparation of the sales budget, preparation of the other operating budgets, coordination of the separate budgets, and final review and approval. These are further described below, with approximate dates, assuming that the budget is to become effective January 1.

Guidelines. In the fall, management holds a series of meetings at which the participants discuss and agree on the principal objectives to be sought during the coming year and the broad outlines of the means to be used in reaching these objectives. They form the basis for *budget guidelines,* which are sent to the operating executives on October 15. These guidelines may be in the form of tentative sales estimates, or they may be more general statements of expectations. Expected changes in price levels and changes in policy are also included. These guidelines are of great interest to competitors, so they are circulated only to those who need to know them. If it is particularly important that a new strategy be concealed, it may be omitted from the statement, with necessary adjustments in the budget being made subsequently at the headquarters level. In the absence of statements to the contrary, the organization customarily assumes that next year will be similar to the current year.

Preparation of Estimates. From October 15 through November 15, each responsible supervisor at the lowest level in the organization prepares estimates of the items for which he is responsible, based on these guidelines. These are discussed with and approved by his immediate superior, who combines them with similar estimates from other supervisors, and then transmits them upward through the organization. Accounting or other staff people assist the supervisors in this work by making detailed calculations, by providing historical data, and by summarizing and recording the estimates; but the line supervisors, not the accountants, make the decisions. Within this period, subsidiary deadlines are established so that those whose budget estimates depend on the estimates of others receive the necessary information in time to meet the overall November 15 deadline.

Coordination and Review. From November 15 to December 15, the budget estimates move up the chain of command. At each level, they are reviewed and either are approved or are changed after discussion with those concerned. At this time also, coordination of the separate budgets occurs. The budget office uses estimates in the responsibility budgets to prepare program budgets, and these are examined for overall balance, feasibility, and desirability. This examination may indicate the need for revision, and such revisions are made after discussion with the persons affected. Unresolved problems are referred to the budget committee for decision. Various summary documents, especially the budgeted balance sheet and budgeted income statement, are also prepared at this time.

Final Approval. On December 15, top management (the president or the board of directors) gives final approval. The approved budget is then transmitted to the organization. This act communicates to the organization the approved objectives and the plans for reaching these objectives during the coming year.

The foregoing description of a timetable and procedures is not intended as being a precise model, but only as suggestive of the steps involved. In the federal government, to take one extreme, the process of preparing an annual budget stretches out over approximately fifteen months, although this long time span is largely a result of the antiquated procedures that are used rather than of inherent difficulties. At the other extreme, a small business may go through the whole process in one afternoon.

Uses of the Budget

The usefulness of the budget in the process of making and coordinating plans is apparent from the above description. The budget is also useful as a communication device and as a standard with which to compare actual performance.

The Budget as a Communication Device. Management's plans will not be carried out (except by accident) unless the organization understands what the plans are. Adequate understanding includes not only a knowledge of programs and objectives (e.g., how many units are to be manufactured, what methods and machines are to be used, how much material is to be purchased, what selling prices are to be) but also a knowledge about policies and restrictions to which the organization is expected to adhere. Examples of these kinds of information follow: the maximum amounts that may be spent for such items as advertising, maintenance, administrative costs, and the like; wage rates and hours of work; desired quality levels; and so on. A most useful device for communicating quantitative information concerning these objectives and limitations is the approved budget.

The Commitment Concept. When a budget is prepared in accordance with the procedures outlined above, the final document may be regarded as a sort of contract or two-way commitment between management and the operating supervisor. By agreeing to the budget estimates, the supervisor in effect says to management: "I can and will operate my department in accordance with the plan described in the budget." By approving the budget estimates, management in effect says to the supervisor: "If you operate your department in accordance with this plan, you will do what we consider to be a good job." Both of these statements contain the implicit qualification of "adjusted for changes in circumstances" since both parties recognize that actual events, such as price levels and general business conditions, may not correspond to those assumed when the budget was prepared and that these changes will inevitably affect the plans set forth in the budget. In judging whether the commitment is in fact being carried out as the year progresses, management must take these changes into account.

The Budget as a Standard. A carefully prepared budget is the best possible standard against which to measure actual performance, and it is increasingly being used for this purpose. Until fairly recently, the general practice was to compare current results with results for last month or with results for the same period a year ago; and this is still the basic means of comparison in many companies. Such a historical standard has the fundamental weakness that it does not take account either of changes in the underlying forces at work or of the planned program for the current year.

EXAMPLE: In a favorable market situation, a certain company increased its selling prices and hence increased its net income in 1963 by 25 per cent over the net income of 1962. If 1963's results are compared with 1962's, there is shown an apparent cause for rejoicing. However, the company had *planned* to increase profits by 35 per cent, and performance when measured against the plan was not so good. The company quite properly took steps to find out, and if possible to correct, the factors accounting for the difference between actual and budgeted results.

In general, it is more significant to answer the question, "Why didn't we do what we planned to do?" than the question, "Why is this year different from last year?" Presumably, the principal factors accounting for the difference between this year and last year were taken into consideration in the preparation of the budget.

The foregoing discussion presupposes a carefully prepared budget. If management does not trust the budget, then there is good reason to use last year's performance as a benchmark, for it at least has the merit of being a definite, objective figure.

An Illustration: The Flight Plan

Rather than attempt to illustrate the budget process by showing the mass of detailed figures that would be collected in an actual company, we shall describe the "flight plan" that is prepared for each airplane flight. In most essential respects, a flight plan is similar to the operating budget in a company, but it relates to a business operation that is started

Illustration 14–1

AMERICAN AIRLINES FLIGHT PLAN

CAPT. *MacKenzie* F/O *White* F/E *Robins* FLT. NO. *2* FROM *LAX* TO *JFK* AIRPLANE TYPE & NO. *707-502* DATE *9/1/*

TO	AIRWAYS	IFR/VFR	ALTITUDE	TEMP	EST. GROSS WEIGHT	WIND	TAS	GAIN/LOSS	GND. SPEED	MILES	TOTAL MILES	TIME	TOTAL TIME	TYPE CRUISE	LBS. FUEL BURN
TOC	JR-64	IFR	27,000	4	207000	1615	326	00	326	190		35		MCT	13000
DGS		↓		-25	204000	2535	435	+35	470	106		14	:49	13.0	3000
ALS			29,000	-29	193400	2240	438	+35	473	389		49	1:38	13.0	10600
PWE				-29	180600	2420	445	+15	460	480		1:02	2:40	12.4	12800
JOT				-28	171000	2620	455	+19	474	369		:46	3:26	12.5	9600
CLE	JR-60			-28	163900	2325	463	+19	482	277		:34	4:00	12.5	7100
JFK	JR60ABE/V-30	↓	↓	-27	152800	2925	467	+25	492	413		:53	4:53	12.6	11100

FUEL		
FROM – TO	LAX/IDL	
ALTERNATE	—	
POINT TO POINT	67200	
(2)TAXI & CLIMB	—	
TO ALTERNATE	—	
INST. APPROACH	—	
RESERVE	7500	
ADDED FUEL	10300	
TOTAL FUEL POUNDS	85000	
TOTAL FUEL GALLONS	—	

① OPTIONAL ENTRY CERTAIN CONDITIONS. REFER SECTION 3, PAGE 15.(FLIGHT MANUAL PART 1)
② 707 OPERATION LEAVE BLANK
REMARKS:

CAPT. *B. MacKenzie* DISP. *B. J. L.*

and finished in a matter of hours. A flight plan for American Airlines Flight 2 is shown in Illustration 14–1. American Airlines has stated in its advertisements: "For your safety, we fly every mile on paper before we fly it in the air," an excellent description of a basic reason for preparing a budget. Some of the things that should be noted about this flight plan are these:

1. The flight plan is a written document. It is prepared in advance by Captain MacKenzie, the person who is responsible for the flight.

2. It is prepared within the framework of decisions made by higher authority. Among these decisions are the following: the objective is to be JFK (Kennedy Airport); the plane is to be of a specified type (a 707 jet); and the crew is to consist of a captain, a first officer, and a flight engineer.

3. The captain describes how he plans to reach the objective (i.e., his altitude and route) and the estimated cost (in terms of gasoline consumption and time) of doing so. In making his plan, he has considered forecasts of wind, temperature, and weather; and in view of these forecast conditions he works out what seems to him to be the best way of getting from Los Angeles to Kennedy Airport.

4. The meteorologist, a staff man, has furnished information that helps the captain to plan, but the captain, not the staff man, is responsible for the plan.

5. The captain signs the plan, indicating that he accepts responsibility for it.

6. The dispatcher, B. H. A. initials the plan, indicating that he approves it, and that management will support and back the captain if he operates according to plan.

7. The plan itself does not fly the plane. Similarly, the budget is an aid to management, not a substitute for management.

Information about the actual performance of Flight 2 is reported by Captain MacKenzie on the reverse side of the form shown in Illustration 14–1. This part of the form, called a "flight log," corresponds to the accounting reports of actual performance. The record shows the time actually taken between each check point, actual altitude and actual fuel consumption, and also the captain's explanation of significant differences between actual and planned performance. If there are no differences, or if the differences are explainable in terms of noncontrollable factors, such as the wind or weather, he cannot be criticized; otherwise, he is legitimately subject to criticism.

The flight log does not show all aspects of the flight, but only those that are reduced to quantitative terms. It does not show, for example, whether the passengers were jounced around or whether the captain almost missed the runway. The factors not shown may be more important than the factors that are shown. The report is therefore not a *complete* record of performance.

A plane is a responsibility center, and the duration of a flight is a "budget" period. Each of the points noted above about the flight plan applies equally well to the preparation and use of a budget in a business. The business budget differs from that shown in Illustration 14–1 in that its figures will be shown in dollar terms. The budgeting process in a business is complicated both by the necessity of fitting many individual segments (e.g., departments) into a plan that is satisfactory for the company as a whole, and by the fact that future events that affect the progress of a business toward its objective are likely to be much less foreseeable than those that affect the flight of a plane.

THE CASH BUDGET

The operating budget is usually prepared in terms of revenues and expenses. For financial planning purposes, it must be translated into terms of cash receipts and cash disbursements. This translation is the *cash budget.* The financial people use the cash budget to make plans to insure that the company has enough, but not too much, cash on hand during the year ahead.

There are two approaches to the preparation of a cash budget:

1. Start with the budgeted balance sheet and income statements and adjust the figures thereon to reveal the sources and uses of cash. This procedure is exactly the same as that described for the cash flow statement in Chapter 12, except that the data are estimates of the future rather than historical. It therefore is not described again here.

2. Project directly each of the items that results in cash receipts or cash disbursements. A cash budget prepared by this means is shown in Illustration 14–2. Some useful points in connection with this technique are mentioned below.

Collections of accounts receivable is estimated by applying a "lag" factor to estimated sales or shipments. This factor may be simply based on the assumption that the cash from this month's sales will be collected next month; or there may be a more elaborate assumption, for example, that 10 per cent of this month's sales will be collected this month, 60 per cent next month, 20 per cent in the second month, 9 per cent in the third month, and the remaining 1 per cent will never be collected.

The estimated amount and timing of *raw materials purchases* is obtained from the purchases budget, and is translated into cash disbursements by applying a lag factor for the time interval that ordinarily elapses between the receipt of the material and the payment of the invoice.

Other *operating expenses* are often taken directly from the expense budget, since the timing of cash disbursements is likely to correspond

Illustration 14–2
CASH FORECAST, 1963
(000 Omitted)

	January	February	March	April	May	June	July	Totals for Year
Gross shipments	1,200	1,987	2,063	1,387	2,363	2,325	1,575	21,000
Cash balance beginning of month	375	396	222	150	257	160	192	375
Add: Cash receipts								
Collections of accounts receivable	1,380	1,350	1,605	1,635	1,680	2,055	2,205	19,305
Miscellaneous receipts	66	81	70	105	105	97	97	1050
Total Receipts	1,446	1,431	1,675	1,740	1,785	2,152	2,302	20,355
Total Cash Available	1,821	1,827	1,897	1,890	2,042	2,312	2,494	20,730
Less: Cash disbursements								
Operating Expenses	810	915	1,035	885	975	1,020	960	10,730
Raw materials purchases	503	570	1,050	600	607	555	345	7,140
Taxes		60	412	13		395	3	1,310
Equipment purchases					100			100
Dividends	112			135			135	517
Pension contribution		210						247
Total Disbursements	1,425	1,755	2,497	1,633	1,682	1,970	1,443	20,044
Cash balance or (deficiency) end of month before bank loans or (repayments)	396	72	(600)	257	360	342	1,051	686
Bank loans or (repayments)		150	750		(200)	(150)	(450)	0
Cash Balance End of Month	396	222	150	257	160	192	601	686

closely to the incurrence of the expense. Depreciation and other noncash expenses are excluded from this item.

The bottom of the cash forecast shows how cash plans are made. In February, for example, cash on hand would drop to $72,000, which is considered to be too low for safety; so the company plans to borrow $150,000 to provide a better safety margin. It plans to borrow $750,000 more in March and to start repaying these bank loans in May, when cash receipts exceed cash disbursements.

A monthly cash forecast, as in Illustration 14–2, is especially useful in planning for short-term, seasonal needs of cash. In order to estimate needs for more permanent capital, such as that obtained from the issuance of stock or bonds, the same general procedure would be followed, but with longer time intervals.

It should be noted that the figures in Illustration 14–2 are rounded. This procedure is customary in budgets. The amounts could be shown to the last penny, but the users of the report do not need such precise estimates. Furthermore, such figures tend to give a spurious impression of accuracy. Two or three significant digits are usually adequate.

THE CAPITAL BUDGET

The capital budget is essentially a list of what management believes to be worthwhile projects for the acquisition of new capital assets together with the estimated cost of each project. Proposals for such projects may originate anywhere in the organization. The capital budget is usually prepared separately from the operating budget, and in many companies it is prepared at a different time and cleared through a capital appropriations committee that is separate from the budget committee.

Each proposal, except those for minor amounts, is accompanied by a justification. For some projects, the expected return on investment can be estimated by methods to be described in Chapter 19. For others, such as the construction of a new office building or remodeling of employee recreation rooms, no estimate of earnings is possible, and these are justified on the basis of improved morale, safety, appearance, convenience, or other subjective grounds. A lump sum usually is included in the capital budget for projects that are not large enough to warrant individual consideration by top management.

As proposals come up through the organization, they are screened at various levels, and only the sufficiently attractive ones flow up to the top and appear in the final capital budget. On this document, they are often arranged in what is believed to be the order of desirability, and the estimated expenditures are broken down by years, or by quarters, so that the funds required in each time period are shown. At the final review meeting, which is usually at the board-of-director level, not only are the individual projects discussed but also the total amount requested on the budget is compared with total funds available. Many apparently worthwhile projects may not be approved, simply because the funds are not available.

Approval of the capital budget usually means approval of the projects *in principle,* but does not constitute final authority to proceed with them. For this authority, a specific authorization request is prepared for the project, spelling out the proposal in more detail, perhaps with firm bids or price quotations on the new assets. These authorization requests are approved at various levels in the organization, depending on their size and character. For example, each foreman may be authorized to buy production tools or similar items costing not more than $100 each, provided the total for the year does not exceed $1,000; and at the other extreme, all projects costing more than $500,000 and all projects for new products whatever their cost may require approval of the board of directors. In between, there is a scale of amounts that various echelons in the organization may authorize without the approval of their superiors.

An increasing number of companies are instituting procedures to follow up on capital expenditures. These include both checks on the spending itself and also an appraisal, perhaps a year or more after the project is completed and under way, as to how well the estimates of costs and earnings actually turned out.

ILLUSTRATION: NATIONAL CASH REGISTER COMPANY

To illustrate the whole process of budgeting we quote a description of how it is done at National Cash Register Company, taken from an article by R. Stanley Laing, now its president.[2]

The system of management control which we use [at National Cash Register] is called "The Profit Plan" and if there is a single word which typifies the Profit Plan at NCR, it is the word "Objectives."

We begin with a top management outline of broad corporate objectives, for we believe that an essential of profit planning is top management participation and support. These broad corporate objectives embrace both short and long term targets and financial and nonfinancial goals. Most important, they represent the

---

[2] R Stanley Laing, "MPC—Key to Profit Growth," *Financial Executive,* February 1963, pp. 32 ff.

considered judgment of top management as to the course the business should take.

At the beginning of each year, our Chief Executive Officer calls together the entire management group and presents, in a detailed set of charts, the Company's Objectives for the year. These objectives cover every major phase of our business and are tied in directly with the approved Profit Plan. This meeting sets the Company's course for the year and provides specific direction to the entire management team.

Consistent with these overriding objectives, each operating division, with the assistance of the financial division, develops its own set of objectives for each year's operation. These division objectives are tied specifically into the Company's Profit Plan for that year. For example, in our 1963 Profit Plan, if we expect to bill fifteen million dollars of new Product "A," the Marketing Vice President assumes responsibility for this result, including the attainment, let us say, of new orders totalling twenty-one million dollars in sales. He also formulates specific supporting plans such as the completion of sales and service training by a definite date within a specific expense budget; the release of the product for sale by a certain date and the attainment of a predetermined rate of incoming orders. These supporting commitments are essential in providing check points against which to measure progress towards the accomplishment of the primary objective.

Nor do we stop here since our Marketing Division can obviously not do this job alone. Our Manufacturing Vice President, for example, must include in his 1963 objectives the production of these units in accordance with a precalculated schedule. This, of course, again contemplates many subsidiary objectives such as the completion of tooling by a certain date for a specific investment, the required factory rearrangement and training, the completion of production models for test purposes, and the attainment of a target production rate by a definite date.

Finally, our Vice President in charge of [Research and Development], commits himself in advance to complete the final design and to release drawings to the Manufacturing Division by a specific date as well as to complete prototype models within a budgeted model-making allocation.

These objectives are established by each of the responsible divisions and become their goals. The Vice Presidents sign their names to documents setting forth these objectives in specific terms. Psychologically we find that this practice materially increases the attention given to the achievement of these results. On a non-psychological basis, year end bonuses are also affected by the achievement of these objectives.

Coordinating the Program

The coordination of this program to achieve consistency is the task of the financial planning department. But we believe that objectives must be established by the man responsible for the results since he knows best the significance of the assignment, the meaning of deviations and ways to correct them. Let me emphasize that the figures entered in the profit plan for the marketing, manufacturing, and R&D divisions do not represent estimates of the financial division. Rather, each expenditure, each cost, each projection represents the considered judgment of the division responsible for carrying out the program.

Division managers are required to be specific in these objectives. It is not enough to say "we must reduce costs." He must say "we will reduce costs on product 'X' by so much." It is not enough to say "we must increase volume." It must be "we will increase volume of product 'Y' by 'Z' units." It is not enough to say "we will tool product 'A.'" We must have a commitment to "complete the tooling of product 'A' by a specific date and for so many dollars."

At this juncture, I should emphasize our experience that we cannot control in any greater degree than we plan. For example, if our sales budget for a period is fifty million dollars and we only achieve forty million dollars, we will be unable to clearly analyze the variances if we have not planned the sale of individual products and recorded the actual results in the same detail.

Once management approves a profit plan and the detailed programs making it up, the financial data becomes an approved budget and an approved target for the operating divisions against which actual results will be measured.

Control by Exception

During the year the financial planning department must provide control reports to measure results and report progress towards the established objectives. Our reports of variance are prompt—they are available before the financial statements. The reports are designed for the managers involved—they do not follow the format of regular accounting statements. The reports include a covering analysis of deviations. Our reports at this level do not go to top management. As we detect variations we either must agree on corrective action or we must, as a management team, make other adjustments to our profit plan. We stress control by exception—we deal with variances from the objectives making up the profit plan.

We do not depend completely on variance reports to identify deviations from our Profit Plan. The responsible parties must report when they know that they are going to miss a particular target for no one knows sooner than they. A variation at this point may cause some unpleasantness with the front office but it is nothing compared to that which occurs if they fail to point out the variance until it is too late to do something about it.

We believe, of course, that tight financial supervision is a key to the Profit Plan. It puts realism, measurability and consistency into the entire Plan. This includes the challenge of putting measurability into the non-financial objectives of the Plan. The purpose of our reporting system is to throw the spotlight on problems as soon as they develop so that the decision-making attention of management may be focused on the specific item causing a major deviation from the profit objective.

SUMMARY

Budgets are used for planning and for control. The underlying principles are psychological and correspond to those discussed in Chapter 13. The *operating budget* usually consists of two parts with identical totals, the program budget and the responsibility budget. The latter, and especially the underlying variable budgets, is the principal basis for subsequent comparisons with actual costs.

The line organization, perhaps headed by a budget committee, makes the decisions on what the plans are to be, and the staff organization, perhaps headed by a budget director in the controller's department, assists the line organization by providing data, by making calculations, and by assembling and transmitting the budget figures. Chronologically, the important steps in the budget process are as follows: setting guidelines, preparation of the sales budget, preparation of other operating budgets, coordination of the separate budgets, and review and approval.

The *cash budget* translates revenues and expenses into receipts and disbursements and thus facilitates financial planning.

The *capital budget* is a priced list of presumably worthwhile projects for the acquisition of new capital assets. Often it is prepared separately from the operating budget. Approval of the capital budget constitutes only approval in principle, and a subsequent specific authorization is usually required before work on the project can begin.

SUGGESTONS FOR FURTHER READING

CHAMBERLAIN, NEIL W. *The Firm: Micro-Economic Planning and Action.* New York: McGraw-Hill Book Co., Inc., 1962.

HEISER, HERMAN C. *Budgeting, Principles and Practices.* New York: The Ronald Press Co., 1959.

WELSCH, GLENN A. *Budgeting: Profit Planning and Control.* 2d ed. New York: Prentice-Hall, Inc., 1963.

CASES

CASE 14–1. SLIQUE HARDWARE, INC.

Mr. Slique, the manager and majority stockholder of Slique Hardware, Inc., had examined the balance sheet and income statement for the year. Mr. Slique felt, on the whole, that the past year had been a satisfactory one; yet, while his profit as a percentage of sales was close to the average for the industry, he felt that it might be improved. The balance sheet and income statement are shown in Exhibits 1 and 2.

The company, located in Dungannon, Ohio, had been founded by Mr. Slique's father before the turn of the century. The store had followed a policy of giving good service and customer satisfaction, so that over a period of years it achieved a wide patronage, both within the city and from the outlying areas.

For many years the policy of the store had been that of cash transactions only. Mr. Slique's father had maintained steadfastly that

Exhibit 1

SLIQUE HARDWARE, INC.

Balance Sheet as of December 31, 1963

ASSETS			EQUITIES		
Cash.................		$ 8,869	Accounts payable............		$ 9,488
Accounts receivable....		4,130	Accrued taxes................		2,113
Inventories...........		94,215	Other accruals...............		863
Prepayments..........		2,837	Current Liabilities........		$ 12,464
Current Assets.....		$110,051			
Fixtures..............	$16,113				
Less: Depreciation....	3,672	12,441	Common stock 1,000 shares		
Delivery equipment.....$ 2,385			$50 par value..............		50,000
Less: Depreciation....	476	1,909	Surplus......................		61,937
Total Assets.....		$124,401	Total Equities..........		$124,401

Exhibit 2

SLIQUE HARDWARE, INC.

Income Statement for 1963

Gross sales..			$246,416
Less: Sales returns and allowances (3%)...................			7,641
Net sales..			$238,775
Cost of goods sold (70%)...............................			164,874
Gross margin...			$ 73,901
Salary expenses:			
Manager's salary...................................$12,000			
Sales salaries...................................... 35,000		$47,000	
Other expenses:			
Advertising...$ 4,537			
Utilities.. 2,268			
Depreciation.. 1,552			
Rent.. 5,400			
Taxes (other than income)............................ 2,865			
Insurance... 1,671			
Unclassified... 6,099		24,392	71,392
Net operating profit.................................			$ 2,509
Cash discounts and other earnings........................			4,535
Net profit...			$ 7,044
Federal income tax....................................			2,113
Net Profit after Taxes...............................			$ 4,931

friends can agree on any subject except money. If, therefore, a person owed you money, he could not be your friend. Prior to World War II, after Mr. Slique and his sister had inherited the business, Mr. Slique permitted the charging of goods to those of his better customers who he believed were credit worthy. These charges were then due in the following month. He found, though, that in the store's experience only about 75 per cent of the accounts receivable due at the beginning of the month were paid in the month. He had maintained a close watch on his accounts receivable over the years, however, with the result that his bad debt experience had been negligible.

Mr. Slique had been considering a plan of extending credit to additional customers. He found that credit transactions were, as a rule, for larger amounts than cash sales. Furthermore, he had become convinced that credit sales were not a complete danger, as his father had believed. He felt that, if the plan was satisfactory at the outset and good supervision was maintained over the accounts receivable, then the losses should not be more than about 2 per cent of such sales.

Mr. Slique considered a number of credit plans and finally decided that the one that appealed to him the most was the budget payment plan. The plan called for the granting of credit to customers in an amount six times larger than the amount that they would agree to pay monthly. For example, a customer would be permitted credit of $150 if he agreed to pay $25 a month on his bill. To cover part of the cost of the plan there was to be a charge of 1½ per cent of the unpaid balance at the beginning of each month. Mr. Slique felt that such a plan would take care of the needs of most customers and might tend to increase sales. He realized, though, that the increase in sales that he might expect was extremely difficult to forecast.

He determined that to examine the plan thoroughly, he would have to hypothesize it over a period of time and that he might best accomplish this by constructing a cash flow budget that would show his costs and expenses under the plan and what he could expect to recover from it. In conjunction with his examination of this budget, he wanted to see year-end financial statements based on his estimates.

Mr. Slique prepared the information shown below. He instructs you to compile the necessary budget, including a projected income statement, and to make recommendations as to whether or not he should use the plan.

He included the following information for your use:

1. Estimated bookkeeping and administrative expenses of the plan would be about $50 a month.
2. Accrued income taxes would have to be paid in equal installments on March 15 and June 15.
3. Dividends of $500 a quarter would be paid on the first of March, June, September, and December.
4. Depreciation on the fixtures would amount to $723; on the delivery equipment, $477.
5. The prepayments and other accruals would remain at the same level as the end of the year 1963.
6. Cash at the beginning of the month should be equal to one half of that

month's sales. At the beginning of the year 1965, cash should be about $8,500.

7. Charge account sales would amount to 20 per cent of each month's sales.
8. Budget payments would be equal to one sixth of the unpaid balance at the beginning of the month after interest was charged.
9. Funds could be borrowed at 5 per cent interest to supplement the cash requirements of the firm.
10. Budget estimates are indicated in Exhibit 3.
11. Purchases were acquired with an average discount of 2 per cent. The discounts allowed on purchases were generally $\frac{2}{10}$ E.O.M. It was Mr. Slique's policy to take the discounts.
12. Accounts payable appearing in the balance sheet for 1963 reflect the purchases for the month of December.

Mr. Slique suggests that you use the following form in setting up the cash budget:

Schedule 1—Cash Sales

Sales monthly
    Less: Credit sales
    Less: Budget sales
    Cash Sales

Schedule 2—Credit Sales and Payments

Cash accounts receivable beginning of month
    Less: 75% paid during month
Balance
    Add: Credit sales for month
        Credit Accounts Receivable End of Month

Schedule 3—Budget Sales Interest and Payment

Budget accounts receivable beginning of month
    Add: Interest $1\frac{1}{2}\%$ per month
Accounts receivable beginning of month with interest
    Less: $\frac{1}{6}$ payment
Accounts receivable after payment
    Add: Budget plan sales for month
        Budget Accounts Receivable End of Month

Schedule 4—Cash Expenses

Other cash expenses
Purchase payments (net of discount)
Budget plan expenses
Income taxes
Dividends
    Total Cash Expenses

Schedule 5—Cash Income

Cash sales (Schedule 1)
Credit payments (Schedule 2)
Budget payments (Schedule 3)
    Total Cash Income

Exhibit 3

SLIQUE HARDWARE, INC.

Budget Estimates for the Year 1964

	Jan.	Feb.	Mar.	Apr.	May	June	July	Aug.	Sept.	Oct.	Nov.	Dec.
Total sales	$16,000	$15,200	$18,200	$19,300	$22,100	$21,700	$20,800	$20,400	$19,600	$20,900	$20,000	$24,700
Budget sales	600	1,260	2,160	3,040	4,480	5,260	5,240	5,120	4,980	5,220	5,000	6,160
Purchases	11,000	13,000	14,000	14,000	13,500	14,000	14,000	15,500	15,000	16,000	17,000	10,500
Expected expenses:												
Manager's salary	$ 1,000	$ 1,000	$ 1,000	$ 1,000	$ 1,000	$ 1,000	$ 1,000	$ 1,000	$ 1,000	$ 1,000	$ 1,000	$ 1,000
Other wages	2,900	2,900	2,900	2,900	2,900	2,900	2,900	2,900	2,900	2,900	2,900	3,000
Rent	450	450	450	450	450	450	450	450	450	450	450	450
Utilities	200	200	200	200	200	200	200	200	200	200	200	200
Advertising	300	400	400	400	400	400	400	300	400	400	400	400
Taxes (other than income)	300	200	300	200	200	300	200	200	300	200	200	300
Depreciation	100	100	100	100	100	100	100	100	100	100	100	100
Insurance		400				500		400				500
Other	500	500	500	500	500	500	500	500	500	500	500	700
Total	$ 5,750	$ 6,150	$ 5,850	$ 5,750	$ 5,750	$ 6,350	$ 5,750	$ 6,050	$ 5,850	$ 5,750	$ 5,750	$ 6,650

Schedule 6—Summary

Cash expenses
Cash income
Surplus or deficiency of receipts over disbursements
Cash at beginning of month
    Total Cash Available
Minimum cash balance required
Amount borrowed to meet month's requirement
Monthly interest payment

CASE 14–2.   SANTA INEZ POULTRY COMPANY

In 1938, George Russo, a recent graduate of the State Agricultural College, took over the management of his father's small poultry hatchery. Up to that time, the hatchery had been merely one of his father's many, not-very-successful, agricultural operations. Through the combination of good management and a booming market for poultry, George Russo had developed the hatchery into the largest of its kind in the region. The tremendous population boom in the area plus high prices of other meats had made the poultry and egg business highly profitable. George decided that, since he controlled the area's largest supply of chicks, he could safely expand his hatchery operations and thus service both his hatchery customers and reserve his additional production for raising broilers on his own account.

By 1950, southern producers, who had lower labor costs and a beneficial climate, had increased the competition. As a result, profit margins in poultry raising had narrowed to the point where the independent grower had, in many cases, become merely an adjunct to a large feed mill. The large, well-financed mill could absorb the volatility of the poultry market, offsetting potential losses in broiler sales with profits from feed production.

This profit squeeze convinced Russo that he would have to go into feed production in order to remain competitive. As a result, in 1950, the Santa Inez Poultry Company constructed a 40,000-ton feed mill. But, in order to utilize fully the output of his own mill, he expanded chick production and broiler production under contract with other hatcheries. By 1955, Santa Inez either produced directly or had under contract 5,700,000 broilers a year. In 1956, production had risen to 7,200,000 birds and, in 1957, to 8,500,000.

Several facts had convinced Mr. Russo in 1956 that his feed production was not adequate. The original mill had been poorly located with regard to receipt of shipments of grains, and he estimated that if he constructed a new mill on a railroad siding, he could save $5.00 a ton in handling and freight alone. Further, since the declining prices of broilers had practically wiped out the profits in broiler production, his only chance of maintaining his high profit level was to produce and sell more feed. He decided to build another feed mill, using the best technological developments, with an 80,000-ton capacity. This would require purchase of a site contiguous to the railroad. He decided that rather than continue operation of the old feed mill when the new mill went into production, he would scrap it even though it was not fully depreciated.[3]

In early 1958, the company had already paid out $379,000 for the new mill plus $40,000 for a plant site.[4] (See Exhibit 1.) It was estimated that an additional $75,000 would be required to finish the feed mill and put it in production. Considering that the new mill would roughly double his present service capacity of 8.5 million birds, hatchery production would have to increase to keep pace. Mr. Russo thought that eight new incubators at $9,000 each plus a new hatchery building costing $50,000 would be adequate to handle all this additional production. However, he felt that if additional bird production were built up to only 48,000 birds a week, he could get along with only four new incubators and that he could house these incubators in some of the service buildings of the abandoned feed mill.

The problems in early 1958 that Mr. Russo had to decide were how much money he needed and how he should raise this money. Of course, his financial needs were dependent upon what additional level of broiler production he attained and how fully he utilized his new feed mill.

In addition to his financial problems, Mr. Russo was bothered by the fact that the size of his organization was growing beyond his ability to control it directly. In 1957, he had over 150 employees. He had as executives under him an executive vice president, a feed mill superintendent, a hatchery superintendent, a sales manager, a supervisor of field service men, and an office manager–controller. He was looking for a young man trained in animal husbandry with financial or business experience who could act as his executive assistant. He was willing to offer a salary of $6,500 to the right man, but found that he could not get any takers at this price. He himself drew $35,000 a year as salary, and his father, as chairman of the board, drew $20,000 but did not contribute to the management of the business. Other Santa Inez executives were drawing from $8,000 to $12,000 a year, and Mr. Russo

---

[3] Scrapping the mill would give the company an $80,000 tax write-off in 1958.

[4] The remaining new investment in land was for farm land owned by Russo's father.

Exhibit 1

SANTA INEZ POULTRY COMPANY
Balance Sheets, December 31
(000 Omitted)

ASSETS	1957		1956		Net Increase
Cash.................................		$ 438		$ 394	$ 44
Accounts receivable.......................		261		250	11
Inventories:............................					
Own broilers............................	$ 370		$325		
Contract broilers.......................	57		54		
Other.................................	75		10		
Total Inventories.......................		502		389	113
Prepaid items...........................		7		9	(2)†
Total Current Assets...................		$1,208		$1,042	$116
Mortgages...............................		84		50	34
Note payable (unsecured).................		32		28	4
Land and improvements....................	$ 179		$ 17	$162	
Machinery and equipment.................	311		304	7	
Buildings...............................	166		186	(20)	
Construction in progress.................	*379		0	379	
	$1,035		$507	$528	
Less: depreciation......................	247		202	45	
Total Net Fixed Assets.................		788		305	483
Reserve fund for construction.............		0		200	(200)†
Total Assets..........................		$2,112		$1,625	$487
LIABILITIES					
Notes payable bank.......................		$ 292		$ 165	$127
Accounts payable.........................		158		216	(58)†
Accrued liabilities......................		150		62	88
Accrued taxes...........................		250		179	71
Total Current Liabilities..............		$ 850		$ 622	$228
Capital stock and surplus.................					
Stock.................................	$ 600		$500		$100
Retained earnings.......................	662		503		159
Total Equity..........................		$1,262		$1,003	
Total Liabilities......................		$2,112		$1,625	$487

*New feed mill
†Decrease

feared that if he brought a new man in at a salary of $10,000, the other executives who had worked up in the company would resent the new man.

Questions

1. Prepare a statement showing how much the company will need to finance its increased production. Give your assumed production figures.

2. How should the increased production be financed?

3. What do you recommend as a means of improving the management of the enlarged company?

Exhibit 2

SANTA INEZ POULTRY COMPANY
Income Statements
(000 Omitted)

	1957	1956
Net sales:		
Broilers..	$4,083	$3,918
Feed..	1,202	1,110
Supplies...	177	122
Chicks..	318	375
Other...	18	23
Total Sales................................	$5,798*	$5,548
Cost of goods sold		
Materials..	$3,916	$3,998
Operating expense†..............................	1,305	1,042
Total..	5,221	5,040
Gross income......................................	$ 577	$ 508
Operating ratio...................................	90%	91%
Selling, general, and administrative expense............	179	174
Income before taxes...............................	$ 398	$ 334
State and federal taxes........................	239	190
Net Income..	$ 159‡	$ 144

* $3,259,000 of own feed, chicks. and other supplies used in broiler operations. These cancel out through broiler sales on own account. Figures not available for 1956.
† Operating expense includes annual depreciation charge of $65,000. Straight line method on all depreciable assets. The average life was 10 years.
‡ The breakdown of profit from the divisions of the company shows that 73 per cent of profit was contributed by the feed mill and 18 per cent by the hatchery. Broiler production and other sales contributed the remainder.

Chapter 15

ESSENTIALS OF COST ACCOUNTING

IN PRECEDING chapters, we have referred to various uses that are made of cost information. The present chapter discusses how such information is collected; that is, it discusses systems of cost accounting. Cost information can be classified into three types according to the purposes for which it is used: (1) for financial accounting, (2) for management control, and (3) for decision making.

The place of cost information in *financial accounting* was set forth in Chapter 7. As products pass through the various stages of a manufacturing process, they accumulate costs. This accumulated cost is the basis for the entries to inventory accounts and for the transfer from finished goods inventory to cost of goods sold, when the products are sold. For this purpose, the guiding principle is this: *Each unit of product should be assigned a fair share of the manufacturing costs incurred in producing it.*

A similar principle governs the costs accumulated for certain related purposes. For example, many products and services are sold for cost plus a predetermined allowance for profits. Such transactions range from the multibillion-dollar "cost-plus-fixed-fee" contracts for the development and production of complete weapons systems down to an order for printing 500 letterheads or repairing an automobile. In these situations, the objective is to assign a *fair share* of costs to the product or service involved.

For *management control,* cost information is used to guide and influence people in the organization to act in a way that is consistent with the organization's goals. Some general considerations relating to cost information used in management control were discussed in Chapter 13, and a more thorough discussion will be found in Chapters 16 and 17.

For *decision making,* cost information shows the cost implications of alternative courses of action and thus helps management to reach a decision as to which choice is the best. The use of cost information for this purpose is discussed in Chapter 18.

The present chapter describes mainly the accumulation of costs for the first purpose, financial accounting. We follow this procedure partly because this makes the description easier to follow than if we attempted simultaneously to describe the different types of cost accumulation appropriate for the three different purposes. There is an even better reason, however; in practice, most cost accounting systems were designed to collect cost information for financial accounting, and information for the other two purposes is obtained by appropriate modifications in this basic system. Thus, one needs to understand the way in which costs are collected for financial accounting purposes in order to appreciate the modifications that are necessary to make them useful for other purposes.

The system used to collect cost information for financial accounting is often called *product costing,* since the emphasis is on building up a cost figure for each product.

PRODUCT COSTING

The student is asked to refer back to the flow chart in Illustration 7–2 (p. 184), which sketched the flow of costs as products (in this case, smoking pipes) moved through goods in process inventory to finished goods inventory, and then out to the customer. (It will be helpful, before going further, if the student traces through each entry in Illustration 7–2 in order to refresh his memory.) Brief mention was made in Chapter 7 of the problem of assigning material, labor, and factory overhead costs[1] to the partially completed pipes in goods in process inventory, to the completed pipes in finished goods inventory, and to cost of goods sold when the pipes are shipped. This is the problem of product costing. Consider the transaction that recorded the transfer of pipes from Goods in Process Inventory to Finished Goods Inventory. (This was Transaction No. 7 in Illustration 7–2 in the amount of $9,000.) The number and types of physical units (pipes) involved in this transfer can be ascertained readily, but in order to assign dollar amounts corresponding to these physical units, a cost per unit must be established.

If the company manufactured only one style of pipe, it would be possible to divide the total amount of debits to Work in Process by the total number of units worked on to obtain an approximation of the cost per unit; this figure could then be used to calculate the amount to be

---

[1] For the purpose of determining inventory valuation and cost of goods sold, it is not necessary to determine the selling, general, and administrative costs applicable to a particular unit of product; nevertheless, such a breakdown is useful for some pricing and other decisions relating to the product. Some cost accounting systems therefore do provide for the collection of these costs by units of product.

transferred from Goods in Process Inventory to Finished Goods Inventory. If the factory made more than one kind of product, however, such a simple calculation would not give results that fitted the facts, since one product probably used more material, labor, or overhead—that is, it cost more—than another. If the entry transferring completed products from Goods in Process to Finished Goods Inventory is to reflect the facts of the situation, there must be some means of taking these differences into account. The two types of methods for doing this are called job costing and process costing.

Job Costing and Process Costing

Essentially, a job cost system collects costs for each physically identifiable job or batch of work as it moves through the plant, regardless of the accounting period in which the work is done, while a process cost system collects costs for all products worked on in an accounting period.

Job Costing. The "job" in a job cost system may consist of a single unit (e.g., a turbine or a house), or it may consist of all units of identical or similar products covered by a single production order (e.g., 1,000 printed books or ten dozen white shirts).[2] Usually costs are collected on a separate form that is set up for each job. This *job cost sheet* contains spaces to record the material, labor, and overhead costs charged to that job, and these costs are recorded as the job moves through the various departments in the factory. Thus, when the job is completed, its costs can be readily totaled. The sum of all the material, labor, and overhead costs charged to all the jobs worked on in the factory during an accounting period is the basis for the entries debiting Goods in Process and crediting Raw Materials Inventory, Wages, and Overhead accounts. When each job is completed, the total cost recorded on the job cost sheet is the basis for the entry transferring the product from Goods in Process to Finished Goods Inventory, and this same cost is the basis for the entry transferring the product from Finished Goods Inventory to Cost of Goods Sold, when the product is sold. The total cost recorded on all job cost sheets for products still in the factory as of the end of an accounting period equals the total of the Goods in Process Inventory account at that time.

In summary—

1. A separate job cost sheet is established for each job or job lot.

---

[2] When the job consists of more than one unit of product, the system is often called "job-lot costing," or simply "lot costing."

2. Labor, material, and overhead costs chargeable to the job are recorded on this sheet, and are also debited to Goods in Process Inventory.

3. When the job is completed and transferred out of the factory, the total cost accumulated on the job cost sheet is the amount used to debit Finished Goods Inventory and to credit Goods in Process Inventory (unless the job is immediately sold, in which case the debit is to Cost of Goods Sold.)

4. The balance in Work in Process Inventory at the end of the accounting period is therefore the sum of the costs accumulated on all jobs still in the factory.

Process Costing. In a *process cost system,* all the costs for a time period, such as a month, are collected, with no attempt to attach these costs to specific units of product. This system is used in a factory making only one product, such as cement, or in a factory where the difference between various types of products is not substantial, that is, where the products are relatively homogeneous. Essentially, in a process cost system the total cost incurred during the period and the total number of units of products worked on during the period are collected. By dividing total costs by total units, one derives the cost per unit; and this cost per unit is used as the basis of valuing the units transferred to Finished Goods Inventory and, later on, from Finished Goods Inventory to Cost of Goods Sold.

The units *worked on* in a period include the following: (1) units that were both started and completed during the period; plus (2) units that were started but not completed; plus (3) units that were started in prior periods and completed in this period. Since 100 per cent of the cost of the first type were incurred in the current period, but only a portion of the costs of the second and third types, production activity for the period cannot be determined simply by adding up the number of units worked on. The three types of units must be converted to a common base, called *equivalent production,* that is, the equivalent of one completed unit. In order to convert the number of uncompleted products into their equivalence in terms of completed units, the assumption is often made that units still in process at the end of the period are 50 per cent complete, and similarly that units in process at the beginning of the period were 50 per cent complete at that time. Thus, in order to calculate the labor and overhead costs per unit worked on, each unit completed would be given a weight of one, each unit in process at the end of the period would be given a weight of one half, and each unit in process at the beginning of the period also would be given a weight of one half.[3]

> EXAMPLE: If 200 units were completed, 50 units were in process at the end, and 10 were in process at the beginning, the number of equivalent production units worked on would be $200 + 50/2 - 10/2 = 220$. If total costs incurred were \$2,200, costs per equivalent unit would be \$10, and each of the 50 partially completed units in process at the end of the month would be costed at \$5.

Raw material would be costed according to its physical flow (unless the Lifo system was used). If material was added evenly throughout the production process, it could reasonably be costed by use of the 50 per cent assumption described above. If, as is perhaps more common, all the raw material for a unit is issued at the beginning of the process, material cost per unit would be obtained by dividing the total cost of material used by the number of units *started* during the period.

In any event, some reasonable assumption has to be made. In a process cost system, there is no precise way of determining the amount of costs attributable to partially completed units.

In summary—

1. Labor, material, and overhead costs incurred during the accounting period are accumulated as debits to Goods in Process Inventory.

2. Production is measured in terms of the number of equivalent units of production.

3. A cost per unit is found by dividing total costs by the number of equivalent units.

4. Finished Goods Inventory is debited and Goods in Process Inventory credited by an amount equal to the number of units completed in the period multiplied by this cost per unit.

5. The balance in Goods in Process Inventory at the end of an accounting period is the material cost of the units still in the factory plus an appropriate share (say 50 per cent) of the labor and overhead cost of these units if they had been completed.

Choice of a System. Since a process cost system requires less record keeping than a job order system, there is a tendency to use it even though the products manufactured are not strictly homogeneous. Thus, many shoe manufacturers use a process cost system, even though there are

---

[3] A more precise procedure would be to estimate the actual stage of completion, but this involves more work. At the other extreme, some companies disregard the units in process and show no Goods in Process Inventory account. If the goods in process inventory is small, or if it remains relatively constant in size, no serious error is introduced. Another variation is to apply the 50 per cent assumption separately to each department through which the product passes rather than to the factory as a whole.

considerable differences in cost among the various sizes, styles, and colors of shoes manufactured; for pricing purposes, these companies measure the approximate effect on cost of these differences by calculations made outside the accounting system itself. If there are important reasons for keeping track of the differences between one product and another, or between one production lot of the same type of product and another, then a job cost system is more appropriate. For example, a job cost system would invariably be used if the customer paid for the specific item or production order on the basis of its cost (as is often the case in so-called "job shop production"). Also, use of a job cost system makes it possible to examine actual costs on specific jobs, and this may help one to locate trouble spots; whereas in a process cost system costs cannot be traced to specific units in this fashion.

For our purposes, there is no need to study differences in the detailed records required for the two types of systems. Both systems are essentially devices for collecting information. Either furnishes the information required for the system shown in Illustration 7–2. In practice, there are many systems that have job costing in some departments or for some types of cost and process costing in other departments or for other types of cost.

Variations in Practice

The accounting system outlined in Illustration 7–2 will probably never be precisely duplicated in actual practice since it is a schematic representation of underlying structures. Companies build on the basic structure by adding accounts that collect the data in more detail so as to meet their particular needs for information. A company may, for example, set up several raw material inventory accounts, each one covering a different type of material, instead of the single account shown in Illustration 7–2. Another common variation is to have several goods in process accounts, one for each main department or "cost center" in the factory. A system using several goods in process accounts is shown in Illustration 15–1. It will be noted that such a system is essentially like that shown in Illustration 7–2 except that work is transferred from one department to another. The finished goods of one department become, in effect, the raw material of the next department.

Problems of Cost Accumulation

Three problems must be solved in the accumulation of a reasonable cost for each product worked on—

Illustration 15-1

COST SYSTEM WITH DEPARTMENTAL ACCOUNTS

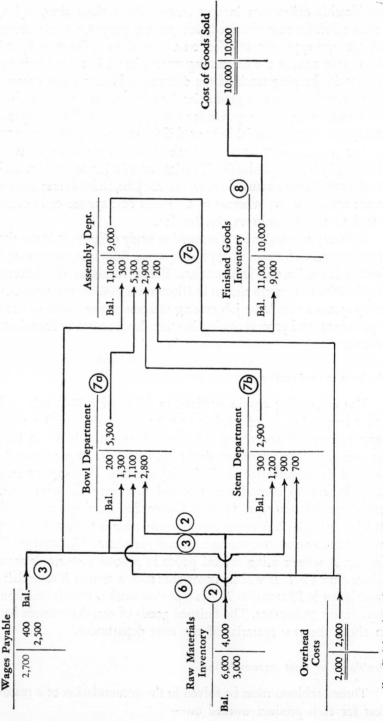

Note: Circled numbers refer to events described in Chapter 7 (pp. 183, 185).

1. *Assignment of costs to accounting periods.* This problem is one of measuring costs incurred, in accordance with the accrual concept. Since this problem was discussed at length in Part I, nothing additional needs to be said here.
2. *Measurement of direct labor and direct material.*
3. *Accumulation and allocation of overhead.*

The second and third problems will be discussed in the following sections.

Direct Labor and Direct Material Costs

Direct Labor. Direct labor costs are the labor costs that can be specifically identified with a product or that vary so closely with the number of products produced that a direct relationship is presumed to exist. There are essentially two problems in the measurement of direct labor cost: measuring (1) the *quantity* of labor effort expended on the product (e.g., the time spent), and (2) the *price* per unit of quantity.

Measuring the quantity of labor effort is relatively easy. In a job-cost system, there is often a timecard, or comparable record, for each direct worker, and on it a record is made of the time he spends on each job. Or, if direct workers are paid a piece rate, the record shows the number of pieces completed. In a process cost system, all that is needed is the total of the time spent by all employees on activities directly related to production; these times appear on their timecards. (Actually, the matter is not quite this simple, for problems arise about the treatment of idle time, personal time, overtime, and so on. These are mostly beyond the scope of this introductory treatment.)

Deciding on the best way to price these labor quantities is conceptually more difficult. The great majority of companies have a simple solution, which is to price direct labor at the amounts actually paid the employees concerned (so much an hour if employees are paid on a day-rate basis; so much a piece if they are paid on a piece-rate basis). Some companies, however, add *labor-related* costs to the basic wage rate. They reason that each hour of labor effort costs the company not only the wages paid to the employee but also the social security taxes, pension contributions, and other fringe benefits that are an inevitable part of the real cost of each employee. In some cases, they even add in a share of the costs of the personnel department and employee welfare programs. Using such a higher figure gives a more accurate picture of true labor costs. It also involves additional record keeping, however, and many companies do not believe the gain is worthwhile.

Direct Material. The measurement of direct material cost (or "raw materials cost") also has the two aspects of the quantity of material used and price per unit of quantity. The quantity is often determined from requisitions or similar documents that order material out of the storeroom and into production. The question of pricing this material is analogous to that already discussed under direct labor. It may be priced at solely its invoice cost, or there may be added some or all of the following *material-related* costs: inward freight, inspection costs, moving costs, purchasing department costs, and interest and space charges associated with holding material in inventory.

Overhead Costs

Overhead costs are those costs not associated directly with the products worked on; included are all manufacturing costs other than those classified as direct material and direct labor. Some costs are classified as overhead because it is *impossible* to associate them directly with products. Who can say how much of building depreciation or of a factory superintendent's salary actually belongs to each unit of product manufactured? Other costs are classified as overhead because it is *not convenient* to trace them directly to products, even though it would be possible to do so. Wage-related costs, as mentioned above, are one example. Furthermore, there are good grounds for differences of opinion as to whether some elements are properly considered as direct costs or as overhead costs. Is a premium payment for overtime work properly a direct labor cost of the products worked on during the overtime period, is it a direct labor cost of the products worked on earlier in the day that may have caused the subsequent overtime, or is it an overhead cost, not directly attributable to any specific product?

Since, by definition, overhead costs are not associated directly with products, it is impossible to measure precisely how much overhead should be charged to a given product. Nevertheless, total overhead is properly part of the cost of the total products worked on, and some reasonable part of the total overhead costs incurred must therefore be charged to each unit of product.

Cost Centers.   A *cost center* is merely an accounting unit for which costs are accumulated. It may be an organizational unit, such as a department, but, as will be seen, there is no necessary connection between cost centers and physically indentifiable organization units.

One type of cost center is a *product center;* that is, a center through which the product passes. Often a product center corresponds to a production department, but a group of similar machines, such as a bank of screw machines, may be a product center, and so may a single machine, such as each printing press in a printing job shop.

A *service center,* another type of cost center, is a department or other unit that incurs costs, but that does not work directly on products, for example, the maintenance department and the general factory offices. If each machine in one department is a product center, then there is also a departmental service center in which the departmental costs not directly traceable to machines are collected.

Steps in Overhead Allocation. The steps in the process are as follows:

1. Estimated overhead costs are accumulated in cost centers.
2. Costs accumulated in service cost centers are transferred to product cost centers.
3. The total cost accumulated in each product center is divided by a measure of activity, giving an overhead rate.
4. Overhead is allocated at this rate to each product passing through the cost center.

Usually, the first three steps leading to the determination of an overhead rate are carried out annually, prior to the beginning of the year, although the overhead rate may be changed more than once a year or even less than once a year, depending on how volatile are the underlying factors. The figures used, therefore, usually are estimates of what the costs will be, rather than historical records of what they actually were. These steps apply to both job and process costing, except that in process costing there is no need to calculate overhead rates for individual units of product.

These steps are described in the following paragraphs, using the pipe factory as an illustration. As shown in Illustration 15–2, our pipe factory has three product centers—the bowl department, the stem department, and the assembly department—and two service centers—occupancy and general. The occupancy center is used to accumulate building depreciation, building maintenance, heat, light, and other occupancy costs. The general center is used to accumulate the costs of factory supervision and miscellaneous general costs not traceable directly to other cost centers.

Cost Accumulation by Cost Centers. The first step in the accumulation of overhead cost is to estimate the amounts that will be spent directly in each of the product centers and service centers. This procedure involves estimating the elements of cost that are traceable to each. Note that in this step, each cost component is recorded in one, and only one, cost center, so that the sum of the costs for all the cost centers exactly equals total overhead costs. These estimates appear in

Illustration 15–2

CALCULATION OF OVERHEAD RATE

Cost Type	Product Centers				Service Centers	
	Total	Bowl	Stem	As-sembly	Occu-pancy	General
Indirect labor..................	$ 9,700	$ 3,100	$ 2,700	$	$	$ 3,900
Indirect supplies...............	4,000	900	600	500	400	1,600
Other........................	12,000	3,900	1,200	700	4,300	1,900
Subtotals...................	$25,700	$ 7,900	$ 4,500	$1,200	$4,700	$ 7,400
Allocation of Service Centers						
Occupancy......................		1,900	1,400	900	(4,700)	500
General.......................		3,600	2,600	1,700		$(7,900)
Total Cost................	$25,700	$13,400	$ 8,500	$3,800	....	....
Direct labor cost...............		$15,800	$10,600	$4,200		
Overhead rate per direct labor dollar......................		$0.85	$0.80	$0.90		

the upper section of Illustration 15–2. Ordinarily, these estimates are based on past experience, adjusted for changes in wage rates, prices, or other factors that may be anticipated for the ensuing year.

Transfer of Service Center Costs. The second step is to transfer all service center costs to product centers, for this is the way in which they become a part of product costs. There are two general ways of doing this: (1) by a direct charge and (2) by allocation.

Some service center costs are charged directly to the product centers. We have already mentioned (on p. 363) the possibility of charging maintenance department costs to operating departments on the basis of the maintenance service actually performed. The same possibility exists for other service activities, although beyond a certain point the rationale becomes so tenuous as not to be practicable. Theoretically, but not practically, the president's time could be charged directly to each of the cost centers he deals with, for example.

Other service center costs are *allocated* to product centers on some basis that seems to have a reasonable relationship to "benefits received," or to a "fair share." The dozens of possible bases of allocations that are used in practice can be grouped into the following principal categories:

1. *Labor related.* Fringe benefits, personnel department costs, and other costs associated with employees may be allocated on the basis of the number of employees. Alternatively, as mentioned above, some or all of these costs may enter into the calculation of direct labor costs and

hence not appear as overhead costs at all. If overhead costs are ultimately charged to products by means of a direct labor rate, the ultimate effect of collecting these labor-related costs in overhead is the same as that of charging them as part of direct labor costs.

2. *Material related.* This category, also discussed above, may be allocated on the basis of the volume of material used in the product center, or, alternatively, it may be excluded from overhead and charged to products as part of direct material cost.

3. *Space related.* These are costs associated with the space that the cost center occupies, and are charged to cost centers on the basis of the relative areas of the centers. Occupancy cost in Illustration 15–2 is an example. Assuming that the bowl center has 40 per cent of the total floor space, the stem center 30 per cent, the assembly center 20 per cent, and the general center 10 per cent, the total occupancy cost of $4,700 is allocated to the other centers according to these percentages.

4. *Activity related.* Some costs are roughly related to the overall volume of activity, or size of the cost center; or at least there is a presumption that the larger the cost center, the more costs are properly chargeable to it. Electrical costs and steam costs fall into this category, and so do a variety of other service center costs which, although not demonstrably a function of activity, are more fairly apportioned in this way than in any other. The measure of activity may be closely related to the item, as, for example, allocating electrical costs on the basis of the total horsepower of motors installed, or it may be an overall measure, such as total labor cost, total direct costs, or sales value of products processed. The general service center in Illustration 15–2 falls in this category. The total cost of $7,900 is allocated to the product centers on the basis of the relative direct material and labor costs of these centers, here assumed to be 46 per cent for bowl, 33 per cent for stem, and 21 per cent for assembly.

Step-down Order. Note that in Illustration 15–2, part of occupancy cost is charged to the general service center. It may be that part of general's cost should be charged to occupancy. When there are a number of service centers, the interrelationships among them could theoretically lead to a long series of redistributions and re-redistributions, but in practice this is avoided by distributing the service center costs in a prescribed order, which is called the *step-down order.* In the illustration, the order is occupancy first, and general second. No additional cost is allocated to a service center after its costs have been distributed. Since the step-down order is adhered to in all calculations, the results are always consistent.

Overhead Rates. Having brought all the costs to product centers, we now seek some equitable means of loading them onto the products passing through the center, step three in the process of calculating overhead. This step applies only in job costing. In process costing, there is no need to calculate an overhead rate, since costs are not traced to individual units of product. Total costs, both costs incurred directly in the product center and a fair share of service center costs, are accumulated in product centers, and this total is the amount used to calculate the cost per unit of equivalent production.

Essentially, the calculation of an overhead rate requires an answer to the question: Why should one unit of product bear more overhead than another? Possible answers are the following: (1) because more work has been done on it; (2) because the product is worth more and therefore is able to bear more overhead; (3) because it requires more labor, and overhead is largely associated with labor; and so on. These answers suggest some quantitative bases of making the charge, respectively: (1) the number of direct labor hours or machine-hours required for the product; (2) total direct costs of the product; (3) direct labor cost; and so on. Of these, the machine-hours basis is common for cost centers that consist primarily of one machine (such as a paper machine) or a group of related machines. The direct labor cost basis is perhaps most frequently used in other situations since it is readily available on the job cost card. Direct labor hours are also often used if the number of hours worked on each job is readily available.

In our pipe factory, let us assume that a direct labor cost basis will be used in each product center. (Actually, the same basis of measurement is not necessarily used in all product centers.) All that remains, therefore, is to estimate the total direct labor cost for each product center in the ensuing year and divide this into the total overhead cost of the center. The result is the amount of overhead that is to be charged to pipes for each dollar of direct labor incurred. In the bowl center, for example, the overhead rate is $0.85 per dollar of direct labor.

Allocation of Overhead. The fourth step in the total process of accumulation and allocation of overhead is to apply the rate calculated above to the products passing through the product center. If for a given lot of pipes the direct labor cost in the bowl center is $100 and the overhead rate is $0.85 per dollar of direct labor, the overhead cost of this lot of pipes is $85.

Because of the nature of the methods used, two observations should be made about the overhead cost: (1) The total amount transferred in this way may not coincide exactly with the total actual incurred costs for the period under consideration. If there are differences, then overhead is under- or overabsorbed, and various accounting techniques are used for handling such amounts. (2) The whole process, being based on subjective judgments of what is a "fair" distribution, cannot result in an *accurate* cost. These points are discussed in the following sections.

Unabsorbed and Overabsorbed Overhead

In any accounting period, the overhead costs charged to pipes worked on in the bowl cost center will equal the total overhead costs charged to the cost center if, but only if, total overhead costs are exactly 85 per cent of total direct labor costs. This is not likely to happen. If more overhead is charged to products than is actually incurred, overhead is said to be *overabsorbed,* and if less, it is *underabsorbed* (or more commonly, *unabsorbed*). For management purposes, a record of the amount of unabsorbed or overabsorbed overhead is a useful piece of information, as will be discussed in Chapter 17.

For financial accounting purposes, this amount can be handled in one of three ways: (1) charge or credit it entirely to the income of the period on the income statement (often as an adjustment to cost of good sold); (2) divide it between inventory and period expense in the proportion that inventory is to cost of goods sold; or (3) do nothing, in the expectation that unabsorbed overhead in one period will be offset by overabsorption in a succeeding period. An argument for the first alternative is that the difference between estimated and actual costs may reflect events occurring in the period and therefore should affect income of the period. An argument for the second alternative is that the difference may reflect an inability to make accurate estimates, and that the estimated costs in inventory and cost of goods sold should be corrected accordingly. The third alternative is not a generally accepted accounting practice for annual financial statements, but it is often used for monthly or other interim internal statements both as a matter of convenience and to avoid having income affected by short-term fluctuations in overhead absorption.

In the interests of simplicity, no account for overabsorbed or unabsorbed overhead was shown in Illustrations 7–1 or 15–1. Such an account could be fitted into the system in either of two places, depending on whether the overhead charged to the cost center was the amount absorbed in the period or the amount incurred. If the cost center was debited for the amount of overhead *absorbed,* then the over- or underabsorbed account would take up the difference between this amount and the total overhead costs incurred as shown in the various overhead cost accounts (i.e., the $2,000 in Illustration 15–1). If the cost center was debited for the overhead cost *incurred*, then the balance in the cost center account would later be adjusted to remove the difference between cost incurred and cost absorbed onto products.

If there are seasonal variations either in costs (as in heating costs) or in the level of activity, the amount of overhead cost charged to the cost center each month is often a *normalized* amount rather than the actual amount of cost incurred. This normalized amount is set in such a way that the unit costs do not vary from month to month because of volume changes or seasonal factors. The difference between the normalized amount and actual costs incurred is held in an overabsorbed or underabsorbed account, with the expectation that over the course of a year, overabsorptions will be washed out by underabsorptions.

Accuracy of Overhead Costs

By definition, overhead costs are not traced directly to products; therefore the overhead cost charged to a product cannot be the "actual" overhead cost incurred in making the product in any literal sense of this word. Through the distribution and allocation mechanism described above, we have indeed succeeded in adding a portion of, for example, building depreciation onto the cost of each unit of product, but judgments as to what is fair and reasonable were involved in each step of this process: in deciding on the costs applicable to the *period* (what really is the depreciation expense of this period?), in deciding how much of this cost is applicable to each *cost center,* and in deciding how much of the cost center's cost is applicable to each *product.* Two equally capable accountants can arrive at quite different amounts of overhead per unit, and there is no way of proving that one is right and the other wrong, that is, that one overhead figure is accurate and the other is inaccurate.

Since all production costs appear on the financial statements as either cost of goods sold or inventory, and since the judgments about allocations may have relatively little effect on the division of total cost between these two categories, many companies do not bother about a refined method of allocation. Often a *plant-wide overhead rate* is used, which is obtained simply by dividing estimated total overhead cost by estimated total direct labor cost for the entire plant. Although the amount of overhead charged to a given product if a plant-wide rate is used will probably differ from the amount charged by a series of cost center rates, these detailed differences may well offset one another in the computation of total inventory and cost of goods sold.

If costs are to be used as a basis for pricing, however, carefully set overhead rates may be important. It may not be appropriate, for example, to charge the same amount of overhead per labor dollar for a product that requires the use of expensive equipment as for a product that involves only the use of hand tools.

A few companies compute what they call "actual" overhead costs by going through the process shown in Illustration 15–2 at the end of the period, rather than prior to the beginning of the period. At the end of the period the actual overhead cost and the actual level of activity are available, and these are used to calculate a rate that, when applied to products, will result in the exact absorption of overhead. Since under this procedure no jobs can be costed until the period has ended, it is rarely used. Furthermore, although this procedure does absorb overhead in total, it does not eliminate the judgment made with respect to the amount of costs applicable to the period, to the product center, or to the individual product, and hence the detailed overhead allocations cannot be said to be, literally, "actual" even under this procedure.

STANDARD COSTS

The basic objective of the system outlined above was to charge units of product with a fair share of the *actual* costs incurred in making these products. Many cost accounting systems, in contrast, are based wholly or in part on the principle that the costs charged to individual products are the costs that *should have been incurred* on those products rather than the costs that *actually were incurred.* Such a system is called a *standard cost system.*[4] The essential nature of standard costs, then, is that they represent costs that should have been incurred rather than costs that actually were incurred.

Each unit of product has a standard material cost, a standard labor cost, and a standard overhead cost for each product cost center. The total standard cost for the month is obtained by multiplying these standard unit costs by the number of units flowing through the cost center in that month.

Illustration 15–3 shows the system for our pipe factory shifted to a standard cost basis. It is the same as the actual cost system shown in Illustration 7–2 except that three *variance accounts* have been added. Standard costs are usually different from the actual costs incurred, and

---

[4] Some accountants limit the term "standard costs" to costs determined on the basis of engineering estimates and use the term "estimated costs" for costs determined on the basis of estimates made by persons who are not engineers. As a practical matter, the distinction is not of great significance.

Illustration 15-3

A STANDARD COST SYSTEM

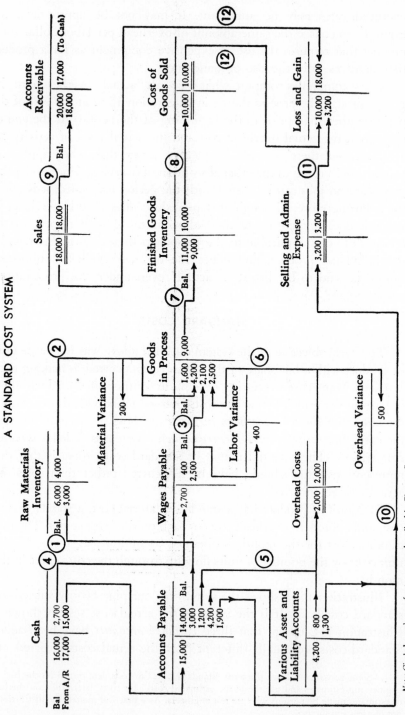

Note: Circled numbers refer to events described in Chapter 7.

Bal. = Net income before taxes

variance accounts are a repository for these differences. For example, if actual labor costs for the month were $2,500, the credit to the liability account Accrued Wages Payable must be $2,500. If the standard labor costs of the operations performed totaled only $2,100, Goods in Process would be debited for $2,100, and the $400 difference would be debited to the Labor Variance account. Entries to variance accounts are debits if actual costs are greater than standard costs, and they are credits if actual costs are less than standard costs.

A standard cost system may have several advantages. First, it is often simpler and requires less work than an actual cost system. This is so because once the standard cost for a unit of product has been determined, this cost remains unchanged for relatively long periods, instead of being recalculated for each separate unit that goes through the plant.

Second, a standard cost system produces the same costs for physically identical units of product, whereas an actual cost system may not. For example, in our pipe factory there may be two equally efficient men making identical sizes and shapes of pipe bowls. If one man, because of seniority or other reasons, has a higher wage rate than the other, under an actual job cost system the pipes that he makes will have a higher labor cost than the pipes the other man makes; yet realistically there is no difference in the finished pipes—no reason why one should be said to "cost" more than another. This fact also makes standard costs a better basis for estimating selling prices than are actual costs.

Third, a standard cost system provides the beginning of a mechanism for checking on the efficiency with which the work was done, in that the balance in the variance account may be an indication of good or bad performance. The validity of this statement depends on the accuracy with which the standard cost actually measures what should have been incurred; this point is discussed in Chapter 17.

Companies which use standard costs do not necessarily use a *complete* standard cost system, that is, a system that treats all elements of cost on a standard basis. Some, for example, use standard labor and overhead costs but use actual material costs.

Standard costs may be inserted into the system at any one of several places. Thus, material may be taken up in Raw Materials Inventory at a standard price, with the difference between actual purchase price and the standard price being entered in a Raw Materials Price Variance account; in Illustration 15–3 this account would be placed to the left of the Raw Materials Inventory account. Another alternative is to charge all elements of cost into Goods in Process at actual; the conversion to a standard cost basis would then be made between Goods in Process and Finished Goods Inventory. In the latter system, the variance account would occur between Goods in Process and Finished Goods Inventory. The essential point is that one or more variance accounts are inserted in the system at whatever point the shift from actual to standard is made.

The variance accounts may or may not be closed at the end of the accounting period. The possibilities are the same as those already discussed with respect to under- or overabsorbed overhead, which is one type of variance account.

JOINT PRODUCTS AND BY-PRODUCTS

In some manufacturing plants, two or more dissimilar end products may be made from a single batch of raw material or from a single production process. The classic example of these *joint products* is the variety of end products—the hide, the many different cuts of meat, and so on—that are made from the single raw material, a steer. Beyond a certain point in the manufacturing process, which is called the *split-off point,* separate end products are identified, and costs are accumulated for each of them. The problem of joint costing is to find some reasonable basis for assigning to the joint products the material, labor, and overhead costs incurred up to the split-off point.

This problem is essentially the same as that of allocating overhead. In both cases, the objective is to assign a fair share of the joint or common costs to the separate end products, and in neither case can the results be scientifically accurate.

One common basis of allocating joint costs is in proportion to the *sales value* of the end products, adjusted for processing and marketing costs incurred beyond the split-off point. If the selling price depends on cost, this method involves a certain amount of circular reasoning, but there may be no better alternative. If gasoline sells for twice the price of kerosene, it is perhaps reasonable that gasoline should bear twice as much of the crude oil and joint refining costs. Another basis of allocation is weight; in the case of the steer, this would assume that the stew meat is as valuable as the tenderloin, which is unrealistic; but in other situations, this might be a reasonable assumption. In any event, the amount charged to each end product must be recognized as an allocation. If some scientifically correct method of apportioning the cost were available, the product would not be a joint product, by definition.

By-products are a special kind of joint product. If management wishes to make Products A and B in some predetermined proportion, or if it wishes to make as much of each as possible from a given quantity of raw material, then they are ordinary joint products. If, on the other hand, management's objective is to make Product A, but its production inevitably results in Product B, then Product A is a main product and Product B is a by-product. The intention is to make from a given amount of joint material as much of the main product and as little of the by-product as possible. As management's intention changes, the classification changes. Kerosene was once the main product made from crude oil; subsequently, with the growth in consumption of gasoline, many petroleum companies considered it a by-product; and currently it has become a main product again, because it is an important component of jet engine fuel. Certain tars and petrochemicals, once by-products, are now main products.

A special accounting procedure is used when by-products exist. All costs are assigned to the main product, and the *sales value* of the by-product is *deducted* from these costs to give the net cost of the main product. The effect of by-product costing, therefore, is to value by-products at their sales value, and a consequence is that no profit or loss appears in the accounting records when these products are sold; the entire profit of the process is attributed to the main product.

DIRECT COSTING

Although not now a generally accepted financial accounting practice, mention should be made of the practice of *direct costing,* which is widely discussed and used by an increasing number of companies in their internal accounting systems.[5] "Direct costs," as used here, are costs that vary with changes in production volume; therefore they correspond to variable costs, and not to direct costs in the sense of traceable costs as the term was used in the preceding section.[6]

In the conventional system, the basic concept is *full costing;* that is, products should bear a fair share of all the costs involved in making them. In the direct cost system, only the variable costs are charged to products and thus pass through inventory accounts; nonvariable costs

---

[5] Of 365 respondents to a 1959 Controllers Institute survey, 77, or 21 per cent, reported a use of direct costing, and nearly half of these had started using the system within the previous five years.

[6] This confusion in terminology is another example of the differences in the definition of cost that cause trouble in practice unless they are recognized.

are charged off as expenses in the period in which they are incurred. Consequently, overhead costs affect net income more quickly in the direct cost system than in a full cost system. This effect can be seen in Illustration 15–4, in which it is assumed that one unit is manufactured each period, but that the unit manufactured in the first period is not sold until the second period. The sales price is $100 per unit, variable costs are $30 per *unit*, and nonvariable overhead is $50 per *period*. In the conventional full cost system, the entire manufacturing cost of $80 is held in inventory at the end of Period No. 1, and is released as cost of goods sold in Period No. 2, along with the cost of the unit made

Illustration 15–4

COMPARISON OF FULL COSTING AND DIRECT COSTING

	Under Full Costing		Under Direct Costing	
	Period No. 1	Period No. 2	Period No. 1	Period No. 2
Activity:				
Units manufactured.................	1	1	1	1
Units sold........................	0	2	0	2
Income Statement:				
Sales............................	$ 0	$200	$ 0	$200
Cost of goods sold.................	0	160	0	60
Manufacturing overhead............	0	0	50	50
Selling and administrative..........	10	10	10	10
Net Income or Loss................	$(10)	$ 30	$(60)	$ 80
Ending Inventory (Balance Sheet)......	$ 80	$ 0	$ 30	$ 0

and sold in that period. In direct costing, only the $30 of variable cost is held in inventory at the end of Period No. 1, and the $50 of fixed overhead is charged as an expense of the period.

The conventional system is also called *absorption costing* because all costs are absorbed by products, in contrast with direct costing, in which nonvariable overhead is not absorbed by products.

In direct costing, nonvariable manufacturing overhead is viewed as being essentially the same as administrative costs; that is, these are costs associated with being in business rather than costs associated with the specific units of product manufactured. Proponents of direct costing assert that management can be misled by the income reported in a period if these costs are hidden away in inventory. This argument, together with the possible advantages of direct costing for other management purposes, is discussed in more detail in Case 15–5, the Beale Company. Direct costing is the extreme case of differences of opinion about which costs are product costs and which are period costs.

Since direct costing is not a generally accepted practice for financial accounting, companies that use it for internal purposes recompute their inventory valuation and cost of goods sold for their published financial statements. They do this by computing an overhead rate, usually on a plant-wide basis, which they use solely for this purpose.

RELATION TO FINANCIAL ACCOUNTING

It should be emphasized that the cost accounting systems described above are an integral part of financial accounting, with the same rules of debit and credit.[7] The accounting entries described in this chapter are made for the same purpose as those described in Chapter 7. The only substantive difference is that in Chapter 7 we assumed that the company did not have a way of obtaining directly the cost of items moving from Raw Materials, through Goods in Process, to Finished Goods, and out to Cost of Goods Sold; we therefore had to find these amounts by the process of deduction. In the present chapter, a method of finding the amounts directly has been described. The other differences, such as the classification of goods in process into cost centers, are merely differences in detail.

RELATION TO MANAGEMENT CONTROL

The systems described above had the objective of assigning products a fair share of the costs incurred in producing them—the financial accounting objective. Although the management control process has a different objective, the same information often can be adapted to meet this objective with relatively little effort, despite the fact that two of the concepts relevant in management control are inherently different from corresponding concepts in financial accounting. These are (1) the responsibility center, as contrasted with a cost center; and (2) controllable costs, as contrasted with total costs. Actually these differences are reconcilable within a single system.

---

[7] Cost information is sometimes collected outside the debit-and-credit structure. Such a system is called a *statistical* cost system, in contrast with a *tied-in* cost system. A statistical system is simpler to operate but does not permit the checks on accuracy that are possible in the tied-in system.

Responsibility Centers

Cost centers are often production departments, and these departments are also responsibility centers since the department foreman is a responsible supervisor. When individual machines or other segments of a department are used as cost centers, costs for the responsibility center can be obtained simply by adding up the relevant costs of these separate cost centers. At the other extreme, if the whole factory is a single cost center (as is the case when a plant-wide overhead rate is used), separate accounts are set up to collect the controllable costs for the individual responsibility centers in the plant. Likewise, if cost centers are departments and responsibility centers are individual work shifts or other departmental subdivisions, separate accounts for these subdivisions are required. In short, costs are collected for the cost center or the responsibility center, whichever is the smaller unit, and costs for the other are obtained by addition. Thus, the fact that a cost center is not necessarily the same as a responsibility center raises no particular problem of cost collection.

Service centers headed by responsible supervisors, such as the maintenance department, the personnel department, the accounting department, and so on, are also responsibility centers. Service centers that are mere aggregates of cost without reference to personal responsibility are not. An example of the latter is the occupancy service center described in a preceding section, which is not in itself a responsibility center, although its costs are part of the responsibility center of the plant manager.

Profit and Investment Centers

If the responsibility center is a *profit center,* then, in addition to accumulation of costs, a revenue figure is also developed. If the profit center actually sells products or services to customers who are outside the company, the sales revenue is easy to measure. For internal transactions, revenue is measured by means of the transfer price discussed in Chapter 13. Note that these internal transactions result both in revenue to the responsibility center that supplies the goods or services and also in cost to the responsibility center that receives them. The cost aspect of the transaction is the "direct charge" that has already been discussed.

In an *investment center,* there is the additional problem of measuring the investment base, or *capital employed,* on which the investment center is supposed to earn a satisfactory return. This base consists of both direct investment and allocated investment, which are concepts essentially similar to those of direct and allocated costs. The investment center concept is so new that there is by no means general agreement on how this problem should be solved. A few matters are mentioned as illustrations. First, consider cash. The cash balance of the company is a safety valve, or shock absorber, protecting the company against short-run fluctuations in funds requirements. An investment center needs very little cash, however, since it can obtain funds on short notice from headquarters. Part of the headquarters cash balance therefore exists for the financial protection of the operating investment centers, and headquarters cash can therefore logically be allocated to the investment centers as part of their capital employed.

Fixed assets raise several problems. Should they be considered at original cost or replacement cost? This is the price level problem described in Chapter 9, but whereas for financial accounting purposes historical costs must be used, for control accounting there is no such mandatory requirement. Should they be counted at gross values (i.e., cost), or at net values (i.e., cost less depreciation)? If at gross values, then the accumulation of depreciation is completely disregarded; but if at net values, then the investment center with the oldest, most fully depreciated assets tends to have the lowest amount of capital employed and hence the highest percentage return.

Other problems involve the allocation of accounts receivable, the treatment of intangible assets, and the question of whether or not current liabilities are to be deducted from gross assets employed.

Controllable Costs

For financial accounting we are interested in the total costs of cost centers, but for control purposes we are primarily interested in those elements of cost over which the responsible supervisor can exercise some significant degree of influence. This fact requires that total costs be segregated between those that are controllable and those that are not. These two requirements can be met within a single system simply by providing a way of segregating the controllable costs from the noncontrollable costs.

In product costing, we need only to know the total cost to be charged to products, but for management control, the total must be broken down in a way that facilitates the analysis of performance. Thus, costs are classified according to *type* (also called "object," or "natural element," or "function"). Indirect labor, supplies, power, heat, overtime premiums, and spoilage are examples from the long list of cost types that might be useful in a given situation.

For analysis purposes, it may also be useful to separate *variable costs* (which are costs that change proportionately with changes in production volume or other measure of activity) from nonvariable costs, but such separation usually requires only that each cost type be designated either as variable or as nonvariable. Variable costs are discussed further in Chapter 16.

In summary, control accounting, or, as it is often called, *responsibility accounting,* requires that costs be classified by (1) responsibility centers, (2) within each responsibility center by whether controllable or noncontrollable, and (3) within the controllable classification by cost types, or natural elements, in a way that provides a useful basis for analysis.

The lowest cost unit, which is the amount of one type of cost in the smaller of a cost center or responsibility center, is often called the cost *building block;* all the summaries of cost information are obtained by combining these building blocks in various ways.

SUMMARY

For financial accounting purposes, each product worked on is charged with what is believed to be a fair share of the total manufacturing costs incurred. Products in inventory are valued at this cost, and this is the cost used in figuring the cost of goods sold. Direct labor and direct material costs applicable to each product can usually be measured with reasonable accuracy; for these costs, the principal problem is the mechanical one of accumulating the various labor and material costs that belong to the product. The remaining cost elements, collectively called overhead, cannot be traced directly to products. These costs are accumulated by cost centers, and the total costs of the cost center are allocated to products going through the center on some reasonable basis. *Whenever allocated costs are involved, the resulting product cost cannot be said to be accurate.*

Also, when joint or common costs are involved there can be no scientifically correct way of splitting them up among time periods, among cost centers, or among products passing through cost centers. A pig is a pig; there is no way of knowing how much of its cost belongs to the hide and how much to the bacon. This is *not* merely difficult; it is impossible.

But the objective of financial cost accounting is not to ascertain a scientifically correct cost; rather it is to charge products with a *fair share* of the total costs incurred in the manufacturing process. This it can do.

Since costs are also used for management control, the elementary building blocks of cost are arranged by type in responsibility units, and by proper combination and summarization they can serve both purposes.

SUGGESTIONS FOR FURTHER READING

DEARDEN, JOHN. *Cost and Budget Analysis.* Englewood Cliffs, N.J.: Prentice-Hall, Inc., 1962.

DICKEY, ROBERT I. (ed.). *Accountants' Cost Handbook.* 2d ed. New York: The Ronald Press Co., 1960.

MATZ, ADOLPH; CURRY, OTHEL J.; AND FRANK, GEORGE W. *Cost Accounting.* 3d ed. Cincinnati: South-Western Publishing Co., 1962.

NEUNER, JOHN J. W. *Cost Accounting: Principles and Practice.* 6th ed. Homewood, Ill.: Richard D. Irwin, Inc., 1962.

NICKERSON, CLARENCE B. *Cost Accounting: Text, Problems and Cases.* 2d ed. New York: McGraw-Hill Book Co., Inc., 1962.

SHILLINGLAW, GORDON. *Cost Accounting: Analysis and Control.* Homewood, Ill.: Richard D. Irwin, Inc., 1961.

THOMAS, WILLIAM E. (ed.). *Readings in Cost Accounting, Budgeting and Control.* 2d ed. Cincinnati: South-Western Publishing Co., 1960.

CASES

CASE 15–1.   BENNETT BODY COMPANY

Mr. Ralph Kern, the controller of the Bennett Body Company, received a memorandum from Mr. Paul Bennett, the company's president, suggesting that Mr. Kern review an attached magazine article and comment on it at the next executive committee meeting. The article described the Conley Automotive Corporation's cost accounting system. The Bennett Body Company was a custom manufacturer of truck bodies. Occasionally a customer would reorder an exact duplicate of an earlier body, but most of the time some modifications caused changes in design and hence in cost.

The Conley System

Mr. Kern learned from the article that Conley also manufactured truck bodies but that these were of standard design. Conley had 12 models that it produced in quantities based upon management's estimates of demand. In December of each year, a plan, or budget, for the following year's operations was agreed upon, which included estimates of costs and profits as well as of sales volume.

Included in this budget were estimated costs for each of the 12 models of truck bodies. These costs were determined by totaling estimated labor at an expected wage rate, estimated material at an expected cost per unit, and an allocation for overhead that was based on the proportion of estimated total overhead costs to estimated total direct labor hours. This estimate for each model became the standard cost of the model.

No attempt was made in Conley's accounts to record the actual costs of each model. Costs were accumulated for each of the four direct producing departments and for several service departments. Labor costs were easily obtainable from payroll records, since all employees assigned to a producing department were classified as direct labor for that department. Material sent to the department was charged to it on the

Exhibit 1

SUMMARY OF COSTS, DEPARTMENT 4, NOVEMBER

Standard	Num- ber of Bodies	Material		Labor		Overhead	
		Per Unit	Total	Per Unit	Total	Per Unit	Total
Model 101...........	10	$150	$ 1,500	$220	$ 2,200	$220	$ 2,200
109...........	8	200	1,600	175	1,400	175	1,400
113...........	11	305	3,355	210	2,310	210	2,310
154...........	20	95	1,900	194	3,880	194	3,880
Total...............	49		$ 8,355		$ 9,790		$ 9,790
Actual costs.........			9,120		10,030		10,030
Variances...........			$— 765		$— 240		$— 240

The overhead rate for Department 4 was 100 percent of direct labor cost.

basis of signed issue slips. Overhead costs were charged to the department on the basis of the same percentage of direct labor as that used in determining the standard cost.

Since Conley's management also knew how many truck bodies of each model were handled by each department monthly, the total standard costs for each department could easily be calculated by multiplying the quantity of that model produced by its standard cost. Management watched closely the difference between the actual cost and the standard cost as the year progressed.

As each truck body was completed, its cost was added to Finished Goods Inventory at the standard cost figure. When the truck body was sold, standard cost became the Cost of Sales figure. This system of cost recording avoided the necessity of accumulating detailed actual costs on each specific body that was built; yet the company could estimate, reasonably well, the costs of its products. Moreover, management believed that the differences between actual and standard cost provided a revealing insight into cost fluctuations that eventually should lead to better cost control. An illustrative tabulation of the costs for Department 4 is shown in Exhibit 1. No incomplete work remained in this department either at the beginning or at the end of the month.

The Bennett System

Because almost every truck body that Bennett built was in some respect unique, costs were accumulated by individual jobs.

When a job was started it received a code number, and costs for the job were collected weekly under that code number. When material (such as wood, metal tubing, steel forms or bars, canvas, paint, etc.) used for a particular job was issued to the workmen, a record of the quantity issued was obtained on a requisition form. This quantity of material—so many units, board feet, linear feet, weight, etc.—was multiplied by the purchase cost per unit to arrive at the actual cost of material used. Maintenance of cumulative records of these withdrawals by code number made the total material cost of each job easy to determine.

Likewise, all labor costs of making a particular truck body were recorded. If a man moved from job to job, a record was made of his time spent on each job, and his week's wages were divided among these jobs in proportion to the amount of time spent on each. Throughout the shop, the time of any person working on anything directly related to an order—Job No. 1375J, for example—was ultimately computed in dollar cost and charged to that job.

Finally Bennett's overhead costs that could not be directly associated with a particular job were allocated among all jobs on the proportional basis of direct labor hours involved. Thus, if in any month 135 direct labor hours were spent on Job No. 1375J, and this was 5 per cent of the 2,700 direct labor hours spent on all jobs at Bennett, then Job No. 1375J received 5 per cent of all the overhead costs—supplies, salaries, depreciation, etc.—for that month.

Under this system Bennett's management knew at the end of each month what each body job in process cost to date. They could also determine total factory cost and therefore gross profit at the completion of each job.

The note that Mr. Bennett attached to the magazine article read:

Ralph:

Please review the system of cost accounting described in this article with the view of possible applications to our company. Aside from the overall comparison, I am interested particularly in your opinion on—

1. Costs of paper work and record keeping, as compared with our system.
2. Possible reasons for cost differences between the actual and standard costs under Conley's system.
3. How do you think Conley develops the standard cost of factory overhead for a particular model for the purpose of preparing the budget?
4. Do you think that we should change our period for determining the overhead allocation rate from monthly to annually? If so, why?

These are just a few questions which might be helpful in your overall analysis. I would like to discuss this question at the next executive committee meeting.

Thank you.

Paul Bennett

Question

As Mr. Kern, what would you be prepared to say in response to Mr. Bennett's memorandum?

CASE 15–2.   DIXON COMPANY

The Dixon Company made metal parts and subassemblies for approximately a dozen manufacturers in the Detroit area. Prior to 1960, it had done all this work on a fixed-price basis. In 1960 the company negotiated a contract with the Mayer Company, a large manufacturing company. Under the terms of this contract, the Dixon Company would devote roughly 40 per cent of its output to parts for the Mayer Company. The exact nature and volume of these parts were to be determined subsequently. Payment was to be made on a basis of cost plus a fixed fee. "Cost" was to be the sum of the direct material, direct labor, and overhead cost of the parts. The overhead cost was to be calculated as that percentage of direct labor that total overhead in the plant bore to total direct labor. A tentative overhead rate was to be set for billing purposes, and an adjustment was to be made at the end of each year after actual overhead costs and actual direct labor costs for the year had been determined.

The Dixon Company used a simple cost accounting system under which most payments to employees were classified as direct labor. This classification was not satisfactory to the representative of the Mayer Company, and he suggested that the classification should be governed by the *Armed Services Procurement Regulation,* which is the principal regulation relating to the determination of costs under U.S. Defense Department contracts. Excerpts from this regulation are quoted below:[8]

15–201.1   Composition of Total Cost.   The total cost of a contract is the sum of the allowable direct and indirect costs allocable to the contract, incurred or to be incurred, less any allocable credits. In ascertaining what constitutes costs, any generally accepted method of determining or estimating costs that is equitable under the circumstances may be used, including standard costs properly adjusted for applicable variances.

*   *   *   *   *

15–201.4   Definition of Allocability.   A cost is allocable if it is assignable or chargeable to a particular cost objective, such as a contract, product, product line, process, or class of customer or activity, in accordance with the relative benefits received or other equitable relationship. Subject to the foregoing, a cost is allocable to a Government contract if it

(i)   is incurred specifically for the contract;

(ii) benefits both the contract and other work, or both Government work and other work, and can be distributed to them in reasonable proportion to the benefits received; or

(iii) is necessary to the overall operation of the business, although a direct relationship to any particular cost objective cannot be shown.

*   *   *   *   *

15–202   Direct Costs.   A direct cost is any cost which can be identified specifically with a particular cost objective. Direct costs are not limited to items which are incorporated in the end product as material or labor. Costs identified specifically with the contract are direct costs of the contract and are to be charged directly thereto. Costs identified specifically with other work of the contractor are direct costs of that work and are not to be charged to the contract directly or indirectly. When items ordinarily chargeable as indirect costs are charged to Government work as direct costs, the cost of like items applicable to other work of the contractor must be eliminated from indirect costs allocated to Government work.

*   *   *   *   *

15–203   Indirect Costs.   An indirect cost is one which, because of its incurrence for common or joint objectives, is not readily subject to treatment as a direct cost. Minor direct cost items may be considered to be indirect costs for reasons of practicality. After direct costs have been determined and charged directly to the contract or other work as appropriate, indirect costs are those remaining to be allocated to the several classes of work.

*   *   *   *   *

---

[8] *Armed Services Procurement Regulation,* Section XV, revised November 2, 1959.

15–205.6 Compensation for Personal Services. Compensation for personal services includes all remuneration paid currently or accrued, in whatever form and whether paid immediately or deferred, for services rendered by employees to the contractor during the period of contract performance. It includes, but is not limited to, salaries, wages, directors' and executive committee members' fees, bonuses (including stock bonuses), incentive awards, employee stock options, employee insurance, fringe benefits, and contributions to pension, annuity, and management employee incentive compensation plans.

The treasurer of the Dixon Company thought that further discussion of this topic would be desirable. Consequently, he prepared, with the assistance of his chief accountant, a list of the types of labor payments likely to be incurred during the life of the contract. Recognizing that the magnitude of the expense would enter into the discussion, he included a rough estimate of the monthly anticipated cost to the Dixon Company for each type of labor. This list, which was to be used as a basis for discussion, follows:

1. Earnings of piece-rate workers (approximately $25,000).
2. Earnings of day-rate workers who worked on productive work (approximately $3,000).
3. Overtime payments (impossible to estimate; depends on delivery requirements of Mayer Company).
4. Payments to workers who for some reason or other were idle (approximately $1,250).
5. Payments for time spent setting up machines (very roughly $2,000).
6. Payments to workers for regular work time used in attending union meetings (approximately $200).
7. Payments to foremen and assistants (approximately $1,800).
8. Payments to inspectors (approximately $600).
9. Payments to office workers (approximately $2,600).
10. Payments to sweepers (approximately $450).
11. Payments to maintenance men (approximately $600).
12. Payments to man employed in the raw material stock room ($275).
13. Allowance for vacation pay (all the above employees had one week's vacation with pay each year).
14. The company's contribution to old-age benefit taxes (approximately 3 per cent of all wages paid).
15. The company's unemployment insurance tax (approximately 2 per cent of all wages paid).

Questions

1. Should the treasurer of the Dixon Company be concerned about this matter? Why?

2. In your opinion, which types of payments on the above list should be classified as direct labor and which should be classified as indirect labor and, therefore, included in overhead?

3. Comment on the usefulness of the definition of direct costs quoted in the case. Should it be made more precise?

CASE 15–3. TREYNOR COMPANY

The Treynor Company had a standard cost system with separate accounts established to record factory variances. Variance accounts were closed at the end of the month to the Loss and Gain account. Two products were made, each with a standard cost as follows:

	Product A	Product B
Direct material cost (at standard cost of $1 per pound)......	$ 5	$ 8
Direct labor cost (at standard rate of $1 per hour).........	20	12
Overhead cost...	10	20
Total..	$35	$40

Raw material cost was debited to the Raw Materials Inventory account at the standard cost of $1 a pound upon delivery, any discrepancy between actual and standard price going to a variance account. All debits to Goods in Process were at standard.

Following are statements relating to operations in September:

1. On September 1, balances in the accounts were as follows:

	Dr.	Cr.
Raw materials..	$ 12,000	
Goods in process....................................	35,000	
Finished goods......................................	43,000	
Other assets...	200,000	
Accounts payable....................................		$ 20,000
Wages payable.......................................		8,000
Other liabilities.....................................		100,000
Stockholders' equity................................		162,000
Total...	$290,000	$290,000

2. During September, the company bought and received 20,000 pounds of material, paying $12,000 cash of the total bill of $23,000, leaving $11,000 still payable as of September 30.

3. Direct labor expense incurred during September was $30,000. Indirect labor expense was $10,000. Wages paid were $38,000 (disregard taxes).

4. Production schedules for September called for 800 units of A and 1,200 units of B to be started through production during the month, and these were, in fact, started. To provide for this volume of production, 15,000 pounds of material were used during the month.

5. Overhead expenses for September other than indirect labor were $25,000. Of this amount, $19,000 was credited to Other Assets and $6,000 to Accounts Payable.

6. Administrative and selling expenses were $20,000. The offsetting entry was to Accounts Payable.

7. Standard cost sheets showed that standard costs were charged to products, representing work done on those products during the month, as follows: labor, $30,400; overhead, $32,000.

8. During September, 1,100 units of A and 1,000 units of B were delivered to the warehouse as finished goods, although some of this production had in fact been started in August.

9. September sales were 1,000 units of A for $53,000 and 1,200 units of B for $65,000. The offsetting entry was to Other Assets.

Questions

1. Set up T-accounts and record the above transactions. Adjust and close the accounts, carrying the process through to the transfer of September's net profit to Retained Earnings.

2. Prepare an income statement for September.

3. Prepare a balance sheet as of September 30.

4. Why is your figure for the profit in September only a rough approximation at best?

CASE 15–4.   LAREN MANUFACTURING COMPANY

In September, Mr. James Laren, Jr., was asked to investigate the possibility of instituting new methods of cost control in the Laren Manufacturing Company, which was owned by his father. Mr. Laren, Sr., keenly felt the need for better cost control because his small plumbing and pipe-fitting equipment firm competed on a price basis with large corporations that were firmly entrenched in the market.

James Laren, Jr., decided to start his investigation in the company's valve department, because this department produced almost one third of the company's total volume of sales. The valve department contained drilling and grinding machines, lathes, welding equipment, and assembly space. In this department all the operations necessary to produce and assemble valves were performed.

The valve department occupied almost one half the total floor space in the Laren company's three-story plant. Section 1, the welding section, was located on the first floor of the plant and occupied about one sixth of the space on that floor. Sections 2, 3, and 4, as well as the office, toolroom and stock room were all located on the third floor. None of these sections occupied more than one fifth of the third floor's space. Section 5, the assembly section, occupied about one half of the second floor and one sixth of the third floor. Exhibit 1 describes the functions of these sections, each of which was under the supervision of a leadman.

Exhibit 1

FUNCTIONS PERFORMED IN VALVE DEPARTMENT

Section 1 Welding	This section repairs casting defects, welds special fittings to valve bodies, and performs other welding operations required in fabrication of valve parts.
Section 2 Grinding	Grinding is done to prepare castings for further machining. Also, various parts which make up valves are ground for precision fit.
Section 3 Machining	All the necessary machining operations to produce various standard valves are done in this section.
Section 4 Special Work	Here, the layout, drilling, tapping, and special machining needed on valves other than the standard line are done.
Section 5 Assembly	This section is responsible for the assembly and testing of all valves produced in the department.

Exhibit 2 indicates the flow of production through the various sections of the valve department. Valves in the standard line went through Sections 1, 2, 3, and 5. Special valves (i.e., valves not in the standard line) went through all five sections. Pieces produced for spare parts inventory did not go through Section 5 (assembly). In addition, any section of the valve department might perform some operations on products for other departments of the Laren Manufacturing Company.

Mr. Laren's investigation showed that all factory costing in the valve department (except material costs) was done on a department-wide, direct-labor-hour basis; that is, each lot of products going through the department was costed at a certain rate for each direct labor hour actually spent on the lot. Exhibit 3 shows the computation made to arrive at the cost figure of $2.88, which was the rate per labor hour in the whole

Exhibit 2

PRODUCTION FLOW THROUGH VALVE DEPARTMENT

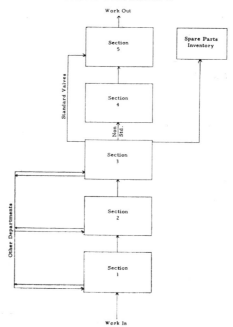

Exhibit 3

CALCULATION OF MANUFACTURING COST PER DIRECT LABOR HOUR IN THE VALVE DEPARTMENT*

(August)

Section	Labor Charge per Month	Burden	Total
1......................	$ 1,535		
2......................	930		
3......................	5,360		
4......................	2,050		
5......................	8,700		
Total...............	$18,575	$30,315	$48,890

Total number of hours worked: 16,970/month
Average hourly charge: $48,890 ÷ 16,970 = $2.88

* Does not include materials.

department in August. Costs were accumulated and allocated to jobs each month.

Mr. Laren, Jr., did not feel that this method of obtaining and apportioning costs was accurate enough. He believed that problems could arise in trying to judge performance and in obtaining the true cost of different products by following this method. He proposed, therefore, that costs be collected monthly for each section of the department and that these costs be apportioned to jobs according to the amount of time spent in each section.

In order to study the effect of this proposal, Mr. Laren recomputed the costs for August so as to show the costs applicable to each section.

Exhibit 4

PROPOSED COST PER DIRECT LABOR HOUR FOR EACH SECTION OF THE VALVE DEPARTMENT*

(August)

Section	Total Hours	Labor Charge per Hour	Burden Charge per Hour	Total Cost per Hour
1....................................	1,370	$1.12	$1.66	$2.78
2....................................	1,000	0.93	1.55	2.48
3....................................	4,000	1.34	3.28	4.62
4....................................	1,800	1.14	2.10	3.24
5....................................	8,800	0.99	1.09	2.08
Total.........................	16,970			

* Does not include materials.

Since direct labor charges were already being collected by sections, no change in procedures was necessary for the collection of labor costs. Some overhead items, such as leadman wages, could be charged directly to the section in which they were incurred. Other overhead charges, such as heating and lighting, were allocated on bases that seemed to Mr. Laren to be reasonable. He divided the total overhead costs charged to each section by the number of labor hours worked in the section, and arrived at costing rates for each section. These are shown in Exhibit 4.

Mr. Laren made the following observations in support of his proposal for revising the costing rates. One of the items produced in largest volume by the department was Valve 301. A standard production run of Valve 301 required the following hours in the different sections of the department:

Section	Hours
1	15
2	10
3	65
5	40

Mr. Laren said that there obviously was a wide difference between the cost for this valve as figured under the present system and the cost as figured under his proposed system. His contention was that the present method led to false conclusions as to the profitability of a line.

Mr. Laren also saw problems in the valuation of the spare parts inventory produced by the valve department. The company produced a wide line of valves, and it was necessary to maintain an inventory of spare parts in order to be able promptly to supply repair parts to customers. The following amounts of time were usually spent on producing spare parts for inventory each month:

Section	Hours
1	160
2	145
3	560

When Mr. Laren's proposal was explained to the heads of the operating departments, it met with immediate and strong opposition. First to voice disapproval were the heads of other departments that had work totaling the following amounts done by the valve department each month:

	Hours
Welding (Section 1)	350
Grinding (Section 2)	250
Machining (Section 3)	1,100

These supervisors thought that is was unfair to change a sizable part of their department's costs, especially since they had no control over the costs incurred in the valve department.

Mr. Ahearn, foreman of the pipe fixture department, was very much against the proposal: "The valve department does the machining work on all the work that my department can't handle. If you raise my costs on this work, I'll never be able sto stay within my budget, because the valve department is already charging me more than I could do the work for in my own department if I had the capacity."

The sales manager was also against the proposal: "If you start monkeying around with our cost system, we'll have to start changing our prices, and we're having enough trouble with price competition from the major companies as it is. After all, our complete valve line is showing a profit. You have to carry some items for sales reasons regardless of their profitability, so why worry about the very small variation in cost between different items."

The foreman of the valve department also opposed the change: "I'm too busy to fool with more paper work. It takes all my time to get the production out without trying to keep up with this stuff, section by section. And my leadmen in the sections don't have time for it either. The department is carrying all its costs now, so why put in an extra gimmick?"

Mr. Laren, Sr., remained neutral on the question. He was most interested in whether or not the added cost and trouble of the proposed system would be justified by the benefits the system would give.

Questions

1. What is the difference in the cost of Valve 301 under the proposed method as compared with that under the present method? In value of spare parts added to inventory each month? In the cost of work done for other departments? Are these cost differences significant?

2. What causes the difference in costs given by the proposed method as compared with the present method?

3. Suppose that the company purchased a new $50,000 machine for Section 4 that both reduced machining time and resulted in higher-quality special valves. As a result, the total time required for valves in Section 4 is reduced by 30 per cent. The extra labor is transferred to other departments. About 10 per cent of the burden in Section 4 is variable with respect to machining time. The engineer's best estimate of the life of the machine is about five years. During August only special valves were worked on in Section 4:

   a) Calculate what the total cost per hour would be after the new machine is in operation if there were only one cost center in the valve department. Assume that operations are the same as actual operations in August in all other respects.

b) Calculate what the total cost per hour would be if Section 4 were a separate cost center.

c) What would happen to the computed costs per month of producing special valves with a single cost center, after purchase of the machine, as compared with the cost before purchase of the machine?

d) What would happen to the computed costs per month of producing special valves with five cost centers, after purchase of the new machine, as compared with the cost before purchase of the machine?

e) What do you conclude about the relative usefulness of the two methods (single cost center versus five cost centers)?

4. What management benefits, if any, would you expect from the proposed system, that is, the allocation and collection of costs by sections? Consider this question from the standpoint of (*a*) product pricing, (*b*) cost control, (*c*) inventory valuation, and (*d*) charges to other departments. Do you think these benefits would outweigh the costs of collection of the necessary data?

CASE 15–5. BEALE COMPANY

Early in November the new president of the Beale Company was eagerly awaiting the completion of the income statement for October. He knew that October sales had exceeded those for September by more than $50,000, and he was anxious to see how much of this increased sales volume was reflected as extra profit. But when the report came in, it showed an overall loss of $5,015. (See Exhibit 1.) In September, profit had been $3,509.

The president immediately thought some mistake had been made and called in the controller for an explanation. The controller said the figures were correct, but that in October the company had not produced anywhere near its normal volume and hence the charge for unabsorbed burden had decreased the profit more than the added sales had increased it. He said that if the rate of sales were always the same as the rate of factory production, the kind of distortion that was bothering the president would not appear. When factory operations were out of phase with sales operations, however, such distortions were almost certain to result, so long as the company followed the commonly practiced accounting convention of charging or crediting periodic under- or overabsorbed factory overhead to the current profit and loss account.

The president reacted strongly to the controller's explanations: "I don't care a hoot for your accounting conventions. But I do know this: when our sales go up, with other things reasonably equal, I expect our profit to increase. If your reports can't show so simple a thing as that, why do we spend so much money on your department?"

As a matter of fact, the controller had been thinking about the problem that disturbed the president. He concluded that the solution was to take a radically different approach to the accounting treatment of overhead, namely, to charge all fixed overhead costs for the month to the current operating statement rather than to absorb them as a part of product costs. If this were done, there would be no problem of heavy over- or underabsorbed overhead as the volume of operations changed. Cost of goods sold would then reflect only the nonfixed factory costs, that is, variable costs, which the controller called "direct costs."

Exhibit 1

BEALE COMPANY

Condensed October Income Statement as Actually Prepared

Sales..	$336,903	
Cost of sales at standard.............................	178,168	
Standard gross margin................................		$158,735
Less: Manufacturing variances:		
Labor...	$ 4,321*	
Material..	3,972	
Overhead:		
Volume...	26,870	
Spending.......................................	1,347	
Net Manufacturing Variances.....................		27,868
Gross profit...		$130,867
Selling costs:		
Selling expenses..................................	$ 84,514	
Sales taxes.......................................	3,236	
Freight allowed...................................	7,195	
Total Selling Costs.............................		94,945
Operating profit before administration costs...........		$ 35,922
Administrative costs:		
General administrative expenses....................	$ 20,640	
Research expenses................................	5,879	
Total Administrative Costs......................		26,519
Operating profit.....................................		$ 9,403
Other income or charges.............................		14,418
Loss, Current Month................................		$ 5,015

* Credit variance.

As an illustration of how his proposal would work out, the controller reworked the company's figures for October with the startling result that instead of a loss of $5,015, the statement showed a profit of $11,028. (See Exhibit 2.) When this revised statement was shown to the president, he first exclaimed, "That's more like it." Then he hesitated and started to speculate: "But this means more taxes and more demands for wage increases and dividends and what-all. Maybe your idea isn't so good after all."

The controller was in favor of the new plan largely because of its simplified accounting procedures. For one thing there would be no fixed overhead costs in the standard cost figures for different products but only the three classes of direct costs: (*a*) raw materials, (*b*) direct labor, and (*c*) the portion of the outlay for manufacturing expenses which varied directly with productive activity. Omission of fixed overhead costs from the individual product costs would mean that the vexing and expensive task of working out an acceptable allocation of overhead to each product would be unnecessary. Inasmuch as many of these prorations had in fact become out of date, the controller was further attracted to his plan by the possibility that the expense of the needed overhauling of the figures might be avoided.

Exhibit 2

BEALE COMPANY

Condensed October Income Statement, Proposed Style

Sales		$336,903	
Standard "variable" cost of sales		123,133	
Gross margin above variable costs			$213,770
Selling expenses		$ 84,514	
Sales taxes		3,236	
Freight allowed		7,195	
Total Selling Expenses			94,945
Merchandising margin			$118,825
Administrative expenses:			
General administrative expenses		$ 20,640	
Research expenses		5,879	
Total Administrative Expenses			26,519
Additional factory expenses:			
Fixed factory overhead		$ 65,862	
Manufacturing variances:			
Labor variance	$4,321*		
Material variance	3,972		
Overhead variance (spending)	1,347	998	66,860
Operating margin			$ 25,446
Other income or charges			14,418
Profit, Current Month			$ 11,028

* Credit variance.

The controller also believed the proposed system would greatly increase management's focus on the *controllable* portion of costs by spotlighting the variable elements. Since the fixed costs pertaining to factory operations tend to fall into quite a different category from that of the variable costs, he thought they should be segregated anyway. By way of analogy he suggested that, like a retail store, a manufacturing company "purchases" its product for a known "direct cost." Consequently the chief difference between the two kinds of business is that to make a profit the manufacturing company has to pay the fixed factory costs in addition to the selling salaries, administration costs, storage, etc. Furthermore, the fixed factory costs are like the occupancy costs (rent, maintenance, etc.) of a retail store. On such a basis the factory's direct costs, that is, variable costs, are similar to the retail store's cost of purchases.

The controller argued that a further advantage of his proposal would be the provision of a more satisfactory basis for making the usual monthly comparison of margin figures in the company's product-by-product gross margin statement. When recast in the new form, with fixed costs excluded, the figures would be much more meaningful. The new margin figures would be much higher all down the line, but the controller was confident that once the management adjusted its thinking to the new basis, the value of knowing how much each product was contributing to fixed costs and profit would be greatly appreciated.

One of the sales executives supported the controller's argument on the usefulness of the new margin figures. He pointed out that if there were two products sold by one of his divisions, Products A and B, and if the situation were as described in the following example, Product B would clearly *appear to be* the more desirable item to sell:

Product	Total Factory Cost per Pound (Std.)	Selling Price	Margin	Percentage of Sales
A..........	$0.897	$1.55	$0.653	42.1
B..........	1.015	1.80	0.785	43.6

If, however, the new margin figures were to work out something as follows, then Product A was by all odds the product on which the company's selling effort really should be concentrated:

Product	Variable Factory Cost	Selling Price	New Margin	Percentage of Sales
A..........	$0.413	$1.55	$1.137	73.6
B..........	0.809	1.80	0.991	55.6

The controller's proposed method of keeping records, the sales executive reasoned, would thus reveal the true opportunities for profit. He cited one company he knew that had adopted a system similar to that proposed by the controller and had so redirected its selling effort that in less than eight months it had shifted from an operating loss to an operating profit and had maintained good profits ever since.

At this point in the discussion the treasurer entered the argument. He observed, cynically, that the first thing anyone knew, the sales department, in its efforts to get business, would be selling at its usual markup over the new standard cost figures (variable costs only). "When that time comes," he snorted, "how are we going to cover the fixed costs? Where do we get our capital replacements? We'll have to pay the piper sooner or later."

Turning to the controller, who had talked of the desired focus of the new system on variable costs, the treasurer gave as his opinion, based on long experience, that it was the lack of control of the long-run costs that really wrecked a company. "You can make mistakes on the direct costs," he said, "but because things in this area are constantly changing and because one never makes much of a commitment anyway, the life of the company is really not seriously hurt. If necessary, a new management could quickly reverse the trend. But once a company lets the long-run costs get out of control, then the fat really is in the fire. I'm opposed to anything that leads us to take a shortsighted view of cost." To this argument the controller had little to say, except that it was a matter of emphasis, and that he still thought the variable costs the more important.[9]

All the group discussing the proposal were aware of the effect of the controller's scheme on the inventory item in the balance sheet. The treasurer, and the president too, were worried about this effect, and both wondered if the possible improvement to the operating statement was worth the price of distorting the balance sheet. The controller proposed that a footnote be carried in the balance sheet calling attention to the matter, and perhaps indicating the extent of the distortion.

When one of the officials asked about the income tax implications, the controller pointed out that the tax return was a special report, that it already differed from the company's operating reports in several respects, and that the reports he was suggesting were monthly profit estimates largely for internal use and not annual reports. Furthermore, if the company wished to do so, it could have the annual reports computed on the more orthodox basis. "But," he insisted, "let's make these monthly reports so that they help us, not handicap us."

Balance sheets for the company are shown in Exhibit 3, together with an indication of how the balance sheet figures would appear had the company used the direct cost method. Income statements for September, under both the present and proposed methods, are shown in Exhibit 4.

---

[9] In the preceding year, variable costs were 67 per cent of total costs.

In this exhibit, nomenclature and arrangement have been changed somewhat in order to facilitate comparison between the present and proposed systems.

Exhibit 3

BEALE COMPANY

Condensed Balance Sheets as Actually Prepared

	As of September 30	As of October 31
ASSETS		
Current Assets:		
Cash	$ 80,560	$ 95,553
Accounts receivable	150,428	178,610
Inventory	573,630	521,822
Total Current Assets	$ 804,618	$ 795,985
Plant and equipment (net)	2,120,450	2,108,788
Total Assets	$2,925,068	$2,904,773
LIABILITIES AND NET WORTH		
Current liabilities	$ 397,480	$ 382,200
Mortgage payable	560,000	560,000
Total Liabilities	$ 957,480	$ 942,200
Net Worth:		
Capital stock	$1,000,000	$1,000,000
Retained earnings	967,588	962,573
Total Net Worth	$1,967,588	$1,962,573
Total Liabilities and Net Worth	$2,925,068	$2,904,773

Effect of "Direct Cost" Method

Had the Beale Company used the direct cost method, its balance sheets would appear as above except for the inventory and retained earnings items. These would appear as shown below:

	As of September 30	As of October 31
Inventory	$401,541	$365,776
Retained earnings	795,499	806,527

Note: In both present and proposed statements, the effect of income taxes is not shown. The Beale Company recorded estimated income tax expense only at the end of the calendar year.

Questions

1. What do you recommend?

2. Approximately how busy (relative to normal volume) was the factory in October?

3. Could the problem in the case ever arise with respect to annual statements of profit?

Exhibit 4

BEALE COMPANY

Condensed Income Statement, September

	As Actually Prepared	Under Proposed Method
Sales	$283,028	$283,028
Cost of sales at standard	152,604	104,662
Gross margin	$130,424	$178,366
Less: Manufacturing variances:		
Labor	$ 5,426*	$ 5,426*
Material	5,081	5,081
Overhead:		
Volume	447*	......
Spending	2,173	2,173
Fixed factory overhead	......	65,862
Subtotal Overhead and Variances	$ 1,381	$ 67,690
Profit before administrative and selling expenses	$129,043	$110,676
Selling expenses (total)	$ 85,482	$ 85,482
Administrative expenses (total)	26,026	26,026
Total Administrative and Selling Expenses	$111,508	$111,508
Operating profit	$ 17,535	($ 832)
Other income or charges	14,026	14,026
Net Profit or (Loss) Current Month	$ 3,509	($ 14,858)

* Credit variance.

CASE 15–6. BLACK METER COMPANY

After his graduation from college, Richard Harrington was employed in the cost department of the Black Meter Company. His duties purposely were made light during the first few days so that he could have time to acquaint himself with the company in general and its cost system in particular. He had been taken on a complete plant trip before having been hired, and he had had a chance to see most of the operations again in the early days of his employment. Also, the assistant controller, Mr. Miller, who was his immediate supervisor, had spent several hours describing the Black cost system to him.

By combining the information gained from these trips and conversations, Mr. Harrington acquired the information summarized below. He expected that Mr. Miller would, in the near future, ask for his opinion about the cost system.

Product

The Black Meter Company manufactured water meters in one standard design but in a wide range of sizes for industrial and residential applications. The water meters installed in the basements of most homes are an example of its product. The meters consisted basically of a hard rubber piston that was put in motion by the flow of water past it, a gear train that reduced this motion and registered it on a dial, and two heavy bronze castings which were bolted together around the measuring device.

Production

The company was organized into several functional departments to manufacture almost all the parts for these meters. The casings and many interior parts were cast in the foundry and then were sent to one of the three machining departments, depending upon their size. The machining departments were equipped with most of the machines which are common to the metalworking industry. Many of the finished parts were sent to a subassembly department to be subassembled into gear trains. The other parts went directly to the meter assembly departments. There were also several departments that provided service to the producing departments.

The Standard Cost System

In describing the cost system to Mr. Harrington, Mr. Miller said:

The Black Meter Company uses a standard cost system to control costs and to obtain monthly operating statements. The basic difference between this standard cost system and an actual cost system lies in the way we value our inventories, from raw materials to finished goods. In an actual cost system the debits for the amounts of materials, direct labor, and manufacturing overhead added to the inventories are made at actual cost. In a standard cost system like ours, normal or standard costs are established for these elements, and every debit to the inventory account is made at standard cost. The fact that all the inventory items are valued at standard costs allows us to forget about the actual cost of every item, thereby greatly simplifying the accounting procedure.

During the month, actual costs are accumulating. Material is purchased, workers are paid, manufacturing overhead items, such as water or electricity, are purchased and paid for at actual cost. But the *values* of these items are debited into inventory at predetermined standard costs for each cost factor. Often the actual cost varies from the standard costs, and this fact causes variations that we journalize and post to variance accounts. At the end of a month we examine the variations between actual and standard; consequently, we are able to control costs by focusing our attention on these variances, or *exceptions,* rather than on the bulk of the cost data.

Setting Up Standard Costs

The first step in setting up standard costs in this company was to establish a standard cost for every type of material that was purchased.

This was done by adjusting the current market price for any irregularities that might not be expected to continue for the following year. For example, if copper at the end of a year cost 30 cents a pound and no change was predicted, the standard cost for copper for the next year would be 30 cents a pound. The same procedure was followed for every purchased item.

Having established standard costs for all materials, the accountants next calculated standard rates for direct labor and manufacturing overhead. They did this on a departmental basis, and set up the rates to be applied according to the number of standard direct labor hours incurred in the processing of each product.

From each department they obtained data for the past few years on the actual direct labor payroll and the number of direct labor hours worked. On the basis of these data and from estimates of future conditions, the accountants selected a figure for total labor cost and a figure of hours worked under normal conditions of activity in each department. By dividing this payroll figure by the normal number of hours, they obtained a standard direct labor rate per standard direct labor hour for each department.

The same type of calculations was made to determine standard manufacturing overhead rates for each department. The procedure was complicated by the necessity of allocating all service department costs to the producing departments. The first step had been to calculate from past records the total cost of each of the service departments at normal volume. Then various methods were used to allocate the service department costs to the producing departments. For example, the total cost of the boiler room was allocated to the producing departments according to the number of square feet of floor space taken up by each. The maintenance department expense was allocated on the basis of the number of hours the maintenance men normally worked for each producing department.

After the cost of the service departments had been allocated to the producing departments, it was necessary to calculate the manufacturing overhead costs that normally were incurred within each producing department. The sum of the allocated and the internal costs gave the total manufacturing overhead cost for each department under normal conditions. These totals were divided by the standard number of direct labor hours for each producing department, the same totals that had been used in calculating the labor rate. In this way, a manufacturing overhead rate per standard direct labor hour was obtained for each department, as shown in Exhibit 1.

The next step in setting up this standard cost system was to apply the standard rates to each of the items manufactured. This was accomplished on the manufacturing orders, examples of which can be seen in Exhibits 2 through 5. The part described was a ⅝ inch chamber ring that was manufactured for assembly into a ⅝ inch HF meter. The standard costs of most parts were calculated on the basis of 100 pieces.

Exhibit 1

STANDARD RATES EFFECTIVE JANUARY 1

Depart-ment No.	Department Name	Labor	Burden	Total Rate
103	Carpenter and pattern shop	$2.06	$1.07	$3.13/hour
104	Toolroom	2.35	1.26	3.61/hour
108	Pattern storage	--	--	0.02/pound
120A	Foundry -- molding	2.50	3.78	6.28/hour
120B	Foundry -- grinding and snagging	1.50	0.90	2.40/hour
122	Small parts manufacture	1.72	1.38	3.10/hour
123	Interior parts manufacture	1.68	1.73	3.41/hour
124	Case manufacture	1.98	4.02	6.00/hour
125	Plating -- rack	--	--	2.50/100 pcs.
130	Train, register, and interior assembly	1.70	1.97	3.67/hour
131	Small meter assembly	1.50	2.01	3.51/hour
132	Large meter assembly	1.90	3.98	5.88/hour
133	Meter testing	2.11	1.56	3.67/hour
134	Meter repair	1.50	1.66	3.16/hour

Exhibit 2

FOUNDRY ORDER											
Drawing No. X-2408			Part 5/8" HF Chamber Rings				Deliveries to Stores		Order No.		
Material Gov't Bronze 100 Pieces 91.0# At 0.3265/#							$29.712				
									Quantity Ordered		
Weight			Plating			Econ. Lot		Pattern Cost 0.02	$1.82		
Rate Number	Std.Man Hrs.Per 100 Pcs.	Std. Basic Rate	Prod. Center	Opr. No.	Operation and Tools		Machine	Man No.	Std. Rate /Hr.	Man No.	Total Cost	Total
	1.76		120 A	1	Mold		Match Plate		6.28		11.053	
	.45		120 B	2	Grind		Wheel		2.40		1.08	
	.68		120 B	3	Snag		Bench		2.40		1.632	
											$45.297	

The standard material cost was figured in the second line of the foundry order (Exhibit 2). These parts were cast from government bronze that had a standard cost of $0.3265 a pound. Since the standard weight of 100 pieces was 91 pounds, the standard material cost was $29.712 as shown in the deliveries-to-stores box. The $0.020 figure in the pattern cost box was a standard pattern cost per pound which resulted in a $1.82 standard pattern charge.

In order to apply the standard direct labor and manufacturing overhead rates to any part, it was necessary to calculate the standard time

Exhibit 3

RR-7					PARTS ORDER				
Drawing No. X-2408			Part 5/8" HF Chamber Rings				Deliveries to Stores	Order No.	
Plating H.T. & E.T.			Material Gov't Bronze 100 Pieces 89#		W'gt per 100		$45.297	Quantity Ordered	
Econ. Lot 2,000					L'gth per 100		Date Wanted		

Rate Number	Hours per 100 pc. St'd	Hours per 100 pc. All'w'd	Set-up St'd	Prod. C't'r	Opr. No.	Operation and Tools	Machine	Man No.	Std. Rate /Hr.	Total
0.75				122	1	Broach out let #734	P.P.		3.10	2.325
0.55				123	2	Finish tap plate bore & face	Heald		3.41	1.876
0.93				123		Drill 6 holes	Drill		3.41	3.171
0.47				123	3	C-Sink 3 holes tap plate side	Drill		3.41	1.603
0.17				123		Tap 3 holes tap plate side	Heskins		3.41	0.560
5.00				123	4	Rough & finish inside & outside	Heald		3.41	17.050
0.20				123		C-Sink 3 holes on bottom	Drill		3.41	0.682
0.30				123	5	Tap 3 holes on bottom	Drill		3.41	1.023
0.47				123		Spline inside	Spliner		3.41	1.603
0.50				123	6	Spline outside	Miller		3.41	1.705
5.80				123		Dress	Bench		3.41	19.778
					7					96.673

Exhibit 4

ASSEMBLY ORDER

Drawing No. 2400		Assembly 5/8" Disc Interior				Sheet No. of				
Used on Assemblies of 5/8' HF & HD Meters						Order No.				
Parts of Assembly		Delivered	Parts of Assembly		Delivered	Quantity Ordered				
K-2408 Chamber Ring		96.673								
K-2414 Chamber Top Plate		43.550				Date Ordered				
K-2418 Chamber Bot. Plate		40.120								
X-2465 Disc Piston Assem.		79.010				Date Wanted				
K-2422 Disc Chbr. Diaphragm		3.660								
			K-4521 Chamber Screws (6)		7.000	Deliveries to Stores				

Rate Number	Std. Man Hrs. Per 100 Pcs.	Std. Basic Rate	Prod. Center	Oper. No.	Operation and Tools	Machine	Man No.	Std. Rate /Hr.	Total No.	Total Cost	Total
2.6			130	1	Assemble Top Plate to Ring	Bench		3.67		9.542	
0.9			130	2	Fit Abutment for Interior	Bench		3.67		3.303	
1.1			130	3	Mill & Scrape Diaphragm for Interior	Bench		3.67		4.037	
3.9			130	4	File Diaphragm Slots in Piston	Bench		3.67		14.313	
											301.208

needed to perform the operations to make that part. This task was simplified for the Black Meter Company because all operations had been time-studied. Using the results of the time studies, the accountants could fill in the first column of the foundry order. For example, the standard time to mold 100 chamber rings was 1.76 hours, to grind them 0.45 hours, and to snag them 0.68 hours. In the first column of figures on the right-hand side of the foundry order, the combined standard direct labor and manufacturing overhead (i.e., burden) rate per standard direct labor hour was recorded for the department in which the operation took place. For example, Exhibit 1 shows the labor and burden rate for molding in Department 120A as $6.28 per standard man-hour. This amount appeared on the foundry order for the molding operation, and multiplied by the standard time gave a standard cost of labor and burden of $11.053. The same procedure was followed for the three foundry operations, and the total standard foundry cost of 100 chamber rings was $45.297.

Exhibit 3 traces these 100 chamber rings through the interior parts manufacture department. They entered the parts department at the standard cost of $45.297—the same cost with which they left the foundry. After 11 operations had been performed on them, they became finished chamber rings with a standard cost of $96.673. As shown in Exhibits 4 and 5 these parts were assembled into ⅝ inch HF disc interiors, and finally, into the ⅝ inch meters. The total cost of the meters was $850.506.

Exhibit 5

ASSEMBLY ORDER

Drawing No. 2735			Assembly	5/8" HF Meter ET FB				Sheet No. of		
Used on Assemblies of								Order No.		
Parts of Assembly			Delivered	Parts of Assembly			Delivered	Quantity Ordered		
2761 Top Case			170.60	K-5030 5/8 HF Dur. Bolt (6)			32.880			
K-2776 Casing Gasket			3.25	K-4630 5/8 HF ac Nut (6)			25.440			
X-2770 Bottom Case			50.14	K-5068 5/8 HF Washers (6)			10.140	Date Ordered		
2779 Casing Strainer			6.95	2782 Chamber Pin			1.966			
3209 5/8 Closed Train			200.01	6172 Misc. Train Conn.			7.120			
2400 5/8 HF Int. Assem.			301.208					Date Wanted		
2412 5/8 HF Sand Plate			5.00							
								Deliveries to Stores		

Rate Number	Std. Man Hrs. Per 100 Pcs.	Std. Basic Rate	Prod. Center	Oper. No.	Operation and Tools	Machine	Man No.	Std. Rate /Hr.	Man No.	Total Cost	Total
4.6			131	1	Assem. Train & Strainer to Case	Bench		3.51		16.146	
5.6			131	2	Assem. Int. & Bottom to Meter			3.51		19.656	
										850.506	

In the same manner, standard costs had been calculated for all the meter sizes that the Black Meter Company manufactured. These standards were revised annually to recognize any significant changes in the costs of labor, materials, or overhead.

Accounting Entries

While talking about the uses of the standard cost system, Mr. Miller said: "Once the standards have been established, all material, direct labor, and manufacturing overhead are charged into the Inventory account at standard costs that do not change. This means that actual costs need only be collected in total for the period, and the actual cost of each individual item in inventory is forgotten. Therefore, the controlling of costs becomes a relatively simple matter."

Material. As soon as any material was purchased, the standard cost of that material was penciled on the vendor's invoice. Each purchase was journalized in an invoice and check register containing columns in which to credit the actual cost of the material to Accounts Payable, to debit an inventory account for the standard cost, and to debit or credit the difference to a variance account called "Purchase Loss or Gain." The company had a single inventory account in its general ledger which lumped together raw materials, work in process, and finished goods inventory; therefore no accounting entry was made when material was issued for use in production.

Exhibit 6

INCENTIVE JOB CARD

MACH. NO.	PROD. CENTER 130	QUANTITY ORDERED 3000 3000	ORDER NUMBER 2I - 86572 1 I- 86572			CLOCK NO. 337
TOTAL FIN. 1250 3000	PART NAME	5/8 " Cl. Trains.				
PREV. QUAN. FIN. 0 1150	OPR. NO. 9	OPERATION NAME Finish Assem.				
QUAN. FINISHED 1250 1850	STD. HOURS PER 100 1 75	STD. HOURS 54 25	STD. RATE 1 70	STANDARD LABOR 92 23		
QUAN. FINISHED 3,100	ALL'D HOURS PER 100 1 75	ALL'D HOURS 54 25	INCENTIVE JOB CARD			NAME
Sept. 20	STOP 40.0	ACTUAL HOURS 40 0	D.W. RATE 1 65	EARNINGS 89 51		
Sept. 20	START 00.0	FOREMAN		GAIN OR LOSS 2 72		

Labor. The basic document for controlling direct labor costs was the incentive job card. Each productive employee filled out a card for each order on which he worked during the week. The card reproduced as Exhibit 6 shows that Mr. Harris had worked all week on one order so that he had turned in only one card for that week. On the card he recorded the quantity finished, the actual hours worked, and the allowed hours, which were usually the same as the standard hours. A payroll clerk entered each employee's daywork rate, the standard direct labor rate for that department, and extended the actual and standard direct labor cost of the work completed.

By totaling all the incentive job cards, the payroll clerk obtained the actual wages accrued for each employee in each department, and the standard labor cost of the work done in each department. He credited accrued wages for the actual amount to set up the liability and debited the Inventory account for the standard amount of direct labor. The variance was closed out to a Direct Labor variance account.

Manufacturing Overhead. The method of handling manufacturing overhead was very similar in each department. A cost clerk multiplied the standard direct labor hours worked by the manufacturing overhead rate for that department (Exhibit 1) to obtain the amount of manufacturing overhead to be absorbed by the department that month. He debited the Inventory account for the total amount of the absorbed manufacturing overhead. During the month actual manufacturing overhead expenses had been accumulating in the invoice and check register and in various adjusting entries. The difference between the sum of the actual expenses and the absorbed manufacturing overhead cost was the under- or overabsorbed manufacturing overhead variance, which was closed to the overhead variance accounts.

Exhibit 7

CARBON COPY OF SALES INVOICE

Village of Vernon, Att. Village Clerk, Vernon, N.Y.	41740 NY 931	9/11/-- 9/10/--			
Village of Vernon, Water Dept., Att: E. J. Blackburn, Mayor Vernon, N.Y.	7/31/-- 8/13/--	Boston			
STIBBS	Prepaid				
10	5/8 x 3/4 Model HF Meters SG SH ET FB & 3/4"		21.80	218.00	
		Cons.			
	#3015331-340				
		40%		130.80	
1	Charge Gear #46X -- shipped 8-10-		.25		
	Plus 10%		.03	.28	131.08
		Meters		130.80	85.05
		Parts		.28	.18
	Ship gear by P. Post				

When these transactions had been made, all material, direct labor, and manufacturing overhead were charged into the Inventory account at standard cost, and three variance accounts were debited or credited for the difference between actual and standard.

A physical inventory was taken every six months, and was valued at standard cost. Any difference between this figure and the total value of the inventory as shown in the Inventory account was debited or credited to an Inventory Adjustment variance account.

Cost of Sales. Before monthly operating statements could be prepared, a cost clerk had to make an analysis of sales for the month. A duplicate copy of each invoice was sent to the cost office where a clerk entered in pencil the standard cost of the items sold (see Exhibit 7). At the end of the month the cost clerk simply totaled the figures on these duplicate invoices to get figures for sales and the standard cost of those sales for the month. The standard cost of sales was a credit to the Inventory account and a debit to the Cost of Sales account. The total sales amount was a credit to Sales and a debit to Accounts Receivable. When this work had been completed, the cost department was in a position to obtain the monthly income statements (see Exhibit 8) by closing the ledger.

Exhibit 8

BLACK METER COMPANY

Income Statement
Six Months Ending June 30

Sales..		$3,148,234.13
Less: Cash discounts.........................		3,030.13
Net sales....................................		$3,145,204.00
Standard cost...............................	$2,045,127.63	
Variances...................................	118,080.55*	2,163,208.18
Gross manufacturing profit...................		$ 981,995.82
Selling expense..............................		504,032.35
Operating profit.............................		$ 477,963.47
Administrative expense.......................		108,236.76
Adjusted operating profit....................		$ 369,726.71
Nonoperating profit..........................		6,415.93
Net Profit...................................		$ 376,142.64

* Variances

Deductions from gross profit:	
Direct labor variance................................	$ 26,389.14
Factory burden unabsorbed...........................	48,137.61
Material price variance..............................	39,298.01
Unused space and equipment.........................	210.00
Inventory adjustments...............................	12,875.30
Loss due to changes in manufacturing methods........	10,146.50
Total Deductions................................	$ 137,056.56
Additions to gross profit:	
Cash discounts taken................................	$ 9,699.60
Gain from sale or salvage............................	9,276.41
Total Additions.................................	$ 18,976.01
Net Variances.......................................	$ 118,080.55

Questions

1. Assuming that you were Mr. Harrington, what evaluation would you have made of the standard cost system employed by the Black Meter Company?

Would you have agreed with the statements made by Mr. Miller to the effect that this system made the controlling of costs "a relatively simple matter"?

2. What questions concerning this cost system would you have wished to ask Mr. Miller at your next conversation with him?

Exhibit 9

FLOW CHART

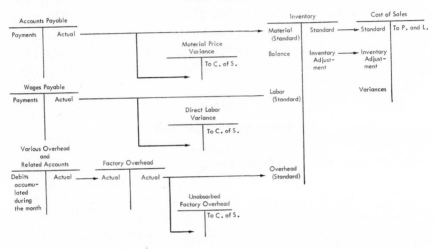

CASE 15–7. CRAIK VENEER COMPANY

The sales manager of the Craik Veneer Company received from the Groton Company an offer to buy 1,000,000 feet per month of sound "backs" of $\frac{1}{24}''$ birch veneer[10] at $8 per thousand surface feet. The sales manager wanted to accept the offer, but the production manager argued that it should not be accepted because the cost of production was at least $10 per thousand feet and probably more.

The Craik company manufactured rotary cut birch veneer from high-grade yellow birch logs bought in Vermont. Selected sections called "blocks" were cut out of those logs, the length of the block varying from 84 inches to 98 inches, depending on the length along the grain of the veneer being produced. These blocks, as cut for the lathe, cost an average of $200 per thousand board feet. A thousand board feet, log measure, was an amount of logs which being sawed would produce a thousand board feet of lumber. (A board foot is one square foot one inch thick.) After being cut, the blocks were put in vats filled with hot water

---

[10] Veneer is a term applied to thin leaves or layers of wood. Generally veneer is made of valuable wood and is laid over a core of inferior wood.

and left there for 24 to 48 hours until the entire log was heated through.

Manufacturing Process

In the rotary veneer process, a block was put in a lathe in which a knife longer than the block, with a heavy frame, guide bars, and pressure bars, was brought against the side of the block so that it cut off a thin slice of wood the entire length of the block. The process was similar to unrolling a large roll of paper held on a horizontal shaft. The process could be controlled with skillful operation so it would produce veneer of uniform thickness. The Craik company produced principally $\frac{1}{24}$ inch veneer, and for the purposes of this case it may be assumed that all of its product was $\frac{1}{24}$ inch.

The sheet of veneer from the lathe, for instance from a 98-inch block, was brought onto a clipping table approximately 60 feet long. This table had rubber belts on its upper surface which moved the veneer along to the clipper. At this point the veneer was like a long sheet of paper moving along the table, the veneer being 98 inches along the grain. The clipper was a long knife extending entirely across the table. The clipper operator was one of the most highly skilled men in the plant. Constantly inspecting the sheet of veneer, he first took one cut to get a straight edge. If the next section of the sheet was of high quality, he advanced the sheet not over 3 feet 8 inches, depending on customers' requirements. If the sheet showed a defect within 3 feet 8 inches, he made his cut just short of the defect. A man called the "off bearer" piled these sheets on a hand truck reserved for high-grade or "face" veneer. If the defect was a knot, the clipper operator then advanced the sheet enough to clear the knot and took another cut, making a piece of waste possibly 3 inches wide. If he decided that a section of the sheet was not of face quality, he cut it off for "backs," either 3 feet 8 inches or in lesser widths. Backs were put on another hand truck.

The clipper operator thus separated the whole sheet of veneer into faces, backs, and waste. The faces consisted of pieces of veneer 98 inches long along the grain and anywhere from 6 inches to 3 feet 8 inches wide. The sound backs were of the same size. The waste went to a chipper and was then burned. The term "faces" came from the fact that these veneer sheets were substantially perfect and could be used on the exposed parts of furniture or on the best face of plywood.[11] The backs had minor

---

[11] Veneer is a single thin sheet of wood. Plywood consists of several sheets (three, five, or nine) glued together with the grain of alternate courses at right angles to add to the strength.

defects and were so called because they were used on the back of plywood panels. The quality required for faces was established by specifications and by the custom of the industry. The dividing line between sound backs and waste was similarly established. The Craik company had a reputation for using high-grade logs and for producing a high grade of veneer both on faces and backs.

Groton Company's Offer

The Groton Company's research and development department had developed two new lines of furniture, one in blond modern and one in colonial, in which the table tops, dresser tops and panels, drawer fronts, and other exposed parts were of birch veneer over lower-grade birch or poplar cores, with table legs, dresser frames, etc., of solid birch. The Groton research people knew that while all sheets of backs contained defects, 50 to 60 per cent of the area of backs as produced by Craik were of face quality. They had discovered that by buying backs 84 inches to 98 inches long they could cut clear face quality veneer in lengths that would match their use requirements: enough 54 inches for their longest dresser tops and enough of other lengths down to 14-inch drawer fronts. The remainder of the veneer that was not of face quality could be used for such purposes as making plywood for drawer bottoms. The methods developed in the research department had been tested by cutting up several carloads of backs bought from Craik and by the manufacture and sale of the furniture.

On the basis of this experience the Groton Company offered Craik $8 per thousand feet for 1,000,000 feet per month of sound backs in $\frac{1}{24}$ inch birch veneer for the next 12 months.

Cost Information

The Craik company cut an average of 12,000 board feet of logs a day in one eight-hour shift. With the high quality of logs it bought, it got a yield of 18,000 surface feet of $\frac{1}{24}$ inch veneer per 1,000 board feet cut; this graded on the average 50 per cent faces and 50 per cent backs.

Labor and factory overhead costs together averaged $8 per thousand surface feet of veneer; selling costs averaged $1.50. Both the cost of the blocks and operating costs for the heating, lathe turning, and clipping operations were joint costs; backs had to be produced in order to get the faces. The remaining operations in drying, a slight amount of reclipping, storing, and shipping were in a sense separate costs as the operations were done on backs separately, although with the same equipment. The labor and factory overhead costs through clipping averaged $6.75 per

1,000 surface feet of veneer; those for drying and later operations, $1.25.

The selling price for $\frac{1}{24}$ inch birch faces 84 inches to 98 inches long was $40 per thousand surface feet. Face veneer 84 inches to 98 inches had a high price because it could be used on large surfaces such as flush birch doors that require lengths up to eight feet. The shorter veneer in length along the grain, made from recutting backs, had a somewhat lower price because it could not be used for these purposes. Unlike faces, the price of backs fluctuated widely. Sometimes Craik could get $10 per thousand feet, but the insistence of the production manager on $10 had led to the accumulation of a heavy inventory of backs. Faces were easy to sell and were shipped substantially as fast as they were produced.

More effort was required to sell backs than to sell faces, although both were sold to the same customers by the same salesmen. Sometimes buyers of faces were required to take a percentage of backs in order to get a carload of faces. For these reasons the offer of the customer was attractive to the sales manager.

Discussion of Offer

When the production manager was first informed by the sales manager of the offer of $8 per thousand surface feet, the production manager contended that "your salesmen are so lazy, they would give veneer away if nobody watched them." The production manager went on to say: "If a birch block cost $200 per thousand and we get 18,000 feet of $\frac{1}{24}$ inch thick veneer from every thousand board feet of the block, the cost of the block to be allocated to a thousand feet of veneer, whether backs or faces, is $200 divided by 18,000 feet, or about $11.11 per thousand feet. Simple arithmetic proves that selling backs at $8 per thousand doesn't even pay for the material, let alone labor and overhead."

The sales manager countered that this argument was fallacious. "Allocating the cost of the block to the veneer in this manner," he said, "implies that backs are as valuable as faces, which is not the case. The $11.11 material figure for a thousand feet of veneer that you get is merely an average of the value of faces and backs. The material for faces is worth considerably more per thousand feet than this figure; the material for backs is worth considerably less."

The sales manager suggested that the proper procedure was to allocate the cost of the block to faces and backs in proportion to the amounts for which the products were sold. Using this method, the ratio that the revenue of one of the two grades of veneer bore to the revenue received from both grades of veneer would be applied to the total cost of the block, the result representing the cost to be allocated to that particular grade. To illustrate this method, assume a block of a thousand board feet cost $200, and the selling prices and quantities of faces and backs are as shown in the following table:

Grade	1/24 Inch Veneer in Feet	Sales Revenue per 1,000 Feet 1/24 Inch Veneer	Net Value	Per Cent of Total	Cost Applicable to Each Product
Faces.........	9,000	$40	$360	83.3%	$166.67
Backs........	9,000	8	72	16.6	33.33
	18,000		$432	100.0%	$200.00

The material cost applicable to each product, then, per thousand feet of 1/24 inch veneer would be $166.67/9,000 feet × 1,000 feet, or $18.52, for faces; and $33.33/9,000 feet × 1,000 feet, or $3.70, for backs.

The production manager again argued that this did not represent the true material cost, which was the same for both products, and added, "Under your method the material cost allocated to either faces or backs would be a function of their relative selling prices. If the selling price of faces fell from $40 per thousand to $20 per thousand and the price of backs remained the same, you would then charge much more material costs to backs, and much less to faces. Your method of allocating cost doesn't make sense."

The sales manager, at this point said, "O.K., if you don't think that method is justified, then let's treat backs as a by-product. I think you'll agree that we would prefer to be making faces all the time, yet we can't. As long as we manufacture faces, we're going to produce backs as an undesirable consequence. Now if we consider backs as a by-product, we can charge all block costs to faces. The net proceeds from the sale of backs, after allowing for all conversion, selling and administrative expenses, can be credited to the raw material cost of faces. All profits and losses of the business would be borne by the main product."

The production manager, however, pointed out again that the cost of material allocated to faces would still be a function of the selling price of backs and, furthermore, there would be some difficulty in trying to value inventories at the end of an accounting period, and that any profits arising from the sale of backs would be hidden since it would be included in the credit to faces. "It is important to determine the profit or loss being realized on the sale of backs so we can establish a firm sales policy," he said.

Because of their inability to resolve this question, the production manager and the sales manager consulted the president of the Craik Veneer Company who, in turn, asked the controller to examine the cost situation to determine whether the $8 per thousand surface feet of $\frac{1}{24}$ inch backs would, or would not, result in a profit.

Questions

1. As controller, what method of allocating raw material costs would you recommend? What similarities and differences would be encountered in allocating labor and overhead costs as compared to material costs?

2. Should the sales manager accept the $8 per thousand feet offer that he received for the $\frac{1}{24}$ inch backs?

3. If a group of blocks containing 1,000 board feet costs $205, what would be the cost applicable to faces and backs under each of the methods of allocating costs described in the case, and other methods that you may devise, if the following conditions existed:

a) The current market price of $\frac{1}{24}$ inch faces is $40 per thousand feet, $\frac{1}{24}$ inch backs are currently selling at $9 per thousand.

b) 10,000 feet of $\frac{1}{24}$ inch faces and 8,000 feet of $\frac{1}{24}$ inch backs were produced from a group of blocks.

c) Factory labor and overhead cost averaged $8 per thousand feet of veneer ($6.75 for operations through clipping and $1.25 for drying and later operations). Selling costs averaged $1.50 per thousand feet of veneer. If backs were not manufactured (i.e., if they were treated the same as waste), labor, overhead, and selling costs amounting to roughly $2.00 per thousand feet of backs might be saved.

Chapter 16

CHARACTERISTICS OF COST

IN THIS chapter we discuss some concepts and techniques that are useful when one is studying the behavior of costs, either for the purpose of estimating what costs will be in the future or for the purpose of analyzing recorded cost performance.

In the beginning, we emphasize again the point that the word "cost" is slippery. It is used indiscriminately with several quite different meanings, and the reader or listener often has difficulty in deducing which meaning is intended. In particular, it is important to remember that there is no such thing as "the" cost of something in any situation in which joint or common costs are involved, and they usually are. When someone refers to "cost" under such circumstances, he may mean full costs, direct costs, variable costs, controllable costs, or whatever.

The appropriate definition depends on the purpose for which the cost is to be used. Consider the factory superintendent's salary. In costing a product for inventory purposes, some fraction of the superintendent's salary is usually included. For overall planning purposes, it is the whole amount of the salary, and not the fractions allocated to individual products, that needs to be studied. As the basis for certain specific decisions (such as whether to buy a new machine), the salary is completely excluded from the figures; for other types of decisions (such as whether to shut down the factory), the salary is an important consideration. In the evaluation of performance, only those costs for which the person being judged is responsible should be taken into account. Thus, in an appraisal of the performance of a departmental foreman, the superintendent's salary is not an element of cost, but in an appraisal of the performance of the whole company, it is. In summary, some of these purposes require the full amount of the actual salary, some require a fraction of that amount, some require an estimate of what the amount (full or fractional) will be in the future, and some require that the amount be completely omitted.

The fact that different purposes require different cost constructions is obvious, but failure to appreciate this fact is perhaps the most important cause both of the misuse of cost figures and of the common but

476

unwarranted criticism that cost accountants can't be pinned down to a definite statement on what "the" cost is.

RELATION OF COSTS TO VOLUME

In general usage, the word "variable" means simply "changeable," but in accounting "variable" has a more restricted meaning. It refers not to changes that take place over time, or to changes associated with the seasons, but only to changes associated with the *level of activity,* that is, with volume. If a cost goes up as volume goes up, it is a variable cost; otherwise, it is not. More specifically, we can distinguish three types of cost patterns: variable, nonvariable, and semivariable.

Variable costs vary directly and proportionately with volume; that is, as volume increases by 10 per cent, the cost also increases by 10 per cent. Direct labor, direct material, lubricants, power costs, and supplies often are examples of variable costs.

Nonvariable costs do not vary at all with volume. Building depreciation, property taxes, supervisory salaries, and occupancy costs (heat and light) often behave in this fashion. These costs are incurred with the passage of time, and are independent of the level of activity within a time period. They are sometimes called "fixed" costs, but this term implies that they cannot be changed, which is not so.

Semivariable costs vary directly, but less than proportionately, with volume; that is, as volume increases by 10 per cent, the cost increases, but by less than 10 per cent. Examples may be indirect labor, maintenance, and clerical costs.

A generalized picture of the behavior of these types of cost is shown in Illustration 16–1. The nonvariable cost is $300 regardless of the level of activity; the variable cost is $0.80 per unit of volume; and the semivariable costs starts at $200 and increases at a rate of $0.20 per unit of volume. Note that the semivariable cost can be broken into two

Illustration 16–1

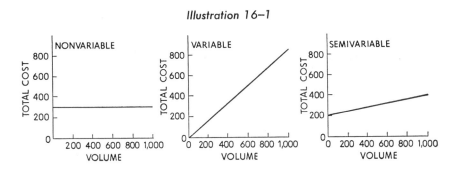

elements, a nonvariable element of $200 and a variable element of $0.20 per unit.

Cost-Volume Diagrams

Certain characteristics of the cost-volume diagrams shown in Illustration 16–1 should be noted, since they are common to all diagrams showing the relationship between cost and volume. In such diagrams cost is always plotted on the vertical, or y, axis, and volume is plotted on the horizontal, or x, axis. A conventional rule in geometry is that the "dependent variable" is plotted on the y axis and the "independent variable" is plotted on the x axis. In the above diagrams, therefore, cost is implicitly assumed to be the "dependent variable" and volume the "independent variable." In these diagrams, the measure of volume is not defined; various possibilities will be described in a subsequent section.

Behavior of Total Costs

If the separate cost elements behave according to one of the three patterns shown above, then the total cost, which is the sum of these separate elements, must vary with volume, as shown in Illustration 16–2, which was constructed by merging the separate elements.

Since the semivariable item can be split into nonvariable and variable components, the *behavior of total costs can be described in terms of only two components—a total amount, and an amount per unit of volume.* In Illustration 16–2, the nonvariable amount is $500 and the

Illustration 16–2

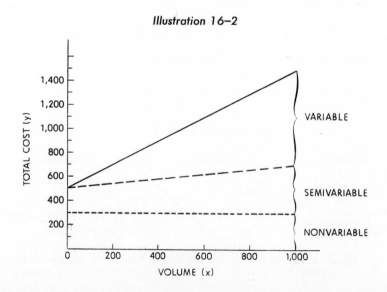

variable amount is \$1 per unit of volume. Since a semivariable cost item can likewise be split into these two elements, there is no need to consider semivariable costs as a separate category; from this point on, we shall consider only the nonvariable and variable components.

Illustration 16–2 is based on several implicit assumptions as to the behavior of costs, of which two are discussed below. The first is usually a reasonable one, but the second is actually quite unrealistic.

The Linear Assumption. One cost behavior assumption is that all overhead costs behave according to one of the three patterns described above. Actually, some costs may vary in steps, as in Illustration 16–3. This happens when the cost occurs in discrete "chunks," as when one indirect worker is added for every 160 additional hours of direct labor per week. Others may vary along a curve rather than a straight line, and others, such as maintenance of idle machines, may actually decrease as volume increases.

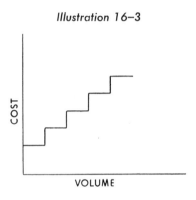

Illustration 16–3

In most situations, however, the effect of these discontinuities and nonlinear cost functions on total overhead costs is minor, and the assumption that total overhead costs vary in a linear relationship with volume is a satisfactory working approximation. This is a most fortunate fact. Many theoretical treatises discuss cost functions with various types of complicated curves. The formulas for these functions are difficult to understand and to work with. Such complicated curves are rarely used in practice, for it is usually found that the simple straight line, although perhaps not a perfect representation of cost-volume relationships, is close enough for practical purposes.

Full-Range Assumption. A second cost behavior assumption implicit in Illustration 16–2 is that overhead costs move along a straight line throughout *the whole range* of volume. This is unrealistic. At zero volume, for example, when the factory is shut down, a special set of conditions operate, and these may make costs considerably higher or considerably lower than the \$500 shown in the diagram. When production gets so high that a second shift is required, costs may behave quite differently from the way in which they behave under one-shift operations. Even within the limits of a single shift, it is to be expected that costs will behave differently when the factory is busy from the way they do when it is operating at low volume levels. In short, a single straight line gives a good approximation of the behavior of costs *only within a certain range of volume.* We can indicate this fact by modifying the cost diagram, as shown in Illustration 16–4.

Illustration 16–4 shows the same cost pattern as Illustration 16–2, but the solid line representing total costs now extends only over a selected range of volume, here 600 units to 1,200 units. The dotted line extending back to zero does not imply that costs will behave in this

Illustration 16–4

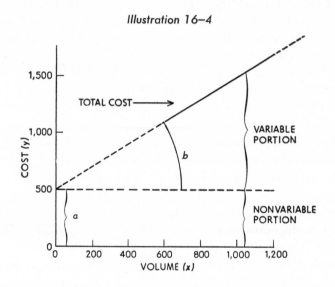

fashion at low volumes; rather it is drawn on the diagram solely as a means of finding the nonvariable component of total costs.

Formula for the Cost Line

As already pointed out, cost at any volume is the sum of the nonvariable component ($500) and the variable component ($1 per unit). For example, at a volume of 1,000 units, cost is $500 + ($1 per unit times 1,000 units) = $1,500. Designating cost as y, volume as x, the nonvariable component as a, and the variable component as b, the cost at any volume can be found from the formula, $y = a + bx$; this is simply the general formula for a straight line.[1] For example, $1,500 = $500 + ($1)(1,000).

If the values of a and b for a given line are not known, they can be found, provided total costs are known for any two points or volume levels on the line. One method of doing this is as follows:

---

[1] In many geometry texts, the notation used is: $y = mx + b$. In such a notation, m represents the slope, or cost per unit, and b represents the nonvariable component.

1. Subtract total cost at the lower volume from total cost at the higher volume, and subtract lower volume from higher volume;
2. Divide the difference in cost by the difference in volume, which gives b, the amount by which cost changes with a change of one unit of volume;
3. Multiply either of the volumes, x, by b and subtract the result from the total cost at that volume, thus removing the variable component and leaving the nonvariable component, a.

Unit Costs

It should be emphasized that the line we are studying shows *total* costs at various volumes. This line should not be confused with a line showing *unit* costs. If total costs have a linear relationship with volume, then unit costs will be a curve, showing how unit costs decrease as volume increases, as in Illustration 16–5, which is a unit cost curve derived from Illustration 16–4.

Estimating Cost-Volume Relationship

In many practical situations costs are expected to vary with volume in the straight-line relationship shown in Illustration 16–4. The formula for this line of expected costs can be estimated by any of the following methods:

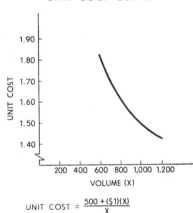

Illustration 16–5

UNIT COST CURVE

$$\text{UNIT COST} = \frac{500 + (\$1)(X)}{X}$$

1. Estimate the cost at any two volumes in order to establish two points on the line. Find the values of a and b by the method described above. (This is sometimes called the "high-low" method because one of the volumes selected is likely to be high, and the other is likely to be low.)

2. Estimate the cost at one volume, and estimate how cost will change with a given change in volume. This gives b directly, and a can be found by subtraction, as described above.

3. Build up separate estimates of the behavior of each of the elements that make up total cost.

4. Make a "scatter diagram" in which actual costs recorded in past periods are plotted against the volume levels in those periods, and draw a line that best fits these observations. Such a diagram is shown in

Illustration 16–6. A statistical technique, called the "method of least squares" may be used to find the line of best fit (see Appendix, p. 496), but in many cases, a line drawn by eye is just as good as, and in some cases it is better than, a mathematically fitted line.

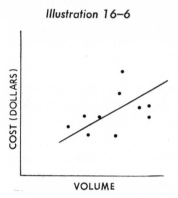

Illustration 16–6

Problems with Scatter Diagrams. Estimating cost-volume relationships by means of a scatter diagram is a common practice, but the results can be misleading. In the first place, this technique shows, at best, what the relationship was in the past, whereas we are interested in what it is now or will be in the future. The past is not necessarily a mirror of the present or the future. Also, the relationship we seek is that obtaining under a *single set of conditions,* whereas each point on a scatter diagram may represent changes in factors other than the two being studied, namely, cost and volume.

Illustration 16–7 shows a common source of difficulty. In this scatter diagram, volume is represented by sales revenue, as is often the case. Each dot is located by plotting the cost for one year on the *y* axis and the sales revenue for that year on the *x* axis. The dots lie along a well-defined path, which is indicated by the straight line, but this line may *not* indicate the present relationship between cost and volume. It may, instead, indicate nothing more than the tendency for both revenue and cost to increase over the past six years because of inflationary factors. If this is the case, then the line shows the trend, or *drift,* of costs *through time,* not the probable relationship between cost and volume *at a given time.* Any scatter diagram covering a period of years in which sales were generally increasing each year, or generally decreasing each year, is likely to have this characteristic, and the longer the period covered, the more unreliable the diagram becomes.

If, in order to avoid this difficulty, the figures for only the most recent years are plotted on the diagram, there may not be enough difference in the volumes of the several periods to indicate a satisfactory line of relationship. The choice of a series of observations that are recent enough so that they do not reflect an obsolete set of conditions, yet which cover a wide enough volume range to permit the drawing of a satisfactory line, is a difficult matter.

Sometimes, statistical techniques are used to adjust, or "deflate," historical observations so as to allow for changes in price and other

Illustration 16–7

SCATTER DIAGRAM, ILLUSTRATING DRIFT

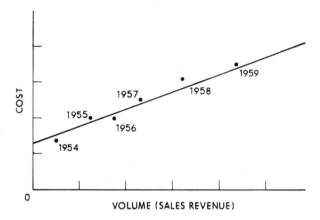

factors. As a minimum, the historical relationship should be adjusted for anticipated changes in the underlying conditions.

Whatever the method used for estimating the relationship, the result is a line, described by the formula $y = a + bx$, which shows how costs are expected to vary with volume.

We have described the line as referring to total costs. The same technique can be used to study various parts of the total. In fact, it is common to restrict analyses of this type to overhead costs, since direct material and direct labor are presumed to be purely variable.

Measures of Volume

Thus far, "volume" has been used as an abstract concept. In a real situation, it must be measured in some concrete fashion. The best measuring stick of volume is one that most closely reflects the conditions that cause costs to change. Two basic questions must be answered: (1) Should the measuring stick be based on input or on output? and (2) Should the measuring stick be expressed in monetary terms or in physical quantities? Within each general category, there are many specific possibilities. The following discussion is limited to overhead costs, for it is here that the choice of the best measure of volume is especially important.

Input measures relate to the effort being expended in the cost center; examples are the number of actual direct labor hours worked, actual machine-hours operated, or the pounds of raw material used. *Output measures* relate to the amount of product coming out of the center; examples are units of product completed or the standard labor costs absorbed by products worked on. Since overhead is itself an input factor, in many situations it tends to vary more closely with other input factors than with output. For example, it is reasonable to expect that overhead cost items associated with direct labor, such as fringe benefits, social security taxes, payroll accounting, tend to vary with the actual quantity of direct labor used more closely than with the standard labor content of products produced. In general, an input measure is likely to be more accurate than an output measure. Some overhead costs, such as inspection costs and plant transportation, however, might vary more closely with the quantity of products produced.

A measuring stick expressed in physical quantities, such as direct labor hours, is often better than one expressed in dollars, such as direct labor cost, because it is unaffected by changes in prices. A wage increase would cause direct labor costs to increase, even though there were no actual increase in the volume of activity. On the other hand, if price changes are likely to affect both labor and overhead to the same degree, the use of a monetary measuring stick may be a means of allowing implicitly for the effect of these price changes.

These theoretical considerations must be tempered by practicality. Total direct labor costs are often available in the cost system without extra calculation, whereas the computation of total direct labor hours, or machine-hours, may require considerable additional work. Also, since the measuring stick of volume for control purposes is often (but not always) the same as that used in allocating overhead costs to products for the purpose of financial accounting, the appropriateness of the measure for that purpose must also be taken into account.

The Overhead Rate and Standard Volume

It will be recalled from Chapter 15 that the overhead rate for product costing purposes is found by dividing total overhead costs by a measure of activity. When the same measure of activity is used in the description of the behavior of costs, total overhead cost is one point on the cost line shown in Illustration 16–4. This point is the total cost expected at *standard volume* (or *normal volume*). Standard volume is defined in one of three ways. In some companies, it is the volume anticipated for the next year or other short period of time; in other companies, it is the average volume expected over a number of years in the future, and in still other companies it is the volume at capacity operations. Overhead costs *per unit* (i.e., the overhead rate) decrease as volume increases because the same amount of nonvariable cost is spread over a larger number of units. Therefore, the overhead rates resulting from the application of one of these three concepts of standard volume can differ substantially from one another.

When the standard volume is taken as the volume expected next year, total overhead costs incurred in the year will be approximately absorbed onto products if the estimates are made with reasonable accuracy. This fact meets the objective of financial accounting. It may, however, cause difficulty if the costs are being used as a basis for pricing, for unit costs will tend to be high in a year of low volume. If the low volume implies a business recession, the high unit cost may lead to an increase in selling prices at the very time when it is probably most unwise to attempt such an increase.

A standard volume based on an average of several years is used by automobile manufacturers and by a number of other leading companies. It avoids the pricing paradox mentioned above, but does result in a large variance in a year of abnormally high or abnormally low volume.

A measure based on capacity is not widely used, except by companies that expect to operate at capacity, and in these situations it is the same as the first method. "Capacity" means not the theoretical maximum amount of product that can be produced if everything goes perfectly, but rather "practical capacity," which is a reasonably attainable amount. It may mean the capacity of one shift, or 168 hours a week, or anywhere in between.

THE PROFITGRAPH

The cost/volume diagram in Illustration 16–4 can be turned into a useful device called the *profitgraph* (or "Profit-Volume graph," or "P/V graph") simply by the addition of a revenue line to it, for a profitgraph is a diagram showing the expected relationship between cost and revenue at various volumes.[2] On a profitgraph, the measure of volume may be the number of units produced and sold, or it may be sales revenue. We have already stated the formula for the cost line. It will be recalled that total cost (y) at any volume (x) equals a nonvariable component (a) plus a variable component (b) times the number of units of volume (x); or, for cost $y = a + bx$.

Revenue is plotted on the assumption of a constant selling price per unit. Assuming that volume is to be measured as units of product, and designating the unit selling price as p, total revenue (y) at any volume

---

[2] This device is also called a "break-even chart," but such a label has the unfortunate implication that the objective of a business is merely to break even.

(x) equals the unit selling price (p) times the number of units of volume (x); or, for revenue $y = px$. For example, if the unit selling price is \$2, the total revenue from 1,000 units will be \$2,000.

A profitgraph of these relationships is shown in Illustration 16–8. Note that as on Illustration 16–4, the lines are dotted at very low and very high volumes to emphasize the fact that the relationships are expected to hold only within a limited volume range (in practice, the lines are usually drawn solid throughout, and it therefore is easy to overlook the fact that the relationship is not valid outside the normal range).

At the *break-even volume,* cost equals revenue. (This is simply a geometric fact; the break-even point is of little practical interest in a profitable company, since attention is focused on the profit area above it.) At lower volumes, a loss is expected; and at higher volumes, a profit is expected. The amount of loss or profit expected at any volume is the

Illustration 16–8

A PROFITGRAPH

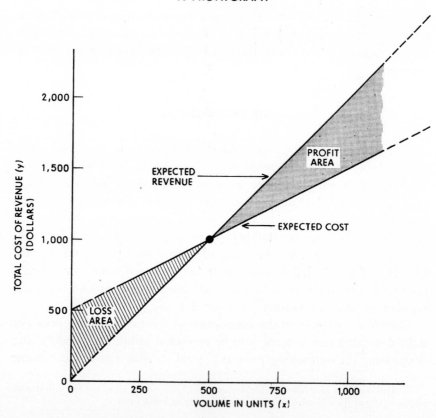

difference between points on the cost and revenue lines at that volume. The break-even volume is not the same as the "normal" volume used as a basis for determining the overhead rate. In a profitable business, normal volume is considerably higher than the break-even volume.

Construction of a Profitgraph

If volume (the x axis) is expressed in terms of sales revenue, the revenue line on a profitgraph is simply the straight line $y = x$. If volume is expressed as number of units sold, revenue at any volume is found from the formula $y = px$, as described above. Sometimes several revenue lines are drawn on a profitgraph, each one showing what revenue would be at one selling price. This procedure helps to show how a change in selling price affects the profit at any given volume.

Interpretation of the Profitgraph

The profitgraph is a useful device for analysis of the overall profit characteristics of a business. To illustrate such an analysis, assume the following situation, which is the same as that shown in previous diagrams:

Nonvariable costs. . . . . : $500
Variable costs. . . . . $1.00 per unit
Normal volume. . . . . 1,000 units
Selling price. . . . . $2.00 per unit

In this situation, total costs at normal volume will be $500 (nonvariable) plus $1,000 (variable), or $1,500. The cost of the product as shown on the accounting records will therefore be $1,500 ÷ 1,000 units, or $1.50 per unit. At a selling price of $2.00 per unit, the normal profit will be $0.50 per unit.

Computation of Break-Even Volume. Recall that the break-even volume is the volume at which cost equals revenue.

Since revenue (y) at any volume (x) is $y = px$
And cost (y) at any volume (x) is $y = a + bx$
And since at the break-even volume, cost = revenue
Therefore the break-even volume is the volume at which $px = a + bx$

If we let x equal the break-even volume, then for the above situation, we have

$$\$2x = \$500 + \$1x$$
$$x = \quad 500 \text{ units}$$

At the break-even volume of 500 units, revenue equals 500 units $\times$ \$2 per unit, and cost equals \$500 $+$ (500 units $\times$ \$1 per unit), both of which equal \$1,000.

Marginal Income. From the relationships of cost and revenue at various volumes, an important conclusion can be drawn: although the normal profit is \$0.50 per unit, this rate of profit will be earned *only* at the normal volume. At lower volumes the profit will be less than \$0.50 per unit, and at higher volumes it will be more than \$0.50 per unit. The relationship between cost, revenue, and volume can be summed up by the statement that for each change of one unit in volume, profit will change by \$1. This \$1 is the *marginal income,* the difference between selling price and *variable cost* per unit. Below the break-even point, losses will be incurred at the rate of \$1 for each unit decrease in volume.

The break-even volume can also be determined by the relationship between nonvariable costs and marginal income. In the illustrative situation where the marginal income is \$1 per unit and nonvariable costs are \$500, 500 units must be sold before enough income can be earned to cover nonvariable costs. After that, a profit of \$1 per unit will be earned.

Improving Profit Performance

These revenue-cost-volume relationships suggest that a useful way of studying the profit factors of a business is to consider not the normal profit per unit (which is different at every volume), but rather the nonvariable costs and the marginal income, which is the difference between selling price and marginal cost. In these terms, there are four, and only four, ways in which the profit of a business can be increased:

1. Increase selling prices per unit.
2. Decrease variable costs per unit.
3. Decrease nonvariable costs.
4. Increase volume.

The separate effects of each of these possibilities are shown in the following calculations and in Illustration 16–9. Each starts from the current situation, assumed to be "normal" (selling price, \$2; variable costs, \$1 per unit; nonvariable costs, \$500; and volume, 1,000 units). The effect of a 10 per cent change in each factor is calculated:

> A. A 10 per cent increase in selling price would add \$200 to revenue and would therefore increase the current profit of \$500 by 40 per cent.

Illustration 16-9

EFFECT OF 10 PER CENT CHANGE IN PROFIT FACTORS

A. Increase Selling Price

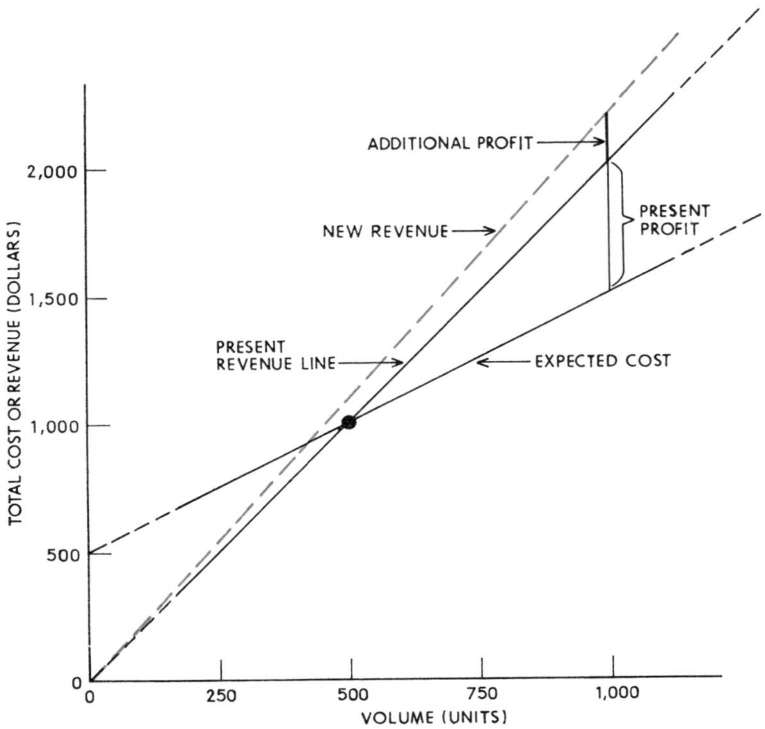

B. Decrease Variable Cost

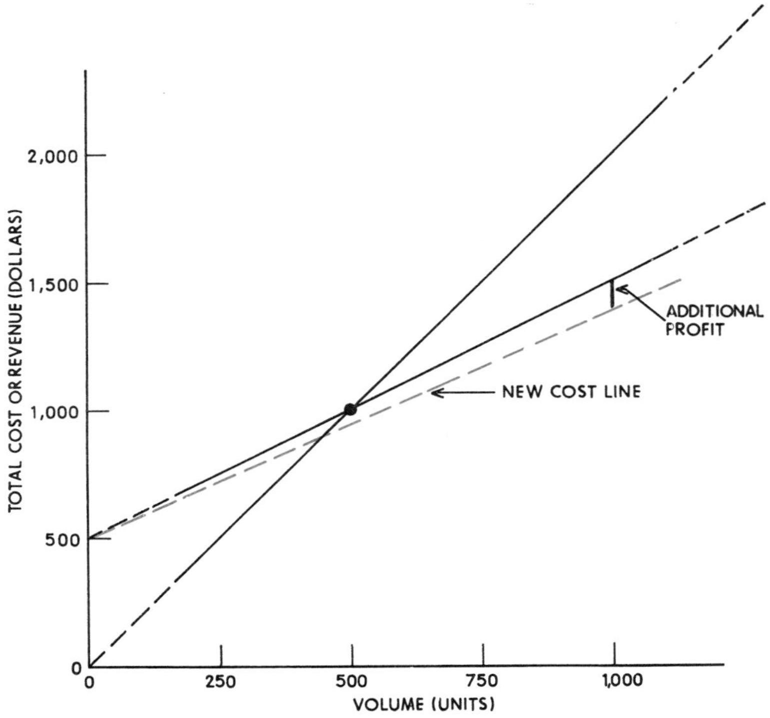

C. Decrease Nonvariable Cost

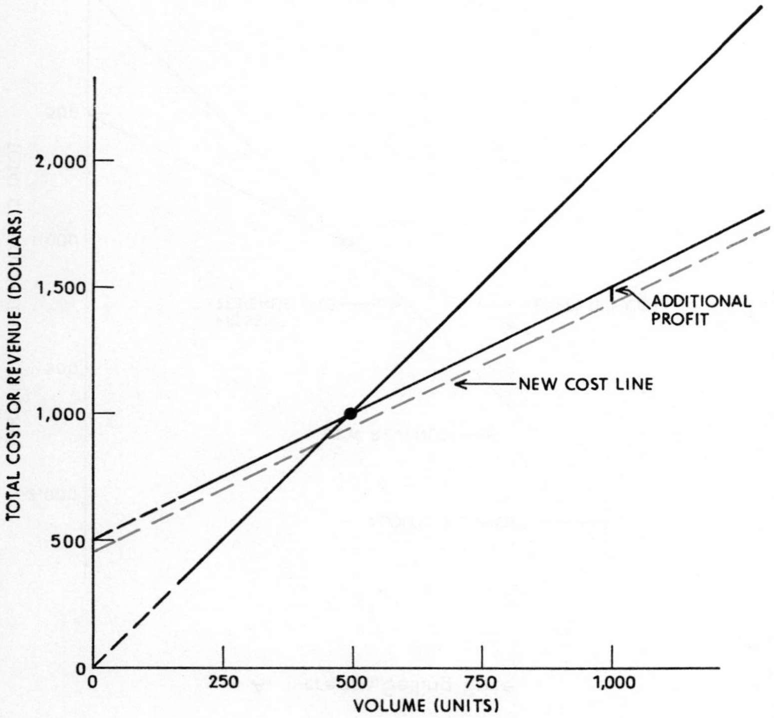

TOTAL COST OR REVENUE (DOLLARS)

2,000

1,500

1,000

500

0

0   250   750   1,000

VOLUME (UNITS)

ADDITIONAL
PROFIT

NEW COST LINE

D. Increase Volume

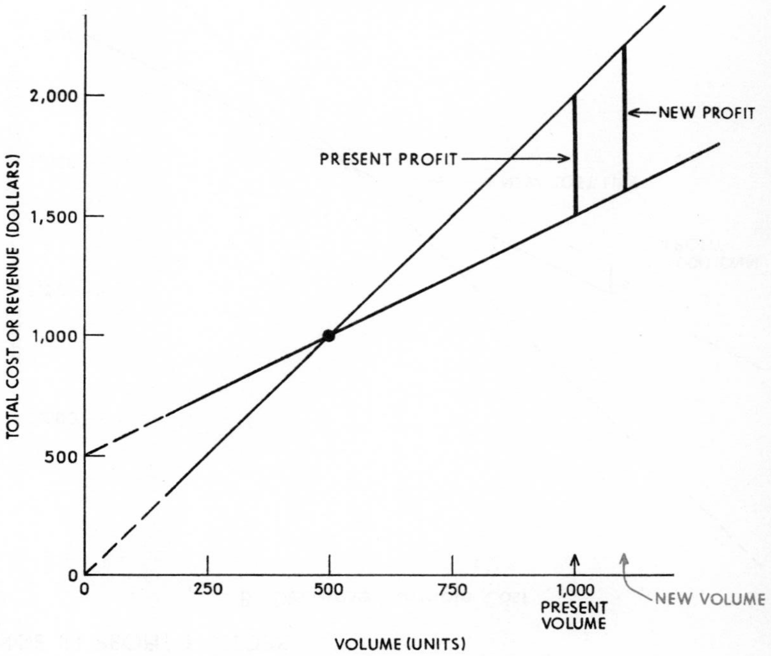

TOTAL COST OR REVENUE (DOLLARS)

2,000

1,500

1,000

500

0

0   250   500   750   1,000
                      PRESENT
                      VOLUME

NEW VOLUME

VOLUME (UNITS)

NEW PROFIT

PRESENT PROFIT

B. A 10 per cent decrease in variable cost would reduce variable costs by $100 and would therefore increase profit by 20 per cent.
C. A 10 per cent decrease in nonvariable cost would amount to $50, an increase in profit of 10 per cent.
D. A 10 per cent increase in volume would increase profit by the marginal income of $1 per unit times an additional 100 units, or $100, an increase of 20 per cent.

If we look at some of the interrelationships, we can calculate, for example, that a 20 per cent (i.e., $100) increase in nonvariable costs could be offset by a 5 per cent increase in selling price, a 10 per cent increase in volume, or a 10 per cent decrease in variable costs.

Another calculation made from a profitgraph is the *margin of safety*. This is the amount or ratio by which the current volume exceeds the break-even volume. Assuming current volume is 1,000 units, the margin of safety in our illustrative situation is 500 units, or 100 per cent, in relation to the break-even volume. Sales volume can decrease by 50 per cent before a loss is incurred, other factors remaining equal.

Limitations on Profitgraph Analysis

The foregoing calculations assume that each of the factors is independent of the others, a situation that is rarely the case. An increase in selling price often is accompanied by a decrease in volume, for example. Changes in the factors must therefore usually be studied simultaneously rather than separately as was done above.

Also, the diagram assumes that the company, in effect, sells only one product. If several products with different marginal incomes are sold, the profitgraph for the whole company shows the average marginal income for all products, and is affected by changes in the mix of products. Under these circumstances, profitgraphs for each product, or for each group of approximately homogeneous products, are more useful for analysis than is the single overall diagram.

The profitgraph analysis also implicitly assumes that changes in the four factors are not accompanied by changes in the amount of capital employed. If a decrease in variable cost arises because of the purchase of a new machine, for example, the effect on the return on investment is not given by the profitgraph. In part, the effect shows up as an increase in the nonvariable depreciation cost, but one cannot tell from this alone what is the effect on the overall rate of return.

MARGINAL INCOME ANALYSIS STATEMENT

The marginal income idea suggests a way of recasting the conventional income statement so as to provide more useful information to

Illustration 16–10

MARGINAL INCOME ANALYSIS STATEMENT

A. Conventional Income Statement for June

Sales..		$3,540
Salaries...	$1,640	
Supplies..	900	
Heat, light, power..	210	
Employer's payroll tax...	89	
Advertising...	88	
Telephone..	66	
Rent..	100	
Depreciation...	483	
Amortization of leasehold improvements............................	140	
Insurance...	95	
Total Expenses..		3,811
Net Loss..		$(271)

B. Same Data Recast in Format of a Marginal Income Analysis Report

	Dry Cleaning		Laundry	
Sales...	$2,800		$740	
Variable costs:				
Salaries..	$ 790		$200	
Supplies..	760		140	
Heat, light, power................................	150		25	
Employer's payroll tax............................	43	1,743	10	375
Contribution to nonvariable costs.....................		$1,057		$365
Less: Depreciation on equipment.....................		200		100
Contribution to unassigned nonvariable costs...........	$1,122	$ 857		$265
Unassigned nonvariable costs:				
Salaries..	$650			
Advertising......................................	88			
Telephone..	66			
Heat, light, power................................	35			
Employer's payroll tax............................	36			
Rent...	100			
Depreciation.....................................	183			
Amortization.....................................	140			
Insurance..	95	1,393		
Net Loss for the Period.........................	$ 271			

Source: Adapted from material collected by Professor W. W. Haynes, University of Kentucky, and Professor J. L. Gibson, Arlington State College, for the Small Business Administration.

management. Illustration 16–10 shows such a recasting for a dry cleaning and laundry business. The top section is the conventional income statement. The lower section shows the same basic information in the form of a "Marginal Income Analysis Report."

To construct this report, the cost elements are first segregated into variable and nonvariable categories. For some items (e.g., heat, light, and power in the illustration), part of the cost is variable and part is nonvariable. For each activity, the variable costs relating to the activity are subtracted from revenue, giving the marginal income, or, as labeled here, "Contribution to nonvariable costs." In the illustration, non-variable costs assignable to each activity (i.e., depreciation on equipment) are also shown, although this is not always done. Then the other nonvariable costs are listed, with no attempt to allocate them among activities.

In the illustration, the revenue and variable costs are broken down by revenue-earning activities. Marginal income analysis statements are also prepared in which the breakdown is by products or product groups.

CONTROLLABLE COSTS

The basic distinction between controllable and noncontrollable costs is that the amount of controllable costs incurred in a given responsibility center can be influenced by the actions of the supervisor responsible for the center, whereas the amount of noncontrollable cost is essentially unaffected by any action he may take. In this section, we shall explore the concept of controllable cost in more depth.

Direct material and direct labor costs are usually controllable. With respect to the overhead costs in a cost center, some are controllable and others are not. Indirect labor, supplies, and electricity are usually controllable. So are charges from service centers based on services actually rendered by the service center. By definition, *an allocated cost is not controllable;* the amount of the charge varies in accordance with the formula used for allocation, not with the actions of the supervisor. This is so unless the cost is actually a direct cost that is allocated only for convenience, as in the case of social security taxes on direct labor that are as controllable as other elements of the direct labor cost.

The distinction between controllable and noncontrollable costs is largely a matter of judgment about the situation in a given responsibility center. It may be affected by the method of charging costs to the center. Referring back to the example of maintenance described on page 363, if maintenance costs are allocated to the responsibility center, they are not controllable; but if the responsibility center is charged on the basis of an hourly rate for each hour that a maintenance man works therein, and if maintenance work is done at the request of the responsible supervisor, then clearly maintenance is a controllable element of his cost.

It is important to recognize that controllable costs and noncontrollable costs are not synonymous with *direct costs and allocated costs.* All controllable costs are direct since by definition an allocated cost is not controllable, but not all direct costs are controllable. For example, depreciation on departmental equipment is a direct cost of the department, but the depreciation charge is often noncontrollable by the departmental supervisor since he may have no authority to acquire or dispose of equipment. The rental charge for rented premises is another example of a direct but noncontrollable cost.

Neither are controllable costs necessarily the same as *variable costs.* Variable costs vary with volume. Some costs, such as indirect labor, heat, light, and magazine subscriptions, may be unaffected by volume, but they are nevertheless controllable. Conversely, some variable costs are noncontrollable. Raw material and parts, whose consumption varies directly with volume, may be entirely outside the influence of the departmental supervisor. For example, in an automobile assembly department, the fact is that the car requires an engine, a body, five wheels, and so on, and there is nothing the supervisor can do about it. He is responsible for waste and spoilage of material, but not for the main flow of material itself. For similar reasons, direct labor may be a noncontrollable cost in certain types of operations.

Engineered Costs and Managed Costs

In the study of the behavior of controllable costs, it is crucial that a distinction be made between engineered costs and managed costs. Both are controllable, but the approach to the control of one is quite different from the approach to the control of the other.

Engineered costs are elements of cost for which the *right* or *proper* amount of costs that should be incurred can be estimated. Direct labor is an example. Given the specifications for a product, engineers can determine the necessary operations to be performed and can estimate, within reasonably close limits, the time that should be spent on each operation. The total amount of direct labor costs that should be incurred can then be estimated by translation of these times into money by means of a wage rate and multiplication by the number of units of product produced. Since production engineering is not an exact science, these amounts are not necessarily the exact amount that should be spent, but the estimates can usually be made close enough so that there is relatively little ground for disagreement as to what the cost should be. In particular, there can be no reasonable ground for denying that there is a direct relationship between volume and costs; two units require more direct labor than does one unit.

Managed costs (or "programed" or "discretionary" costs), on the other hand, can be whatever management wants them to be, within wide limits. There is no scientific way of deciding what the "right" amount should be, or at least there is no scientific basis that the management of the particular company is willing to rely on. How much should we spend for research and development? for public relations? for employees' parties and outings? for donations? for the accounting department? No one knows. In most companies, the managed cost category includes all general and administrative functions, all order-getting costs, and a great many items of factory overhead cost.

In the absence of an engineering standard, the amount to be spent must be a matter of judgment. Usually, this judgment is arrived at by joint agreement between the supervisor concerned and his superior, as part of the budgeting process. Indeed most of the discussion in the budgeting process occurs with respect to the permitted level of managed costs.

It should be pointed out that although there is no "right" level for the total amount of a managed cost item, there may be usable standards for controlling some of the detail within it. Although no one knows the right amount to spend for accounting, it is nevertheless possible to measure the performance of individual clerks in the accounting department in terms of number of postings or number of invoices typed per hour. And although we cannot know the "right" amount of total travel expense, we can set standards for the amount that should be spent per day or per mile.

Furthermore, new developments in management accounting result in a gradual shift of items from the managed cost to the engineered cost categories. Several companies have recently started to use what they believe to be valid techniques for determining the "right" amount that they should spend on advertising in order to achieve their sales objectives, or the "right" number of salesmen.

Analysis of Performance. With respect to engineered costs, the general rule is "the lower they are, the better." The objective is to spend as little as possible, consistent with quality standards, safety standards, and so on. The supervisor who reduces his engineered costs usually should be congratulated.

With respect to managed costs, the situation is quite different and much more complicated. Often, optimum performance consists of *spending the amount agreed on,* for spending too little may be as bad as, or worse than, spending too much. A factory supervisor can easily reduce his costs by skimping on maintenance or on training; a marketing manager can reduce his advertising or sales promotion expenditures; top management may eliminate research. None of these actions may be in the overall best interest of the company, although all of them result in lower costs on the current income statement.

Spurious Relationships. The decision on how much to spend for a managed cost item may take several forms, such as "spend the same amount as we spent last year," or "spend *x* per cent of sales," or "spend *x* dollars plus *y* per cent of sales." These decision rules result in historical patterns which, when plotted against volume have the same superficial appearance as the patterns of engineered cost. The first rule gives a nonvariable cost line, the second a variable cost line, and the third a semivariable cost line.

These relationships are fundamentally different from those observed for engineered costs, however. For engineered costs, the pattern is inevitable; as volume increases, the direct labor cost *must* increase. For managed costs, the relationship exists only because of the management decision, and it can be changed simply by changing the management decision. For example, a company may decide that research and development cost should be 3 per cent of sales. There can be no scientific reason for such a decision, for no one knows the optimum amount that should be spent for research; in all probability, such a rule exists primarily because management thinks that this is what the company can afford to spend. In such a situation there will be a linear relationship between sales volume and research/development costs. There is, however, little significance to such a relationship, and no reason to believe that research/development costs in the future should follow the same pattern.

Order-getting Costs. Order-getting costs are those incurred in order to make sales. They include the costs of the selling organization, advertising, sales promotion, and so on. These costs may vary with sales volume, but the relationship is the reverse of that for factory costs: order-getting cost is the independent variable, and sales volume is the dependent variable. Order-getting costs vary not in response to sales volume but rather *in anticipation of* sales volume, according to decisions made by management.[3] They are therefore managed costs.

---

[3] Exceptions are salesmen's commissions and other payments related to sales in that sales is the basis of figuring the cost. These of course vary directly with sales.

If management has a policy of spending more for order-getting activities when sales volume is high, then a scatter diagram of the relationship between selling costs and sales volume will have the same appearance as the diagram for production costs and production volume, Illustration 16–6. The two diagrams should be interpreted quite differently, however. The production cost diagram indicates that cost *necessarily* increases as volume increases, while the selling cost diagram shows that cost has been *permitted* to increase with increases in volume; there is no necessary relationship in the latter case. Further, subject to some qualifications, it may be said that for total factory overhead costs, the lower they are the better; but lower selling costs may reflect inadequate selling effort. The "right" level of selling costs is a judgment made by management.

Nor is there always a direct relationship between order-getting cost and sales volume. Taking advertising as an example, management may decide either (1) to increase advertising expenditures when sales *increase,* on the theory that the company can afford to spend more when revenue is high; (2) to spend the same amount for advertising, regardless of sales volume; or (3) to increase advertising expenditures when sales *decrease,* in the belief that additional effort is necessary to regain lost volume. Each of these policies gives a different line of relationship, and the pattern is further obscured by the fact that sales volume is influenced not only by advertising, or indeed sales effort in total, but also by general business conditions and other factors outside the company's control.

SUMMARY

The word "cost" has many meanings, and care must always be taken to make sure that the context applying to a given situation is understood.

Variable costs are those that vary with volume. Although some costs are semivariable, they usually can be decomposed into variable and nonvariable components. The relationship between costs and volume is usually linear within a normal range of volume.

When a revenue line is added to a diagram showing the cost-volume relationship, the diagram is called a profitgraph, an important tool in analysis of the factors that affect profit. Marginal income, which is the difference between revenue and variable cost, is a significant concept in such an analysis.

Controllable costs may be classified as either engineered costs or managed cost. The methods for estimating and analyzing the former are fundamentally different from those applicable to the latter.

APPENDIX

Fitting a Straight Line by Least Squares

If the variable measured on the vertical axis is designated y and that on the horizontal axis x, then *any* straight line is described by the general formula, $y = a + bx$. In order to describe a *specific* straight line, we must assign specific numerical values to the two constants (or "parameters"), a and b.

These two numbers have very simple meanings: a is the *ordinate* ("height") at which the line cuts the y axis (at the y axis $x = 0$ and therefore $bx = 0$ and therefore $y = a$); b gives the *slope* of the line, the amount by which y increases when x increases by one unit. (When b is negative, y *decreases* when x increases.)

Illustration 16–11

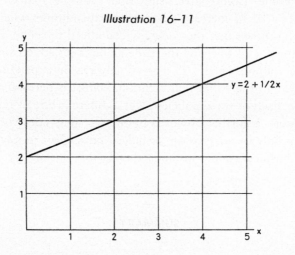

EXAMPLE: Illustration 16–11 shows the line $y = 2 + \frac{1}{2}x$. Notice that the line cuts the y axis at a value of 2, and that for each unit increase in x, y increases $\frac{1}{2}$ unit.

The technique of fitting a straight line by the method of least squares makes use of this formula for a straight line. We assume here that the distances from the point to the line are measured *vertically*, that is, parallel to the y axis. We write down in two adjacent columns every value of x and beside each value of x the corresponding actual value of y. In a third column we put the square of each value of x, and in the fourth, the product of each x times the corresponding y. We total each column and use the symbol Σx^2 to denote the total of the squares of the x values, Σxy to denote the total of the products of x times the corresponding y, etc. (Notice that Σx^2 does *not* denote the square of the sum of the x's, nor does Σxy denote the total of the x's times the total of y's.) We then determine the constants a and b in the equation for a straight line by solving the two simultaneous "normal equations":

$$Na + b\,(\Sigma x) = \Sigma y$$
$$a\,(\Sigma x) + b\,(\Sigma x^2) = \Sigma xy$$

N is the number of items, that is, the number of x, y pairs.

Suppose we have the following data (simplified for the purpose of illustration):

Visits	Sales
0	10
1	12
2	13
3	15

We write the figures:

(1) x	(2) y	(3) x^2	(4) xy
0	10	0	0
1	12	1	12
2	13	4	26
3	15	9	45
6	50	14	83

Therefore,

$$\Sigma x = 6 \quad \Sigma y = 50, \quad \Sigma x^2 = 14, \quad \Sigma xy = 83, \quad N = 4;$$

and the normal equations given above become

$$50 = 4a + 6b$$
$$83 = 6a + 14b \,.$$

To solve for a and b, multiply the first equation by 3 and the second equation by 2 and get—

$$150 = 12a + 18b$$
$$166 = 12a + 28b \,.$$

Subtract the first equation from the second and get—

$$16 = 10b$$
$$b = 1.6 \,.$$

Therefore, $50 = 4a + 9.6$ (from the first normal equation with 9.6 written in place of $6b$):

$$4a = 40.4$$
$$a = 10.1 \,.$$

Therefore, the equation of the least-squares regression line is:

$$y = 10.1 + 1.6x \,.$$

CASES

CASE 16–1.   SCANNELL APPLIANCE COMPANY

When the Scannell Appliance Company, a manufacturer of household electrical appliances, began to lay the foundations for a comprehensive program of cost control in its manufacturing departments, one of the most important problems was believed to be the education of the plant foremen in what kinds of costs were necessary to do the various departmental jobs and how much these costs should be in a well-run department. Also it was felt desirable to discuss in a preliminary way the design and use of techniques of cost control that might be useful to the foremen in accomplishing what the management had in mind. As a first step, the company prepared the following material and distributed it to its supervisory organization in pamphlet form.

"TIPS FOR FOREMEN"

A Few Facts on Product Costs and Budgetary Control

The Cost of Our Product

In all industrial enterprises management is constantly faced with the problem of so controlling the various operations that the finished product will be of a designated quality and produced by the best and most economical methods in a definite and required time. To do this, management must operate under carefully made and efficiently executed plans. Regardless of whatever plan is devised for the control of any operation, the element of *cost* must be a vital part of it, and the budget is used as a guide or measure of these operating costs.

According to the best authorities, four fifths of the industrial failures in this country are directly the result of faults of incompetence of one kind or another. Ignorance of the *true costs* of production is without doubt one of the most common of the shortcomings.

Predetermined standards and methods of operation and performance are essential in order that a hit-or-miss type of operation may be avoided. Improvement and advancement have been made largely through our system of records from which information of past experiences and results is obtainable. This is the guide to our future planning. It is from our records of past performance, adjusted for known changes in conditions, that the budget is established.

"Thoroughly effective control of plant expense begins right at the *source* of the expenditure—that is *with you, the foreman.*" This statement is true because it places responsibility where it belongs. It gives foremen greater vision and insight of their duties and utilizes the ingenuity of each foreman in stopping the many small "leaks" now occurring in the department.

This is the thought which has prompted the preparation of this pamphlet. It is realized that this pamphlet is not a treatise on budget or costs. It is not intended as such. However an effort has been made to bring out a few facts on the control of costs that will aid you in your efforts toward the efficient management of your department. It is the hope of management that you will examine this pamphlet frequently.

In any industry no doubt one often wonders just what items are included in manufacturing costs. Exhibit 2 will give you a vivid picture of many of the items included in the cost of our products.

You will notice that the total manufacturing costs are built up on (1) direct material, (2) direct labor, and (3) expense. Each of these divisions is made up of many items. We have listed the most important of them under their proper heading for your observation.

1. *Direct Material.* In the manufacturing of our line of products certain of the materials used are issued on regular material lists. These materials or piece parts pass through the various departments of the factory with the flow of production. Replacements should not have to be made except through the process of the scrap ticket which cost is included in the budget and not applied directly to product costs. This cost also vitally concerns you.

2. *Direct Labor.* Direct labor has been defined as "that labor that is directly applied to the product on routings." This labor of course fluctuates as does the schedule. However you, as foremen, must at all times keep direct labor costs under control. This can best be accomplished by having only the exact number of people required to do the job as set up in the routings.

The biggest contribution of the department manager or foreman in keeping direct labor costs under control is to be found in the methods used in keeping

Exhibit 1

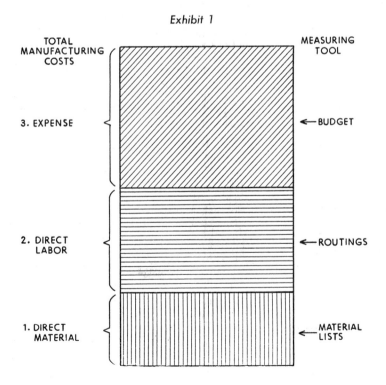

Exhibit 2

3. Expense.   *Measuring Tool: Budget*

Indirect Labor

Supervision	Buildings	Janitors, sweepers
Clerical	Furniture and fixtures	Policemen, watchmen, fire
Material handlers, truckers	Labor allowance on scrap	protection
Metal washers	Reoperation	Elevator men
Paint mixers	Manufacturing delays	Tool attendants
Oven tenders	Waiting for repair and tools	Drafting and engineering
Learner's allowance	Waiting for orders	Inspection—all except that
Unauthorized labor	Waiting for stock	on routings
Overtime premiums	Waiting for power	Sundry and miscellaneous in-
Maintenance and repair labor	Earnings equalization	direct labor
Machinery and equipment	Experimental work	
Tools	Rearrangements	

Indirect Materials

Processing supplies	Stationery and office supplies	Special tools—replaced or re-
Plating supplies	Packing and shipping supplies	paired
Cleaning materials	—not on parts list	Scrap
Carbide and oxygen	Fuel—gas, coal, etc.	Maintenance and repair ma-
Lubricants and cutting com-	New perishable and permanent	terial for equipment, build-
pounds	tools	ings, tools, furniture, and
Testing supplies		fixtures

Utilities

Power	Light	Process steam
Heat	Water	

Fixed Charges

Taxes	Employees groups, fire, tor-	Depreciation—buildings and
Insurance compensation	nado, public liability, etc.,	equipment
	insurance	

2. Direct Labor.   *Measuring Tool: Routings*

Shearing	Grinding	Soldering
Punch press	Annealing	Assembling
Automatics	Plating	Painting and enameling
Machining	Polishing	Inspection (on routings)

1. Direct Material.   *Measuring Tool: Material Lists*

Cast iron	Brass	Paint
Steel bars and sheets	Wood	Purchased parts

conditions in the department in such shape that the labor can be performed most efficiently. Careful study of the operations of the department including the layout, the sequence of operations, the proper placement of the operators for the particular job together with *adequate* supervision will do much in keeping direct costs in line with the actual standard that has been established for it.

3. *Expense.* Expense includes all items which cannot be definitely charged to the product by one of the two mediums enumerated above, that is, labor routings or material lists. It is under the classification of expense that some of the largest of all losses occur.

In the whole manufacturing setup, there is no one who realizes any better than the foreman what the absolute requirements in respect to these expense

Exhibit 3

LAST YEAR'S EXPENSES PLOTTED, SHOWING TREND

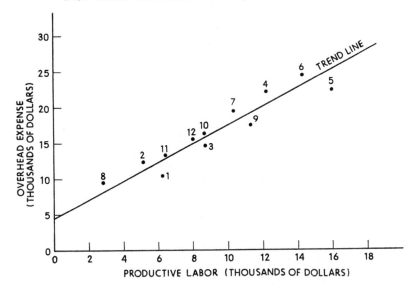

PRODUCTIVE LABOR (THOUSANDS OF DOLLARS)

items might be at the various levels of a fluctuating production schedule. To assist you, upon whom rests the responsibility for the control of expense, the manufacturing expense budget has been put into use.

Snap judgment and guessing cannot be relied upon in the complex nature of present-day manufacturing conditions. Forecasts and comparisons must be continuously made. You have at your command, through budgetary methods only, a means of fulfilling the requirements of the complete job of (1) getting the required production, (2) meeting the necessary requirements as to quality, and (3) doing these within the expense limits.

Allowances consistent with good operations must therefore be established and met. Direct labor, being the true measure of activity within any department, has been chosen as the basis for establishing the expense allowances for any period.

Our management makes available to us, through the budget reports, forecasts, daily and semiweekly comparisons, and monthly analysis, information without which we would be at a loss in the efficient operation of our portion of this business. This is the measuring stick by which we can make decisions, by which we can prove our efficiency, and by which we are and will be judged by those who are looking to us for results.

Serious consideration of, and constant attention to, this angle of our three-sided job is therefore of absolute importance.

To illustrate the development of a flexible budget for expense control we have shown in Exhibit 3 actual monthly expenses of one department plotted against its own productive labor. Point number one represents January, point number two February, and so on. It is noticeable that a definite trend of expense exists over the whole period of high and low production months, higher expense resulting from increased requirements in the months of large volume production, and lower expense in the less active months. This is as it should be, and with this experience as a guide a "trend line" can be drawn as the beginning of a budget.

Exhibit 4

THE TREND CHART AS A TOOL FOR BUDGETING

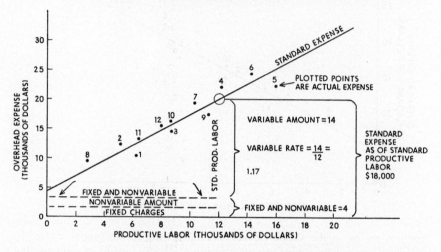

Fully developed, the information available from Exhibit 4 can be seen to furnish all the factors required in a complete expense budget. The point at which the "trend line" meets the expense scale at the left is known as the non-variable and fixed amount for this department, which is $4,000. Fixed charge items were enumerated in Exhibit 2. The remaining portion of the lower block includes those few items which actually exist whether the department functions or not, designated "nonvariable." The triangle above the fixed and nonvariable line is a measure of the expense which should be normal at any given volume of production. At the productive labor of $12,000 the variable portion amounts to $14,000. The fixed and nonvariable portion remains $4,000—total budget, $18,000.

When *your* department exceeds its expense allowance at any given productive labor, by that same amount is the overall cost of the product which we manufacture exceeded, and a definite *loss* in manufacturing cost is the result.

When expense can be kept under the budget, the saving is reflected in the overall cost, thus bringing our products within the reach of more people, which means increasing our total volume of business.

How well or how poor the showing of your department will be in the future is strictly up to you. We hope that you will become cost and budget conscious for the future mutual benefit of the company and yourself.

Questions

1. Consider first the technical matters discussed in the pamphlet. Are the statements made therein correct, insofar as you can determine?

2. How effective do you think the pamphlet will be in educating the foremen?

CASE 16–2. BILL FRENCH

Bill French picked up the phone and called his boss, Wes Davidson, controller of Duo-Products Corporation. "Say, Wes, I'm all set for the meeting this afternoon. I've put together a set of break-even statements that should really make the boys sit up and take notice—and I think they'll be able to understand them, too." After a brief conversation about other matters, the call was concluded and French turned to his charts for one last check-out before the meeting.

French had been hired six months earlier as a staff accountant. He was directly responsible to Davidson and, up to the time of this case, had been doing routine types of analysis work. French was an alumnus of a liberal arts undergraduate school and graduate business school, and was considered by his associates to be quite capable and unusually conscientious. It was this latter characteristic that had apparently caused him to "rub some of the working guys the wrong way," as one of his co-workers put it. French was well aware of his capabilities and took advantage of every opportunity that arose to try to educate those around him. Wes Davidson's invitation for French to attend an informal manager's meeting had come as some surprise to others in the accounting group. However, when French requested permission to make a presentation of some break-even data, Davidson acquiesced. The Duo-Products Corporation had not been making use of this type of analysis in its review or planning programs.

Basically, what French had done was to determine the level at which the company must operate in order to break even. As he phrased it, "The company must be able at least to sell a sufficient volume of goods so that it will cover all the variable costs of producing and selling the goods; further, it will not make a profit unless it covers the fixed, or nonvariable, costs as well. The level of operation at which total costs (that is, variable plus nonvariable) are just covered is the break-even volume. This should be the lower limit in all our planning."

The accounting records had provided the following information that French used in constructing his chart:

Plant capacity—2,000,000 units
Past year's level of operations—1,500,000 units
Average unit selling price—$1.20
Total fixed costs—$520,000
Average variable unit cost—$0.75

From this information, French observed that each unit contributed $0.45 to fixed overhead after covering the variable costs. Given total fixed costs of $520,000, he calculated that 1,155,556 units must be sold in order to break even. He verified this conclusion by calculating the dollar sales volume that was required to break even. Since the variable costs per unit were 62.5 per cent of the selling price, French reasoned that 37.5 per cent of every sales dollar was left available to cover fixed costs. Thus, fixed costs of $520,000 require sales of $1,386,667 in order to break even.

When he constructed a break-even chart to present the information graphically, his conclusions were further verified. The chart also made it clear that the firm was operating at a fair margin over the break-even requirements, and that the profits accruing (at the rate of 37.5 per cent of every sales dollar over break-even) increased rapidly as volume increased (see Exhibit 1).

Shortly after lunch, French and Davidson left for the meeting. Several representatives of the manufacturing departments were present, as well as the general sales manager, two assistant sales managers, the purchasing officer, and two men from the product engineering office. Davidson introduced French to the few men whom he had not already

Exhibit 1

BREAK-EVEN CHART—TOTAL BUSINESS

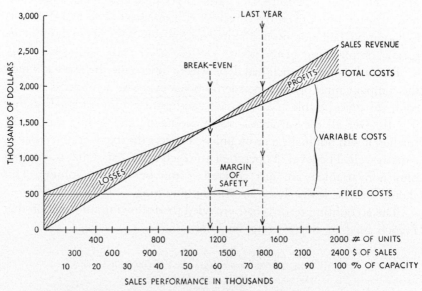

BREAK-EVEN VOLUME = 1,156,000 UNITS, OR
$1,387,000

met, and then the meeting got under way. French's presentation was the last item on Davidson's agenda, and in due time the controller introduced French, explaining his interest in cost control and analysis.

French had prepared enough copies of his chart and supporting calculations for everyone at the meeting. He described carefully what he had done and explained how the chart pointed to a profitable year, dependent on meeting the volume of sales activity that had been maintained in the past. It soon became apparent that some of the participants had known in advance what French planned to discuss; they had come prepared to challenge him and soon had taken control of the meeting. The following exchange ensued (see Exhibit 3 for a checklist of participants with their titles):

COOPER (production control): You know, Bill, I'm really concerned that you haven't allowed for our planned changes in volume next year. It seems to me that you should have allowed for the sales department's guess that we'll boost sales by 20 per cent, unit-wise. We'll be pushing 90 per cent of what we call capacity then. It sure seems that this would make quite a difference in your figuring.

FRENCH: That might be true, but as you can see, all you have to do is read the cost and profit relationship right off the chart for the new volume. Let's see—at a million-eight units we'd . . . .

WILLIAMS (manufacturing): Wait a minute, now! ! ! If you're going to talk in terms of 90 per cent of capacity, and it looks like that's what it will be, you had better note that we'll be shelling out some more for the plant. We've already got okays on investment money that will boost your fixed costs by ten thousand dollars a month, easy. And that may not be all. We may call it 90 per cent of plant capacity, but there are a lot of places where we're just full up and we can't pull things up any tighter.

COOPER: See, Bill? Fred Williams is right, but I'm not finished on this bit about volume changes. According to the information that I've got here—and it came from your office—I'm not sure that your break-even chart can really be used even if there were to be no changes next year. Looks to me like you've got average figures that don't allow for the fact that we're dealing with three basic products. Your report here (see Exhibit 2) on costs, according to product lines, for last year makes it pretty clear that the "average" is way out of line. How would the break-even point look if we took this on an individual product basis?

FRENCH: Well, I'm not sure. Seems to me that there is only one break-even point for the firm. Whether we take it product by product or in total, we've got to hit that point. I'll be glad to check for you if you want, but . . . .

BRADSHAW (assistant sales manager): Guess I may as well get in on this one, Bill. If you're going to do anything with individual products, you ought to know that we're looking for a big swing in our product mix. Might even start before we get into the new season. The "A" line is really losing out and I imagine that we'll be lucky to hold two thirds of the volume there next year. Wouldn't you buy that Arnie? [Agreement from the general sales manager.] That's not too bad, though, because we expect that we should pick up the 200,000 that we lose, and about a quarter million units more, over in "C" production. We don't see anything that shows much of a change in "B." That's been solid for years and shouldn't change much now.

WINETKI (general sales manager): Bradshaw's called it about as we figure it, but there's something else here too. We've talked about our pricing on "C" enough, and now I'm really going to push our side of it. Ray's estimate of maybe half a million—four hundred fifty thousand I guess it was—up on "C" for next year is on the basis of doubling the price with no change in cost. We've been priced so low on this item that it's been a crime—we've got to raise, but good, for two reasons. First, for our reputation; the price is out of line class-wise and is completely inconsistent with our quality reputation. Second, if we don't raise the price, we'll be swamped and we can't handle it. You heard what Williams said about capacity. The way the whole "C" field is exploding, we'll have to answer to another half million units in unsatisfied orders if we don't jack that price up. We can't afford to expand that much for this product.

At this point, Hugh Fraser (administrative assistant to the president) walked up toward the front of the room from where he had been standing near the rear door. The discussion broke for a minute, and he took advantage of the lull to interject a few comments.

FRASER: This has certainly been enlightening. Looks like you fellows are pretty well up on this whole operation. As long as you're going to try to get all the things together that you ought to pin down for next year, let's see what I can add to help you.

Number One: Let's remember that everything that shows in the profit area here on Bill's chart is divided just about evenly between the government and us. Now, for last year we can read a profit of about $150,000. Well, that's right. But we were left with half of that, and then paid out dividends of $50,000 to the stockholders. Since we've got an anniversary year coming up, we'd like to put out a special dividend about 50 per cent extra. We ought to hold $25,000 in for the business, too. This means that we'd like to hit $100,000 *after* the costs of being governed.

Number Two: From where I sit, it looks like we're going to have to talk with the union again, and this time it's liable to cost us. All the indications are— and this isn't public—that we may have to meet demands that will boost our production costs—what do you call them here, Bill—variable costs—by 10 per cent across the board. This may kill the bonus-dividend plans, but we've got to hold the line on past profits. This means that we can give that much to the union only if we can make it in added revenues. I guess you'd say that that raises your break-even point, Bill—and for that one I'd consider the company's profit to be a fixed cost.

Number Three: Maybe this is the time to think about switching our product emphasis. Arnie Winetki may know better than I which of the products is more profitable. You check me out on this Arnie—and it might be a good idea for you and Bill French to get together on this one, too. These figures that I have

Exhibit 2

PRODUCT CLASS COST ANALYSIS

(Normal Year)

	Aggregate	"*A*"	"*B*"	"*C*"
Sales at full capacity (units).............	2,000,000			
Actual sales volume (units)..............	1,500,000	600,000	400,000	500,000
Unit sales price........................	$1.20	$1.67	$1.50	$0.40
Total sales revenue....................	$1,800,000	$1,000,000	$600,000	$200,000
Variable cost per unit..................	$0.75	$1.25	$0.625	$0.25
Total variable cost....................	$1,125,000	$ 750,000	$250,000	$125,000
Fixed costs...........................	$ 520,000	$ 170,000	$275,000	$ 75,000
Net profit............................	$ 155,000	$ 80,000	$ 75,000	......
Ratios:				
Variable cost to sales.................	0.63	0.75	0.42	0.63
Variable income to sales..............	0.37	0.25	0.58	0.37
Utilization of capacity................	75.0%	30.0%	20.0%	25.0%

(Exhibit 2) make it look like the percentage contribution on line "A" is the lowest of the bunch. If we're losing volume there as rapidly as you sales folks say, and if we're as hard pressed for space as Fred Williams has indicated, maybe we'd be better off grabbing some of that big demand for "C" by shifting some of the facilities over there from "A."

That's all I've got to say. Looks to me like you've all got plenty to think about.

DAVIDSON: Thanks, Hugh. I sort of figured that we'd get wound up here as soon as Bill brought out his charts. This is an approach that we've barely touched, but, as you can see, you've all got ideas that have got to be made to fit here somewhere. I'll tell you what let's do. Bill, suppose you rework your chart and try to bring into it some of the points that were made here today. I'll see if I can summarize what everyone seems to be looking for.

First of all, I have the idea buzzing around in the back of my mind that your presentation is based on a rather important series of assumptions. Most of the questions that were raised were really about those assumptions; it might help us all if you try to set the assumptions down in black and white so that we can see just how they influence the analysis.

Then, I think that Cooper would like to see the unit sales increase taken up, and he'd also like to see whether there's any difference if you base the calculations on an analysis of individual product lines. Also, as Bradshaw suggested, since the product mix is bound to change, why not see how things look if the shift materializes as sales has forecast.

Arnie Winetki would like to see the influence of a price increase in the "C" line, Fred Williams looks toward an increase in fixed manufacturing costs of ten thousand a month, and Hugh Fraser has suggested that we should consider taxes, dividends, expected union demands, and the question of product emphasis.

I think that ties it all together. Let's hold off on our next meeting, fellows, until Bill has time to work this all into shape.

With that, the participants broke off into small groups and the meeting disbanded. French and Wes Davidson headed back to their offices and French, in a tone of concern asked Davidson, "Why didn't you warn me about the hornet's nest I was walking into?"

"Bill, you didn't ask!"

Exhibit 3

LIST OF PARTICIPANTS IN THE MEETING

Bill French............................staff accountant
Wes Davidson.........................controller
John Cooper...........................production control
Fred Williams.........................manufacturing
Ray Bradshaw.........................assistant sales manager
Arnie Winetki.........................general sales manager
Hugh Fraser..........................administrative assistant to president

Questions

1. What are the assumptions implicit in Bill French's determination of his company's break-even point?

2. On the basis of French's revised information, what does next year look like:

a) What is the break-even point?

b) What level of operations must be achieved to pay the extra dividend, ignoring union demands?

c) What level of operations must be achieved to meet the union demands, ignoring bonus dividends?

d) What level of operations must be achieved to meet both dividends and expected union requirements?

3. Can the break-even analysis help the company decide whether to alter the existing product emphasis? What can the company afford to invest for additional "C" capacity?

4. Is this type of analysis of any value? For what can it be used?

CASE 16–3.   DAVIGO FOODS COMPANY

The Davigo Foods Company, located in a tomato-growing section, had for many years produced tomato specialties such as tomato juice cocktail, tomato paste, and ketchup. In 1953 it was able to extend its production season from four to nine months by the addition of various types of prepared spaghetti dinners and ravioli. In order to keep certain skilled personnel, the company had found a place for five men in the shipping department during the three months when the remainder of the plant was closed.

These men had been earning a wage of $1.30 an hour at their regular work, but they were willing to accept $0.97 an hour for the time they were in the shipping department. This meant that during the three months that they were in the shipping department the five men had collectively received $860 less than they would have received at their regular rate of pay. However, the regular wage rate in the shipping department was $0.80 an hour, and the shipping department therefore had been charged with $440 more than it ordinarily would have paid for this type of work.

The head of the shipping department was indignant that his costs were increased by this amount and contended that he should be charged at a rate not higher than the regular $0.80 rate for his department and that a fairer rate would be the beginners' rate of $0.65, since these men were not so efficient as his experienced work force.

Question

How would you account for the $0.97 an hour paid the five men when they worked in the shipping department?

CASE 16–4.   AZIENDA VINICOLA ITALIANA

Azienda Vinicola Italiana produced and bottled wines. A large percentage of its sales were of a special table wine. Most of its customers, located in the principal Italian cities, were served through local representatives. Its prices were in line with those of competitors.

In 1956 the firm sold 704,000 liters[4] of wine, in 871,850 bottles. In recent years demand had been increasing, and the firm had approached the limit of its productive capacity, which was estimated to be 900,000 bottles a year.

The production process was not complicated since the firm did not buy grapes but rather bought either mosto[5] or bulk wine. This policy had the disadvantage that the firm could not assure itself of a consistently high-quality product. Moreover, it was estimated that if grapes were purchased, the price of raw material would be reduced by about Lit.[6] 10 per bottle. On the other hand, the purchase and installation of equipment needed for pressing grapes would require an additional investment of about Lit. 50,000,000. No significant increase in labor costs was anticipated under such a practice.

In the production department there were 40 employees who worked

---

[4] One liter is slightly more than one United States liquid quart.

[5] Mosto is the juice of grapes before the fermentation process takes place. The fermentation process takes about one month. During this process carbon monoxide develops, and the sugar is converted into alcohol. Therefore, mosto is an unstable product, and wine is a stable product.

[6] In 1956, 100 Italian Lira (abbreviated "Lit.") equaled approximately U.S. $0.16.

a total of about 90,000 hours in 1956 and whose average wage per hour, including fringe benefits, was Lit. 365. The administrative manager was of the opinion that 40 per cent of this labor expense should be considered as being fixed, while the remainder could be considered as varying proportionally with production volume.

In 1956, production had required 700,000 liters of mosto and bulk wine, purchased at a total cost of Lit. 54,752,000. The average cost incurred for auxiliary materials (bottles, stoppers, neckbands, labels, etc.) was about Lit. 41 per bottle.

The income statement for 1956 is shown in Exhibit 1.

Exhibit 1

AZIENDA VINICOLA ITALIANA

Income Statement for 1956 in Lira

Sales.		174,670,000
Costs:		
Labor.	32,467,000	
Raw materials.	54,752,000	
Auxiliary materials.	35,774,000	
General manufacturing expenses (including pay of two cellar foremen). . . .	4,795,000	127,788,000
Manufacturing gross profit.		46,882,000
General administrative expenses (including the salary of a person skilled in the art of making and preserving wine).	16,745,000	
Depreciation.	10,540,000	
Interest.	7,500,000	
Advertising.	7,900,000	42,685,000
Net Profit.		4,197,000

The administrative manager wished to reorganize the firm in order to exploit its productive capability to the utmost and, above all, to increase the net profit, which the owners did not consider satisfactory. They were of the opinion that a net profit of 8 per cent or 9 per cent of sales could be realized.

As a basis upon which to make decisions, the administrative manager intended to use charts of costs and revenues that he had seen other firms use and that he considered helpful. The first step in this graphic analysis was a study of costs, separating fixed costs from variable costs. For that purpose, he examined the income statements of preceding years and came to the conclusion that the figures for 1956 were representative. He also noticed that the different types of wine had been sold in more or less the same relative proportions each year, despite large fluctuations in the total volume of business, and this fact confirmed his belief that the figures for 1956 were representative. He therefore prepared the following analysis:

a) *Fixed Costs*

40% of labor cost	12,987,000
Staff salaries	10,745,000
General manufacturing expenses	4,795,000
General administrative expenses	6,000,000
Advertising expenses	7,900,000
Interest	7,500,000
Depreciation	10,540,000
	60,467,000

b) *Variable Costs*

60% of labor cost	19,480,000
Raw materials	54,752,000
Auxiliary materials	35,774,000
	110,006,000

The administrative manager assumed a maximum capacity of 900,-000 bottles a year. At current prices he estimated this would produce sales revenue of Lit. 180,000,000.

With the present structure of costs and revenue, the profits resulting from an annual production of 900,000 bottles would be small. The administrative manager decided, therefore, to try to discover a way to change costs and revenue so as to obtain a profit of Lit. 16,000,000 a year, which would be 9 per cent of sales of Lit. 180,000,000.

Questions

1. Accepting the distribution between fixed and variable elements as estimated by the administrative manager, prepare a chart of costs and revenues. Determine the volume of production at which the firm reaches its break-even point and the profit at capacity operation.

2. Draw three other charts, each constructed so that a production of 900,-000 bottles will produce a profit of Lit. 16,000,000, one in which selling price is assumed to increase, another in which fixed costs are assumed to decrease, and a third in which variable costs are assumed to decrease. What are the break-even points in each of these situations?

3. What are the most likely alternatives to consider so as to achieve a profit of Lit. 16,000,000?

CASE 16–5.   TRACY MANUFACTURING COMPANY

In the summer of 1947 there was considerable feeling among the executives of the Tracy Manufacturing Company that costs were out of line. The company had made good profits for several years, and it was believed that under such conditions laxity in cost control had developed.

Exhibit 1

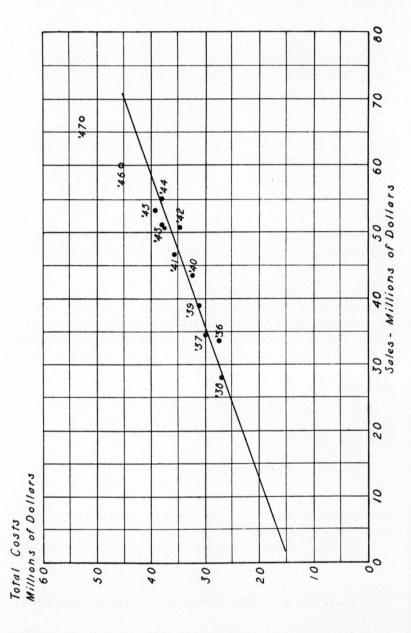

Total Costs
Millions of Dollars

Sales - Millions of Dollars

'30 '36 '37 '39 '40 '41 '43 '45 '42 '44 '46 '47

The end of World War II in 1945 and the sharp increases in prices in 1946 also had created problems.

The Tracy Manufacturing Company made a variety of tools. Although the company concentrated on small tools that it sold through mail-order houses and hardware stores, it also manufactured larger tools sold directly to manufacturers. The company used a well-developed cost accounting system.

In an effort to determine whether the cost-sales relationship had changed, the treasurer had an assistant plot the total cost of sales for each of the years 1936–45, taken from income statements, against net sales for each of those years. (See Exhibit 1.) A trend line was then fitted to these points by the method of least squares; that is, the line was drawn in such a way that the squares of all deviations of actual points from the line were at a minimum. When, however, the actual cost for 1946 and the budgeted cost for 1947 were plotted against actual and projected sales, the points were found to fall well above the previous line of relationship. On seeing the chart, some of the executives were quick to point out that here was proof of the company's growing inefficiency. The treasurer, however, believed that more study was needed before any such conclusion could be reached.

The treasurer asked his assistant to initiate a study that would, among other things, answer the following questions.

1. Are the 1946 and 1947 points out of line?

2. If so, why are they out of line?

3. If volume declines, what line of relationshipcan cost be expected to follow? What has happened to the break-even point?

Questions

1. What was the approximate break-even point under the 1936–45 relationship?

2. What are some of the possible reasons why the 1946 and 1947 points departed from the 1936–45 line of relationship?

3. What steps would you take in order to answer the treasurer's questions?

CASE 16–6.   REED PAINT COMPANY

C. H. Macrae had recently been elected president of the Reed Paint Company to fill the vacancy created by the retirement from active business life of the former chief executive. Mr. Macrae had been with the company for 15 years, and for the preceding six years he had been vice president in charge of manufacturing. Shortly after taking over his new position, Mr. Macrae held a series of conferences with the controller in which the general subject under discussion was budgetary control technique. The new president thought that the existing method of planning and checking on selling costs was particularly unsatisfactory, and he asked the controller to devise a system that would provide better control over these costs.

The Reed Paint Company manufactured a complete line of paints that its branch office salesmen sold to wholesalers, retailers, builders, and industrial users. Most of the products carried the Reed brand name, which was nationally advertised. The company was one of the largest in the industry.

Current Budgeting Procedure

Under the procedure then being used, selling expenses were budgeted on a "fixed" or "appropriation" basis. Each October the accounting department sent to branch managers and to the other executives in charge of selling departments a detailed record of the actual expenses of their departments for the preceding year and for the current year to date. Guided by this record, by estimates of the succeeding year's sales, and by his own judgment, each department head drew up and submitted an estimate of the expenses of his department for the succeeding year, detailed as to main items of expense. The estimates made by the branch managers were sent to the sales manager, who was in charge of all branch sales. He determined whether or not they were reasonable, and cleared up any questionable items by correspondence. Upon approval by the sales manager, the estimates of branch expenses were submitted to the manager of distribution, Mr. Campbell, who was in charge of all selling, promotional, and warehousing activities.

The manager of distribution discussed these figures and the expense estimates furnished by the other department heads with the executives concerned, and after differences were reconciled, he combined the estimates of all the selling departments into a selling expense budget. This budget was submitted to the budget committee for final approval. For control purposes, the annual budget was divided into 12 equal amounts, and actual expenses were compared each month with the budgeted figures. Exhibit 1 shows the form in which these monthly comparisons were made.

Mr. Macrae believed that there were two important weaknesses in this method of setting the selling expense budget:

1. It was impossible for anyone to ascertain with any feeling of

certainty the reasonableness of the estimates made by the various department heads. Clearly, the expenses of the preceding year did not constitute adequate standards against which these expense estimates could be judged, since selling conditions were never the same in any two years. One obvious cause of variation in selling expenses was the variation in the "job to be done," as defined in the sales budget.

2. Selling conditions often changed substantially after the budget was adopted, but there was no provision for making the proper corresponding changes in the selling expense budget. Neither was there a logical basis for relating selling expenses to the actual sales volume obtained or to any other measure of sales effort. The chief executive believed that it was reasonable to expect that sales expenses would increase, though not proportionately, if actual sales volume were greater than the forecast volume; but that with the existing method of control it was impossible to determine how large the increase in expenses should be.

Exhibit 1

BUDGET REPORT CURRENTLY USED

BRANCH SALES AND EXPENSE PERFORMANCE					
DATE: October		BRANCH A		Mgr: H. C. Obermeyer	
	This Month				Over*—Under Year to Date
	Budget†	Actual	Over* Under	Per-centage of Sales	
Net sales	190,000	160,000			
Executive salaries	2,000	2,000	....	1.25	....
Office salaries	1,150	1,134	16	0.71	1,203
Salesman's compensation	11,400	9,600	1,800	6.00	2,802*
Traveling expense	3,420	3,127	293	1.95	1,012*
Stationery, office supplies, and expense	1,042	890	152	0.56	360
Postage	230	262	32*	0.16	21
Light and heat	134	87	47	0.05	128
Subscriptions and dues	150	112	38	0.07	26
Donations	125	....	125	0.00	130
Advertising expense (local)	1,900	1,800	100	1.12	1,200*
Social security taxes	291	205	86	0.13	27*
Rental	975	975	....	0.61	....
Depreciation	762	762	....	0.48	....
Other branch expense	2,551	2,426	125	1.52	247*
TOTAL	26,130	23,380	2,750	14.61	3,420*

† ¹⁄₁₂ of annual budget.

Proposed Procedure

As a means of overcoming these weaknesses the president suggested setting standards for the selling cost budget on a fixed and variable basis, a method similar to the techniques used in the control of manufacturing expenses. The controller agreed that this approach seemed to offer the most feasible solution to the problem, and he therefore undertook, with the cooperation of the sales department, a study of selling expenses for the purpose of devising a method of setting reasonable standards. In recent years, the accounting department had made many analyses of selling costs, the results of which had been used to determine the proper bases for allocating costs to products, customers, functions, and territories. These studies also were used in the solution of certain special problems, such as that of determining how large an individual order must be to yield a profit for the company. Many of the data that had been accumulated for these purposes were helpful in the controller's current study.

The controller was convinced that the fixed portion of selling expenses—in other words, the portion that was independent of any fluctuation in volume—could be established by determining the amount of expenses that had to be incurred at the minimum sales volume at which the company was likely to operate. He therefore asked Mr. Campbell to suggest a minimum volume figure and the amount of expenses which would have to be incurred at this volume. A staff assistant was assigned the task of studying the past sales records of the company over several business cycles, the long-term outlook for sales, and sales trends in other companies in the industry. From the report prepared by his assistant, Mr. Campbell concluded that sales volume would not drop below 45 per cent of the current capacity of the factory.

Mr. Campbell then attempted to determine the selling expenses that would be incurred at the minimum volume. With the help of his staff assistant, he worked out a hypothetical selling organization that in his opinion would be required to sell merchandise equivalent to 45 per cent of factory capacity, complete as to the number of persons needed to staff each branch office and the other selling departments, including the advertising, merchandise, and sales administration departments. Using current salary and commission figures, the assistant calculated the amount of money that would be required to pay salaries for such an organization. The manager of distribution also estimated the other expenses, such as advertising, branch office upkeep, supplies, and travel, that he thought would be incurred by each branch and staff department at the minimum sales volume.

The controller decided that the variable portion of the selling expense standard should be expressed as a certain amount per sales dollar. He realized that the use of the sales dollar as a measuring stick had certain disadvantages in that it would not reflect such important influences on costs as the size of the order, the selling difficulty of certain territories, changes in buyer psychology, etc. The sales dollar, however, was the measuring stick most convenient to use, the only figure readily available from the records then being kept, and also a figure that all the individuals concerned thoroughly understood. The controller believed that a budget that varied with sales would certainly be better than one that did not vary at all. He planned to devise a more accurate measure of causes of variation in selling expenses after he had had an opportunity to study the nature of these factors over a longer period.

As a basis for setting the initial variable expense standards, the controller prepared a series of charts on which the actual annual expenditures for the principal groups of expense items for several preceding years were correlated with sales volume for the year. Using these charts, which showed to what extent the principal expense items had fluctuated with sales volume in the past, and modifying them in accordance with his own judgment, the controller determined a rate of variation for the variable portion of each item of selling expense. The controller thought that after the new system had been tested in practice, it would be possible to refine these rates, perhaps by the use of a technique analogous to the time-study technique employed to determine certain expense standards in the factory.

At this point the controller had both a rate of variation and one point (i.e., at 45 per cent capacity) on the selling expense curve for each expense item. He was therefore able to construct a formula for each item by extending a line through the known point at the slope represented by the rate of variation. He determined the height of this line at zero volume and called this amount the fixed portion of the selling expense formula. The diagram in Exhibit 2 illustrates the procedure, although the actual computations were mathematical rather than graphic.

The selling expense budget for the following year was determined by adding to the new standards for the various fixed components the indicated flexible allowances for the year's estimated sales volume. This budget was submitted to the budget committee, which studied the fixed amounts and the variable rates underlying the final figures, making only minor changes before final approval.

The controller planned to issue each month reports showing for each department actual expenses compared with budgeted expenses. The variable portion of the budgeted allowances would be adjusted to correspond to the actual volume of sales obtained during the month. Exhibit 3 shows the budget report that he planned to send to branch managers, with figures for the same month as those in Exhibit 1.

One sales executive privately belittled the controller's proposal. "Anyone in the selling game," he asserted, "knows that sometimes customers fall all over each other in their hurry to buy, and other times, no matter what we do, they won't even nibble. It's a waste of time to make fancy formulas for selling cost budgets under conditions like that."

Exhibit 2

BUDGET FOR "OTHER BRANCH EXPENSE," BRANCH A

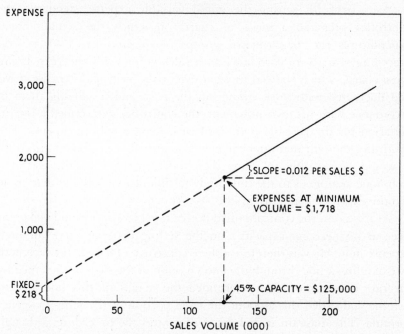

Questions

1. From the information given in Exhibits 1 and 3, determine, insofar as you can, whether each item of expense is (*a*) nonvariable, (*b*) partly variable with sales volume, (*c*) variable with sales volume, or (*d*) variable with some other factor.

2. What bearing do your conclusions in Question 1 have on the type of budget that is most appropriate?

3. Should the proposed sales expense budget be adopted?

4. If a variable budget is used, should dollar sales be used as the measure of variation?

Exhibit 3
BUDGET REPORT PROPOSED BY CONTROLLER

<table>
<tr>
<td colspan="7">Expense Budget Report   BRANCH: A
MANAGER: H. C. Obermeyer
DATE: October</td>
</tr>
<tr>
<td rowspan="2"></td>
<td colspan="2">Budget Factors</td>
<td colspan="3">This Month</td>
<td rowspan="2">Year to Date</td>
</tr>
<tr>
<td>Fixed</td>
<td>Variable</td>
<td>Budget</td>
<td>Actual</td>
<td>Over* Under</td>
<td>Over* Under</td>
</tr>
<tr>
<td>Net sales</td>
<td></td>
<td></td>
<td></td>
<td>160,000</td>
<td></td>
<td>†</td>
</tr>
<tr>
<td>Executive salaries</td>
<td>2,000</td>
<td>. . . .</td>
<td>2,000</td>
<td>2,000</td>
<td>. . .</td>
<td></td>
</tr>
<tr>
<td>Office salaries</td>
<td>110</td>
<td>0.0051</td>
<td>926</td>
<td>1,134</td>
<td>208*</td>
<td></td>
</tr>
<tr>
<td>Salesman's compensation</td>
<td>. . . .</td>
<td>0.0600</td>
<td>9,600</td>
<td>9,600</td>
<td>. . .</td>
<td></td>
</tr>
<tr>
<td>Traveling expense</td>
<td>·568</td>
<td>0.0142</td>
<td>2,840</td>
<td>3,127</td>
<td>287*</td>
<td></td>
</tr>
<tr>
<td>Stationery, office supplies, and
  expense</td>
<td>282</td>
<td>0.0042</td>
<td>954</td>
<td>890</td>
<td>64</td>
<td></td>
</tr>
<tr>
<td>Postage</td>
<td>47</td>
<td>0.0010</td>
<td>207</td>
<td>262</td>
<td>55*</td>
<td></td>
</tr>
<tr>
<td>Light and heat</td>
<td>134</td>
<td>. . . . .</td>
<td>134</td>
<td>87</td>
<td>47</td>
<td></td>
</tr>
<tr>
<td>Subscriptions and dues</td>
<td>10</td>
<td>0.0008</td>
<td>138</td>
<td>112</td>
<td>26</td>
<td></td>
</tr>
<tr>
<td>Donations</td>
<td>20</td>
<td>0.0005</td>
<td>100</td>
<td>. . . .</td>
<td>100</td>
<td></td>
</tr>
<tr>
<td>Advertising expense (local)</td>
<td>150</td>
<td>0.0100</td>
<td>1,750</td>
<td>1,800</td>
<td>50*</td>
<td></td>
</tr>
<tr>
<td>Social security taxes</td>
<td>42</td>
<td>0.0013</td>
<td>250</td>
<td>205</td>
<td>45</td>
<td></td>
</tr>
<tr>
<td>Rental</td>
<td>975</td>
<td>. . . . .</td>
<td>975</td>
<td>975</td>
<td>. . .</td>
<td></td>
</tr>
<tr>
<td>Depreciation</td>
<td>762</td>
<td>. . . . .</td>
<td>762</td>
<td>762</td>
<td>. . .</td>
<td></td>
</tr>
<tr>
<td>Other branch expense</td>
<td>218</td>
<td>0.0120</td>
<td>2,138</td>
<td>2,426</td>
<td>288*</td>
<td></td>
</tr>
<tr>
<td>TOTAL</td>
<td>5,318</td>
<td>0.1091</td>
<td>22,774</td>
<td>23,380</td>
<td>606*</td>
<td></td>
</tr>
</table>

† The controller had not recalculated budgets for previous months, and figures were therefore not available for this column.

Chapter 17

THE ANALYSIS OF DIFFERENCES

ALL ANALYSES of accounting data involve comparisons. We make judgments about current performance, not by using some abstract or absolute criterion, but rather by comparing data on current performance with some other data. The basis for comparison may be historical data for the same company, it may be data from another company, or it may be a predetermined yardstick, such as a budget.

We shall refer to the data we are analyzing as the *actual* data, and to the data used as a basis for comparison as the *standard* data. As used here, therefore, the word "standard" has a broader connotation than in the phrase "standard cost," it includes *any* figure with which actual performance is compared.

In cost accounting, the difference between actual and standard is called a *variance*.[1] We shall use the words "variance" and "difference" interchangeably.

It is of little use to know only the amount by which actual profit differs from standard profit. In order to take effective action, we need to know what factors accounted for the difference. This chapter discusses techniques for decomposing a total difference into the elements that account for it.

In a given company the techniques actually used will depend on management's estimate of the value to be derived from them. Some companies use no formal techniques, others use only a few of those described here, and still others use even more complicated techniques. There is no prescribed pattern beyond the general rule that any technique should be worth more than the costs involved in using it.

Presumably, we choose a certain standard because it is the best measure we can find of the job that should have been done; yet a standard is rarely, if ever, perfect. Thus, although it is often convenient to refer to "favorable" and "unfavorable" variances, these words imply value judgments that are valid only to the extent that the standard is a valid measure of what should have been done. Some of the limitations of

---

[1] Note that this word has quite a different meaning in statistics.

various types of standards have been discussed in Chapters 11, 13, and 15.

Even a standard cost may not be an accurate estimate of what costs "should have been under the circumstances." This situation can arise for either or both of two reasons: (a) the standard was not set properly, or (b) although set properly in the light of conditions existing at the time, those conditions have changed so that the standard has become obsolete. An essential first step in analysis of a variance, therefore, is an examination of the accuracy of the standard. Judgments made on the basis of the variance must be tempered by the results of this examination. The importance of this first step cannot be overemphasized, but we must assume for the purpose of describing other analytical techniques that the standard has been properly set.

Even though the standard is accurate, a variance may not reflect the performance of a responsible supervisor since it may result from a combination of causes, some of which he can control and some of which he cannot. Analytical techniques make it possible to separate out, at least approximately, the controllable portion. These techniques are strictly mechanical, and at best provide a starting point for solution of the problem of performance evaluation.

STRUCTURE OF ANALYSIS

The operations of a business can be examined in terms of its accomplishments, i.e., its outputs, and the resources it uses, i.e., its inputs. Outputs are measured in terms of revenue, and inputs in terms of cost or expense; profit is the difference between them. The difference between actual and standard profit is explainable principally by the existence of some or all of the following factors:

1. Noncomparable data.
2. Inherent product or service characteristics.
3. Price per unit of input.
4. Quantity of input.
5. Mix.
6. Price per unit of output.
7. Volume.
8. The measuring stick.
9. Assets employed, if the comparison is for return on investment, rather than profits alone. (This factor will not be discussed further here.)

These factors explain the profit variance for a whole company. Some or all of them also explain the variance for any department or other organization unit within the company. Even though a department does not have revenue as such, it does have an output—that is, it *does* something—and if this output can be measured, the analysis holds. Also, the analysis is applicable not only to profit but also to any difference between an actual and a standard.

NONCOMPARABLE DATA

For many reasons, the data used as the standard may not be strictly comparable with the actual data. Possible differences in the accounting rules used and in the definition of terms have been discussed at length in previous chapters. It is also possible that simple arithmetic errors have crept into one or the other set of data. Before proceeding with the detailed analysis, therefore, it is important that one examine the data carefully, and adjust them to remove such sources of noncomparability whenever possible.

PRODUCT CHARACTERISTICS

In many situations, there is no numerical way of measuring the differences in quality or other characteristics between the standard and the actual output, and the significance of this factor must therefore be judged intuitively. In some cases, it can be brought into the analysis explicitly. For example, if we are analyzing the differences between two bids to build a house, the fact that one contractor includes certain features that the other omits is an obvious factor to be taken into account.

PRICE AND QUANTITY OF INPUTS

In order to decompose variances in input factors into price and quantity elements, we must have available, for both standard and actual, the number of units and the price per unit. The procedure will be discussed first in terms of direct labor and then in terms of material.

Direct Labor

The standard labor cost of a unit of product is constructed essentially by multiplying the standard time (e.g., number of hours) required to produce that unit by a standard rate per unit of time (e.g., standard wage rate per hour). Total standard labor cost for an accounting period is found by multiplying the standard labor cost per unit by the number of units of product produced. When employees are paid on an hourly basis, actual labor cost for the period is the product of actual hours worked times the actual labor rate per hour. These relationships suggest that it is possible to break the variance between actual and standard labor costs into two components: (1) the variance caused by the fact that actual *time* differed from standard time, and (2) the variance caused by the fact that actual *rates* differed from standard rates. The former is the input quantity variance, and the latter is the input price variance.

A commonly used pair of rules for isolating the effects of these components follows:

1. The *time* variance is the difference between standard hours and actual hours, priced at the standard rate per hour. (This variance is also known as a "usage," "spending," or "efficiency" variance, although the latter two terms connote too strong an inference as to the meaning of the results.)
2. The *rate* (or "price") variance is the difference between the standard rate per hour and the actual rate per hour multiplied by the actual numbers of hours.

The *net* variance (or *total* variance) in labor costs is the algebraic sum of the time and rate variances. It follows that having found one variance, the other can be found by subtracting this variance from the net variance. The net variance is also the difference between actual cost and standard cost.

The application of these rules is illustrated in Illustration 17–1, which is a diagram of this situation:

	Actual	Standard
Hours to produce one unit............................	6	8
Wage rate per hour....................................	$ 3	$ 2
Cost of one unit (rate times hours).....................	$18	$16

Illustration 17–1

ILLUSTRATION OF COMPUTATION OF TIME AND RATE VARIANCES

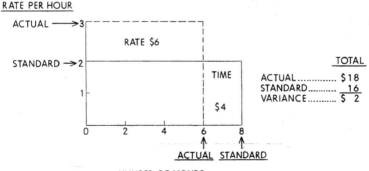

In the diagram, the solid rectangle indicates the standard cost (8 hours × $2 = $16), and the dotted rectangle indicates actual cost (6 hours × $3 = $18). The variances are the areas where the two rectangles do not coincide. The *time* variance is 2 hours times $2 per hour, or $4, it is favorable because actual time is less than standard time. The *rate* variance is $1 per hour times 6 hours, or $6; it is unfavorable because the actual wage rate exceeds the standard rate. The net variance is the algebraic sum of these two variances, or $2, unfavorable; this is also the difference between actual cost and standard cost.

The calculations are repeated in terms of the rules given above:

1. (STD. HOURS − ACTUAL HOURS) × STD. RATE = TIME VARIANCE
   (8   −   6   ) × $2   = $4

2. (STD. RATE − ACTUAL RATE) × ACTUAL HOURS = RATE VARIANCE
   ($2   − $3   ) ×   6   =   −$6

3. STD. COST − ACTUAL COST   = NET VARIANCE
      $16   − $18   =   −$2

These equations are set up in such a way that a plus answer means a favorable variance and a minus answer means an unfavorable variance, but it often is easier to find by inspection whether the variance is favorable or unfavorable than to remember this fact.

When both the time and rate variances are favorable, or when both are unfavorable, the above rules do not give so clear-cut a result. The difficulty is demonstrated in Illustration 17–2, which shows the following situation:

	Actual	Standard
Hours to produce one unit	10	8
Wage rate per hour	$ 3	$ 2
Cost of one unit	$30	$16

Illustration 17–2

COMPUTATION OF TIME AND RATE VARIANCES

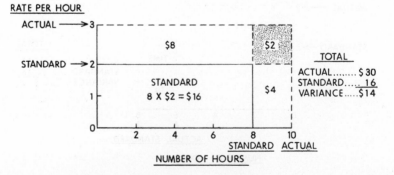

In this situation, the unfavorable net variance of $14 is partly the result of the high wage rate and partly the result of the longer time required. Clearly, at least $8 of the variance is a rate variance resulting because the work was done at a rate that was $1 per hour higher than standard, and at least $4 results because actual hours exceeded standard hours. But the remaining $2 is a *gray area;* it is an inextricable combination of the influence both of the high rate and the long time. The above rules have the effect of assigning the entire $2 as *rate variance.* Other possibilities would be just as logical, but in practice the rules given are usually used. The calculation is:

1. (Std. Hours − Actual Hours) × Std. Rate = Time Variance
   (8   −   10   ) × $2   =   −$4
2. (Std. Rate − Actual Rate) × Actual Hours = Rate Variance
   ($2   − $3   ) ×   10   =   −$10

Interpretation of the Labor Variance. The reason for attempting to break down the total labor variance as described above is that the rate variance is often evaluated differently from the time variance. The rate variance may arise because of a change in wage rates for which the foreman cannot be held responsible, whereas the foreman may be held entirely responsible for the time variance, because he should control the time spent on a given job.

This distinction cannot be made in all cases, for there are many situations in which the two factors are interdependent. For example, the foreman may find it possible to complete the work in less than the standard time by using men who earn a higher than standard rate, and he may be perfectly justified in doing so. Even so, the use of the technique described above may lead to a better understanding of what actually happened.

The technique described provides only a partial explanation of the cause of the labor variance. It does not isolate any of a great number of other factors that may cause a difference between actual and standard labor costs. An incomplete list of such factors follows:

1. A standard labor cost per unit is valid only if labor costs vary proportionately with the number of units produced. Labor costs, in fact, may not vary proportionately with volume at all levels of production.
2. The measure of volume (e.g., number of units, pounds of product, etc.) may not be an accurate indication of the amount of direct labor required. For example, a standard labor cost of $1 a pound implies that each pound of product requires the same amount of labor, which, in fact, may not be the case.
3. The volume figure used to compute total standard costs may not corre-

spond exactly to the volume figure that generated the actual labor costs, because of the nature of the system.

4. The elements included in standard cost (e.g., overtime, fringe benefits, shift premium) may differ from the elements included in actual costs.
5. Spoilage may not have been allowed for properly.
6. Quality may have suffered or improved.
7. Labor performance may have affected, or may have been affected by, factors that are reflected in material or overhead costs.
8. There may have been changes in morale that have not affected current costs but which may have an important effect on future costs.
9. The total actual costs and the total standard costs for a period may be influenced by offsetting forces for individual products or individual responsibility centers. The totals conceal these underlying forces.

Since the objective is to isolate that portion of the variance that is the result of efficiency or inefficiency and to hold the supervisor responsible for this portion, factors of the type mentioned above must be considered.

Material Cost Variances

The variance between actual and standard direct material costs can be broken down into what are commonly called *material usage variance* and *material price variance* by the same technique as that described above for direct labor. The diagram in Illustration 17–1 is made applicable to material costs simply by changing the names:

	Actual	Standard
Quantity (pounds) used to produce one unit...............	6	8
Price per pound..	$ 3	$ 2
Material cost for one unit.............................	$18	$16

The *usage* variance, or *yield* variance, is 2 pounds times $2 a pound, or $4; and the *price* variance is $1 a pound times 6 pounds, or $6.

In some companies, the cost accounting system is constructed so that the price variance is removed as a part of the regular accounting entries; if such a system is used, there may be no need to separate out the price variance by the method described above. For example, if a company takes raw material into inventory at a standard price, the price variance is set up at the time the purchase is recorded. Raw Materials Inventory is debited at standard cost, Accounts Payable (or Cash) is credited at actual cost, and the difference is debited or credited to Material Price Variance. Even in such a case, a kind of price variance may later appear if material of a different *quality* from standard (hence, with a different standard cost) is used in the production process.

Spoilage and Rework. The material usage variance shows the difference between the actual and standard quantities of material *put into* the manufacturing process. If the product itself does not pass inspection at the end of the process or at some intermediate stage, it must either be discarded or sent back to have the defect corrected. If discarded, the labor, material, and overhead costs accumulated on it up to that point constitute *spoilage*. If sent back for correction, the extra *rework* cost is also a cost associated with substandard products.

Spoilage and rework costs can be handled in any of several ways, only one of which is described here. A standard allowance for spoilage may be established for each responsibility center, and the responsibility center charged for the material, labor, and overhead cost accumulated on defective products for which it is responsible; the offsetting credit is to Goods in Process Inventory. Note that the charge is made to the responsibility center where the defect occurred, which is not necessarily the same as the center in which the defect was discovered. Rework costs are also charged to the center whose poor work occasioned the rework; this center is not necessarily the one doing the rework. Spoilage and rework costs, then, are costs of the center that caused them to occur. In a standard cost system, there is often a standard allowance for spoilage and rework, in which case the variance between actual and standard represents a difference from the standard amount, not the total cost of spoiled work.

MIX

When the process uses several different materials, or several grades of the same material, that are supposed to be combined in a standard proportion, it is possible to compute a *mix variance* that shows the effect on cost of variations from the standard proportions. The mix variance for each item of material is the difference between the actual quantity of material used and the standard proportion (i.e., the quantity that would have been used if the standard proportions were adhered to), priced at the standard price. If a mix variance is calculated, the price variance is also calculated for each item of material separately.

To illustrate the calculation of the mix variance, we shall use a situation similar to that described in Illustration 17–1. We shall shift the situation from labor costs to material costs, simply to highlight the fact that the technique applies equally well to either type of cost; and instead of a single quantity and a single unit price, we shall assume that there are three items of material, each with its own quantity and unit price. The total amounts for the three items correspond to the totals shown on

Illustration 17—1, signifying that the mix variance is a further decomposition of the differences analyzed there.

The calculation of the mix variance is shown in Illustration 17—3. As shown in the top block of the illustration, a standard unit of product consists of Materials A, B, and C in the proportions $\frac{4}{8}$, $\frac{2}{8}$, and $\frac{2}{8}$,

Illustration 17—3

MIX, PRICE, AND USAGE VARIANCES

A. Assumed Situation

	Standard			Actual		
	Quantity (Lbs.)	Unit Price	Total	Quantity (Lbs.)	Unit Price	Total
Material A..............	4	$1.00	$ 4.00	2	$3.50	$ 7.00
Material B..............	2	2.00	4.00	1	2.00	2.00
Material C..............	2	4.00	8.00	3	3.00	9.00
Total.................	8	$2.00	$16.00	6	$3.00	$18.00

B. Computation of Mix Variance

	Standard* Mix	−	Actual Quantity	=	Differ- ence	×	Std. Price	=	Mix Variance
Material A.................3			2		+1		$1.00		$1.00
Material B.................1.5			1		+0.5		2.00		1.00
Material C.................1.5			3		−1.5		4.00		− 6.00
Total....................6			6						−$4.00

*This is the standard proportions $\frac{4}{8}$, $\frac{2}{8}$, and $\frac{2}{8}$ applied to the actual total quantity.

C. Computation of Price Variance

	Std. Price	−	Actual Price	=	Differ- ence	×	Actual Quantity	=	Price Variance
Material A..........$1.00			$3.50		−$2.50		2		−$5.00
Material B.......... 2.00			2.00		. . .		1		. . .
Material C.......... 4.00			3.00		+1.00		3		+ 3.00
Price Variance......									−$2.00

D. Computation of Usage Variance

$$(\text{Standard Quantity} - \text{Actual Quantity}) \times \text{Standard Price} = \text{Usage Variance}$$
$$(\qquad 8 \qquad - \qquad 6 \qquad) \times \qquad \$2 \qquad = \$4$$

respectively. In the next block, these fractions are applied to the *actual* total quantity, 6 pounds, to give the standard mix of the three materials in such a quantity: namely, 3 pounds of A, 1.5 pounds of B, and 1.5 pounds of C. The difference between the actual quantity of each material and its standard mix, priced at its standard price, and totaled is the mix variance.

The price variance on each material is computed according to the rule already given: the difference between standard price and actual price, times the actual quantity. Note that the *sum* of the mix variances and price variances computed in this manner equals the price variance computed from the total quantity and average price given above, that is $(-\$4) + (-\$2) = -\$6$. The usage variance and the net variance are not affected.

Computation of the mix variance and price variance in this manner, although a little complicated, reveals information that might otherwise be concealed. It shows the effect of changes in the price of each material, which is hidden if averages are used. It also shows the effect of varying the mix of materials. These two may be interrelated; for example, it is quite possible that a higher than standard proportion of one material was used in an attempt to offset the effect of an increased price of another material. The mix variance may also be related to the quality of the product, although this does not appear in the calculation; if one material is a low grade and another is a high grade, then the increase in the proportion of the lower-grade material may have had an adverse effect on quality.

General Use of the Mix Concept

The mix phenomenon arises whenever a cost or revenue item is analyzed by components, rather than in total. The price and quantity variances obtained from an analysis of each of the components will not add up to the price and quantity variance of the whole item if the actual proportions of the components differ from the standard proportions. Thus, if labor cost is being analyzed by employee skill classifications, if revenue is analyzed by individual products, or by individual geographic regions, a mix variance inevitably arises. Failure to appreciate this fact can lead to great frustration in trying to make the figures add up properly.

OUTPUT PRICE AND VOLUME

The sales revenue variance can be decomposed into a price factor and a quantity or volume factor. The *price variance* is the difference between the standard price per unit and the actual price per unit multiplied by the actual quantity sold. The *quantity variance* is the difference between standard quantity and actual quantity sold priced at the standard price per unit. Note the similarity between these rules and the rules for deriving the labor time and rate variances; whenever a total variance is to be broken down into a quantity element and a price element, the same general approach is used.

If revenue is analyzed by individual products or product lines, a mix variance will emerge, as described in the preceding section.

In many situations, it is more informative to analyze output in terms of gross margin, rather than in terms of sales revenue. The procedure is the same, except that gross margin per unit is used instead of selling price per unit. Such an analysis implies that the output of the sales organization is more usefully viewed as dollars of gross margin, rather than as dollars of sales revenue.

VOLUME AND COSTS

Direct labor and direct material costs usually vary directly and proportionately with volume. Consequently, *unit* direct labor and direct material costs are the same at all volume levels within the normal range; they are unaffected by volume. By contrast, overhead costs vary with volume but less than proportionately, as we saw in the diagrams presented in Chapter 16. This being so, *unit* overhead costs are inevitably higher at low volumes than they are at high volumes.

EXAMPLE: If the formula for the overhead cost line is $500 plus $1 per unit, overhead costs at various volumes are expected to be as follows:

Volume (in Units)	Total Overhead Cost	Unit Overhead Cost
800	$1,300	$1.62
900	1,400	1.56
1,000	1,500	1.50
1,100	1,600	1.45
1,200	1,700	1.42

Since the unit selling price presumably does not fluctuate with volume, whereas unit costs change with volume as seen above, unit profits are different at different volumes. Thus, if actual volume is different from standard volume, a volume variance results.

In order to measure this variance, we shall make use of the cost-volume relationship developed in Chapter 16. On Illustration 17–4,

Illustration 17–4

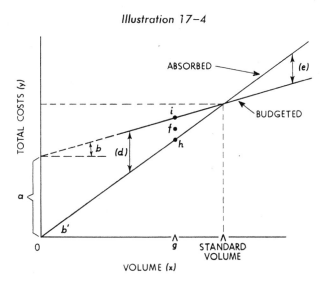

the line marked "budgeted" cost shows this direct, but less than proportional, relationship between costs and volume. Costs at any volume are expected to be the nonvariable amount, *a,* plus the variable rate, *b,* times the number of units of volume.

Recall that the overhead rate was set by choosing one level of volume, the *standard volume,* and dividing total costs at that volume by the number of units of volume. Thus, if the formula for the budgeted cost line is $500 + $1 per unit, and if standard volume is 1,000 units, total budgeted costs at 1,000 units are $1,500, and the overhead rate is $1.50 per unit.

At any volume, overhead costs would be *absorbed* into products at the rate of $1.50 per unit. The line of "absorbed" cost on the diagram shows the total costs that would be absorbed at any volume. At standard volume, budgeted costs equal absorbed costs, but at any other volume budgeted costs are different from absorbed costs, as indicated by the spread between the two lines. At lower volumes, costs are *underabsorbed,* as indicated by the amount *d,* and at higher volumes they are *overabsorbed,* as indicated by the amount *e.* They are underabsorbed or overabsorbed *because* actual volume differs from standard volume; hence, this amount is the volume variance. The volume variance results solely from the fact that actual volume in a given period differed from the standard volume that was used, *prior to the beginning of the year,* in setting the overhead rate.

If everything went as expected during an accounting period, actual costs incurred would coincide with budgeted costs at the level of activity prevailing in the period. For a variety of reasons, actual costs will probably be different from budgeted costs; the difference is called the *spending variance.* For control purposes, the spending variance is of particular interest as a starting point in appraising the supervisor's performance. It is only a starting point, since the variance may be the result of any of a number of uncontrollable factors, such as changes in prices, the method of overhead allocation, the rate and direction of change in volume, and changes in methods.

The overhead variance, as shown in the accounting records, is the algebraic sum of the volume variance and the spending variance. It is therefore useful to break down this *net variance* into its two components. The method for doing this is shown in Illustration 17–4 in a period when actual costs are at the point marked *f* and actual volume is *g.* Absorbed cost at this volume is the amount *h,* and budgeted cost the amount, *i.* Note that budgeted cost is the amount of cost budgeted for the volume level actually attained in the period. The following relationships will hold:

The *net variance* is the difference between actual cost, *f,* and absorbed cost, *h.* In the example, cost is underabsorbed.

The *volume variance* is the difference between budgeted cost, *i,* and absorbed cost, *h.* In the example, this variance is unfavorable.

The *spending variance* is the difference between actual cost, *f,* and budgeted cost, *i.* In the example, this variance is favorable.

The accounting variance is also the algebraic sum of the volume variance and the spending variance. (The "favorable" and "unfavorable" variances can be designated by + or − signs, but it is usually easier to insert the proper signs from a consideration of the relationships than by memorizing the algebraic formulas.)

EXAMPLE: Assume that—

　　Actual volume in an accounting period is 900 units.
　　Actual cost is $1,380.
　　The budget formula is $500 plus $1 per unit.
　　The overhead rate is $1.50 per unit.

　Then:

Budgeted cost at the actual volume	=	$1,400
Absorbed cost at the actual volume	=	1,350
Net variance (underabsorbed)	=	1,380 − $1,350 = 30
Volume variance (unfavorable)	=	1,400 − 1,350 = 50
Spending variance (favorable)	=	1,380 − 1,400 = 20

Interpretation of the Variances

Presumably, the supervisor is responsible for the spending variance that arises in his responsibility center. Because the budgeted cost line cannot take account of all the noncontrollable factors that affect cost, there may be a reasonable explanation for the spending variance. The existence of an unfavorable variance is therefore not, by itself, grounds for criticizing performance. Rather, it is a signal that investigation and explanation are required.

In some situations the supervisor may also be responsible for the volume variance. Failure to obtain standard volume may result from his inability to keep products moving through his department, for example. The volume variance is more likely to be someone else's responsibility, however. It may result because the sales department was unable to obtain the required volume of orders, or because some earlier department in the manufacturing process failed to deliver materials as they were needed.

In appraising spending performance, the analyst will go behind the total spending variance and examine the individual overhead items of which it consists. The total budgeted cost is the sum of the allowances for each of the separate items. A spending variance can be developed for each item, being the difference between actual cost incurred and the budget allowance for the item; attention is focused on significant spending variances for individual items.

In terms of the structure established at the beginning of this chapter, the spending variance is a composite of input price and input quantity factors. After it has been separated from the volume variance, it could conceivably be broken down into its price and quantity elements, as was done for direct labor, but in practice the analysis is usually not carried this far.

It should be emphasized that the volume variance arises only from differences in the *level* of volume. The *speed* of change in volume from one level to another also can have an effect on costs. So can the *direction* of change, for actual costs often tend to be below the line of budgeted costs when volume is increasing and above the line when volume is decreasing. This phenomenon, which is called *lag* or *hysteresis,* shows up in the spending variance, not the volume variance.

MEASURING STICK VARIANCE

If the measure of volume is an input factor, such as actual direct labor hours, rather than an output factor, such as units of products produced or the standard direct labor hours in these products, then an additional complication arises. To illustrate it, let us assume that the unit of volume in Illustration 17–4 was actual direct labor hours, but that overhead costs were absorbed into products on the basis of $1.50 per *standard* labor hour in these products.

Assume further that actual direct labor in a month totaled 900 hours and that standard direct labor totaled only 820 hours, other conditions remaining as in the above illustration. The amount of overhead costs absorbed will then be 820 hours times $1.50 per hour equals $1,230. If standard hours had totaled 900, then $1,350 (900 × $1.50) would have been absorbed. The difference of $120 between this $1,350 and $1,230 actually absorbed arises because the direct labor force worked at less than standard efficiency. This variance is therefore called the *efficiency variance,* although it can be seen that the word "efficiency" relates to the ultilization of direct labor, and not to overhead itself. It is the difference between actual hours and standard hours, priced at the standard rate per hour.

> EXAMPLE: The complete analysis of this new situation is as follows:
>> Actual overhead cost incurred = $1,380
>> Budgeted cost at actual volume = 1,400
>> Absorbed cost, 820 standard hours × $1.50 = 1,230
>> Net variance (underabsorbed) = 1,380 − $1,230 = 150
>> Volume variance (unfavorable) = 1,400 − 1,350 = 50
>> Spending variance (favorable) = 1,380 − 1,400 = 20
>> Efficiency variance (unfavorable) = (820 − 900) × $1.50 = 120

The efficiency variance is not present in many situations, but only in those in which there is a difference in the way volume is measured for control and the way costs are absorbed for product costing.

AN ILLUSTRATIVE ANALYSIS

As a way of summarizing the techniques described in this chapter, we show the complete analysis of a simple hypothetical situation in Illustration 17–5. Although the company in this example manufactures three products, we have treated them as only one product in calculating manufacturing variances by making standard unit manufacturing cost the same for all products; this is simply for the purpose of avoiding numerous computations of mix variance. For further simplification of the arithmetic, we have assumed that only one kind of material and one class of labor are used. In the examination of revenue variances, we have carried through the three-product analysis in order to illustrate the calculation of a mix variance.

The income statement (Section A) shows a variance between actual and standard profit of $55. The question is: What accounts for this variance? The answer to this question is given in Section B, which decomposes the total variance into elements. The remainder of the illustration shows how these elements were found.

Illustration 17–5

COMPUTATION OF VARIANCES

A. Income Statements

	Standard	Actual	Variance
Sales..	$540	$555	
Less standard cost of sales....................	440	418	
Gross margin at standard cost...............	$100	$137	$ 37
Less manufacturing variances.................	0	82	(82)
Gross margin...........................	$100	$ 55	$(45)
General and admin. expense...............	40	50	(10)
Operating Profit before Taxes...............	$ 60	$ 5	$(55)

B. Summary of Variances

Sales volume.............................	$(5)
Sales mix................................	3
Sales price...............................	39
Net marketing...........................	$ 37
Material price............................	$(16)
Material usage...........................	4
Labor time...............................	(24)
Labor price...............................	(8)
Overhead volume.........................	(15)
Overhead spending.......................	(23)
Net manufacturing.....................	$(82)
General and admin.	$(10)
Net Profit Variance.....................	$(55)

( ) = unfavorable

C. Underlying Data, Marketing Area

	Standard			Actual		
	Quan-tity	Unit Price	Total	Quan-tity	Unit Price	Total
Product A.....................	100	$2.60	$260	80	$2.50	$200
Product B.....................	60	2.80	168	60	3.00	180
Product C.....................	40	2.80	112	50	3.50	175
Total.................	200	$2.70	$540	190		$555

Illustration 17–5 (continued)

D. Computation of Marketing Variances

(1) *Volume Variance*

Actual Vol.	—	Std. Vol.	=	Diff.	×	Std. Gross Margin		
190	—	200	=	−10	×	$0.50	=	$−5.00

(2) *Mix Variance*

Actual Quantity	—	Std. Quantity*	=	Diff.	×	Std. Gross Margin	=	Variance	
80	—	95	=	−15	×	$0.40	=	$−6.00	
60	—	57	=	+ 3	×	0.60	=	+1.80	
50	—	38	=	+12	×	0.60	=	+7.20	
Total 190		190				Mix Variance =			$+3

*Based on standard proportions of $\frac{100}{200}, \frac{60}{200}, \frac{40}{200}$.

(3) *Selling Price Variance*

Actual Selling Price	—	Std. Selling Price	=	Diff.	×	Actual Quantity	=	Variance
$2.50	—	$2.60	=	− 0.10	×	80	=	$ − 8
3.00	—	2.80	=	+ 0.20	×	60	=	+ 12
3.50	—	2.80	=	+ 0.70	×	50	=	+ 35
						Price Variance =		$ + 39

E. Underlying Data, Manufacturing Area

Item	Standard	Actual
Volume.....................	200 units	170 units
Direct material...............	2 lbs./unit at $0.20/lb.	320 lbs. at $0.25 = $ 80
Direct labor.................	0.4 hrs./unit at $2.00/hr.	80 hrs. at $2.10 = 168
Overhead...................	$100 + $0.50 per unit	$208

F. Computation of Manufacturing Variances

(1) *Material Price Variance*

Std. Price	—	Actual Price	=	Diff.	×	Actual Quantity	=	Material Price Variance
$0.20	—	$0.25	=	$−0.05	×	320	=	$−16

Illustration 17–5 (continued)

(2) *Material Usage Variance*

Std. Quantity		Actual Quantity		Diff.		Std. Price		Material Usage Variance
340	−	320	=	20	×	$0.20	=	$+4

(3) *Labor Time Variance*

Std. Hours		Actual Hours		Diff.		Std. Rate		Labor Time Variance
68	−	80	=	−12	×	$2.00	=	$−24

(4) *Labor Price Variance*

Std. Rate		Actual Rate		Diff.		Actual Hours		Labor Price Variance
$2.00	−	$2.10	=	$−0.10	×	80	=	$−8

(5) *Overhead Variances*

Net Variance   = $170–$208 = $−38
Volume Variance   = $170–$185 =   −15
Spending Variance = $185–$208 =   −23

Marketing Variance

The first step in the computation is to make a breakdown of the variance for which the marketing department is held accountable. The basic data required for this part of the analysis are shown in Section C and the computations are made in Section D. Mix, volume, and price variances are calculated, their algebraic sum totaling the $37 shown as a revenue variance on the income statement. In calculating marketing variances, notice that gross margin, not selling price or total revenues, is used. This is because the contribution of the marketing department is best measured by the gross margin it generates, rather than by sales revenue. Gross margin is found by subtracting *standard* cost of sales (which is $2.20 per unit) from selling prices. Using the *standard* cost of sales figure means that the marketing department is not held accountable for any manufacturing expense variances; rather, these are the responsibility of the manufacturing organization.

The volume variance is the loss or gain in gross margin that results from a difference between actual and standard sales volume. The mix variance is figured by multiplying the standard gross margin for each product by the difference between the actual and standard quantity. The selling price variance is determined by multiplying the actual sales quantities for each product by the difference between actual and standard selling price.

Note that revenue variances are favorable when actual is greater than standard, which is of course the opposite situation from expense variances. Here, as always, logical reasoning rather than memorization of rules seems to be the best approach in determining whether a variance is favorable or unfavorable.

Manufacturing Variances

Next we turn to an analysis of the manufacturing expense variances. Note that, as shown in Section E, actual production volume is less than actual sales volume, the difference being made up out of inventory which is carried at standard cost. Carrying the inventory at standard cost means that expense variances are treated as period costs and charged directly to cost of sales during the period in which they occur and not put into inventory.

The labor, material, and overhead variances described earlier in the chapter are calculated in Section F. Their algebraic sum equals the $82 unfavorable variance noted on the income statement. This is charged directly to cost of sales.

An examination of the $10 unfavorable variance in general and administrative expenses completes the analysis of the net profit variance. This is not shown; it would consist of an analysis by class of expense of the amount of and reasons for differences between the budgeted expense and the actual expense.

SUMMARY

The difference between actual and standard performance can be separated into a number of variances which provide useful information to management. The total difference is explained principally by some or all of the following factors: noncomparable data, inherent product or service characteristics, price per unit of input, quantity of inputs, mix, price per unit of output, volume, and the measuring stick employed.

Analytical techniques are available to show the magnitude of these factors in a specific situation. These techniques never provide a complete answer to the question, "Why?" At best, they show the areas toward which further investigation should be directed in order to find the answer.

CASES

CASE 17–1.   DAVISON MANUFACTURING COMPANY

The Davison Manufacturing Company, manufacturer of electric light fixtures, operated under a standard cost accounting system. Labor data for the four production departments for the month of June (with numbers slightly rounded for ease of computation) were as follows:

Department	Direct Labor Cost		Hours of Direct Labor		Rate per Hour	
	Actual	Standard	Actual	Standard	Actual	Standard
A............	$2,227.50	$2,231.00	990	970	$2.25	$2.30
B............	1,056.00	1,071.00	480	510	2.20	2.10
C............	1,935.50	2,132.00	790	820	2.45	2.60
D............	1,828.50	1,650.00	690	660	2.65	2.50
Total.......	$7,047.50	$7,084.00	2,950	2,960		

Questions

1. Prepare a journal entry recording the direct labor cost. The company used an account called Work in Process, and direct labor was charged to this account at standard. The difference between actual cost and standard cost was carried to an account called Labor Variance.

2. For each department, determine how much of the difference between actual and standard cost was caused by differences between actual and standard hours and how much was caused by differences between actual and standard rates of pay.

3. What additional information, if any, would be required in order to explain the significance of the differences?

CASE 17–2.   PROBLEMS IN THE ANALYSIS OF OVERHEAD COST

PROBLEM A

The overhead rate is $2 a ton. Budgeted overhead cost at 3,000 tons a month is $8,000 and at 7,000 tons is $12,000. Actual overhead cost in September is $9,000, and actual volume is 5,000 tons.

Required:
1. Show graphically absorbed costs and expected costs.
2. State the following:

    a) Standard volume.
    b) Budgeted nonvariable cost.
    c) Budgeted variable cost per ton.
    d) Costs absorbed in September.
    e) Volume variance in September.
    f) Spending variance in September.
    g) Net variance in September.

PROBLEM B

The formula for budgeted overhead costs is $y = \$5{,}000 + \$1$ per unit. Standard volume is 5,000 units a month. Actual overhead expense in March is $11,500, and output in March is 6,000 units.

Required:

1. Standard volume.
2. Budgeted nonvariable cost.
3. Budgeted variable cost per unit.
4. Cost absorbed in March.
5. Volume variance in March.
6. Spending variance in March.
7. Net variance in March.

PROBLEM C

The forecast year's overhead expense for an expected volume of 180,000 pounds of a product is as follows:

Nonvariable overhead	$ 36,000
Variable overhead	108,000

In May, output was 10,000 pounds and actual overhead expense was $7,700. Determine (*a*) the budget line, (*b*) standard volume, (*c*) standard overhead per unit, and (*d*) the overhead variances.

PROBLEM D

In June overhead volume variance was 0 and "spending" variance was a debit of $600. In July overhead volume variance was a debit of $800, but "spending" variance was 0. June actual overhead expense was $7,000 for an output of 800 tons. July's expense was $5,600, and output was 600 tons. In August output was 900 tons and actual overhead expense was $7,100. What was the budget figure for August? How much was absorbed in August? What can you say of variances for August?

PROBLEM E

Overhead was charged to product at 75 per cent of direct labor dollars. According to the budget, overhead should be $5,600 for a direct labor payroll of $8,000 and $6,800 for a direct labor payroll of $10,000. If actual overhead costs turned out to be $6,000 and $7,000, respectively, at these two volumes, what were the variances? What was standard volume for the company?

PROBLEM F

Budgeted overhead costs per month are $2,000 plus $0.60 per actual direct labor hour. The overhead rate is $0.80 per standard direct labor hour. In November, standard direct labor hours totaled 11,000, actual direct labor hours totaled 11,500, and actual overhead costs totaled $9,000. Compute the overhead variances.

PROBLEM G

Department 12 of the Hudson Company manufactured rivets and no other products. All rivets were identical. In August Department 12 made 4,000,000 rivets. The company used a standard cost system plus a variable budget for overhead expense. Standard unit overhead charges (i.e., standard unit costs for overhead) were determined by dividing budgeted costs at an expected average volume by the number of rivets (in thousands) which that volume level (i.e., rate of capacity) represented.

Certain cost information is shown in the following table, and you are requested to fill in the blank spaces. The clue to the expected average volume necessary to fill in the blanks in line 3 can be found by a close analysis of the relationships among the figures given for allocated service and general overhead.

Dept. 12	Actual Cost, August	Std. Chg. per 1,000 Rivets	Total Std. Cost, August*	Overhead Budget, August	Overhead Budget Formula
Direct labor............	$10,500	$3.00	$	Not Used	
Direct material.........	22,000	5.00	20,000	" "	
Department direct overhead expense........	9,500	...	.....	$ 9,200	$6,000 per month plus $0.80 per thous. rivets
Allocated service and general overhead.....	5,000	1.00	4,000	5,000	$5,000 per month
Total.............	$47,000	$ ...	$	$14,200	

*Standard charge per one thousand rivets times August volume of 4,000,000 equals total standard cost.

Required:

1. Fill in the blanks.

2. What was the expected average volume (in terms of rivet output) at which the standard unit overhead charge was determined?

3. Explain as much of the difference between total actual costs and total standard costs as you can on the basis of the information given.

CASE 17–3.   LOTSACAL SUGAR COMPANY

The Lotsacal Sugar Company produced a compound which was sold as a "body-builder." The standard cost card per 100 pounds of this product, Lotsacal, is given in Exhibit 1. These standard costs were

Exhibit 1

STANDARD COST CARD

Lotsacal—100 Lbs.

Materials:			
Refined sugar	50 lbs. at $0.05	$ 2.50	
Dextrose	40 lbs. at $0.09	3.60	
Malt	10 lbs. at $0.07	0.70	
			$ 6.80
Labor:			
Mixing	8 hrs. at $2.00	$16.00	
Cooking	8 hrs. at $1.50	12.00	
			28.00
Overhead:			
Mixing	8 hrs. at $1.25	$10.00	
Cooking	8 hrs. at $1.50	12.00	
			22.00
Total Standard Cost per 100 lbs.			$56.80

established at a normal volume for the year of 220,000 pounds of Lotsacal. At this level of volume, variable overhead costs should amount to $11,440 in the mixing department and $10,560 in the cooking department. Fixed overhead costs amount to $10,560 in the mixing department and $15,840 in the cooking department.

During the week of May 22, 1961, 4,400 pounds of Lotsacal were produced. Actual costs for this production were accumulated as follows:

Refined sugar used	2,350 lbs. at $0.04
Dextrose used	1,850 lbs. at $0.08
Malt used	400 lbs. at $0.08

Direct labor hours worked in the mixing department: 350 hours at $2.05 an hour.

Direct labor hours worked in the cooking department: 370 hours at $1.40 an hour.

At December 31, 1961, production records revealed that 200,000 pounds of Lotsacal had been produced during the year with 15,000 hours of direct labor in the mixing department and 16,500 hours of direct labor in the cooking department. The actual overhead costs for the year amounted to $20,300 in the mixing department and $25,000 in the cooking department.

Question

Prepare an analysis of actual and standard costs reflecting a price and mix variance for each material, a total material usage variance, a time and rate variance for labor in each department, and as complete an analysis of overhead costs as you can.

CASE 17–4.   RETALLACK COMPANY

The Retallack Company manufactured pennants on a customer-order basis for local organizations, such as schools, fraternities, and yacht clubs. Because there was considerable variation in the quantities ordered, the quality of material used, and the sizes and patterns, the company prepared a separate job cost sheet for each order.

Costs of materials and direct labor applicable to each order were recorded directly on the appropriate job cost sheet. Manufacturing overhead was allocated to each order on the basis of a standard overhead rate per unit. The standard overhead rate was determined before the beginning of each year for each size of pennant by dividing the estimated overhead costs for the coming year chargeable to that size by the estimated sales of units of that size. Overhead costs were divided into two components, variable and fixed.

In December 1954, the accountant was working out for the following year the overhead rates to be applied per unit for each of the four sizes of pennants manufactured by the company. The estimated number of pennants of each size to be sold in 1955 was as follows:

Size	Estimated Quantity to Be Sold
A	15,000
B	20,000
C	10,000
D	5,000
Total	50,000

On the basis of the sales forecast, the accountant estimated that the overhead costs chargeable to each size of pennant would probably be as follows:

1955 Estimated Components of Overhead Cost

Size	Fixed*	Variable (per Pennant)
A....................	$3,300	$0.08
B....................	4,000	0.06
C....................	1,500	0.05
D....................	850	0.03
Total...............	$9,650	

* Fixed overhead costs, both estimated and actual, were allocated to each size of pennant on the basis of direct labor-hours, raw material quantity, floor space required, and other reasonable bases of allocation.

Questions

1. What is the estimated total overhead cost per pennant (i.e., the standard overhead rate) for each of the four sizes?

2. Using the standard overhead rate found in Question 1, determine the overhead variances attributable to volume and the variances attributable to "spending" or "efficiency" if the actual units produced and sold in 1955 and actual overhead costs were as follows:

a) 15,000 units of size A produced and sold. Actual overhead cost was $4,700.
b) 18,000 units of size B produced and sold. Actual overhead cost was $5,080.
c) 9,000 units of size C produced and sold. Actual overhead cost was $1,825.
d) 7,000 units of size D produced and 6,500 units sold. Actual overhead cost was $975.

3. When the accountant calculated the overhead per pennant to be allocated on customers' orders for the following year, should he have included the fixed element of the overhead?

CASE 17–5. DAWKINS MANUFACTURING COMPANY

Early in January 1959, the cost report shown in Exhibit 1 was submitted to Mr. Peter Dawkins, president of the Dawkins Manufacturing Company. This report was for the frame department, which was one of the primary producing departments in the company. Mr. Dawkins was alarmed by the report because of the increase in cost. He commented that the only area of efficiency seemed to be in the use of indirect labor. Mr. Dawkins requested an investigation of the situation, which produced the following additional information.

The department made two types of metal frames that were used in the construction industry. The primary difference in the types was their size. The larger size, called the J frame, required more material than the smaller S frame, but less direct labor time was required because of the

Exhibit 1

COMPARISON OF MANUFACTURING COSTS

Metal Frame Department

	1957	1958	Variance, 1958 over 1957
Raw materials.................	$535,000	$616,000	$81,000
Direct labor....................	130,000	135,000	5,000
Department overhead:			
Indirect labor................	50,000	10,000	(40,000)
Supervision..................	10,000	10,000	. . .
Power.......................	4,000	4,750	650
Depreciation.................	15,000	50,000	35,000
General burden................	116,000	132,250	16,250
Total......................	$860,100	$958,000	$97,900

use of an automatic assembly process that had not yet been adapted to the small frames. The department supervisor said that the J frame required about two units of raw material (primarily metal stripping), whereas the S frame required only one unit. The supervisor indicated that these quantities were based on normal operating efficiency. An investigation of the storeroom records showed that 560,000 units of raw materials had been issued during 1958, whereas 535,000 units had been issued during 1957.

The direct labor requirement was the opposite of the raw material. A J frame required about one half the amount of labor time required by the S frame. The foreman estimated that, under normal working conditions, the department should produce about ten J frames per labor hour. The level of skill required by direct labor in the department was about the same for each type of frame, and the average wage rate per hour was $2.50. Failure to schedule work properly and failure to provide adequately for absenteeism (primarily the responsibility of the personnel department) sometimes resulted in a night shift, which was paid a 10 per cent premium. The policy of the company was to avoid night shift work if at all possible.

Whereas the price of raw materials had gone up in 1958 about 10 per cent (a unit of raw material cost $1 in 1957), the basic direct labor rate stayed about the same. An investigation of the payroll showed that about 52,000 direct labor hours actually were paid for during 1958, and about 50,500 hours had been paid for in 1957. The actual direct labor rate varied from the $2.50 rate because of some night shift work and also because in February 1958 some workers were transferred into the frame department to cover excess absenteeism due to a mild influenza epidemic. These transferred workers received a wage rate somewhat higher than the average for the frame department.

An investigation of the general burden revealed that this cost was an assigned cost. The company's practice was to assign the general administration burden (the cost of such departments as accounting, personnel, general factory management, engineering, etc.) to producing departments on the basis of total direct and indirect labor dollars (excluding supervision). The total general burden for the company was $575,000 in 1958 and $580,000 in 1957. The total direct and indirect labor cost for all producing departments was $900,000 in 1957 and $630,000 in 1958.

During 1958, the company purchased and installed portable conveyers that made it possible to release several material handlers, who made up the largest element of indirect labor. The desirability of the equipment had been assessed by use of a ten-year economic life, and this period was chosen for depreciation purposes. A full year's depreciation had been included for 1958.

The power cost was assigned to the frame department by using the unit cost of power as determined by the power service department. In 1957, this cost was 0.8 cents ($0.008) per kw-hr, whereas the rate went up to 0.9 cents in 1958 because of an increase in the cost of fuel used to make the power. The foremen of the power department and the frame department agreed that power consumption was highly dependent on direct labor hours. The frame department foreman said that a fairly good rule of thumb that had been used in the past was ten kw-hrs of power for every hour of direct labor. He said that if power was used efficiently this rate of consumption should be attainable.

A check of the production reports showed that production of completed frames for each of the two years was as follows:

	1957	1958
S Frames	150,000	150,000
J Frames	180,000	200,000

Questions

1. Explain, insofar as possible, the significance of and reasons for the increase in costs.

2. In general, how would you rate the efficiency of the metal frame department in 1958?

3. Can you suggest a better way of reporting costs for the department in the future?

CASE 17–6. STALCUP PAPER COMPANY

. In March 1935, the president of the Stalcup Paper Company, while examining a group of charts regarding unit costs submitted to him by the cost department, noted that the unit costs of sorting rags had been rising for approximately two years. In order to determine the reason for this increase, he invited the foreman of the rag-sorting department and the head of the cost department to his office to discuss the matter. The head of the cost department submitted three exhibits, shown as Exhibits 1, 2, and 3, giving the details of the upward trend in costs shown in the charts. The foreman of the rag-sorting department said that his costs were lower rather than higher than they had been in past years, and that the basis of the cost department's estimates was unsound. He submitted Exhibit 4 in support of this contention.

The Stalcup Paper Company used old rags, new rags, and pulp in manufacturing its papers. The proportions in which these materials were mixed were varied in accordance with the requirements for different grades and types of paper. New rags, which were purchased from textile converters, cost substantially more per pound than did old rags, which were purchased from junk dealers. The old rags usually were received in the form of garments, from which it was necessary to remove carefully all foreign materials such as buttons, rubber, and metal. New rags were mostly remnants containing only a small percentage of foreign matter requiring removal; consequently, they could be sorted much more rapidly than could old rags.

The sorters sat at benches. Their task was to remove all foreign matter from the material placed before them and to distribute the usable cloth, according to quality, into containers placed beside them. The sorters processed, on the average, 55 pounds of old rags per hour or 575 pounds of new rags per hour. They were paid on a day-rate basis, the

Exhibit 1

OUTPUT OF RAG-SORTING DEPARTMENT IN POUNDS

	1932	1934	Change
Old rags.	3,220,000	2,460,000	− 23.6%
New rags.	810,000	2,520,000	+211.1
	4,030,000	4,980,000	+ 23.6%
Percentage old rags.	79.9%	49.4%	
Percentage new rags.	20.1	50.6	

Exhibit 2

EXPENSES OF

RAG-SORTING DEPARTMENT

	1932		1934	
		% of Direct Labor		% of Direct Labor
Direct labor.............	$20,965		$17,185	
Rag-sorting department burden:				
Indirect labor..........	$ 8,533		$ 9,540	
Repair labor...........	610		508	
Repair materials.......	123		271	
Supplies...............	156		160	
Power.................	612		553	
Investment............	15,549		15,204	
	25,583	122	26,236	153
General overhead........	19,128	91	15,186	88
	$65,676		$58,607	

Exhibit 3

RAG-SORTING DEPARTMENT,

COSTS OF SORTING OLD AND NEW RAGS

(As Shown in Cost Records)

	1932		1934	
	Dollars	Cents per Pound	Dollars	Cents per Pound
Old rags:				
Wages..............	$20,475	0.636	$15,645	0.636
Department overhead.....	24,985*	0.776	23,885†	0.971
General overhead........	18,681	0.580	13,825	0.562
	$64,141	1.992	$53,355	2.169
Increase..............				0.177
New rags:				
Wages.................	$ 490	0.0605	$ 1,540	0.0611
Department overhead.....	598*	0.0738	2,351†	0.0933
General overhead........	447	0.0552	1,361	0.0540
	$ 1,535	0.1895	$ 5,252	0.2084
Increase..............				0.0189

* 122 per cent of wages.
† 153 per cent of wages.

Exhibit 4

RAG-SORTING DEPARTMENT,

COSTS OF SORTING OLD AND NEW RAGS

(As Estimated by Foreman)

	1932		1934	
	Dollars	Cents per Pound	Dollars	Cents per Pound
Old rags:				
Wages..................	$20,475	0.636	$15,645	0.636
Department overhead.....	20,441	0.635	12,960	0.527
General overhead........	15,285	0.475	7,502	0.305
	$56,201	1.746	$36,107	1.468
Decrease...............				0.278
New rags:				
Wages..................	$ 490	0.060	$ 1,540	0.061
Department overhead.....	5,142	0.635	13,276	0.527
General overhead........	3,843	0.475	7,684	0.305
	$ 9,475	1.170	$22,500	0.893
Decrease.............				0.277

management having discovered by experience that payment on a piece-rate basis resulted in their picking over rags less carefully.

Between 1932 and 1934 the composition of rags purchased by the Stalcup Paper Company changed considerably, as shown in Exhibit 1. The percentage of old rags to the total dropped from approximately 80 per cent to approximately 50 per cent. During the same interval the total quantity of rags handled increased by nearly 25 per cent. In spite of the large increase in total volume, labor costs declined over the period because of the smaller quantity of old rags handled.

Costs charged to the rag-sorting department were of three types: first, direct labor in the department; second, overhead charged directly to the department; and third, general factory overhead. The amount of general factory overhead charged to a department was obtained by multiplying the direct labor in the department by the ratio of total general overhead to total direct labor in the entire plant.

Both departmental overhead and the department's share of general factory overhead were charged to products processed by the department as a percentage of the direct labor applied to these products. This percentage was obtained by dividing total overhead by total direct labor in the department.

The items included in the overhead of the rag-sorting department were as shown in Exhibit 2. The most important of these were indirect labor, including the salary of the foreman and wages of employees engaged in taking material to and from the sorters, and investment, which included the charge against the department for taxes, depreciation, and insurance on the premises and equipment it used. General overhead included miscellaneous factory labor, building repair labor and materials, manufacturing executive salaries, and expenses of functional departments, such as planning, costing, and research.

The head of the cost department pointed out to the president that between 1932 and 1934 the overhead charge of the rag-sorting department had increased from 122 per cent of direct labor to 153 per cent and that the difference in the cost of rag sorting in the two years was, as shown in Exhibit 3, almost entirely attributable to this increase.

The foreman differed with the cost department's estimated unit costs and pointed out that it was hard to conceive of unit costs increasing while total costs were diminishing and while volume of output was rising. He stated that the cost department was not charging the proper proportion of overhead charges to the new rags and that therefore old rags were taking more than their share of total department overhead. He said that, in his opinion, a much sounder method of allocating overhead charges would be on a per-pound basis rather than on the percentage-of-direct-labor basis previously used, and he recommended that costs in the rag department in the future should be calculated on the basis shown in Exhibit 4.

The unit costs for old and new rag sorting, as calculated by the cost department, were used in setting up standard costs. These standard costs, however, were used only rarely in setting prices of finished paper, since most of the company's paper was sold in a competitive market at prices established by competition. The company used the standard costs mostly to determine the relative profitability of the various lines of paper manufactured. When the plant was being operated at capacity and orders were being refused, the relative profitability of lines was a factor in determining what lines should be discontinued. In 1935, the Stalcup Paper Company was operating at about 55 per cent of capacity.

Questions

1. What is your assessment of performance in 1934?

2. Discuss the validity of the points made by the foreman and by the head of the cost department.

CASE 17-7. STORROW COMPANY

Mr. George Jessup was one of the junior managers in an operating division of Storrow Company, which did a mail-order business in women's clothing. Mr. Jessup was supervisor of a unit engaged in the inspection and preparation for stock of women's coats. It was his job to see that the work of his examination and preparation unit, as it was called, was done carefully yet efficiently and economically.

Functions of the Examination and Preparation Unit

The procedure of examining and checking shipments of new merchandise in Mr. Jessup's unit was elaborate, particularly in the early part of each season. For a period of two or three weeks a thorough examination was conducted of all coats received, regardless of the manufacturer or the type of coat. The examination routine consisted of a careful inspection of the stitching, the condition of the cloth and lining, the evenness of hems, and other features. Comparison was made with a sample approved by the Storrow buyer. Each coat was placed on a model so that inspectors could see if it fitted properly; sometimes live models were used. If a manufacturer's shipments were consistently satisfactory as the season progressed, a less thorough examination of each coat, called a spot check, was made. The spot check was a quick, overall inspection of the quality of the garment and a check on the presence of all accessories. Substantially the same procedure was followed for merchandise returned by customers.

In the examination and preparation unit, operators were stationed at work tables, and floor boys were employed to bring in merchandise and later to remove it to stock, or wherever it was to go. Every afternoon each girl reported, on a specified form, the number of coats she had handled and the number of hours she had spent on the work. Each girl filled out her daily report at about half an hour before closing time, including thereon her estimate of work for the remainder of the day. These forms were then countersigned by the floor supervisor, whose responsibility it was to see that the work was done by the close of the day.

There were three classes of employees in Mr. Jessup's unit. The first was a group of "basic regular" operators, who were guaranteed 38 hours a week for 50 weeks in the year. This group was ordinarily limited to the minimum number of employees required to handle the lowest weekly volume in the year. The second group of workers, known as "nonbasic," was guaranteed 30 hours of work a week. Finally, there were temporary workers who were employed to meet peak demands. The only requirement of their use was that if a girl was taken on, she had to be given at least four hours of work for that day.

Budget Procedure

At the beginning of the spring season, which ran from February through July, the company prepared a six-month key budget of revenue, expense, and net profit by months. This general budget was based on all known factors, including national and local economic conditions, anticipated trends, and planned company policies. Based on the sales estimate in this budget, Mr. Jessup made up a budget for his unit showing the number of hours of labor that would be required in the various activities under his charge and also the expected rate of output per man-hour. In addition, on the fifteenth of each month Mr. Jessup prepared a budget for each week of the coming month. In preparing these weekly budgets he used the estimates of the merchandisers as to the volume of shipments to be received into the examination and preparation unit, and also the recorded performance for the corresponding period in the preceding year. Both the semiannual budget and the weekly budgets were submitted to the expense controller, who either approved them as presented or discussed revisions with Mr. Jessup.

Every Wednesday morning Mr. Jessup prepared a revised weekly budget for the coming week, again showing the expected hours of work to be spent in the several lines of activity in his department. This revised weekly budget, which also had to be approved by the expense controller, set the standard against which the performance of Mr. Jessup's unit would be judged by his superiors. After his weekly budget had been approved, Mr. Jessup divided his week's estimate according to days, in order to follow daily performance. Whereas he might be in the red on any one day, it was expected that at the end of the week the total hours spent would not exceed his budget.

The expense control department maintained a budget book that showed for each unit the total hours worked each day and the budgeted hours for that day, with summary figures for each week. A copy of this book was in the office of the superintendent of operations, and a copy of his own record, day by day and week by week, was also available to the head of each unit. The management believed that effective control required good planning and a careful watch on daily performance, and it therefore wanted results and not excuses. It approved prompt corrective action taken in order to attain an objective; it did not approve the use of unproductive time spent in explanation of why the objective had not been reached.

Performance Reports

For comparison with his budget, daily performance reports of output and hours worked in Mr. Jessup's unit were compiled by one of his clerks from the daily work reports filed every afternoon by each of the operators. The ratio of total output to total hours worked provided a measure of output per man-hour, after an adjustment had been made by applying a weighting factor that reflected the amount of work involved in the several operations.

Exhibits 1 and 2 show budgeted and actual performance reports, respectively, for the week ended May 15. In column 1 is listed the budgeted or actual output, in number of coats, of Mr. Jessup's unit. In column 2 is listed the budgeted or actual number of hours worked.

Lines 1–6 and 10 relate to direct labor used in the examination and the preparation for stock of both new and returned merchandise. Other lines relate to the activities of floor boys and other service employees,

Exhibit 1

LABOR BUDGET FOR EXAMINATION AND PREPARATION UNIT
WEEK ENDING MAY 15
(Revised Figures in Parentheses)

APPROVED BUDGET ESTIMATES

		1	2	3	4	5	6
		ACTUAL OUTPUT	HOURS WORKED	OUTPUT PER MAN HOUR (1 ÷ 2)	WEIGHTING FACTOR	WEIGHTED OUTPUT (1x4)	CARRY- OVER
1	EXAMINATION OF NEW MERCHANDISE	*(10000)* 5970	*(286)* 171	35.0	.63	*(6300)* 3761	
2	PREPARATION OF NEW MERCHANDISE	*(9000)* 4220	*(300)* 141	30.0	.73	*(6570)* 3081	
3	INSPECTION OF CUSTOMER RETURNS	*(3100)* 3600	*(140)* 163	22.0	1.00	*(3100)* 3600	
4	PREP. & LISTING OF CUSTOMER RETURNS	*(3100)* 3600 *(2790)* 3240	*(12)* 14 *(96)* 112	257.0 29.0	.09 .76	*(279)* 324 *(2118)* 2462	
5	IRREGULARITY HANDLING	*(700)* 520	*(30)* 23	22.6	.94	*(658)* 489	
6	R.G. & JOB SALE MDSE. HANDLING	*(1000)* 880	*(20)* 18	48.9	.44	*(440)* 387	
7	UTILITY		*(148)* 105				
8	CLERICAL		*(79)* 63				
9	SUPERVISION - INSTRUCT. TIMEKEEPING		*(90)* 78				
10	*Sign-up*	*(1860)* 2160	*(124)* 144	15.0	1.47	*(2734)* 3175	
11	*Additional*	100	*(3)* 3	35.0	.63	63	
12	TOTAL		*(1328)* 1035	16.76		*(22262)* 17342	

Exhibit 2

ACTUAL LABOR PERFORMANCE, EXAMINATION AND PREPARATION UNIT
WEEK ENDING MAY 15

ACTUAL PERFORMANCE

Receipts 6463	1 ACTUAL OUTPUT	2 HOURS WORKED	3 OUTPUT PER MAN HOURS (1 ÷ 2)	4 WEIGHTING FACTOR	5 WEIGHTED OUTPUT (1x4)	6 CARRY-OVER
1 EXAMINATION OF NEW MERCHANDISE	7042	224 6/12	31.2	.63	4427	12991
2 PREPARATION OF NEW MERCHANDISE	9023	278 3/	32.4	.73	6587	11620
3 INSPECTION OF CUSTOMER RETURNS	4046	156 7/	26.0	1.00	4046	
4 PREP. & LISTING OF CUSTOMER RETURNS	4603 5219	12 7/ 160 8/	358. 32.6	.09 .76	414 3967	
5 IRREGULARITY HANDLING	120	3 9/	31.7	.94	113	
6 R.G. & JOB SALE MDSE. HANDLING	2833	65 4/	43.3	.44	1247	
7 UTILITY		167 7/				
8 CLERICAL		164 10/				
9 SUPERVISION - INSTRUCT. TIMEKEEPING		119 9/				
10 Sign-up	1761	122 5/	14.4		2589	
11 Additional		19				
12 TOTAL		1495 3/	15.6		23390	

clerical help, and the various supervisors including Mr. Jessup. Since supervisors on the floor were required to do some of the routine work themselves when they were not busy otherwise, Mr. Jessup was restricted in the number of hours he could budget for supervision. When the department was busy, it was presumed that there would be more time spent in supervision than when work was slack.

The weighting factors in column 4 reflect the relative amounts of time normally required to do the several operations. The figures are not in units of time but are in relative units, the activity taking the longest time (excluding "sign up") being expressed as 1.00. For example, the activity reported on line 1 was supposed to take 63 per cent as much time as the activity reported on line 3. The entries in column 5 are the measures of weighted output obtained by multiplying output figures by the weighting factors. The outputs per man-hour in column 3 are the simple ratios of output to hours worked. The overall output per man-hour figure (16.76 budgeted and 15.6 actual) is derived from the total weighted output figure of column 5.

Column 6 was used to record the quantity of work on hand, that is, carry-over, at the end of the week. Inasmuch as shipments of new merchandise did not arrive every day, a stock of unexamined merchandise was ordinarily kept in Mr. Jessup's unit in order to even out his daily work load. Ordinarily this unexamined stock amounted to one or two days' work. As indicated on Exhibit 2, the unit received 6,463 new coats during the week ended May 15.

The reports shown in Exhibits 1 and 2 were sent to Mr. Phillips, superintendent of Division 10 of Storrow, who was Mr. Jessup's immediate superior. Since performance of the examination and preparation unit for the week was below the budget, Mr. Jessup was required to make a written explanation. This accompanied the reports and read as follows:

The following factors were responsible for the failure to meet budget requirements:

The transfer to the division of the handling of even exchanges (customers' returns). Time had to be spent explaining the new procedure to all sign-up clerks as well as the additional time required to handle the added activity.

The transfer to the examination and preparation payroll of two employees (Brown and Swenson). Since no provision had been made for training during this week, examination output suffered. Assuming that the new examiners produced 50 per cent of normal output, 40 hours additional were required, plus instruction time.

Twenty-four hours spent by Jones preparing drawings of the new preparation and examination fixtures and having them priced by the plant engineer.

Questions

1. What aspects of Mr. Jessup's job (speed, quality, cost, etc.) should Mr. Phillips be interested in controlling?

2. Insofar as you can determine, how well did Mr. Jessup perform each of these aspects during the week ended May 15? With respect to his cost performance:

   a) What exactly was the standard to which Mr. Jessup was expected to adhere? (Hint: Trace through exactly how the figures in Exhibit 1 were reached; the process was *not* that of working from left to right.)

   b) By how many *hours* was actual performance over or under standard on each line?

3. Are you satisfied with Mr. Jessup's explanation of his performance?

4. What action, if any, should Mr. Phillips take?

5. Can you suggest a better way of presenting the information on performance?

CASE 17–8. SAMUEL BREESE CORPORATION

When Mr. Lewis, sales manager of Samuel Breese Corporation, returned from a sales convention early in April, he told the controller,

Mr. Morse, about an address in which a financial officer of a competing company strongly recommended the break-even chart as a device for indicating the approximate profit to be expected at various levels of output. Mr. Morse said that such a chart could be prepared for the Samuel Breese Corporation without much difficulty, and within a few days gave Mr. Lewis the chart reproduced as Exhibit 1. In its cost

Exhibit 1

BREAK-EVEN CHART

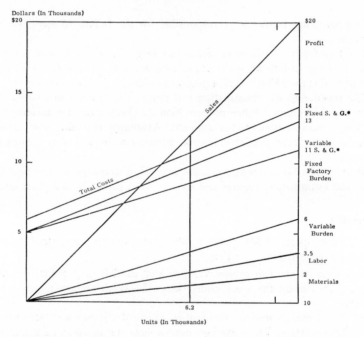

*S. & G. = selling and general expense.

accounts, the corporation treated 10,000 units a month as normal (practical) capacity.

On June 1, as soon as he learned that 6,200 units had been sold in May, Mr. Lewis drew the line at 6.2 on the chart and from it estimated that the net profit (before income tax) for May would be between $1,400 and $1,500. He was pleasantly surprised, therefore, when he got the May income statement on June 8 and saw that the book profit was $2,500. (See Exhibit 2.) Whereas he could not complain about the reported profit, he did want to know why it was some 70 per cent higher than he had expected.

Exhibit 2

SAMUEL BREESE CORPORATION
Income Statement for May

Sales (6,200 units)..		$12,300
Expenses:		
Standard cost of goods sold...........................$6,820		
Manufacturing variances:		
Volume (debit).................................	400	
All other* (debit)................................	280	
Selling and general................................	2,300	9,800
Net Profit before Income Tax...........................		$ 2,500

* There were no labor or burden efficiency variances.

Questions

1. What was the break-even point for the Samuel Breese Corporation?

2. What was the exact profit indicated by the break-even chart for sales of 6,200 units?

3. How many units were produced in May?

4. Reconcile the profit found in the answer to Question 2 with the profit of $2,500 shown on the income statement, giving the amount of each item that accounts for the difference.

Part

IV

ACCOUNTING IN BUSINESS DECISIONS

Chapter 18

DECIDING AMONG ALTERNATIVE COURSES OF ACTION

BUSINESSMEN make decisions by choosing what they believe to be the best of the possible alternative[1] courses of action. Problems in this area are therefore often called "alternative choice problems."

In a great many business problems, the decision is made intuitively; that is, there is no systematic attempt to define, measure, and weigh the advantages and disadvantages of each alternative. A person who makes an intuitive decision may do so simply because he is not aware of any other way of making up his mind, or he may do so for the very good reason that the problem is one in which a systematic attempt to weigh alternatives is either not useful or not possible. No mathematical formula will help to solve a problem in which the attitudes or emotions of the individuals involved are dominant factors, nor is there much point in trying to make calculations if the available information is so sketchy or so inaccurate that the results are completely unreliable.

In many other situations, however, it is possible to reduce at least some of the anticipated consequences of the alternatives to a quantitative basis and to weigh these consequences in a more or less systematic manner. Usually, this process involves a consideration of accounting data, particularly cost data. Some of the problems that managers face in using costs as an aid in making business decisions are discussed in this chapter.

APPROACH TO ALTERNATIVE CHOICE PROBLEMS

Criteria

We have assumed that, insofar as it is measured quantitatively, the objective of a business is to earn a satisfactory return on its investment. We now expand this concept by adding the common-sense idea that if two alternative courses of action are being considered, the business will

---

[1] Grammarians state that there can be only two "alternatives." As used here, the word alternative often refers to more than two; this definition is more convenient for our purposes.

select the one that is likely to lead to the higher return on investment, or if no investment is involved, the one with the higher profit.

The fact that this criterion is limited to measurable objectives should again be emphasized. In many practical problems, personal satisfaction, friendship, patriotism, self-esteem, or other considerations may be much more important than return on investment. Or, the company may have other measurable objectives, such as maintenance of its market position, stabilization of employment, or avoidance of undue risk. When these considerations are important or dominant, the solution to the problem cannot be reached by the techniques discussed here. The most these techniques can do is show the effect on return on investment of seeking some other objective. The problem then becomes one of deciding whether the attainment of the other objective is worth the cost.

Outline of Approach

Return on investment may be expressed as the ratio:

$$\frac{\text{REVENUE} - \text{COSTS}}{\text{INVESTMENT}}$$

Although the general approach to all alternative choice problems is similar, it is useful to discuss three types separately. First, there are problems that involve only the cost element of the ratio. Since revenue and investment are unaffected, the best alternative is the one with the lowest cost.[2] Problems of this type are discussed in the next section. Second, there are problems in which both revenue and costs are involved. These are discussed in the latter part of this chapter. Third, there are problems that involve both the numerator and the denominator of the ratio. These are discussed in Chapter 19.

Before a separate discussion of these types is given, some general comments about approaching alternative choice problems are in order. Following is a list of steps that are useful for most problems:

1. Define the problem.
2. Define the most likely alternative solutions.
3. Measure and weigh those consequences of each alternative that can be expressed in quantitative terms.
4. Evaluate those consequences that cannot be expressed in quantitative terms and weigh them against each other and against the measured consequences.
5. Reach a decision.

Definition of the Problem and of Alternative Solutions

Unless the problem is clearly and precisely defined, quantitative figures that are relevant to it cannot be computed. In many situations,

---

[2] Herbert Simon calls this the "criterion of efficiency," an excellent description.

the definition of the problem, or even the recognition that a problem exists, may be the most difficult part of the whole process. In most of the cases accompanying this chapter, the nature of the problem is reasonably evident. Even so, it is useful to state the problem as precisely as possible before proceeding further.

Quite often, the possible alternative solutions to the problem are by no means clear at the outset. For example, suppose that the factory manager, having listened to a machinery salesman's story of the advantages of using his machine to manufacture a part that is now being made by manual methods, is now trying to decide what to do about the salesman's proposal. At first glance, the alternatives may appear to be (a) buy the new machine or (b) continue to perform the operation by hand. Actually, however, several additional alternatives should perhaps be considered, such as these: (c) buy a machine other than the one recommended by the salesman, (d) improve the present method of making the part, or even (e) eliminate the manufacturing operation altogether and buy the part from another manufacturer. Some thought should be given to these other possibilities before attention is focused too closely on the original proposal.

On the other hand, the more alternatives that are considered, the more complex the analysis becomes. For this reason, having thought about all the possible alternatives, the analyst should eliminate without more ado those that are clearly unattractive, leaving only a few for detailed analysis. In the simplest situation, only two alternatives are examined closely. These can be described in general terms as follows: (a) the continuation of what is now being done or (b) the adoption of a proposed change—a new machine, a new process, a new selling price, and so on. Note that there must always be at least two alternatives. If only one course of action is open, the company literally has "no choice," and hence no analytical problem.

Weighing and Measuring the Quantitative Factors

There are usually a number of advantages and a number of disadvantages associated with each of the alternative solutions of a problem. The task of the analyst is to evaluate each of the relevant factors and to decide, on balance, which alternative has the largest *net* advantage.

If the factors are stated solely in words, such an evaluation is an exceedingly difficult task. For example, consider the statement that a proposed manufacturing process will save labor but that it will require increased power consumption and additional insurance protection. Such a statement provides no way of weighing the relative importance of the saving in labor against the increased power and insurance costs. If, by contrast, the statement is made that the machine will save $1,000 in labor, that increased power will cost $200, and that increased insurance will cost $100, the net effect of these three factors can easily be estimated; that is, $1,000 − $200 − $100 is a net advantage of $700 for the proposed process.

The reason why we try to express as many factors as possible in quantitative terms is made clear in the above illustration: once we have done this, it becomes easy to find the net effect of these factors by the simple arithmetic operations of addition and subtraction. The measurement of those quantitative factors that are relevant for a given problem is the subject of the bulk of this chapter.

Evaluating and Weighing the Unmeasured Factors

For most problems there are important factors that are not measurable; yet the final decision must take into account *all* differences between the alternatives being considered, both those measured and those not measured. The process of weighing the relative importance of these unmeasured factors, both as compared with one another and as compared with the net advantage or disadvantage of the measured factors, is solely a judgment process.

It is easy to underestimate the importance of these unmeasured factors. The numerical calculations for the measured factors often require hard work, and they result in a figure that has the appearance of being definite and precise; yet all the factors that influence the final number may be collectively less important than a single factor that has not been measured. For example, there are many persons who could meet their transportation needs less expensively by using public conveyances rather than by operating an automobile, but who nevertheless own an automobile for reasons of prestige, convenience, or other unmeasured factors.

As another example, an analysis of trucking costs and freight movements indicated that a company could save $14,260 a year by operating its own truck instead of using common carriers. Nevertheless, the decision was made to continue using common carriers, and the reasons given were as follows:[3]

1. The difference in the densities of the products carried would complicate the truck loading.
2. The problem of scheduling the routing of the truck to insure maximum utilization would be difficult. What happens if the truck is needed when it is on the road?

---

[3] From Norwalk Screw Company, a case prepared by Professor Harold Bierman, Jr.

3. The length of the round trip (approximately 280 miles) would result in the truck's visiting some locations after working hours, thus missing the pickup or delivery.

4. Our company is not unionized. The question of unionization of the truck driver would be troublesome.

5. The cost figure of $0.06 a mile is questionable.

6. Is December a typical month? [The analysis was based on December traffic data.]

7. It may be possible to have the suppliers absorb the freight, thus eliminating the transportation cost entirely.

8. Who will administer the operation of the truck? The traffic manager has only one clerk.

9. How are the common carriers going to treat the company on the remainder of the items that cannot be carried on the company truck.

10. Freight rates and truck operating costs are subject to change.

11. The supply points may change.

12. Since there is only one truck and one driver, the risk of truck breakdown and illness of the driver would be too great.

Note that this list includes both factors that probably were unmeasurable (e.g., the consequences of unionization) and factors that could have been measured, but in fact were not (e.g., the cost of administering the operation of the truck).

Cost calculations make it possible to express as a single figure the net effect of many factors bearing on the decision. They therefore reduce the number of factors that must be considered separately in the final judgment process that leads to the decision; or, as is often said, they narrow the area within which judgment must be exercised. Rarely, if ever, do they eliminate the necessity for this final judgment process.

Reaching a Decision

Having gone through the above process, the analyst has only two choices: to seek additional information or to reach a decision and act on it. Most decisions could be improved by making the former choice; in a complicated business situation, it is usually possible to obtain more information than that available when the analysis begins. However, obtaining this information always involves effort and, what is more important, it involves time. There comes a point, therefore, when the analyst concludes that he is better off to act than to defer a decision until more data have been collected.

PROBLEMS INVOLVING COSTS

In the first class of problems we shall discuss, the difficult part of the quantitative analysis involves costs; that is, revenue is either unaffected by the alternative or is affected in an obvious way that does not result in analytical problems. Illustrative of these problems are the following questions: Will a proposed new method of doing something cost less than the present method? Which of several proposed methods is the better? Should we manufacture a certain part or buy it from an outside vendor? Shall we discontinue a department that is apparently losing money? Shall we produce on one shift or two shifts? Shall we shut down the plant temporarily? Problems of this type are often called *trade-off problems:* we wish to find out whether one alternative has an acceptable trade-off compared with another in terms of its costs and the advantages that we hope to obtain from adopting it.

The types of cost that are relevant in problems of this type can be summed up in two brief statements: (1) they are *future* costs and (2) they are *differential* costs.

Future Costs

No decision made by man can change what has already happened. The past is history; decisions made now can affect only what *will* happen in the future. It follows that the only relevant cost figures are estimates of what costs will be in the future.

The difficulty in applying this obvious statement arises from the fact that in many instances our best information about future costs is derived from an analysis of historical costs. One can easily lose sight of the fact that historical costs per se are irrelevant. These historical costs, often obtained from the accounting records, may be a useful guide as to what costs are likely to be in the future, but using them as a guide is basically different from using them as if they were statements of what the future costs are in fact *going* to be.

Except where costs are determined by long-term contractual arrangements, future costs are necessarily estimates, and they usually cannot be close estimates. An estimated labor saving of $1,000 a year for five years, for example, implies assumptions as to future wage rates, future fringe benefits, future labor efficiency, future production volume, and other factors that cannot be known with certainty at the time the estimate is prepared. There is therefore ordinarily no point in carrying computations of cost estimates to several decimal places; in fact, there is a considerable danger of being misled by the illusion of precision that such meticulous calculations give.

Book Value of Fixed Assets. A historical cost that seems to cause considerable difficulty is the book value of fixed assets. Suppose that a new production process is proposed as a substitute for operations now performed on a certain machine. The machine was purchased six years previously for $10,000, and depreciation on it has been charged at $1,000 a year, a total of $6,000 to date. The machine therefore has a book value of $4,000. Assume that it has no market value, that is, the cost of removing it just equals its value as scrap metal, and assume that it would be of no further use to the company. If the new process requires additional labor and related costs of $600 a year, one could argue that in spite of this increase, adoption of the process would save a net of $400 a year, since the depreciation charge of $1,000 a year would no longer be a cost. The fact is, however, that the remaining book value must be

Illustration 18–1

COMPARATIVE INCOME STATEMENTS ILLUSTRATING
IRRELEVANCE OF SUNK COSTS
(For Four Years)

	A. If New Process Is Adopted	B. If New Process Is Not Adopted
Sales.	$1,000,000	$1,000,000
Cost and expenses:		
Costs unaffected by the decision.	$700,000	$700,000
Additional labor, etc.	2,400	0
Depreciation on machine.	0	4,000
Book loss on disposal of machine.	4,000	0
Total Costs and Expenses.	706,400	704,000
Profit before income taxes.	$ 293,600	$ 296,000
		− 293,600
Loss if New Process Is Adopted.		$ 2,400

written off the books; and this amount, of course, exactly offsets the total depreciation charge over the remaining life of the machine. Thus the depreciation charge is *not* relevant to the problem. It is a *sunk cost,* arising from actions taken in the past, and unaffected by any subsequent decision. Adoption of the proposed process would in fact result in a *loss* of $600 a year.

The irrelevance of sunk costs can be demonstrated by comparison of two income statements for the complete time periods of the remaining life of the machine, one showing the results of operations if the new process is adopted and the machine is scrapped, and the other showing the results if the process is continued on the present equipment, as in Illustration 18–1. This illustration demonstrates that there would be a loss of $2,400 over a four-year period if the new process were adopted.

If the machine had a *market value,* this fact would be a relevant consideration, since its disposal would then bring in additional cash. If the *tax effect* of writing off the loss on disposal were different from the tax effect of writing off depreciation over the four-year period, which is often the case, the effect on taxes is relevant. The book value of the machine itself is not relevant. Ultimately, the book value is going to be charged against income, but whether this is done through the annual depreciation charge or through a lump-sum write-off makes no ultimate difference. The facts given indicate that the new process should not be adopted.

Differential Costs

A great many cost items will be unaffected by the alternatives under consideration, and these may be disregarded. Attention is focused on items whose costs will be *different* under one alternative from what they will be under the others. Suppose, for example, that a company is considering the possibility of buying Part No. 101 from an outside supplier instead of manufacturing the part as it is now doing. In this case the alternatives are either: (*a*) to continue manufacturing Part No. 101 or (*b*) to purchase Part No. 101 from the outside supplier. All revenue items, all selling and administrative expenses, and all production expenses other than those directly associated with the manufacture of Part No. 101 will probably be unaffected by the decision. If so, there is no need to consider them.

In some calculations, a listing of some or all of these unaffected costs may be useful, so as to insure that all relevant cost items have been considered. This was done, for example, in Illustration 18–1, and there is no harm in doing so, provided the unaffected costs are treated exactly the same way under each of the alternatives. The *net difference* between the costs of the two alternatives, which is the figure we seek, is not changed by adding equal amounts to the cost of each alternative.

Variable Costs. The term "variable costs" is not necessarily the same as the term "differential costs." Variable costs are those that vary directly with, and roughly proportionately to, changes in the *volume of output;* that is, if output increases 50 per cent, variable costs will increase approximately 50 per cent. Differential costs are related to the specific alternatives that are being analyzed. If, in a specific problem, one of the alternatives involves a change in output, then differential costs may be the same as variable costs. Depending on the problem, however, the differential costs may include nonvariable items. A proposal to change the number of plant watchmen and their duties, for example, involves no elements of variable cost.

Synonyms. *Opportunity cost* is a synonym for differential cost. Opportunity cost is the sacrifice involved in accepting the alternative under consideration rather than the next best opportunity. This is a precise concept of the relevant costs in an alternative choice problem, but it is more roundabout than the differential cost concept. *Incremental cost* and *marginal cost* are usually used in the sense of differential cost, so they are usually synonyms. In any event, it is the behavior of the cost element that is important, not the name attached to it.

Costs from a Cost Accounting System. In considering "costs that make a difference," figures drawn from a cost accounting system may be misleading, since differences in such figures may not reflect actual differences in cost arising because of the alternative under consideration. For example, for cost accounting purposes, the "cost" of Part No. 101 may include charges for rent, heat, light, and other occupancy costs that are prorated to this product on the basis of the number of square feet of floor space occupied by the department in which it is manufactured. If Part No. 101 were purchased from an outside vendor, the floor space formerly used in its manufacture would be saved. It does not necessarily follow, however, that the *costs* prorated to Part No. 101 on the basis of floor space used would actually be saved. The costs for rent, heat, light, and so on might not be changed at all by the decision not to manufacture the part. Unless there is some real saving in cash outlays (or their equivalent) or some real additional revenue possibilities resulting from the use of the freed floor space (e.g., renting it, or manufacturing some revenue-producing item in it), the "cost" of floor space should be ignored.

In general, when estimating differential costs, *allocated or prorated accounting charges should be viewed with skepticism.* In a cost accounting system, each unit of product manufactured is charged with its fair share of all manufacturing costs, including costs that are not directly caused by or traceable to the product. Such cost figures are not intended to show, and in fact do not show, the differential costs that are relevant in most alternative-choice problems. A company may allocate overhead as 100 per cent of direct labor; but this does *not* mean that if direct labor cost is decreased $575 by purchasing Part No. 101, there will be a corresponding decrease of $575 in overhead costs. Overhead costs may not decrease at all; they may decrease, but by an amount less than $575; or they may even increase, as a result of an increased procurement and inspection work load resulting from the purchase of Part No. 101. In order to estimate what will happen to overhead costs, we must go behind the overhead rate and analyze what will actually happen to the various elements of overhead under each of the alternatives being considered.

Fringe Benefits. Labor costs are one of the important considerations in many business decisions. In many problems an allowance for fringe benefits should be added to the actual amount of wages earned for the work done. Fringe benefits include such items as taxes for old-age and unemployment compensation; insurance, medical, and pension plans; vacation and holiday pay; and the like. For business in general, these benefits average about 25 per cent of wages earned, although there is so wide a variation among different companies that an overall average is unlikely to be reliable in a specific situation. To the extent that the cost of these fringe benefits varies directly with wages paid, they are relevant when costing an alternative that involves a change in labor costs.

Imputed Costs. Most, but not all, relevant cost figures are represented by real cash outlays. In some cases, however, the concept of cost should be broadened to include sacrifices that are not immediately reflected in the cash account; in other words, it is sometimes desirable to include certain *imputed* costs. The floor space item mentioned above provides an example. If the floor space required to make Part No. 101 can be used for some other revenue-producing purpose, then the sacrifice involved in using it for Part No. 101 is a cost of making that part. Note that this cost is measured by the income sacrificed if the floor space is used for Part No. 101; this is not necessarily the same as the allocated cost per square foot of floor space as developed in the cost accounting system.

Importance of the Time Span. The question of what costs are relevant depends to a considerable extent on the time span of the problem. If the proposal is to make only one unit of Part No. 101, only the direct material costs may be relevant; the work could conceivably be done without any differential labor costs if, for example, workers were paid on a daily basis and had some idle time. At the other extreme, if the proposal is to make Part No. 101 over the foreseeable future, practically all the elements of manufacturing costs may be affected. In general, *the longer the time span of the proposal, the more items of cost are differential.* In the very long run, all costs are differential. Thus, in very long-run problems, differential costs include the same elements as the conventional accounting "full costs," for in the long run one must consider even the replacement of buildings and equipment, which are sunk costs in the short run. (Although the *elements* are the same, the amounts are different, since alternative choice problems involve future costs, not historical costs.) In the short run, relatively few cost elements may be subject to change by a management decision.

General Characteristics of Differential Costs. Few specific suggestions can be made as to what costs should be included in an alternative choice calculation, because there is a wide variety of problems, each with its own characteristics. In general, we are looking for costs that *would* be incurred if the alternative were adopted but that *would not* be incurred if the alternative were not adopted. Labor costs are relevant in many problems; but if in a specific situation people are going to be employed regardless of which alternative is adopted, labor costs may not be relevant. For example, it can be demonstrated that a given quantity of material can be typed in less time with an electric typewriter than with a nonelectric typewriter, but an actual saving in labor costs will result from the purchase of an electric typewriter only if the time thus freed is used productively for some other purpose.

Mechanics of the Calculation

Any of several devices can be used for combining the various cost elements that are relevant to each alternative. Costs may, for example, be listed separately under each alternative, viz.:

	If Part No. 101 Is Manufactured	If Part No. 101 Is Purchased
Purchased material...................	$ 572	$1,700
Labor..............................	600	25*
Power.............................	98	0
Other costs........................	150	0
Total...........................	$1,420	$1,725
Difference (Disadvantage of Purchasing)..		$305

* Estimated handling cost.

Or, exactly the same result can be obtained by figuring the net differences between the alternatives, viz.:

Purchase price of Part No. 101...................	$1,700
Costs saved by not manufacturing Part No. 101:	
Raw material..............................$572	
Labor.................................... 575	
Power.................................... 98	
Other costs.............................. 150	
Total Costs Saved.........................	1,395
Net Disadvantage in Purchasing.................	$ 305

The same result can also be obtained by preparing a complete income statement for each alternative for the total time period involved in the proposal, as was done in Illustration 18–1. This requires more work than either of the other two types of calculations shown above, but it provides assurance that some cost or revenue elements have not been overlooked, and it may also provide a useful explanation of the calculations to someone else.

The Margin of Error

Cost figures used in alternative choice problems are estimates, and in many cases they are very rough estimates. In some calculations, an attempt is made to express the margin of error in these estimates by making two sets of calculations, one in which costs are estimated on the high side and the other in which they are estimated on the low side. Even though the range between these two estimates is wide, the rough estimates may be more useful than none at all, since they set boundaries on the net influence of the factors that are contained in them.

Sometimes the high and low estimates are combined into a single "compromise" figure by averaging them. This is often a useful device, but it should be recognized that the compromise is not necessarily a more correct estimate than either the high or the low figure. The reliability of the estimate depends on the uncertainties involved, and there may be no way of eliminating or minimizing these uncertainties.

Example: Operating an Automobile

As an example of the fact that the cost elements that are relevant in an alternative choice problem vary with the nature of the problem, let us consider the costs that are relevant for various decisions that may be made about owning and operating an automobile. A study made by Runzheimer and Company and published by the American Automobile Association gives the national average cost in 1963 of operating a 1963 eight-cylinder Chevrolet Bel Air, four-door sedan, as follows:

Variable Costs:	Average per Mile
Gasoline and oil	2.61 cents
Maintenance	0.68
Tires	0.41
Total	3.70 cents

Nonvariable Costs:	Annual
Fire and theft insurance	$ 30.00
Property damage and liability insurance	117.40
License and registration	23.60
Depreciation	621.00
Total	$792.00

What costs are relevant? In answering this question, we shall assume that the car in question is comparable with that for which the averages were computed; that gasoline prices, insurance rates, and the like are "average" in the locality in which the automobile is to be operated; that the AAA figures are reliable; that the classification of certain costs as variable and others as nonvariable is valid; and that costs during the period in which the automobile will be operated will be the same as they were in 1963. Unless each one of these assumptions is reasonable, the figures given above cannot be used. Accepting these assumptions, we can make the following statements about relevant costs:

1. When you own the automobile, already have it registered, and are deciding whether it is worthwhile to make a proposed trip, the relevant costs are 3.70 cents a mile times the estimated mileage of the trip. The nonvariable costs are not relevant since they will continue whether or not the trip is made. (Costs are shown here exactly as reported in the AAA table above; actually, you would undoubtedly round off the numbers rather than showing them to hundredths of a cent.)
2. When you own the automobile and are deciding whether to (a) register it for a year or (b) leave it idle and use some other form of transportation, the relevant costs are the insurance and fees of $171 plus 3.70 cents a mile times the number of miles you expect to travel by automobile during the year. The $171 has become a cost because it is affected by the decision as to registration.
3. When you are deciding whether to (a) buy an automobile or (b) use some other means of transportation, the relevant costs are $792 a year plus 3.70 cents a mile times the number of miles you expect to drive. (Actually, in this case you probably would have a closer estimate for depreciation for the specific automobile under consideration than the average figure of $621.)

Other statements can be made for the costs relevant to other contemplated uses of the automobile. These illustrations may help to clarify the basic point that the relevant costs for a given decision are the costs affected by that decision; other costs can be ignored.

Example: Economic Lot Size

When manufacture of a product involves setup costs that are incurred once for each lot manufactured, the question arises of how many units should be made in one lot. If the demand is predictable and if sales are reasonably steady throughout the year, the optimum quantity to manufacture at one time, called the *economic lot size* or *economic order quantity,* is arrived at by considering two offsetting influences—setup costs and inventory costs. Consider an item with annual sales of 1,200 units. If the whole 1,200 were manufactured in one lot, only one setup a year would be necessary, but inventory costs would be high, since the inventory would start with 1,200 units and would average 600 units over the year. By contrast, manufacture of 12 lots of 100 units each (i.e., one lot a month) would involve 12 setups but a low inventory carrying cost, since there would be a maximum of 100 units, and an average of 50 units, in inventory at any one time.

Given this set of relationships, the mathematician can easily construct a formula from which the economic lot size can be found. His reasoning is as follows: Let:

Q = Economic lot size (number of units in one lot)
S = Setup costs, for one setup
R = Annual requirements in units
K = Inventory carrying charge, expressed as a percentage of average inventory value
C = Factory cost per unit

Then:

Number of lots made in one year $= \dfrac{R}{Q}$

Annual setup cost = setup cost for one lot times number of lots made per year $= S\left(\dfrac{R}{Q}\right) = \dfrac{SR}{Q}$

Average number of units in inventory $= \dfrac{Q}{2}$

Average value of inventory = average units in inventory times unit cost $= \left(\dfrac{Q}{2}\right) C = \dfrac{QC}{2}$

Annual carrying cost = Average inventory value times $K = \left(\dfrac{QC}{2}\right) K$

$= \dfrac{QCK}{2}$

Total cost will be at a minimum when the increase in carrying cost resulting from adding one more unit to a lot is equal to the corresponding decrease in setup costs. Using calculus, we can show that this minimum occurs when annual setup cost equals annual carrying cost,[4] or when—

$$\frac{SR}{Q} = \frac{QCK}{2}$$

Solving for Q gives the desired formula:

$$Q = \sqrt{\frac{2SR}{CK}}$$

---

[4] It is not *generally* true that when it is desired to find a minimum total cost point for two costs, one of which is increasing and the other decreasing, the minimum will be found at the point where the two totals are equal. It happens to be true for the specific cost functions being considered here.

At this point, the mathematician loses interest. As far as he is concerned, the problem has been solved, and all that remains is to insert the relevant numbers in the formula and do the arithmetic. But the important practical question is: what numbers? What are the setup costs that are relevant to this problem? Clearly, they include the differential labor costs involved in making the setup, they include fringe benefits on this labor, they include any differential overhead costs, and they also include such costs as moving the products to inventory if these are a function of the number of lots manufactured, even though these are not labeled as setup costs. Deciding which costs vary with the number of lots produced and are therefore differential setup costs is a difficult matter. Similarly, the unit cost used in valuing the inventory involves problems. Essentially, we need to know how much funds will be tied up in inventory, and for this purpose it may be necessary to adjust the cost-accounting unit cost of the products to eliminate elements such as depreciation that do not represent current outlays of funds. Finally, the calculation of the inventory carrying charge includes an estimate of interest costs, and of the costs associated with the occupancy of warehouse space.

The point is that in this, and many other types of business problems involving costs, the general approach to the problem may be quite simple and definite, but estimating the relevant cost figures may be exceedingly difficult.

PRICING

The second class of problems involves revenue considerations as well as cost considerations. The discussion here will focus on the pricing problem; that is, how much should we charge for our products? This is the most common problem in this category.

Theoretical Considerations

Some economics texts state that the selling price of a product should be set so as to maximize the difference between revenue and costs. In order to do this, one needs to be able to estimate (1) the demand schedule, which is the number of units that would be sold at each possible selling price; and (2) variable costs, which in this context is what economists mean by *marginal* costs. Variable costs can of course be estimated by techniques already discussed, but estimating the demand schedule is a much more difficult matter. Who can estimate what quantity of product will be sold at one price, let alone at all possible prices? Indeed, the difficulty is so great that few companies ever attempt to estimate a demand schedule, and few managers have ever even seen one.

Without a demand schedule, the elaborate diagrams and equations that economists have built up cannot be used to solve real-world pricing problems (although they are useful for classroom analysis).

Not only is the maximization approach to pricing unworkable, but also it leads to "gouging," "profiteering," "charging all the traffic will bear," and other unethical practices. A discussion of pricing that is built on the maximization foundation would therefore be both impractical and ethically indefensible.

This fact is one of the reasons why this book is not based on the profit maximization concept. (A second reason has to do with the cost-of-capital approach to investment decisions, discussed in Chapter 19.) But if we do not use profit maximization as an underlying premise, we must have an alternative concept to replace it. Some have advocated "long-run profit maximization," but this is too vague a concept to serve as a basis for the solution of practical problems.

The concept that probably underlies the actions of most responsible businessmen is that of *satisfactory profit,* or satisfactory return on investment; that is, they have a notion of a fair or reasonable profit that should be earned in their business, and they strive to earn such a profit. This is the one we shall use.

The satisfactory profit concept leads to what is called *full-cost pricing,* as the normal approach to pricing problems, and to *contribution pricing* in certain unusual situations. These two types of pricing practices will be discussed separately.

Full-Cost Pricing

Many companies have no pricing problem. A market price exists, customers will not pay more than this price, and there is no reason why the product should be sold for a lower price. Wheat and other products traded on commodity markets are the classic examples, but the situation also exists for companies in many other industries, such as small companies in industries where a few companies exercise price leadership. Under such circumstances, a company makes no pricing calculations; it simply charges the market price.

If a company does have the problem of determining its selling prices, the usual practice is to compute the full cost of the product and add to this a profit margin, figured either as a percentage of cost or preferably as a percentage return on the investment involved in making the product.

Note that the relevant costs are *full costs,* which are the direct costs plus a fair share of allocated costs; they are not the differential costs discussed in the preceding section. The result of this calculation is a *first approximation* to the price; it is modified to take into account the strength of competition, the necessity of fitting the price into customary price lines (such as $9.98 dresses), and many other marketing considerations. Consequently, actual prices and hence actual profit margins on specific products may differ widely from this first approximation. The company plans, however, that overall it will obtain the desired profit, with extra profits on high-margin products offsetting thin profits on low-margin products. It will achieve this goal if a fair share of total costs is allocated to each product, and if it obtains a satisfactory profit margin above this cost, on the average, for the products it actually sells.

Adjustments to this first approximation may take the form of changing costs as well as changing profit margins. If it is thought that the computed price is too high, then the product may be redesigned to bring its costs down so that a satisfactory profit can be made at the attainable price. In this process, it is full costs rather than differential costs that are considered.

Profit Margin. In many companies, the profit margin is expressed as a percentage of cost. Increasingly, however, companies are figuring the profit margin as a return on the assets employed in manufacturing and selling the product. This newer practice relates prices to the overall objective of earning a satisfactory return on investment.

Assume, for example, that a company manufactures two products, A and B, the manufacturing cost of each being $6 per unit. At a markon of 50 per cent of cost (33 per cent of selling price), the normal selling price of each product would be $9, and if 100,000 units of each are sold, the total margin would be $600,000. Under return-on-investment pricing, the company would first estimate the total assets employed for the two products. Assume that this works out to $3,000,000 or $30 per unit, for Product A and $1,000,000, or $10 per unit, for Product B. If the company desires 15 per cent return on its investment, the normal margin would be $4.50 for Product A and $1.50 for Product B, making the normal selling price $10.50 and $7.50 respectively. These prices produce the same total margin, $600,000, as the alternative prices calculated as a 50 per cent markon on cost. Product A's higher price reflects the fact that more assets are required to make a unit of Product A than a unit of Product B.

Adding or Dropping Products. In making decisions about whether or not to add a new product and whether or not to discontinue an existing product, similar considerations normally govern. A new product is normally added to the line only if it is expected to produce a satisfactory return on the investment. If an existing product has a low margin, and if the situation cannot be corrected by increasing prices or reducing costs, then the product normally is replaced with a more profitable one. Again, marketing considerations may dictate departures from the normal procedure. Many low-margin products are retained so that the company may offer its customers a full line, equipment may be sold at a low margin in order to induce the sale of high-margin accessories and supplies,[5] no replacement product wth an adequate margin may be known, and so on.

Price Regulations.   A further reason for basing price on full costs rather than on differential costs is the fact that the Robinson-Patman Act prohibits differentials in the prices charged competing customers unless these differentials "make due allowance for differences in the cost of manufacture, sale, or delivery resulting from the differing methods or quantities in which commodities are to such purchasers sold or delivered." The Federal Trade Commission and the Courts have interpreted these "due allowances" as related to full costs, and they have uniformly rejected defenses that are based on differential cost calculations. Many states prohibit the sale of certain products or services below cost, with "cost" either specified as, or interpreted as meaning, the full cost.

Time and Material Prices.   One of the commonly used pricing formulas based on full costs is the *time and material* price. This price consists of a charge for material plus a charge per labor hour. Profit may be included as part of the material element, or the labor element, or both of them. The usual price for repairing an automobile consists of the material priced at cost plus a profit margin, plus labor priced at an hourly rate that includes the direct labor cost, a fair share of overhead, and profit. Most other service work (television repair, plumbing, carpentry, electrical work, etc.) is priced on this basis. In job shops, where each job is done according to the customer's specifications, this is a common basis for pricing.

Contribution Pricing

Although the full cost is the normal basis for pricing, and although a company must recover its full cost or eventually go out of business, there are many situations where differential (i.e., variable, or incremental)

---

[5] A company cannot *compel* its customers to buy its own accessories and supplies. Such "tie-in" agreements are illegal.

costs are appropriately used. In general, these may be described as *crisis* situations. In normal times, a company may refuse to take orders at prices that will not yield a satisfactory profit, but if times are bad, such orders may be accepted if the differential revenue obtained from them exceeds the differential costs involved. The company is better off to receive some revenue above its outlays than to receive nothing at all. Such orders make some contribution to profit,[6] and the selling price is therefore called a *contribution price,* to distinguish it from a normal price. Here, differential costs are the same as those discussed in the preceding section; that is, the costs that will be incurred if the order is accepted and that will not be incurred if it is not accepted.

Dumping, which is the practice of selling surplus quantities of a product in a selected marketing area at a low price, is another version of the contribution idea. However, dumping may violate the Robinson-Patman Act in domestic markets, and may be prohibited or unwise for other reasons in foreign markets.

In times of crisis a product may be retained in the line if it makes some contribution to profits, even though it has such a low profit margin that in normal times it would be dropped.

It is difficult to generalize on the circumstances that determine whether full costs or differential costs are appropriate. Even in normal times, an opportunity may be accepted to make some contribution to profit by using otherwise idle facilities. Conversely, in crisis times the contribution concept may be rejected on the grounds that the low price may "spoil the market," or that orders can in fact be obtained at normal margins if the sales organization works hard enough. Finally, it must be recognized that some companies do not price on the basis of full costs simply because they do not know what their full costs are. Dun & Bradstreet's annual analysis of bankruptcies invariably lists inadequate knowledge of costs as one of the principal factors responsible for business failure.

SUGGESTIONS FOR ATTACKING CASES

The following points may be helpful to an analyst attacking specific cases and also real-life alternative choice problems:

1. Use imagination in choosing the possible alternatives to be considered, but don't select so many alternatives that you bog down before you begin. There is only a fine line between the alternative that is

---

[6] Some prefer to regard this as a contribution to *overhead,* which is merely another way of looking at it.

a "stroke of genius" and the alternative that is a "harebrained idea," but it is a crucial one.

2. Don't yield to the natural temptation to give too much weight to the factors than can be reduced to figures, even though the figures have the appearance of being definite and precise.

3. On the other hand, don't slight the figures because they are "merely" approximations. A reasonable approximation is much better than nothing at all.

4. Often, it is easier to work with total costs rather than with unit costs. Unit cost is a fraction in which total cost is the numerator and number of units the denominator, that is,

$$\frac{\text{Total Cost}}{\text{Number of Units}} = \text{Unit Cost}.$$

Changes in either the numerator or the denominator result in changes in unit costs. An error is made if one of these changes is taken into account and the other is overlooked.

5. There is a tendency to underestimate the cost of doing something new because all the consequences often are not foreseen.

6. The *number* of arguments is irrelevant in an alternative choice problem. A dozen reasons may be, and often are, advanced against trying out something new, but all these reasons put together may not be so strong as a single argument in favor of the proposal.

7. Be realistic about the margin of error in any calculation involving the future. Fancy figures cannot be made out of rough estimates, nor is an answer necessarily precise or valid simply because you spent a long time calculating it.

8. Despite uncertainties, you should make a decision if as much information is available as you can obtain at reasonable cost and within a reasonable time. Postponing action is the same as deciding to perpetuate the existing situation, which may be the worst possible decision.

9. Show clearly the assumptions you made and the effect of these on your estimates so that someone going over your analysis can substitute his own judgments if he wishes.

10. Do not expect that everyone will agree with your conclusion simply because it is supported with carefully worked-out figures. Think about how you can sell your conclusion to those who must act on it.

SUMMARY

Differential costs are the costs that are incurred if a project is undertaken that would not be incurred if it is not undertaken. When an alternative choice problem involves changes in costs but not changes in revenue or investment, the best solution is the one with the lowest differential costs, insofar as cost information bears on the solution.

When the problem involves both cost and revenue considerations, full costs are often a useful first approximation in normal times, but differential costs are used in times of crisis. Managements differ as to their opinion of the circumstances under which each is appropriate.

Cost calculations alone rarely provide the answer to any business problem, but they facilitate comparisons and narrow the area within which judgment must be applied.

CASES

CASE 18–1.　HARCORD WHOLESALE GROCERS, INC.

Prior to 1962, Harcord Wholesale Grocers, Inc., had kept no departmental income statements. In order to control operations more effectively, the management decided at the beginning of that year to install departmental cost accounts. At the end of 1962, the new accounts showed that although the business as a whole had a gross margin of 13.1 per cent and a net profit of 1.1 per cent on net sales of $2,408,000, the fresh fruit and produce department had shown a substantial loss, with a gross margin of only 9.8 per cent of its $416,000 net sales, against an expense rate of 12.3 per cent. The income statement for this department is shown in Exhibit 1.

Exhibit 1

HARCORD WHOLESALE GROCERS, INC.

Income Statement, Fresh Fruit and Produce Department

		Per Cent
Net sales	$416,016	100.0
Cost of sales	375,246	90.2
Gross margin	$ 40,770	9.8
Expenses:		
Payroll, direct labor, and supervision in the department...$ 20,640		
Salesmen's commissions (fruits sold by general salesmen selling for all departments on straight, uniform, commission basis)	6,396	
Rent (charged to department on basis of yearly rental per square foot occupied; the company rented and occupied an entire building)	16,440	
Taxes (assessed by state on average value of inventory)	600	
Insurance (for protection of inventory)	480	
Depreciation (basis: 5 per cent on departmental equipment)	1,560	
Administration and general office (allocated on basis of departmental sales)	12,824	
Interest on inventory (an accounting charge; actually there was no outside borrowing for working capital)	235	
Total Expenses	$ 59,175	14.2
Net Loss	$ 18,405	4.4

This loss led one executive to argue that the department should be discontinued. The executives agreed that, so far as the factor of customer satisfaction with the completeness of the company's line was concerned, it was not essential to continue selling fresh fruits and produce. Elimination of this department, in other words, was not expected to result in loss of sales by other departments.

After several protracted discussions of the proposal, one of the executives sought to end the controversy by saying that the company should discontinue either the department or the new accounting system.

Question

What action should be taken?

CASE 18–2.   LIQUID CHEMICAL COMPANY

The Liquid Chemical Company manufactured and sold a range of high-grade products throughout Great Britain. Many of these products required careful packing, and the company had always made a feature of the special properties of the containers used. They had a special patented lining, made from a material known as GHL, and the firm operated a department especially to maintain its containers in good condition and to make new ones to replace those that were past repair.

Mr. Walsh, the general manager, had for some time suspected that the firm might save money, and get equally good service, by buying its containers from an outside source. After careful inquiries, he approached a firm specializing in container production, Packages, Ltd., and asked for a quotation from it. At the same time he asked Mr. Dyer, his chief accountant, to let him have an up-to-date statement of the cost of operating the container department.

Within a few days, the quotation from Packages, Ltd., came in. The firm was prepared to supply all the new containers required—at that time running at the rate of 3,000 a year—for £12,500 a year, the contract to run for a term of five years certain and thereafter to be renewable from year to year. If the number of containers required increased, the contract price would be increased proportionally. Additionally, and irrespective of whether the above contract was concluded or not, Packages, Ltd., undertook to carry out purely maintenance work on containers, short of replacement, for a sum of £3,750 a year, on the same contract terms.

Mr. Walsh compared these figures with the cost figures prepared by Mr. Dyer, covering a year's operations of the container department, which were as follows:

	£	£
Materials....................................		7,000
Labour......................................		5,000
Department overheads:		
Manager's salary...........................	800	
Rent......................................	450	
Depreciation of machinery...................1,500		
Maintenance of machinery...................	360	
Other expenses.............................1,575		
		4,685
		16,685
Proportion of general administrative overheads...		2,250
Total Cost of Department for Year........		18,935

Walsh's conclusion was that no time should be lost in closing the department and in entering into the contracts offered by Packages, Ltd. However, he felt bound to give the manager of the department, Mr. Duffy, an opportunity to question this conclusion before he acted on it. He therefore called him in and put the facts before him, at the same time making it clear that Duffy's own position was not in jeopardy; for even if his department were closed, there was another managerial position shortly becoming vacant to which he could be moved without loss of pay or prospects.

Mr. Duffy looked thoughtful and asked for time to think the matter over. The next morning, he asked to speak to Mr. Walsh again, and said he thought there were a number of considerations that ought to be borne in mind before his department was closed. "For instance," he said, "what will you do with the machinery? It cost £12,000 four years ago, but you'd be lucky if you got £2,000 for it now, even though it's good for another four years at least. And then there's the stock of GHL (a special chemical) we bought a year ago. That cost us £10,000, and at the rate we're using it now, it'll last us another four years or so. We used up about one fifth of it last year. Dyer's figure of £7,000 for materials probably includes about £2,000 for GHL. But it'll be tricky stuff to handle if we don't use it up. We bought it for £50 a ton, and you couldn't buy it today for less than £60. But you wouldn't have more than £40 a ton left if you sold it, after you'd covered all the handling expenses."

Walsh thought that Dyer ought to be present during this discussion. He called him in and put Duffy's points to him. "I don't much like all this conjecture," Dyer said. "I think my figures are pretty conclusive. Besides, if we are going to have all this talk about 'what will happen if,' don't forget the problem of space we're faced with. We're paying £850 a year in rent for a warehouse a couple of miles away. If we closed

Duffy's department, we'd have all the warehouse space we need without renting."

"That's a good point," said Walsh. "Though I must say, I'm a bit worried about the men if we close the department. I don't think we can find room for any of them elsewhere in the firm. I could see whether Packages can take any of them. But some of them are getting on. There's Walters and Hines, for example. They've been with us since they left school 40 years ago. I'd feel bound to give them a small pension—£150 a year each, say."

Duffy showed some relief at this. "But I still don't like Dyer's figures," he said. "What about this £2,250 for general administrative overheads. You surely don't expect to sack anyone in the general office if I'm closed, do you?" "Probably not," said Dyer, "but someone has to pay for these costs. We can't ignore them when we look at an individual department, because if we do that with each department in turn, we shall finish up by convincing ourselves that directors, accountants, typists, stationery, and the like don't have to be paid for. And they do, believe me."

"Well, I think we've thrashed this out pretty fully," said Walsh, "but I've been turning over in my mind the possibility of perhaps keeping on the maintenance work ourselves. What are your views on that, Duffy?"

"I don't know," said Duffy, "but it's worth looking into. We shouldn't need any machinery for that, and I could hand the supervision over to a foreman. You'd save £300 a year there, say. You'd only need about one fifth of the men, but you could keep on the oldest. You wouldn't save any space, so I suppose the rent would be the same. I shouldn't think the other expenses would be more than £650 a year." "What about materials?" asked Walsh. "We use about 10 per cent of the total on maintenance," Duffy replied.

"Well, I've told Packages, Ltd., that I'd let them know my decision within a week," said Walsh. "I'll let you know what I decide to do before I write to them."

Questions

1. Assuming no additional information can be readily obtained, what action should be taken?

2. What, if any, additional information do you think is necessary for a sound decision?

CASE 18–3. HANSON MANUFACTURING COMPANY

In February 1955, Mr. Herbert Wessling was appointed general manager by Mr. Paul Hanson, president of the Hanson Manufacturing

Company. Mr. Wessling, age 56, had wide executive experience in manufacturing products similar to those of the Hanson Company. The appointment of Mr. Wessling resulted from management problems arising from the death of Mr. Richard Hanson, founder and, until his death early in 1954, president of the Hanson Company. Mr. Paul Hanson, who then was 34 years old, had only four years' experience with the company. His father had hoped to train him over a ten-year period, but his untimely death had cut this seasoning period short. The younger Hanson became president when his father died and exercised full control until he hired Mr. Wessling.

Mr. Paul Hanson knew that during 1954 he had made several poor decisions and noted that the morale of the organization had suffered, apparently through lack of confidence in him. When he received the profit and loss statement for 1954 (Exhibit 1), the net loss of over

Exhibit 1

HANSON MANUFACTURING COMPANY

Profit and Loss Statement for Year Ending December 31, 1954

Gross sales..		$10,589,405
Less: Cash discount..............................		156,578
Net sales...		$10,432,827
Cost of manufacturing.............................		7,529,758
Manufacturing profit...............................		$ 2,903,069
Less: Selling expense............................	$1,838,238	
General administration....................	653,020	
Depreciation..............................	458,440	2,949,698
Operating loss......................................		$ 46,629
Less: Other income...............................		21,065
Net loss before bond interest.....................		$ 25,564
Add: Interest on bonds............................		145,283
Net Loss after All Charges........................		$ 170,847

$170,000 during a good business year convinced him that he needed help. He attracted Mr. Wessling from a competitor by offering him a stock option incentive in addition to salary, knowing that Mr. Wessling wanted to acquire a financial competence for his retirement. The two men came to a clear understanding that Mr. Wessling, as general manager, had full authority to execute any changes he wished. In addition, Mr. Wessling would explain the reasons for his decisions to Mr. Hanson and thereby train him for successful leadership upon Mr. Wessling's retirement.

The Hanson Manufacturing Company made only three industrial products, 101, 102, and 103. These were sold by company salesmen for use in the processes of other manufacturers. All the salesmen, on a salary basis, sold the three products but in varying proportions. The Hanson

Exhibit 2

HANSON MANUFACTURING COMPANY

Analysis of Profit and Loss by Departments, Year Ending December 31, 1954

	Product 101 (Thousands)	Product 101 ¢ per Cwt.	Product 102 (Thousands)	Product 102 ¢ per Cwt.	Product 103 (Thousands)	Product 103 ¢ per Cwt.	Total (Thousands)	Direct	Allocated	Basis of Allocation
Rent	$ 587	27.55	$ 457	44.43	$ 388	39.25	$ 1,432		x	Sq. ft.
Property taxes	62	2.93	50	4.85	40	4.05	152		x	Sq. ft.
Property insurance	52	2.45	40	3.87	53	5.33	145		x	Val. of equip.
Compensation insurance	83	3.87	57	5.58	45	4.55	185		x	Direct labor
Direct labor	1,293	60.63	890	86.42	687	69.65	2,870	x		
Indirect labor	398	18.65	273	26.48	212	21.52	883		x	Direct labor
Power	22	1.05	25	2.42	30	3.05	77		x	Machine hrs.
Light and heat	15	0.70	13	1.23	10	1.02	38		x	Sq. ft.
Building service	10	0.47	8	0.75	7	0.75	25		x	Sq. ft.
Materials	978	45.85	280	27.20	287	29.12	1,545	x		
Supplies	52	2.45	48	4.62	35	3.55	135	x		
Repairs	18	0.83	15	1.45	10	1.03	43	x		
Total	$3,570	167.43	$2,156	209.30	$1,804	182.87	$ 7,530			
Selling expense	910	42.70	458	44.45	470	47.62	1,838		x	$ val. of sales
General administrative	345	16.17	130	12.63	178	17.98	653		x	$ val. of sales
Depreciation	165	7.75	127	12.37	165	16.73	457		x	Val. of equip.
Interest	52	2.45	40	3.88	53	5.32	145		x	Val. of equip.
Total Cost	$5,042	236.50	$2,911	282.63	$2,670	270.52	$10,623			
Less: Other income	10	0.48	5	0.50	5	0.50	20		x	$ val. of sales
Sales (net)	$5,032	236.02	$2,906	282.13	$2,665	270.02	$10,603			
	5,167	242.35	2,599	252.28	2,667	270.27	10,433			
Profit or loss	$ 135	6.33	$ 307*	29.85*	$ 2	0.25	$ 170*			
Unit sales (in cwts.)	2,132,191		1,029,654		986,974					
Quoted selling price	$2.45		$2.58		$2.75					
Cash discounts taken (% of sales)	1.08%		2.03%		1.72%		1.48%			

* Loss.

Note: Figures may not check exactly because of rounding.

Company sold throughout New England and was one of eight companies with similar products. Several of its competitors were larger and manufactured a larger variety of products than did the Hanson Company. The dominant company was the Samra Company, which operated a branch plant in the Hanson Company's market area. Customarily, the Samra Company announced prices annually, and the other producers followed suit.

Price cutting was rare, and the only variance from quoted selling prices took the form of cash discounts. In the past, attempts at price cutting had followed a consistent pattern: all competitors met the price reduction, and the industry as a whole sold about the same quantity but at the lower prices. This continued until the Samra Company, with its strong financial position, again stabilized the situation following a general recognition of the failure of price cutting. Furthermore, because sales were to industrial buyers and because the products of different manufacturers were very similar, the Hanson Company was convinced that it could not individually raise prices without suffering a volume decline.

During 1954 the Hanson Company's share of industry sales was 12 per cent for type 101, 8 per cent for 102, and 10 per cent for 103. The industry-wide quoted selling prices were $2.45, $2.58, and $2.75, respectively.

Mr. Wessling upon taking office in February 1955 decided against immediate major changes. Rather he chose to analyze 1954 operations and to wait for results of the first half of 1955. He instructed the accounting department to provide detailed expenses and earnings statements by products for 1954 (see Exhibit 2). In addition, he requested an explanation of the nature of the costs including their expected future behavior (see Exhibit 3).

To familiarize Mr. Hanson with his methods, Mr. Wessling sent him copies of these exhibits, and they discussed them. Mr. Hanson stated that he thought Product 102 should be dropped immediately as it would be impossible to lower its expenses as much as 30 cents per cwt. In addition, he stressed the need for economies on Product 103.

Mr. Wessling relied on the authority arrangement Mr. Hanson had agreed to earlier and continued production of the three products. For control purposes he had the accounting department prepare monthly statements using as standard costs the costs per cwt. taken from the analytical profit and loss statement for 1954 (Exhibit 2). These monthly statements were his basis for making minor sales or production changes during the spring of 1955. Late in July 1955, Mr. Wessling

Exhibit 3
ACCOUNTING DEPARTMENT'S COMMENTARY ON COSTS

Direct Labor: Variable. Union shop at going community rates. No abnormal demands foreseen.

Compensation Insurance: Variable. Five per cent of direct and indirect labor is an accurate estimate.

Materials: Variable. Exhibit 2 figures are accurate. Includes waste allowances. Purchases are at market prices.

Power: Variable. Rates are fixed. Use varies with activity. Averages in Exhibit 2 are accurate.

Supplies: Variable. Exhibit 2 figures are accurate. Supplies bought at market prices.

Repairs: Variable. Varies as volume changes within normal operation range. Lower and upper limits are fixed.

General Administrative, Selling Expense, Indirect Labor, Interest, and Other Income: These items are almost nonvariable at levels of operation between $5 and $15 million.

Cash Discounts: Almost nonvariable. Average cash discounts taken are consistent from year to year. Percentages in Exhibit 2 are accurate.

Light and Heat: Almost nonvariable. Heat varies slightly with fuel cost changes. Light is a fixed item regardless of level of production.

Property Taxes: Almost nonvariable. Under the lease terms Hanson Company pays the taxes; assessed valuation has been constant; the rate has risen slowly. Any change in the near future will be small and independent of production volume.

Rent: Nonvariable. Lease has 12 years to run.

Building Service: Nonvariable. At normal business level variances are small.

Property Insurance: Nonvariable. Three-year policy with fixed premium.

Depreciation: Nonvariable. Fixed dollar total.

received from the accounting department the six months' statement of cumulative standard costs including variances of actual costs from standard (see Exhibit 4). They showed that the first half of 1955 was a successful period.

During the latter half of 1955 the sales of the entire industry weakened. Even though the Hanson Company retained its share of the market, its profit for the last six months was small. In January 1956, the Samra Company announced a price reduction on Product 101 from $2.45 to $2.25 per cwt. This created an immediate pricing problem for all its competitors. Mr. Wessling forecast that if the Hanson Company held to the $2.45 price during the first six months of 1956, its unit sales would be 750,000 cwt. He felt that if it dropped its price to $2.25 per cwt., the six months' volume would be 1,000,000 cwt. Mr. Wessling

Exhibit 4

HANSON MANUFACTURING COMPANY

Profit and Loss Statement by Departments, at Standard, Showing Variations from January 1 to June 30, 1955

	Product 101		Product 102		Product 103		Total Standard (Thousands)	Total Actual (Thousands)	Variations + = Standard Exceeds − = Actual Exceeds
	Unit* Standard	Total at Standard (Thousands)	Unit* Standard	Total at Standard (Thousands)	Unit* Standard	Total at Standard (Thousands)			
Rent	¢ 27.55	$ 275	¢ 44.43	$ 316	¢ 39.25	$ 197	$ 788	$ 715	$ + 73
Property taxes	2.93	29	4.85	35	4.05	20	84	77	+ 7
Property insurance	2.45	25	3.87	28	5.33	27	80	73	+ 7
Compensation insurance	3.87	39	5.58	40	4.55	23	102	102	
Direct labor	60.63	604	86.42	615	69.65	349	1,568	1,582	− 14
Indirect labor	18.65	186	26.48	188	21.52	108	482	448	+ 34
Power	1.05	10	2.42	17	3.05	15	42	42	
Light and heat	0.70	7	1.23	9	1.02	5	21	20	+ 1
Building service	0.47	5	0.75	5	0.75	4	14	10	+ 4
Materials	45.85	457	27.20	194	29.12	146	797	788	+ 9
Supplies	2.45	24	4.62	33	3.55	18	75	75	
Repairs	0.83	8	1.45	10	1.03	5	23	25	− 2
Total	¢167.43	$1,669	¢209.30	$1,490	¢182.87	$ 917	$4,076	$3,957	$ + 119
Selling expense	42.70	426	44.45	317	47.62	239	982	923	+ 59
General administrative	16.17	161	12.63	90	17.98	90	341	328	+ 13
Depreciation	7.75	77	12.37	88	16.73	84	249	227	+ 22
Interest	2.45	25	3.88	28	5.32	26	79	73	+ 6
Total Cost	¢236.50	$2,358	¢282.63	$2,013	¢270.52	$1,356	$5,727	$5,508	$ + 219
Less: Other income	0.48	5	0.50	4	0.50	2	11	11	
Actual sales	¢236.02	$2,353	¢282.13	$2,009	¢270.02	$1,354	$5,716	$5,497	$ + 219
	242.35	2,416	252.28	1,796	270.27	1,355	5,567	5,567	
Profit or loss	¢ 6.33	$ 63	¢ 29.85†	$ 213†	¢ 0.25	$ 1	$ 149†	$ 70	$ + 219
Unit sales	996,859		712,102		501,276				

* Unit = Cwt.
† Loss.

knew that competing managements anticipated a further decline in activity. He thought a general decline in prices was quite probable.

The accounting department reported that the standard costs in use would probably apply during 1956, with two exceptions: materials and supplies would be about 5 per cent below standard; and light and heat would decline about one third of 1 per cent.

Mr. Wessling and Mr. Hanson discussed the pricing problem. Mr. Hanson observed that even with the anticipated decline in material and supply costs, a sales price of $2.25 would be below cost. Mr. Hanson therefore wanted the $2.45 price to be continued since he believed that the company could not be profitable while selling a key product below cost.

Questions

1. Is Exhibit 4 the most useful form in which to present information to management?

2. Was Mr. Wessling correct in his decision not to drop Product 102 in the spring of 1955?

3. In January 1956, should the company have reduced the price of Product 101 from $2.45 to $2.25 or to an intermediate figure?

CASE 18–4.   ATHERTON COMPANY

Early in January 1956, the sales manager and the controller of the Atherton Company met for the purpose of preparing a joint pricing recommendation for Item 345. After the president approved their recommendation, the price would be announced in letters to retail customers. In accordance with company and industry practice, announced prices were adhered to for the year unless radical changes in market conditions occurred.

The Atherton Company was the largest company in its segment of the textile industry; its 1955 sales had exceeded $6 million. Company salesmen were on a straight salary basis, and each salesman sold the full line. Most of the Atherton competitors were small. Usually they waited for the Atherton Company to announce prices before mailing out their own price lists.

Item 345, an expensive yet competitive fabric, was the sole product of a department whose facilities could not be utilized on other items in the product line. In January 1954, the Atherton Company had raised its price from $1.50 to $2.00 a yard. This had been done to bring the profit per yard on Item 345 up to that of other products in the line. Although the company was in a strong position financially, it would require considerable capital in the next few years to finance a recently approved long-term modernization and expansion program. The 1954 pricing decision had been one of several changes advocated by the directors in an attempt to strengthen the company's working capital position so as to insure that adequate funds would be available for this program.

Competitors of the Atherton Company had held their prices on products similar to Item 345 at $1.50 during 1954 and 1955. The industry and Atherton Company volume for Item 345 for the years 1950–55, as estimated by the sales manager, is shown in Exhibit 1. As

Exhibit 1

ITEM 345, PRICES AND PRODUCTION, 1950–55

Year	Volume of Production (Yards)		Price	
	Industry Total	Atherton	Charged by Most Competitors	Atherton Company
1950........	610,000	213,000	$2.00	$2.00
1951........	575,000	200,000	2.00	2.00
1952........	430,000	150,000	1.50	1.50
1953........	475,000	165,000	1.50	1.50
1954........	500,000	150,000	1.50	2.00
1955........	625,000	125,000	1.50	2.00

shown by this exhibit, the Atherton Company had lost a significant portion of its former market position. In the sales manager's opinion, a reasonable forecast of industry volume for 1956 was 700,000 yards. He was certain that the company could sell 25 per cent of the 1956 industry total if it adopted the $1.50 price. He feared a further volume decline if it did not meet the competitive price. As many consumers were convinced of the superiority of the Atherton product, the sales manager reasoned that sales of Item 345 would probably not fall below 75,000 yards, even at a $2 price.

During the pricing discussions, the controller and sales manager had considered two other aspects of the problem. The controller was concerned about the possibility that competitors would reduce their prices below $1.50 if the Atherton Company announced a $1.50 price for Item 345. The sales manager was confident that competitors would not go below $1.50 because they all had higher costs and several of them were in tight financial straits. He believed that action taken on Item 345 would not have any substantial repercussions on other items in the line.

The controller prepared estimated costs of Item 345 at various volumes of production (Exhibit 2). These estimated costs reflected

Exhibit 2

ESTIMATED COST PER YARD OF ITEM 345 AT VARIOUS VOLUMES
OF PRODUCTION

	75,000	100,000	125,000	150,000	175,000	200,000
Direct labor..............	$0.400	$0.390	$0.380	$0.370	$0.380	$0.400
Material.................	0.200	0.200	0.200	0.200	0.200	0.200
Material spoilage.........	0.020	0.020	0.019	0.019	0.019	0.020
Department expense:						
Direct*................	0.060	0.056	0.050	0.050	0.050	0.050
Indirect†..............	0.400	0.300	0.240	0.200	0.180	0.150
General overhead‡........	0.120	0.117	0.114	0.111	0.114	0.120
Factory cost..............	$1.200	$1.083	$1.003	$0.950	$0.943	$0.940
Selling and administrative						
expense§.............	0.780	0.704	0.652	0.618	0.613	0.611
Total Cost.........	$1.980	$1.787	$1.655	$1.568	$1.556	$1.551

*Indirect labor, supplies, repairs, power, etc.
†Depreciation, supervision, etc.
‡30 per cent of direct labor.
§65 per cent of factory cost.

current labor and material costs. They were based on past experience except for the estimates of 75,000 and 100,000 yards. The company had produced more than 100,000 yards in each year since World War II, and prewar experience was not applicable because of equipment changes and increases in labor productivity.

Questions

1. How, if at all, did the company's financial condition relate to the pricing decision?

2. Should $1.50 or $2.00 have been recommended?

CASE 18–5. BELTON WOOLEN MILLS, INC.

In January 1958, executives of Belton Woolen Mills, Inc.—a firm that had held its own in the New England textile race for more than 50 years—found itself facing the typical question: How do we adjust to competitive pressures?

Word from the sales personnel in New York City had been received the afternoon before to the effect that Pattern 7031, priced by the company at $3 a yard, had aroused much interest on the part of buyers as they examined samples; in fact, this reception at the showing indicated that such a style would probably become a best seller in the current cloth season for eventual display at retail in the autumn of 1958 in women's coats.

The fly in the ointment was that a competitor was showing, at a price less by 20 cents a yard, or at $2.80, a fabric that seemed to be almost the same, having virtually the same distinctive pattern. In the judgment of sales personnel, who had sent a sample of the cloth from New York, the fabrics were so nearly alike that Belton Mills would have to match the $2.80 price if it expected to reap much benefit from the pattern's appeal to buyers.

At this time operations were on what was essentially a three-shift basis. Approximately 525 people were employed by the concern, about 485 in production. Seventeen shifts were worked during each week, only two reporting on Saturday. This was the level at which the firm preferred to work when orders permitted. In some parts of the plant, however, a third daily shift was not employed because of the great importance in these areas of supervision, both costly and difficult to obtain. Dyeing and finishing operations were in this category. Careful planning and an adequate amount of machinery in these processes kept them from becoming bottlenecks, however.

Cost Estimating

The firm's management of costs was built around a cost estimate sheet set up for each style or pattern in the process of planning its production. Essentially, the estimates were developed from actual historical costs of producing similar cloth; however, they reflected departures from historical data which were known or could be anticipated. For example, material estimates were stated at current or expected market price. Labor and operating cost estimates were regularly based on prior cost experience for similar operations, with allowance for expected rates in different operations. Burden cost estimates generally were not based entirely on either expectations or recent experience, but rather on rates developed in the relationship between production and estimated burden cost if activity should be at the 15-shift level (five-day week) for the year, on the average. This allocation procedure gave a burden estimate on cloth that was lower than expected-actual in cases in which the operating level was expected to average less than 15 shifts during the year, as was generally the case.

Burden was applied in cost estimates on the basis of the number of spinning units, for example, at $5 per spinning unit of 100,000 yards of yarn. For each pattern the number of ends (the individual threads of yarn running lengthwise and making up the full width of the cloth) and the number of picks (the number of individual threads of yarn running crosswise in a yard of finished cloth) were specified on the cost estimate sheet. To determine the number of yards of yarn in a yard of the fabric, the number of picks was multiplied by the number of yards of yarn in the pick, or width of the fabric; to this product was added the number of ends in the fabric. This sum then was multiplied by $5 (the assumed burden rate) and divided by 100,000, the spinning unit, to secure the burden cost of a yard of the cloth. Thus, for yarn of the same size and weight, the burden cost was estimated actually on the basis of cloth weight; and generally a weight basis would give substantially the same result. The burden item included both factory overhead and general and administrative expenses.

In decisions involving idle-capacity cost (as in changes in the number of shifts), it was generally assumed that burden costs, including general and administrative expense, were 55 per cent variable and 45 per cent fixed. The controller expressed the opinion, however, that the proportion was more nearly fifty-fifty for reductions in activity below 12 shifts a week. Also, certain variable-burden inefficiencies tended to develop at levels below 12 shifts.

The sum of material, labor, and burden was called Total Mill Cost. Normal percentages were added in sequence for selling expense, returns and allowances, and cash discounts. Each of these was computed as a percentage of selling price. The addition of estimated net profit before income taxes gave the accumulated total, or the planned selling price. In general, the planned percentage for net profit, based on sales, was approximately the same for all styles.

Selling expense was considered a fixed cost for the year, no decline being expected when volume of production or sales decreased. This fixed cost was expressed as a percentage of expected annual sales volume to determine the percentage figure to be used for selling expense on the cost estimate sheet. The figure for returns and allowances was based on the past relationship between total sales and these deductions from sales. The allowance element was important in the woolen industry. Contracts generally provided for arbitration procedures in case the buyer considered the cloth delivered not up to specifications. Although the Belton management agreed that it could predict roughly the risk of allowances for a certain pattern and that this risk was much greater for some items than others, it did not consider it worthwhile to attempt to allow for this variation in estimating originally the cost of a certain pattern; therefore, the same average rate was used for all estimates in the season's planning. Since sales were made on terms of $1/10$, $n/60$ from date of billing, the discount was estimated at 1 per cent of selling price.

Pricing

As was customary in the woolen industry, numerous patterns of Belton Woolen Mills were grouped together and assigned the same "range number" and sales price. A range included cloth styles that were similar in fabric, pattern, production operations, and estimated cost. Ordinarily the estimates of cost for the specific items in a range varied not more than 10 per cent from the average cost of the range.

Situation 1

With respect to the problem of Pattern 7031, Mr. Lincoln, general manager of the mill, made the decision at once that it would not be possible simply to meet the $2.80 price: "If we can't figure some way to cut the fabric's cost, the sales office will just have to push something else." He was convinced, however, that in view of the urgent appeal from New York, this settlement of the issue would create some real danger of Belton's securing a significantly smaller share of the total market for the year.

"Of course, nobody can be certain of the ultimate effect," commented another executive sympathetically, "for New York has weathered such storms before."

But Mr. Lincoln knew immediately that he wanted some cost estimating work done before he and his group tried to reach a decision: "We've got to decide whether we can get into the market on this popular style or stay out. Let's find a way to do it if we can, boys."

This instruction meant that George Buchanan, a technical assistant, who actually compiled the firm's cost estimates, had a job to do. He found that Pattern 7031 was in Range 253 and that Range 253, priced at $3.00 a yard, showed an average estimated total mill cost of $2.58 for a margin of 42 cents, or 14 per cent, based on sales price, and an average net profit of 12 cents, or 4 per cent. He found the highest total mill cost in the range to be $2.68, and the lowest to be $2.52. He pulled the cost estimate sheet for Pattern 7031 and found the following summary of the cost elements:

```
Raw materials.....................$1.40
Dyes.............................. 0.12
Emulsions and chemicals........... 0.05
Labor............................. 0.54
Burden*........................... 0.44
                                  ─────
    Subtotal......................$2.55
5⅔% selling expense.............. 0.17
3⅓% returns..................... 0.10
1% discount...................... 0.03
Net profit....................... 0.15
                                  ─────
    Selling Price................$3.00
```

* Burden in this summary includes general and administrative expense.

Mr. Buchanan worked for hours on the problem, gathering information to present to the executives, in the form of a new cost estimate sheet, for the decision as to whether "to get into the market." He compiled the following notes on his findings, including reactions he received from key personnel:

1. The competing fabric weighs 19½ ounces as compared with our 20-ounce cloth. Both are all wool.
2. The price of raw wool is now approximately 1½ per cent lower than it was when pre-season estimates were made.
3. I know that the yarn yield would be slightly higher than average on this particular fabric if its current popularity should increase the average lot size materially—maybe a saving of 2 to 3 cents a yard.
4. Our cloth has a brighter color, which is obvious when the samples are compared closely. We can save at least a penny on dyes, for brightness is costly.
5. The competing fabric is not as well finished as ours is. If we match the finishing of the other fabric, our labor saving will be negligible, but the saving in machine time (largely in napping) will justify a 3 to 4 per cent saving of the variable burden.
6. Neither Harris (vice president, dyeing and finishing) nor Lynn (vice president, other manufacturing) thinks we should try to further cheapen the fabric by blending with nylon.
7. This fabric is not the sort on which we will have much trouble with returns and allowances. Mr. Harris says this loss can probably be cut to 2 per cent of sales.
8. We already have a plain color blend in a range priced at $2.75; we have nothing priced between that amount and $3.00.
9. Mr. Lynn says these fabric adjustments should put us in as good position as the competitor to get the business if we quote the same price. Generally we consider our line more popular than the competitor's.
10. Mr. Winthrop (controller) wonders if we can actually get larger production lots than average in this fabric if we have to share the market with the competitor.
11. Mr. Lynn and the production people think these changes are simple enough that they can be made quickly.

Situation 2

Six months after the executives of Belton Woolen Mills made the decision called for above on Pattern 7031, Mr. Lincoln returned from a trip to the New York sales office and greeted Mr. Winthrop, the controller, with a request for more cost information. A firm known to buy exceptionally large quantities of cloth for manufacture in large lots for a chain of stores had offered to negotiate with the New York office, just the day before, with regard to Belton's best price on 12 samples, delivery to be required not before July 1, 1959, with billing to be made as of that date regardless of actual delivery time, which could be on any date after January 1, 1959.

The controller knew that the president was fearful of a repetition of the experience of some previous fall quarters when the operating level had fallen below eight shifts a week on the average. He knew that Mr. Lincoln wanted to take some action to avoid this decline during the slow season and that many competing firms also would be trying to get volume business during the slow season, a fact well known to large-lot buyers also.

It was clear to Mr. Winthrop that he should set up the lowest possible costs for the specific patterns, cost figures which the president could use as a basis for discount negotiation, knowing that at these figures his firm could at least cover extra costs of production. In other words, he wanted to estimate those costs that would not be present at the eight-shift level, which was considered attainable without these special orders.

Belton Mills normally gave discounts for large orders, but if the orders for the chain of stores were received, they would be much larger than the orders the firm usually received for regular season work.

Mr. Winthrop and Mr. Buchanan, with others, spent many hours discussing their cost-volume relationships and other problems raised by the assignment. Buchanan made the following notes concerning cost figures to be submitted to the president with respect to Pattern 7031:

1. If we get orders of the size indicated on the 12 patterns, we can operate at about a 12-shift level all fall except for the two-week closing for vacations.
2. Let's assume that we get enough extra business out of this negotiation to hold at the ten-shift level. At lower levels of operation we are not quite so efficient on variable burden costs as at the 15-shift level. Mr. Winthrop says that on ordinary lots our costs per unit should run 8 per cent above the comparable 15-shift variable burden cost, as an approximation.

3. Raw wool prices will be figured 4.3 per cent above the original estimates on 7031, prices having risen.
4. Labor cost can be cut by 5 per cent.
5. Because of the larger-lot sizes, yarn wastage should decrease and savings of 6 per cent should be realized.
6. A given amount of cloth can move through machine operations at a faster rate per unit in a large lot than in a small lot. Because of this, we should be able to make savings of 5 per cent in total burden over the amount indicated on the cost estimate sheet.
7. If the buyer changes no specifications, returns and allowances can probably be held to 2 per cent.
8. As we plan to schedule the production, we will have to carry the receivable about seven months before billing. Money is worth 5 per cent per annum to us.
9. Mr. Lincoln wants a report showing all costs applicable to the expected order and relevant to this pricing decision. He will decide later how much more than this minimum amount he should try to secure.

Questions

1. What action do you think should be taken on Situation 1?
2. Prepare the estimate called for in Situation 2.

CASE 18–6. HELVIN BLANKET COMPANY

The Helvin Blanket Company was a large producer of cotton blankets. Since the company performed all the operations from the baled cotton to the finished blankets, and since a market existed for cotton in various stages of manufacture, an ever-present problem before its management was at what point in the manufacture of a blanket the alternative of selling the uncompleted product was more profitable than continuing with the manufacturing process toward a later market. In the spring of 1956, during a period of undercapacity operations, an incident occurred that raised the question of the validity of using the familiar total average cost accumulations and prorations of the accounting department as a basis for deciding at which point to terminate manufacturing and to sell the product in process.

At a meeting of the principal executives in the spring of 1956, the sales manager proposed that the carding and spinning capacity of the mill be used to produce warp yarn which, he said, the company could sell currently at a profit. The production manager, on the other hand, contended that the loom capacity of the plant rendered it desirable to continue all yarn operations through to the stage of blankets. The sales manager defended his position with the following figures, which the cost office had prepared for him on the basis of current standard costs:

	Cost per Pound, Warp Yarn	Cost per Blanket
Labor........................	$0.1316	$0.2937
Overhead.....................	0.1053	0.2327
Processing materials...........	0.0083	0.0521
Raw materials.................	0.3812	1.1436
Cost at standard..............	$0.6265	$1.7221
Current selling price...........	0.6450	1.7000
Profit or (Loss)...............	$0.0185 per lb.	($0.0221) per blanket

Each blanket contained one pound of warp yarn and two pounds of filling yarn. The figures for cost per blanket were cumulative. Thus, the $0.2937 labor item under cost per blanket included the $0.1316 labor cost of making one pound of warp yarn, plus the labor cost of making two pounds of filling yarn and the labor cost of weaving the blanket.

The production manager challenged the validity of any figures that indicated that the optimum move for the management was to shut down the greater part of the mill in the face of a reasonably favorable market demand for blankets. He argued that the plant was set up to manufacture blankets, not yarn, and to sell yarn was, in effect, to get out of the blanket business, in which the company had made its name. Moreover, he wasn't sure but that the company, despite the generally weak market, might do better financially by keeping the blanket room open.

The head of the cost office stated that the figures presented by the sales manager had been based on painstaking studies of labor and material costs and of methods of distributing overhead to products. He admitted that certain allocations were rough and that different kinds of costs were reported together. On being questioned, he said that for both yarn and blankets about 15 per cent of the labor cost was fixed and that about 60 per cent of overhead was fixed.

The executives had to reach a decision on the issue. The sales manager was opposed to selling blankets at a loss when he could be selling yarn at a profit. The production manager certainly did not want to close his blanket mill.

Questions

1. What different courses of action might be taken, and what arguments can be made to support them?

2. What information or forecasts might be useful to round out the story?

3. On balance and in the light of the probable state of affairs, what would you decide?

4. If the current selling price of warp yarn was $0.725 a pound, instead of $0.645, as given in the case, would your decision be changed?

CASE 18–7. MARTALL BLANKET COMPANY

In the spring of 1941, the Martall Blanket Company was negotiating a large contract for blankets with the U.S. Navy. A question arose as to the method that the company should use in estimating the price that it would ask for these blankets.

In January 1941, the production manager prepared an estimate of production for the 1941–42 season. This estimate, shown in Exhibit 1,

Exhibit 1

PRODUCTION ESTIMATE 1941–42

Style	Size	Quantity
Ashmont	72 × 90	12,000
Velona	72 × 90	26,000
Fairfax	72 × 90	22,000
Total Domestic		60,000
Army	66 × 84	75,000
Navy	66 × 90	25,000
Total		160,000

was made on the assumption that the mill would be operated at three-shift capacity. There was general agreement in the company that demand was strong enough to warrant capacity operations for the foreseeable future. Production facilities could be used to make any of the blankets shown on Exhibit 1 interchangeably.

The production estimate was sent to the cost department, which prepared cost and selling price estimates for each blanket appearing thereon. Raw material prices were obtained by averaging the prices of wool on hand and the prices of expected purchases for the period of the budget. Standard costs for labor, factory expense, and processing materials were added to raw material costs so as to arrive at a total manufacturing cost per blanket. These standard costs had been estimated in 1938 but had been corrected subsequently for actual cost experience through ratios applied to labor, factory expense, and processing materials. Selling, advertising, administrative, and interest charges were added at $24 per loom.[7] (At $24 a loom it was possible to absorb these charges at 85 per cent of three-shift capacity.)

Profit was also computed on a similar loom basis at $60 a loom. This

---

[7] As a measure of output, a "loom" meant the number of blankets that could be produced on one loom running for 40 hours.

$60 rate was set so as to return to the blanket division $162,000 profit for the year at three-shift operations. This was considered a "reasonable return" on investment and management. Thus the cost and pricing sheet submitted by the cost department, Exhibit 2, furnished the prices at which the various types of blankets would have to be sold in order to realize the budgeted total profit.

The Units per Loom column in Exhibit 2 showed the number of blankets that could be produced on one loom running for 40 hours.

The vice president in charge of government contracts questioned the selling price that the cost department had calculated for Navy blankets. He pointed out that at this price, profit on Navy blankets would be 13.5 per cent of cost, whereas the profit on Army blankets would amount to only 12.3 per cent of cost. Furthermore, the profit margin on Navy blankets was higher, both in absolute terms and as a percentage of cost, than the profit on any of the domestic blankets. The Army contract had already been negotiated at $7.83 per blanket, and the vice president knew that the Navy would be most reluctant to pay a price that was out of line with the price the Army paid. The company gave the government negotiators full access to all its cost information.

The vice president realized that the difference in profit margins arose because of the manner in which selling and administrative cost and profit were allocated. He asked the controller either to provide an adequate justification of the price computed in Exhibit 2 or to recalculate the price. The controller replied with a memorandum, which included the following:

The problem of overhead (used hereafter to include selling, administrative, advertising, and interest charges) and profit distribution is probably the most important source of possible error. While the loom basis of allocation of these items is arbitrary in certain respects and may therefore be misleading, it is certainly not without logical foundation.

The fair basis of allocating profit and overhead apparently depends upon the market conditions existing at the time. If the division can produce more than can be sold, profit and overhead may well be distributed on a per-blanket basis; that is, we could add a certain per cent to each type of blanket for overhead and profit, as you suggested. On the other hand, if the mill is operating at capacity in the sense that total capacity can be sold, the distribution on some measure of capacity, such as loom hours, will provide the fair answer, for such a method takes into account the time required to produce each blanket.

In allocating overhead and profit on a loom basis we have assumed that total blanket division capacity would be completely sold out for the coming fiscal year. For this reason I feel that the blanket prices previously submitted to you are justified.

Exhibit 2

COMPUTATIONS OF COSTS AND SELLING PRICES FOR 1941–42

Style	Size (Inches)	Weight (Pounds)	Raw Material ($)	Labor ($)	Expense ($)	Processing Materials ($)	Total Mfg. Cost ($)	Units per Loom	Selling Admin. Interest, Adv. Per Loom ($)	Per Blanket ($)	Total Cost Sold ($)	Profit per Loom ($)	Profit per Blanket ($)	Net Selling Price ($)	Invoice Selling Price ($)	Retail Price 40% ($)
Ashmont	72 × 90	3.75	4.12	0.93	0.66	0.58	6.29	64	24.00	0.38	6.67	60.00	0.94	7.61	7.76	12.94
Velona	72 × 90	4.00	4.39	0.94	0.66	0.58	6.57	60	24.00	0.40	6.97	60.00	1.00	7.97	8.13	13.55
Fairfax	72 × 90	5.00	5.43	1.03	0.74	0.59	7.79	56	24.00	0.43	8.22	60.00	1.07	9.29	9.48	15.80
Army	66 × 84	3.75	4.83	0.99	0.63	0.18	6.63	70	24.00	0.34	6.97	60.00	0.86	7.83		
Navy	66 × 90	4.25	5.85	1.08	0.64	0.19	7.76	54	24.00	0.44	8.20	60.00	1.11	9.31		

Questions

1. Assume that Martall was considering the possibility of making Blanket X, on which the following information was available. (Items correspond to column headings in Exhibit 2.)

Size............72 × 90 inches		Expense..................$0.59	
Weight.........3.75 lbs.		Processing materials......$0.57	
Raw material....$4.38		Total manufacturing cost..$6.37	
Labor.........$0.83		Units per loom..........84	

Complete the columns in Exhibit 2 for Blanket X, including the retail price necessary to give the desired markup.

2. At what price should Navy blankets be sold?

3. How should the vice president explain this price in his contract negotiations?

CASE 18–8. LACKLIN AIRCRAFT COMPANY

On several occasions since late 1950 the Lacklin Aircraft Company had renewed contracts with the government for the manufacture of BF 2C bombers. In March 1953, Mr. Fred Hill, one of the buyers for the Lacklin Aircraft Company, was trying to decide upon a fair price to offer the Heyler Company, a subcontractor, for the manufacture of guide strips for the bomb-bay doors, one of the many parts for the BF 2C bomber.

The guide strips, made of a special alloy steel, required difficult machining operations, first to fit the guide strips to the contour of the plane's fuselage, second to provide a groove along which rollers traveled, and third to cut down the weight of the guide strips by boring holes. Unusual accuracy was demanded in order to prevent the bomb-bay doors from jamming.

The Heyler Company had been subcontracting the manufacture of the guide strips since December 1950, at which time its bid of $253 per ship set[9] for the 120 ship sets required was the lowest of the several bids considered. With each new order for the BF 2C bomber that the Lacklin company received from the government, Mr. Hill successfully negotiated new contracts for the manufacture of the guide strips with Mr. Wright, the Heyler Company salesman. During this period the Heyler Company continued to meet all quality standards and delivery schedules.

On each successive contract after the original one signed in December 1950, Mr. Hill had applied an 80 per cent learning curve[10] to the price of the previous order, excluding the cost of raw material and also exclud-

---

[9] A "ship set" is the set of guide strips required for one bomber.

[10] See Appendix, p. 608, for a description of learning curves.

ing profit. Mr. Hill assumed that the tooling cost incurred by the Heyler Company in manufacturing the guide strips was amortized over the cost of the original contract, and therefore he made no allowance for tooling cost in estimating the price of subsequent contracts. Although it appeared to Mr. Hill that Mr. Wright was not familiar with the use of learning curves in purchase contracting, Mr. Wright agreed to manufacture the guide strips at the prices quoted by Mr. Hill. As a result, the price paid per unit for the guide strips was lowered on each successive contract. The Heyler Company's production rate of guide strips was held essentially constant at eight ship sets a month. Application of the learning curve would not be valid if production was not reasonably steady.

In making his calculations of the price to offer the Heyler Company for the guide strips after the first contract had been fulfilled, Mr. Hill had to rely on his own estimates of the raw material price, the tooling cost, and the Heyler Company's profit. Mr. Hill knew from his previous experiences with the Heyler Company that this company would refuse to reveal its cost and profit figures. Because of his past experience in purchasing and the use of the learning curve, however, Mr. Hill was confident that his estimates were fairly accurate. The Lacklin Company's own man-hour records showed that an 80 per cent curve was appropriate for the production of similar guide strips for another type of bomber made in the immediate postwar period, and this led Mr. Hill to conclude that the same 80 per cent curve was applicable to the Heyler Company.

Breaking down the original bid of $253 per ship set, Mr. Hill estimated the profit was around $23, which was 10 per cent of total cost, and the raw material was about $40 per ship set. He estimated that the Heyler Company's tooling cost was in the neighborhood of $3,600 and that this had probably been amortized over the 120 ship sets ordered under the first contract.

In order to set up his 80 per cent curve to find the cumulative average price on which he could base his future price offers, Mr. Hill made the following calculations:

Original price..........................		$253 per ship set
Less: Profit at 10 per cent of cost..........$23		
Tooling cost on first order $3,600 ÷ 120 units........................	30	
Raw material cost per unit..........	40	
Items not subject to learning curve....	93	
Costs Subject to Learning Curve...........	$160	

The adjusted costs of $160 per ship set for 120 units was plotted on log-log graph paper (see Exhibit 1). Mr. Hill then took double the quantity of the original order (or 240 units) and 80 per cent of the unit price ($128) and plotted his second point on the log-log graph paper. Through these two points he drew a straight line.

When the Lacklin company signed the second contract calling for 40

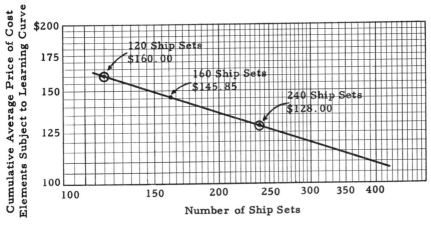

Exhibit 1

EIGHTY PER CENT LEARNING CURVE—BF 2C BOMBER GUIDE STRIPS

more BF 2C bombers, Mr. Hill looked at his graph to find the new cumulative average price of cost elements subject to the learning curve for the total quantity of the old and new orders, which amounted to 160 ship sets. The new cumulative average price, as indicated by the graph, was $145.85 per ship set (see Exhibit 1). Using this information, Mr. Hill continued his calculations:

160 ships sets at $145.85 per set average for cost elements sub-
  ject to learning curve..................................$23,336
Less: 120 units purchased at $160 per set average for cost ele-
  ments subject to learning curve......................... 19,200
    Total Price to Be Paid on New Order for Cost Elements Sub-
    ject to Learning Curve..............................$ 4,136

The new average price per ship set to be paid on the new order for the cost elements subject to the learning curve was found to be $4,136 ÷ 40 new ship sets, or $103.40. To this new price of $103.40 per ship set Mr. Hill added back in the cost items not subject to the curve which previously had been subtracted:

Cost elements subject to learning curve.....................$103.40
Plus: Raw material... 40.00
Average price per unit before profit........................$143.40
Plus: Profit at 10 per cent of cost......................... 14.34
    Total Price per Ship Set on the New Order.............$157.74

Mr. Hill believed that this figure of $157.74 per ship set was quite adequate, and he used it in his negotiations with Mr. Wright, who finally, but grudgingly, accepted this figure.

In subsequent negotiations, the prices Mr. Hill offered to the Heyler Company on successive contracts for the guide strips became lower and lower. Mr. Wright became more emphatic in his objections and warned Mr. Hill that "this learning curve business is going too far." However, each time Mr. Hill asked to see the Heyler Company's cost data to justify some other price, Mr. Wright would give the same answer: "Our cost data is none of your business!"

On February 2, 1953, about one month before the final delivery of the latest order of guide strips, which had been contracted for in November 1952, Mr. Wright complained that the Heyler Company had recently experienced an increase in raw material cost which added $2 to the cost per ship set. Furthermore, Mr. Wright stated that modifications in the design of the guide strips since the original contract had been signed had increased the raw material cost per ship set by another $3. These modifications in design, however, had not increased labor or overhead costs. Mr. Wright stated that because of these increased costs and the low $148 per ship set price paid by the Lacklin company for the currently produced guide strips, he was quite skeptical as to whether his company would take on any further contracts for guide strips, especially since at that time it could get all the business it wanted. He went on to say that his company was "sick and tired of producing guide strips at a loss for Lacklin and having to make up these losses out of contracts with other companies." While Mr. Hill believed that the raw material cost increases mentioned by Mr. Wright were correct, he did not have any way of appraising the validity of Mr. Wright's statements about the Heyler Company's losing money on this contract with the Lacklin Aircraft Company.

Two weeks after this conference between Mr. Hill and Mr. Wright, the Lacklin Aircraft Company negotiated a new contract with the government for additional BF 2C bombers, which would require 100 more ship sets of guide strips. Again Mr. Hill was confronted with the task of securing more guide strips. From December 1950 to March 1953, the Heyler Company would have produced 210 ship sets of guide strips. Over this period the price paid for the guide strips had decreased from $253 per ship set on the first order to $148 per ship set on the current order contracted for in November 1952 and scheduled for completion within the next two weeks. The total price of the 210 ship sets *for the cost elements subject to the learning curve* was $28,060.20.

This sum compares to $33,600 which would have been paid on 210 ship sets for these same cost elements if the learning curve had not been applied. A further saving to the Lacklin Company was realized because the profit which the Heyler Company received per unit was a fixed percentage of cost. Thus with the lower calculated cost per ship set based on the learning curve, the profit to the Heyler Company was cut substantially.

Despite these savings that had resulted from dealing with the Heyler Company, Mr. Hill realized that it was important to continue dealing with this particular company for the additional 100 ship sets of guide strips. Mr. Hill recalled that at 1950 price levels the Heyler Company's first bid of $253 per ship set was the lowest of the several bids submitted; the next lowest bid at that time was $272. If the Heyler Company refused to accept any more orders, dealing with a new subcontractor would probably result in a substantial increase in price. Mr. Hill estimated that the lowest price for which he could currently purchase guide strips from another subcontractor would be in the neighborhood of $280 per ship set (including the amortized cost, over 100 ship sets, of new tooling). Furthermore, Mr. Hill considered the Heyler Company an excellent source of supply because it produced a satisfactory product and always met its delivery schedule.

On the other hand, Mr. Hill knew that the validity of the learning curve had been widely accepted in the aircraft industry and that it was especially applicable to the manufacture of parts such as guide strips, for which direct labor was the major cost component. Furthermore, it was his job as a purchasing agent for the Lacklin Aircraft Company to get as low a price as possible commensurate with a satisfactory product.

Mr. Hill had an appointment with Mr. Wright the next day, at which time they would open negotiations for the 100 additional ship sets of guide strips. Mr. Hill knew that Mr. Wright would suggest a substantial upward revision in the price.

Questions

1. If he used the 80 per cent learning curve, what price would Mr. Hill calculate for the new order of 100 ship sets?

2. What is the highest price that the Lacklin Company should pay to the Heyler Company for the guide strips?

3. What price *should* Mr. Hill use as a basis for his negotiations?

4. What are the implications of the use of learning curves in purchase contracting to both the prime contractor and the subcontractor?

5. In what situations would the use of the learning curve in purchase contracting not be appropriate?

APPENDIX

The Use of Learning Curves in Purchase Contracting

The basis for negotiating a lower price on each successive contract for a specific product rests on the assumption that certain costs decrease as the workers and their supervisors become more familiar with the work; as the flow of work, tooling, and methods improve; as less scrap and rework result; as fewer skilled workers need to be used; and so on. The decreasing costs are a function of the learning process, which results in fewer and fewer man-hours being necessary to produce a unit of product as more units of the same product are completed. It should be noted, however, that not all costs decrease; for instance, material costs are not usually subject to the learning process, although they may decrease to the extent to which waste is eliminated. Packaging and trucking costs are other examples of costs that usually are not subject to the learning process.

Studies have been made of this decreasing cost concept, and the results have shown that in certain industries over a period of time an average rate of decrease for costs which vary with the learning function is fairly typical of the experience of the individual companies making up that industry. This average industry rate, however, may not be an accurate rate for specific products.

In the aircraft industry, which is continually involved in new and redesigned planes and parts, the use of the principle of decreasing costs based on the learning function is widely regarded as being appropriate in many situations. The job of estimating future costs and prices on new and modified aircraft components is difficult because of the scarcity of usable historical cost data, and for this reason the aircraft industry has done some research in the use of learning curves for estimating costs in setting purchase contract prices. Besides their use in negotiating purchase contracts, learning curves have been used for other planning purposes, such as scheduling and developing labor loads, area and equipment requirements, shop efficiency measures, budgets, and sometimes standards.

The research done in the aircraft industry indicates that there is probably an average learning curve rate that can be applied to the increase in production efficiency, insofar as costs subject to the learning function are concerned. This rate approximates an "80 per cent curve," which means that when quantities of production are doubled on an item, cumulative average man-hours per unit should be reduced 20 per cent. As an illustration of this concept, assume that a company has purchased 250 machined castings at $50 each from XYZ Company. To simplify this case, assume further that material costs are insignificant and that the elements of labor, overhead, selling, and administration expense and profit, which make up the $50 per unit price, all vary in relation to the man-hours required to produce one machined casting; that is to say, all the elements of the $50 price are subject to the learning curve. Before production of the 250 castings has been completed, another 400 castings of the same type are ordered from the XYZ Company. What price should be paid for the additional 400 castings?

Assuming that an "80 per cent curve" can be applied in this situation, the $50 price is plotted at the 250-unit quantity level on log-log graph paper (see Exhibit 2). The second point on the graph is established at double the quantity and 80 per cent of the price of the first order. A straight line is drawn through and extended past these two points. (Log-log graph paper shows the 80 per cent curve as a straight line, whereas arithmetic graph paper shows the 80 per cent curve as a complex curve that is difficult to plot.) The point on this line that locates the sum of the quantities of the old and new orders (250 plus 400 units) indicates also the cumulative average unit price for the total units, or $36.76, as indicated on Exhibit 2. Multiplying the total quantity of 650 units by the new cumulative average price of $36.76 gives the *total price* for *both* orders, $23,894. Because the first order of 250 castings cost in total $12,500, this is subtracted

Exhibit 2

EIGHTY PER CENT LEARNING CURVE—MACHINED CASTINGS

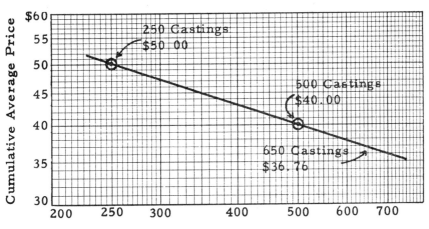

Number of Castings

from the total price of both orders. The remaining $11,394.00 is divided by the number of units to be purchased in the new order (400) to give the unit price of $28.48 to be paid for the new castings.

While it may be demonstrated in many situations that the learning curve applies to direct labor costs,[11] it usually cannot be applied to raw material costs. Overhead costs present another problem. Many overhead costs are allocated to specific jobs on a per-labor-hour basis, and the allocated cost therefore varies with direct labor hours. On the other hand, certain overhead costs, such as tooling,[12] crating, and shipping costs, do not vary with direct labor hours and therefore are not subject to the learning curve. The per-unit costs of these latter items should be subtracted from the total per-unit cost of the product before any calculations are made with the other costs that *are* subject to the learning process.

Selling and administrative costs present similar problems. Many selling and administrative costs vary roughly in relation to direct labor hours or are allocated to products on the basis of direct labor hours. All selling and administrative costs are often assumed to be subject to the learning curve.

---

[11] Direct labor costs usually vary proportionately with direct labor hours except where piece rates or other incentive plans are in effect.

[12] It is common in the aircraft industry to purchase tooling separately.

In the case of both overhead costs and selling and administrative costs, the costs actually incurred may not vary with direct labor hours even though they are allocated on this basis. Nevertheless, if the allocated costs are used as a basis for pricing, as is often the case, it can be argued that it is proper to treat them as variable for the purpose of pricing decisions.

The procedure for handling the items of cost *not* subject to the learning curve, such as raw material, tooling (if any), and shipping costs, is to deduct these items from the total contract price prior to making any computations using the learning curve. The remaining costs, then, can be subjected to the calculations using the learning curve (as explained above). When the new figure for the cost elements subject to the learning curve is calculated, the fixed unit cost elements, previously subtracted, are added back in to arrive at a total cost figure.

With regard to the profit element, the usual procedure is to deduct the amount from the total selling price, along with the raw material and other fixed unit costs, before making the computations based on the learning curve. After the new figure for the cost elements subject to the learning curve is derived, the profit per unit is added back to make up the rest of the total unit price along with the other fixed unit costs (e.g., raw material, etc.). The profit figure added back in is not necessarily the same amount as the profit figure previously subtracted. It would be reduced in amount if the customary practice was followed of calculating profit as a percentage of cost.

Chapter 19 | PLANNING CAPITAL ACQUISITIONS

OF THE SEVERAL types of alternative choice problems, those involving the investment of funds in new assets are both the most important and the most difficult. These problems are important not only because they involve large sums of money but also because the decision may influence the whole conduct of the business for years to come. A decision to build a new plant, for example, tends to commit a company to a certain locality and to a certain character and scale of manufacturing activity for the life of the plant. The special difficulty of capital investment problems arises because of the necessity of making allowances for differences in the timing of the various cost and revenue elements.

Any investment involves the commitment of funds *now* with the expectation of earning a satisfactory return on these funds over a period of time in the future. The word "investment" immediately calls to mind the commitment of funds to stocks or bonds. The commitment of funds to land, building, equipment, inventory, and other types of assets has the same essential characteristic as these financial investments: namely, that the commitment is made with the expectation of earning a satisfactory return on the investment in the future.

Illustrative of these *capital budgeting* problems are the following:

1. *Expansion.* Shall we build or acquire a new plant? (The expected earnings on this investment are the profits from the products produced in the new plant.)
2. *Replacement.* Shall we replace existing equipment with more efficient equipment? (The expected earnings on this investment are the savings resulting from lower operating costs, or the profit from additional volume produced by the new equipment, or both.)
3. *Choice of Equipment.* Which of several proposed items of equipment shall we purchase for a given purpose? (The choice often turns on which item is expected to give the largest return on the investment made in it.)
4. *Buy or Lease.* Having decided to acquire a building or a piece of equipment, should we lease it or should we buy it? (The choice turns on whether or not the investment required to purchase the asset will earn an adequate return as compared with leasing.)

There are two general types of investment problems. First, there is the *screening* problem: an investment is proposed, and the problem is to decide whether it will provide a satisfactory return or not; that is, the problem is to screen out the satisfactory proposals from all the investment proposals that are made. Second, there is the *preference* problem, also referred to as the *ranking* problem: which of several proposals is the best? which the next best? and so on. The screening problem is conceptually simpler, and the first part of this chapter will be restricted to a discussion of this problem. The preference problem will be discussed in the last section of the chapter.

The comments in Chapter 18 about the types of costs and revenues that should be used in alternative choice problems are equally relevant in capital budgeting problems. As also noted in that chapter, the techniques are applicable only to those problems or parts of problems for which quantitative information is available and important. In nearly every problem, there are important unmeasured considerations that must be weighed in order to make a final decision, and in many problems these considerations are so important that calculations of the type described here are not even made. Decisions regarding investments in employee recreational facilities, or in research equipment, or in office furniture ordinarily are not based on an estimate of the return on investment.

GENERAL FRAMEWORK OF ANALYSIS

Essentials of a Business Investment

If the company purchases a machine, the funds so invested are tied up, or frozen, until they can be gradually liquidated through the profitable operation of the machine. Any investment involves a risk, and even if the money to finance the purchase is borrowed, it is the owner of the machine who incurs the risk. A businessman will ordinarily not risk funds in an investment unless he believes that he will obtain a satisfactory return on these funds.

Since the purchase of proposed equipment will presumably result in additional earnings, the issue to be resolved in an investment problem is *whether the proposed investment is justified by the earnings it will create over its life.* The techniques to be described are methods for comparing these essentially unlike elements: (1) a stream of future earnings, and (2) a single lump-sum investment made now.

Concept of "Return on Investment"

When a bank lends $1,000 and receives interest payments of $80 at the end of each year for five years with the loan being repaid at the end of the fifth year, the bank is said to earn a return of 8 per cent on its investment of $1,000. Note that the percentage is always expressed on an annual basis and that it is found by dividing the annual return by the amount of the investment outstanding during the year.

If a bank lends $1,000 and is repaid $250 at the end of each year for five years, the problem of finding the return becomes more complicated; for in this situation, only part of the $250 represents interest, and the remainder is a repayment of the principal. By a method to be described below, it turns out that this loan also has a return of 8 per cent, in the same sense as the loan described in the preceding paragraph: namely, the $250 annual payments will repay the loan itself and in addition will provide a return of 8 per cent of the *amount still outstanding each year*. This is demonstrated in Illustration 19–1. Of the $250 earned in the first

Illustration 19–1

DEMONSTRATION OF MEANING OF RETURN ON INVESTMENT

Year	Total Earnings (a)	Return at 8% of Investment Outstanding (b)	Balance, to Apply against Investment c = (a − b)	Investment Outstanding End of Year (d)
0...........	$...	$..	$...	$1,000
1...........	250	80	170	830
2...........	250	66	184	646
3...........	250	52	198	448
4...........	250	36	214	234
5...........	250	19	231	3

year, $80, or 8 per cent of the $1,000 then outstanding, is the return, and the remainder, or $170, goes to reduce the investment, making it $830. In the second year, $66 is a return of 8 per cent on the $830 then outstanding, and the remainder, $184, reduces the investment to $646. And so on. (The residual of $3 at the end of the fifth year arises because the true return is not exactly 8.000 per cent.)

Thus, when an investment involves annual interest payments with the full amount of the investment being repaid at its termination date, the computation of the return is simple and direct; but when the annual payments combine both principal and interest, the computation is more complicated. Some business problems are of the simple type. If a business buys land for $1,000, for example, and rents it for $80 a year for five years, selling the land for $1,000 at the end of five years, its return is 8 per cent. Many business investment decisions, on the other hand, relate to depreciable assets, whose characteristic is that they have no, or very little, resale value at the end of their useful life. The earnings on these investments must therefore be large enough for the investor both to recoup the investment itself during its life and to earn a satisfactory return on the amount not yet recouped, just as in the situation shown in Illustration 19–1.

The Concept of Present Value

A businessman will not invest $1 today unless he expects to get back somewhat more than $1 later on; that is, he expects to earn a return on the investments he makes. By the same token, if a certain proposal will produce earnings of $1 at the end of one year, the businessman will be willing to invest only somewhat less than $1 in it today. The expectation of receiving $1 at the end of the year therefore has a *present value,* a value today, of somewhat less than $1. How much less depends on how much the businessman expects to earn on money he invests. If he expects to earn 10 per cent, for example, the expectation of receiving $1 a year from now has a present value of $0.909, since if he invested $0.909 today for one year at a rate of 10 per cent, he would earn $0.091 on the investment and have $1 at the end of the year.

The present value for a payment of $1 to be received n years hence at any rate of return (i) can be found with the formula:

$$\frac{1}{(1 + i)^n}$$

The formula itself need not be used, however, since present values computed from it are given in Table A (p. 742). It is important that the meaning of the numbers in this table be clearly understood. Note, for example, that the first figure in the 10 per cent column is the same 0.909 used in the preceding paragraph. It means that, at a rate of 10 per cent, the expectation of receiving $1 a year from today has a present value of $0.909.

The next figure in the 10 per cent column, $0.826, means that the expectation of receiving $1 *two* years from today has a present value of $0.826. This can be checked, as follows: for each $0.826 invested today, at 10 per cent, $0.0826 would be earned during the first year, and the total amount would therefore increase to $0.9086; during the second year, 10 per cent of the $0.9086, or $0.09086, would be earned, so that by the end of the second year, the total would have increased to $0.99946, or practically $1.[1] Tracing through any other figure in Table

---

[1] The difference of $0.00054 arises from rounding.

A will produce the same result; namely, the final figure will be practically $1.

Table A shows the present value of $1. The present value of any amount other than $1 can be found simply by multiplying that amount by the appropriate figure in the table. Thus the present value of $1,000 to be received two years hence at a rate of 10 per cent is $826.

Present Value Method

The foregoing concepts can be used to construct methods for making decisions about investment proposals, always keeping in mind the fact that these methods are necessarily limited to those aspects of the proposal that can be reduced to money amounts. One such method is called the *present value* method. The rule here is: *Neglecting nonmonetary considerations, an investment proposal should be accepted if the present value of its earnings equals or exceeds the amount of the investment required.* Earnings are *cash flow* earnings; that is, they are the cash or cash equivalent amounts which are relevant in alternative choice problems, as explained in Chapter 18. The cash flow earnings are *discounted* at a specified rate of return, using the numbers in Table A. This rate will henceforth be referred to as the *required earnings rate.*

EXAMPLE 1. Should a proposed investment of $1,000 with expected earnings of $1,080 one year hence be accepted if the required earnings rate is 8 per cent? In Table A, we find that the present value of $1 to be received one year hence at 8 per cent is $0.926. The present value of $1,080 is therefore $1,080 × $0.926 = $1,000. The proposal should be accepted.

EXAMPLE 2. Should a proposed investment of $1,000 with expected earnings of $250 a year for five years be accepted if the required earnings rate is 8 per cent? The present value of the earnings is found as follows:[2]

Year	Earnings (a)	Present Value of $1 at 8% (b)	Total Present Value (a × b)
First..........................	$250	0.926	$230
Second........................	250	0.857	214
Third.........................	250	0.794	198
Fourth........................	250	0.735	184
Fifth..........................	250	0.681	172
		Total Present Value..$998	

---

[2] Calculations in all examples are rounded to emphasize the fact that the numbers are only estimates. In real problems, results that came so close as those in these two examples would certainly be decided on other grounds than results of the arithmetic calculations, because of the inevitable margin of error in the estimates.

The present value being slightly less than $1,000, the proposal is not acceptable, neglecting nonquantitative considerations.

Present Value of a Stream of Payments

Table B (p. 743) has, for many problems, a more convenient set of present value figures than those in Table A. It shows the present value of $1 to be received annually for *each* of the next *n* years. Each figure on Table B was obtained simply by cumulating, that is, adding together, the figures for the corresponding year and all preceding years in the same column on Table A. Table B can be used directly to find the present value of a stream of equal payments received annually for any given number of years, and therefore reduces considerably the arithmetic required in problems of the type worked in Example 2 above.

> EXAMPLE: Same question as in Example 2, page 615. The present value of $1 *a year* for five years at 8 per cent, as shown in Table B, is $3.993; therefore the present value of $250 a year for five years is 250 × $3.993 = $998, which is the same result as in Example 2.

Although the values in Table B are cumulative from year 1, they can be used to find the present value of a stream of earnings between any two points in time. The procedure is to subtract the value for the year *preceding* the first year of the flow from the value for the last year of the flow.

> EXAMPLE: What is the present value of $250 a year to be received for five years starting in year 6, if the discount rate is 8 per cent? Solution:
>
> Present value of $1 a year for 10 years at 8 per cent.............. $6.710
> Less: Present value of $1 a year for 5 years at 8 per cent.......... −3.993
> Difference (equals present value; years 6–10)................... $2.717
> 250 × $2.717 = $679.

Other Present Value Tables

Tables A and B are calculated on the assumption that earnings are received once a year and on the last day of the year. For many problems this is not a realistic assumption, for earnings in the form of increased revenues and lower costs are likely to be incurred throughout the year. Nevertheless, annual tables are customarily used in business investment problems, on the grounds that they are easier to understand than tables constructed on other assumptions, and are good enough considering the inevitable margin of error in the basic estimates.

Annual tables *understate* the present value of earnings if earnings are in fact received throughout the year rather than entirely on the last day of the year. The amount of the understatement can be seen in Illustration 19–2. Other tables are available showing the present values of earnings

Illustration 19-2

EFFECT OF RAPID RECEIPTS

Approximate Ratio of Present Value of Faster Receipts to Present Value of Annual Receipts at Various Discount Rates

Frequency of Receipt	Discount Rates			
	6%	10%	15%	25%
Semiannually..................	1.01	1.03	1.04	1.06
Monthly.....................	1.03	1.05	1.07	1.11
Continuously.................	1.03	1.05	1.08	1.12

flows that occur quarterly, monthly, or even continuously, but they are not commonly used. Close results often can be obtained from a table that is based on the assumption that the amount is received at the *middle* of the year rather than at the *end* of the year.

The discussion here will be restricted to the annual tables: *Table A* for a single amount to be received *n* years from now, and *Table B* for a stream of uniform amounts to be received for each of the next *n* years. The two are often used in combination, as illustrated in the next example, which also relates the mechanism discussed here to the basic meaning of return on investment discussed at the beginning of this section.

EXAMPLE: Should a proposed investment of $1,000 with annual earnings of $80 a year for the next five years with the $1,000 to be repaid at the end of five years be accepted if the required earnings rate is 8 per cent? Solution: As shown by the following calculation, the earnings have a present value of $1,000, so the proposal is acceptable:

Year	Payment	8% Discount Factor	Present Value
1-5.............	$80/year	3.993 (Table B)	$ 319
End of 5........	1,000	0.681 (Table A)	681
		Total Present Value....$1,000	

Unadjusted Return on Investment

Since the depreciation mechanism provides, in a sense, for the recovery of the cost of a depreciable asset, one might suppose that the return on an investment could be found by relating the investment to its income after depreciation, but such is *not* the case. In our illustrative situation, if a depreciation allowance of $200 is subtracted from the gross annual earnings of $250, and the net amount of $50 is divided by the investment of $1,000, the indicated return is 5 per cent. Note that this differs substantially from the 8 per cent that we now know to be the true return. The return figured in this manner is called the "accounting" return or the "unadjusted" return. It is unadjusted in the sense that it makes no allowance for the differences in present values of the earnings of the various years; that is, it treats each year's earnings as if they were as valuable as those of every other year, whereas actually the prospect of earning $250 next year is more attractive than the prospect of earning $250 two years from now, and *that* $250 is more attractive than the prospect of earning $250 three years from now, and so on.

The unadjusted return method, computed as above, will always understate the true return. The shorter the time period involved, the more serious is the understatement. For investments involving very long time periods, the understatement is insignificant. An unadjusted return can be computed in other ways, such as using one half the investment as the divisor. All these variations have the same conceptual error, although some of them yield a close approximation to the true return under certain conditions.

ESTIMATING THE VARIABLES

In order to make the calculation described above, four types of estimates must be made: (1) the required earnings rate; (2) the amount of earnings in each year; (3) the economic life, which is the number of years for which earnings are anticipated; and (4) the amount of investment. Each is discussed below. The examples will be limited to the *equipment replacement* problem, although the same considerations apply to problems of all types. Essentially, the alternatives in this problem are (1) to continue to use the present equipment or (2) to replace it, with the expectation that savings in operating costs or other factors will be sufficient to recoup the investment and earn a satisfactory return on the funds that have been frozen in the new equipment.

Required Earnings Rate

The selection of the appropriate earnings rate is a crucial matter of top-management judgment. The problem can usefully be subdivided into two parts: (1) selection of the average rate required on all investments and (2) consideration of factors that make the proposed investment different from the average.

Average Earnings Rate. In many companies, the choice of an average required earnings rate is largely subjective. Management decides that a sufficient amount of investment opportunities can be found that will earn 10 per cent, 15 per cent, or some other number, and this percentage becomes the prescribed minimum below which the company refuses to make investments of average risk.

Formula Approaches. Attempts to devise formulas that will yield the appropriate required earnings rate for a given company have so far not produced very satisfactory results. Perhaps the best approach is to construct a *pro forma* balance sheet and income statement for a "satisfactory" situation. The balance sheet will show the real values of the assets (as distinguished from their book value), perhaps using half the current cost of fixed assets as an indication of their average value. It will show a proportion of fixed debt to equity capital that management considers satisfactory. The income statement will show the profit that management considers as being an acceptable level of earnings for such assets. The required earnings rate is then the sum of net profit after taxes plus interest on long-term debt, divided by the sum of long-term debt plus owners' equity. Interest is calculated at one half the actual interest cost so as to allow for the effect of income taxes. The procedure is shown in Illustration 19–3.

Illustration 19–3

ESTIMATING THE REQUIRED EARNINGS RATE

A.   "Satisfactory" Balance Sheet

(000 Omitted)

ASSETS			EQUITIES	
Working capital.......		$ 2,000	Long-term debt (4%)..........$ 4,000	
Fixed assets, gross......$16,000			Owners' equity................ 6,000	
Less: Average				
depreciation.....	8,000	8,000		
Total Assets.......		$10,000	Total Equities.............$10,000	

B.   "Satisfactory" Income Statement

Revenue........	.$11,000
Less all costs except interest and taxes............	9,000
Profit before interest aud taxes........	.$ 2,000
Interest........	160
Profit before taxes........	.$ 1,840
Income taxes (50%)........	920
Profit after Taxes........	.$ 920

C.   Calculation of Required Earnings Rate

$$\frac{\text{Interest} + \text{Profit}}{\text{Debt} + \text{Equity}} = \frac{80 + 920}{4,000 + 6,000} = 10 \text{ per cent}$$

Cost of Capital. Some people argue that the required earnings rate should be equal to the company's *cost of capital,* which is the after-tax cost of debt capital plus the cost of equity capital, weighted by the relative amount of each in the normal capital structure (the after-tax cost of debt is used because interest on debt is a tax deductible expense); thus:

Type	Cost	Weight	Weighted Total
Debt (bonds).....	2%	40%	0.008%
Equity (stock)...	15	60	0.09
Total........		100%	0.098%

The indicated cost of capital is 9.8 per cent or, rounded, 10 per cent. The trouble with the cost-of-capital approach is that the cost of equity capital is extraordinarily difficult to estimate.[3] One starts with the market price of the stock, and then tries to estimate what fraction of the market price is attributable to the market's judgment of profits on the present equity and what fraction is attributable to the market's judgment of future profits that will be earned on retained earnings. Few people have much confidence in the results of such estimates. The discussion here has been cursory for this reason.

Lacking a formula, companies essentially arrive at a satisfactory rate by trial and error. If a given rate results in the rejection of projects that management intuitively feels are desirable, there is an indication that the rate is too high, and it is lowered. An average required rate of 10 per cent after taxes is found in many industrial companies, with lower rates in public utilities, say 8 per cent, and in government agencies, say 6 per cent, and higher rates in companies in industries where profit opportunities are unusually good or risks are unusually high.

Sometimes, income taxes are ignored, in which case the rate is a pretax rate, which is higher than the after-tax rate in the same company.

Interest Rate. Whatever the rate selected, it is almost certain to be considerably higher than an *interest* rate, that is, the rate for borrowing money (say, 4 per cent to 7 per cent before taxes). The required earnings rate includes interest, but it also includes an additional allowance for risks that are borne by the business rather than by the lender of money, and for which the business expects compensation.

---

[3] See Hunt, Williams, and Donaldson, *Basic Business Finance: Text and Cases* (rev. ed.; Homewood, Ill.: Richard D. Irwin, Inc., 1961), chap. xxi, "The Cost of Capital." The economists' profit maximization model requires that a cost-of-capital figure be esti mated. This is the second reason why this book is not based on the profit maximization assumption. The other reason was discussed on page 576.

Adjustment of the Average Rate. The required earnings rate for the whole business reflects the average risk of investments in various classes of assets. This average results from a composite of many different types of risks, ranging from investments in government bonds, where the risk is very low, to investments that may be almost pure gambles, such as those in untried new products. The earnings rate required on the particular investment under consideration should reflect, if feasible, the relative risk of this investment compared to the average.

It may also reflect the uncertainty that the estimated savings will actually be realized. The figures on costs, savings, and economic life are *estimates* of what will happen in the future. Often, a higher than average earnings rate is used when these uncertainties are believed to be great. (Uncertainty can also be allowed for by arbitrarily shortening the estimate of economic life. Care should be taken not to *overallow* for uncertainty by using both a short life and a high required earnings rate.)

Finally, the required earnings rate is sometimes adjusted to compensate for the "administrative bother" that may be entailed in going into the venture—the unmeasured, but sometimes significant, cost of the additional management headaches and worry that may be a consequence of making the proposed investment.

Financial Problems. In some problems, the issue is not whether to acquire an asset, but rather the manner in which to finance it; or a certain method of financing may be an integral part of the proposal. In these situations, the relevant required earnings rate must be tailored to the facts of the problem. If a company has already decided to acquire a building, and the issue is whether to buy it with borrowed funds or to acquire it through a long-term noncancelable lease, the required earnings rate is close to the cost of borrowing funds rather than the overall earnings rate for the whole company.

Unless the method of financing is closely related to the proposition itself, it is usually better to consider finance as a separate problem. Ordinarily, the question of whether the proposed investment is or is not desirable is an operating matter, decided by operating people; the question of how to finance it is a financial matter, decided by financial people.

Earnings

The earnings from an investment are essentially the additional cash that the company estimates it will earn from the investment as compared with what its earnings would be if it did not make the investment. The *differential* concept emphasized in Chapter 18 is therefore equally applicable here. Consider, for example, a proposal to replace an existing machine with an even better machine. We note first that the existing machine must still be usable, for if it can no longer perform its function, there is no problem; it *must* be replaced. The existing machine has a certain set of labor, material, power, repair, maintenance, and other costs associated with its future operation. If the proposed machine is under consideration as a means of reducing costs, there will be a different, lower set of costs associated with its use. The difference between these two sets of cost is the *earnings* anticipated if the new machine is acquired. These earnings are figured on an annual basis.

If the proposed machine increases the company's productive capacity, and if the increased output can be sold, the incremental profit on this increased volume is earnings arising from acquisition of the proposed machine. Incremental profit is the difference between added sales revenue and incremental costs, which usually include direct material, direct labor, direct selling costs, and any other costs that will not be incurred if the increased volume is not manufactured and sold.

Depreciation on the proposed equipment is not a relevant cost item, since the present value tables automatically provide for recouping the investment itself, and to include a depreciation charge would be counting this recoupment twice. Depreciation on the existing equipment is likewise not relevant because, as explained in Chapter 18, this represents a sunk cost that is unaffected by the present decision.

In general, the earnings are cash flows. As explained in Chapter 18, changes in prorated or allocated costs are not relevant unless they actually represent differential costs.

Income Taxes. Presumably, the purpose of making an investment is to increase the owners' equity. Owners' equity will not be increased by the full amount of the cost savings or additional revenue resulting from the investment, however, since a substantial fraction of these savings or revenues usually will be paid to the government in the form of additional income taxes. Owners' equity will be increased only by the amount remaining after these additional taxes have been deducted.

If "earnings," as defined above, were the same as "additional profit subject to income tax," then profit after taxes could be found simply by multiplying the profit by the complement of the estimated future tax rate (i.e., 1 minus the tax rate). Thus, if 50 per cent is accepted as a reasonable estimate of future applicable tax rates, the profit after taxes would be one half the profit before taxes.

In estimating earnings, however, depreciation was intentionally omitted from the calculations. Since depreciation is an allowable expense for tax purposes, "additional profit subject to income tax" will therefore not correspond to earnings in any problem where depreciation is a significant factor. In effect, the depreciation on the equipment being purchased provides a "tax shield"; it shields earnings from the full impact of income taxes.

> EXAMPLE: A proposed machine costing $1,000 is expected to result in cash savings of $320 a year for five years. Assuming a required earnings rate of 10 per cent, is it a good investment?
>
> The additional income subject to taxes will be not the whole $320, but rather $320 less the depreciation charge. If straight-line depreciation is used, this will be $200 a year ($1,000 ÷ 5 years). The additional income subject to tax will be $320 − $200 = $120. At a tax rate of 50 per cent, income taxes will be increased half of this, or $60, so the net savings will be $320 − $60 = $260. Savings of $260 a year for 5 years at 10 per cent has a present value of 260 × $3.791 = $986. Since this is less than the $1,000 investment, the machine is not a good investment.

Accelerated Depreciation. In the preceding example we assumed that depreciation would be calculated on a straight-line basis for tax purposes. Many companies use one of the accelerated bases of depreciation, however (see p. 158 for description). Assuming the sum-of-years' digit basis is used, the tax deductible depreciation each year and the earnings after taxes would be as follows:

Year	Cash Earnings (a)	Depreciation (b)	Earnings Subject to Tax (c = a − b)	Tax at 50% (d)	Cash Earnings after Tax (e = a − d)
1............	$ 320	$ 333	$−13	$−6	$ 326
2............	320	267	53	26	294
3............	320	200	120	60	260
4............	320	133	187	94	226
5............	320	67	253	126	194
Total......	$1,600	$1,000	$600	$300	$1,300

We could then find the present value of the earnings by discounting each of the five after-tax cash earnings amounts in the last column, as follows:

Year	Earnings after Tax	Discount at 10%	Present Value
1.........................	$ 326	0.909	$ 297
2.........................	294	0.826	243
3.........................	260	0.751	195
4.........................	226	0.683	154
5.........................	194	0.621	121
Total.................	$1,300		$1,010

Table C. There is a way of greatly simplifying the above calculation. It involves the use of Table C, page 744, which shows the present value of a stream of depreciation charges figured by the sum-of-years' digit method. (Double declining balance, which is the other commonly used accelerated method, gives practically the same results.) Using this table, the total present value of the depreciation tax shield can be figured easily in a single computation, and this amount can then be added to the present value of the after-tax cash earnings to give the total present value of the earnings.

EXAMPLE: Same problem as above, but using Table C.

The cash earnings after taxes, but *neglecting depreciation*, are 50 per cent of $320, or $160 a year. The present value of $1 a year for five years at 10 per cent is $3.791; therefore the present value of the cash earnings is 160 × $3.791　　= $　607
The present value of depreciation of $1 of investment spread over five years is, from Table C, $0.806. For an investment of $1,000, it is therefore 1,000 × $0.806 = $806. The present value of the depreciation tax shield is $806 times the tax rate, 50 per cent,　　　　　　　=　　403
The total present value therefore equals　　　　　$1,010

Note that the result in the above example is exactly the same as in the year-by-year calculation. Note also how the use of accelerated depreciation increases the attractiveness of the investment; its present value rises from $948 under straight-line depreciation to $1,010, and the proposal now meets the criterion that the present value of its earnings exceeds the investment. This result occurs because a larger fraction of the depreciation tax shield occurs in the early years; it is the reason why accelerated depreciation has become so popular for tax purposes.

If the proposed machine is to replace a machine that has not been fully depreciated for tax purposes, then the tax shield is only the differential depreciation, that is, the difference between depreciation on the present and that on the new machine, because if the new machine is purchased, the old machine will presumably be disposed of so its depreciation will no longer provide a tax shield. In this case, the present value of the tax shield of the remaining depreciation on the old machine must be calculated (usually year by year), and this amount must be subtracted from the present value of the depreciation tax shield on the proposed machine.

Omission of Tax Calculation. In many types of alternative choice problems, the question of income taxes may be omitted entirely, since the alternative that produces the most profit *before* taxes will also produce the most profit *after* taxes. This is the case with pricing problems and many make-or-buy problems. In problems involving depreciable assets, however, there is unlikely to be a simple relationship between savings before taxes and savings after taxes, and the above calculation is therefore necessary.

Tax Effect of Interest. Interest actually paid (as distinguished from imputed interest) is an allowable expense for income tax purposes; therefore, if interest costs will be increased as a result of the investment, it could be argued that interest provides a tax shield similar to depreciation and that its impact should be estimated by the same method as that shown for depreciation, above. Customarily, however, interest is *not* included anywhere in the calculations either of earnings or of taxes. This is because we usually seek the overall rate of return on the investment, without regard for whether the funds required for the investment are borrowed (which involves interest) or whether they come from the stockholders (which does not involve interest).

In problems where the method of financing is an important part of the proposal, the tax shield provided by interest may appropriately be considered. In these problems, the rate of return that results from the calculation is a return on that part of the investment which was financed by the stockholders' equity, not a return on the total funds committed to the investment.

For example, suppose a company is considering an investment in a parcel of real estate, and intends to finance perhaps 70 per cent of the investment by a mortgage loan on the property, then it may wish to focus attention on the return on its own funds, namely, the remaining 30 per cent. It would be appropriate to include in the calculation of such a return both the interest on the mortgage loan and the effect of this interest on taxable income.

Economic Life

The cash flow analysis is carried out for the time period corresponding to the life of the proposed project, the period over which benefits can be estimated. The end of this period is called the *horizon* for the project, the word suggesting that beyond this point earnings are not visible. When the proposed project involves the purchase of equipment, this time period corresponds to the economic life of the equipment.

There are at least three ways of defining the "life" of equipment:

1. Its physical life.
2. Its technological life.
3. Its product-market life.

The economic life, which is the relevant life for the problem we are studying, is the *shortest* of these three types of life. Economic life can rarely be estimated exactly; nevertheless, making the best possible judgment of the economic life is extremely important.

Physical Life. There is a tendency, when thinking about the life of a machine, to consider primarily its *physical life;* that is, the number of years the machine will probably be of use to the company in performing the technical job for which it was purchased. This concept of life is sometimes used in calculating depreciation for accounting purposes and for income tax purposes.[4] It is of little use in investment decisions.

Technological Life. This refers to the period of time that elapses before a new machine comes out that makes the present machine obsolete. It is this life that, for most companies, corresponds to the economic life. Improvements will almost certainly be made sometime in all machines now in existence, but the question of *which* machines will be improved and *how soon* the improved machines will be on the market is a most difficult one to answer. Unless special information is available, the answer can be little more than a guess. Yet it is a guess that must be made, for the investment in a machine will cease to earn a return when and if this machine is replaced by an even better machine.

Product-Market Life. Although the machine may be in excellent physical condition, and although there may be no better machine available, its economic life has ended, as far as the owner is concerned, as soon as the company ceases to market the product made on the machine. The "product-market" life of the machine may end because the particular operation performed by the machine is made unnecessary by a change in style or a change in process, or because the market for the product itself has vanished. A machine for making buggy whips may last physically for 100 years, and there may be no possibility of making technological improvements in it; yet such a machine cannot earn a return on its investment if the buggy whips produced on it cannot be sold.

The product-market life of a machine also ends if the company goes out of business. Most managements quite properly operate on the premise that the company will be in business for a long time to come. There are instances, however, when a businessman foresees an end to his business, or to a particular part of it, in the relatively near future. In such

---

[4] Although both accounting principles and income tax laws permit equipment to be depreciated over its "useful life," which means economic life, some accountants and internal revenue agents rely heavily on estimates of physical life.

a case, the economic life of a machine *to him* is limited to the period during which he believes his business is going to operate.

Uneven Lives. For many types of equipment, it is reasonable to assume that the present machine can be used, physically, for a period of time at least as long as the economic life of the proposed machine. In situations in which this assumption is not valid, however, earnings on a proposed machine purchased now will not in fact occur each year of the period being considered, for a new machine must be purchased anyway when the physical life of the present machine ends. Thereafter, there may be no difference in the annual cost of the two alternatives (buy now versus don't buy now), since the same machine will be involved in both of them.

If the expected physical life of the present machine is significantly shorter than the expected economic life of the proposed machine, some way must be found of making an equivalence between the time periods covered by the two alternatives. For example, if the proposed machine has an economic life of ten years but the present machine has a remaining physical life of only six years, the relevant earnings will occur for only six years. This fact raises the difficult question of treating the situation that will exist at the end of the sixth year.

Since the purchase of a new machine now eliminates the need of purchasing another one six years from now, this future purchase price will have been saved and its present value can therefore be counted as a cash inflow in the sixth year. However, the machine purchased now will presumably have to be replaced at the end of ten years, whereas if a machine is not purchased until six years from now, it will last until 16 years from now. So, if the proposal is accepted, there will be an additional cash outflow at the end of the tenth year. This intricate reasoning can be extended indefinitely through later replacement cycles. Estimates of these distant values are tenuous, and this whole procedure is based on the assumption that there will be no further changes in technology or price levels, but the roughness of the estimates is somewhat mitigated by the fact that the present values become low as the time span increases; therefore, the calculations need not be carried out indefinitely.

Another approach is to estimate the remaining value of the new machine at the end of the sixth year of its life. The analysis would then cover only the six-year period, with this remaining value being treated as a residual value, or implicit cash inflow at the end of the period. Such an estimate is extremely difficult to make, however.

The problem of uneven lives does not arise often, and this is fortunate because the timing and consequences of the future replacements under each alternative are difficult to visualize.

Investment

The amount of the investment is the amount that the company risks if it accepts the proposal.

The relevant investment costs are the differential or incremental costs. These are the outlays that will be made if the project is undertaken and that will not be made if it is not undertaken. The cost of the machine itself, its shipping costs, cost of installation, and the cost of training operators are examples. These outlays are part of the investment, even though some of them are not capitalized in the accounting records.

Investment Credit.   At present a company may receive an "investment credit" of up to 7 per cent of the cost of a new machine, which reduces its income taxes. The amount of company funds involved may therefore be only 93 per cent of the invoice cost of the machine.

Existing Equipment.   If the purchase of new equipment makes possible the sale of existing equipment, the proceeds from the sale may reduce the amount of incremental investment. In other words, the investment represents the total amount of *additional* funds that must be committed to the operation. To subtract this resale value from the gross investment, however, is to assume implicitly that (*a*) if the proposed machine is not purchased, the present machine will continue to be used, and its resale value will decrease to zero through its continued use; and (*b*) if the proposed machine is purchased, the present machine will in fact be sold or converted to some other productive use. If either of these assumptions is not valid, and if the amount involved is significant, the resale value of the present machine should be treated separately as a cash inflow in some subsequent year, not netted against the gross investment in the proposed machine.

Tax Effects.   The disposition of the present machine may involve a write-off of undepreciated book values or a sale at a price above book value. In either of these cases, special tax considerations may apply, since the write-off may give rise to a capital loss and the sale to a capital gain. The capital gains rate is, in effect, 25 per cent. Nevertheless, under most circumstances, gains and losses on the disposition of machinery and equipment (not buildings) are taxed at the regular rate of approximately 50 per cent. No tax gain or loss arises if the new machine replaces one of "like kind." Expert tax advice is needed on problems involving gains and losses on the sale of depreciable assets, for the line between the assets giving rise to capital gains or losses and other assets is difficult to define. In any event, when existing assets are disposed of, the relevant amount by which the net investment is reduced is the proceeds of the sale, adjusted for taxes.

Sunk Costs. As emphasized in Chapter 18, sunk costs are irrelevant. If $100,000 has been sunk in research leading to a new product, and if the new product will require an additional investment in new facilities of $10,000 and is expected to generate profits of $5,000 a year for five years, the relevant investment figure is $10,000, not $110,000. The $100,000 may be regretted, but it cannot be recouped.

Investments in Working Capital. An investment is the commitment, or locking up, of funds in any type of assets. Although a machine has here been used as an example, land and buildings also are investments, and so are commitments of funds to additional inventory and other current assets. In particular, if the new equipment is to produce a new product, additional funds will probably be tied up in inventories, accounts receivable, and increased cash needs. Part of this increased working capital will be supplied from increased accounts payable and accrued expenses. The net increase in working capital is as much an investment as the equipment itself, although in a more liquid state. Often it is reasonable to assume that the residual value of investments in working capital items is approximately the same as the amount of the investment; that is, that at the end of the project, they can be liquidated at their cost. Under these circumstances, the amount of working capital is treated as a cash inflow in the last year of the project, and its present value is found by discounting at the required earnings rate.

Residual Value. A machine may have a salvage or resale value at the end of its useful life. In a great many cases, the estimated residual value is so small and occurs so far in the future that it has no significant effect on the decision. Moreover, any salvage value that is realized may be almost, or completely, offset by removal and dismantling costs.

In situations where residual value is significant, the net residual value (after removal costs) is a cash inflow in the year of disposal, and is included with the other cash inflows. Other assets, such as repair parts or inventory, may also be released at the end of the project, and these are treated in the same fashion.

Several Alternatives. Some proposals involve a choice among several alternatives, each involving a different amount of investment. A useful way of approaching such problems is to start with the alternative that requires the smallest investment and to analyze the next most expensive alternative in terms of its *incremental* investment and its *incremental* earnings above those of the least expensive alternative. In other words, this question is asked: Is the *additional* investment in the second alternative justified by the *additional* earnings that are expected from it, over and above the earnings expected from the least expensive alternative? If it is not, the proposal with the smaller investment should be accepted.

Deferred Investments. Many projects involve a single commitment of funds at one moment of time, which we have called "the present." For some projects, on the other hand, the commitments are spread over a considerable period of time. The construction of a new plant may require disbursements over several years, or it may involve the construction of one unit now and a second unit five years later. In order to make the return-on-investment calculations, these investments must be brought to a common point in time, and this is done by the application of discount rates to the amounts involved. In general, the appropriate rate depends on the uncertainty that the investment will be made; the lower the uncertainty, the lower the rate. Thus, if the commitment is an extremely definite one, the discount rate may be equivalent to the interest rate on bonds (which also represents a definite commitment), whereas if the future investments will be made only if earnings materialize, then the rate can be the required earnings rate. In effect, in the latter case, the future investment is treated as a cash outflow.

Summary of the Process

Following is a summary of the steps involved in using the present value method:

1. Select a required earnings rate. Presumably, once selected this rate will be used for all proposals in the same risk category.

2. Estimate the differential cash inflows, or "earnings," for each year or sequence of years; including:

a) The cash earnings, neglecting depreciation, after taxes, for each year of the economic life.

b) The depreciation tax shield, using Table C.

c) Residual values at the end of the economic life, consisting of disposal value of equipment, plus working capital that is to be released.

3. Estimate the cash outflows other than the investment itself, if there are any, for the year in which they occur.

4. Find the net present value of all future inflows and outflows by discounting them at the required earnings rate, using Table A or Table B.

5. Find the net investment, which includes the additional outlays

made at "the present time," less the proceeds from disposal of existing equipment (adjusted for tax consequences), plus the present value of investment outlays made at some time other than the present. Use a low discount rate if these future outlays are quite certain to be made.

6. If the present value of the cash flows exceeds the amount of the net investment, decide that the proposal is acceptable, insofar as the monetary factors are concerned. This comparison is often made by treating the net investment as a cash outflow in year 0; i.e., with a present value of 1.000. When this is done, adding the numbers algebraically gives the result directly. A positive sum indicates an acceptable proposal; a negative sum an unfavorable one.

7. Taking into account the nonmonetary factors, reach a final decision. (This part of the process is at least as important as all the other parts put together, but there is no way of generalizing about it, other than to offer the list of suggestions given in Chapter 18, page 579.)

As an aid to visualizing the relationship, it is often useful to make a rough diagram of the flows, such as that shown in Illustration 19–4.

Illustration 19–4

CASH FLOW DIAGRAM

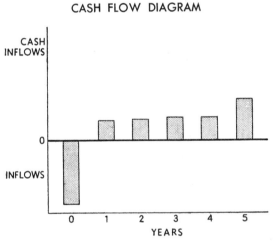

The diagram is for the same situation given in the example on page 623, with the addition of an estimated residual value of $200; namely, a machine costing $1,000, and estimated cash earnings (say from savings in labor costs) of $320 a year for five years. As an illustration of the whole process, the analysis of this proposal will be described, arranged according to the steps given above.

1. The required earnings rate is 10 per cent. (The company has arrived at this rate by one of the methods described above.)

2. The differential cash inflows are:
   a) The cash earnings of $320 a year, after adjustment for an estimated income tax of 50 per cent, becomes $160 a year for five years.
   b) The depreciation tax shield, assuming the whole investment of $1,000 is subject to depreciation for tax purposes, has a present value of $403, as calculated in the preceding example.
   c) The residual value at the end of the fifth year is $200.
3. There are no noninvestment cash outflows in this problem.
4. The net present value of the cash flows, other than the investment are the sum of (a) the aftertax cash earnings of $160 a year for five years, which has a present value, already calculated, of $607; plus (b) the present value of the depreciation tax shield of $403; plus (c) the present value of the residual value of $200, which discounted at 0.621 (from Table A), amounts to $124. These amounts total $1,134.
5. The net investment is the gross investment of $1,000, less the investment credit, here assumed to be 2 per cent, a net of $980. (The investment credit is not always 7 per cent; the amount varies, depending principally on the estimated life of the asset.)
6. Since the present value of the inflows, $1,134, exceeds the net investment, $980, the indication is that the proposal is acceptable insofar as the monetary factors are concerned.
7. The final decision would also take into account nonmonetary factors which, although not discussed here, may be as important as or more important than the monetary factors.

OTHER METHODS

Time-Adjusted Return

With the present value method, the required earnings rate must be selected in advance. There exists an alternative method, which finds the earnings rate at which the present value of the earnings equals the amount of the investment. This rate is called the *time-adjusted return,* or *internal rate of return,* or *project rate of return.* The method is called by one of the above names and also by the terms "discounted cash flow method" and "investor's method." We shall refer to it as the time-adjusted return method.

Level Earnings. If the earnings are level—that is, the same amount each year—the process is simple. It will be illustrated by a proposed investment of $1,000 with estimated earnings of $250 a year for five years. The procedure is as follows:

1. Divide the investment, $1,000, by the annual earnings, $250. The result, 4.0, is called the "factor."
2. Go across the five-year row of Table B. The column in which the figure closest to 4.0 appears shows the rate of return. Since the closest figure is 3.993 in the 8 per cent column, the return is slightly less than 8 per cent.

3. If management is satisfied with a return of slightly less than 8 per cent, then it should accept this project (neglecting nonquantitative considerations); if it requires a higher return, then it should reject the project.

The factor 4.0 is simply the ratio of the investment to the annual earnings. Each figure on Table B shows the ratio of the present value of a stream of earnings to an investment of $1 made today, for various combinations of discount rates and numbers of years. The number, 4.0, opposite any combination of years and discount rates means that the present value of a stream of earnings of $1 a year for that number of years discounted at that rate is $4. The present value of a stream of earnings of $250 a year is in the same ratio; therefore it is $250 times 4, or $1,000.

In this procedure, it is usually necessary to interpolate, that is, to estimate the location of a number that lies between two figures appearing in the table. There is no need to be precise about these interpolations because the final result can be no better than the basic data, and the basic data are ordinarily only rough estimates. A quick interpolation, made visually, is usually as good as the accuracy of the data warrants. Computations of fractions of a per cent are rarely, if ever, warranted.

Computing Several Returns. Since the most uncertain estimate of all is often the number of years during which there will be earnings, it is often useful to locate several combinations of years and rates that have the specified factor. For example, an investment of $20,000 and annual earnings of $4,000 give a factor of 5.0. Some of the combinations found on Table B for a factor of 5.0 are as follows:

If the Life Is—	Then the Rate of Return Is about—		If the Required Rate of Return Is—	Then the Life Must Be at Least—
6 years.....	6%	Or	6%.......	6+ years
8 years.....	12%	figured	10%.......	7+ years
10 years.....	15%	another	15%.......	10 years
12 years.....	17%	way:	18%.......	14 years

If the proposed investment is expected to have a longer life, *and* if the required earnings rate is lower than any one of the combinations selected, the investment is attractive; otherwise, it is not attractive.

Payback. The figure referred to above as the "factor" is also called the "payback" because it is the number of years over which the investment outlay will be recovered or paid back from earnings *if* the estimates turn out to be correct; that is, the project will "pay for itself" in this number of years. The payback figure is often used as a quick but crude method of appraising investments. If the payback period is equal to or only slightly less than the estimated life of the project, then the proposal is obviously a poor one. If the payback period is considerably less than the estimated life, then the project begins to look attractive.[5]

If several investment proposals have the same general characteristics, then the payback period can be used as a valid way of screening out the acceptable proposals. For example, if a company finds that production equipment ordinarily has a life of ten years, and if it requires a return of at least 15 per cent, then the company may specify that new equipment will be considered for purchase only if it has a payback period of five years or less; Table B shows that this payback period is equivalent to a return of approximately 15 per cent if the life is ten years. Stating the criterion in this fashion avoids the necessity of explaining the present value concept to the members of the operating organization.

The danger of using the payback figure is that it gives no consideration to differences in the lives of various projects. There may be a tendency to conclude that the shorter the payback period, the better the project; whereas the project with the longer payback may actually be better if it will produce earnings for a longer period of time.

Uneven Earnings. If earnings are not the same in each year, the time-adjusted return must be found by trial and error; that is, the earnings for each year and the residual values are listed, and various discount rates are applied to these amounts until a rate is found that makes their total present value equal to the amount of the investment. This rate is the time-adjusted return.

This method is illustrated by a problem in which it is assumed that the net investment is $1,000 and that earnings are estimated to be $300 a year for the first five years but only $100 a year for the sixth through the tenth year.

As a first trial, the present value of these earnings will be computed at an earnings rate of 18 per cent. From Table B, we find that the present value of $1 a year for the next five years at 18 per cent is $3.127. Table B does not tell us directly the present value of an amount to be received from the sixth through the tenth year, but, as already explained, this can easily be found by subtraction. The amount for ten years is $4.494, and

---

[5] Professor Myron Gordon has shown that the reciprocal of the payback (i.e., 1/payback period) is a close approximation of the time-adjusted return IF the estimated life of the project is somewhat more than twice the payback period and IF earnings are level. The return found by this simple method slightly overstates the true return (*Journal of Business,* October 1955, p. 253).

the amount for the first five of these years is $3.127; therefore, the amount for the sixth through the tenth years must be the difference between these figures, or $1.367. The present value of the estimated earnings can be computed by use of these factors, as follows:

Time Period	Earnings	Factor at 18%	Present Value
Years 1– 5.......	$300/year	3.127	$ 938
6–10.......	100/year	1.367	137
Total.....			$1,075
Investment.....			1,000
Difference.....			+$ 75

When the present value exceeds the net investment, a higher earnings rate is used on the next trial; when the present value is less than the net investment, a lower rate is used.

In this case, therefore, a higher rate must be used, and 20 per cent is selected. Another trial is made, as follows:

Time Period	Earnings	Factor at 20%	Present Value
Years 1– 5........	$300/year	2.991	$ 897
6–10........	100/year	1.201	120
Total.....			$1,017
Investment.....			1,000
Difference.....			+$ 17

This calculation gives a present value very close to the net investment, which indicates that the time-adjusted return is slightly more than 20 per cent.

In a similar fashion, all the elements involved in an investment can be compared with all the elements involved on the earnings side of the equation, with the difference in the timing of the money flows being recognized by the application of a trial discount rate. Eventually a rate will be found that makes the present value of the outflows approximately equal to the present value of the inflows. Usually, a satisfactory approximation to this rate can be found in two or three trials.

MAPI Method

Dr. George Terborgh of the Machinery and Allied Products Institute (MAPI) has developed a method that is specifically intended to help decide whether a machine should be replaced now or whether replacement should be deferred until some future time. Special forms and charts make this method quite easy to use. The charts are constructed in accordance with certain assumptions, the most important of which is that earnings will decline each year as the machine ages, in accordance with a prescribed pattern. Doctor Terborgh asserts that this is the typical situation with respect to replacement equipment, both because equipment becomes less efficient and requires higher maintenance costs with the passage of time and because the probability of obsolescence increases as time goes on.

If this and the other assumptions built into the method fit facts of the situation being analyzed, then the "urgency rating," which is the end product of the MAPI method, is a close approximation to the time-adjusted return. This method is fully described in the third reference at the end of this chapter.

Comparison of Methods

Given the same set of raw data, the time-adjusted return method will produce the same results as the present value method in the class of problems we have called screening problems; that is, if one method signals that a proposal is acceptable, so will the other. Under most circumstances, the MAPI method will also give the same signal if the special assumptions built into this method are used in the other methods. As will be seen, this similarity of results does not hold true in the other class of problems, called preference problems.

PREFERENCE PROBLEMS

So far, the discussion has been limited to *screening* or go, no-go problems, where this is the question: Is the proposal acceptable, or isn't it? We turn now to the more difficult *preference* problem, where we must decide which of two competing proposals is preferable, or where we must rank a series of proposals in order of their attractiveness. The time-adjusted return and the present value methods are used for this purpose.

If the time-adjusted return method is used, the preference rule is as follows: the higher the return, the better the project. A project with a return of 20 per cent is said to be preferable to a project with a return of 19 per cent.

Profitability Index

If the present value method is used, the present value of the earnings of one project cannot be compared directly with the present value of the earnings of another unless the investments are of the same size. Most people would agree that a $1,000 investment that produces earnings with a present value of $2,000 is better than a $1,000,000 investment that produces earnings with a present value of $1,001,000. In order to compare two proposals, we must relate the size of the earnings to the amount of money that is risked. This is done simply by dividing the present value earnings by the amount of investment, to give a ratio that is called the *profitability index*. The preference rule is as follows: the higher the index number, the better the project.

Comparison of Preference Rules

Conceptually, the profitability index is superior to the time-adjusted return as a preference device, for the time-adjusted return method will not always give the correct preference as between two projects with different lives or with different patterns of earnings.

As an example, consider two proposals. Proposal A involves an investment of $1,000 and earnings of $1,200 received at the end of one year; its time-adjusted return is 20 per cent. Proposal B involves an investment of $1,000 and earnings of $300 a year for five years; its time-adjusted return is only 15 per cent. But Proposal A is *not* necessarily preferable to Proposal B. It is preferable only if the company can expect to earn a high return during the following four years on some other project in which the funds released at the end of the first year are reinvested. Otherwise, Proposal B, which earns 15 per cent over the whole five-year period, is preferable.[6]

The error illustrated above is not present in the profitability index method. Assuming a required earnings rate of 10 per cent, the two proposals described above would be analyzed as follows:

Proposal (a)	Earnings (b)	Discount Factor (c)	Present Value (d = b × c)	Investment (e)	Index (f = d ÷ e)
A.................	$1,200—1 yr.	0.909	$1,091	$1,000	1.09
B.................	$ 300—5 yrs.	3.791	1,137	1,000	1.14

The index signals that Proposal B is better than Proposal A, which is in fact the case if the company can expect to reinvest the money released from Proposal A so as to earn only 10 per cent on it.

Although the profitability index method is conceptually superior to

---

[6] Note that this problem arises when a choice must be made between two competing proposals, only one of which can be adopted. If the proposals are noncompeting and the required earnings rate is less than 15 per cent, then *both* of them are acceptable.

the time-adjusted return method and although the former is also easier to calculate since there is no trial-and-error computation, the time-adjusted return method is more widely used in practice. There seem to be two reasons for this. First, the profitability index requires that the earnings rate be established before the calculations are made, whereas many analysts prefer to work from the other direction; that is, to find the return and then see how it compares with their idea of the earnings rate that is appropriate in view of the risks involved. Second, the index is an abstract number that is difficult to explain; whereas the time-adjusted return is similar to interest rates and earnings rates with which every businessman is familiar.

Concluding Comment

Not every businessman uses a discounting technique in analyzing investment proposals. In some cases, this is because the businessman is not familiar with the techniques. But there is a much better reason than this in many instances. Some businessmen, having studied the approach carefully, have concluded that it is like trying to make a silk purse out of a sow's ear; that is, in their opinion the underlying estimates are so rough that the refinement of discounting them is more work than it is worth. They therefore use a payback method or some alternative that does not involve discounting.

Those who do use one of the discounting methods argue that the extra work involved is small, and that the results although admittedly rough are nevertheless better than not even attempting to allow for the time element.

SUMMARY

The capital investment problem is essentially that of determining whether the anticipated earnings from a proposed project are sufficiently attractive to warrant risking the investment of funds in the project. The investment is typically made at one moment of time, whereas earnings flow in over a period of time in the future. The analysis technique must take this difference in timing into account.

For screening purposes, that is, for deciding whether a proposal is or is not attractive, two techniques are available. In the present value method, the *present value* of the earnings is found by discounting earnings at a required rate. If this present value equals or exceeds the amount of the investment, the proposal is acceptable. In the *time-adjusted return* technique, a discount rate is found that makes the present value of the earnings equal to the investment. If this rate equals or exceeds the required earnings rate, the proposal is acceptable.

Similar techniques may be used to establish preferences. The *profitability index* derived from the present value method is conceptually superior to the time-adjusted return method in signaling preferences, but it is less widely used in practice.

These techniques can be used only to the extent that the facts of a proposal can be reduced to dollar amounts for investment and earnings. For many proposals, nonquantitative considerations are dominant, and the techniques are not applicable. In nearly every problem there are some nonquantitative considerations, and these must be used to temper the numerical result.

SUGGESTIONS FOR FURTHER READING

GRANT, EUGENE L., AND IRESON, WILLIAM G. *Principles of Engineering Economy.* 4th ed. New York: The Ronald Press Co., 1960.

SOLOMON, EZRA (ed.). *The Management of Corporate Capital.* Glencoe, Ill.: The Free Press, 1959.

TERBORGH, GEORGE. *Business Investment Policy.* Washington, D.C.: Machinery and Allied Products Institute, 1958.

CASES

CASE 19–1.   RE-EQUIPMENT PROBLEMS

A. Equipment Replacement

The Parsons Company is considering the purchase of new equipment to perform operations currently being performed on different, less efficient equipment. The purchase price is $10,000, delivered and installed.

A Parsons production engineer estimates that the new equipment will produce savings of $2,000 in labor and other direct costs annually, as compared with the present equipment. He estimates the proposed equipment's economic life at ten years, with zero salvage value. The present equipment is in good working order and will last, physically, for at least 20 more years.

The company can borrow money at 5 per cent, although it would not plan to negotiate a loan specifically for the purchase of this equipment. The company requires a return of at least 20 per cent before taxes on an investment of this type. Taxes are to be disregarded.

Questions

1. Assuming the present equipment has zero book value and zero salvage value, should the company buy the proposed equipment?

2. Assuming the present equipment is being depreciated at a straight-line rate of 10 per cent, that it has a book value of $4,800 (cost, $8,000; accumulated depreciation, $3,200), and has zero net salvage value today, should the company buy the proposed equipment?

3. Assuming the present equipment has a book value of $4,800 and a salvage value today of $3,000, and that if retained for ten more years its salvage value will be zero, should the company buy the proposed equipment?

4. Assume the new equipment will save only $1,000 a year, but that its economic life is expected to be 20 years. If other conditions are as described in (1) above, should the company buy the proposed equipment?

B. Replacement Following Earlier Replacement

The Parsons Company decided to purchase the equipment described in Part A (hereafter called "Model A" equipment). Two years later, even better equipment (called "Model B") comes on the market and makes the other equipment completely obsolete, with no resale value. The Model B equipment costs $20,000 delivered and installed, but it is expected to result in annual savings of $5,000 over the cost of operating the Model A equipment. The economic life of Model B is estimated to be ten years. Taxes are to be disregarded.

Questions

1. What action should the company take?

2. If the company decides to purchase the Model B equipment, a mistake has been made somewhere, because good equipment, bought only two years previously, is being scrapped. How did this mistake come about?

C. Effect of Income Taxes

Assume that the Parsons Company expects to pay income taxes of 50 per cent and that a loss on the sale or disposal of equipment is treated as an ordinary deduction, resulting in a tax saving of 50 per cent. The Parsons Company expects to earn 10 per cent on its investment after taxes. Depreciation for tax purposes is computed on the sum-of-years' digits basis.

Questions

1. Should the company buy the equipment if the facts are otherwise as described in Part A (1)?

2. If the facts are otherwise as described in Part A (2)?

3. If the facts are otherwise as described in Part B?

D. Change in Earnings Pattern

Assume that the savings are expected to be $2,500 in each of the first five years and $1,500 in each of the next five years, other conditions remaining as described in Part A (1).

Questions

1. What action should the company take?
2. Why is the result here different from that in Part A (1)?

CASE 19–2.   ECONOMY MANUFACTURING COMPANY

The Economy Manufacturing Company owns a truck that is six years old. The production vice-president has decided to replace the old truck with a new truck, since he feels that it is uneconomical to operate equipment older than six years. The truck is fully depreciated, as of December 31, 1958. It can, though, be sold for $500. Its estimated operating expenses for the next six years (excluding depreciation and income taxes) are estimated as follows:

Year	Operating Expenses
1959	$2,800
1960	2,800
1961	2,850
1962	2,850
1963	2,900
1964	3,100

By December 31, 1964, the truck would have a scrap value of $50.

The operating expenses of the new truck, which would cost $4,000, are estimated to be (exclusive of depreciation and income taxes):

Year	Operating Expenses
1959	$1,800
1960	1,800
1961	1,900
1962	1,900
1963	2,000
1964	2,100

The estimated resale value of the new truck will be $1,000 at December 31, 1964.

The company also is considering leasing the new truck on either of two plans. Under both plans, the company would have to pay all operating expenses, just as if it owned the vehicle. From Leasing Company A, Economy could lease the truck for $900 a year for six years, with an option to buy the truck at the end of the six years for $500. From Leasing Company B, the rent would be $800 a year for six years, with an option to buy for $1,000. Both leases are noncancelable.

The company has a required earnings rate of 10 per cent and an estimated income tax rate of 50 per cent. If the truck is purchased, the company would be able to write off in the year of purchase 20 per cent of the cost of the truck. It would take depreciation on the remainder of the truck cost on a declining-balance method, using a rate of twice the straight-line rate, based on an estimated useful life of eight years from January 1, 1959. Assume that salvage value need not be considered in computing depreciation.

Questions

1. Should the company acquire the new truck?
2. If the new truck is acquired, should it be purchased, leased from Company A, or leased from Company B?

CASE 19–3. STANDEEN MANUFACTURING COMPANY

The Standeen Manufacturing Company, which produced oil burners, had followed a policy of purchasing the metal cabinets required in the assembly of its burners. In 1939, however, the executives were considering whether the company should continue to purchase the metal cabinets or whether it should make them. The cost of the cabinets represented about 15 per cent of the total cost of the completed oil burners.

The cabinets were purchased from a single supplier, who had always made delivery on time. Early in the spring the company contracted for a full year's requirement, ordinarily between 1,500 and 2,000 units. The Standeen Company did not pay for the cabinets until delivery, but it was financially committed for the number ordered.

The cabinet supplier made the cabinets during the off-peak season and held them until Standeen asked for them. Then the supplier crated the cabinets and sent them directly to the Standeen dealers for installation with the Standeen burner that was on the customer's premises. Standeen's peak production was in August, September, and October. As a result of this method of off-peak production and the large volume of business that the cabinet manufacturer obtained from Standeen and others, he had quoted a price lower than that of any competitors that Standeen's purchasing agent had discovered.

Nevertheless, in the opinion of the management of the Standeen Manufacturing Company, the purchase arrangement had certain unsatisfactory aspects. For one thing, the supplier did not provide full inspection at the time of crating; occasionally not all necessary parts were included, or the cabinets had defects such as scratches that had developed during storage in the supplier's warehouse. The supplier made good any defects, but in order to provide full inspection at the factory at the time of shipment, the supplier estimated that he would have to charge $1 more for each cabinet.

Another difficulty arose from the method of mass production used by the cabinet supplier. Each cabinet was composed of several pieces, including side panels and top. In order to obtain low costs, the manufacturer made large lots of each individual piece. These pieces were painted and baked in lots, and often there was some slight variation in the color of different lots. Thus, when the individual pieces were assembled into a cabinet, the side panels did not always match the top.

One Standeen executive believed the present purchasing arrangements slowed up the adoption of new cabinet models. The company first had to submit the specifications to the cabinet manufacturer and have a model made. This model then had to be inspected by the Standeen company's sales department, a process that necessitated either shipping the model cabinet to the company or sending a Standeen representative to the supplier's plant. Additional negotiations often were necessary after the model had been inspected.

In the event that the Standeen Manufacturing Company did decide to manufacture its own cabinets, the executives expected that certain disadvantages of the present arrangement would be overcome. They were of the opinion that a better inspection job would be possible at a total cost not much more than now was being paid to the supplier. They were not bothered by the fact that the general practice in the industry was to purchase finished cabinets. One executive argued that if Standeen withdrew its business, the supplier's costs would rise and so would the price at which Standeen's competitors bought cabinets.

If the company were to produce its own cabinets, it would have to take certain steps. It would be necessary to clear space in the factory, and to purchase some new equipment. Experienced men would have to be obtained and trained in the company's methods. Detailed production plans would have to be developed.

Investigation revealed that sufficient factory space could be made available for the needed equipment by means of plant rearrangement. This was true despite the fact that the company had recently started to produce equipment for the United States Army in its rearmament program. There was adequate capital to meet the anticipated financial requirements. The corporation was currently estimating its income tax expenses as 20 per cent of its net income before taxes. The manufacturing processes required for the cabinets were somewhat similar to those already familiar to the company's workers, and some of the needed equipment was already at hand. It was estimated that other needed skilled and semiskilled men could be hired and trained within 30 days.

The experience of the company was that, if it purchased cabinets on the basis of annual contracts for 1,000 or more, it could obtain them at a price of $35 a unit. The company's accounting department made cost estimates for making cabinets on the basis of a volume of 1,000 units. Estimated costs for a unit were as follows:

Material..	$17.30
Direct labor..................................	11.25
Overhead, at 100 per cent of direct labor..........	11.25
Total Unit Cost..........................	$39.80

The Standeen Manufacturing Company followed the practice throughout its operations of charging overhead at a standard rate of 100 per cent of direct labor; it was roughly estimated that half the overhead represented variable costs. Executives estimated that the company would have to spend $10,000 for new equipment and for the rearrangement of the plant in order to make cabinet production possible. This new equipment would be subject to depreciation at a rate of 15 per cent a year.

Question

Should the Standeen Manufacturing Company manufacture its cabinets?

CASE 19–4. PHILLIPS LAUNDRY

In January 1954, the Phillips Laundry, of Boston, installed a new shirt-pressing unit. The results obtained from operation of this unit were so satisfactory that early in 1955 Mr. Howard Phillips, president of the laundry, was considering the purchase of a second new shirt-pressing unit.

For the preceding several years Phillips' sales had amounted to roughly $130,000 each year. Mr. Phillips, owner of the laundry, thought that sales probably would not change much during 1955, but he hoped eventually to increase sales volume. The business was subject to slight seasonal fluctuations, which necessitated employment of part-time labor during parts of the year.

The laundry had always operated profitably, although since 1945 the shirt-laundering section had done no better than break even. Inasmuch as shirts made up an important part of the laundry's business, Mr. Phillips was extremely anxious to make this operation profitable. He had considered the possibility of raising shirt-laundering prices to the customer but had rejected this alternative because of the intense competitive conditions that existed in the area.

In order to determine where costs might be reduced, Mr. Phillips in 1953 had made a careful analysis of the operations performed on shirts. He concluded that high costs in the pressing department were his principal problem. At that time the shirt-pressing department included three separate but similar pressing units, called here Units A, B, and C. Each unit consisted of four presses. In each of Units A and B, a cuff and collar press and a front press were operated by one girl, a back press and a sleeve press were operated by a second girl, and two other girls did touch-up ironing and the folding of the finished shirts. Each of these two pressing units had a capacity of 90 shirts an hour. Unit C had four basically similar presses, but it was operated only when there were more shirts to be pressed than the other two units could handle. Two girls employed on a part-time basis operated Unit C and turned out 40 shirts an hour.

Both the full-time and part-time employees were paid 95 cents an hour; social security taxes and fringe benefits increased this expense to almost exactly $1 an hour. The company did not have a piecework incentive plan, but the girls were free to leave the plant when they finished a day's work. Full-time girls were guaranteed and paid for a 40-hour week. In practice, however, they averaged only 27.5 hours of actual work a week; they had one hour off for lunch and two 15-minute rest periods daily. The remaining five hours a week was accounted for by their practice of leaving early. Part-time help was employed to operate the third unit rather than work the full-time girls over 27.5 hours.

In order to reduce shirt-pressing costs, Mr. Phillips made a major change in the shirt-pressing department in January 1954. At that time, he replaced Unit A with a new Ajax pressing unit. The Ajax Model 70, only recently announced, represented the first major technological advance in shirt-pressing equipment in ten years.

Each of the old units had cost $1,200 when purchased, and installation charges for all three units had amounted to $300. They were 18 years old, however, and had been fully depreciated on the laundry's books. With periodic replacement of parts and routine maintenance, they probably could have been kept in operating condition indefinitely, but Mr. Phillips thought that the new type of press had made them obsolete. The old presses had no resale value.

The new Ajax pressing unit consisted of only three presses. It occupied only about half the space of one of the old four-press units. Building depreciation, light, and other space costs allocated to each press unit were approximately $1,000 a year. Thus, this saving in space was worth $500 a year.

On the Ajax pressing unit, one girl operated both a collar and cuff press and also a new type of machine that pressed the bosom and body of the shirt in one operation. This girl was able to operate these two presses simultaneously because of automatic timers that made it unnecessary to watch one press while inserting or removing a shirt from another press. A second girl operated the sleeve press and did all the folding for the unit. The touch-up, hand-ironing operation was completely eliminated. Even without this touch-up operation, there was a marked improvement in the appearance of shirts turned out by the new Ajax unit as compared with those turned out on the old units. The capacity of the Ajax unit operated by two girls was 70 shirts an hour.

Under the revised setup, then, the shirt-pressing department consisted of (a) the new Ajax unit, which was operated by two girls on a full-time basis and which had a capacity of 70 shirts an hour; (b) one old unit, which was operated by four girls on a full-time basis and had a capacity of 90 shirts an hour; and (c) a second old unit, which was operated only when needed by two girls on a part-time basis, with a capacity, when operated in this manner, of 40 shirts an hour. Mr. Phillips continued his policy of using Unit C on a part-time basis rather than have his employees work over 27.5 hours a week. Exhibit 1 shows the number of hours the presses of each unit were in operation in 1954, the number of shirts each unit pressed, and the number of hours for which the operators of each unit were paid.

The cost of the three new presses of the Ajax unit was $7,935 f.o.b. the factory. Freight to Boston was $455, and installation charges were $100. There was no disruption of work while the presses were being installed over a weekend, but there was some slowdown while the girls became accustomed to the new methods and procedures used. The slowdown resulted in an increase in labor cost for the period of about $100. Power costs were increased by the cost of electricity for a five-horsepower motor that powered the bosom and body press. The motor used one kilowatt of electricity an hour at a cost of 4½ cents a kilowatt-hour. Also, it was estimated that costs of operating the boiler and air compressor used to produce steam would increase about $5 a month.

Exhibit 1

SELECTED DATA FROM THE PRESSING DEPARTMENT FOR 1954

Unit	Capacity in Shirts/ Hour	No. of Hours in Operation in 1954	No. of Shirts Pressed in 1954	No. of Hours for Which Each Operator Was Paid
A. Two-girl unit—full-time basis....	70	1,375*	96,250	2,080
B. Four-girl unit—full-time basis....	90	1,375*	123,750	2,080
C. Two-girl unit—part-time basis....	40	900	36,000	1,350†

* There were 250 working days in 1954. The presses were actually in operation about 5.5 hours a day.
† Part-time help were paid for their lunch hour and rest periods.

During 1954 the Ajax unit performed much as expected. Mr. Phillips was pleased with the results and therefore was led to consider a second change in February 1955. At about that time, the manufacturer of Ajax machines brought out a new model, Model 85, which was equipped with an automatic folding table. The capacity of this unit, which also was operated by two girls, promised to be 85 shirts an hour. In the new setup, as Mr. Phillips conceived it, a Model 85 unit would replace Unit B, the pressing unit then being operated by four girls. The two Ajax units would then be operated on a full-time basis, 1,375 hours each a year, and the remaining old unit, Unit C, would be operated only when necessary by two girls on a part-time basis. This arrangement would give Mr. Phillips one Ajax unit with a potential capacity of 85 shirts an hour, one Ajax unit with a capacity of 70 shirts an hour, and one old unit with a capacity of 40 shirts an hour when operated by two girls, or 80 shirts an hour when operated by four girls.

The Ajax Model 85 would cost $9,030 f.o.b. the factory; freight would be $525; and the installation cost would be $120. The bosom and body press of the second Ajax unit would have its own five-horsepower motor. Costs of operating the boiler and air compressor would be increased about $5 a month by use of the Ajax Model 85 in place of the old equipment in Unit B.

An income statement for 1954 and a year-end balance sheet with figures rounded to hundreds of dollars are shown in Exhibits 2 and 3.

Exhibit 2

PHILLIPS LAUNDRY

Balance Sheet, December 31, 1954

ASSETS

Current Assets:

Cash	$ 4,100	
Accounts receivable	5,500	
Prepaid expenses	2,700	
Total Current Assets	$ 12,300	

Fixed Assets:

Machinery and equipment (net)	60,400	
Building (net)	45,800	
Total Assets	$118,500	

LIABILITIES AND NET WORTH

Current Liabilities:

Accounts payable	$ 3.200	
Accrued expenses	1,100	
Total Current Liabilities	$ 4,300	

Long-Term Liabilities:

Mortgage loan	31,400	
Total Liabilities	$ 35,700	

Net Worth:

Capital stock	40,000	
Surplus	42,800	
Total Liabilities and Net Worth	$118,500	

Exhibit 3

PHILLIPS LAUNDRY

Income Statement, Year Ending December 31, 1954

Net sales			$131,000
Laundry operating costs:			
Productive labor	$46,500		
Productive supplies	12,400		
Power	4,200		
Plant overhead	17,100		
Total Operating Costs		$80,200	
Collection and delivery		18,200	
Sales promotion		4,500	
Executive salaries		7,100	
Office and administrative		8,400	
Total Costs			118,400
Net profit before taxes			$ 12,600
Federal income tax (30%)			3,800
Net Profit after Taxes			$ 8,800

Question

Should the Phillips Laundry buy an Ajax Model 85 for use in Unit B?

CASE 19–5.   WILSON COMPANY

In March 1960, the Wilson Company was considering a proposal to replace four hand-loaded transmission case milling machines with one automatic machine. The company operated a large machine shop that did machining work on a subcontract basis for local industries in the Detroit area. One of the contracts was to machine transmission cases for truck engines for the Maynard Automobile Company. The Wilson Company had negotiated such a contract with the Maynard Automobile Company for each of the previous 14 years. For the last few years, the contract had been for 60,000 transmission cases annually.

The unfinished cases were supplied by Maynard. With a hand-loaded machine, all the faces could not be machined at the same time. Each machine required the constant attention of one skilled machine operator.

The machines used by Wilson were only three years old. Each had an annual output of approximately 15,000 cases on a two-shift, five-day week basis; therefore, four machines had been purchased at a total cost of $147,500.

The useful life of a hand-loaded machine on a two-shift, five-day week basis was estimated to be 15 years. Its salvage value at the end of its useful life was estimated to be $1,000. Depreciation of $29,500 had been built up for the four machines, representing three years' accumulation. The purchase of the machines had been financed by a 5 per cent bank loan, and $45,000 of this loan had not yet been repaid. It was estimated that the four machines could be sold in their present condition for a total of $60,000, net, after dismantling and removal costs. The book loss resulting from the sale would be a deductible expense for income tax purposes and would therefore result in a tax saving of 52 per cent of the loss.

The machine being considered in 1960 was a fully automatic transfer-type milling machine, equipped with four machining stations. Automatic transfer equipment on this machine moved the part progressively from one station to the next and indexed at each station, finishing a complete case with each cycle of the machine. One skilled machine operator was required to observe the functioning of the machine and make any necessary adjustments.

An automatic transfer-type machine with an annual output of 60,000 transmission cases on a two-shift basis would be specially built by a machine tool manufacturer at an estimated cost of $170,000, delivered and installed. The useful life of this machine was estimated to be 15 years. No reliable estimate of scrap value could be made; a rough estimate was that it would approximate the removal costs.

The Wilson Company's engineering department was asked to prepare a study for the executives to use in deciding what action to take. Its findings were as follows: The direct labor rate for milling machine operators was $2.50 an hour, including provision for social security taxes and fringe benefits, which varied with the payroll. There would be a saving in floor space amounting to $400 annually on the basis of the charge made in 1960 for each square foot of floor space used. However, the factory layout was such that it would be difficult to use this freed space for some other purpose, and no other use was planned. Out-of-pocket savings of $5,000 a year for other cost items were estimated if the automatic machine was purchased.

Exhibit 1

WILSON COMPANY

Selected Financial Information

Condensed Income Statement, 1959

Net sales.................................	$5,364,213
Less: All costs and expenses................	4,138,647
Profit before taxes.........................	$1,225,566
Provision for income taxes.................	622,715
Net Income................................	$ 602,851

Condensed Balance Sheet, December 31, 1959

Current assets...........	$3,051,349	Current liabilities.......	$ 930,327
Fixed assets (net).......	4,239,210	4% mortgage bonds.....	500,000
Other assets...........	151,491	Capital stock..........	1,000,000
		Surplus...............	5,011,723
	$7,442,050		$7,442,050

The Wilson Company planned to finance any new equipment purchase with a bank loan at a rate of 5 per cent.

Selected financial data for the company are shown in Exhibit 1. The company considered the picture given by these statistics to be normal and expected the same general pattern to prevail in the foreseeable future.

Question

What action, if any, would you recommend? Why?

CASE 19–6.   BISBO A.G.

Mr. Aschinger, managing director of Bisbo A.G., a large German manufacturer of biscuits, was concerned about sales of two types of cream-filled crackers, "Cocktail" and "Picknick." Although Bisbo's total sales volume had been growing steadily for the last several years, the sales volume of Cocktail and Picknick had remained static for some time. Moreover, recent cost calculations indicated that the company was losing money on both items. In 1956 total Bisbo sales amounted to DM 49,740,000,[7] of which sales of Cocktail and Picknick were approximately DM 320,000 each.

The sales manager, Mr. Stark, believed that the poor sales record on Cocktail and Picknick resulted from the fact that competing firms had recently introduced crackers similar in quality and taste but wrapped in cellophane rolls, ten crackers to a roll. Cocktail and Picknick were at present sold loose. Mr. Stark was convinced that Bisbo A.G. could increase sales considerably if it offered Cocktail and Picknick packed in cellophane rolls. On the basis of a careful analysis of dealers' reports and market research information, he estimated that if the products were so wrapped, 1957 sales of the two items would increase to DM 1,045,000.

Mr. Stark had been with Bisbo A.G. for eight years and was thoroughly familiar with the German biscuit market. He made sales estimates for each product annually by months, based on dealers' reports and recommendations of his market analyst. In a typical recent monthly forecast, covering 87 items, actual sales of 72 items were within 20 per cent of his estimate, sales of 11 were 20 per cent to 70 per cent below the forecast, and sales of 4 exceeded the forecast by from 20 per cent to 100 per cent. Mr. Stark considered that his market analyst, who had been with the company for three years, was very competent.

The technical department made a study of the wrapping proposed by Mr. Stark. A new packing machine costing DM 31,000 and having a physical life of ten years would be required. Installation costs would add a further DM 1,200. At the volume of 376,000 kg. of crackers with the new cellophane wrapper predicted by Mr. Stark for 1957, operating

---

[7] In 1957 one Deutsche mark (DM) equaled approximately U.S. $0.24. One kilogram (kg.) equals 2.2 pounds. One square meter (m²) equals 1.2 square yards.

costs were estimated to be DM 7,886 a year, as shown in Exhibit 1.

At the same time, the cost department prepared an estimate of the 1957 product costs of Cocktail and Picknick. With the present method of packaging, annual sales for 1957 had been estimated at DM 325,-000 (117,000 kg.) of each of the two items. The manufacturing di-

Exhibit 1

ESTIMATED OPERATING COSTS OF THE NEW PACKING MACHINE AT A TOTAL ANNUAL PRODUCTION OF 376,000 KG. COCKTAIL AND PICKNICK, IN DM

Labor..1,000
Material (48,200 m² of cellophane at 0.13 DM/m²).....6,266
Electricity, maintenance........................... 600
    Total..7,866

rect cost of this quantity was estimated to be DM 299,617 for Cocktail and DM 320,158 for Picknick. Overhead, allocated at the plant-wide rate of 14.38 per cent of estimated sales, was DM 46,735 for each item. Thus total costs of the two items in 1957 were expected to exceed total revenue by DM 63,245, or 9.73 per cent of sales (see Exhibit 2).

Exhibit 2

ABSORPTION OF FIXED OVERHEAD BY COCKTAIL AND PICKNICK AT A PRODUCTION OF 117,000 KG. EACH

	Manufacturing Cost*	Total Cost	Estimate of Sales	Unabsorbed Fixed Overhead		Absorbed Fixed Overhead	
	DM	DM	DM	DM	%	DM	%
Cocktail........	299,617	346,352	325,000	21,352	6.57	25,383	7.81
Picknick........	320,158	366,893	325,000	41,893	12.89	4,842	1.29
Total........	619,775	713,245	650,000	63,245	9.73	30,225	4.65

* Manufacturing direct cost included all costs of production, with the exception of fixed factory overhead and other overhead costs listed in Exhibit 3.

Exhibit 2 also indicates that Cocktail and Picknick together would absorb overhead only at a rate of 4.65 per cent (14.38 — 9.73 per cent) at a production rate of 117,000 kg. each.

Mr. Sager, head of the costing department, explained the method of allocating overhead. Prior to the beginning of the year, sales estimates for all products were collected. Fixed costs for the total forecast volume were then estimated. These two estimates were used to calculate the plant-wide overhead rate, which was allocated to individual products on the basis of actual individual sales. For 1957, total fixed costs were estimated at DM 7,967,000, as shown in Exhibit 3, and total sales were

Exhibit 3

ESTIMATE OF TOTAL FIXED OVERHEAD IN 1957 IN DM

Fixed plant overhead	2,554,000
Sales force	1,245,000
Advertising	410,000
Interest	80,000
Depreciation	976,000
General costs	2,702,000
Total	7,967,000

estimated to be DM 55,400,000; thus the overhead rate was 7,967,-000 ÷ 55,400,000, or 14.38 per cent.

Mr. Aschinger, who did not usually see complete cost figures for individual products, was surprised to learn that Cocktail and Picknick were not covering their full costs. He discussed with Mr. Stark the possibility of dropping these items entirely, but they agreed this was not feasible, because the products were essential to Bisbo's full product line. Nevertheless, Mr. Aschinger questioned whether it was prudent to buy a new machine, since this would result in additional costs that would have to be charged against an already unprofitable line.

However, since he knew that increased production volume meant an increase in the absorbed amount of overhead, Mr. Aschinger continued his investigation. His calculations were based on the estimates of Mr. Stark, which he agreed were the best that could be made, that sales of Cocktail and Picknick if offered in the new cellophane rolls would go up to a total of 376,000 kg., or DM 1,045,000. Mr. Aschinger reasoned that the expected increased sales of DM 395,000 would result in a considerable increase in the amount of overhead absorbed. Even if this was not at the rate of 14.38 per cent, which was the rate needed to cover the fixed overhead, but only at the rate of 4.65 per cent, which was the rate at which overhead currently was being absorbed, his calculations showed an increase in fixed overhead absorption of DM 18,370 (4.65 per cent of DM 395,000).

The company wished an average return of at least 20 per cent before taxes on investments in capital assets.

Question

What action should Mr. Aschinger take?

CASE 19–7.   BURTON CHEMICAL COMPANY

The Burton Chemical Company was a medium-size producer of industrial chemicals. In November 1958, the company was in the process of expanding its production. This expansion created the need for additional capacity for an intermediate product that was currently being manufactured in the company's plant. The required increment was 300,000 pounds a year, which the plant could produce only if it installed

Exhibit 1

INITIAL CALCULATION OF RETURN ON INVESTMENT

Additional quantity of intermediate product required:		300,000 lb./year
Investment required to manufacture:		
Equipment....................................	$100,000	
Inventory (raw materials).........................	50,000	
Total..	$150,000	
Manufacturing costs, per pound of intermediate product:		
Raw materials (current prices)......................	$ 0.50	
Labor..	0.04	
Utilities and supplies............................	0.01	
Depreciation...................................	0.05	
Total..	$ 0.60	
Analysis of savings, per pound of intermediate product:		
Purchase price from supplier (estimated).............	$ 0.70	
Less: Manufacturing costs........................	0.60	
Saving.......................................	$ 0.10	
Less: Tax at 50%..............................	0.05	
Net Saving...................................	$ 0.05	

$$\text{Return on investment: } \frac{\text{Net saving per pound}}{\text{Investment per pound}} = \frac{\$0.05}{\$0.50} = 10\%.$$

additional facilities. On the other hand, the increment could be purchased from the major supplier of the raw materials which went into the intermediate product. Mr. Burton, the president, asked the company's controller, Mr. Scott, to investigate these alternatives and to determine the return on investment that could be expected if additional facilities were installed.

Mr. Scott gathered the data shown in Exhibit 1. An increase in the plant's manufacturing capacity to produce the 300,000-pound annual increment would require an investment of $100,000 in equipment (to be depreciated at a rate of 15 per cent) and $50,000 in raw materials inventory. On a unit basis, therefore, Mr. Scott figured the investment to be 50 cents a pound. Manufacturing costs, including depreciation, would be 60 cents a pound. If the product were purchased from the supplier, Mr. Scott estimated the price at 70 cents a pound. Thus by manufacturing the increment, the company would realize an after-tax saving of 5 cents a pound. The controller's final calculation—saving per pound over investment per pound—indicated an expected return on investment of 10 per cent. He considered this return to be barely sufficient to justify the installation of facilities.

Before reporting to the president, Mr. Scott asked the purchasing department to solicit a bid price on the intermediate product from the

Exhibit 2

REVISED CALCULATION OF RETURN ON INVESTMENT

Current production of intermediate product: 900,000 lb./year
Raw material price saving on current level of annual production of
    intermediate product (900,000 × $0.07)......................$63,000
    Less: Additional costs to produce 300,000-pound increment . . .
        labor, supplies and utilities, depreciation (300,000 × $0.10) 30,000
Net saving...$33,000
    Less: Tax at 50%... 16,500
Net Saving after Tax..$16,500
Investment required to manufacture 300,000-pound increment: $150,000

$$\text{Return on investment:} \frac{\text{Net saving after tax}}{\text{Investment}} = \frac{\$\,16,500}{\$150,000} = 11\%.$$

supplier. To the controller's surprise, the price quoted was 55 cents a pound. Since this was below the company's own manufacturing costs, it now appeared more advantageous to purchase the 300,000-pound increment. However, Mr. Scott could not see why the raw material supplier should be able to produce and sell the intermediate product at such a low price. He ran a check on his manufacturing cost estimates and found them to be quite accurate. This led him to conclude that the price the company was currently paying for raw materials might be excessive. Further negotiations with the supplier confirmed this conclusion, and the company was able to secure a price reduction on raw materials of 7 cents a pound of intermediate product.

Under these new circumstances, Mr. Scott prepared a revised calculation of the return on investment that could be expected if the company were to manufacture the 300,000-pound increment. His calculations, shown in Exhibit 2, indicated a return of 11 per cent on the $150,000 investment required to increase plant capacity. His reasoning was as follows: Current annual production of the intermediate product was 900,000 pounds. The 7-cent price reduction in raw materials would generate annual savings of $63,000. From these savings he subtracted the additional costs to manufacture a 300,000-pound increment (i.e., labor, utilities and supplies, and depreciation) at 10 cents a pound, or $30,000. This produced net savings of $33,000, or $16,500 after tax. The ratio of net annual savings after tax to the initial investment showed a return of 11 per cent.

Mr. Scott reported the results of his investigation to Mr. Burton and recommended that the company increase plant capacity to produce the 300,000-pound increment of intermediate product. He stated that the anticipated 11 per cent return in investment would justify such a decision.

Questions

1. Comment on the strengths and weaknesses of the approach used by Mr. Scott.

2. Should the product in question be purchased or manufactured?

CASE 19–8.   NATIONAL BRAKELINE DIVISION

In August 1950, Mr. James Cornell, divisional sales manager of the National Brakeline Division of the Consolidated Metals Corporation, was approached by the Auto-Lease Sales Company with a proposal that Mr. Cornell lease automobiles for Brakeline Division salesmen who were located outside Detroit, headquarters of the division. The Brakeline Division sold automotive parts. The 1949 sales volume of the division was approximately $8,000,000; 95 per cent of this volume represented the sale of brake linings.

The headquarters of the Consolidated Metals Corporation were in New York City. Its sales volume, which in 1949 exceeded $91,000,-000, was derived from a variety of products sold to railroads and other industries. Each of the ten divisions in the company operated relatively independently.

In addition to giving thought to leasing cars, Mr. Cornell was also considering the possibility that the company buy the cars to be used by his sales force. At present, the division paid its salesmen 7 cents a mile for the use of their own cars. The average mileage driven on company business was 20,500 miles per car per year.

Brakeline Division products were sold nationally by a sales force of 36 men stationed in major cities throughout the country. Salesmen were paid a straight salary and had an expense account; average earnings were $7,000 annually.

The Leasing Company's Proposal

The Auto-Lease Sales Company offered Mr. Cornell an arrangement whereby it would provide the automobiles (1950 Ford or other similar vehicles) with standard equipment such as heater, windshield defrosters, spare tire, and spare tube. The term of the agreement was for one year and was to continue from year to year unless and until terminated by one of the parties. The Brakeline Division would pay $55 a month rental fee for each car it leased and would assume the public liability, property damage, and fire and theft insurance cost on the automobiles. The division would also purchase all the gasoline used.

The Auto-Lease company would pay for oil and for the cost of repairs and service. These were to include not more than four new tires and tubes, and not more than one oil change and lubrication for each 2,000 miles per car. "Repairs and service" excluded storage, washing, and polishing. Whenever the lessee (Brakeline Division) found it necessary to have an automobile repaired and serviced, this was to be done at the shop of an authorized dealer of the make of the automobile. The lessee was to pay for any repairs or damages to the automobiles resulting from an accident or collision, and the leasing company was not responsible for any loss of business or other damage caused by time lost in repairing or replacing the automobiles, or by the leasing company's failure to deliver the vehicles by reason of strikes or other causes beyond its control. The leasing company would provide the lessee with another automobile in the event that a car was stolen or a repaired car was not returned within a reasonable time. If the lessee was deprived of the use of a car for more than seven days, no rental would be charged after the seventh day until a replacement was delivered to the lessee.

The terms of this proposal were as good as, or better than, those of any other Mr. Cornell had seen. The fee for each car was not dependent upon the number of cars to be leased by Mr. Cornell.

Mr. Cornell was also informed by the representatives of the leasing company that the Brakeline Division could keep some cars for a second year at reduced cost. After studying other conditions surrounding such an arrangement, he dismissed this idea as not being suitable for the Brakeline Division.

Mr. Cornell understood that the leasing agreement would not preclude the use of leased cars by persons in the immediate families of employees if these persons were qualified drivers.

Information from the New York Office

Mr. Cornell wrote to the New York office of Consolidated Metals Corporation for information about the experience of other divisions. Mr. Dudley, sales assistant to the president, provided average costs of operating the cars leased by the Eastern Wheel Division and estimates of costs of operating cars owned by the company based on the experience of the Eastern Wheel Division. These data are shown in Exhibits 1 and 2.

Exhibit 1

AVERAGE COSTS OF OPERATION OF CARS LEASED BY THE EASTERN WHEEL DIVISION*

	Cents per Mile	Dollars per Year
Gasoline	1.33	$ 309
Insurance (public liability, property damage, fire, and theft)	0.40	90
Accident repairs	0.20	45
Rental	3.05	708
Total	4.98	$1,152

* Based on 28 cars traveling at an average annual rate of 23,200 miles each.

Exhibit 2

ESTIMATED COSTS OF OPERATING CARS OWNED BY THE COMPANY*

	Cents per Mile	Dollars per Year
Gasoline	1.33	$309
Oil and lubrication	0.11	25
Repairs and maintenance	0.35	81
Tires and tubes	0.06	12
Licenses and fees	0.14	32
Insurance (public liability, property damage, fire, and theft)	0.40	90
Accident repairs	0.20	45
Depreciation	1.04	241
Interest on investment at $3\frac{1}{2}$ per cent	0.18	42
Total	3.81	$877

* Assumes average mileage traveled to be 23,200 a year.

Mr. Dudley explained that depreciation in Exhibit 2 was based on insurance company records that he thought represented the consensus as to average first-year depreciation cost on cars in the low-price field. The figure thus estimated was 25 per cent, but since Mr. Dudley anticipated that he could buy automobiles at a 10 per cent fleet discount, he estimated the actual net first-year depreciation at 15 per cent. This depreciation was figured on an average list price of $1,600 per automobile. Although his estimates given in Exhibit 2 pertained to first-year operation of new cars, he thought that savings could be made by keeping company cars for two years or more, provided that the total mileage did not get so high that the cars would not be dependable or maintenance would be prohibitively expensive.

Purchasing Considerations

The purchasing department of the Brakeline Division informed Mr. Cornell that 1950 Fords, similar to the cars Auto-Lease could deliver, could be bought for an average delivered price of around $1,900. A fleet discount was not obtainable on any of the major makes of low-priced cars.

For tax purposes, rental payments could be deducted from income as an operating expense if the cars were leased; whereas depreciation and interest on financing could be deducted if the cars were owned. Mr. Fox, controller of the Brakeline Division, thought that company ownership of cars would tie up cash that would not be required under either a leasing plan or the present plan of salesmen's ownership. The cash required for the purchase of cars could either be obtained from funds that were available for investment in equipment, or it could be borrowed.

Company-Owned Cars—Arrangement for Personal Use

Mr. Cornell thought that if he decided to lease or purchase automobiles for his salesmen, he would have to make some arrangement to provide for their personal use of the cars. The Eastern Wheel Division required each man to keep an account of the miles he drove that were not on company business and to credit the company with that mileage at 2 cents a mile. On the basis of his conversations with the salesmen, Mr. Cornell made a rough estimate that each of them put about 3,000 miles a year on his car on nonbusiness trips, and he concluded that the salesmen would be willing to accept either of the two alternatives (i.e., leased or company-owned cars) provided they could use the cars for personal traveling.

Question

What action do you recommend?

CASE 19–9. MORRISVILLE HARDWARE COMPANY

Early in the summer of 1958, Mr. Albert Foster, executive vice president and chief operating officer of the Morrisville Hardware

Company, was concerned with the amount and cost of subcontracted services that the company was regularly procuring from other nearby manufacturers.

The Morrisville Hardware Company had been in operation for more than a half century as a manufacturer of hardware apparatus used to actuate, lock, control, weatherstrip, and mount all types of residential windows. It had long been one of the largest of the 17 or so firms that competed for this specialized market on a national basis. The company's current sales were approximately $1,500,000 a year.

In addition to the national firms, the company also faced competition from approximately 18 other hardware manufacturers, many quite small, which operated on a local or regional basis. These firms usually concentrated on only a few types of window hardware. Morrisville's product line currently consisted of 15 major items, including locks, handles, sash balances, and actuators for casement units. It manufactured each of these in a variety of sizes. Morrisville officials believed that this was one of the most complete lines in the industry, permitting their company to service any conventional need for window hardware apparatus.

The company distributed its product through a dozen salesmen to about 250 active accounts, consisting of jobbers, window manufacturers, and retail lumberyards. Jobbers accounted for approximately 80 per cent of the company's volume, with the balance being divided about equally between the other two channels.

The company conducted its manufacturing operations in a 55-year-old two-story plant on the outskirts of an industrial city of about 300,000 persons. Its work force numbered about 100 employees, some three quarters of whom were production workers who averaged $1.75 an hour, largely on piece rate incentives. The raw materials used by the company were chiefly steel and aluminum. These were formed or machined into the various hardware units through a variety of manufacturing processes. These required operations on punch presses, screw machines, slitting machines, rolling mills, plating tanks, etc. The company also maintained a large assembly department and a tool and die shop equipped with all the basic machine tools. Except for the rolling mills, which were on two shifts, all the production departments were currently operating on a one-shift basis. Two of the departments (plating and punch presses) were, in fact, operating at slightly less than half of their one-shift capacity.

In 1954, after an extended period of declining sales and serious operating losses, the once highly profitable company had been acquired by a new owner group. Since that time several sweeping changes had been inaugurated. These included the production of numerous new window hardware items, extensive changes in management personnel, new operating procedures (particularly in factory operations), and the ouster of the union formerly representing the company's production employees. This latter move had resulted in a six-month strike in 1954, in which the union attempted unsuccessfully to be reinstated as the bargaining agent for the work force.

The various steps taken by the new management group had achieved significant improvements, but in 1958 the firm still had not succeeded in regaining a profitable position. In January of that year, therefore, further management changes were effected. Mr. Foster, who had been general manager of a large integrated lumber mill before joining the company, was convinced that major cost improvements were imperative. In the course of launching an extensive campaign of cost reductions, his attention was drawn to the company's subcontracting practices.

In commenting on the general situation to one of his associates, Mr. Foster said:

> We're in a peculiar spot. Clearly we are faced with an urgent need to reduce costs. Our present use of subcontractors looks like it may be an area for real savings. On the other hand, our financial position is exceptionally tight. This makes the acquisition of any new equipment for these purposes particularly difficult, although not entirely impossible as long as the investment is modest. But we cannot afford to be unrealistic about hidden bugs or headaches that we might encounter when taking on an unfamiliar process. In short, we need to be darned sure about the size and attainability of any savings we go after.

Of the several services being subcontracted by the company, Mr. Foster was currently directing primary attention to spring winding and spring flocking.

Two of the company's principal items employed coil springs as the means of holding open, at any desired level, each of the sashes of an installed double-hung[8] window. The coiled springs were encased in narrow aluminum channels situated in the sides of the window housing. When the sash was raised, the springs were contracted; when the sash was lowered, they were expanded.

At 1958 sales volume, the company required roughly 104,000 of these springs a month, divided about equally among the 14 different lengths (from 9 to 31 inches) that were necessary to accommodate the

---

[8] A double-hung window consists of two sashes, top and bottom, which slide vertically past each other, and which are held in position by means of weights, balances, or springs.

numerous standard sizes of double-hung windows employed in residential construction. The springs were manufactured from high-grade steel wire, approximately 0.018 inches in diameter, by use of coil winding machines. Since the company did not possess such machines, it had always subcontracted the coil winding to two local firms, giving each about half of the work in order to avoid dependence on a single source of supply. The Morrisville Hardware Company itself purchased the necessary wire, delivered it to the subcontractors in its own truck, and subsequently picked up and returned the finished springs to the Morrisville factory.

Exhibit 1
SPRING FLOCKING INSTALLATION

Both subcontractors had proven entirely satisfactory. They invariably met delivery promises and turned out springs of excellent quality.

In addition to forming the springs, the subcontractors put them through a "flocking" operation. This consisted of spraying each spring with a liquid adhesive and then coating it thoroughly with tiny felt-like fibers that were then baked onto the springs in special ovens. A typical installation for performing a flocking operation is shown in Exhibit 1. The coating of flocking served to dampen down the humming sounds created by the vibrations of the springs when they were extended or contracted in the aluminum channels of installed window units.

Company sales personnel were certain that unless these sounds were reduced by flocking, their products would have been placed at a severe competitive disadvantage.

The current charges being made by each of the two subcontractors for the winding operation on the various lengths of springs were identical. See Exhibit 2. In addition, the subcontractors charged $25 a thousand for the flocking operation, regardless of spring length.

Exhibit 2

SUBCONTRACTORS' CHARGES
FOR SPRING WINDING

Spring	Spring Winding Price per Thousand
9"	$31.00
11"	37.00
13"	43.00
15"	49.00
16"	52.00
18"	58.00
19"	61.00
21"	67.00
23"	73.00
24"	76.00
26"	82.00
27"	85.00
29"	91.00
31"	97.00

The Morrisville Company's accounting department estimated that additional charges of $1.47 a thousand should be made to reflect the cost incurred in transporting the springs to and from the subcontractors' plants. This charge included allocations to cover such items as the wages of the driver during the time required for the trip, depreciation on the company's truck, and the operating and fixed costs connected with the vehicle.

In his investigations Mr. Foster had determined that coil winding machines could be purchased for approximately $3,000 each, installed. Two would be needed to produce the company's current requirements on a one-shift basis. The type of unit he was considering is shown in Exhibit 3.

With the advice of the company's production supervisor, Mr. Foster had concluded that if purchased, the two machines could be located in the company's screw machine department, where there was ample room for them without any rearrangement of existing equipment.

Mr. Foster also had ascertained that the job of operating a spring winding unit was not particularly complex. Setup for a specific length, diameter, and gauge of spring was not difficult, and once it was accomplished machine operations were largely automatic other than for frequent checking to assure that the machines did not require adjustment. A single operator usually was in charge of two (or even more) units. Mr. Foster also learned that the going rate in the community for operators skilled in setting up and operating such equipment was around $1.80 an hour, and that such men were usually available in the local area.

Exhibit 3
COIL SPRING WINDER

In regard to the flocking operation, Mr. Foster's investigations established that the materials required were readily obtainable from several suppliers. At current price levels, the flocking and adhesive for the company's average monthly requirements of approximately 104,000 springs would cost between $350 and $375 a month.

The cost of the equipment required for the operation, including spraying devices (for both the adhesive and flocking) and a baking room, would be dependent upon the extent to which the company wished to mechanize the process. For about $13,000, installed, the company could obtain a unit equipped with an automatic conveyor, thus permitting a team of two operators to turn out the company's requirement on a one-shift basis. On the other hand, for approximately $6,300 installed, the company could purchase a unit that would be almost entirely dependent upon manual operations. In this case, four operators would be needed, on one-shift operation, to achieve the necessary production rate. The work was not especially skilled, and Mr. Foster believed that operators could be hired for such work for $1.55 an hour.

With either type of installation, it would be necessary for the flocking unit to be located in a partitioned area, of at least 300 square feet, preferably in an isolated part of the shop. This was to minimize the fire hazard and to prevent the unpleasant adhesive odors and the small fibers of excess flocking from being carried throughout the plant.

After careful investigation, Mr. Foster and the production supervisor concluded that the only feasible location that met these requirements was the area on the first floor currently used as the employees' cafeteria. This space was of sufficient size, was already partitioned, and was also somewhat removed from the main flow of plant operations. At the same time it was still only 50 feet from the screw machine department, where the spring winding machines would be located if the company decided to undertake that operation.

Mr. Foster was convinced that, if the cafeteria was utilized for the flocking installation, the only available site in which dining facilities could be reestablished was a small enclosed area currently unused and located near the punch press department on the first floor. This location would provide only about one quarter of the space available in the present cafeteria and would permit seating of only about 60 persons at a time. It would also not be possible in this space to arrange for any extensive kitchen facilities. The hot food dishes currently offered for sale at cost to employees would, therefore, no longer be available. In the past, about half of the plant's personnel had regularly purchased such items. The remainder brought their lunches from home, although some of them purchased supplemental items, such as beverage or ice cream, at the plant.

If the area in question was converted into a lunchroom, it would still be possible to offer hot and cold beverages, sandwiches, ice cream, pie, cake, and other items that did not require preparation on the premises. The room was lined with windows along the entire length of one wall. Mr. Foster was confident that, with painting and decorations, the room could be made into an attractive area at negligible out-of-pocket cost.

Mr. Foster thought it likely that both the spring winding machines

Exhibit 4

MORRISVILLE HARDWARE COMPANY

Balance Sheet—June 30, 1958

ASSETS

Current Assets:

Cash..	$ 22,732	
Accounts receivable—net	215,801	
Inventories..................................	401,539	
Prepayments................................	33,870	
Total Current Assets........................		$ 673,942

Other Assets:

Notes receivable.............................	$ 2,774	
Accounts receivable...........................	6,494	
Cash surrender value—officers' insurance..........	9,297	
Investment in subsidiaries......................	135,837	
Total Other Assets.........................		154,402

Fixed Assets:

Machinery and equipment—net..................	$149,241	
Dues, patterns and fixtures—net................	69,367	
Patents—net.................................	11,573	
Tools and equipment—net.....................	11,465	
Leasehold improvements—net..................	1,799	
Automobiles and trucks—net..................	3,421	
Furniture and fixtures..........................	10,862	
		257,728
Total Assets............................		$1,086,072

LIABILITIES

Current Liabilities:

Notes payable—bank...........................$156,000		
Notes payable—others......................... 41,977	$197,977	
Accounts payable..............................	214,711	
Fed. income tax witheld.......................	3,769	
Social security taxes payable...................	840	
Accruals......................................	25,016	
Reserves......................................	5,580	
Total Current Liabilities....................		$ 447,893

Fixed Liabilities:

Notes payable—bank..........................	$ 63,000	
Notes payable—others........................	401,937	
Accounts payable..............................	50,000	
Total Fixed Liabilities.....................		$ 514,937

Net Worth:

Capital stock	$200,000	
Surplus—November 1, 1957....................($65,635)		
November 1—June 30.................(11,123)	(76,758)	
Total Net Worth............................		123,242
Total Liabilities and Net Worth...........		$1,086,072

and the flocking installation would have a production life of at least ten years. The design of window hardware, however, was currently in a state of rapid technological change. For planning purposes Mr. Foster therefore thought it wise to assume that any new equipment purchased for specialized purposes should justify its existence in not more than two years of operations.

In assessing all the various cost savings possibilities that he was currently considering, Mr. Foster usually employed a figure of $4.50 an hour to reflect the total charge for labor cost, fringe benefits, and overhead. Actual overhead charges were currently averaging about 165 per cent of direct labor.

Although he had not discussed the matter directly with the subcontractors, Mr. Foster had been advised that both firms had some customers for whom they performed solely spring winding operations and others for whom they performed only spring flocking. Mr. Foster therefore believed that it was not necessary that he limit his choice either to undertaking both operations or neither of them. Instead, he believed that if his analysis suggested that it would be preferable to do so, his company would wind its own springs but continue to subcontract for the flocking operation, or vice versa.

The company's most recent balance sheet is shown in Exhibit 4.

Question

What action should Mr. Foster take?

CASE 19–10.   FAIRLANE COMPANY

Introduction

In July 1957, the treasurer of the Fairlane Company, Mr. Barton, described a problem that he faced in his accounting section.

In our billing department we have five machines that are 13 years old and fully depreciated. For the last five years the manufacturer has been unwilling to write a service contract on them, since it will write such contracts for a total of only eight years after machines are purchased new.

All things considered, the machines are still doing a reasonably good job for us. But less than two years ago we sent all five machines back to the manufacturing plant for what might be called a minor overhaul. This overhaul cost us $225 a machine. We have had a few little difficulties since then, and we have incurred service charges that are probably normal for machines of their age. That is, we ordinarily spend less than $50 a year for services and repairs to each machine. But last week a pin sheared way down in the middle of one of the machines, and it cost us $285 to get the machine back in operation. If these breakdowns continue, we shall probably be forced to pay increasingly high repair bills, and the machines will probably be out of working order more than they are now. Thus we shall probably get less work out of the department than we do now.

Our board of directors has asked me to make a recommendation as to what we should do about the machines, but I know that they will be reluctant to undertake any plan that will require a large outlay of cash.

Operations of Fairlane Company

Fairlane Company was the wholesale distributor for a company producing an exclusive line of hosiery, underwear, and knitwear. Fairlane also sold a limited number of apparel items under its own private label. The company was founded in the 1870's by Mark Harrington, who in two decades succeeded in making his company one of the country's largest apparel wholesalers. In the early 1900's he changed the organization of his business from a proprietorship to a corporation in which he held controlling interest. By 1957, members of his family owned a majority interest in the common stock of the corporation, with Mark Harrington's grandson, Steve, serving as president and chairman of the board of directors. In July 1957, the company conducted its business from a modern one-story warehouse and office building that contained over 100,000 square feet of floor space. Total employment exceeded 170 people, including salesmen.

The company sold men's, women's, and children's apparel to retail outlets in all 48 states. Sales of 15 product lines were made through 55 salesmen who were paid on a straight commission basis. The salesmen tended to specialize on a single line, such as hosiery, so that it was not uncommon for two or three of the company's salesmen to sell to the same large retail store, but through different store buyers. On the other hand, a salesman typically sold more than one product line.

It was not unusual for Fairlane's sales of a given product to any one store to vary in volume from one year to the next. However, an unusual decrease in a salesman's volume to a particular store usually suggested to management that it should investigate the salesman, his product lines, and the customer, to see what corrective action could be taken. Conversely, an unusual increase in the volume of sales to any store normally led management to study the situation, so that any resulting suggestions about how to improve sales could be passed on to the other salesmen.

"This company has been in the wholesale apparel business for many years," said Mr. Barton. "We are an 'independent' distributor and in common with most 'independents' have seen our sales volume and profits shrink during the last few years.[9] Our sales dropped from $9.0

---

[9] Fairlane was considered an independent because it produced none of the merchandise that it sold.

million in 1950 to $7.5 million in 1953. By 1955 our sales were down to $7.0 million. We hope we have finally been able to stabilize sales near the $7.0 million level."

Fairlane had been investing heavily in warehouse space, office space, and office equipment since World War II, with the result that the percentage of total assets represented by plant and equipment was well above what was considered normal for apparel wholesalers. Several of

Exhibit 1

FAIRLANE COMPANY

Comparative Balance Sheets, December 31

ASSETS		1956		1955
Current Assets:				
Cash...........................		$ 495,000		$ 570,000
Net receivables...................		825,000		740,000
Inventories......................		1,110,000		1,080,000
Total Current Assets........		$2,430,000		$2,390,000
Fixed Assets:				
Real estate, equipment............$920,000			$850,000	
Less depreciation................. 180,000			150,000	
Net property.....................		740,000		700,000
Other assets......................		15,000		15,000
Deferred charges..................		50,000		40,000
Total Assets................		$3,235,000		$3,145,000
LIABILITIES AND NET WORTH				
Current Liabilities:				
Accounts payable.................		$ 520,000		$ 560,000
Mortgage payable................		8,000		20,000
Dividends payable................		20,000		20,000
Taxes and accruals................		130,000		80,000
Total Current Liabilities........		$ 678,000		$ 680,000
Mortgage payable...................		182,000		150,000
Net Worth:				
Common stock....................		1,500,000		1,500,000
Retained Earnings................		875,000		815,000
Total Liabilities and Net Worth................		$3,235,000		$3,145,000

the board members contended that Fairlane should now try to "get by" on existing equipment, or with minimum equipment expenditures, until it could see what its sales future was likely to be. These board members suggested that management do as much as possible to maintain or improve the company's liquid position. (See Exhibit 1 for recent balance sheets of the company.)

In spite of this attitude on the part of a majority of the board, Mr. Barton believed that he could get the board to approve any reasonable program that offered significant operating savings or expanded services.

At the same time, his personal pride would suffer if he were forced to admit within the next two or three years that he had made a mistake, even though the board would probably accept some of the responsibility.

The Billing Department

The billing department was responsible for the accurate invoicing of customers' orders that had been filled and shipped. Five or six people worked in this department, using four billing machines and one duplex calculator, which in 1956 turned out 85,000 invoices, with the monthly volume ranging (as sales volume fluctuated) from a low of 6,000 invoices to a high of 9,600. Five workers were sufficient to handle the work load when the monthly volume was below 7,000 invoices. In those months in which volume exceeded 7,000 invoices, it was necessary to hire an additional employee on a part-time basis.

The work was described by Mr. Barton as monotonous. For example, the pricing clerk simply had to verify the accuracy of the prices written on the original order before releasing the order to one of the four billing clerks for invoicing.

A billing clerk prepared an invoice on the billing machine by typing the customer's name, address, and account number, along with shipping information and terms of sale, across the top of the invoice. The clerk then itemized the merchandise by product order number, style, and size, without a written description. The price per dozen was then entered, and the calculator section of the billing machine was used to calculate and print extensions, subtotals for each product line, and the total amount of the invoice. If the order was too long to permit inclusion of all the items on one page, the customer's name, address, account number, shipping information, and terms of sale had to be repeated on a second invoice page before the clerk could continue with the itemized listing. It was not uncommon for one invoice to contain more than one page, since some product lines contained many styles and sizes.

After the invoice had been prepared, a clerk auditor used a duplex calculator to verify the accuracy of the extensions, subtotals, and total selling price on the invoice. Each day this duplex calculator produced a tape showing the total amount of sales invoiced on that day. The original invoice was mailed to the customer, one copy was sent to the accounts receivable department with the original customer's order, and another copy was sent to the statistical department. Partly because of the age and limited capacity of the machinery in the billing department, that department nearly always took two or three days after the goods had been shipped before it could get invoices prepared and in the mail.

Consequently, the company received numerous complaints from customers who had received shipments but had no invoice from which to prepare inventory and pricing records. Mr. Barton had made a study of the operations of the billing department, and concluded that, with the equipment it had, the department was handling its work as expeditiously as could reasonably be expected.

The Statistical Department

The invoices prepared in the billing department were used by the statistical department to provide basic information for the sales management group, especially for purposes of market research and the computation of salesmen's commissions.

The statistical department in the summer of 1957 consisted of two full-time clerks, who occasionally borrowed the clerk from the accounts payable department to help out during periods of peak load. When the volume of invoices to be processed exceeded 7,000 a month, these clerks used three distributor machines in their work of preparing the daily and monthly reports for sales management. When the volume fell below 7,000 invoices a month, only the two regular clerks and two machines were used. When the girls received their copies of the sales invoices from the billing department, they sorted the invoices by salesmen. Since sales commissions varied from one product line to the next, it was necessary for the clerks to distribute the amount of the invoice among the several product lines. The machine printed a wide tape that showed the salesman's number, invoice numbers, and the total of his day's sales according to product line. At the end of a day's run the total amount of sales that had been distributed among the salesmen was compared with the tape prepared by the billing department covering the same batch of invoices, to make certain that the invoicing had been accurate.

Breakdowns of the dollar volume sold by each of the 55 salesmen, and in each of the 15 product lines they sold, were prepared daily by the statistical department. The department also calculated monthly sales summaries, for compilation of income statements and for the final determination of salesmen's commissions.

Although the distributor machines used in the statistical department were also 13 years old and had been fully depreciated, they continued to operate with only an occasional breakdown. These breakdowns were relatively expensive when they did occur, however, because of the complexity of the machines. Mr. Barton estimated that Fairlane spent a total of about $900 annually in repairing the three distributor machines.

The Semiannual Report

Every six months Fairlane arranged for the preparation of reports that showed for each salesman just how much each of his customers bought of each product line during the preceding six months. Sales figures for the comparable period in the preceding year were also provided in the same report. Mr. Barton thought that this semiannual report was quite important, because from it the sales management could spot significant changes in sales patterns and attempt to find out why the change took place. Mr. Barton stated that, since this industry was so competitive, he thought that the information contained in the semi-annual report should be summarized even more often, perhaps every three months.

In preparation for the semiannual reports, the company had, prior to 1955, employed in the statistical department two girls who worked full time posting product line sales from the invoices to customers' cards in a Kardex file. These customers' cards provided spaces to show how the total amount invoiced was divided among the various product categories. If the customer was one of those called on by several salesmen, a separate card was included for each salesman. Then every six months the two girls went through the complete file, which contained several thousand cards, to summarize sales for the preceding six-month period. The report prepared from this summary showed for the preceding six months:

1. The customers' purchases in total.
2. The customers' total purchases for each of the 15 product lines.
3. Salesmen's total sales by customer.
4. Salesmen's total sales of each of the 15 product lines by customer.

(As noted above, sales from the preceding year's report were included in the new report to provide a basis for comparison of sales efforts.)

Prior to 1955, a semiannual report covering the first six months of the calendar year had almost never been ready for management's study before November of the same year. In 1955 Mr. Barton made an arrangement with a local service bureau to provide the same report at a cost of from $2,000 to $3,000 a year, depending on the number of invoices to be processed. Under this arrangement, the statistical department simply accumulated all the invoices that it received during each six-month period, and at the end of the period it sent the accumulated invoices to the service bureau, which processed them quickly with special equipment, and returned both the invoices and the finished report to

Fairlane. This arrangement worked so well that the report covering the first six months of 1957 was ready for company use by July 15.

Replacement Equipment Available for the Billing Department

Mr. Barton had talked with several business machine manufacturers and their salesmen. He had also visited other companies with new equipment installations, in an effort to see what system would be most suitable for Fairlane. He found that Fairlane could replace the four billing machines and the one duplex calculator with three new billing machines and one duplex calculator from the same manufacturer that had built the machines being used at present. These four new machines together would cost $11,700 and could be delivered in 30 days. Only four new machines would be needed, and they would require only four operators, one of whom would assume supervisory responsibility, since the new machines would operate at higher speeds than the ones being used at present. The manufacturer would provide free installation and free service for the first 12 months, and would make a total service charge of $550 a year for the succeeding seven years. For federal income tax purposes these machines could be depreciated over an eight-year period, with no scrap value remaining at that time. Labor costs in the billing department, which at present totaled $20,000, would be lower with the new machines; they would total $15,000 annually for the four regular employees who would be needed.

Mr. Barton believed that these machines would enable the department to handle, without additional personnel, up to 9,600 invoices a month. He also believed that, with their greater speed, these machines might enable the billing department more effectively to keep abreast of the flow of invoices that resulted from sales.

Replacement Equipment Available for the Statistical Department

If the three distributor machines in the statistical department were replaced with newer model distributor machines, two new machines, which could do the work currently being done by the three older and slower machines, would cost $22,000 and for tax purposes could be written off over the next eight years. These distributor machines were not built by the same company that produced the billing machines, but the same free installation and approximately the same service arrangements were offered as for the billing machines. Thirty-day delivery was promised, with free service for the first year, and a service contract for the following seven years was available. This service contract would cover both machines and would cost $750 a year. Total payroll costs in the statistical department were currently about $9,000 a year. These costs would probably be cut to $8,000 a year if the new model machines were purchased, since part-time assistance from the accounts payable clerk would no longer be necessary.

Even with new equipment in the statistical department, Fairlane would still need to send its invoices to the service bureau, in order to be able to expect the semiannual report approximately 15 days after the termination of any six-month period.

Data-Processing Equipment Available

Mr. Barton had in the past been reluctant to investigate the possibilities of using a punched-card data-processing system, even though salesmen from two companies that offered punched-card systems had called on him several times over a period of years. However, he had recently seen a fairly complex data-processing installation being used for control purposes in a wholesale auto parts company with annual sales of only $2.5 million. That experience led him to consider seriously whether Fairlane could make use of such a system. Accordingly, he had conducted an inquiry into the possibilities that would be offered by the installation of such equipment. After discussing the matter with salesmen representing a number of producers, he concentrated his attention on the proposal of the manufacturer who offered the most attractive terms.

Mr. Barton found that this manufacturer would sell him the basic installation outright for $76,000. The equipment could be depreciated for tax purposes over an eight-year period. The same equipment could be leased for a minimum of eight years, at a rental of $1,200 a month. At the end of the eight-year period, the rental contract could be renewed for successive additional periods of four years each, but Mr. Barton considered it possible that the rent might be increased in any renewal of the contract. Under either the purchase or the rental plan, the seller would install the equipment free of charge; he would make no charge for servicing purchased equipment for eight years, and he would service the equipment without charge for the entire period during which a rental agreement was in force. In addition, he would without charge train Fairlane employees to use the equipment.

Mr. Barton discovered that, once installation had started, it might take two months to get all the components into place and operating correctly. There would, however, be no need to stop or slow down present bookkeeping and statistical operations while the machinery was being installed.

It was estimated by Mr. Barton that the data-processing system would require no more than four trained people in all, a working supervisor and three clerks, whose total wage cost would amount to about $17,000 a year. This system, with the four operators, could do in less than two hours all the daily work currently being performed by both the billing and the statistical departments. The remaining working time of each of these four employees could be utilized on other work currently being performed by other employees. The system would also replace the one girl and machine that made up the accounts payable department. The total annual savings on the portion of her salary charged to accounts payable, and on maintenance of the machine that she operated, would approximate $3,000. The machine currently being used in the accounts payable department had been fully depreciated, but it was operating satisfactorily and was incurring no more annual maintenance costs than the billing machines.

The basic installation of the data-processing system included the absolute minimum number of components required to make the system effective. Even if Fairlane's sales volume were to be cut to 20 per cent of the 1956 volume, all this equipment would still be required; whereas it would be possible with present machinery and operations to reduce both the amount of equipment in use and the number of employees, as sales volume declined.

According to Mr. Barton, the data-processing system could provide management with the reports currently being prepared by the service bureau by the next day after the closing date of the period under study. Another advantage of the system was the ease with which Fairlane could use it to install a perpetual inventory control at a later date; only one component would need to be added.

Mr. Barton knew that the system would be fast and flexible, and that it would be capable of providing management with a substantial amount of information in a fairly short time. He recognized, however, that with the rapid growth of knowledge about data-processing techniques, the rate of technical obsolescence on equipment was quite high. More efficient machines and installations were continually being designed and marketed. He did not know how significant for Fairlane the risk of obsolescence on such equipment would be. Mr. Barton believed that, whether he rented or purchased the data-processing equipment, installation could not start until November 1958. He knew, however, that if he decided in July 1957 to order the equipment, he would have to sign a firm rental or purchase agreement to accept installation as soon as the manufacturer was in a position to install it.

Mr. Barton believed that the depreciated equipment that Fairlane was now using probably could not be resold, and that its scrap value was minimal. He realized that, if Fairlane was to install any new equipment, the company would in effect eliminate the jobs of one or more employees of long standing, but that it might be able to create positions for them elsewhere in the company.

Question

As Mr. Barton, what recommendation would you make to the board of directors?

ADVANCED CONCEPTS
AND TECHNIQUES

MANAGEMENT accounting is a large subject, and there is much more to it than the material given in this book. Also, it is a rapidly evolving subject; a great many new concepts and techniques are being developed and applied. In this chapter, we describe some aspects of the subject that we omitted or touched on only briefly in the preceding chapters, and speculate on developments that seem likely to occur in the near future. Our purpose is not to make the reader familiar with these topics, but merely to indicate what they are, in the hope that this will help him in planning further study in the field.

Management accounting is used in connection with the management functions of planning and control. We shall organize this chapter according to the principal processes into which these functions may be divided, namely, (1) strategic planning, (2) management control, (3) operational control, and (4) information handling.

STRATEGIC PLANNING

Strategic planning is the process of deciding on the changes in the objectives of the organization, in the resources that the business is to use in attaining these objectives, and in the policies that are to govern the acquisition and use of these resources. The word "strategy" is used here in its usual sense of combining and employing resources. Thus, strategic planning is a process having to do with the formulation of long-range, strategic, policy-type plans that change the character or direction of the organization. In an industrial company this includes planning that affects the objectives of the company; policies of all types (including policies as to management control and other processes); the acquisition and disposition of major facilities, divisions, or subsidiaries; the markets to be served and distribution channels for serving them; the organization structure (as distinguished from individual personnel actions); research and development of new product lines (as distinguished from modifications in existing products and product changes within existing lines); sources of new permanent capital; dividend policy; and so on. Strategic planning decisions affect the physical, financial, and organizational framework whithin which the firm operates.

The discussion of the cost constructions useful in decision making in Chapter 18 and the techniques for analyzing proposed investments in Chapter 19 are relevant to the strategic planning process. There is a large body of literature on the subject matter of both these chapters. Much of it is classified in the field called microeconomics, or economics of the firm. In particular, techniques for analyzing proposed investments have been improved considerably in recent years and although Chapter 19 gives the main outlines of the principal approaches, many of the ramifications and several variations of these approaches were omitted. For example, a whole book, *Leasing of Industrial Equipment*[1] has been written on a topic mentioned only briefly in Chapter 19.

Two other topics will be mentioned here, probability theory and mathematical models. These are relevant both to strategic planning and to the other processes.

Probability Theory

All the figures used in making business plans and business decisions are estimates of what will happen in the future. In discussing the techniques of planning, we have assumed that these estimates were "single valued," that is, that each of them was a single number representing someone's best guess as to the future situation. Some companies are experimenting with extimates made in the form of probability distributions. For example, instead of stating, "I think sales of Item X will be $100,000 next year," the estimator states a range of possibilities, together with his estimate of the probability that each will occur. The sum of these separate possibilities, weighted by the probability that each will occur, is called the *expected value* of the probability distribution. It is computed as in the following example:

Possible Sales (a)	Estimated Probability (b)	Weighted Amount (a × b)
$ 60,000	0.1	$ 6,000
80,000	0.1	8,000
100,000	0.4	40,000
120,000	0.2	24,000
140,000	0.2	28,000
	Expected Value....$106,000	

[1] Richard F. Vancil, *Leasing of Industrial Equipment* (New York: McGraw-Hill Book Co., Inc., 1963).

The probability, 0.1, means that there is one chance in ten that sales will be about $60,000. The sum of the probabilities always adds to 1.0.

Businessmen do not find it easy to state their estimates in the form of probability distributions; but if they can do so, the usefulness of the estimates can be greatly increased. For one thing, probability distributions tend to fall into a limited number of patterns. Many of them, for example, are the familiar "normal," or bell-shaped, curves. These patterns are described by mathematical equations, and important characteristics of the distributions may be inferred from them. Historical data can often be fitted into the same patterns, and used more powerfully than hitherto to improve the accuracy of the estimates.

Growing out of probability theory is the *theory of sampling.* Sampling theory has been used in market research and statistical quality control for years, and is currently being extended to other areas. Application of the theory of sampling makes it possible either to state the limits within which the results of a sample of a specified size are probably correct or to tell whether the results observed from a sample are significantly different from some given norm, standard, or other sample. Sampling theory is therefore beginning to be used in auditing to determine, for example, how many accounts receivable records the auditor should verify in order to conclude that the accounts receivable amount is probably reasonably correct. Since the actual cost incurred for an item in a period can be considered as one sample result out of all the possible cost amounts that might have been incurred, sampling theory is also being considered as a means of deciding whether or not the difference between actual costs and standard or budgeted costs is significant.

The most important developments in the application of probability theory to business problems have occurred since the late 1940's. Although much of the work is currently at the experimental level, there is a strong likelihood that it will have great practical significance and that its use will grow rapidly.

Mathematical Models

A mathematical model is a set of equations or other expressions that states what are believed to be the significant factors in a situation and the relationships among them. A balance sheet is a mathematical model, with the relationships among the balance sheet items being governed by the principles of financial accounting. A budget is also a model, and probably a more useful one than a balance sheet. A profitgraph is a model, and so is the equation that states the relationship between investment and the present value of earnings in a capital budgeting problem. Thus, the basic idea of the model is not new.

The preceding examples illustrate two types of models, those for a whole business (the balance sheet and the budget) and those for some specific problem or facet of the business (the profitgraph and the capital budgeting model). The former type is especially significant in strategic planning.

Overall Models. In the budget, individual revenue and expense items are combined by the arithmetic operations of addition and subtraction to give anticipated net income. The newer models attempt to describe or simulate the basic forces at work in the business (or, rather, as many as can be reduced to quantitative terms) and the interrelationships among them in much more elaborate manner. For example, whereas the variable budget may state that a $10,000 increase in sales will result in a $4,000 increase in labor costs, the more sophisticated model may relate labor costs not solely to sales volume but also to the desired level of inventory, the cost of hiring and training an additional worker, other costs associated with changing the level of produccion, and so on. Furthermore, the model may take into account the delay, or lag, that occurs between the receipt of a sales order and the actual incurrence of labor costs to fill the order.

As these models become more accurate simulations of the real situation, it becomes possible to use them to try out proposed policies and see the effect of these policies on the balance sheet and income statement; thus models will become increasingly useful in the strategic planning process. If the proposal is not sound, it is obviously much better to find this out by making some mathematical calculations rather than from actual experience. This type of model serves the same function as a pilot plant; it permits inexpensive experimentation with various proposals so that mistakes in full-scale operation can be avoided. Since a single experiment often involves many millions of separate calculations, these models require the use of a computer.

A model is necessarily a simplification of the real situation because the real situation is too complex to be handled on even the largest computers, but if it is *over*simplified, it is useless. Very few companies have, up to the present, devised a model of their overall situation that is both sufficiently simple to be manipulated and also sufficiently realistic so that they trust it as an aid for making decisions. Many companies are working on this problem however.

Model building will become increasingly important to business. As Dr. Oskar Morgenstern has said: "The penetration of mathematics into new fields has, without exception, brought about profound changes. Whenever mathematics has entered, it has never again been pushed out by other developments."

MANAGEMENT CONTROL

Social Psychology

Although in the section on management control we discussed a number of techniques for collecting and analyzing costs, we tried to emphasize the point that the central ideas of management control are psychological. The purpose of a management control system is to motivate managers to take actions that are in the best interests of the company. Thus, management control is related to the field of social psychology.

Until recently, research that could lead to formulation of principles about the way men can work together effectively in business organizations has been practically nonexistent. Psychologists and other social scientists have confined their experiments largely to animals, and although they wrote extensively on how businesses should be organized and controlled, they had little clinical or experimental evidence to support their conclusions. Much of this writing was based on the now discredited image of the "economic man," a person who always acts intelligently and rationally. Businessmen have quite properly paid little attention to theories based on this assumption and have continued to rely on intuition and common sense. It should be emphasized again that the principles stated in Chapter 13 are not supported by experimental evidence and are therefore extremely tentative.

Experiments that involve people working in a business are difficult, for they must be conducted with full regard for the rights of individuals, and they must not disrupt the functioning of the organization. Despite these difficulties, in recent years some useful work has been done. Attention was focused initially on the individual worker: on methods of selecting the right man for the job, on factors that contribute to worker productivity, and so on. Research on the problems of supervision, among which is the management control problem, is relatively new. Such research will probably increase and become more effective as time goes on.

Related Disciplines

Cybernetics is a new and only vaguely defined discipline dealing with control processes wherever they are found, ranging from the single cell through the individual animal, the group, and organizations such as businesses, to whole societies. Similarities in control in these different environments have been found, and these provide a basis for thinking about the problem of control in a business.

Information theory is also a new discipline, so closely related to cybernetics, that the two may merge. It seeks general principles of communication that are applicable to such apparently different activities as the communication of information within a business and the propagation of a voice along a telephone wire.

Profit Centers and Investment Centers

The role of profit centers and investment centers in management control was described briefly in Chapter 13, but most of the problems involved in these concepts are beyond the scope of this introductory book. There are three fundamental questions: (1) Under what circumstances should a given responsibility center be made into a profit center or investment center, rather than an expense center; that is, when should we attempt to measure profit or return on investment, rather than simply expenses? (2) What principles should govern the setting of the transfer prices that are used to measure intracompany transactions? (3) How should the investment base, or "assets employed," in an investment center be measured? At present, there is no general agreement on answers to any of these questions, and they are interesting subjects for research and discussion.

New Planning Devices

In Chapter 14 the budget was described as the principal tool for making and coordinating plans for future operations. Recently, other techniques have come to be used as an aid to planning in certain types of activities, principally those in which operations are complex and non-repetitive and in which activities are interdependent; that is, where one activity cannot start until another has been completed. These techniques are known by such names as PERT, PERT/COST, Line of Balance, and Critical Path methods.

Essentially, the procedure is as follows: (1) the total job to be done is broken down into a number of small pieces (called "events" or "milestones"); (2) the activities required to accomplish each such event is identified; (3) the time, and sometimes the cost, of each activity is estimated; (4) a network is constructed, showing the relationship between activities and events, and this network is analyzed to find which of the activities are critical in determining the total time that the whole job will require. The network can be used to study more efficient ways of scheduling the activities, thus resulting in a better plan, and it also can be used to control the progress of work.

Although used originally for such extraordinarily complex activities as the development of a new weapons system or the construction of a ship, the techniques are being used increasingly in similar, but less gigantic, activities.

Cost Accounting

Only the elements of cost accounting were discussed in Chapter 15. There is much more to the subject than given there, as indicated by the fact that the *Accountants' Cost Handbook*[2] contains 940 pages.

OPERATIONAL CONTROL

Operational control is the process that is related to specific tasks or operations, as contrasted with management control, which is related to broader types of activities. Inventory control and production scheduling and control are examples of operational control techniques. In recent years, developments in this area have been great.

Operations Research

A relatively new discipline, operations research, is concerned with the development of new techniques, or the improvement of old techniques, for operational control. Operations research is also concerned with the strategic planning process. The technique for deciding on the optimum amount of material or products to order, called economic order quantity (see Chapter 18), is an example of an old technique that has been made more powerful by the addition of better rules for determining the relevant costs and for estimating the rate at which inventory will be used up.

The operations researcher develops mathematical models. Not all his models have proved to be useful, however, and the person interested in practical applications has the difficult task of deciding which of the new techniques are useful and which are not. To illustrate the difficulty, let us consider *linear programing* and the *theory of games,* both of which were first talked about in the early 1950's.

Linear programing is a type of model that was first used for what is known as the "transportation problem." A company has orders from customers in various cities, which it fills from a number of warehouses, each of which contains a specified quantity of merchandise; there is a

---

[2] Robert I. Dickey, *Accountants' Cost Handbook* (New York: The Ronald Press Co., 1960).

known transportation cost for shipments from any warehouse to any customer. Use of the linear programing technique makes it possible to find which warehouses should be used to fill each customer's order so as to minimize total transportation cost, and it demonstrates that the best solution is *not* in all cases to ship from the warehouse nearest the customer.

It was quickly found that this same technique could be used to determine the best way of scheduling production orders through a factory when there was a choice as to which part should be made on which machine, or to determine the optimum mix of petroleum products that should be made in a refinery, and for a number of other apparently dissimilar problems. Thus linear programing is finding wide acceptance for use in several types of problems that previously were thought to have nothing in common, and its use is being constantly extended. The equations are long but relatively simple, the most complicated mathematical operation involved in them being multiplication. The trick is to fit the facts of a particular situation into the equations, a task that depends on common sense and a knowledge of the business rather than on advanced mathematical ability.

The theory of games has had quite a different development. This theory attempts to state the best strategy for one to follow in competing with someone else. Thus, it might be thought to have wide application in planning marketing strategy. As is the case with linear programing, several books and hundreds of articles have been written about it. By contrast with linear programing, however, there have been only a few practical applications of the theory of games to business problems.

As new techniques are developed, there is a tendency for more and more activities to become susceptible to operational control techniques. In the factory, the production schedule that was formerly set according to the foreman's intuition is now derived by linear programing. And although not very long ago it was believed that operational control techniques were appropriate only for factory operations, we now see models and formulas being used for certain marketing decisions, such as planning salesmen's calls and planning direct mail advertising. This tendency probably will continue; it is a large part of what people have in mind when they say, "Management is becoming increasingly scientific."

INFORMATION HANDLING

Information handling is the process of collecting, manipulating, and transmitting information, whatever its use is to be. In this book we have said little about this important subject, other than to give some brief descriptions in Chapter 4 of the techniques used to collect and summarize accounting data. There is a large body of knowledge that we have not touched on, ranging from the proper arrangement of blank spaces on a form, through techniques for insuring accuracy and minimizing the possibility of theft and fraud (called internal auditing and internal control), and including the use of various types of equipment. Of these, the development of automatic data-processing equipment has had the greatest impact on management accounting.

Automatic Data Processing

Although less than 25 years have elapsed since the first electronic computer began operation, and despite a number of mistakes and misuses at the beginning, enough is now known about the capabilities of computers so that there can be no question of their importance to business management. Their uses can be divided into two categories: the "data-processing" uses and the "decision-making" uses.

For data processing, computers permit information to be processed at less cost, with greater accuracy, and with greater speed. They also facilitate rearrangement of data in various ways, and thus help to solve the problem of recording data in a form that permits their use for different purposes. More data will become available to management as a consequence of these developments, but whether this result means more of the *right kind* of data depends on the system designers. Unless they understand management's needs, vast quantities of useless information will be spewed out.

With respect to decision making, the fact that computers can be programed to perform a long sequence of operations rapidly, inexpensively, and without human intervention, means that it is now feasible to use quantitative techniques for many types of problems for which their use has not hitherto been practical; and the fact that the computer can be programed to make choices means that machines can now make certain types of decisions formerly made by humans. For example, the computer can be programed to decide when a purchase order should be placed to replenish a routine item carried in inventory, the quantity that should be ordered, and the date when the new stock should arrive; and it can even write the purchase order without human intervention, although humans are necessary to supervise the operation and to make certain that the transaction is actually "routine." The computer can do this job better than people can do it, "better" in the sense that if its program truly expresses what management wants done, the computer will carry out these intentions more accurately and more consistently than the humans normally employed for these routine operations.

Fortunately for us humans, the computer is limited to repetitious tasks that can be specifically described. It cannot consider the un-measured factors that are crucial in many decisions, and the development of a computer program is economically justified only if the same data-processing operation is repeated a large number of times.

Partly as a consequence of the development of computers, the concept of management accounting becomes increasingly broad. As several of the cases in this book indicate, it already includes various types of nonmonetary data. Efforts are also under way to combine cost accounting, inventory control, production control, payroll, and other separate, duplicating, and sometimes conflicting systems into a single *integrated data-processing* system.

The person interested in management accounting must learn what automatic computers can do and continue to keep abreast of new uses as they come along. He does not need to know much about *how* they operate, any more than he needs to know how a television set operates in order to use it.

CONCLUSION

There is much more to be learned about management accounting than is described in this book. In part, it can be learned by further study, but only in part, for as is the case with most subjects, there is no adequate substitute for actual experience.

In addition to experience with things as they are now, the mana-ger must also be alert to promising new techniques and concepts. The person who understands these new developments will have an advantage over a person who does not, assuming they both have good judgment and common sense. Thus, the successful person will keep alert for those developments that are likely to have practical significance, attempting to extract these from the undigested mass of untried theories. A good maxim is this: "Be not the first by whom the new is tried, nor yet the last to cast the old aside," especially when this is coupled with G. K. Chesterton's advice: "Let us look to the future, for that is where we are going to spend our lives."

REVIEW CASES

CASE 21–1. C. F. CHURCH MANUFACTURING COMPANY

The C. F. Church Manufacturing Company was established in 1898 for the purpose of manufacturing toilet seats. The executives had devoted considerable effort to the development of a quality product, to widespread advertising of the product, and to the realization of economical manufacturing methods.

The manufacturing processes were quite simple. First, the seats were shaped out of wood at a branch plant. They were then shipped to the main plant, where they underwent the particular finishing processes required. Some units were sprayed with paint, but the best seats were coated with cellulose nitrate sheeting. After the seats were coated, the rough edges were filed and the seats were sanded, buffed, and polished. Finally, hinges and rubber bumpers were added, and the seats were packed for shipment. Most operations were performed by hand with the aid of small machines, such as paint spray guns and buffing wheels.

1. Accounting

Collection of Material and Labor Cost

A major part of the work required in the cost system was the orderly accumulation of data on actual and standard costs. The procedure in regard to materials used was as follows. When an order for a particular style of finish was started through the factory, the foreman of the department that performed the first operation received a manufacturing order (Exhibit 1). On the basis of this order, the foreman filled out a stores requisition slip (Exhibit 2) for the materials necessary to manufacture this order. Items listed on this requisition subsequently were priced, and their purchase cost was entered on the requisition by the cost department on a last-in, first-out basis. (Inasmuch as raw material was purchased infrequently in large contract lots, this procedure was not difficult.) When seats were ready to be assembled and packed, the foreman in the assembly department made out an assembly order (Exhibit 3), which

Exhibit 1

```
MANUFACTURING ORDER
STANDARD SHEET COVERED PRODUCTION
```

DATE August

QUANTITY	PLATE NO.	
	SEAT	COVER
100	2000	2000

HINGE	COLOR
2000	917

SPECIAL INSTRUCTIONS

W 2068   **ASSEMBLE-PACK**

TIME ALLOWED   **DAYS**

MOVED - DATE	A.M.	P.M.

DELAY REPORT NO.   BY

W 2068   **SAND**

TIME ALLOWED   **DAYS**

MOVED - DATE	A.M.	P.M.

DELAY REPORT NO.   BY

W 2068   **TOP-COAT**

TIME ALLOWED   **DAYS**

MOVED - DATE	A.M.	P.M.

DELAY REPORT NO.   BY

W 2068   **BOTTOM COAT-TRIM**

TIME ALLOWED   **DAYS**

MOVED - DATE	A.M.	P.M.

DELAY REPORT NO.   BY

START

Exhibit 2

GEN 8 STORES REQUISITION		Date August	No. 2068		
QUANTITY ORDERED	UNIT OR PART NUMBER	DESCRIPTION		UNIT COST	AMOUNT
100	580	Color 917			
100	520	" "			
100	570	" "			
100	51	" "			
CHARGE TO Work in Process		ISSUED BY	APPROVED	DELIVERED BY	

Exhibit 3

ASSEMBLY ORDER No. 6291
Coated

Date __August__ Plate No. __2000__

Shipping Order No. _____

Work Order No. _____ Quantity __100__

Seats 2,000 - 917

Covers 2,000 - 917

Hinges 2,000

Special Instructions

FOR COST DEPT. ONLY	UNIT COST		AMOUNT	
Material	5	51	551	00
Labor		92	92	00
Burden	1	90	190	00
Total Cost	8	33	833	00

REQUISITION No. 6291
Hinges – Screws – Bumpers

Date __August__

DESCRIPTION	QUANTITY
Hinges 2,000	100
Screws 3/4 x 7	
Screws 5/8 x 7	
1 1/4 x 8	400
Brass Ferrules	200
Bar Bumpers	200
Tack Bumpers	200

Delivered by

	UNIT COST	AMOUNT
Hinges		
Screws		
Screws		
Ferrules		
Bar Bumpers		
Tack Bumpers		

REQUISITION No. 6291
Cartons – Fillers

Date __August__

DESCRIPTION	QUANTITY
Cartons 25	100
Fillers	200
800	100
214	
105	
Blocks	

Delivered by

	UNIT COST	AMOUNT
Cartons		
Filler No. 1		
No. 105		
No. 800		
No. 214		
Blocks		

included a requisition for hinges, screws, bumpers, cartons, and fillers. These issues of materials were also costed at "last-in, first-out." The totals of the requisition slips for the month served as the basis for credits to the respective materials inventory accounts and a debit to the Work in Process account for the cost of material put into process.

The direct labor debit to Work in Process was equally straight-forward. Daily, each productive employee made out a time and production report (Exhibit 4) on which he recorded the factory order number,

Exhibit 4

FORM C-STR 7918		C. F. CHURCH MFG. CO.							
		Time and Production					Date August —		
Employee No. 3/3		Name							
Order No.	Oper. No.	TIME			Labor or Piece Rate	No. Pieces	Cost		✓
		Started	Finished	Elapsed					
2068	31	7:20	12:00	4.8	2.30	350	8	05	
2068	31	1:00	4:20	3.4	2.30	250	5	75	
							13	80	

the operation, the time spent on each operation, and the number of pieces that he had finished. A clerk in the payroll department entered the correct piece rate or hourly rate and made the proper extension. The total of the direct labor thus computed provided the credit to the Accrued Wages account and the debit (for direct labor) to Work in Process.

Standard Burden Schedule (Annual)

The debit to Work in Process for manufacturing expense was based on annual estimates of the relation of burden expenses to direct labor costs for each department. These annual estimates were made so that for each department there was available a schedule of standard burden expenses at varying possible rates of capacity utilization. Exhibit 5 illustrates such a schedule for the coating department, Department No. 3.

Exhibit 5

BURDEN DEVELOPMENT, DEPARTMENT NO. 3

	100%	95%	90%	85%	80%	75%	70%	65%	60%	50%	40%
Indirect Labor:											
01 Supervision	775.00	775.00	775.00	775.00	775.00	775.00	775.00	775.00	775.00	775.00	775.00
08 General labor	625.00	595.00	565.00	530.00	500.00	470.00	440.00	405.00	375.00	315.00	250.00
10 Idle and lost time											
11 Guaranteed rate cost	375.00	356.00	338.00	319.00	300.00	281.00	263.00	244.00	225.00	188.00	150.00
16 Overtime bonus	100.00	100.00	95.00	90.00	85.00	85.00	80.00	75.00	50.00	25.00	25.00
19 Repairs and maint.—M and E	175.00	175.00	165.00	165.00	160.00	160.00	160.00	150.00	150.00	100.00	100.00
Total Indirect Labor	2,050.00	2,001.00	1,938.00	1,879.00	1,820.00	1,771.00	1,718.00	1,649.00	1,575.00	1,403.00	1,300.00
Indirect Supplies:											
31 Repairs and maint.—M and E	25.00	25.00	25.00	20.00	20.00	20.00	20.00	20.00	15.00	15.00	10.00
35 Acetone and isotone	1,625.00	1,545.00	1,465.00	1,380.00	1,300.00	1,220.00	1,140.00	1,055.00	975.00	815.00	650.00
37 Sandpaper and sandbelts	11.00	10.00	10.00	9.00	9.00	8.00	8.00	7.00	7.00	5.00	4.00
38 Glue and cement	775.00	736.00	700.00	660.00	620.00	580.00	540.00	500.00	465.00	385.00	310.00
41 Consumable supplies	125.00	120.00	112.00	106.00	100.00	94.00	88.00	81.00	75.00	63.00	50.00
42 Loose and hand tools	50.00	48.00	46.00	43.00	40.00	38.00	35.00	33.00	30.00	25.00	20.00
46 Miscellaneous	15.00	14.00	14.00	13.00	12.00	11.00	10.00	9.00	9.00	7.00	6.00
Total Indirect Supplies	2,626.00	2,498.00	2,371.00	2,231.00	2,101.00	1,971.00	1,841.00	1,705.00	1,576.00	1,315.00	1,050.00
Fixed Charges:											
65 Insurance—bldgs. and equip.	21.58	21.58	21.58	21.58	21.58	21.58	21.58	21.58	21.58	21.58	21.58
66 Insurance—L. and C.	161.00	152.00	145.00	137.00	128.70	121.00	113.00	105.00	97.00	80.00	64.00
68 Power	27.00	26.00	24.00	23.00	21.60	21.00	19.00	18.00	16.00	14.00	11.00
69 Water	17.25	17.25	17.25	17.25	17.25	17.25	17.25	17.25	17.25	17.25	17.25
70 Taxes—city and town	28.68	28.68	28.68	28.68	28.68	28.68	28.68	28.68	28.68	28.68	28.68

71 Taxes—social security	530.00	504.00	477.00	450.00	424.27	398.00	371.00	345.00	318.00	265.00	212.00
72 Depreciation	81.25	81.25	81.25	81.25	81.25	81.25	81.25	81.25	81.25	81.25	81.25
73 Provision for vacations	725.40	725.40	725.40	725.40	725.40	725.40	725.40	725.40	725.40	725.40	725.40
78 Group insurance	112.70	112.70	112.70	112.70	112.70	112.70	112.70	112.70	112.70	112.70	112.70
80 Pensions	420.36	420.36	420.36	420.36	420.36	420.36	420.36	420.36	420.36	420.36	420.36
Total Fixed Charges	2,125.22	2,089.22	2,053.22	2,017.22	1,981.79	1,947.22	1,910.22	1,875.22	1,838.22	1,766.22	1,694.22
Total Direct Expense	6,801.22	6,588.22	6,362.22	6,127.22	5,902.79	5,689.22	5,469.22	5,229.22	4,989.22	4,484.22	4,044.22
Charges from other depts	9,435.37	9,333.33	9,240.12	9,140.56	9,032.28	8,945.27	8,826.90	8,751.83	8,630.42	8,440.11	8,235.38
Total Expense	16,236.59	15,921.55	15,602.34	15,267.78	14,935.07	14,634.49	14,296.12	13,981.05	13,619.64	12,924.33	12,279.60
Direct labor dollars	9,375.00	8,906.00	8,437.00	7,969.00	7,500.00	7,031.00	6,562.00	6,094.00	5,625.00	4,687.00	3,750.00
Burden rate	173%	179%	185%	191%	200%	208%	218%	229%	242%	276%	327%

The process used to prepare the standard burden schedules was as follows:

1. Determine 100 per cent capacity of each department in terms of direct labor hours and direct labor dollars by theoretically loading each unit of productive machinery and equipment with the number of men required to operate it, together with the necessary productive employees on floor or bench work. Consider, however, the normal sales volume of different types of products and limitations as to type of equipment in any one department that affect the capacity of the plant as a whole. For example, output might be limited to the capacity of the coating and spraying departments.

2. Establish burden expense allowances for each department, considering four general classifications: indirect labor, indirect supplies, fixed charges, and charges from nonproductive departments.

3. Base allowance for indirect labor and indirect supplies on the past year's experience, making adjustments if necessary for changes in wage rates and the prices of supplies. Compute these projections first for the 100 per cent capacity determined above, and from this point use a sliding or graduated scale for the lower percentages of capacity. Give due recognition to the fact that some of these costs do not vary at all with production, that others vary in the same ratio as production, and that others, although variable, do not move proportionately with the rate of actual plant activity.

4. Prorate power expense according to the number of horsepower hours used and metered in the respective departments; water expense (after consideration is given to any special demands for water in particular departments such as steam) according to the number of employees; insurance, taxes, and depreciation with reference to the net book value of buildings and equipment. Charge directly to the department involved specific insurance that definitely can be allocated to an individual department, such as automobile insurance on trucks in the shipping department or boiler indemnity for the steam department.

5. Distribute the total expense of nonproductive departments such as steam, general plant, shipping, and plant administration to the productive departments on the most logical basis: steam according to floor area, general plant and plant administration according to direct labor hours, and shipping according to direct labor dollars. The estimated cost of defective work for the whole plant was distributed to operating departments on the basis of the expected distribution of direct labor dollars. This item of expense was included in the total of "Charges from other departments," shown at the bottom of Exhibit 5.

6. Revise the standard burden schedules only for a general increase or decrease in wage rates or material costs or an important change in the manufacturing processes.

Standard Burden Rate

After the burden expense schedule was prepared, executives estimated the percentage of capacity utilization expected during the coming year. The standard burden rate was the rate shown on Exhibit 5 for the estimated percentage of capacity. For example, it was estimated that during the year the coating department would operate at an average of 80 per cent of capacity. The standard burden rate for the coating department was therefore 200 per cent of direct labor, as shown at the bottom of the 80 per cent column in Exhibit 5. The other columns in Exhibit 5 were used for control purposes, as described subsequently.

Actual Burden Costs (Monthly)

Actual burden costs incurred during the month were charged to the Burden account in the general ledger and to an appropriate detail account in a burden subsidiary ledger. There was a detail account for each item listed on Exhibit 5 (supervision, general labor, etc.) in each department. Service department and other overhead costs were allocated to the producing departments. At the end of the month, the amount of "absorbed burden" was calculated by multiplying the burden rate for each department by the actual direct labor cost of the department for the month. In the coating department, for example, the actual direct labor for August was $5,915.60, and this multiplied by 200 per cent gave $11,831.20, the absorbed burden. (Note that the rate used was the burden rate determined annually, *not* the burden rate under the column in Exhibit 5 that relates to the actual volume of the current month.)

The absorbed burden for all departments was debited to Work in Process and credited to the Burden account. Any balance remaining in the Burden account was then closed to Loss and Gain. In August, for example, actual burden was $45,914.98, absorbed burden was $45,-904.44, so $10.54 was debited to Loss and Gain.

Standard Product Costs

Deliveries from work in process to finished goods were recorded by completion in the factory of the assembly order (Exhibit 3). On the lower left corner of that form there was space for the cost department to fill in the standard cost per unit and the total amount of standard cost for the order, and the total of these standard costs entries for a month was credited to the Work in Process account and debited to Finished Goods Inventory.

The standard costs per unit mentioned in the previous paragraph were prepared for each product in the form illustrated in Exhibit 6.

Exhibit 6

STANDARD COST				
DATE January 1			PLATE NO. 2000	
Description	Material	Labor	Burden	Total
Receive woodwork	1.17	0.004	0.008	1.182
Insp. and hand sand		0.012	0.024	1.218
Bottom coat	0.542	0.038	0.076	1.874
Trim T.B. and O.F. seats		0.011	0.022	1.907
Sand edges T.B.C.F. out		0.003	0.008	1.918
Sand edges T.B.C.F. in.		0.003	0.008	1.929
Inspect		0.012	0.024	1.965
Top coat	0.543	0.079	0.158	2.745
Shave		0.010	0.020	2.775
Sand edges—upright belt		0.005	0.014	2.794
Sand seats and covers		0.039	0.107	2.940
Inspect and file		0.015	0.030	2.985
Dope		0.004	0.008	2.997
Buff seats and covers		0.108	0.208	3.313
Inspect		0.012	0.024	3.349
Buff repairs		0.044	0.085	3.478
Trade-mark		0.007	0.014	3.499
Drilling		0.004	0.008	3.511
Total seat	2.255	0.410	0.846	3.511
Total cover No.	1.983	0.399	0.826	3.208
Total seat and cover	4.238	0.809	1.672	6.719
Assemble		0.032	0.064	6.815
Cleanup polish		0.033	0.066	6.914
Seal end of carton		0.006	0.012	6.932
Inspect and wrap		0.034	0.068	7.034
Seat, label, and pack		0.010	0.020	7.064
Bar bumpers	0.043			7.107
Tack bumpers	0.019			7.126
Screws 1¼–8	0.047			7.173
Hinge	1.04			8.213
Carton and filler 2—No. 1	0.125			8.338
Total Cost	5.512	0.924	1.902	8.338

Because the lines on the standard cost sheets were arranged by successive operations, they showed the cumulative cost of a product at the completion of every operation as well as the final cost at which the product was delivered to finished goods inventory. For each operation and for the total cost there was a breakdown that showed separately the standard costs of materials, labor, and burden. The method of arriving at these costs is described below.

Standard materials costs consisted of a predetermined physical amount per unit priced at the expected purchase price for each classification of raw stock or of finished parts stock. Standard labor costs for the various piece-rate operations were simply the current piece rates; in the case of daywork operations, they were the quotients obtained by dividing the daywork rate by an estimated attainable average output. Standard burden costs were found by multiplying the departmental burden rate selected for the year by the standard labor cost for the operation concerned. For example, the standard cost sheet for a style calling for a coated finish might show for an operation in the coating department a standard labor charge of $0.079. As indicated above, operations in the coating department for the year were estimated to be at 80 per cent of capacity, which for the coating department meant a burden rate of 200 per cent of productive labor. Thus, the standard burden cost for the operation with a labor charge of $0.079 was set at 200 per cent of this amount, or $0.158.

These standard product costs were used to price deliveries into finished stock, to cost work in process inventory, and to transfer production between accounts. Once the standard costs were prepared, it was expected that they would remain constant except for alterations necessary to reflect a significant change in the manufacturing process, a change in wage rates or in the price of materials, or the selection of a new normal percentage of operating activity that determined the unit allowance for burden.

Variances

At the end of each month's accounting period, a physical inventory of raw materials, supplies, work in process, and finished goods was taken. For this inventory, raw materials and supplies were priced on the basis of last-in, first-out purchase cost, and work in process and finished goods were priced according to the standard cost sheets described above. The difference between the inventory thus determined and the book balance of each inventory account was closed into Cost of Goods Sold. The most important of these differences was for work in process inventory.

A work in process statement (Exhibit 7) was prepared each month. This report showed the beginning inventory at standard cost plus actual direct materials, actual labor, and actual absorbed burden added during the period in each department. From this total cost figure, there were subtracted the actual deliveries to finished goods as indicated on the completed assembly orders, less products transferred from Finished Goods back to Work in Process for reworking, both costed at standard cost. The resulting Balance in Process was the book value of work in process and was compared with the figure obtained by valuing, at standard, the results of the physical inventory. Any difference indicated by this comparison constituted the variance of actual cost from standard and was closed to Cost of Goods Sold. The physical inventory balance at standard constituted the debit to Work in Process at the beginning of the

Exhibit 7
WORK IN PROCESS

Period Ending August   Order No. GENERAL

Detail			Amount			
Balance from Last Period			158	597	19	
DIRECT MATERIALS			76	338	21	
DIRECT LABOR						
1 Varnish						
2 Spray	2	990	25			
3 Coating	5	915	60			
4 Filing		998	83			
5 Sanding	1	637	53			
6 Buffing & Polishing	6	175	78			
8 Assembling and Packing	4	788	60			
Total Direct Labor			22	506	59	
BURDEN						
1 Varnish						
2 Spray	6	180	50			
3 Coating	11	831	20			
4 Filing	1	937	73			
5 Sanding	4	489	05			
6 Buffing & Polishing	11	888	76			
8 Assembling and Packing	9	577	20			
10 Shipping						
Total Burden			45	904	44	
TOTAL COST			303	346	43	
Less Deliveries at Cost			222	386	74	
BALANCE IN PROCESS			80	959	69	

DELIVERIES AT COST

Date			Amount		Date		Amount		Date			Amount	
8/31	Del.	220	876	63									
	Var.	1	259	07									
	Defect.		251	04									
	Net	222	386	74									

Exhibit 8

SUMMARY OF ENTRIES TO INVENTORY ACCOUNTS FOR AUGUST

Raw Materials

(Several accounts according to nature of material)

$151,204 Balance	$76,318.21 Requisitions, priced at last-in, first-out cost (debit to Work in Process).
$343,640.19 Purchases at invoice cost (credit to Accounts Payable).	$138.32 Adjustment to physical inventory (Dr. or Cr.).
$1,101.67 Materials salvaged from returned goods (credit to Cost of Goods Sold).	

A physical inventory of all raw materials was taken each month and the difference between inventory and book balance written off to Cost of Goods Sold.

Work in Process

$158,597.19 Balance	$220,894.24 Deliveries to finished goods at standard costs (debit to Finished Goods).
$76,318.21 Direct materials from requisitions priced at last-in, first-out cost (credit to Raw Materials).	$251.04 Defective work, from defective work order (debit to Burden).
$22,506.59 Direct labor from payroll summary (credit to Accrued Wages).	$1,259.07 Adjustment to physical inventory (Dr. or Cr.).
$20.00 Materials purchased not usually carried in inventory (credit to Accounts Payable).	
$17.61 Transfers from finished goods for reworking or alteration, at standard cost (credit to Finished Goods).	
$45,904.44 Absorbed expense (earned burden) from burden summary sheet (credit to Burden).	

A physical inventory was taken of all work in process every month. This was priced and totaled according to standard costs at last operation performed; the difference between the inventory and balance in the Work in Process account, representing the cost variation, was written off to Cost of Goods Sold.

Finished Goods

$429,682.73 Balance	$400,954.09 Shipment at standard costs (debit to Cost of Goods Sold).
$220,894.24 Deliveries to finished goods at standard costs (credit to Work in Process).	$17.61 Transfers to work in process for reworking or alteration at standard cost (debit to Work in Process).

next month. If this Work in Process variance was large, its causes were investigated and action was taken accordingly.

A descriptive summary of the inventory accounts is given in Exhibit 8.

2. Control of Burden Expenses

Budgeted Burden Expenses

The Church company used the departmental burden schedules to set bogeys for the foremen and supervisors who were responsible for incurring expenses. A knowledge of the actual amount of direct labor for each productive department made it a simple matter to determine which column of figures to use as the bogey standard for evaluating the spending performance of each foreman. For example, the coating department (Exhibit 5) might be expected to operate, on the average, at 80 per cent of capacity, but in any one month the actual operations might vary considerably from this average. Thus, if direct labor dropped to $7,031, the foreman would be expected to spend only $580 for glue and cement rather than $620 allowable at the average operating level. For the nonproductive departments the column selected was the one that listed the expenses expected for the percentage of capacity nearest the average operating level of all productive departments.

Comparison of Actual and Budget

The departmental comparisons of the actual burden expenses, by accounts, with the appropriate budgeted allowance for that volume, are illustrated in the departmental budget sheet, Exhibit 9. The August budgeted expense figures for the coating department are based upon an output level of 65 per cent of capacity. This figure was arrived at by comparing the actual direct labor expense for the month, amounting to $5,915.60, to the closest corresponding direct labor expense, $6,094, which is under the 65 per cent column shown on Exhibit 5. (Exhibit 9 is a standard form, and only those lines that are pertinent to the operations of the coating department are filled in on the example shown.)

Exhibit 9 also showed two items over which the foreman had no control. Other Overhead expenses was the total amount of fixed charges allocated to the department on the basis of the percentage distributions described earlier. Defective Work was the total amount of defective work budgeted ($600) and actual ($251.04) for the *entire plant,* and it bore no relation to the work done in the coating department. The amount allocated to each department for defective work was not shown on Exhibit 9 because the basis of allocation was considered too arbitrary. The amounts for both Other Overhead expenses and for Defective Work were shown in the Analysis of Overhead Expenses principally as a matter of information for the foreman. They were not considered as being controllable by the foreman.

Exhibit 9

C. F. CHURCH MFG. CO.
HOLYOKE
Analysis of Overhead Expenses

DEPARTMENT #3 Coating   Month August

		Budget	Actual Expense	Over or Under Actual
1	INDIRECT LABOR			
2	01 Supervision	775 00	756 00	19 00
3	04 Truck Drivers & Helpers			
4	06 Shipping			
5	08 General Labor	405 00	171 22	233 78
6	09 Repair and Rework			
7	10 Idle and Lost Time		1 77	(1 77)
8	11 Guaranteed Rate Cost	244 00	28 14	215 86
9	16 Overtime Bonus	75 00	32 98	42 02
10	19 Repairs & Maint. & Mchy. & Equip.	150 00	38 26	111 74
11	17 Vacations		46 00	(46 00)
12	21 Paid Holidays			
13	Total	1649 00	1074 37	574 63
14	INDIRECT SUPPLIES			
15	31 Repairs & Maint.--Mchy. & Equip.	20 00	360 18	(340 18)
16	33 Repairs & Maint. Trucks			
17	35 Acetone & Isotone	1055 00	739 48	315 52
18	36 Buffing Compounds & Buffs			
19	37 Sandpaper & Sandbelts	7 00	9 60	(2 60)
20	39 Labels, Tape, etc., Glue & Cement	500 00	734 71	(234 71)
21	40 Shipping Cartons			
22	41 Consumable Supplies	81 00	55 54	25 46
23	42 Loose & Hand Tools	33 00	13 55	19 45
24	46 Miscellaneous	9 00	7 51	1 49
25	Total	1705 00	1920 57	(215 57)
26	OTHER OVERHEAD expenses:			
27	Insurance, power, taxes, social			
28	security, depreciation, group			
29	insurance & pension	1875 22	1472 46	402 76
30				
31	DEFECTIVE WORK	600 00	251 04	348 96
32				
33	DIRECT LABOR	6094 00	5915 60	178 40
34				
35				
36				
37				
38				
39				
40				

Exhibit 10

BURDEN SUMMARY AND STATISTICS

Plant—Holyoke   Period Ending—August 31

Dept. No.	Description	Direct Labor	Actual Expense	Budgeted Expense	Loss or Gain on Budget	Absorbed Expense	Over- or Under-absorbed
1							
2	Spray	2,990.25	6,464.64	7,103.64	639.00	6,180.50	(284.14)
3	Coating	5,915.60	12,829.53	13,981.05	1,151.52	11,831.20	(998.33)
4	Filing	998.83	2,590.83	2,190.20	(400.63)	1,937.73	(653.10)
4–I							
4–C							
4–5							
5	Sanding	1,637.53	3,907.74	5,243.47	1,335.73	4,489.05	581.31
6	Buffing	6,175.78	11,275.76	10,750.25	(525.51)	11,888.76	613.00
7							
8	Assemble and pack	4,788.60	8,846.48	8,998.58	152.10	9,577.20	730.72
9							
10							
11							
12							
14							
15							
	Total Plant	22,506.59	45,914.98	48,267.19	2,352.21	45,904.44	(10.54)

YEAR TO DATE

Dept. No.	Description	Direct Labor	Actual Expense	Budgeted Expense	Loss or Gain on Budget	Absorbed Expense	Over- or Under-absorbed
1							
2		22,071.46	44,718.50			45,643.78	925.28
3		50,512.16	104,611.39			101,024.32	(3,587.07)
4		9,077.03	21,509.51			17,618.52	(3,890.99)
4–I							
4–C							
4–5							
5		13,660.61	35,648.86			37,443.73	1,794.87
6		51,978.12	98,119.96			100,057.88	1,937.92
7							
8		30,878.48	62,125.19			61,756.96	(368.23)
9							
10							
11							
12							
14							
15							
	Total Plant	178,177.86	366,733.41			363,545.19	(3,188.22)

Each month the accounting department prepared Exhibit 10, summarizing the actual, budgeted, and absorbed burden costs for each operating department. The amount shown as Actual Expense was obtained by adding the Charges from Other Departments ($8,362.13 for the coating department) to the other burden items shown in Exhibit 9 (excluding defective work). The Budgeted Expense was the total burden for each department as shown on the burden development sheets (Exhibit 5) at the applicable level of operations (65 per cent for the coating department in August).

The amount of Absorbed Expense was computed by applying the *annual* burden rate to the direct labor in each productive department, as explained in the preceding section.

In the opinion of the management the entries in the column headed Loss or Gain on Budget could be considered a measure of the effectiveness of departmental supervision, whereas the amount of Over- or Underabsorbed was influenced both by efficiency and by the volume of production.

The departmental overhead budget constituted the point of real control over expenditures. At the end of each month, the president met with the cost supervisor and the foremen to discuss spending. At these meetings the foremen were encouraged to discuss their performance as indicated by the budget report. When the system was first installed, the cost supervisor did most of the talking, but with increasing familiarity with the costs for which he was responsible, each foreman gradually became "cost conscious," and after a short time each foreman knew approximately what his monthly performance would be, even before he saw the budget comparison report.

The foreman in charge of the coating department was particularly interested in controlling the overhead costs under his jurisdiction. Every month he discussed the analysis of overhead expenses with the factory manager and the cost supervisor to evaluate with them the performance of his department. During the first week of September, he received the analysis of overhead expenses for August (Exhibit 9), and he checked all the items carefully to learn if there were any costs out of line with his expectations for that month. He copied the August figures onto a sheet (Exhibit 11) on which he had previously summarized the figures for recent months (except for July, which included a vacation shutdown). After he felt that he had a good idea of his cost position, he arranged for a meeting with the factory manager and the cost supervisor to review the situation with them.

Exhibit 11

SUMMARY OF PERFORMANCE IN THE COATING DEPARTMENT

	April		May		June		August	
	Actual	(Over) or Under	Actual	(Over) or Under	Actual	(Over) or Under	Actual	(Over) or Under
Indirect Labor:								
01 Supervision	811	(36)	782	(7)	756	19	756	19
08 General labor	654	(124)	558	(28)	418	22	171	234
10 Idle and lost time								2
11 Guaranteed rate cost	313	6	154	165	50	213	28	216
16 Overtime bonus	63	27	45	45	37	43	33	42
19 Repairs and maint.—mchy. and equip.	89	76	30	135	35	125	38	112
17 Vacations							46	(46)
Total	1,930	(51)	1,569	310	1,296	422	1,074	575
Indirect Supplies:								
31 Repairs and maint.—mchy. and equip.	5	15	85	(65)	176	(156)	360	(340)
33 Repairs and maint.—trucks								
35 Acetone and isotone	1,300	80	1,134	246	1,031	109	739	316
36 Buffing compounds and buffs								
37 Sandpaper and sandbelts	10	(1)	14	(5)	5	3	10	(3)
39 Labels, tape, etc., glue and cement	575	85	462	199	182	358	735	(235)
40 Shipping cartons								
41 Consumable supplies	66	40	116	(10)	48	40	56	25
42 Loose and hand tools	37	6	14	29	10	25	14	19
46 Miscellaneous	27	(14)	9	3	9	1	8	1
Total	2,020	211	1,834	397	1,461	380	1,922	(217)
Other Overhead Expenses: Insurance, power, taxes, social security, depreciation, group insurance, and pension	1,456	561	2,014	3	1,836	74	1,472	403
Defective work	391	209	656	(56)	594	6	251	349
Direct labor	7,812	157	8,024	(55)	6,599	(36)	5,916	178

Questions

1. What are the major purposes of the standards developed by the company?

2. How does the company develop standard burden rates? How often do *you* think they should be changed?

3. What steps are involved in the development of the standard cost sheet (Exhibit 6)? How accurate do you judge the figures to be?

4. What are the possible causes of the $1,259.07 credit to Work in Process labeled "adjustment to physical inventory" in Exhibit 8?

5. Explain so as to distinguish them clearly from one another the figures $12,829.53, $13,981.05, and $11,831.20 shown for the coating department on Exhibit 10.

6. If you were the cost supervisor, what evaluation would you make of the performance of the foreman in the coating department in controlling his overhead costs? About which items in Exhibits 9–11 would you be likely to question him?

7. In the coating department for the month of August, what is the variance attributable to "Charges from Other Departments"? Of what significance is this variance to (*a*) the coating department, and (*b*) the service departments that created these charges? Should this variance be included in the burden summary and statistics report?

CASE 21–2. CLIMAX SHIPPING COMPANY

In the spring of 1950, the controller of the Climax Shipping Company, located in Pittsburgh, was preparing a report for the executive committee regarding the feasibility of repairing one of the company's steam river boats or of replacing the steamboat with a new diesel-powered boat.

The Climax Shipping Company was engaged mainly in the transportation of coal from the nearby mines to the steel mills, public utilities, and other industries in the Pittsburgh area. The company's several steamboats also, on occasion, carried cargoes to places as far away as New Orleans. The boats owned by the Climax Company were all steam powered. All were at least ten years old, and the majority were between 15 and 30 years old.

The steamboat the controller was concerned about, the Cynthia, was 23 years old and required immediate rehabilitation or replacement. It was estimated that the Cynthia had a useful life of another 20 years provided that adequate repairs and maintenance were made. Whereas the book value of the Cynthia was $39,500, it was believed that she would bring somewhat less than this amount, possibly around $25,000, if she were sold in 1950. The total of immediate rehabilitation costs was estimated to be $115,000. Of this amount, $55,000 was for general overhaul, reconversion, and repairs, exclusive of work on the hull. It was estimated that these general rehabilitation expenditures would extend the useful life of the Cynthia, exluding the hull, for a period of about 20 years. The remaining $60,000 was for a new hull, which would last approximately ten years. At the end of this ten-year period another new hull costing $60,000 at current costs would be required.

New, spare parts from another boat that had been retired in 1948 were available for use in the rehabilitation of the Cynthia. An estimate of the fair value of these parts if used on the Cynthia was $43,500. Their use would, in effect, decrease by $7,500 the $60,000 cost of hull replacement and decrease by $36,000 the $55,000 cost required for general overhaul, reconversion, and repairs. It was believed, however, that if these parts were sold on the market they would bring only around $30,000. These parts could not be used on any of the other Climax steamboats.

It was estimated that at the end of the Cynthia's useful life the cost of dismantling and scrapping the boat would be offset by the value of the scrap and used parts taken off the boat.

The controller was also concerned at this time with a city smoke ordinance signed in 1948 to take effect in 1952 that applied to hand-fired steamboats. To comply with the regulations of the ordinance, all steamboats had to be converted from hand firing to stoker firing. Several of the Climax Company's steamboats were already stoker-fired; the Cynthia, however, was hand-fired. The additional cost of converting the Cynthia to stoker firing was estimated to be $40,000, provided it was done at the same time as the general rehabilitation. This $40,000 included the cost of stokers and extra hull conversion and was not included in the $115,000 rehabilitation figure. The controller was not certain at this time just when stoker firing of the Cynthia would become necessary, since some local industries owning steamboats had already been granted relief from the ordinance for a period of several years beyond the effective date initially established. The controller also knew that if $115,000 were spent currently in rehabilitating the Cynthia and it was found out later that no relief or only temporary one- or two-year relief was granted under the smoke ordinance, the cost of converting to stoker firing would no longer be $40,000, but around $70,000. The higher cost would be due to rebuilding that would not be necessary if the Cynthia were converted to stoker firing at the time of her general rehabilitation.

Currently, the annual operating costs for the 20-man crew on board the Cynthia amounted to around $110,200 for wages, $1,880 for vacation and sickness benefits, $2,400 for social security payments, $1,800 for life insurance, and $15,420 for commissary supplies, a total of $131,700. If the Cynthia were stoker-fired, two less crew members would be necessary. It was estimated that the annual operating costs for an 18-man crew would amount to around $100,650 for wages, $1,650 for vacation and sickness benefits, $2,200 for social security payments, $1,620 for life insurance, and $13,880 for commissary supplies, a total of $120,000.

The other annual operating costs of the Cynthia, whether it had an 18- or 29-man crew, were approximately $71,450, consisting of repairs and maintenance, $24,400; fuel, $34,500; lubricants, $550; and miscellaneous service and supplies, $12,000.

An alternative to rehabilitating the steamboat was the purchase of a diesel-powered boat. The Quapelle Company, a local boat manufacturer, quoted the price of $325,000 for a diesel boat. An additional $75,000 for a basic spare parts inventory would be necessary to service a diesel boat and would be sufficient to service up to three such boats; however, if four or more diesels were purchased, it was estimated that additional spare parts inventory would be necessary. The length of life and the cost of replacing a diesel boat hull were estimated to be the same as for a steamboat; that is, $60,000 about every ten years. The useful life was estimated to be 25 years, at the end of which time the boat would be scrapped or completely rehabilitated at a cost approximately that of a new boat. The possibility of major diesel engine overhaul during the 25-year life was not contemplated by the controller, since information he had obtained from other companies having limited experience with such river boats did not indicate that such overhaul would be necessary.

One of the features the Quapelle Company pointed out was the 12 per cent increase in average speed of diesel-powered boats over the steamboats. The controller of the Climax Company discounted this feature, however, because the short runs and lock-to-lock operations involved in local river shipping would prohibit the diesel boats from taking advantage of their greater speed, since there was little opportunity for passing and they would have to wait in turn at each lock for the slower steamboats. In 1950 only two diesel boats, out of about 40 boats, were operating on the river. The controller felt it would be many years, if at all, before diesel boats displaced the slower steamboats.

After consulting the Quapelle Company and other companies operating diesel-powered boats, the controller of the Climax Company estimated that the annual operating cost of such boats would total $156,640, broken down as follows: wages, for the 13-man crew, $77,300; vacation and sickness benefits, $1,320; social security payments, $1,680; life insurance, $1,170; repairs and maintenance (excluding possible major overhaul of diesel engines), $21,700; extra stern repairs, $2,000; fuel, $28,000; miscellaneous service and supplies, $12,650; and commissary supplies, $10,020.

All operating data the controller had collected pertaining to crew expenses were based on the regular two-shift, twelve-hour working day, which was standard on local river boats. The controller had been informed, however, that the union representing crew members wanted a change to a three-shift, eight-hour day. If the union insisted on an eight-hour day, accommodations on board the steamers or the diesels would have to be enlarged. The controller was perturbed by this fact, because he knew the diesels could readily be converted to accommodate three crews whereas steamers could not. How serious the union was in considering the change, when it would be put into effect if ever, and how strongly the union would insist on the change, were questions for which the controller could get no satisfactory answers. The controller believed that the union would have a difficult time in getting acceptance of a demand for three eight-hour shifts on steamers, since it would be very difficult, if not impossible, to convert the steamers to hold a larger crew, because of space limitations. The controller thought that the union might succeed in getting its demands accepted, however, in the case of diesel-powered boats. One of the diesel boats currently operating in the Pittsburgh area had accommodations for three crews, although it was still operating on a two-shift basis. The diesel boats that the Quapelle Company offered to build for Climax could be fitted to accommodate three crews at no additional cost.

Another factor the controller was considering at this time was alternative uses of funds. The Climax Shipping Company had sufficient funds to buy four diesel-powered boats; however, there were alternative uses for these funds. Some of the other projects that the Climax Company was considering at this time had an estimated return of at least 10 per cent after taxes. The income tax rate at the time was 48 per cent.

Question

What action do you recommend?

CASE 21–3. CAMEO DEPARTMENT STORE

The Cameo Department Store consists of four selling departments. Departments I, II, and III are located in the main store, whereas department IV is located in a smaller building next to the main store. Until three years ago (January 1, 1958) the building occupied by department IV had been used as a warehouse. At that time alternative warehouse space was rented at a total annual rental of $11,000 and the warehouse was converted into a selling area at a cost of $12,000 excluding furnishings, which cost $9,000. Department IV has been used to display and sell seasonal merchandise, such as toys at Christmas, lawn and garden products in the spring and early summer, etc.

Financial data for the past three years consists of the following:

SELLING DEPARTMENTS

1958	I	II	III	IV
Sales	$335,000	$398,000	$257,000	$156,000
Cost of goods sold	181,000	205,000	173,000	121,000
Purchases	185,000	210,000	165,000	90,000
Salaries	10,000	13,000	8,500	8,200
Supplies	2,500	2,650	2,300	1,900

1959	I	II	III	IV
Sales	343,000	405,000	265,000	158,000
Cost of goods sold	185,000	208,000	177,000	123,500
Purchases	190,000	206,000	168,000	116,000
Salaries	10,000	130,000	8,500	8,200
Supplies	2,450	2,700	2,100	1,950

1960	I	II	III	IV
Sales	351,000	408,000	268,000	153,000
Cost of goods sold	186,000	208,000	178,000	119,000
Purchases	180,000	205,000	182,000	113,000
Salaries	10,000	13,000	8,500	8,200
Supplies	2,600	2,700	2,250	

Sales commissions are 1 per cent of sales in each department, and estimated uncollectible accounts average one half of 1 per cent of sales.

Nonselling activities of the Cameo Department Store are divided into purchasing, sales promotion, and general administration. These costs for the past three years were as follows:

PURCHASING

	1958	1959	1960
Salaries	$10,500	$10,500	$10,500
Supplies	1,325	1,300	1,370

SALES PROMOTION

	1958	1959	1960
Salaries	$14,000	$14,000	$14,000
Newspaper ads	9,800	10,400	12,100
Handbills	525	485	540
Price reductions on sales promotion	4,800	5,300	5,800
Other sales promotion costs	400	380	405
Supplies	1,480	1,535	1,600
	$31,005	$32,100	$34,445

GENERAL ADMINISTRATION

	1958	1959	1960
Salaries	$29,000	$29,000	$29,000
Supplies	2,900	2,870	2,920

OTHER COSTS FOR THE THREE YEARS

	1958	1959	1960
Delivery costs	$11,780	$12,125	$12,320
Heat	8,575	8,225	8,380
Light and power	10,580	11,120	10,975

The main store building had a book value of $300,000 on January 1, 1958. Estimated useful life of the building as of that date was 20 years. The building occupied by department IV had a book value of $80,000, excluding renovation costs, and an estimated useful life of 20 years as of January 1, 1958. No extensive renovations are planned for department IV for at least 20 years.

Furnishings in each of the selling and nonselling departments remained constant during the past three years. The cost of furnishings in each department is as follows:

SELLING DEPARTMENTS

I	$15,000
II	15,000
III	12,000
IV	9,000

NONSELLING DEPARTMENTS

Purchasing	$2,500
Sales Promotion	4,000
General Administration	8,400

Estimated useful life for all furnishings is five years.

Three fourths of the floor space in the main building is shared equally by the selling departments, whereas the other one fourth is divided equally among the nonselling departments. The smaller store building contains one half the floor space of department I. Electrical equipment in the selling departments is of the same variety and amount, whereas the nonselling departments each had approximately one half as much electrical equipment as department I.

On the average, departments I and II use about an equal amount of space in handbills and newspaper advertising, and about twice that of departments III and IV. Warehousing costs include the annual rental of $11,000, a foreman's salary of $6,000 a year, and a helper's wage of $300 a month. The warehousing function includes receiving of all purchased merchandise, storage, and transferring of stored merchandise to the selling departments when needed.

Questions

1. Prepare departmental income statements for department IV for 1958, 1959, and 1960. Use whatever reasonable assumptions are necessary to distribute expenses to departments.

2. Prepare a list of the cost and revenue items that would be included in a statement that attempts to measure the contribution of department IV to the profit of the firm (dollar amounts not necessary). Is it possible that some of the individual expense items included in the departmental income statement will be only partially includable in the contribution statement? Explain.

3. Prepare a list (dollar amounts not necessary) of the cost and revenue items that would be included in a statement that attempts to measure the financial performance of the manager of department IV. With what type of data might we compare the present performance of department IV in order to judge more adequately the financial performance of the manager? What other data might be useful in attempting to measure the financial performance of the department IV's manager? Generally speaking, what has to be added to financial performance in order to build up to total performance?

4. A member of the board of directors has asked this question: In view of the losses shown in department IV would it possibly be wise to discontinue the department? Alternative uses of the building occupied by department IV are as follows:

    a) Convert the building back into warehouse space at a cost of $10,000. Sell the furnishings for $8,000 and dispose of the warehouse space costing $11,000 a year.

    b) Sublease the building, including furnishings, at an annual rental of $12,000, all utilities to be provided.

    c) Sell the building, including all fixtures and equipment, for $200,000.

Prepare a schedule of cost and revenue data that will facilitate making a decision. Cite the limitations of these data (if any) as well as other factors that should be considered before the board of directors makes its decision. Make any assumptions you feel are necessary.

CASE 21–4. MOULDING MOTORS, INC.

In February 1956, Mr. Richard Todd, the chief purchasing agent for the Mercobile Division of Moulding Motors, called in one of his buyers, Mr. Tom Roswald, to discuss Mr. Roswald's purchasing performance. Mr. Todd had just received the January report of buyers' performances, which indicated that Mr. Roswald had incurred a $500,-000 loss on a seat-spring-assembly contract. This report was prepared by the estimators of the parts-cost-control department, who measured a buyer's performance by differences between negotiated prices and the so-called "price objectives" for purchased parts.

Organization of the Company

Moulding Motors, Inc., was a large, decentralized, multiplant manufacturer of automobiles and trucks. Each division manager was considered to be operating an autonomous unit, and was responsible to an executive vice president for his division's profitability.

Sales of the Mercobile Division, which assembled and sold the medium-price line of Mercobiles, were approximately $1.8 billion in 1955. The division operated several assembly plants located throughout the country. Parts and subassemblies, amounting to about $1.2 billion in 1955, were purchased either from other divisions of Moulding Motors or from outside vendors. The division had no facilities for manufacturing these parts and subassemblies.

Parts-Cost-Control System

The highly competitive automobile market required that Mercobile maintain close control over costs. Annually Moulding's top management established total price objectives for the new Mercobile models based on the price bracket in which they were to be sold and on anticipated market conditions. Mercobile Division management then broke down the total price objective for each model into percentages for material, assembly, distribution and other costs, and profit.

To control material costs, a system had evolved of continual cost and price estimates through the annual cycle of planning new models and engineering, developing, and procuring the parts for these models. Mr. Todd's parts-cost-control department was responsible for this task. Of the 97 employees in the department, 80 were estimators or supervisors, each of whom had several years of machine shop or time-study experience. These men maintained their familiarity with production processes, material market information, price trends, labor rates, and other pertinent data through reading a number of current periodicals in these fields. The estimators were responsible for providing cost estimates for important body and chassis parts, which, although they comprised only 21 per cent of the total number of such parts, amounted to 94 per cent of the cost of the body and chassis. They were also responsible for cost estimates for the tooling. Virtually all the tooling necessary for the fabrication of body and chassis parts was designed and purchased by the Mercobile Division. This tooling was provided the division's suppliers once contracts were signed. Cost control of engine parts was not the Mercobile Division's responsibility. This work was performed by an engine engineering division.

Each year the estimators provided tentative cost estimates of future models based upon clay models. Working only with what they could see of the interior and exterior body mock-ups and their knowledge of current costs, they developed detailed estimates of the cost *differences* between the proposed model's parts and the same parts for the current model. These "variance estimates" were based on operational changes that the estimators thought would be necessary, that is, changes in either the type, quantity, or cost of the material or labor required, and changes in labor times, labor rates, and overhead rates.

After the clay model had been approved, parts-cost estimates of the variances were refined, based first on broad structural drawings and, later, on detailed engineering drawings. During these development and engineering phases, variances for one item were typically estimated from five to seven times.

In the final phase, that of actual procurement, the estimators provided the buyers with individual part price objectives, which were the actual costs of the part on the current model plus or minus the estimated variances based upon the final engineering drawings.

The Buyer's Use of Estimates

Once a buyer received notification to purchase specific parts, he initiated requests for bids for the parts from suppliers, stating the specifications and anticipated monthly demand; at the same time he requested a price estimate from the parts-cost-control department.

The parts-cost-control department then completed and sent back to the buyer a price estimate sheet showing the part number, the actual price currently being paid for the same part, and the price that the estimating department thought should be paid in the coming year. The price estimate sheet did not show a detailed cost breakdown but indicated the extent to which the estimated price varied from the actual price as a result of either a design change or a change in the anticipated price level. Thus, if the current actual price for a particular part was $0.75 per unit and the estimated price was $0.72 per unit, the price estimate sheet would show whether a design change and/or price level change caused the difference. In this case, the estimate sheet might show that a design change was expected to decrease the unit price by 4 cents and that an increase in price levels was expected to increase the unit price by 1 cent, resulting in a net unit cost decrease of 3 cents.

In negotiations with vendors, the buyer used the estimate as his target price, although he attempted to negotiate a lower price. The estimates were particularly useful to the buyers when only one or two vendors supplied particular parts and components. In these cases, the buyers were handicapped by not being able to undertake comparative price analyses. Since the Mercobile Division bought parts or components from the manufacturing divisions of Moulding Motors, and since in some cases these divisions were the only possible suppliers, the Mercobile buyers found the estimates of particular help in negotiating the price at which to procure parts from these divisions.

When the buyer completed a transaction, he recorded the price he paid for the part or component on the price estimate sheet. The estimate sheet was then returned to the parts-cost-control department, where a record was kept, showing for each buyer the past month's negotiated savings or losses compared with the estimated price objectives. Once a month a report of each buyer's performance was sent to Mr. Todd, the Mercobile Division's chief purchasing agent.

Special Pricing Studies

Whenever a buyer or a member of the parts-cost-control department thought that an estimated price was out of line, as occurred when over a period of three or four years the accumulated variances for annual changes did not accurately reflect the current manufacturing costs, a special estimate was made that resulted in a new cost figure and price objective. Such studies differed from the typical estimates of variances in that the latter merely considered the cost variances attributable to design or price level changes.

In making a special pricing study, the estimator studied the engineering prints and then carefully defined each operation required for the fabrication. When possible, the estimator visited the manufacturer of the part or component. During these visits the estimator gathered as much information as possible about the operations performed, the type of equipment used, the operating time, and so on. However, even the manufacturing divisions of Moulding Motors refused to permit estimators to time operations or to obtain cost information; the manufacturing divisions, being autonomous, were in the same position as that of other vendors in selling their products to the Mercobile Division.

After he had picked up as much information as he could from the plant visit, the estimator proceeded to fill out a work sheet, entering the type, quantity, and price of material; the labor time, allowances, and rate; and the overhead charges. After he had estimated the costs for each part, he estimated the costs for any assembly operations. Finally, the cost of the individual parts and the cost of any assembly operations were totaled. To this total were added freight costs, general and administrative expenses, and profit, to give a final price.

The prices developed from these special studies were then sent to the buyer as his price objective.

The Seat-Spring Study

In December 1955, when the procurement of parts for the 1957 Mercobiles was being initiated, Mr. Tom Roswald, a buyer of special assemblies, received a price objective from the parts-cost-control department of $14 a set for front- and back-seat-spring assemblies, one of the many items that he procured. Mr. Roswald decided that, since no new estimates of this assembly had been made for several years, the price might possibly be out of date. He therefore requested the parts-cost-control department to study the seat-spring-assembly manufacturing processes and determine a new price objective.

In December, after a careful study of engineering drawings for the seat-spring assembly, the section supervisor of the body cost-estimating section and two of his estimators spent a day at the plants of each of the two suppliers of these assemblies. The three men were particularly interested in the vendors' facilities, their method of fabricating and assembling the seat springs, the manpower required, and the time of the production cycle. After they had concluded these plant visits, the two estimators, with some assistance from their supervisor, spent three weeks in developing a new price objective. Work sheets were made out detailing each fabrication operation for the several side members of the frames, for the springs, and for the assembly of side members and springs into a completed unit. The estimators used as a basis the same production processes and equipment the two vendors were using. (Only in exceptional instances when the vendor was grossly inefficient would an estimator suggest changes in production methods.) Exhibit 1 is a work sheet showing in detail the material, labor, and overhead cost for each operation in the fabrication of one of the side members for the seat-spring assembly.

Once the detailed work sheets had been completed, they were summarized on a final work sheet to which was added freight, general administrative expenses, and profit to arrive at the purchase price objective. The revised purchase price objective for the seat-spring assemblies indicated that each set should cost $11.50, in contrast to the prior estimated cost of $14 a set.

When Mr. Roswald received the new purchase price objective, he contacted the two vendors and explained that the price his division was

Exhibit 1

ESTIMATED COST ANALYSIS

	MATERIAL COST SUMMARY							
DATE OF EST.	MATERIAL DESCRIPTION AND SPECIFICATION	ROUGH PIECE WEIGHT	% SCRAP REJECT	MATERIAL COST		F.C.A. DEDUCTION		
				PER UNIT OF WEIGHT	$ PER PIECE	%	$
1-12	.075 C.R.C.Q. 21" Coil x 14 3/8" = 2	3.289	—	.0602	.1980	—	—

		DESCRIPTION OF EQUIPMENT AND OPERATIONS					LAB
DATE OF ESTI-MATE	OPER. NO.	EQUIPMENT	OPERATION	NO. OF MEN	HOURLY PROD.	BASIC MINUTES	E OF
1-12	10		Blank (R.H. + L.H. Attached)	1	1,667	.036	
1-12	20		First form (R. + L. Attached)	1	950	.063	
1-12	30		Separat + partial trim (R.+L.)	1	950	.063	
1-12	40		Restrike (R. + L.)	1	732	.082	
1-12	50		Pierce (R. + L.)	1	732	.082	
1-12	60		Cam pierce pin holes (R. + L.)	1	732	.082	
1-12	70		Flange rear (R.+ L.)	1	732	.082	
			TOTAL			.490	

| PART NUMBER | BAC-7060356-7-A |

PART NAME _Member- Frt. Seat Cushion Frame Side - Upper_

SOURCE	MAKE	BUY
AUTHORITY _AH 1 # 621 (12-16-55)_	PPC CODE _3D46_	
NEXT ASSEMBLY _BAC-7360336-A_	SHEET _1_ OF _1_	

NET MATERIAL PIECE COST · 1980

MODEL YEAR	ALL	6	8	70A	70D	73A		70B	73B		70C	73C	58A	58B	64A	64B
		✓	✓			1EA			1EA				1EA	1EA		
	64C	63A	57A	76B	51A	57B	79F	59A	59B	59C	79B	79C	79D	79E	77A	78A	40A	40D
			1EA			1EA	1EA					1EA	1EA	1EA			
	F-100 83-110	F-100 82-110	F-250 83-118	F-350 83-130	F-500 81-154			F-600 81-154	C-600 81-158	B-600 84-192	F-750 81-144		F-800 81-144	C-800 81-118	T-800 81-144			F-900 81-144

TIME AND COST				BURDEN		TOTAL MFG. COST $	MARK UP FOR "BUY" ITEMS			
ALLOWANCE	MINUTES INCL. ALL ALLWS.	LABOR RATE PER MINUTE	LABOR COST	%	$		TOTAL COST INCLUDING A & C		TOTAL COST INCLUDING PROFIT	
OFF STD.							@ RATE	$	@ RATE	$
5	·040	·0333	·0013	300	·0039	·0052				
5	·069	·0333	·0023	300	·0069	·0092				
5	·069	·0333	·0023	300	·0069	·0092				
5	·090	·0333	·0030	300	·0090	·0120				
5	·090	·0333	·0030	300	·0090	·0120				
5	·090	·0333	·0030	300	·0090	·0120				
5	·090	·0333	·0030	300	·0090	·0120				
	·538		·0179		·0537	·0716				

willing to pay for the seat springs in the coming year would be substantially less than the price paid in the past year. The larger vendor of the two, the Bornley Company, agreed to review its past year's price. In mid-January 1956, the buyer and four estimators visited the Bornley Company and spent two days comparing their material, labor, and overhead cost data with data of the Bornley Company. On the basis of this review, the Bornley Company representatives agreed that they could reduce the price of seat-spring assemblies to $13.35 a set. At the same time, the purchase price objective developed by the Mercobile estimators was adjusted upward to $11.60 a set on the basis of the additional information they had received during the talks.

Because of the still existing spread in price, further negotiations were conducted the following week at the Mercobile Division's buying offices. After two days of negotiations, the Bornley Company finally reached an agreement with Mr. Roswald to supply the seat-spring assemblies for $12.50 a set. In the meantime, the Mercobile Division estimators had increased their purchase price objective to $11.75 a set.

Once the Bornley Company had agreed to the $12.50 figure, Mr. Roswald reached a quick settlement with the second vendor to supply seat-spring assemblies at the same price.

In February 1956, after he had received the January report showing the performance of his buyers, Mr. Todd, the Mercobile Division's chief purchasing agent, called in Mr. Roswald. Mr. Todd explained to Mr. Roswald that his purchasing performance for the month of January had been fine except for the seat-spring-assembly procurement. "According to my monthly report on buyers' performance," Mr. Todd said, "on the seat-spring assembly you lost over $500,000 compared with your purchase price objective. What I want to know is how this happened? Was it a poor job of estimating or was it a poor job of buying?"

Questions

1. Appraise the parts-cost-control system at the Mercobile Division of Moulding Motors.

2. How effective is the system of reporting negotiated gains or losses in procurement as a means of appraising buyers' performance?

3. Is Mercobile's system of providing price objectives to buyers applicable to other industries?

4. Did Mr. Roswald do a poor job of procuring the seat-spring assemblies, or was there a poor job in estimating the price?

CASE 21–5. SEAGER BROTHERS

Early in January 1956, Robert Thompson, the manager of the Eastern Divison of Seager Brothers, wholesale grocers, proposed that the firm establish a cash-and-carry operation in the commercial section of Hastings, a city with a population of 35,000, in which the Eastern Division had its warehouse. When apprised of Mr. Thompson's suggestion, George Fleming, the president of Seager Brothers, expressed the opinion that the question of the Hastings branch should be included in an evaluation of the whole cash-and-carry operation.

In method of operation a cash-and-carry outlet resembled a supermarket, but it served the small grocer rather than the ultimate consumer. As in a supermarket, the customer waited on himself, placing his selections in a vehicle that he pushed, in this case a small hand truck; when he reached the exit he had the merchandise checked and totaled, paid for it in cash, and carried it away in his own car or truck. Although a vigorous effort was made to keep the shelves of the cash-and-carry well stocked, the aisles clear, and the overall appearance tidy, the interior of the cash-and-carry looked more like a warehouse than a retail store. Contributing to the warehouse-like appearance was the necessity of using large walk-in refrigerators for frozen foods and certain produce and dairy products.

Cash-and-carry operations were one of a number of innovations in grocery wholesaling that Seager Brothers had adopted in the postwar period. The first Seager cash-and-carry had been opened in February 1946, in Walton, as a means of servicing at a lower-than-usual markup small grocery stores in the vicinity, which up to that time had been supplied only by old-line wholesalers operating on a higher margin. Executives of Seager Brothers had, of course, no intention of refusing business from larger grocers, but in their opinion it was unlikely that proprietors of such stores would buy from cash-and-carries. The executives reasoned that operators of larger stores would not have the time to spend and would find it too much of a burden to transport the larger quantities of merchandise that their stores required.

Seager opened its first cash-and-carry in the commercial section of Walton, in a building adjacent to its main warehouse, and established similar operations in Smithville (late 1946), in Lawrence (1947), and in Beltown (1953). These other three towns were much smaller than Walton, which had a population of 140,000 in its metropolitan area, but with the exception of Beltown they were among the larger communities in the region. Smithville had a population of approximately 21,000, and Lawrence, 20,000; Beltown itself had a population of only 3,000, but it was not more than five miles from a city of about 18,000. In both Smithville and Lawrence, Seager had selected locations in the commercial sections, but in Beltown the company had rented a building on a main highway leading to the larger community five miles away.

Besides competing with the old-line wholesalers in Walton for the business of cash-and-carry customers, Seager competed with a small cash-and-carry operated by one of its competitors. In the opinion of management, however, this cash-and-carry did not constitute effective competition.

One of the principal attractions of the cash-and-carry for the small grocer was price. The typical markup taken by the old-line wholesaler who supplied small grocers on a service basis was 8 per cent to 10 per cent of the wholesale selling price. Seager Brothers' cash-and-carries, however, sold groceries and dairy products at a markup averaging approximately 6 per cent and produce at a markup of slightly over 10 per cent. Special offerings, advertised in the mailing piece (called a "flier") sent every week to the customers and potential customers of the cash-and-carries, frequently carried even lower markups.

Many customers were undoubtedly attracted to the cash-and-carries also by the wide variety of merchandise available. The Seager cash-and-carries stocked between 2,000 and 2,500 items, a much greater number than were available from most of the old-line wholesalers.

Although the four cash-and-carries of Seager Brothers had achieved a substantial volume of sales, Mr. Fleming and Mr. Goode, the executives in charge of this part of the business, questioned the feasibility of continuing to operate them at the current low markup; indeed they entertained some doubts about the current and future profitability of this kind of business, and were hesitant to make any further investment in cash-and-carries.

Walter Goode maintained that it was the small grocer himself who was making it unprofitable to operate the cash-and-carries at current margins. According to Mr. Goode, the typical small grocer, who came from as far away as 25 or 30 miles, was a shopper. That is, instead of buying most of his requirements from one source, and utilizing the time formerly spent on shopping to improve the operation of his store, he chose to visit several sources hunting for bargains. As a result of this tendency to shop, Mr. Goode alleged that virtually 50 per cent of the cash-and-carry customers purchased principally the specials and only a little of the regular merchandise, and went elsewhere for much of the merchandise that they required. Mr. Goode said also that 75 per cent of all customers purchased only half-cases of most items.[1] Although Seager offered customers half-cases in order that they might have an adequate

---

[1] Depending on the item and size of container, a case (which was the unit of purchase in transactions between manufacturers and wholesalers) contained anywhere from 6 to 96 cans or jars.

variety of merchandise without carrying an excessive inventory, Mr. Goode was of the opinion that cash-and-carry customers were taking unwarranted advantage of the half-case privilege in order to reduce their inventory investment to the very minimum. From Seager Brothers' standpoint, half-case sales not only required labor to cut the cases in half but also resulted in increased shortages, since cans or jars often were found to be missing from a split case. That cash-and-carry customers were buying from hand to mouth, a practice frequently necessitated by lack of funds, was indicated by the amount of the average purchase, which, at the end of 1955, was in the neighborhood of $32 (see Exhibit 1). Many cash-and-carry customers shopped two and three times

Exhibit 1

SUMMARY OF RESULTS OF FOUR-WEEK SURVEY OF SALES OF GROCERIES AND DAIRY PRODUCTS AND OF PRODUCE, TOTAL NUMBER OF TRANSACTIONS, AND AVERAGE SALE FOR EACH OF THE CASH-AND-CARRIES

Cash-and-Carry	Sales			Trans-actions	Average Sale
	Groceries and Dairy	Produce	Total		
Walton.................	$80,662	$6,233	$86,895	2,500	$35
Lawrence...............	39,163	2,203	41,366	1,439	29
Smithville..............	33,735	1,698	35,433	1,277	27
Beltown................	24,466	2,897	27,363	851	32

a week; and, in fact, proprietors of the very small stores not infrequently visited the cash-and-carries six days a week.[2] Furthermore, although customers knew that the cash-and-carries operated on the basis of self-service, they frequently asked for assistance in finding the items that they wanted and in loading their purchases into their cars and trucks.

Of concern also to Mr. Fleming, Mr. Goode, and other executives in the organization was the size of the profit that the cash-and-carries had been earning in recent years (see Exhibit 2). For the year ending December 31, 1955, the total profit before taxes of the cash-and-carries had been only $20,000, and actually two of the four, namely, those located at Walton and at Smithville, had produced virtually all the profit. George Stone, the company treasurer, however, was not sure that the income statements of the cash-and-carries accurately measured their contribution to the profitability of the organization. He pointed out

---

[2] The cash-and-carries opened for business at 7:00 A.M.; they closed at 3:00 P.M. Monday through Friday and at noon on Saturday.

Exhibit 2

SEAGER BROTHERS

Profit and Loss Statements for the Four Cash and Carries, Year Ended December 31, 1955

	Walton		Smithville		Lawrence		Beltown	
	Dollars	Net Sales = 100%	Dollars	Net Sales = 100%	Dollars	Net Sales = 100%	Dollars	Net Sales = 100%
Sales:								
Grocery and dairy	$1,164,665	92.4%	$519,370	93.9%	$607,853	73.8%	$343,817	79.2%
Fruits and vegetables	95,490	7.6	33,686	6.1	215,366	26.2	90,201	20.8
Total Sales	$1,260,155	100.0%	$553,056	100.0%	$823,219	100.0%	$434,018	100.0%
Gross profit:								
Grocery and dairy	$ 66,999	5.7%	$ 26,404	5.0%	$ 28,265	4.6%	$ 23,907	7.0%
Fruits and vegetables	9,331	9.8	2,381	7.1	26,197	12.2	7,985	8.9
Total Gross Profit	$ 76,330	6.0%	$ 28,785	5.2%	$ 54,462	6.6%	$ 31,892	7.4%
Operating expense:								
Advertising	$ 817	0.1%	$ 815	0.1%	$ 820	0.1%	$ 799	0.2%
Warehouse	40,797	3.2	17,544	3.2	32,656	4.0	19,772	4.5
Delivery	2	0.0	19	0.0	5,121	0.6	942	0.2
Administrative	3,688	0.3	2,827	0.5	9,172	1.1	3,829	0.9
Turnover	3,715	0.3	497	0.1	1,551	0.2	460	0.1
Occupancy	3,991	0.3	4,206	0.8	7,065	0.8	5,081	1.2
Total Operating Expense	$ 53,010	4.2%	$ 25,908	4.7%	$ 56,385	6.8%	$ 30,883	7.1%
Provision for bad debts			301	0.0	366	0.0		
Bonuses paid	3,311	0.3	462	0.1	483	0.1	371	0.1
Net profit before taxes	20,010	1.6	2,114	0.4	(2,772)	(0.3)	638	0.2
Grocery and dairy inventory, end of year	102,365	...	57,429	...	69,705	...	63,545	...

that, in the statements, the cash-and-carries had not been credited with any share of the 2 per cent cash discount earned on purchases. He also had some doubt as to the equitableness of the warehouse expense charged to the cash-and-carries, which consisted of a "warehouse" charge for merchandise obtained from the Seager warehouses plus a charge for delivery of the merchandise from the warehouse to the cash-and-carry. The warehouse charge, which was based on the billed cost of the merchandise to Seager Brothers, was 1.5 per cent for groceries and dairy products and 3 per cent for fruits and vegetables.

Each of the cash-and-carries, furthermore, received a substantial quantity of merchandise direct from suppliers; on this, therefore, there was no warehouse charge. In determining the percentage of direct delivery merchandise to be carried by each of the cash-and-carries, executives calculated the transportation costs incurred on merchandise shipped direct and compared these costs with the warehouse and transportation costs incurred on merchandise shipped from the main warehouse; they also gave consideration to the question of whether the cash-and-carry could take advantage of quantity discounts offered by the supplier without having to stock an excessive quantity of merchandise. Currently the cash-and-carries were receiving about 33 per cent of their merchandise direct from suppliers, but Seager executives hoped to increase the average to 50 per cent within the near future.

The transportation charges for shipping merchandise from the main warehouse to the cash-and-carries were based on distance from the main warehouse. This charge was 6 cents a hundred pounds for merchandise shipped to the Walton cash-and-carry, 15 cents a hundred pounds for the Smithville cash-and-carry, and 25 cents a hundred pounds for those located at Lawrence and Beltown. Company executives estimated that the average cost of a hundred pounds of merchandise to a cash-and-carry was between $25 and $33.

Charged also to the cash-and-carries was the expense of delivery to customers other than the cash-and-carry customers serviced. Although the cash-and-carries had originally been opened to service only their own self-service customers, occasionally they were called upon to service other customers, such as institutions, independent grocers, and, in the case of the Lawrence cash-and-carry, even voluntary group members.[3] When this occurred, the sale was credited to the cash-and-carry involved,

---

[3] Only the Lawrence cash-and-carry regularly serviced accounts other than cash-and-carry customers, and even there noncash-and-carry business accounted for no more than 10 per cent of volume.

and charged to it was the cost of transporting the merchandise to the customer and an appropriate provision for bad debts.

The administrative expense incurred by each of the cash-and-carries included such items as telephone, travel, stationery, payroll taxes, and group insurance. It also included a share of the salary of the supervisor responsible for all four cash-and-carries and an appropriate part of the remuneration of the two employees who worked on the cash-and-carry books in the main office.

Turnover expense, another of the items on the income statement, included a share of municipal personal property taxes attributable to inventories and also the cost of fire insurance on the inventories.

In addition to being concerned about low profits, some Seager executives were disturbed by what they considered the inadequate turnover of grocery and dairy inventories. On the basis of year-end figures, they estimated that for 1955 the stock turn of the average Seager cash-and-carry was 8.5 times, the lowest being that of the Beltown operation, 5.0 times, and the highest that of the Walton cash-and-carry, 10.7 times. They realized, of course, that the stock-turn figure would be even lower if it reflected the stocks in the main warehouse that were needed to support the cash-and-carries. The stock turn of the entire organization during 1955 had been approximately 13 times.

Concerned though Mr. Goode and Mr. Fleming were about the current profits of the cash-and-carries, they were somewhat more apprehensive about the future of these operations. Census data indicated that from 1948 to 1954 in the counties in which the four Seager cash-and-carries were operating, the number of retail outlets that sold food had declined, although in three out of four of these counties dollar food sales had increased substantially and in the other county had remained relatively stable. (See Exhibit 3.) Mr. Fleming theorized that the decline in number of retail food stores revealed by the census data indicated that many small stores were going out of business and thus that cash-and-carry business would decline. Mr. Stone, however, argued that Seager Brothers' sales represented only about 40 per cent of the wholesale food business in the state and that some of the wholesalers who had the other 60 per cent of the volume were finding it unprofitable to remain in business. He reasoned that the demise of other wholesalers would leave many small stores without a wholesale source of supply and that these stores would have to trade with the cash-and-carries.

It was Robert Thompson's argument that many of the small grocers who needed the services of a cash-and-carry were within Hastings County. The Census of Business data indicated that from 1948 to 1954 the number of retail food stores in the county had declined from 395 to 346 but that retail food sales had increased from $24,790,000 to $30,610,000. Mr. Thompson estimated that slightly less than half of this business was done by about 35 markets, all of which either were affiliated with one of the two large chains operating in the territory or were members of one of the two voluntary groups operating in the county. The other half of the retail food business in the county was done by approximately 310 smaller stores.

Exhibit 3

NUMBER OF FOOD STORES AND ANNUAL SALES OF
THOSE STORES IN COUNTIES WHERE SEAGER CASH
AND CARRIES WERE LOCATED, 1948 AND 1954

	Number	Sales (in Millions)
Walton:		
1948..........................	675	$48.3
1954..........................	548	48.3
Smithville:		
1948..........................	419	22.5
1954..........................	395	27.3
Lawrence:		
1948..........................	326	19.2
1954..........................	277	22.7
Beltown:		
1948..........................	335	19.5
1954..........................	319	25.3

Thompson pointed out that the company already owned in the commercial section of Hastings a building that could easily be made into a cash-and-carry at a cost of no more than $15,000. Currently this building was occupied by a tenant who paid a rental of $2,400 a year. Mr. Thompson thought that other occupancy expenses of the proposed Hastings cash-and-carry would be no more than $2,000 a year. He believed that in expense categories other than occupancy the experience of the Hastings operation would parallel that of existing cash-and-carries. He thought, however, that warehouse expense, because of the proximity of the Hastings cash-and-carry to the Eastern Division warehouse, would be fully as low as at Walton.

Questions

1. State, as accurately as possible, the actual profitability of the four cash-and-carries in 1955.

2. Should any of the existing cash-and-carries be closed?

3. Should the recommendation for a new cash-and-carry in Hastings be accepted?

CASE 21–6. APPERSON CORPORATION

Executives of the Apperson Corporation were considering the installation of a high-speed electronic computer in its Michigan plant. In this plant 350 persons were engaged in processing the payroll of 25,000 employees. Although additional uses for a computer were contemplated, it was the possibility of its use to reduce payroll costs that Apperson executives had focused their attention.

The Apperson Corporation had conducted a detailed study of existing payroll procedures in order to estimate the savings from eliminating existing operations and to judge the feasibility of applying electronic methods to the payroll problem. Considerations of reliability, accuracy, speed, service, and applicability to commercial data-processing problems in general and the payroll job in particular had eliminated from study all machines but two.

Equipments Being Considered

The equipments considered were the National Computers Corporation Model 240 and the Winchester Electric Model 404. Annual rental for the Model 240 was $275,000; for the Model 404, $320,500. The outright purchase price of the Model 404 was $1,210,000; the Model 240 was not being considered for outright purchase.

Installing the components of the Model 240 would entail extensive remodeling (including floor strengthening, etc.), the installation of 50 tons of air conditioning, and the assignment to the newly created computer room of office furniture, file cabinets, and peripheral equipment peculiar to the computer. Remodeling costs would approach $100,000.

Apperson executives were satisfied that the claims of the respective manufacturers for accuracy, speed of arithmetic and memory access operations, and general electronic and mechanical reliability were well supported. It was known, however, that several other manufacturers were developing computers that might be significant improvements over existing machines in speed, space required for information storage, reliability, and adaptability to a variety of applications. Unfortunately, experience had shown that a computer's performance on a specific job could be appraised only in an application on that job.

Although the Apperson Corporation had spent considerable time and money analyzing the payroll application, executives still were not convinced that acquiring a computer was the proper course of action. Among the possible alternatives were the extension of the existing punched-card system and the institution of a thoroughgoing analysis and revision of systems and procedures. Apperson executives also were considering extending the analysis of the computer application before making a decision.

The Computers and Their Components

Like all general-purpose (i.e., capable of doing more than one job) computers, the Models 240 and 404 had in common certain basic functions. Although the Models 240 and 404 differed in some technical aspects, the problems of adapting the two machines to the payroll processing job were similar. Detailed discussion is therefore restricted to the Model 240.

The Model 240 components proposed by National Computer Corporation representatives utilized magnetic tape. Information recorded on magnetic tapes could be read into the internal memory on the main frame of the computer, or read (via the printer synchronizers) into the tape printers. Information could be recorded onto the magnetic tapes from the internal memory of the computer and from the punched-card reader. Model 240 could digest only information which was suitably coded and in the proper physical form.

In addition to the computer's internal memory, the main frame contained the operating component and the control component of the computer. The operating component was capable of performing any of a few dozen basic operations, such as transferring information from one "address" in the internal memory to another, transferring information to magnetic tape from the internal memory, or adding two numbers together and storing the result in an address indicated by instructions from the control unit. Like the numbers on which the computer operated, the instructions that determined the order of operations were read into the Model 240's internal memory from an input tape. The Model 240 could perform over 1,000 operations serially before transferring results to output tapes and returning to the input tapes for fresh blocks of data. The absence of human intervention and the characteristically high speed of the computer's electronic components together made possible the computer's dramatic capacity for processing great volumes of data. However, like all other computers, the Model 240 could do only what it was told to do.

Processing the Payroll

At Apperson Corporation, quantities and hours for hourly employees were recorded on piecework vouchers and daywork vouchers, respectively. Clock cards showed times in and out for each employee. Information from these basic source documents was transferred to punched cards. Each week, voucher file and clock card file tapes would be prepared from the punched cards to serve as inputs for the computer.

A limitation of the Model 240 was that the limited internal memory and the limited number of distinct elementary operations available in the operating component would make it necessary to break down the payroll job into parts: "gross pay" and "net pay" calculations. Five separate runs through the computer would be required to produce the finished payroll, as follows:

Run 1: Sort and extend piecework, daywork, and special-payment vouchers by department, sections, and clock number. The clock number served to identify each employee.

Run 2: Calculate gross pay for day workers, incentive workers, and salaried workers.

Prepare a new master file tape.

Prepare the labor distribution file, which accumulated voucher extensions preparatory to the classification and summary of labor costs by account in Run 4.

Run 3: Calculate withholding tax, F.O.A.B. tax, pension contributions, and net earnings, etc., and prepare the check record file from which the checks were printed.

Accumulate dollars and hours for piecework, daytime work, and overtime; accumulate eight separate year-to-date totals.

Accumulate balances for U.S. savings bonds, stock bonus plan, garnishees, etc.

Prepare a revision of the new master file.

Run 4: Distribute labor cost to various cost accounts.

Run 5: Produce 11 reports.

Differences between the Model 240 and the Model 404

Having analyzed the payroll job in some detail, Apperson executives concluded that the five runs would require 14 hours each week on the Model 240, not including time for routine maintenance and preparation of input tapes. The payroll operation in the Model 404 was estimated to require only 11 hours. More time thus would be available for jobs that Apperson executives had not yet analyzed for computer solution.

Some Apperson executives believed that the greatest potential savings from use of a computer lay in applications of inventory and production control and receivables accounting. Although none of these applications had been analyzed, the time was visualized when a computer would be worked to capacity. The rental of the additional equipment estimated as necessary to bring the time required for payroll operation by the Model 240 down to the time required for the same operation by the Model 404 was $20,000 a year.

The Model 404 and Model 240 differed chiefly in the physical form of their internal memories, the way in which information within the respective computers was coded and transferred, and in the fact that the functions described above were physically unitized in the Model 240 to a degree that promised significantly greater interchangeability than characterized components of the Model 404.

The Model 240 was a new machine on which the shortest promised delivery time was a year and nine months. The Model 404, on the other hand, had been in operation in some applications for almost three years and according to its manufacturer could be installed soon enough to be in operation by the time detailed programing and personnel training were completed. Thus, if the decision was made to use the Model 404, it could reasonably be expected to be in operation a whole year sooner than the Model 240.

The actual time required to run the only payroll application of the Model 404 known to the investigators had been four times as great as originally had been estimated. The erroneous prediction had been based on a flow diagram that it was felt had failed to indicate the actual complexity of the payroll operation.

The Model 240, on the other hand, had yet to be tested. Although the National Computer Corporation had engineered many data-processing systems, it had never attempted the application of a high-speed computer to payroll.

Short of actually testing the programed payroll, no alternative for Apperson executives existed that could supply reliable data on the Model 240's performance. The problems peculiar to each computing job were so important in determination of the success of a given application that probably the only reliable impression to be gained from other companies' experiences was the generally unfavorable disparity between estimated and actual performance.

The Apperson Corporation's Analysis

In order to estimate operating times for payroll processing, several distinct steps were required. To meet the problems created by a variety of work situations and compensation agreements, the Apperson Corporation had developed a variety of payroll procedures. The analysis described above was based on a standardized payroll procedure adopted merely to explore the possibilities of a Model 240 installation. It was thought that the standardized procedure was sufficiently general to cover all the special payroll problems arising in the plant. No attempt, however, at simplifying or improving the standardized procedure was made.

Working closely with representatives of National Computers Corporation, Apperson men made estimates of the time required to collect, organize, and compute source documents, and to record source information on punched cards under the contemplated system.

Exhibit 1 shows estimated gross savings from the elimination of

Exhibit 1

CALCULATION OF THE NET ANNUAL SAVINGS ANTICIPATED FOR THE APPLICATION OF THE MODEL 240 TO PAYROLL PROCESSING

SAVINGS RESULTING FROM ELIMINATION OF EXISTING OPERATIONS

Personnel (185)	$704,000	
Punched-card equipment rentals	46,000	
Furniture and office equipment depreciation	37,200	
Space (allocated cost)	39,000	
		$826,200

ADDITIONAL COSTS OF OPERATING THE MODEL 240

Equipment rentals:*		
Main frame	$130,000	
Tape drives, synchronizers	60,200	
Tape-operated printer, synchronizer	54,500	
Card reader, synchronizer	18,000	
Punched-card equipment	12,300	
Personnel:		
Manager (1)	10,000	
Programers (2)	12,500	
Computer operators (3)	14,000	
Keypunch operators (2)	6,700	
Others (3)	9,500	
Tape costs	7,400	
Space (allocated cost)	11,600	
Departmental costs:		
Personnel (23)	82,300	
Punched-card equipment rentals	9,800	
Furniture depreciation	600	
Space (allocated cost)	4,800	
Punched cards	10,000	
Total		$454,200
Net Operating Savings		$372,000

INITIAL COSTS (NOT INCLUDING MONEY ALREADY SPENT)

Personnel training	$100,000	
Flow charting, programing, and coding	65,000	
Remodeling, installation	100,000	
	$265,000	

existing operations, estimated additional costs of operating the Model 240, and the net operating savings. The same figure for net operating savings could have been found by a comparison of the total cost of payroll processing under existing procedures with the total cost of payroll processing under the proposal involving rental of the Model 240. Those who prepared the figures for Exhibit 1 believed that the differences in costs between the two should be highlighted and therefore that costs common to both should be omitted from the comparison. An exception to this policy was made in the case of punched-card equipment rentals, for which it was considered desirable to show the amount of such rentals in conjunction with the operation of Model 240, even though the same equipment might be in use under the existing procedures. Thus the rental on all existing punched-card equipment was treated as a saving and the rental of punched-card equipment in conjunction with Model 240 was shown as an additional cost.

Of the 350 positions currently required for payroll processing, 185 would be eliminated under the proposal. The remaining 165 positions would continue to be necessary for checking and extending source documents, processing exceptional claims and payments, handling journal entries and control reconciliations, typing reports, and other miscellaneous duties.

As noted in Exhibit 1, the staff contemplated for the computer center, including the operation of Model 240, numbered 11; additional departmental personnel required to produce the punched payroll cards from which the magnetic input tapes were prepared would number 23. It was probable that the majority, if not all, of these 34 people would be obtained from the 185 whose positions would be eliminated. Thus in terms of numbers of employees there would be 185 less 34, or a net of 151 employees, eliminated under the proposal.

In addition to the continuing operating costs of Model 240 there would be initial costs of training the computer staff and departmental workers (the 34 people noted above) estimated at $100,000. These costs would, of course, be greater if extensive changes in departmental clerical procedures involving the 165 other persons were instituted. This cost estimate did not include the cost of retraining the estimated net 151 employees whose jobs were to be eliminated if the contemplated installation was successful. It was expected that normal attrition among clerical workers throughout the company would provide employment opportunities for these people and therefore that no one would be discharged as a result of the Model 240 installation.

Four highly paid systems analysts worked four months to develop the above information. There were, however, two major qualifications to their conclusions. In the first place, estimates of manning requirements, and consequent savings in personnel, were based on estimates of time required to perform departmental payroll tasks. The total man-hours required per year for these tasks divided by the average hours of work per year expected from a clerical worker gave the number of man-years per year involved. No attempt was made to convert these time requirements for *tasks* to specific *jobs* for which existing personnel could successfully be retrained. When the time came, therefore, to lay out the work in terms of jobs there might well be more jobs, and to some extent different people involved, than contemplated in Exhibit 1. Furthermore, it might take longer than anticipated for normal attrition to absorb employees displaced by the installation.

The other qualification refers to the estimate of running time required on the computer proper. Actual operating problems and the time required for individual runs could not be predicted in detail from the analysis. For this purpose a detailed *flow charting* of the arithmetical and logical operations of the computer was necessary. Flow charting would pave the way for programing the computer. It was estimated, however, that flow charting would take several man-years, require additional training for Apperson's staff, and cost as much as $30,000.

One analyst suggested that the payroll job be programed and tested on a computer already in existence before a final decision was made. Programing, however, might require several man-years. Together with testing and the correction of errors, programing could scarcely be compressed into less than six calendar months. The cost of programing might exceed $50,000.

Systems Analysis

Some specialists in the application of computers to business problems insisted that at least as much could be saved by analyzing and improving a company's systems and procedures as by introducing electronic equipment. One company had analyzed savings to be expected from the application of each of several computers and also from the application of punched cards. The punched-card application, which entailed some systems analysis and consequent improvements, indicated savings comparable to the several computer applications.

It will be recalled that the Apperson Corporation analysis of data processing had been based on a standardized payroll procedure. Furthermore, the need for existing reports was not questioned. If flow charting, programing, and coding proceeded on this basis, it was feared that existing inefficiencies would be incorporated into the mechanized process. Such inefficiencies would result partly from intrinsically wasteful procedures under the old system, which mechanization would perpetuate, and partly from failure to adapt procedures to the potential reduction in the number of records created and handled, which was peculiar to a properly integrated electronic data-processing system.

On the other hand, the improvements that might result from systems analysis would depend largely on the time and expense that Apperson was willing to devote to such a study. An ambitious program might take many man-years and cost hundreds of thousands of dollars. One company was known, however, to have cut running time on its computer roughly in half by effecting improvements in procedures.

Questions

1. Should the Apperson Corporation commit itself to a program leading to the acquisition of either computer? If so, what additional steps should it take before deciding which computer to acquire and whether to lease or purchase? Should the Model 404, if recommended, be leased or purchased?

2. What course of action should the Apperson Corporation take if it decides not to acquire a computer at the present time?

CASE 21–7. BIRCH PAPER COMPANY

"If I were to price these boxes any lower than $480 a thousand," said Mr. Brunner, manager of Birch Paper Company's Thompson division, "I'd be countermanding my order of last month for our salesmen to stop shaving their bids and to bid full cost quotations. I've been trying for weeks to improve the quality of our business, and if I turn around now and accept this job at $430 or $450 or something less than $480 I'll be tearing down this program I've been working so hard to build up. The division can't very well show a profit by putting in bids which don't even cover a fair share of overhead costs, let alone give us a profit."

Birch Paper Company was a medium-size, partly integrated paper company, producing white and kraft papers and paperboard. A portion of its paperboard output was converted into corrugated boxes by the Thompson division, which also printed and colored the outside surface of the boxes. Including Thompson, the company had four producing divisions and a timberland division, which supplied part of the company's pulp requirements.

For several years each division had been judged independently on the basis of its profit and return on investment. Top management had been working to gain effective results from a policy of decentralizing responsibility and authority for all decisions except those relating to overall company policy. The company's top officials felt that in the past few years the concept of decentralization had been successfully applied and that the company's profits and competitive position had definitely improved.

Early in 1957 the Northern division designed a special display box for one of its papers in conjunction with the Thompson division, which was equipped to make the box. Thompson's package design and development staff spent several months perfecting the design, production methods, and materials that were to be used; because of the unusual color and shape, these were far from standard. According to an agreement between the two divisions, the Thompson division was reimbursed by the Northern division for the cost of its design and development work.

When the specifications were all prepared, the Northern division asked for bids on the box from the Thompson division and from two outside companies, West Paper Company and Erie Papers, Ltd. Each division manager normally was free to buy from whichever supplier he wished; and even on sales within the company, divisions were expected to meet the going market price if they wanted the business.

Early in 1957 the profit margins of converters such as the Thompson division were being squeezed. Thompson, as did many other similar converters, bought its board, liner or paper, and its function was to print, cut, and shape it into boxes. Though it bought most of its materials from other Birch divisions, most of Thompson's sales were to outside customers. If Thompson got the order from Northern, it probably would buy its linerboard and corrugating medium from the Southern division of Birch. The walls of a corrugated box consist of outside and inside sheets of linerboard sandwiching the corrugating medium.

About 70 per cent of Thompson's out-of-pocket cost of $400 a thousand for the order represented the cost of linerboard and corrugating medium. Though Southern division had been running below capacity and had excess inventory, it quoted the market price, which had not noticeably weakened as a result of the oversupply. Its out-of-pocket costs on both liner and corrugating medium were about 60 per cent of the selling price.

The Northern division received bids on the boxes of $480 a thousand from the Thompson division, $430 a thousand from West Paper Company, and $432 a thousand from Erie Papers, Ltd. Erie Papers offered to buy from Birch the outside linerboard with the special printing already on it, but would supply its own inside liner and corrugating medium. The outside liner would be supplied by the Southern division at a price equivalent of $90 a thousand boxes, and would be printed for $30 a thousand by the Thompson division. Of the $30, about $25 would be out-of-pocket costs.

Since this situation appeared to be a little unusual, Mr. Kenton, manager of the Northern division, discussed the wide discrepancy of bids with Birch's commercial vice president. He told the commercial vice president, "We sell in a very competitive market, where higher costs cannot be passed on. How can we be expected to show a decent profit and return on investment if we have to buy our supplies at more than 10 per cent over the going market?"

Knowing that Mr. Brunner had on occasion in the past few months been unable to operate the Thompson division at capacity, the commercial vice president thought it odd that Mr. Brunner would add the full 20 per cent overhead and profit charge to his out-of-pocket costs. When he asked Mr. Brunner about this over the telephone, his answer was the statement that appears at the beginning of the case. Mr. Brunner went on to say that having done the developmental work on the box, and having received no profit on that, he felt entitled to a good markup on the production of the box itself.

The vice president explored further the cost structures of the various divisions. He remembered a comment the controller had made at a meeting the week before to the effect that costs that for one division were variable could be largely fixed for the company as a whole. He knew that in the absence of specific orders from top management, Mr. Kenton would accept the lowest bid, namely, that of the West Paper Company for $430. However, it would be possible for top management to order the acceptance of another bid if the situation warranted such action. And though the volume represented by the transactions in question was less than 5 per cent of the volume of any of the divisions involved, other transactions could conceivably raise similar problems later.

Questions

The whole concept of decentralized management depends, among other things, on being able to construct a useful income statement for the decentralized component. When intracompany transactions are involved, this requires that valid transfer prices be established. Presumably, the division manager wants his income statement to show as much profit as possible. This is the central question: How can the transfer price be set so that actions taken by the division manager in his own best interest will also be in the best interest of the whole company?

A specific question in this case is as follows: Does the system motivate Mr.

Brunner in such a way that actions he takes in the best interests of the Thompson division are also in the best interests of the Birch Paper Company? If your answer is "no," give some specific instances related as closely as possible to the type of situation described in the case. Would the manager of *other* divisions be correctly motivated?

CASE 21–8.   EASTERN LOCK COMPANY

Robert Burns, production engineer of the Eastern Lock Company, asked one of his assistants, John Hawkins, to write a report analyzing the advisability of purchasing some new drilling equipment. Mr. Burns told him that this equipment might be valuable in reducing the cost of manufacturing bases and plungers[4] for certain styles of padlocks. The management of the company was anxious to make cost reductions wherever possible. Mr. Burns told Mr. Hawkins that he expected the report to include specific recommendations supported by a concise but comprehensive analysis. The report would be used as a basis for further study of the proposal by officials responsible for equipment purchases and would serve as the file record of the plan.

Over a period of 70 years the Eastern Lock Company had become known as a large and dependable manufacturer of high-quality locks of several hundred styles. Currently, sales amounted to over $4 million. Eastern Lock Company was the only lock-making plant in the area. It was operating close to capacity, whereas other metal products concerns in the vicinity were laying off workers. Business conditions were generally uncertain throughout the country.

The new machinery could be used to make parts for 13 standard styles of padlocks that the company had been manufacturing for more than 40 years. It sold these locks largely to organizations that required the same style of lock throughout all their plants and buildings. The sale of all styles of locks was fairly steady throughout the year; annual sales of the 13 styles of locks in recent years had been approximately as follows:

Style A,	3,000 units	Style G,	12,000 units
B,	12,000 "	H,	6,000 "
C,	18,000 "	I,	6,000 "
D,	60,000 "	J,	4,000 "
E,	48,000 "	K,	4,000 "
F,	42,000 "	L,	30,000 "
		M,	12,000 "
		Total	257,000 "

---

[4] The base (also called the shell) is the body to which the main working parts of the lock are attached. The base is inserted into the outside case of the lock. The plunger (also called the bolt) is the small piece that moves against the notch in the shackle and holds it locked.

The equipment that Mr. Burns was considering was of two types. One type was semiautomatic equipment for performing the 12 drilling operations required on lock bases. The other type was automatic equipment for drilling lock plungers. For many years, lock bases and plungers both had been drilled on general-purpose machines.

Drilling Bases

Under the company's existing method, the drilling operations on the bases were performed by semiskilled men who on piecework earned an average of $1.32 an hour for a 40-hour week. Output per man varied somewhat with the particular style of lock base being drilled. On the basis of total annual production figures for the 13 styles of lock bases, output had averaged 33 pieces per worker per hour, exclusive of the setup time. Setup of the machines required very little time and was performed by the operatives, who received no payment for this work.

The semiautomatic machine being considered for the drilling of the lock bases could perform six of the twelve drilling operations at a rate of 225 units an hour; after another setup, the other six drilling operations could then be performed. Or two machines could perform the 12 drilling operations simultaneously, at the rate of 225 completed units an hour; these two machines would easily provide capacity for all 13 styles. Each machine could be operated by a girl who would be paid about 80 cents an hour. Changing the setup of a machine from the drilling (six holes) of one style of lock base to the drilling of another style would require a skilled mechanic and would take an average of five hours. Skilled mechanics in the Eastern Lock Company received $1.80 an hour. In addition, a charge of 100 per cent of the mechanic's wages was made against setup operations to allow for overhead; this charge was included in the standard overhead for the valuation of inventories and the cost of goods sold.

To operate the machines advantageously, the company would have to produce each style of lock in large lots in order to spread the setup costs over a large number of units. On the other hand, the larger the lot produced, the larger would be the inventory of bases and the longer would be the average time a base remained in inventory. Thus, the inventory-carrying costs per unit would increase. In figuring overhead, Eastern Lock charged 4 per cent a year for capital tied up in inventories and 4 per cent of the value of inventories for space, handling, and so forth. Since the company was operating close to capacity, storage space was limited. It was believed, however, that if some rearranging were done in the stock room, sufficient space would be available to store the additional inventory. The handling of the additional inventory was expected to require extra labor, and although no close estimate had been made of the cost of this labor, it was estimated that perhaps a half (i.e., 2 per cent) of the 4 per cent space and handling charge might represent out-of-pocket costs of handling the inventory.

If large lots were manufactured, the parts would have to be moved into the stock room, entered on the inventory cards, tagged, and shelved. When these parts were removed from inventory, it would be necessary to record their withdrawal on the inventory cards and then move them out of the stock room to the place where they would be needed. Under the company's current method of operation, bases and lock plungers were drilled only as required by the assembly line. They were then moved directly over to the next operation without going through the extra handling and record-keeping procedures of the stock room.

The company could purchase from the Thompson Machine Company two identical semiautomatic machines for drilling lock bases at a cost of $8,000 each. A separate set of tools and fixtures would be required for the drilling of each of the 13 styles of lock bases. The Thompson company would produce sets of tools and fixtures at a cost of $2,500 a set. Thus, to buy complete equipment for drilling the 13 base styles would require $16,000 for machines and $32,500 for tools and fixtures.

Drilling Plungers

Although the drilling of plungers consisted of only one operation, this operation could not be performed on automatic equipment as long as the present general-purpose machines were used for the 12 drilling operations on the bases. The positions of the holes drilled in the lock bases by general-purpose machines frequently varied slightly, and plungers had to be inserted in lock bases and drilled with general-purpose machines in order that all holes in the finished lock might be in correct alignment. The use of semiautomatic equipment would enable the company to maintain much closer tolerances in the drilling of bases, and plungers could be drilled on automatic equipment prior to their insertion without the danger that the holes in the finished lock would be out of alignment.

If the lock plungers were drilled on automatic machinery, the direct labor cost of this operation could be reduced from the existing figure of $1 per 100 plungers to 20 cents per 100. The automatic equipment, which could be quickly set up for the drilling of any type of lock plunger, would cost $11,000. This price included fixtures for drilling all types of plungers used by the company. Drilling was the last one of three machining operations performed on plungers; total labor cost of the three operations was $1.45 per 100.

Other Considerations

Thompson Machine Company was the only concern represented in Eastern Lock's area that sold this type of equipment. Over the years, Eastern Lock had bought considerable equipment from Thompson and had always been satisfied with the quality of the machinery and with Thompson's service.

Eastern Lock was currently short of cash because of recent expenditures made in connection with a cost-reduction program, and for this reason Mr. Hawkins thought that new equipment would have to be financed through bank loans. Mr. Hawkins, on consulting with the company treasurer, thought that Eastern Lock could arrange a bank loan at an interest rate of around 6 per cent.

Thompson listed the expected life of the new drilling equipment as 20,000 to 25,000 hours. Eastern Lock's policy was to depreciate such machinery over 15 years. Though he had no evidence of a high obsolescence rate on this equipment, Mr. Hawkins knew that the management would expect it to pay for itself in less than the expected usable life. The company expected to earn at least 15 per cent before taxes on its investments.

The five general-purpose machines being used to drill bases and plungers were about ten years old. They were originally worth $2,000 each and currently had a depreciated value of $675 each. Their scrap value was $50 each. The plant recently had been largely reequipped so that there was little chance that this equipment could be used elsewhere or that excess time on new equipment could be used. The new equipment would be suitable for only a few other operations in the plant.

Mr. Hawkins realized that the drilling of lock bases with semiautomatic machinery and the drilling of lock plungers with automatic equipment might increase the amount of waste. If a machine was not properly adjusted, a large number of bases or plungers might be drilled before the error was recognized. Under the company's existing method of production, waste had amounted to not more than 1 or 2 per cent of total production cost.

For the 13 styles A–M, the average manufacturing cost of locks was computed to be as follows:

Manufacturing Costs per 100 Units

	Bases*	Plungers*	Others	Complete Locks
Material..........................	$14.30	$0.98	$ 11.42	$ 26.70
Direct labor.......................	4.40	1.45	37.95	43.80
Factory overhead..................	4.80	1.45	33.14	39.40
Total Factory Cost................	$23.50	$3.89	$ 82.51	$109.90
General overhead..................	9.40	0.86	19.34	29.60
Total Cost......................	$32.90	$4.75	$101.85	$139.50

*Up to and including the drilling operation only.

Questions

1. What would be the most efficient lot size for the production of base styles A, B, and D using the semiautomatic drilling equipment for bases, and assuming that only one machine is purchased?

2. Assume that the economic lot sizes of the other base styles are as follows:

Style C, 6,600 units	Style I, 3,800 units
E, 10,700 "	J, 3,100 "
F, 10,000 "	K, 3,100 "
G, Same as B	L, 8,500 "
H, 3,800 units	M, Same as B

What action do you recommend?

APPENDIX TABLES

Table A

PRESENT VALUE OF $1

Years Hence	1%	2%	4%	6%	8%	10%	12%	14%	15%	16%	18%	20%	22%	24%	25%	26%	28%	30%	35%	40%	45%	50%
1	0.990	0.980	0.962	0.943	0.926	0.909	0.893	0.877	0.870	0.862	0.847	0.833	0.820	0.806	0.800	0.794	0.781	0.769	0.741	0.714	0.690	0.667
2	0.980	0.961	0.925	0.890	0.857	0.826	0.797	0.769	0.756	0.743	0.718	0.694	0.672	0.650	0.640	0.630	0.610	0.592	0.549	0.510	0.476	0.444
3	0.971	0.942	0.889	0.840	0.794	0.751	0.712	0.675	0.658	0.641	0.609	0.579	0.551	0.524	0.512	0.500	0.477	0.455	0.406	0.364	0.328	0.296
4	0.961	0.924	0.855	0.792	0.735	0.683	0.636	0.592	0.572	0.552	0.516	0.482	0.451	0.423	0.410	0.397	0.373	0.350	0.301	0.260	0.226	0.198
5	0.951	0.906	0.822	0.747	0.681	0.621	0.567	0.519	0.497	0.476	0.437	0.402	0.370	0.341	0.328	0.315	0.291	0.269	0.223	0.186	0.156	0.132
6	0.942	0.888	0.790	0.705	0.630	0.564	0.507	0.456	0.432	0.410	0.370	0.335	0.303	0.275	0.262	0.250	0.227	0.207	0.165	0.133	0.108	0.088
7	0.933	0.871	0.760	0.665	0.583	0.513	0.452	0.400	0.376	0.354	0.314	0.279	0.249	0.222	0.210	0.198	0.178	0.159	0.122	0.095	0.074	0.059
8	0.923	0.853	0.731	0.627	0.540	0.467	0.404	0.351	0.327	0.305	0.266	0.233	0.204	0.179	0.168	0.157	0.139	0.123	0.091	0.068	0.051	0.039
9	0.914	0.837	0.703	0.592	0.500	0.424	0.361	0.308	0.284	0.263	0.225	0.194	0.167	0.144	0.134	0.125	0.108	0.094	0.067	0.048	0.035	0.026
10	0.905	0.820	0.676	0.558	0.463	0.386	0.322	0.270	0.247	0.227	0.191	0.162	0.137	0.116	0.107	0.099	0.085	0.073	0.050	0.035	0.024	0.017
11	0.896	0.804	0.650	0.527	0.429	0.350	0.287	0.237	0.215	0.195	0.162	0.135	0.112	0.094	0.086	0.079	0.066	0.056	0.037	0.025	0.017	0.012
12	0.887	0.788	0.625	0.497	0.397	0.319	0.257	0.208	0.187	0.168	0.137	0.112	0.092	0.076	0.069	0.062	0.052	0.043	0.027	0.018	0.012	0.008
13	0.879	0.773	0.601	0.469	0.368	0.290	0.229	0.182	0.163	0.145	0.116	0.093	0.075	0.061	0.055	0.050	0.040	0.033	0.020	0.013	0.008	0.005
14	0.870	0.758	0.577	0.442	0.340	0.263	0.205	0.160	0.141	0.125	0.099	0.078	0.062	0.049	0.044	0.039	0.032	0.025	0.015	0.009	0.006	0.003
15	0.861	0.743	0.555	0.417	0.315	0.239	0.183	0.140	0.123	0.108	0.084	0.065	0.051	0.040	0.035	0.031	0.025	0.020	0.011	0.006	0.004	0.002
16	0.853	0.728	0.534	0.394	0.292	0.218	0.163	0.123	0.107	0.093	0.071	0.054	0.042	0.032	0.028	0.025	0.019	0.015	0.008	0.005	0.003	0.002
17	0.844	0.714	0.513	0.371	0.270	0.198	0.146	0.108	0.093	0.080	0.060	0.045	0.034	0.026	0.023	0.020	0.015	0.012	0.006	0.003	0.002	0.001
18	0.836	0.700	0.494	0.350	0.250	0.180	0.130	0.095	0.081	0.069	0.051	0.038	0.028	0.021	0.018	0.016	0.012	0.009	0.005	0.002	0.001	0.001
19	0.828	0.686	0.475	0.331	0.232	0.164	0.116	0.083	0.070	0.060	0.043	0.031	0.023	0.017	0.014	0.012	0.009	0.007	0.003	0.002	0.001	0.001
20	0.820	0.673	0.456	0.312	0.215	0.149	0.104	0.073	0.061	0.051	0.037	0.026	0.019	0.014	0.012	0.010	0.007	0.005	0.002	0.001	0.001	0.001
21	0.811	0.660	0.439	0.294	0.199	0.135	0.093	0.064	0.053	0.044	0.031	0.022	0.015	0.011	0.009	0.008	0.006	0.004	0.002	0.001		
22	0.803	0.647	0.422	0.278	0.184	0.123	0.083	0.056	0.046	0.038	0.026	0.018	0.013	0.009	0.007	0.006	0.004	0.003	0.001	0.001		
23	0.795	0.634	0.406	0.262	0.170	0.112	0.074	0.049	0.040	0.033	0.022	0.015	0.010	0.007	0.006	0.005	0.003	0.002	0.001			
24	0.788	0.622	0.390	0.247	0.158	0.102	0.066	0.043	0.035	0.028	0.019	0.013	0.008	0.006	0.005	0.004	0.003	0.002	0.001			
25	0.780	0.610	0.375	0.233	0.146	0.092	0.059	0.038	0.030	0.024	0.016	0.010	0.007	0.005	0.004	0.003	0.002	0.001	0.001			
26	0.772	0.598	0.361	0.220	0.135	0.084	0.053	0.033	0.026	0.021	0.014	0.009	0.006	0.004	0.003	0.002	0.002	0.001				
27	0.764	0.586	0.347	0.207	0.125	0.076	0.047	0.029	0.023	0.018	0.011	0.007	0.005	0.003	0.002	0.002	0.001	0.001				
28	0.757	0.574	0.333	0.196	0.116	0.069	0.042	0.026	0.020	0.016	0.010	0.006	0.004	0.002	0.002	0.001	0.001	0.001				
29	0.749	0.563	0.321	0.185	0.107	0.063	0.037	0.022	0.017	0.014	0.008	0.005	0.003	0.002	0.002	0.001	0.001	0.001				
30	0.742	0.552	0.308	0.174	0.099	0.057	0.033	0.020	0.015	0.012	0.007	0.004	0.003	0.002	0.001	0.001	0.001					
40	0.672	0.453	0.208	0.097	0.046	0.022	0.011	0.005	0.004	0.003	0.001	0.001										
50	0.608	0.372	0.141	0.054	0.021	0.009	0.003	0.001	0.001	0.001												

Table B

PRESENT VALUE OF $1 RECEIVED ANNUALLY FOR N YEARS

Years (N)	1%	2%	4%	6%	8%	10%	12%	14%	15%	16%	18%	20%	22%	24%	25%	26%	28%	30%	35%	40%	45%	50%
1	0.990	0.980	0.962	0.943	0.926	0.909	0.893	0.877	0.870	0.862	0.847	0.833	0.820	0.806	0.800	0.794	0.781	0.769	0.741	0.714	0.690	0.667
2	1.970	1.942	1.886	1.833	1.783	1.736	1.690	1.647	1.626	1.605	1.566	1.528	1.492	1.457	1.440	1.424	1.392	1.361	1.289	1.224	1.165	1.111
3	2.941	2.884	2.775	2.673	2.577	2.487	2.402	2.322	2.283	2.246	2.174	2.106	2.042	1.981	1.952	1.923	1.868	1.816	1.696	1.589	1.493	1.407
4	3.902	3.808	3.630	3.465	3.312	3.170	3.037	2.914	2.855	2.798	2.690	2.589	2.494	2.404	2.362	2.320	2.241	2.166	1.997	1.849	1.720	1.605
5	4.853	4.713	4.452	4.212	3.993	3.791	3.605	3.433	3.352	3.274	3.127	2.991	2.864	2.745	2.689	2.635	2.532	2.436	2.220	2.035	1.876	1.737
6	5.795	5.601	5.242	4.917	4.623	4.355	4.111	3.889	3.784	3.685	3.498	3.326	3.167	3.020	2.951	2.885	2.759	2.643	2.385	2.168	1.983	1.824
7	6.728	6.472	6.002	5.582	5.206	4.868	4.564	4.288	4.160	4.039	3.812	3.605	3.416	3.242	3.161	3.083	2.937	2.802	2.508	2.263	2.057	1.883
8	7.652	7.325	6.733	6.210	5.747	5.335	4.968	4.639	4.487	4.344	4.078	3.837	3.619	3.421	3.329	3.241	3.076	2.925	2.598	2.331	2.108	1.922
9	8.566	8.162	7.435	6.802	6.247	5.759	5.328	4.946	4.772	4.607	4.303	4.031	3.786	3.566	3.463	3.366	3.184	3.019	2.665	2.379	2.144	1.948
10	9.471	8.983	8.111	7.360	6.710	6.145	5.650	5.216	5.019	4.833	4.494	4.192	3.923	3.682	3.571	3.465	3.269	3.092	2.715	2.414	2.168	1.965
11	10.368	9.787	8.760	7.887	7.139	6.495	5.937	5.453	5.234	5.029	4.656	4.327	4.035	3.776	3.656	3.544	3.335	3.147	2.752	2.438	2.185	1.977
12	11.255	10.575	9.385	8.384	7.536	6.814	6.194	5.660	5.421	5.197	4.793	4.439	4.127	3.851	3.725	3.606	3.387	3.190	2.779	2.456	2.196	1.985
13	12.134	11.343	9.986	8.853	7.904	7.103	6.424	5.842	5.583	5.342	4.910	4.533	4.203	3.912	3.780	3.656	3.427	3.223	2.799	2.468	2.204	1.990
14	13.004	12.106	10.563	9.295	8.244	7.367	6.628	6.002	5.724	5.468	5.008	4.611	4.265	3.962	3.824	3.695	3.459	3.249	2.814	2.477	2.210	1.993
15	13.865	12.849	11.118	9.712	8.559	7.606	6.811	6.142	5.847	5.575	5.092	4.675	4.315	4.001	3.859	3.726	3.483	3.268	2.825	2.484	2.214	1.995
16	14.718	13.578	11.652	10.106	8.851	7.824	6.974	6.265	5.954	5.669	5.162	4.730	4.357	4.033	3.887	3.751	3.503	3.283	2.834	2.489	2.216	1.997
17	15.562	14.292	12.166	10.477	9.122	8.022	7.120	6.373	6.047	5.749	5.222	4.775	4.391	4.059	3.910	3.771	3.518	3.295	2.840	2.492	2.218	1.998
18	16.398	14.992	12.659	10.828	9.372	8.201	7.250	6.467	6.128	5.818	5.273	4.812	4.419	4.080	3.928	3.786	3.529	3.304	2.844	2.494	2.219	1.999
19	17.226	15.678	13.134	11.158	9.604	8.365	7.366	6.550	6.198	5.877	5.316	4.844	4.442	4.097	3.942	3.799	3.539	3.311	2.848	2.496	2.220	1.999
20	18.046	16.351	13.590	11.470	9.818	8.514	7.469	6.623	6.259	5.929	5.353	4.870	4.460	4.110	3.954	3.808	3.546	3.316	2.850	2.497	2.221	1.999
21	18.857	17.011	14.029	11.764	10.017	8.649	7.562	6.687	6.312	5.973	5.384	4.891	4.476	4.121	3.963	3.816	3.551	3.320	2.852	2.498	2.221	2.000
22	19.660	17.658	14.451	12.042	10.201	8.772	7.645	6.743	6.359	6.011	5.410	4.909	4.488	4.130	3.970	3.822	3.556	3.323	2.853	2.498	2.222	2.000
23	20.456	18.292	14.857	12.303	10.371	8.883	7.718	6.792	6.399	6.044	5.432	4.925	4.499	4.137	3.976	3.827	3.559	3.325	2.854	2.499	2.222	2.000
24	21.243	18.914	15.247	12.550	10.529	8.985	7.784	6.835	6.434	6.073	5.451	4.937	4.507	4.143	3.981	3.831	3.562	3.327	2.855	2.499	2.222	2.000
25	22.023	19.523	15.622	12.783	10.675	9.077	7.843	6.873	6.464	6.097	5.467	4.948	4.514	4.147	3.985	3.834	3.564	3.329	2.856	2.499	2.222	2.000
26	22.795	20.121	15.983	13.003	10.810	9.161	7.896	6.906	6.491	6.118	5.480	4.956	4.520	4.151	3.988	3.837	3.566	3.330	2.856	2.500	2.222	2.000
27	23.560	20.707	16.330	13.211	10.935	9.237	7.943	6.935	6.514	6.136	5.492	4.964	4.524	4.154	3.990	3.839	3.567	3.331	2.856	2.500	2.222	2.000
28	24.316	21.281	16.663	13.406	11.051	9.307	7.984	6.961	6.534	6.152	5.502	4.970	4.528	4.157	3.992	3.840	3.568	3.331	2.857	2.500	2.222	2.000
29	25.066	21.844	16.984	13.591	11.158	9.370	8.022	6.983	6.551	6.166	5.510	4.975	4.531	4.159	3.994	3.841	3.569	3.332	2.857	2.500	2.222	2.000
30	25.808	22.396	17.292	13.765	11.258	9.427	8.055	7.003	6.566	6.177	5.517	4.979	4.534	4.160	3.995	3.842	3.569	3.332	2.857	2.500	2.222	2.000
40	32.835	27.355	19.793	15.046	11.925	9.779	8.244	7.105	6.642	6.234	5.548	4.997	4.544	4.166	3.999	3.846	3.571	3.333	2.857	2.500	2.222	2.000
50	39.196	31.424	21.482	15.762	12.234	9.915	8.304	7.133	6.661	6.246	5.554	4.999	4.545	4.167	4.000	3.846	3.571	3.333	2.857	2.500	2.222	2.000

Table C

PRESENT VALUE OF SUM-OF-YEARS' DIGIT DEPRECIATION

Years of Useful Life	2%	4%	6%	8%	10%	12%	14%	15%	16%	18%	20%	22%	24%	26%	28%	30%	35%	40%	45%	50%
3	0.968	0.937	0.908	0.881	0.855	0.831	0.808	0.796	0.786	0.764	0.745	0.726	0.707	0.690	0.674	0.658	0.621	0.588	0.558	0.531
4	0.961	0.925	0.891	0.860	0.830	0.802	0.776	0.763	0.751	0.728	0.706	0.685	0.665	0.646	0.628	0.611	0.572	0.538	0.507	0.479
5	0.955	0.914	0.875	0.839	0.806	0.775	0.746	0.732	0.719	0.694	0.670	0.647	0.626	0.606	0.588	0.570	0.530	0.494	0.463	0.435
6	0.949	0.902	0.859	0.820	0.783	0.749	0.718	0.703	0.689	0.662	0.637	0.613	0.591	0.570	0.551	0.533	0.492	0.456	0.425	0.398
7	0.943	0.891	0.844	0.801	0.761	0.725	0.692	0.676	0.661	0.633	0.606	0.582	0.559	0.538	0.518	0.500	0.458	0.423	0.392	0.366
8	0.937	0.880	0.829	0.782	0.740	0.702	0.667	0.650	0.635	0.605	0.578	0.553	0.530	0.508	0.488	0.470	0.429	0.394	0.364	0.338
9	0.931	0.869	0.814	0.765	0.720	0.680	0.643	0.626	0.610	0.580	0.552	0.527	0.503	0.482	0.462	0.443	0.402	0.368	0.338	0.313
10	0.925	0.859	0.800	0.748	0.701	0.659	0.621	0.604	0.587	0.556	0.528	0.502	0.479	0.457	0.437	0.419	0.378	0.345	0.316	0.292
11	0.919	0.848	0.786	0.731	0.682	0.639	0.600	0.582	0.565	0.534	0.506	0.480	0.456	0.434	0.415	0.397	0.357	0.324	0.297	0.273
12	0.913	0.838	0.773	0.715	0.665	0.620	0.580	0.562	0.545	0.513	0.485	0.459	0.435	0.414	0.394	0.376	0.338	0.306	0.279	0.257
13	0.907	0.828	0.760	0.700	0.648	0.602	0.562	0.543	0.526	0.494	0.465	0.439	0.416	0.395	0.376	0.358	0.320	0.289	0.264	0.242
14	0.902	0.818	0.747	0.685	0.632	0.585	0.544	0.525	0.508	0.476	0.447	0.421	0.398	0.377	0.358	0.341	0.304	0.274	0.250	0.229
15	0.896	0.809	0.734	0.671	0.616	0.569	0.527	0.508	0.491	0.459	0.430	0.405	0.382	0.361	0.343	0.326	0.290	0.261	0.237	0.217
16	0.890	0.799	0.722	0.657	0.601	0.553	0.511	0.492	0.475	0.443	0.414	0.389	0.367	0.346	0.328	0.312	0.277	0.248	0.225	0.206
17	0.885	0.790	0.710	0.644	0.587	0.538	0.496	0.477	0.460	0.428	0.400	0.375	0.352	0.332	0.315	0.298	0.264	0.237	0.215	0.196
18	0.880	0.781	0.699	0.631	0.573	0.524	0.482	0.463	0.445	0.413	0.386	0.361	0.339	0.320	0.302	0.286	0.253	0.227	0.205	0.187
19	0.874	0.772	0.688	0.618	0.560	0.510	0.468	0.449	0.432	0.400	0.372	0.348	0.327	0.308	0.291	0.275	0.243	0.217	0.196	0.179
20	0.869	0.763	0.677	0.606	0.547	0.497	0.455	0.436	0.419	0.387	0.360	0.336	0.315	0.296	0.280	0.265	0.233	0.208	0.188	0.171
21	0.863	0.754	0.666	0.594	0.535	0.485	0.442	0.424	0.406	0.376	0.349	0.325	0.304	0.286	0.270	0.255	0.224	0.200	0.181	0.164
22	0.858	0.746	0.656	0.583	0.523	0.473	0.431	0.412	0.395	0.364	0.338	0.315	0.294	0.276	0.260	0.246	0.216	0.193	0.174	0.158
23	0.853	0.738	0.646	0.572	0.511	0.461	0.419	0.401	0.384	0.354	0.327	0.305	0.285	0.267	0.252	0.238	0.208	0.186	0.167	0.152
24	0.848	0.729	0.636	0.561	0.500	0.450	0.409	0.390	0.373	0.344	0.318	0.295	0.276	0.258	0.243	0.230	0.201	0.179	0.161	0.147
25	0.842	0.721	0.626	0.551	0.490	0.440	0.398	0.380	0.364	0.334	0.308	0.286	0.267	0.250	0.236	0.222	0.195	0.173	0.156	0.142
30	0.818	0.683	0.582	0.504	0.442	0.393	0.353	0.336	0.320	0.292	0.269	0.249	0.232	0.216	0.203	0.191	0.167	0.148	0.133	0.120
35	0.794	0.648	0.542	0.463	0.402	0.355	0.317	0.300	0.286	0.260	0.238	0.220	0.204	0.190	0.178	0.168	0.146	0.129	0.116	0.105
40	0.771	0.616	0.507	0.428	0.368	0.323	0.286	0.271	0.257	0.233	0.213	0.196	0.182	0.170	0.159	0.149	0.129	0.114	0.102	0.093
45	0.749	0.586	0.476	0.397	0.339	0.296	0.261	0.247	0.234	0.212	0.193	0.178	0.164	0.153	0.143	0.134	0.116	0.103	0.092	0.093
50	0.728	0.559	0.448	0.370	0.314	0.272	0.240	0.227	0.214	0.194	0.176	0.162	0.150	0.139	0.130	0.122	0.106	0.093	0.083	0.083

Source: From tables computed by Jerome Bracken and Charles J. Christenson. Copyright © 1961 by the President and Fellows of Harvard College. Used by permission. See page 624 for explanation of use of this table.

INDEX

INDEX

A

Absorbed cost, 438–39; *see also* Standard cost
Absorption costing, 438–39
Accelerated depreciation, 158–60, 235, 623–24, 744
Account, 94–95
  adjusting, 128
  balance, 94
  classifications, 42
  clearing, 103
  closing, 128
  control, 111
  inventory, 182
  nominal and real, 102
  permanent, 102
  ruling and balancing, 103–4
  temporary, 102
  trading, 103
  variance, 433–36
Account balance, 94
Account classifications, 42
Account flow chart, 182–83
Accountant, expert knowledge of, 269–70
Accountants' Cost Handbook, 683
Accounting
  basic concepts, 27–52, 257–59
  contrast with economics, 71
  contrast with law, 32, 39
  conventions, 37–39
  differences in practice, 264–66
  double-entry, 37, 95–96
  evolution of, 29
  feasibility criterion, 30
  as a language, 28
  limitations of, 259–66
  objectivity criterion, 30, 258
  principles, 29–31, 257–72
    lack of agreement on, 260
  records, 93–109
  single-entry, 37
  systems, 93, 109–115
  usefulness criterion, 29
  uses, 2, 3
Accounting information, management's use of, 1–10
Accounting machines, 670
Accounting period, 63–64
Accounting practice, diversity in, 264–66
Accounting Principles, 56

Accounting Research Bulletins (AICPA), 30
  No. 33, 247, 251–54
  No. 43, 44, 45, 47, 77, 156, 168, 170, 182, 251–54
  No. 47, 140
Accounting Research Studies, No. 6, 237 n
Accounting Review, The, 65, 142
Accounting Series Releases (SEC), 30
Accounting Terminology Bulletins (AICPA), 29
Accounting Trends and Techniques (AICPA), 264
Accounting variance, 532
Accounts payable, 47
Accounts receivable, 129–30
  aging, 132, 149
  budgeted, 403
  definition, 45
  other, 45
  trade, 45
Accretion, 169
Accrual concept, 37, 61–70, 258–59
Accrued expenses, 48
Accrued revenue, 69
Accumulated depreciation, 101, 166, 167
Acid-test ratio, 300
Activity-related costs, 429
Adjusting entries, 99–102, 109, 132–33; *see also* Depreciation
  for bad debts, 102, 132
  for manufacturing companies, 185–93
Administration costs, 181
Aging accounts receivable, 132
Allocated cost; *see* Overhead *and* Cost
Allocation of costs, 430–31
Allowance for depreciation; *see* Depreciation
Allowance for doubtful accounts, 131–33
Allowance for uncollectible accounts, 131
Alternative choice problems, steps in solving, 561–80, 611
American Accounting Association, 237
  Standards Committee, 30, 65, 142
  price level study, 235
American Airlines flight plan, 401–3
American Appraisal Company, 233
American Automobile Association, 572–73
American Institute of Certified Public Accountants, 29, 30, 114, 247–48, 266,

This book has been set on the Linotype in 12 and 10 point Garamond No. 3, leaded 1 point. Chapter numbers are in 18 point Spartan Heavy italics with 30 point Spartan Heavy figures, and chapter titles are in 16 point Bulmer caps. The size of the type page is 27 by 46½ picas.